MONUMENTS OF SYRIA

MONUMENTS OF SYRIA

An Historical Guide

ROSS BURNS

I.B.Tauris *Publishers*

LONDON • NEW YORK

Revised edition published in 1999 by I.B.Tauris & Co Ltd
Victoria House, Bloomsbury Square, London WC1B 4DZ
175 Fifth Avenue, New York NY 10010
Website: http://www.ibtauris.com

In the United States and Canada distributed by St. Martin's Press
175 Fifth Avenue, New York NY 10010

First published in 1992 by I.B.Tauris & Co Ltd
Paperback edition published in 1994

ISBN 1 86064 244 6

A full CIP record for this book is available from the British Library
A full CIP record for this book is available from the Library of Congress

Library of Congress catalog card: available

Printed in Syria

Contents

List of Plates

List of Maps & Plans

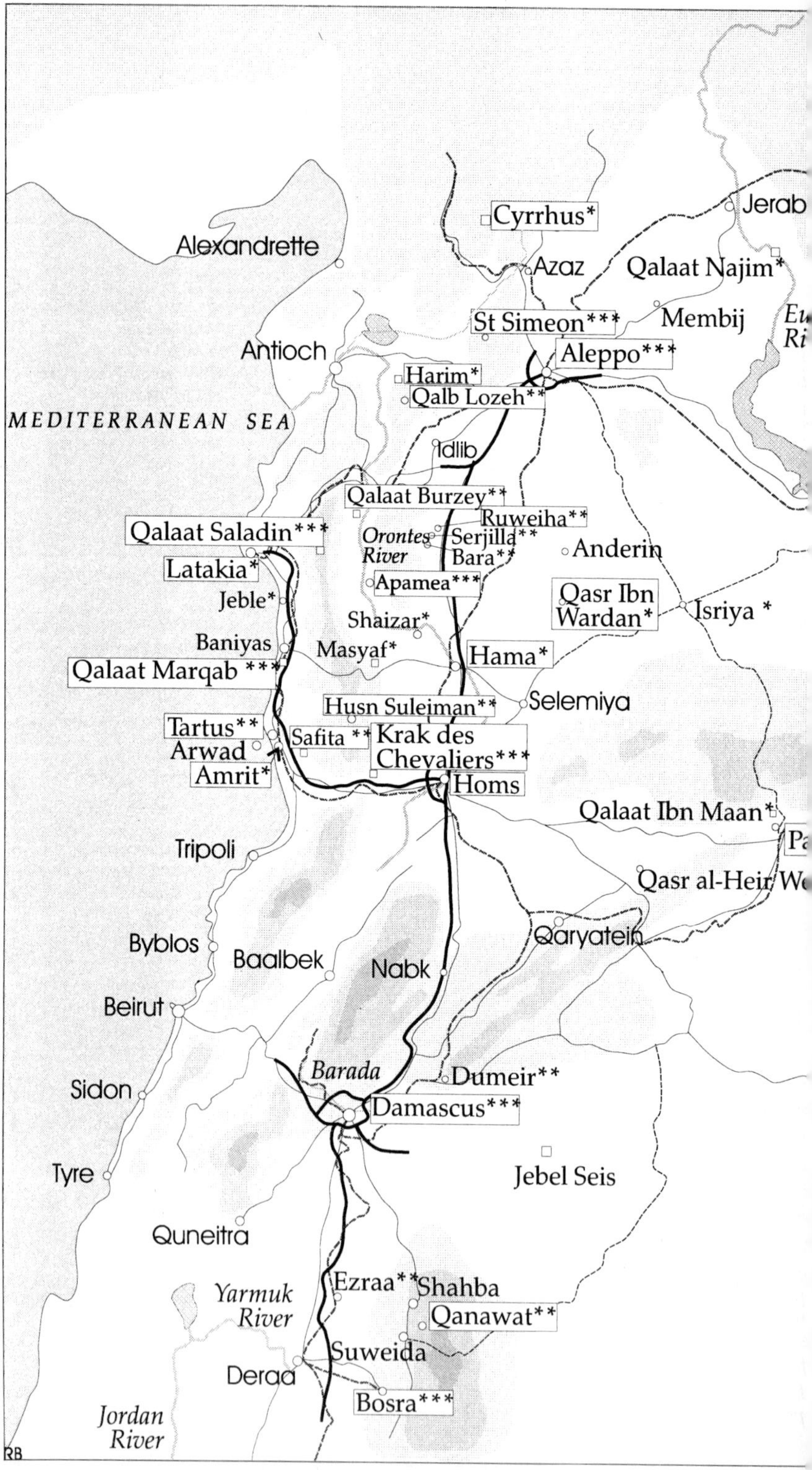

Cyrrhus*

Jerab

Alexandrette

Azaz

Qalaat Najim*

St Simeon***

Membij

Eu
Ri

Antioch

Aleppo***

Harim*
Qalb Lozeh**

MEDITERRANEAN SEA

Idlib

Qalaat Burzey**

Ruweiha**
Serjilla**

Qalaat Saladin***

Orontes
River

Bara**

Anderin

Latakia*

Apamea***

Jeble*

Qasr Ibn
Wardan*

Isriya *

Shaizar*

Baniyas

Masyaf*

Hama*

Qalaat Marqab ***

Husn Suleiman**

Selemiya

Tartus**

Safita **

Krak des
Chevaliers***

Arwad

Qalaat Ibn Maan*

Amrit*

Homs

Pa

Tripoli

Qasr al-Heir W

Byblos

Qaryatein

Baalbek

Nabk

Beirut

Sidon

Barada

Dumeir**

Damascus***

Tyre

Jebel Seis

Quneitra

Yarmuk
River

Ezraa**

Shahba

Qanawat**

Suweida

Deraa

Bosra***

Jordan
River

RB

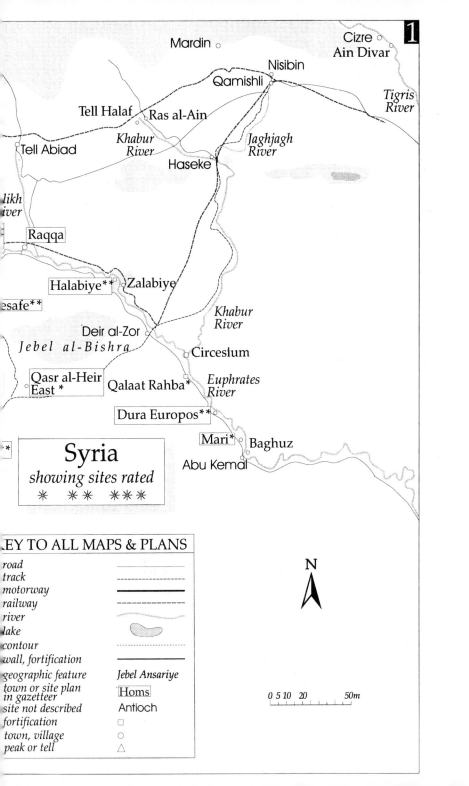

Mardin ○

Cizre ○
Ain Divar

1

Nisibin ○
Qamishli ○

Tigris River

Tell Halaf ○ Ras al-Ain

Khabur River

Jaghjagh River

Tell Abiad ○

Haseke ○

Jikh iver

Raqqa

Halabiye***** ○ Zalabiye

esafe**

Khabur River

Deir al-Zor ○

Jebel al-Bishra

Circesium ○

Qasr al-Heir East * ○

Qalaat Rahba* □

Euphrates River

Dura Europos**

Mari* ○ Baghuz

*

Abu Kemal ○

Syria
showing sites rated
✳ ✳✳ ✳✳✳

ΕΥ TO ALL MAPS & PLANS

road	——————
track	- - - - - - -
motorway	▬▬▬▬▬
railway	┼┼┼┼┼┼┼
river	〰〰〰
lake	🝰
contour	· · · · · · ·
wall, fortification	▬▬▬▬▬
geographic feature	*Jebel Ansariye*
town or site plan in gazetteer	Homs
site not described	Antioch
fortification	□
town, village	○
peak or tell	△

N

0 5 10 20   50m

Foreword

The exploration of Syria is one of the most satisfying pleasures that remain in the field of travel. Though 'Syria is the world's richest resource in terms of the number, variety and scientific interest of its archaeological remains[1]', it is poorly exploited even in an age of mass tourism. Egypt may out-class Syria in its spectacular efflorescence at several periods, but Syria has preserved a rich sample of all the major cross-currents from Early Bronze Age to the Turkish period. Its Byzantine sites, for example, are of exceptional interest and survive in a virtually unspoilt condition, usually unvisited by bus tours and trinket sellers. Two other periods are of exceptional interest - the Roman era (known principally to the world through the desert caravan city, Palmyra); and the Crusades which left Syria an incomparable collection of mediaeval fortifications, of which the Krak des Chevaliers is the best known.

In this living museum, some sort of handbook is needed to guide the visitor through the layers of history, to link the sites to the deeds of men such as Alexander or Saladin and to convey the fact that these are not just pretty stones but remarkable signposts to a complex past. That is what this book aims to do, to make history come alive through the monuments of Syria.

Although this book arose out of the lack of a reference work on Syria's monuments to guide the interested traveller or resident in Syria, it is not intended simply as a guide book. It aspires to explain Syria's history and its place in a region of bewildering cross-currents through its monuments and historic sites. Though it does not claim the authority of an encyclopedia, it should be used in the same way - to be dipped into at need for those interested in a particular site or area; but with a framework for the reader provided by the sections on overall historical and architectural developments.

The book consists at its core of a gazetteer of all the main sites and monuments of historic interest. This is surrounded by aids to understanding the framework of Syria's past - the introductory chapters on the history of the region, the architectural influences to which

Syria has been exposed and a chronology. In addition there are explanations of the main architectural and foreign language terms employed, suggestions for further reading and an index.

A few words of explanation. I have attempted no new solution to the problems of transliterating from Arabic. I have instead adopted several basic rules, not all of which can be applied consistently:

- use the simplest commonly-accepted versions even when they are not necessarily the most accurate - hence Latakia, not Ladhiqiye. (I adopted the 1965 English edition of the Hachette World Guide 'Middle East' as a benchmark but there are a few variations where later more accurate versions have become accepted usage - eg Arwad, not Ruwad; Muhammed, not Mohamed.);
- keep to 'al-' as the Arabic definite article (rather than confuse the reader by trying to represent the pronunciation slide in, for example 'Deir ez-Zor') but use the article only where it is clearly common practice;
- as no single method reconciles the differing requirements of spoken and written Arabic in rendering the final -a (nisba or ta marbuta) I have followed the Blue Guide's practice in rendering it variously as -a, -eh, -e. The Blue Guide is also followed with regard to medial vowels;
- not to include the ''ain' except where illustrating Arabic pronunciation or in the now-common anglicism, 'Shi`ite''; and
- where monuments have passed into history under a non-Arabic name, leave it that way (Krak des Chevaliers in lieu of the modern Arabic Qalaat al-Hosn; Palmyra, not Tadmor).

For dates before the Persian or Greek periods I have usually taken as my guide the chronologies used by the most recent researchers, there being usually only minor discrepencies between the schema adopted for the Bronze Age sites involved.

The visitor to Syria should be aware that my maps and plans are somewhat stylized and represent my best endeavours to reduce the ever-evolving Syrian road pattern to some sort

---

[1] Introduction by Tate to Contribution française à l'archéologie syrienne 1969-1989 Damascus 1989 p IX

of comprehensible system. While I lived in Syria, one could return to a site after a few months and find that an entirely new road had appeared to eliminate some of the tortuous back roads or hiking across country. The motorway system has now stabilised the basic network but I cannot swear that several new local roads may not have sprung up since my surveying. Published maps have the same trouble in keeping up and distances are sometimes approximate. In virtually all cases, there is one rule in Syria - ask and keep on asking! No one minds helping a stranger and don't assume a non-local guide or driver are any more familiar with the back-blocks than you are.

Access to monuments in Syria which are not official museums is something of a lottery. I have not cluttered the gazetteer with notes on how and when access to particular buildings may be secured. The general rule is looked perplexed and someone will offer advice as to who might have the key. In the case of a private house of historic interest, politely indicate your intentions and if the family is not likely to be inconvenienced, they will often be happy to let you look around. Smaller mosques are closed between prayer times. Keys for churches can usually be hunted down from the priest living nearby or a local shopkeeper. Official monuments are much more predictable. Although their hours tend to be standardised (most monuments and sites maintained by the Antiquities Department are closed on a Tuesday), there are local variations regarding the choice of summer and winter hours, the afternoon break and Friday prayers. I have only listed below those cases where the museum hours are fairly fixed and unlikely to change significantly from year to year.

I have not exhaustively chronicled my sources through footnotes. The main works consulted for each site or walking tour are given in the REFS section at the end of each gazetteer entry and a list of further reading is given in the Bibliography section. No student of Syria's past can avoid giving tribute to the enormous achievement of the French *savants* who fanned out over Syria in the twenty years of the Mandate period and researched it in loving detail. The new crop of foreign researchers (the greatest effort is being made by the French, closely followed by the Germans but there are many others from as far afield as Australia) may question some of the *savants'* conclusions but no one could question their enthusiasm and rigourous devotion to the task.

The task of preparing this text from the Antipodes would have been impossible but for the access I enjoyed to the University of Sydney's Fisher Library, in particular the collection bestowed by the former Professor of Archaeology, Professor J R B Stewart.

Finally, if this labour has yielded anything, it has been an immense sense of satisfaction in understanding a little better the history of a region that has funnelled so many of the great forces which played themselves out (not yet to any conclusion, in many cases!) over the past five thousand years. I am grateful for the encouragement, advice and assistance of family, friends and numerous academic and research contacts in this task. But above all, I cannot over-estimate the stimulus that came from living in Syria, finding at every turn villagers and wayfarers who encouraged the visitor to go wherever he or she might choose.

Paris,
October 1991

Foreword to the new paperback edition

I have taken the opportunity of the preparation of a French edition of *Monuments* and of this smaller-format English edition to include a number of changes to the text and some updating of the bibliography. These reflect the enormous range of research and scholarship which continues on Syria both by Syrian researchers and by a range of foreign missions including the resident French and German schools.

At no stage could one be confident that a definitive picture of Syria's past has emerged. New fragments to the mosaic are always being found and if sometimes I have been too hasty in fashioning others' research into conclusions, that is an inevitable hazard of writing a book which tries to cram 3000 years of rich history into 300 pages. A full scale revision of the text might already warrant the inclusion of sites that have been newly explored and made more easily accesible by the development of the road network. However, a complete revision of the text, of the logistics of getting to each site and of the most up to date references will probably have to wait for a few years. Meanwhile I ask the reader to bear with the present survey and its imperfections.

Both the first edition of this work and the present updating would have been impossible without the support, advice and encouragement of many people. Some were named in the 'Acknowledgments' section of the first edition. It might be invidious now simply to reprint that list when others have subsequently given their advice or support. Let me therefore list those for whose assistance over the years I am deeply appreciative with the usual disclaimer absolving the scholars among them of any responsibility for the imperfections in my synthesis:

Khaled Alas'ad, Sarab Atassi, Afif Bahnassi, Janine Balty, Annie Caubet, Margaret Cazabon, Graeme Clarke, Jacqueline Dentzer-Feydy, Jean Pierre Dummar, David and Patricia Ellis, Jorge Ivan Espinal, Georges Jabbour, (the late) William Jobling, Chantal Jouffroy, Brigid Keenan, David Kennedy, Mahat Khouri, the Majloumian family, J.-Cl. Margueron, Fergus Millar, Roger Muller, Victoria Owen, Jennifer Rawson, (the late) Gabriel Sa'adé, Kassem Toueir, Tony Touma, Thilo Ulbert, Alan Warmsley.

Athens,
March 1999

Abbreviations, Ratings & Symbols

ABBREVIATIONS

Abd	Abbasid (750-968)
AH	after *Hijra* (Islamic calendar)
Alt	altitude (metres)
anc	ancient
Arb	Arabic; Arabic periods (includes Ayyubids (1176-1260), Mamelukes (1260-1516))
Ayy	Ayyubid (1176-1260)
b	born (year)
BA	Bronze Age
bib	biblical
Byz	Byzantine (395-636)
C	century (eg 12C = 12th century)
c	*circa* (about)
Cru	Crusader (1097-1292)
d	died (year)
EBA	Early Bronze Age (c3000 – 1900 BC)
Fr	French
Grk	Greek
ha	hectare
IrA	Iron Age (early first millennium BC)
Ism	Ismaeli (mid 12C-mid 13C)
Itn	Italian
km	kilometre(s)
Lat	Latin
LBA	Late Bronze Age (c1550-1200 BC)
m	metre(s)
m^2	square metre(s)
Mam	Mameluke (1260-1516)
MBA	Middle Bronze Age (c1900-550 BC)
Ott	Ottoman (1516 -1919)
Phn	Phoenician (early first millennium BC)
Refs	references (main sources used in compiling gazetteer entry)
r	ruled (dates)
Rom	Roman (64 BC-395 AD)
Sem	Semitic
Tur	Turkish
Umd	Umayyad (661-750)

RATINGS (<u>after</u> a place name)

***	essential
**	well worthwhile
*	worth a detour if time allows
-	limited or specialised interest
T	of interest for historical topography of site

SYMBOLS

*	<u>before</u> a place name indicates a separate gazetteer entry under that title
+	<u>before</u> a number indicates '.. km (or m) further on"
+	<u>after</u> a number means 'more than .. km (or m)"
?	<u>before</u> a name indicates a doubtful identification (eg place name variants);
??	indicates an unlikely identification

OTHER

- for the purpose of establishing alphabetical order in gazetteer entries, the definite article 'al-' before an Arabic place name is ignored
- Map or plan numbers distinguish between
  - *plans* of buildings or urban areas in Section 3 – Gazetteer (in italics) and
  - maps usually in Section 4 - Itineraries (non-italics)
- key to maps and plans is given on the end-paper map of Syria
- all dates are AD unless otherwise indicated
- abbreviations in Refs are listed under Bibliography

Attribution of the Photos

R.Burns   1a, 2b, 3a, 4a, 5a, 5b, 5c, 6a, 7a, 8a, 9b, 10a, 10b, 11a, 13a, 13b, 14a, 14b,
                 15b, 16a, 16b, 16c, 17a, 18a, 18b, 20a, 20b, 21a, 22a, 22b, 23a, 24b.

M.Roumi   1b, 4b, 6b, 11b, 19a, 19b.

J.P.Dummar   9a, 12b, 17b.

M.Balty   3b, 3c, 21b.

D.Jouffroy   12a, 24a.

R.Keseybeh   7c, 8b.

A.Dummar   15a.

I.Touma   2a.

1. SYRIA – HISTORICAL SKETCH

1- SYRIA   HISTORICAL SKETCH

PRELUDE

For a piece of land which has been fought over for millennia, Syria[2] hardly gives the impression of a lush prize. In shape, present-day Syria is a distorted quadrilateral, pushed out to the north east to take in a small portion of the Tigris River. The coastline is short (160 km), sandwiched between Turkey and Lebanon. Much of the land is barren or semi-arid with the central Syrian Desert (a rocky steppe, alt 700-1000 m) opening towards the great historical chasm of the Arabian Desert to the south. Along the edges of the Orontes and Euphrates valleys, there is some pasturage but much of the area near the coast that benefits from the winter Mediterranean rains is occupied by steep and rocky mountainsides (Jebel Ansariye), leaving little room for the coastal plain.

Yet Syria lies within the crescent that has seen most of the great breakthroughs in agricultural, economic and social life that propelled the key historical changes of the past six millennia. This Fertile Crescent extends from Iraq's irrigated lands in the east to the Nile Valley to the south, taking in its sweep the edges of the hill country in south eastern Turkey and the mountains that hug the Mediterranean coastline between Antioch and Jerusalem. At its heart lie the pastures, orchards and grainfields of Syria.

If today, exhausted as much as anything by the surfeits of history, this land looks at times bleak and unyielding, it occupies a strategic position of incomparable value. Syria bears the traces of many caravan routes, Roman roads, pilgrimage trails and superhighways that testify to its role as a corridor for east/west trade. Across its plains, the rich valley of the Tigris/Euphrates system was linked to the outer world that began at the Mediterranean. Across these steppes, as stability and secure trade developed, goods from as far away as China and India were exchanged. When the Persian conquests of the sixth century BC broke down the east/west barriers further, Alexander crossed Syria in his efforts to develop a new order based on an amalgam of Greek and Oriental. Through Roman and Byzantine times, Syria became the focal point in efforts to maintain a universal empire.

Possession of Syria was essential to any power that wished to control the arteries of history. The task was complicated in that Syria has little in the way of natural borders to ensure its security. To the east, the Euphrates is a highway into Mesopotamia that has never bothered potential aggressors. To the south east, the great Arabian desert has historically funnelled its excess energies in the direction of Syria, causing population changes that have marked several of its major historical eras. The northern plains have likewise been a magnet for the disaffected, marginalised by successive changes in Turkey. Much of the historical channelling of forces has focussed on the north west of Syria at the point where the natural corridor between Europe and Asia spills out onto the plains after negotiating the uplands and circuitous coast of Asia Minor. Here the Greeks and Romans placed their major urban centre, Antioch (now in the Hatay province of Turkey), Alexander defeated the massed armies of Darius and the Crusaders first realised what they had taken on in challenging Muslim supremacy.

But beyond the natural chokepoint in the north west, Syria is an open land without doors. It has learnt to survive on its wits - by trading and statecraft rather than closing itself off as a fortress land. It has been the classic buffer, though not in the sense of having little substantial coherence of its own and thus perpetually at the mercy of others. It has learnt to transmit rather than to block - to absorb the first ethnic waves from the steppes and desert to the south; to pass on the great themes and ideas that have moved between east and west; to provide a footing between the religious currents that have swept the region.

As this study is concerned with the buildings and monuments that remain in recognisable condition, we will pass over Syria's role in prehistory and its central part in the rise of the methods of agriculture, domestication of animals and development of urban life that first brought this area out of the obscurities of pre-urban civilisation.

---

[2] As if Syrian history weren't complicated enough, there is no general agreement even on the origin of the country's name. While Herodotus, in my view, came up with the best explanation (a corruption of 'Assyria' misleadingly applied only to the Western reaches of the Assyrian lands), this has not prevented modern commentators devising a variety of exotic explanations involving Egyptian, Hittite or local origins.

Early Bronze Age (c3100-2150 BC

When the earliest written records emerge in the **Early Bronze Age** (third millennium BC), Syria shared in the development of city states that arose in the **Sumerian** lands to the east, along the Tigris/Euphrates system in Mesopotamia. Though of different (Semitic) origins to the Sumerians, the population of the mid-Euphrates city, *****Mari**, based its social structures on analogous systems. Literacy, through the development of a system of cuneiform writing (wedge-shaped markings in soft clay), stimulated complex legal and trading practices, the local monarchs' power depending on the effectiveness of their control of irrigation and trade. The end of Mari's early phase coincided with the rise of the first truly imperial power in the region, the **Akkadian Empire** (2340-2150) under the leadership of Sargon whose conquests reached from Mesopotamia both towards the Persian Gulf and the Mediterranean coast were consolidated by his grandson, Naram-Sin.

To the west, Mari enjoyed close relations with another trading centre of major importance, *Ebla. It had a Semitic population and by 2400 BC had created a complex web of political links across much of northern Syria though it lacked the basic underpinning that irrigation control gave to other city-states. Under the subsequent rule of the Dynasty of **Ur**, Mari retained a degree of importance under the Shakkanaku dynasty while Ebla became a subsidiary state.

Middle Bronze Age (c2150-1600 BC)

By 2100, the early experiments in urban societies were disturbed by new population movements that brought **Amorite** people (of Semitic stock) from the Syrian desert into the settled lands of the Fertile Crescent. This period of urban decay and disruption initially brought an end to much of the pattern of regional trade on which Ebla had thrived and the city fell into decline. After the initial disruption of the Amorites' invasion, many towns absorbed the new population and the development of urban civilisation resumed. The Kingdom of Yamkhad (Aleppo) became a major power in this period, absorbing Ebla into its orbit. Mari enjoyed some independence 19th-18th century BC as an Amorite city. The **Babylonian** leader to the south, Hammurabi (another Semitic ruler, c1792-50) ruled with reformist zeal at home (he promulgated a codified system of law in his name) but this did not distract him from developing an appetite for conquests which caused him to raze Mari around 1759 BC thus terminating the precarious balancing act that the

ruler of Mari, Zimri-Lim (r 1775-60), had maintained between Babylon and Aleppo.

For much of northern Syria, this new golden age brought a flowering of international trade (19th-18th centuries BC). The **Amorite kingdoms** of the north managed to resist direct Babylonian rule but traded extensively to the east - Yamkhad, Alalakh (Tell Achana in the Amuq Plain east of Antioch), Zalmaqum (Harran) and Qatna (the modern Mishrifeh north of Homs).

Late Bronze Age (c1600-1200 BC)

The next major change to the regional power game came from the north west. The Hittites (Indo-Europeans by origin) had installed themselves in central Anatolia and brought an end to Babylonian power c1595. To the south, Egypt was thrown into chaos for two or more centuries by the secondary effects of this movement. The Hyksos, a people whose roots are still unexplained but who may have been related to the Amorites or the Canaanite inhabitants of the coastal mountains of Syria/Palestine, were pushed south by Indo-European pressure.

A non-Semitic people (with Indo-European connections) called the Hurrians had been moving into Syria in large numbers from the north. A second analogous wave, the Mitanni people, soon arrived to blend with the Hurrians to form a federation of Hurrian principalities, the Kingdom of Mitanni (16th to 14th centuries BC), centred on the present North East Province around the Khabur River with links to the 'land of Amurru' to the east. Their region (including the vassal kingdoms of Yamkhad and Alalakh) pressed against the area of Hittite dominance in the north west. They installed themselves firmly enough to form part of the triangle of powers that fought for dominance in Syria in the 15th-14th centuries BC - Egypt, Hittites and Mitanni - until they were made a client state of the Hittites after a series of marriage alliances in the late 14th century .

Egypt had sought tentatively since the Middle Kingdom (20th-18th centuries) to extend its influence in Syria especially to cultivate the coastal cities for the access they gave to important inland sources of timber for shipbuilding. After the disruption of the Hyksos period, the Pharaohs returned under the more grandiose pretensions of the New Kingdom in the great campaigns of Thutmose III (early 15th century), Amenhotep II (mid 15th century), Thutmose IV (late 15th century), Seti I and Ramses II (early to mid 13th century). By the 14th century, their main foe in Syria was the

Hittite Empire which had come to dominate the local city states (Damascus was taken c1360) who did their best, however, to play the powers off against each other. The chaos of the Amarna period in Egypt helped their purpose. In the end, even the vainglorious Ramses II met his match when ambushed by the Hittite cavalry under Hattusilis II at Qadesh (*Tell Nebi Mend) c1286.

At about this time to the south, the tribe of the Israelites was moving into Palestine from the east with consequences still to be resolved 3000 years later.

The Mediterranean coast as a whole enjoyed a more prosperous and untroubled life based on the sea trade routes built up by the Phoenicians - peoples of Semitic origin who had moved into the region at the beginning of the second millennium and had established a culture that blended Mesopotamian, Anatolian, Aegean and Egyptian influences. In this zone of relative prosperity, the port cities of Ugarit, Gabala (*Jeble) and Arwad were left to get on with the business of making money. Some especially privileged enclaves like **Ugarit**, which benefited from the copper trade with nearby Cyprus, had succeeded in working for both Egypt and the Hittites against each other or a third party. Their trading contacts brought wider connections including with Mycenae (after 1500) and the Aegean. The tradition was continued in the next millennium by their Canaanite descendants to the south, the Phoenicians, whose 50 plus colonies around the Mediterranean served to spread the alphabet in the Semitic and Greek worlds.

Iron Age (1200-539 BC)

Syria's ethnic and political chess board, however, was again scattered by the arrival of the Sea Peoples around 1200. Moving in from the west, possibly from the Aegean, the Sea Peoples' invasion brought an end to the apogée of Ugarit as well as to the Hittite Empire; they were only stopped at the edge of the Nile Valley by the land and sea campaigns of Ramses III (r 1198-66).

In the confusion left by the Sea Peoples' passing, further Semitic population movement arrived from the south in the form of the Arameans,[3] a Bedouin people who concentrated particularly in the north where around twenty so-called 'Neo-Hittite' principalities had arisen - Halab (*Aleppo), Arpad (30 km north of Aleppo), Tell Barsip, *Tell Halaf, Hattina and *Hamath (Hama). Except for some continuity in dress and

language, there was, in fact, no link between the Hittite Empire and the principalities whose original leadership was probably Luwian-speaking (from southern Asia Minor). The arrival of the Arameans from the desert further scrambled the mix. The art of northern Syria post 900 reflects this diversity of origins in a clumsy attempt to rival the monumentality of their Assyrian adversaries to the east. In the south, the city-state of Aram-Damascus led a coalition of forces that checked the ambitions of the kingdoms of Israel and Judeah. On the coast, the Phoenician cities survived the dark age that followed the Sea Peoples' invasions and continued to serve as a conduit for products and ideas between Greece, Egypt and the Asian mainland.

The fragmented Aramean states, however, were unable to maintain their autonomy in the face of new and vigorous forces from the east. The **Assyrian** Empire (1000-612) under Shalmaneser took permanent control of parts of northern Syria and Phoenicia from 856 and was confronted by a coalition of Aramean states at the Battle of Qarqar in 853. Under Tiglath-Pilaser (r 744-27 BC), the Assyrians pushed even more firmly into Syria, ending Damascus' independence in 732. But it required further action by Sargon II (r 721-705), after renewed unrest in Syria and Palestine, to confirm the submission of Damascus.

The Assyrians imposed a skeletal administration in their western lands, being largely content to exploit them for opportunistic booty and slave labour. The spoils and tribute from their raids adorned the palaces of Nineveh and Khorsabad which so fascinated 19th century archaeologists. Even centres such as *Arwad and Sidon (Southern Lebanon) could not escape the vehemence of the late Assyrians' ambitions though Sidon resisted even when Assurbanipal came down on it 'like a wolf on the fold' in 668. Eventually it fell, not to the Assyrians, but in 587 to Nebuchadnezzar, one of the first of the **Chaldean** rulers whose short-lived dominance in Syria (605-539) followed their defeat of the Assyrians (they took Nineveh in 612) after a long period of rivalry in their common home territory in Northern Mesopotamia. This was the era of the legendary Babylon, the Chaldean capital, with its palaces and hanging gardens.

Persian Period (539-333 BC)

The **Achaemenid Persians** annexed much of Syria as a consequence of their move westwards and their defeat of the Neo-Babylonians with the capture of Babylon by Cyrus in 539. Syria was made their fifth satrapy or province (Abar Nahara

---

[3] The word Aramean is coined from the geographical description for Syria in Aramaic, 'Aram Naharain' or 'land of the rivers'.

- 'beyond the river') with its capital possibly at Damascus. They recognised the pervasive spread of the Aramean language and its neo-Phoenician script by adopting it as the *lingua franca* of their empire, ensuring its survival well into the Roman period. The Persians brought a regular and comparatively benevolent system of administration to their 23 provinces but above all the integration of the Syrian coast into the network of exchanges across the east Mediterranean to Greece heralded the first of the great east/west clashes that have focussed on Syria. In their efforts to find a sphere of influence in the eastern Mediterranean, countered so arduously by the Greeks (eg the Battle of Marathon in 490), they focused in Syria much of the struggle for supremacy throughout the sixth and fifth centuries BC, bringing a uniquely Persian element to the land, of which only a few traces remain (*Amrit).

Hellenistic Period (333-64 BC) (Thematic Map - 76)

This Greek-Persian contest was decided in the great battles (the first at Issus in 333) in which Alexander the Great defeated the forces of Darius III. Issus lies just to the north of the pass in the Amanus Mountains (south eastern Turkey) called the Syrian Gates. After Alexander's death at Babylon in 323, it took some time to settle the apportioning of his lands between the generals. Syria was contested, with northern Syria falling to Seleucos II Nicator (who had already been assigned Mesopotamia) after his victory over Antigonus at the Battle of Ipsus (Phrygia) in 301. The south (including Damascus) and the regions of Lebanon and Palestine were seized by Ptolemy I Soter who had already been given command of Egypt. The **Seleucid Kingdom** began on an ordered and rational basis but never succeeded in welding Syria into a secure base for the Macedonian dynasty. Applying the principles of government and administration found elsewhere in Alexander's domains, new satrapal headquarters were established - Antioch, Seleucia (now Suweida at the mouth of the Orontes in Turkey), *Apamea, and Laodicea (*Latakia) were the major centres. Subsidiary centres settled included *Cyrrhus, Chalcis ad Belum (*Qinnesrin), Beroia (*Aleppo), Arados (*Arwad), Hierapolis (*Membij), and *Dura Europos, the latter to defend the connection between the two main Seleucid domains, Syria and Mesopotamia.

While the Greek soldier/settler element was probably no more than 50,000, the Hellenization of the region was firmly set in process. Many of the city states, however, preserved a high degree of independence and, though they shed their local dynasties to become republics loosely affiliated to the Seleucid Kingdom, retained an increasing degree of freedom of manoeuvre as the Seleucid hold on Syria weakened in the second century. The Ptolemies lost control of southern Syria by 198 BC when it fell to the Seleucid King, Antiochos III Megas (the Great) (r 223-187 BC). This marked the beginning of a temporary resurgence of the Seleucid dynasty which resulted in the Romans (recent masters of Greece) checking Antiochos' forces at Magnesia, obliging him under the terms of the Treaty of Apamea (188 BC) to cede all his conquests across the Taurus. A successor, Antiochos IV Epiphanes (r 175-164 BC) was forced to withdraw from Egypt, again following Roman intervention (168 BC). Attempts to force a policy of Hellenization on the Jews (including the profanation of the Jerusalem temple by setting up of an altar to Zeus - the 'abomination' referred to in Daniel 9,7) brought a fierce resistance, including the Maccabees' role in fostering the post-166 BC resurgence of a Jewish state in Palestine. By the beginning of the first century BC, Seleucid Syria was fraying badly at the edges with inroads by the Armenians to the north, the Parthians to the east and the Arab Nabateans to the south.

Roman Syria (64 BC-395 AD) (Thematic Map - 77)

The **Romans**, who since their conquest of Greece had shown interest in the fate of Syria, became increasingly involved. In 64 BC, the Roman legate, Pompey, formally abolished the Seleucid Kingdom and created the Roman province of Syria with its principal city (*metropolis*) at Antioch. For a time, Syria became part of the setting for the great leadership struggle that brought an end to the Roman Republic. The main centres played with relish the game of switching allegiance between Augustus Caesar and Mark Antony as fortunes changed. The Augustan peace and the era of consolidation and prosperity that followed advantaged Syria which became one of the principal provinces of the Empire, remaining under the Emperor's jurisdiction, locally represented by a legate of consular rank. Antioch particularly flourished to become the third imperial city after Rome and Alexandria but other centres such as Damascus, Beroia, and the trading hub of Palmyra, also benefited greatly. Under Augustus, four legions came to be stationed in Syria, the level of threat being considerably less, for example, than Germany which garrisoned eight.

ROMAN PROVINCIAL DIVISIONS

The following summarises the administrative divisions under which the broader region of Syria was ruled in Roman and Byzantine times. The original province of Syria did not include a number of principalities or city-states which the Romans allowed to continue within its provincial bounds, including the cities of the Decapolis (Canatha(*Qanawat) and Damascus within present-day Syria) and Emesa. These were gradually absorbed under direct rule from Augustus' principate until Trajan's incorporation of the Nabatean kingdom in 106.

DATE	EMPEROR	PROVINCES	CAPITALS	
64 BC	[Republic]	Syria	Antioch	
AD 69	Vespasian	Syria	Antioch	
			Judaea* Caesaria	
106	Trajan	Syria	Antioch	
		Judaea[1]	Aeolia Capitolina	
		Arabia*	Bostra	
194	Septimius Severus	Coele Syria*	Laodicea 194-202	(later Antioch)
		Syria Phoenice*[2]	Tyre	
		Arabia	Bostra	
		Syria Palaestina	Aeolia　　Capitolina	
		Mesopotamia	Nisibis	
295	Diocletian	Arabia	Petra	
		Augusta Libanensis*	Bostra	
		Syria Palaestina	Caesarea (after 365)	
		Phoenice	Tyre	
		Syria Coele	Antioch	
		Augusta Euphratensis*	Cyrrhus	
		Osrhoene	Edessa	
		Mesopotamia	Nisibis	
c395	Arcadius	Syria Prima	Antioch	
		Syria Secunda[3]	Apamea	
		Phoenice Maritima	Tyre	
		Phoenice Libanensis[4]	Damascus/Emesa?	
		Palaestina	(three provinces)	
		Arabia	Bostra	
		Mesopotamia		
		Euphratensis	Cyrrhus	
		Osrhoene	Edessa	

In many cases, provinces cover only limited parts of present-day Syria.

NOTES: (1) Renamed *Syria Palaestina* in 135 when Jerusalem (*Aeolia Capitolina*) became the capital; (2) Included the main towns of southern Syria – Damascus, Emesa, Palmyra; (3) Justinian (mid sixth century) created a third Syrian province (*Theodorias* in honour of his wife) out of the coastal area around Laodicea; (4) Chief towns were Damascus, Emesa, Heliopolis (Baalbek) and Palmyra.

Roman administration in Syria gradually took more direct control with previously semi-independent city-states such as Arados, Emesa (*Homs), and members of the loose confederation called the Decapolis (eg Abila, Damascus and Canatha (*Qanawat)) quietly brought under direct rule by the early first century AD. The process was more slow-moving in Palestine where the collaborative Hasmoneans had been permitted by the Senate to carve out their own kingdom under Roman protection, partly at the expense of the Nabateans in southern Syria. (The Nabateans were also dislodged from Damascus and retreated to semi-independent status in the fastness of Petra (in southern Jordan), fitfully retaining control as far north as Bosra.) The Hasmoneans were succeeded by the sometimes more rowdy line of Herod the Great (r 39-4 BC) but the Romans took the opportunity of the death of Herod's heirs, Agrippa II in 92/3, to integrate Palestine into the province of Syria.

Economically, Syria flourished and became not only an entrepot zone of central importance in the east/west trade in luxuries (from China, India and Trans-Oxiana) but a major agricultural area whose grain and wine supplied a good share of the Roman market. To service this commerce, trade routes were systematised through the building of roads, including the north/south *Via Maris* and *Via Nova Traiana* and the east/west route through Palmyra that saved considerable time and effort over the northern route following the Euphrates. Settlement and agricultural activities were pushed out into new

such as Apamea, Palmyra, Laodicea-ad-Mare (Latakia), Canatha (*Qanawat) and Bostra (*Bosra) were given similar treatment. The latter two were re-planned after Trajan's more aggressive policy of direct control resulted in the annexation of the Hauran in 106 and the creation of the province of Arabia (in the area south of Damascus and west of Palestine). Rome regarded Syria as a prized province and the position of legate was a valued appointment. Visits by several Emperors brought particular privileges to cities such as Bostra (capital of the new province of Arabia), Damascus (raised to

ROMAN SYRIA - ROUTES AND LIMES

Roman control of Syria was based on a highly developed system of roads and frontier forts which reflected both defensive and commercial needs. After the mid second century, the main axes were thoroughly re-planned. North/south communication along the traditional *Via Maris* following the coasts of Syria and Phoenicia was supplemented by the new north/south routes - the *Strata Diocletiana* which ran from Sura on the Euphrates to Damascus via Resafe, Palmyra and Dumeir and the *Via Nova Traiana* which continued the axis southwards via Bosra to Aila (modern Aqaba, Jordan's port). East/west routes either crossed the desert on partly-improved carriageways (provisioned with milestones and watering points) or skirted it along the fertile lands to the north (eg the route via Cyrrhus and Zeugma and on to present North East Syria; or further south via Chalcis ad Belum (Qinnesrin)). Within the bounds (*limes*) of the closely administered province, roads were now constructed to a high standard of durability (*Roman Road, Bab al-Hawa) better able to negotiate difficult and circuitous terrain (*Roman Road, Wadi Barada). Most roads, however, were of loosely compacted stones with a surface of gravel, on an average 6 m wide and slightly sloping from the centre. In steppe areas, a border of stones sufficed to mark a carriageway cleared of protrusions.

While the initial deployment of four Roman legions reflected as much internal security as frontier defence[1], by the end of second century AD, the military deployments and creation of a fixed line of forts reflected the shift of priority to the east. The system of forts was generally aligned along the eastern frontier zone with a particular concentration in the north east to meet the Parthian (later Sasanian) threat. The thick clustering of forts and sub-forts in the Euphrates/Tigris zone was intensified by the fourth to sixth centuries though most of the remains of this activity are identifiable only by aerial photography. By the Byzantine period, the major building effort shifted further to the west and sites such as Resafe or Halebiye were re-constructed under Justinian's great defensive works program.

Roman forces in Syria rose to a total of six or seven legions (30-40,000 troops?) by the end of the second century supplemented by provincial auxiliaries, many of them locally recruited.

(1) The legions and their probable bases were as follows: *VI Ferrata*, Latakia; *X Fretensis*, Cyrrhus; *XII Fulminata*, Raphanea; *III Gallica*, Zeugma. See Sartre *Orient* p 72.

areas such as the rocky hill country between Antioch and Beroia (*Dead Cities), the marginal zone south of Beroia or the region south of Damascus known as Auranitis (box on Hauran under *Suweida page 228). The cities were upgraded to reflect this prosperity and the energy of the urban upper classes who underpinned it (largely Greek-speaking, though of varied origins). Thus Damascus, already replanned by the prosaic Greek military, was given a more monumental appearance through the provision of a widened and arcaded axial thoroughfare (later to be immortalised in the New Testament as Straight Street) and a vastly enhanced sacred precinct for the Temple of Jupiter/Hadad (*Damascus - Umayyad Mosque). Other cities

metropolis by Hadrian, 117) and Palmyra (renamed *Palmyra Hadriana* in 129).

The second century AD was an era of unparalleled stability with Syria particularly favoured by contrast with the troubles that still beset the Romans in the Province of Judaea to the south where, after the first Jewish/Roman war of 66-70, a second revolt under Bar Cochba in 132 brought an even more vehement Roman campaign to efface the insurrection and scatter the Jewish population. Syria's eastern borders took on an increasingly strategic significance to the Romans in the face of the perceived threat from the Parthians whose presence across the Euphrates had resulted in successive Roman attempts to dominate the Parthian heartland since the late first century BC. As the Parthians hit back into Roman territory, the campaigns in the east became more vigorous and draining, requiring imperial command from the early second century. The military presence in the region grew and with it the influence of Syrians in Rome itself became more direct not the least through links formed by Roman commanders on station in Syria, such as the future Emperor, Septimius Severus. His marriage in 187 to Julia Domna, the daughter of the High Priest of Emesa (Homs), brought a line of 'Syrian' emperors which reached its nadir in 218-22 in the alarming eccentricities of Elagabalus.

By the late second century, the Parthian wars were a dominant pre-occupation with Parthia the only organised power able to conduct a centralised campaign against the Empire's might anywhere along its frontiers. The challenge began to affect the prosperity even of such a flourishing centre as Palmyra which had successfully lived off its ability to act as a go-between in trade across hostile frontiers. The permanent military presence was pushed out as far as the Khabur River by the mid second century. Palmyra came under direct Roman rule (*colonia* from 212) and the sleepy local garrison at remote *Dura Europos on the mid-Euphrates was reinforced with imperial forces.

The sporadic confrontation with Parthia became more persistent by the end of the second century and turned into a more aggressive and focussed Sasanian threat following the takeover of Persia after 224 by Ardashir and particularly under his successor, Shapur I. Successive Emperors over four centuries were to pit themselves against the Sasanian determination directly to challenge Rome's presence. By the mid third century, the situation on the east frontiers of Syria was parlous, the low points being the fall of Dura Europos in 256 and the capture in 260 of the Emperor Valerian in person by Sasanian forces at Edessa (south eastern Turkey), in spite of the presence of a Roman force of 70,000.

The humiliation of Valerian's capture, his torture and subsequent death were telling blows to Roman pride but symbolic of the general loss of authority at many points on the imperial *limes* by the mid third century. The Sasanians had already challenged Rome as far west as Antioch and the Romans were happy to exploit any assistance they could get to hold the situation. They thus eagerly backed the ambitions of a Palmyrene prince, Odenathus, who campaigned on Rome's behalf deep into Sasanian territory (Ctesiphon 262) but who was unfortunately

murdered in 266. His wife, Zenobia, carried on but had a rather different view of the relative power of Rome and Palmyra. She sent forces to Egypt and tried to engineer the takeover of Antioch in 271. The Emperor Aurelian clearly felt the challenge to central authority had gone too far and took to the field to check Zenobia. She fled Antioch, her forces failing to put up any challenge to Aurelian's outside Emesa in 272. Back in Palmyra, she again decided confrontation was best avoided and slipped out of the besieged city towards the Euphrates. Captured by the Romans in her attempt to cross the river, she was led off to Rome to grace Aurelian's triumph; Palmyra, after a second revolt against its occupying forces, was razed.

Syria's agricultural base was not fundamentally undermined by the repercussions of these events to the east and the building programs of the third century in much of Syria reflected the continued prosperity of the region, now divided further with the creation of the new province of Coele Syria after 194.

Christianity

By the time the Emperor Constantine gave official recognition to **Christianity** after 313, increasingly encouraging it as the state religion, Syria (and particularly Antioch) was already an area of intense Christian activity going back as far as the missions of St Paul in the mid first century. Christianity with its blending of Jewish and Greek influences, was at first one more element, albeit a powerful one, in the Syrian melting pot. Before the Christianity became part of public life in the fourth century, churches (as in the house-church unearthed at Dura Europos) were merely adapted dwelling places. After the official recognition of Christianity, they took on the form and scale of Roman public buildings. The pilgrimage phenomenon sponsored by Constantine's mother, St Helen, with her visit to the holy sites of Jerusalem in 324 later proliferated in Syria, complemented by the arrival of the monastic tradition (from Egypt) and the veneration of places associated with ascetic and saintly figures. By the fifth/sixth century, Syria was dotted with countless village, monastic churches and major pilgrimage centres such as those honouring the ascetic, Saint Simeon Stylites or Saint Sergius in northern Syria.

But the diverse ingredients in the Syrian church were never totally at rest with each other. The philosophical debate over subjects as arcane as the division between Christ's physical and divine natures became overriding pre-occupations that divided eastern and western strands within the Church (Monophysites-

Oriental versus Orthodox-Western), often seemingly becoming codeword debates with deep political and social undercurrents.

Byzantine Era (395-636)

The adoption of Byzantium as the second capital of the Empire under Constantine (later renamed Constantinople) foreshadowed the final transfer of the Roman capital to the East in 395, the start of the Byzantine era. Under Theodosius II (r 408-50), a '100 year peace' with the Sasanians brought some respite from the debilitating eastern wars but they became a major distraction again by the mid sixth century, absorbing much of the resources of **Justinian's** reign (r 527-65).

In spite of the troubles on the frontiers and the deep divisions that rent the Church (the Arian heresy in the fourth century; Nestorianism in the fifth century; and the dogged controversy over Monophysitism that continued from the fifth to the seventh century), it was a time of continued prosperity in the more settled parts of Syria. The area of limestone country west of Aleppo (the Romans gave it the name Belus) continued to prosper, based on its olive oil exports; the Hauran was intensely exploited; the cities remained thriving. Church and monastic projects abounded and Syrian builders developed a repertoire of styles (see Churches under 2. Architectural Styles on page 22) that adapted metropolitan and neo-classical models and blended them with elements from the east, often achieving a rather bizarre local mix whose remains are richly evident. In fact, no area of the Mediterranean world contains such a wealth of evidence of this period as can be found in the many churches, village and monastic remains of Syria.

For all its efforts to marry the eastern and western elements in Syrian society, continuing the process which had begun even before Alexander, Byzantine rule by the sixth century had begun to run out of solutions. The controversy over Monophysitism had become a corrosive element provoking intense local resentment against the imposition of orthodoxy from Constantinople. The Sasanian Persians made increasing inroads into Syria, their destructive raids punctuated by a devastating series of earthquakes. In spite of the efforts of Justinian and later Emperors to stabilise the Eastern frontiers, by the early seventh century, Syria was virtually incapable of putting up serious resistance to the prolonged occupation by Chosroes II who brought his presence in Antioch to a climax with the slaughter of 90,000 of its inhabitants. The Byzantines had tried diplomacy

under Maurice (r 582-602) but were subsequently divided by their leadership struggles. By the time they rallied themselves to recover Syria (626), the country was so perpetually wearied by war, famines, earthquakes and plagues that it seemed virtually indifferent to its fate. After centuries of warfare, the Roman and Persian worlds had fought each other to a standstill.

Arab Conquest (632-61)

Into this near-vacuum came the armies of early Islam. After the death of the Prophet Muhammed in 632, his successor in the leadership of the faithful (the Caliphate), Abu Bakr, encouraged his forces to take further steps beyond the tentative moves begun by Muhammed himself to find new outlets to the north for the military, religious and commercial energies of the new Arab leadership. Few Syrian centres put up much resistance. Damascus surrendered twice, the second time in 636 after the crucial defeat of the Byzantine forces at Yarmuk. The small element of new population that the desert Arabs initially introduced - gradually blended with the existing Semitic-based people, the distinctions further blurred by the unhurried process of conversions to the new faith of Islam. In contrast to the often heavy-handed imposition of Byzantine orthodoxy, Islam's introduction depended more on tax incentives than active coercion and thus aroused little active resentment from the local (and for many centuries, still basically Christian) population.

For almost two decades, the new leadership remained based in Medina and Southern Iraq. After Abu Bakr, the Caliphate passed to Umar (Caliph 634-44), Othman (Caliph 644-56) and then Ali (Caliph 656-61), the four comprising the group of *Rashidun* or 'right-guided' Caliphs. Ali's leadership, however, was challenged by Moawiya, the leader of the Umayyad faction who believed Ali had not sufficiently dissociated himself from the murderers of Othman. Ali was murdered by a disaffected former supporter. Of Ali's two sons, Hassan and Hussein, Hassan did not press his claim to the succession. Moawiya had already taken the Caliphate and promptly decided to move the capital to Damascus (where he had built up his power base as Governor).

Umayyads (661-750)

The Umayyad Caliphate brought in what is perhaps one of the most fertile and inventive periods of Syrian history. The perpetual search for an east/west balance was given a new and vigorous interpretation in an eclectic blending of Byzantine, Persian, Mesopotamian and local elements. This inter-action resulting from the collapse of the antique world and the rise of Islam is still not fully explored or explained but the snapshot we are provided in the remains of the period attest to the complexity of forces at play in Umayyad Syria. The establishment of the supremacy of Arabic and the centrality of Islam within the Empire was done with a skilful hand. It was a period of great intellectual curiosity which flourished in an atmosphere of *laissez-faire* under Moawiya's judicious and moderate political leadership. The warrior-aristocracy of the Umayyads readily absorbed ideas from Syria's rich mixture of cultures and aspired to be the successors of the Romans and Byzantium. Damascus became a major centre (the Umayyads' realms eventually stretched from the Indus to Spain), a focus of political, religious and artistic creativity that gave the city a dynamism it had rarely enjoyed.

Gradually, however, the Umayyads' focus turned away from the larger Mediterranean world. Not only did they find few interlocutors interested in dealing with the new power (western Europe had not even begun to emerge from barbarian night; Byzantium was still struggling to hold itself together in its remaining lands) but it had to meet to the east a new trend towards a much harder-edged form of islamicisation. The germ was sown as early as Moawiya's reign (661-80). His assumption of power had exacerbated the split between the Umayyad clan and the followers of Ali, led by Ali's remaining son, Hussein, on the death of Hassan in 669. Moawiya was succeeded by his son, Yazid (r 680-3). Pro-Yazid forces drew the small band of Hussein and his followers into battle at Kerbala (southern Iraq) on 10 Muharram 61 AH (680), slaughtering Hussein and all but a few of his companions. Among those taken into captivity in Damascus was **Zainab**, sister of Hussein. The tragedy of Kerbala was to rankle for centuries. Eventually it would perpetuate the division between orthodox followers of the Umayyad Caliphate (later to be called Sunnis) and the unrequited supporters of the house of Ali (Shi'ites); it gradually deflected the focus of the Umayyad world towards the challenges to its cosmopolitanism that were germinating to the east.

At first, however, the opposition to their caliphate having been driven underground, the Umayyads embarked on the most confident period of their administration. This was marked by major building projects at home and expansion abroad, especially under Abd al-Malik (r 685-705) and al-Walid (r 705-15). The latter was responsible for the immense project of the new congregational mosque in Damascus (*Damascus - Umayyad Mosque) which 1200 years later still bears striking witness to the richness and variety of the Umayyads' inspiration.

After the defeat of the Umayyad attempts to dislodge the Byzantines from Asia Minor, the Empire turned increasingly away from attempts to seek a place in the hostile or indifferent Mediterranean world to address the challenges from the east. Hisham (r 724-43) was the last of the great Umayyad rulers. After him the dynasty declined, exhausted by Shi'ite disaffection and the military incursions from Central Asia, Byzantium, and in North Africa. The line petered out in a succession of debauched or incompetent Caliphs, palace tensions and rebellions in the provinces of Persia and Iraq. A pretender, Abu al-Abbas, emerged in Iraq and marched on Damascus in 750. The Umayyads were eliminated, one grandson of Hisham fleeing to Spain where the Umayyad line survived for a further 500 years.

The new dynasty, the Abbasids, represented the eastern (Persian) tradition and a more theocratic version of the Caliphate, consciously spurning the attempts of the early Umayyads to marry eastern and western influences. The Abbasids transferred the Caliphate to Iraq (Kufa, until the founding of Baghdad in 762) and Syria became merely a neglected backwater, punished for its adherence to the corrupt and lax line of the Umayyads.

Abbasids (750-968)

The **Abbasids** never matched the vigour or the territorial spread of Umayyad power. The promise held out in the plan of Caliph Mansur for a new capital on the Tigris banks at Baghdad (built on a bold circular plan) was never carried through by his successors. Only Harun al-Rashid (Abbasid Caliph 786-809) had the flair to give the Caliphate wider status. He attracted an embassy from Charlemagne, the latter gaining from his gesture the right to protect Christian pilgrims to Jerusalem.

But the Abbasids failed to give sustained momentum to the development of a unified Islamic polity. Within two centuries, the heartland was increasingly invaded by Turkish nomads who displaced the Arab-Persian political elites. Regimes based on alien leadership now became the rule that marked virtually every era until modern times. The Turkish and other successive infiltrations prevented efforts to restore a Mid-East wide empire (a situation which was only securely reversed with the rise of the Mameluke system in the 12th and 13th centuries). The process began in the mid ninth century with the Abbasid domains fragmenting through independent dynasties assuming power in provinces such as Egypt (Tulunids after 868; Fatimids after 905) and Persia (Sasanids after 874). The Caliphs themselves became hostage in Baghdad to foreign 'protectors' such as the Seljuq Turks from 1037.

Syria, once again, was contested from many directions. In this period of unparalleled confusion, the struggle for political dominance was matched by a resurgence of the Shi`ite/Sunni tensions as various factions fought to impose their views on an increasingly Islamicised population. Heterodox sects of all persuasions sprang up in this no-man's-land of empires with Shi`ism (and its Ismaeli variant) the dominant trend even in the cities (especially Aleppo). Rebellions and disaffection abounded and many sects simply retreated to the mountainous and desert areas, there preserving a separate identity which is evident today in the country's ethnic and religious complexity. (It was at this time that the Maronite sect took refuge in the mountains of Lebanon, illustrating that diversity and fragmentation were not the sole prerogative of Muslims).

Syria's political history during this period can only be traced at the local level, separate lines of political succession being established in northern and southern Syria, depending on their degree of exposure to events in Egypt, Iraq (especially Mosul, the seat of Seljuq power), Byzantium and Turkey. Aleppo was controlled by the Hamdanid dynasty (944-1003) whose impetuous adventurism only served to make Aleppo a virtual protectorate of the Byzantines and later of the Fatimids. The Bedouin Mirdasid family then nominally ruled the city (1023-79) in a balancing act that recognised Fatimid suzerainty without provoking Byzantine intervention. The **Seljuq Turks** who had extorted from the putative Abbasid Caliph a mandate to govern northern Syria effectively took over under Alp Arslan as Sultan (1070-2). The Byzantines had been seeking to profit from this instability by intermittently seizing parts of Northern Syria under Emperors Nicephorus II Phocas (r 963-9) and John I Tzimisces (r 969-76) but their campaign had petered out with the signing of a treaty in 997 accepting Fatimid supremacy in Syria.

Damascus, like Aleppo, experienced in the ninth to 11th centures a time of anarchy, with a period of rule in the ninth century by the Cairo-based **Ikhshidid** dynasty. After 961, the **Fatimids**, a Shi`ite dynasty, supplanted them in Cairo. Though the Ikhshidids paid nominal allegiance to the Abbasid Caliphs in Baghdad, the Fatimids set up a rival Caliphate. The significance of this Baghdad/Cairo polarisation was to make Syria a battleground for inter-Muslim tensions, a situation which prevailed until tne centre of power was effective in uniting the Middle East.

The continued rise of the Seljuqs (nominally subservient to the Baghdad Caliphate) now brought the struggle for Syria to a new phase. The supremacy of the Seljuq Turks was sealed at the Battle of Manzikert (in Eastern Turkey) in 1071 which saw their victory over the Byzantine forces of Romanus IV Diogenes who was taken prisoner. They went on to take most of Syria, including Damascus in 1075 and by 1078 were in Jerusalem. By the late 11th century, under Alp Arslan and Malik Shah I (Sultan 1072-92), the Seljuqs were sufficiently strong in Syria to block the Fatimid dynasty's efforts to maintain control of Southern Syria, though Damascus oscillated between the two centres for some time. The Seljuq supremacy began to ring alarm bells in Europe, particularly given the apparent weakness of the Byzantines, and was in large part the stimulus that led to the 12th-13th century crusading movement which called for the recovery of the Holy Places by Christian arms.

The Crusades (Thematic Map - 79)

After centuries of comparative isolation, the **Crusades** brought to Syria another of the great clashes of worlds which have marked its history. After Pope Urban II (1088-99) made his stirring appeal to arms at the Council of Clermont-Ferrand (1095) in 1095, the Christian army that poured into Syria in 1097 found that the Seljuq leadership had disintegrated and that the land lacked any unified command for resistance. Not that the Christian armies were much more united, rent by serious problems of leadership and disputes over tactics. During the nine month seige which resulted in the brutal taking of Antioch (when little respect was paid to the city's still-considerable Greek Orthodox population), the armies divided. Baldwin of Boulogne headed east to set up a separate principality at Edessa (south eastern Turkey). Bohemond was made Prince of Antioch while Raymond, Count of Toulouse set out for Jerusalem with what remained of the largely rabble army. Their taking en route of *Maarat al-Numan produced another gross massacre but still there was no concerted Muslim resistance.

From Maarat, the Crusaders marched south along the Orontes Valley and then turned towards the coast again through the Homs Gap, taking on the way the Kurdish fort which was to become the site of the great castle now known as the Krak des Chevaliers. Tripoli (northern Lebanon) was the next major objective but the city put up a fierce resistance and had to be by-passed while the army went on to take Jerusalem in 1099. It took some time for the various Crusader princes to consolidate their hold on the Syrian coastal areas. Tripoli was finally taken in 1109 but smaller centres such as *Latakia and *Tartus as well as the mountainous region around *Masyaf fell earlier. But the Crusader domains were never a compact and tightly defended entity. The division of control between various families - Raymond, Count of Toulouse now installed in Tripoli; Bohemond and later Tancred, in Antioch; Baldwin in Edessa - their mutual rivalries and separate designs on the Jerusalem Kingdom and their lack of sizeable or professional standing armies meant that many compromises had to be made with the Syrian environment. The divisions between the Muslim cities and leaderships, the fact that the Muslim/Christian gulf was often less important than the temptation to make alliances of convenience in pursuit of local power struggles, the ambiguous position of local Christian communities - these factors and more blurred the great faultline that theoretically ran between the Muslim and Christian worlds.

Yet the confrontation ran on for almost two centuries. To the Muslims, the Crusaders' religious pretext for intervention was never credible, Christian subjects of the Islamic states rarely suffering any distinct disadvantages and Christian pilgrims having long been accepted in the Holy Land. The Crusaders' presence was thus seen as a straight invasion in which religion was a veil cast over territorial motives.

The Franks, as they were known to the Muslims, stayed on in their main bastions, controlled some areas of countryside and precarious communication routes between, brought in fresh recruits through renewed crusade campaigns in Europe, married, died and constructed castles and churches. Though they held on to the slender coastal strip, their hold inland (even when consolidated after 1150 by the transfer of key fortresses to the Hospitaller and Templar orders) was at best precarious given the lack of manpower and popular support in the countryside. They rarely managed to threaten the main Muslim population centres. They got little help from - and did little to advance the position of - local Christians (usually Greek Orthodox and thus aloof from the aspirations of the Westerners). As the Muslim forces rallied to the new centres of Sunni power in Damascus and Aleppo, the process of slow attrition of the Crusaders' positions set in.

The Islamic Resurgence

Aleppo was the first centre for Muslim consolidation under the **Zengid** regents (Atabeqs), Zengi (r 1128-46) and his second son, Nur al-Din (r 1146-74), nominally subservient to the Seljuq Sultan of Mosul and through him to the Caliph in Baghdad. They continued the Seljuq policy of restoring Sunni orthodoxy, rolling back the gains made by Shi`ism under Fatimid encouragement and through the Persian-inspired Ismaelis. Sunni Islam became a more distinct rallying point against the alien threat, its concepts of inner character and righteous living being embodied in the Sharia (Islamic law code) and systematised through the work of the urban religious leadership, the *ulama* and a new network of educational and religious foundations.

The Zengids complemented this consolidation of the spiritual defences of their realms with a consolidation of their physical preparedness. They regained the Crusader outpost at Edessa (1144) and destabilised the Crusader presence in the Orontes Valley. By 1154, they had brought Damascus under their control, uniting for the first time the resistance to the Crusades in Syria into a single front and thus refining the concept of *jihad*.

But the consolidation of orthodoxy and the encirclement of the Crusader forces took most of the century to complete before Muslim forces in Egypt and Syria were linked under one command (thus· denying the Crusaders the capacity to play off Cairo against Damascus). Nur al-Din completed the process, making serious inroads into the Crusader presence in the Syrian coastal mountains but it was taken further by his nephew, Saladin. Although a protege of his uncle, Saladin (a Kurd by origin) was invited to take the succession from Nur al-Din's infant son in 1176, having earlier (1171) ended the Fatimid era in Cairo by nominally restoring the authority of the Abbasid Caliphate. But Damascus, for long the frontline centre of resistance to the Crusader presence in Jerusalem, was his forward base and there he initiated the line of **Ayyubids** (1176-1260 - after his family name) which later took the form of separate dynasties in Damascus and Cairo. From there he completed the unification of Syria, taking full control of Aleppo in 1183 and thus securing strategic depth for a vigurous campaign against the Crusader forces. By 1187 he had lured King Guy of Jerusalem into the disastrous battle at Hattin in Galilee which saw the mass destruction of the Christian army and brought the fall of Jerusalem to the Muslim forces.

Crusader Syria withstood the loss of Jerusalem. The concept of a *jihad* to unite Muslim ranks rarely had much currency outside the areas directly affected by the Crusaders' depredations. Even Saladin's brilliant campaign in 1188 (see box right) did not touch off a consolidated effort to dislodge them from the great fortresses at the Krak or Marqab or from the cities of Tartus, Latakia or Antioch. After Saladin died in 1193, the inspiration had gone. Disputes resulted in the fragmentation of his realm between rival sons and it took nine years before the Ayyubid lands came together again under his brother, al-Adil (Sultan in Damascus, 1196-1218; in Cairo 1200-18). One of his successors in Cairo, al-Kamil I Nasr al-Din (1218-38), even handed back Jerusalem to the Crusaders by treaty with Frederick II in 1229, a move that provoked outrage and rebellion in Damascus. (It was recovered by the Muslims after falling to a Turkish marauding army in 1244.) The Ayyubids' line petered out by 1260, crippled by squabbles between Saladin's many descendants, though there were occasional signs of local vigour, for example the rule of his third son, al-Zaher Ghazi as Governor at Aleppo (1936-1215).

The Mamelukes

By the mid 13th century, the focus of the Muslim/Crusader struggle had moved to Egypt which became the target of the later Crusades. From Cairo came the second great Muslim revival with the rise to open political power of the **Mamelukes** (professional guards usually of central Asian or Turkish background) in a palace coup of 1250. The first of the Mongol invasions of Syria, under Hulaga, inspired the Mamelukes to rally the flagging forces of Islam (Battle of Ain Jalud - 'Goliath's Fountain' - on 3 September, 1260) and to take over Damascus from the last Ayyubid, al-Malik al-Nasr II. The ruthless leadership of the Mameluke Sultan, al-

Malik al-Zaher Baibars (r 1260-77), gave renewed momentum to the anti-Crusader cause and the debilitated Christian presence was rapidly dislodged from Antioch (1268) and from the bastions at the Krak and nearby *Safita (1271). The concurrent campaign against heterodox Shi`ites brought the Ismaeli castles of the coastal mountains under Sunni rule

---

SALADIN'S CAMPAIGN OF 1188

After Hattin and the taking of Jerusalem, Saladin spent the next campaign season in a series of whirlwind strikes against Crusader positions in Syria. His main concern was to block the incursion of a German crusading army then en route through Asia Minor and to complement his diplomatic contacts with the Byzantines aimed at discouraging them from giving the Germans access through Byzantine territory. His tactical objectives were not to drive the Crusader presence in Syria into the sea but to reduce the extent of territory they could make available to a German force. Thus he decided against any frontal assaults on the main Crusader strongholds where resistance developed but rather to roll up their weakly manned positions inland and bottle up the Christian forces in major centres - Tortosa, the Krak, Marqab and Antioch.

His tactics were a brilliant success. The taking of over 50 Crusader positions (for the moment, reducing the Kingdom of Jerusalem to a small enclave around Tyre) fatally weakened the Crusader presence, denying them control of extensive territory and the capacity to interdict major north/south routes inland. The weak Crusader response to his campaign justified his assumptions about the capacity of an alien force to maintain its presence on hostile territory. The last gesture of Saladin, the occupation of the Castle of Baghras, virtually under the nose of the Antioch Prince, Bohemond, showed the ultimate powerlessness of the Frankish forces. What is perhaps most remarkable, however, was that it took almost another century for the Muslim successors of Saladin to capitalise on this realisation and nudge the remaining Crusader forces out of the East.

LIST OF MAIN ENGAGEMENTS

1187

4 July	Battle of Hattin
2 October	Jerusalem falls

1188

30 May	arrives at Krak - decides not to attack
3-8 July	sacking of Tortosa - passes Marqab - burning of Baniyas
16 July	takes Jeble
23 July	siege of Latakia succeeds
29 July	Château de Saône ('Saladin's Castle') falls after three days
1 August	Balatonos (Qalaat al-Mehelbeh) falls
5 August	Bakas falls
12 August	Shugur falls
20 August	arrives at Qalaat Burzey
23 August	Burzey falls
28 Sept	Baghras (Beylan Pass) besieged - later dismantled

(*Masyaf). The process continued under Sultan Qalaun (r 1280-90) who routed the remaining Crusader forces with their successive retreats from Marqab (1285), Latakia (1287), Tripoli (1289) and Tartus (1291).

The Mamelukes, though aliens, rapidly built themselves networks of alliances with the principal families and religious establishments (*ulama*) of the main Syrian cities. Under their guidance and with the aid of the endowments often funded by their governors, the early Mameluke period was another golden age for Damascus. Though not the centre of the Mameluke realms (that remained Cairo), it was made the second capital by the early 14th century, greatly favoured by the early Sultans as demonstrated in the 171 building projects undertaken during the period. Its governors were highly connected and often very effective (most notably Tengiz, Governor of Damascus 1312-39) - r 1312-39). Elaborate chains of command were set up to ensure that they did not arrogate independent authority. By 1312, the Mamelukes had largely achieved all they had set out to gain and a period of sustained prosperity set in for most of the century. After 1380, however, a series of disastrous civil wars weakened the leadership and renewed threats of bedouin and Tartar assaults. After the last, and most disastrous, Mongol invasion of 1400-1 under Timur (Tamerlaine), the Mameluke Sultans never quite recovered their stride.

In 1390, the succession of Bahri Mamelukes (1260-1382 - mainly Turks or Mongols) had been replaced by a largely Circassian line of Burji Mamelukes (1382-1516). A period of consolidation began in 1422 and the long rule (1468-95) of Sultan Qait Bey brought renewed stability to Syria. But the most notable reminders of the late Mameluke period are the numerous mausoleums. (Elisséeff[4] notes that the Mamelukes 'who lived uncertain of what the next day would bring, tried at least to secure themselves a sepulchre'.) In the end, Mameluke rule collapsed as much from its unpopularity (due to the extortionate demands placed on its Syrian subjects) as from the swift inroads of a new Turkish incursion, this time in the form of the Ottoman military.

Ottomans (1516-1918)

The Ottoman Turks had already taken much of Asia Minor (including Constantinople from the Byzantines in 1453) before they moved in on Syria. Many of the upper class rallied spontaneously to them in 1516, the Mameluke garrison quietly slipping out of Damascus to allow the new Sultan to make his entrance. Shortly after, under the long reign of Suleiman (known to Europe as Suleiman the Magnificent - r 1520-66), the administration of Syria was systematised, its population counted and its

revenues stabilised. The early Ottoman period (especially the 16th to 17th centuries) brought a new impetus to the development of the three Syrian provinces (*vilayat*) - Aleppo, Damascus and Raqqa. The role played by the Syrian provinces in the administration and provisioning of the annual pilgrimage (*haj*) to Mecca did much to advance the economy and external trade grew. Under the provisions of the Ottoman 'capitulation' treaties with European powers, Aleppo became the base for a substantial foreign trading presence, a role that Damascus shared only to a limited extent.

Ottoman rule was a reasonably loose arrangement, considerable power being devolved to the local governors (*wali*, holding the rank of Pasha), as long as the central coffers were supplied with tax revenue, the *haj* provisioned and the security interests of the Empire respected. The Sultan's role as Caliph was broadly accepted by Sunnis and helped confer legitimacy on Ottoman rule. There was little attempt to impose a Turkish cultural identity and what borrowing there was of ideas and projects from the capital often became modified in local detail. The *millet* system which ruled minority communities through their religious leaders tended to reinforce the existing forces which had set up distinctive minority quarters in the cities and enclaves in the more remote parts of the countryside. The minorities largely thrived under Turkish rule, the Christians in particular playing an intermediary role in the rise of external commerce under the watchful eye of the Western powers. By the 18th century, however, Turkish rule was stagnating and the economic fortunes of Syria began to diminish with more intense competition from trade routes via the north or via the sea routes to Asia.

The 19th century was again a troubled period for Syria. The 1831 expedition of Ibrahim Pasha, the son of Muhammed Ali who had set up his own power base in Egypt in defiance of Ottoman authority, forced the Ottoman forces back across the Taurus. Egyptian rule brought in a more tolerant dispensation that saw the first European residents of Damascus and encouraged the Christian communities to play a more assertive role in public life. Ibrahim Pasha was forced out in 1840 and Ottoman rule uneasily restored. In 1860, partly as a result of the Druze/Christian troubles in Lebanon, a terrible massacre broke out in Damascus after a Muslim attack on the Christian quarter. The Ottomans restored calm but the situation provoked the landing of French forces on the Lebanese coast. By now, Syria was considerably more open to foreign influence and European educational institutions began to operate in the second half of the 19th century but

4 'Dimashk' *EI* p 286.

much of the initiative had already been lost to the more outward-looking cities of the coast, notably Beirut.

Damascus was thus slow to adopt the Arab nationalist sentiments that were encouraged in the case of Cairo, for example, by the development of the Arabic-language press. (There was no Arabic newspaper in Damascus until 1897.) Some reformist Ottoman Governors such as Midhat Pasha (1878-80) were well in advance of most of their subjects and introduced on their own initiative civic improvements that enhanced the amenities and sanitation of the main cities. The first paved road for wheeled traffic since Roman times was opened between Beirut and Damascus in 1863. A railway from Beirut to Damascus and the Hauran was opened in 1894 and a supplementary line from Rayyak (in the Beqaa Valley in Lebanon) north to Homs and Aleppo was later completed. In 1908, the German-built **Hijaz Railway** was built to connect Damascus with Medina.

Syria anticipated a new deal for the Arab subjects of the Empire with the overthrow of the Ottoman Sultan Abd al-Hamid II in 1909 by the Young Turks. Disappointment at the continuation of Turkish rule and the imposition of policies of 'Turkification' gave new stimulus to Arab nationalism. In 1914, Damascus was made the general headquarters of German and Turkish forces in Syria, Lebanon and Palestine. Damascus became a base for rising Arab feeling against Turkish domination, focussing particularly on the aspirations of Emir Feisal, son of Hussein, the Sharif of Mecca, to liberate the Muslim holy places. World War I was a time of extreme privation in Syria and Lebanon with

Turkish indifference and maladministration aggravating the effects of food shortages, leading to starvation and serious epidemics.

French Mandate

Allied (and Arab nationalist) forces entered Damascus on 1 October 1918, the city having been abandoned the day before by its Turkish garrison. Elections to a National Syrian Government the next year and the appointment of Feisal as King cut across British and French ambitions and were overturned by the establishment under the provisions of the Versailles Conference of a French mandate in Syria (along with a corresponding French mandate in an enlarged Lebanon and British mandates in Palestine and Trans-Jordan). The mandate was imposed by force of arms in 1920 and was accepted at best grudgingly thereafter.

But not for long. France faced a hostile population and wearying resistance. In 1925, a serious revolt broke out in the Hauran and spread to Damascus where the French resorted to the first mass bombardment of the city. Having tried to break Syria up into more malleable portions (separate 'states' were declared in the Hauran, the Alawi area and northern Syria), the French succumbed to rising nationalist agitation with limited constitutional independence in 1943, the Vichy French by then having been dislodged in favour of the Free French with the help of Allied forces. The Mandate formally ended in April 1945 with Syria's admission to the United Nations, though that outcome did not constrain French forces from a final bombardment of Damascus the next month. French forces finally withdrew in late 1946.

2. DEVELOPMENT OF ARCHITECTURAL FORMS IN SYRIA

2- DEVELOPMENT OF ARCHITECTURAL FORMS IN SYRIA

Bronze and Iron Ages – buildings

Although Syria is of critical importance in the scientific study of the remains of the Bronze and Iron Ages and provides an extraordinary range of sites that have been researched over the last century, the scope of this book is restricted to remains that are recognisable as buildings or as monuments to the past. Only a limited number of remains of these early periods are covered in this volume namely those of major historical importance (*Ebla, *Tell Halaf) or where the physical remains uncovered by researchers provides unusually rich evidence of the architectural practices of the period (especially *Ugarit, *Mari, *Ain Dara).

The early sequence of buildings does not represent in itself a continuous tradition, the pattern was continually disrupted by the waves of invasions and cross-currents of influences that washed over Syria. While the remains of temples at sites such as Ugarit do show the beginnings of an architectural style that will emerge later as a steady trend (box on Syro-Phoenician Temples below), most of the architectural development is only broadly related to common themes such as the development of the internal courtyard as the basis of palace design. If the results are thus ad hoc and cumulative, the effects are nevertheless striking when seen on the scale achieved in the Palace of Zimri-Lim at Mari with its 275 rooms or in the main palace of Ugarit with 90 or more rooms on the lower (stone-built) floor plus upper storeys. Major settlements were generally fortress-cities, walled for defence against the newly-developed weapons such as cavalry (based on the horse-drawn light chariot) and archers. A citadel was located on the highest ground, defended by two or three outer walls of beaten earth or stone, surrounded by a moat, intended to resist siege devices such as moveable towers and battering rams. Within the walls, houses were usually of mud brick, some with an upper storey.

The development of decorative elements in palace and temple design is likewise only randomly visible in our survey. At Mari, there are fragments of wall-painting and the use of orthostats to line gateways or courtyards is evident by the early Iron Age, developing into the bold use of stone-carved panels or free-standing sculptures at Tell Halaf (*Aleppo - Museum) or *Ain Dara.

SYRO-PHOENICIAN TEMPLES

Several temples in Syria which are variously described as Roman, Palmyrene, Phoenician or in the style of Baalbek, actually bear many traces of a common lineage which is largely local in inspiration, but takes on many Roman or classical attributes. What is common to the Allat, Bel and Baalshamin temples at *Palmyra, the Phoenician/Persian temple at *Amrit, the Roman temple compound at *Husn Suleiman and even the temple of Jupiter in Damascus (*Damascus - Umayyad Mosque) is a common Syro-Phoenician ancestry.

The idea of isolating the temple cella from the clutter of the surrounding courtyard and locating it in an open compound is an idea that first appeared in Syria (Ugarit temples) and later gave rise to the fully free-standing Greek version. The earliest clear example is the late fifth or fourth century compound at Amrit, a curious site just south of Tartus which betrays an eclectic mixture of influences from local Phoenician to Mesopotamian/Persian. Here can be seen the basic idea of a large open temple compound at the centre of which stands a small *naos* or *cella*. The areas for public assembly are kept open and the room reserved for the image and priestly worship of the gods is enclosed in a relatively small space. (The same idea can be seen in reconstructions of Old Testament religious buildings). In front of the *naos* are an altar for public sacrificial rites and a small pool for lustrations. The provision at Amrit of a sacred lake around the central island is not found at any other sites.

In later examples, the *naos* increases in size, even taking on some of the appearance of the classical temple itself (surrounding colonnade etc) but is still small compared to the vast spaces of the walled and/or arcaded enclosure. The altar and lustral pool survive (Palmyra and Husn Suleiman). So too does the corner tower, a format found in the *Palmyra - Bel temple as well as in the curious building at *Dumeir. The most flamboyant achievement is the Temple of Jupiter Heliopolitan at Baalbek (Lebanon) which is outside the scope of this book but which represents an overblown version of forms found in the major classical and Phoenician sites of the region.

Seleucids

Virtually all of Seleucid Syria has been lost to posterity in later re-building, though the tendency in the Roman period to respect the Greek town plan (based on the Hippodamian grid - *Damascus - Straight Street) means that the principles used in planning Greek cities endured even if the actual fabric was considerably embellished (usually on a grandiose scale - *Palmyra, *Apamea). *Dura Europos is a good example of a Greek fortress later adapted to Persian and Roman needs later. In fact, until

ROMAN THEATRES

SITE	DIAMETER	CAPACITY	ROWS	CENTURY
Apamea	139 m		14+?	late 2C
Bosra	102 m	6-9,000	14+18+5	late 2C?
Cyrrhus	115 m		14+11	c 150
Jeble	90 m	7,000	11+12+?	-
Palmyra	90 m		12 (+18?)	2C?
Shahba	42 m		18	mid 3C

recently there was no evidence of a major Hellenistic fortress that was not rebuilt by the Romans[5] indicating that at least the Greeks' capacity to pick strategic sites could not be improved on even if some of their cities (eg Beroia - *Aleppo) failed to prosper as major civilian centres in Roman times.

Roman Period

Though remains of the early imperial period are scarce, in architecture the second century AD seems to have seen a drift away from the orientalising trends of the Hellenistic and early Roman periods and a closer observance of imperial norms. The mixture of styles that marked the vast project developed from the late first century, the *temenos* of the Palmyra Bel temple, is a last throw in terms of the heavy use of the orientalising repertoire for major projects. But local preoccupations survived at the level of individual sponsorship, for example in the rectangular tower tomb and in funerary art at Palmyra (see box under *Palmyra – page 174).

Syria is well furnished with 12 examples of Roman theatres (of which at least six are preserved in substantial form), including one of the most intact in the Mediterranean world, at *Bosra. Although its construction in sombre basalt gives a different impression from the dazzling stone of Leptis Magna (Libya) or Aspendos (Turkey), its survival virtually intact (only the *scaenae frons* had to be reconstructed) and the sweep of its nearly intact *cavea* make it a monument of singular significance. Though not the largest in Syria (see box at left), other examples only manage to suggest their former proportions, though the small examples at *Jeble and *Shahba are reasonably well preserved.

The theatre boom in Syria does not seem to have begun until the mid second century, reflecting the increasingly prosperous basis of the communities and their acquisition of more distinctly Roman tastes. We have no evidence of theatre construction in the Hellenistic period (though Damascus and Antioch are reported, from written evidence, to have had theatres in the early first century AD). The remaining examples follow Roman models though the Syrian builders were more inclined to chose sites on flat ground

ROMAN CITY PLANS

CITY	MAIN AXIS	WIDTH	GRID ELEMENTS	DATE
Aleppo (Beroia)	1.00 km	20-25 m	120 by 46 m	?
Apamea	1.85 km	37.5 m	105 by 53 m	115-180
Bosra	900 m	23 m	V	105+
Cyrrhus	400+ m	7 m*	?	?
Damascus	1.35 km	26 m	100 by 45 m	late 2/3C
Latakia (Laodicea)	1.50 km	5-7 m*	112 by 57 m	192-211?
Palmyra	1.20 km	25m	V	mid/late 2C

* = between columns only	? = not known	V = variable

(eschewing the advantages of building the huge structure into a hillside) and construction is almost always in stone (as opposed to brick used in the Roman world to the west).

City plans

Other manifestations of the classical period can be found in diverse forms in Syria. The expansion of cities generally respected the basic Hippodamian grid of Hellenistic times (see box above). To this was added, however, a specifically Syrian embellishment - the principal axis (*decumanus* or *cardo maximus*) was considerably enlarged and lined with arcading to

---

[5] A French team has excavated the hellenistic fortress at *Ras al-Basit. An extensive citadel has also been found by an Australian team working at Jebel Khalid, on the Euphrates west of Membij.

shelter pedestrians from the sun, frame the commercial booths or shops to the rear and provide a sumptuous setting to major civic buildings. The effect is still observable at *Palmyra and on an even grander scale at *Apamea but was a widely followed practice at most major Roman centres. Few new cities were founded under the Romans. An exception is Philippopolis (*Shahba), a curious attempt to establish a later Roman 'model town' to commemorate the local ancestry of the reigning Emperor, Philip the Arab (r 244-9).

Temples and Civic Works

Roman temples are found in various locations, mostly remote from population centres which might have re-used their stone for subsequent construction. There are several examples of Roman **baths** (*Barad, *Shahba, *Bosra) but few extant examples of houses. Some prosaic but impressive engineering accomplishments survive (eg *Harbaqa Dam; sections of stone-clad Roman roads - *Roman Road - Bab al-Hawa; the bridges east of *Cyrrhus; the cistern at *Bosra), attesting to the intensive nature of Rome's development of this prized and largely peaceful province. Perhaps most impressive, though, are the lonely sentinels on the outer frontier - the outposts at *Dura Europos and *Cyrrhus, both fortress cities of Greek origins. But the centre-piece of Rome's accomplishment in stabilising the area is Palmyra which also bears witness to the intense (and finally tragic) attempt to build from an isolated society a culture blending eastern and western styles bound together by recognition of the commercial advantages of the *Pax Romana*.

Byzantine Period

The transition to the Byzantine period with its emphasis on architecture in the service of Christianity is the theme of the fourth to fifth centuries in Syria. Leaving aside the notable fortresses of *Resafe, *Qasr Ibn Wardan and *Halebiye, the Byzantine period is largely measured by its extraordinary variety of churches, with which Syria is exceptionally well endowed. (For this reason, and given the profusion of sites in this category, the architectural development of church styles is examined here in some detail.)

Churches

Syria being a crossroads of diverse influences, more than one tradition is reflected in the evolution of architectural styles of **early Christian churches**. Influences include: the

Roman basilica model, adapted to religious use; local domestic architecture; eastern styles (including the surmounting dome); and temple architecture. Also to be factored in are regional variations, often reflecting availability of materials, and (after the fourth century) liturgical and doctrinal fissures within the Christian hierarchy which influenced architectural practice.

Early Styles

The earliest churches of which we have evidence were converted **private houses**. The example at *Dura Europos is the most remarkably preserved (it was transported in the 1930's to a museum at Yale University) and the earliest (early third century) - before the official recognition of the Church under Constantine. From the next century comes the house converted to a church in the village of *Kirkbizeh.

The tradition subsequently became more evidently diverse, the availability of **building materials** playing a large role in regional variations. In the north, the chalky local limestone was easily worked. Usually the basic plan followed the basilica tradition. In the Hauran, the local basalt was heavy and unyielding. The lack of wood and the need to work basalt into roofing slabs no longer than 2 to 3 m imposed a different range of technical needs including the transverse arch and the centralised dome plan. This gave rise to an inventive local tradition different from that of the north and remote from any major metropolitan centre such as Antioch.

Evolution of Church Plans

Most of Syria's early churches are dated, making it relatively easy to trace the variations in their design. Some even record the name of the architect. By the end of the fourth century, church design had become highly ambitious, for example the cathedral at *Barad (built by the architect Julianos - 27 m wide by 39 m). The buildings may lack the refinement of design of counterparts in the area of Antioch, more readily influenced by imperial and metropolitan styles, but the construction is solid and precise.

By the second half of the fifth century, Syrian churches are beginning to show signs of the bold **experimentation** that is evident in other parts of the Mediterranean world. At *Qalb Lozeh, the plan has become so big in scale that new structural devices are needed, especially in order to allow for the opening up of the side aisles. Whereas the outer aisles were previously divided from the central nave by a row of columns, the latter are replaced by broad squat piers which support wide sweeping arches, with added devices such as the dramatic archway enclosing the apse and solid towers flanking the west entrance (an idea which has precedents in Hellenistic buildings).

St Simeon's Church

Shortly after, a project of massive proportions was undertaken a little to the north at *Saint Simeon to commemorate the monk who had spent the later part of his life as a hermit on a small platform atop a pillar. The pilgrimage to commemorate St Simeon had taken off with great vigour even before his death. The imperial authorities probably sought to use it to divert the local population from their heretical attachment to Monophysitism and thus poured funds into the ambitious project - a four-basilica pilgrimage centre, constructed in the last decades of the fifth century. This gigantic construction re-introduced many aspects of classical decoration to the Syrian repertoire, probably via architects and craftsmen imported from Antioch or further afield.

Pilgrimages to the shrines of martyrs inspired many of the churches constructed during the remainder of the Christian period in Syria. The cathedral dedicated to St Sergius at *Resafe represents the 'final stages of majestic authority' of the basilica plan[6]. Dating from the sixth century, it typifies the bold concepts employed post-Qalb Lozeh to divide the centre from the side aisles by means of leaping arches carried on stout piers. The same principle is employed in the Church of Bissos at *Ruweiha (sixth century) though both show the structural weakness of a design which failed to provide sufficient lateral support to hold the towering arches and their surmounting masonry clerestories.

Materials, Decoration

The use of stucco and plaster provided a finish to most churches quite different to that now conveyed by the mellowed and mottled stone. In the south, most were plastered inside and out; internal plastering (and probably the application of frescoes) was employed in the north. Traces of floor mosaics have been found in some churches and transferred to museums for preservation.

The use of external ornamentation in stone is, in the early period, restrained. In the south, external appearance and proportions are not considered important, basalt being the sole structural and decorative resource. In the north, the limestone is carved and moulded to elaborate shapes from the mid-sixth century on, either in the classical repertoire (*St Simeon) or in multitudinous examples of the flamboyant

---

CENTRALISED CHURCHES

In a different stream is the tradition of centralised churches, usually based on a circular domed structure placed on top of square lower walls. The earliest dated example found in Syria is the Cathedral at *Bosra (511-2). The basic method of resolving a round room within a square building by the use of corner *exedra* flanked by niches had been used in Roman architecture, particularly in the construction of baths (as at Bosra itself) but its translation into Christian buildings is a southern Syrian initiative. Later examples were found at Jerash (nearby in northern Jordan) and at Constantinople (Church of Sts Sergius and Bacchus (518-27); Baptistery of Hagia Sophia).

The second notable element of the Bosra design is the central circular arcade, technically called a colonnaded quatrefoil. The device also came from classical sources and had already passed into church architecture by the time the Bosra cathedral was built. Such examples are found in the Church of San Lorenzo in Milan, the martyrium at Seleucia ad Pieria (near Antioch) and (later) in the centralised churches at *Resafe and *Apamea.

The Bosra church thus has clear roots in the hellenized traditions of the Mediterranean world and the local tradition of centralised dome structures. The trend was taken much further in, for example, Hagia Sophia once the technical problems of expanding the centralised design had been resolved by the later development of pendentives and flying buttresses to spread the excessive weight bearing down on vulnerable points.

Another remarkable non-basilica design is the Church of St George at *Ezraa in Southern Syria, probably the oldest continually-used church in Syria whose origins go back to AD 515. It differs from other centralised churches in that its basic shape is octagonal, thus rendering the problem of resolving the transition to the circular dome less formidable. The shape is heavy and solid, the effect inside sombre with little natural light but the impression is remarkable for the sheer survival power of the building.

---

[6] Milburn p 126.

local taste for swooping moulded decoration, linking door and windows frames along entire facades, like festooned spaghetti.

Monasteries

On the whole, monasteries were more sober and practical buildings reflecting particularly the monastic boom that developed in the Antiochene hinterland after the middle of the fourth century. (There were 60 in the area by the end of the sixth century.) There was no standard plan but elements that were often included were a chapel, a monastic tower, a dormitory building up to three storeys high and a collective tomb, usually arranged around a courtyard.

The Muslim conquests of the 630's brought an end to new church building in Syria for many centuries though a few of the churches were later adapted as mosques (eg Cathedral of St

fortification program to contain the revived Persian threat - the palace/barracks complex at *Qasr Ibn Wardan, the fortified/pilgrimage centre at *Resafe, and the fortress at *Halebiye, still grimly maintaining its watch over the mid-Euphrates. A number of other centres were up-graded during the same period including Balis (*Meskene), *Qasr al-Heir West, *Palmyra, *Circesium, *Anderin and *Cyrrhus.

Islamic Architecture

Islamic architecture in Syria burst into flower with extraordinary vigour within decades of the establishment of the Umayyad Empire. There is no single monument in Syria which rivals the Umayyad Mosque in its capacity to sum up the energy and cross-currents of an era the way this building does, for all the imperfections visited on it by subsequent sackings, earthquakes, fires and reconstructions. It is virtually the history of

---

SYRO-BYZANTINE CHURCH PLANS

By the early fifth century, the elements of the typical northern Syrian church plans from this heyday of Christianity were largely in place. The design, repeated in scores of villages of the 'dead cities' zone, comprised a basilica plan with the nave terminating to the east in a semi-dome over the sanctuary housed in the half-circular apse. On either side of the sanctuary was a small chamber - on the north, the diaconicon or sacristy/vestry and south a room often used as a martyrium for the veneration of saints' relics. (One of these chambers might support a tower.) The roof above the nave was usually of pitched timber, avoiding the arched stone or domes found in the south. In many churches, the centre of the nave was occupied by a horseshoe-shaped bema, a raised platform or tribunal, perhaps intended to serve for the celebration of the Liturgy of the Word.

The entrance to the church was often through a doorway on the south side, especially in early examples. Later there was a tendency to develop the west front with either a wide narthex or vestibule or a narrower one enclosed between flanking towers. Social convention prescribed in many areas (but especially in the neighbourhood of Antioch where greater orthodoxy prevailed) the separation of women and men, the former being confined either to the west end of the church or in a separate gallery above the nave.

Helen at Aleppo - * Aleppo - Great Mosque). Many of the older churches, however, remained in use and were constantly adapted and expanded throughout the centuries (eg St Elian's at *Homs; the monastery of *Mar Mousa near Nabk). Most of the larger churches and cathedrals now in use, however, were constructed during the 19th and 20th century.

Justinian's Defensive Works

A major and increasing preoccupation of the Byzantine period after the fifth century was the defense of Syria against the Persian threat from the east. After a relative lull in the fifth century, by the time of Justinian (r 527-65), the need to stem incursions against the Empire on several fronts led to a major commitment of resources in Syria where a strategic plan was entrusted to his general, Belisarius. The results are seen today in the remains of Justinian's fortification or re-

Syria in less than a hectare. However much it was a synthesis of existing architectural and decorative influences, its main purpose was to bear witness to the glories of the new faith and to islamicise the forms of old in a brilliant, new and monumental structure. The fact that many of its parts (the outer structure, the mosaics, the concept of the basilica prayer hall and the transept dome) were taken from an older repertoire is part of the conscious purpose of the building, absorbing the past into a new order.

Umayyads

Apart from the Umayyad Mosque, the architecture of the early Islamic centuries is largely a mystery to which few clues are available. The Abbasids effaced most of the tombs and palaces of their predecessors and sought to leave Syria a wilderness. Fortunately they neglected to obliterate the evidence of the

Umayyads' castles or model settlements in remote desert regions as illustrated in the two *Qasr al-Heir (East and West) and in the more fragmentary remains at *Jebel Seis. The most interesting aspect of these secular projects is not their basic plan, which is largely derived from Roman military models but the eclectic, incessant nature of the decoration, the best examples we have of the budding Islamic decorative style. The concern seems to be to cover every part of the surface in a restless repertoire of diamonds, false arches, rosettes, frieze bands and triangles, drawing on every tradition known locally from Roman to Sasanian - an effect most readily seen on the reconstructed facade of Qasr al-Heir West which forms the main entrance to the *Damascus - National Museum.

Abbasid Period

Since the Abbasids adopted a conscious policy of neglecting Syria, their architecture is absent from the main towns, the most notable exception being *Raqqa which was re-colonised in an effort to revive the Jazira's central role linking the horns of the fertile crescent.

Likewise, the centuries of confusion from the ninth to 11th centuries resulted in little which has survived beyond a few remains of Seljuq fortification works that were incorporated in later reconstructions. The first notable example of the emergence of a new Syrian style is the minaret of the *Aleppo - Great Mosque. But it is only towards the end of the Ayyubid period (particularly with the emergence of the madrasa - see box next page) that we find a substantial range of buildings that remain intact.

Crusades

In the 12th and 13th centuries, Syria's remains bear withness to the intensity of the great struggle between the Crusaders and the Islamic dynasties that established in Syria their forward bases against the Frankish presence.

The Crusaders came with little in the way of an active tradition of fortification in stone but within decades established a formidable range of fortresses based on Byzantine precedents as well as new ideas concurrently tried out in 12th century France. Syria has preserved virtually intact one of the greatest examples of medieval fortification, the *Krak des Chevaliers, rarely equalled in thoroughness of design and construction. Other examples such as the Château de Saône (*Qalaat Saladin) reveal a more varied ancestry but few match the grim steadfastness of the massive fortifications of

*Qalaat Marqab, overlooking the Mediterranean and guarding the coastal route, the precariously held thread that joined Europe and the Holy Land.

Islamic Resurgence

The great struggle between Europe and the east stimulated the development of Arab military architecture, largely a Syrian adaptation of Turkish, Persian and domestic precedents. The walled enclosures of Damascus and Aleppo were rebuilt under the Zengids and Ayyubids, the most spectacular result being the monumental gateway to the Aleppo citadel (built under al-Zaher Ghazi, early 13th century) which remains the supreme example of the Arab style. The fortress at *Bosra was built by surrounding the extant Roman theatre with towers and bastions. Arab military architecture on a smaller scale can be found at *Harim, *Qalaat Rahba, *Qalaat Najim, *Qalaat Jaber and the citadel at Damascus (*Damascus - Citadel, North Walls).

The Minaret

The origins of the minaret is a contested issue among experts, accounts giving different weight to the precedents set by Christian church towers, lighthouses or signal towers. One of the first uses of the tower was at the Umayyad Mosque in Damascus. It was several more centuries before the attachment of towers to mosques became the invariable practice.

During the period of Shi`ite expansion (tenth to eleventh centuries), the mosque tower was not favoured but with the resurgence, under Seljuq influence, of Sunni orthodoxy, the minaret returned with renewed vigour. The tower of the Great Mosque in Aleppo (late 12th century) noted earlier is the first example that proudly proclaimed the local mastery of an assured Islamic style. From then on, minarets are found in virtually every conceivable style in Syria, from the varied confections of the Mamelukes to the severe simplicity of the Ottoman pencil version, often deployed in multiple formations.

Materials, Decoration

The materials used in construction depended, once again, on the local sources. Brick was common in areas influenced by the Mesopotamian tradition (Raqqa, Qalaat Jaber) but masonry was more prevalent elsewhere. Pointed arches are found as early as the eighth century and were virtually universal by the tenth century with the use of elaborate juggled voussoirs for decorative effect being highly

THE MADRASA

The promotion of Sunni orthodoxy (which began in the late tenth century) reached a new peak of energy under the Zengids and Ayyubids (12th to 13th centuries). This era saw the introduction of the *madrasa*, a school-cum-mosque, established by a civic or political leader for the promotion of Islamic exegesis or jurisprudence. The arrangement was funded by an endowment *(waqf)*, usually the income from an area of land, an orchard, a market (*suq*) or a bath (*hammam*). (The corresponding institution for the *sufi* mystics was the *khanqah* of which few have survived into modern Syria). 82 were constructed in Damascus and 47 in Aleppo during this period but the earliest example is found in the additions to the Mabrak Mosque in *Bosra (1134-6).

The *madrasa* in its classic form (derived from tenth century Persia) followed a cruciform plan with four *iwan* facing an internal courtyard but there was no strict adherence to this model in the many variations developed in Syria. Early examples included rooms for the living quarters of the students and teachers, though in the later Mameluke period, the living quarters were usually in a separate commercial building which generated the income for the religious institution. By then, the *madrasa* as a propaganda weapon had fallen into disuse. It tended now to have a broader civic function, serving as a congregational mosque for the quarter, the earlier fashion for a large central congregational mosque by now being replaced by neighbourhood mosques throughout the cities. The *madrasa* often included the mausoleum of the benefactor, separated from the street by a large grilled window to attract the blessings of passers-by.

Although *madrasas* are found in some form throughout much of the Muslim world, their prevalence in Syria was particularly marked. The scale of the *madrasa*, however, was relatively small and their location discreet, perhaps reflecting the fact that it was often not the wealthiest members of the elite who funded them but the local leadership or their wives or mothers and for genuinely pious reasons rather than prestige.

The revival of the *madrasa* as in institution into Ottoman times is illustrated in Syria by the more consciously prestigious aims of the Tekkiye Mosque.

developed by the Zengid period. For non-prestige jobs, such as the vaults of caravanserais or fortresses, rubble in mortar was the common technique.

Domes were adopted in Syria from a variety of sources, not least the local tradition dating from the Christian/Byzantine period where Roman and Persian techniques were used. The basic concept of dome-on-cube proliferated in a variety of uses ranging from multiple arrays for the prayer rooms of major mosques to solitary and undecorated examples serving as simple tombs of holy men.

In the Ayyubid period, builders began to use the **muqarnas** as a device to convert the traditional squinch or pendentive into a more complex and architecturally harmonious means of reconciling the round base of the dome to the square plan of the supporting walls. Muqarnas was also used as a stylized stalactited decoration around portals, first developed in an elaborate way in Syria in 12th century, probably through Mesopotamian influence transmitted via northern Syria. Likewise the use of striped or *ablaq* stonework (contrasting black and white/cream bands) originally came into fashion in Syria in the 13th century and from there became part of the repertoire of the Mameluke style. Arabic calligraphy, often in highly stylized patterns, was used for decorative effect, usually as bands around or on top of doorways or windows. Decoration in carved stone, encrusted marble or stucco was remarkably restrained, being confined to areas such as windows, doorways, stylized bands of inscription or *mihrabs*.

On the whole, pre-Mameluke Islamic architecture in Syria avoided the over-striving for effect that is found elsewhere with the use of multiple decoration and contorted shapes. Buildings were usually on a human scale, not seeking to dominate their surroundings as in some of the more prestigious projects in Cairo. Decoration was confined to a few surfaces or areas and ornamentation usually restricted to interlace devices, mosaic or muqarnas effects. Given the sustained influence of the Umayyad Mosque on the Syrian creative repertoire, the survival of the Hellenistic tradition in decoration continued through much of the Islamic period.

Specialised Buildings

Mashhads, essentially a Shi'ite phenomenon in the form of commemorative foundations dedicated to descendants of the Prophet, are represented in Syria, among traditional buildings, by the 12th-13th century Mashhad al-Hussein and the nearby Mashhad of Sheikh Muhassin.

Other notable building forms of the Islamic middle ages which survive in recognisable form are the hospital-cum-medical school or *maristan* (Maristan Nur al-Din in *Damascus - Khans) and the public bath or *hammam*. Of the latter, virtually none have kept their original decoration given later reconstructions but good examples which preserve much of their original plans can be found in the Hammam Nur al-Din (*Damascus - Khans) and the Hammam al-Nasri (*Aleppo - South Quarter).

Mameluke Period

During the Mameluke period, the indigenous Syrian style became more clearly subordinated to the leadership's Cairo-based tastes. Syrian craftsmen were less free to pick and choose from the traditional range of local styles and were under greater pressure to imitate the more ostentatious repertoire of the Mamelukes in a gimmicky and thus provincial way. On the whole, they brought little that was new or inventive to the city, preferring towards the end of their rule to plumb for the picturesque. 'Everything was sacrificed to outward appearances and the monument was no more than a support for showy ornamentation'[7].

Ottoman Period

The **Ottomans**, their styles based largely on those prevalent in Turkey, introduced for a time a cleansing influence with the preference for simpler, cleaner shapes, particularly in minarets. But most of the examples of Ottoman building in Syria were also provincial in both scale and inspiration. The exceptions, in the area of public buildings, are the projects partly transplanted from the metropolitan context, for example the **Tekkiye Mosque** (*Damascus - Tekkiye Mosque) by the renowned court architect, Sinan. The *tekkiye*, the successor to the Mameluke *khanqah*, returned to the tradition of a series of cells around a courtyard with a central pavilion for the conduct of lessons.

Khans/Caravanserais

For the Ottomans, the importance of Syria lay in its export opportunities and its entrepot role in the Levant trade as well as its part in provisioning and protecting the annual *haj* from Asia Minor to Mecca. Thus much of the Ottoman period survives in the *suqs* (markets) and *khans* (depots/hostelries) of Damascus and Aleppo and in the sequence of **caravanserais** (overnight accommodation for travelling caravans) that dot the north/south route. The latter can still be seen in centres such as *Latakia, *Maarat al-Numan

and *Apamea where they have been turned into museums. But many suqs and khans are still part of the commercial infrastructure of the towns and it is often difficult to pick out from the work-a-day world of the modern suqs the functional 'monuments' described in our walking tours. The best examples of the *suqs* of the Muslim middle ages are in Aleppo whose walled city houses one of the most active market areas in the Middle East. The heavily-vaulted thoroughfares still follow the pattern of the Hellenistic grid (with many subsequent amendments and narrowing of the axes). The present structure of the vaulted *suq* area dates from the 12th to the 16th centuries.

The Ottoman *khan* is on a considerably more monumental scale than its predecessors of the Mameluke period where the central courtyard was left open to the sky. Generally, in the Ottoman period, the court (where goods were stored and bartered) was originally covered either with one or two domes or a series of domes surrounding a central cupola, as in the impressive Khan Assaad Pasha in Damascus (*Damascus - Khans). The storage rooms around the court were supplemented by further rooms off upper galleries, often used to accommodate travelling merchants. While some of the decorative treatment shows Syrian origins, the basic design of the larger scale halls derived from metropolitan Ottoman precedents. Sadly many of the domed spaces now lie uncovered, the roofing having succumbed to weather and earthquake damage but some of the scale of these virtual 'temples of commerce' can be seen in the recent restoration of the Khan Assaad Pasha.

Houses

In the field of private housing, the Ottoman period is also more resourceful. For the elite families favoured by the Ottomans, the opportunities of successive periods as *Wali* or Governor of the main cities inspired the construction of homes on a grand scale. The Azem Palace in Damascus, its counterpart in *Hama (now the city museum) or the houses of the Jdeide quarter in Aleppo are good examples of the blending of Syrian and Turkish practices in domestic architecture with the common emphasis on the internal courtyard with its fountain and the adaptation of the *iwan* as an open reception area (usually on the south of the courtyard, with a winter reception room (*qaa*) on the north). The rest of the ground floor would comprise a study, office and service rooms/kitchen with bedrooms on the upper floor. All domestic architecture followed the Arab pattern of a plain facade to the street with walls

[7] Elisséeff *Dimashk* p 286

high enough to preserve privacy though windows off the upper storey became relatively common in the late 19th century. Wealthier Muslim houses provided a separate area (*selamlek*) for the reception of male visitors, apart from the family quarters (*haremlek*).

Twentieth Century

Our survey closes with the start of the French period. This saw the continuation of the attempts during the late Ottoman era to improve public amenities, open the cities to public transport and to develop new quarters for the operations of government and the needs of the defence forces. Fortunately, much of this development was done on the margins of the older cities, preserving the walled centres (or, rather, often leaving them to decay) while the newer facilities opened out into 'garden suburbs' that still lend grace and a sense of spaciousness to Damascus and Aleppo.

3. GAZETTEER OF SITES

3- GAZETTEER OF SITES

A

Ain Dara (Plate 1a)

VARIANTS: Kinalua (?IrA); Gindaros (?Grk)
PERIOD: IrA RATING: * MAP: 68 ITIN: 10a

LOCATION: 10 km south of Afrin in the valley of the Afrin River (classical Oinoparas), a picturesque orchard area near the Turkish border. You can either: take the Afrin road north from Aleppo (60 km) then south down the river valley after passing the town; or combine your visit with some of the sites near *Saint Simeon. From the south flank of Saint Simeon, take the road that forks left of the hill and runs through the ruins of Deir Semaan. At 17 km north, mound is on the left across fields (track from Ain Dara village).

Ain Dara has remains from many periods including Seleucid, Greek and Arab (with a gap during Roman times) but its main interest lies in the 'Neo-Hittite' period at the beginning of the first millennium BC when Ain Dara was one of the fragmented principalities established following the Sea Peoples' invasion of the Levant. It seems to have been incorporated into the Seleucid domains, lying on the direct route from Antioch to *Cyrrhus (and on to the Euphrates crossing at Zeugma).

The eclectic nature of the Neo-Hittite period is reflected in the temple which is the main point of interest on the mound. It dates from the tenth to ninth centuries BC and continues several traditions from Bronze Age Syria and Turkey though its layout is simpler than the contemporary temple at *Tell Halaf. As you approach from the south entrance to the temple, the steps are flanked by two carved lions, a common Hittite theme continued in the frieze of lions and sphinxes that runs across the lower facade and vestibule. Note the four huge footprints (each 1 m long) carved into the paving of the entrance as if left by some giant extra-terrestrial visitor. (There are other Iron Age manifestations of such footprints, perhaps intended to indicate that the god has graced the precinct with his/her presence.) Abu Assaf cites recent evidence that the temple was devoted to Ishtar, the Semitic goddess of fertility for whom the lion is often a symbol. Since 1994, a Syro-Japanese project is seeking to consolidate and restore the relief panels of the temple base.

While it is difficult to distinguish the various levels of occupation on the rest of the sizeable mound, the site is littered with carvings. The city remained occupied in the Greek and later in the Umayyad periods and was walled for defence. (It was still occupied in the 16th century). The defences were rounded off by a citadel or acropolis at the highest point. There are beautiful views from here of the Afrin Valley which flows away to the south to join the Orontes at the Plain of Amuq behind Antioch.

REFS: Abu Assaf `Ain Dara`; Abu Assaf *Tempel*; Grainger pp 107-8.

Ain Divar (Arab Bridge

VARIANTS: Sapha (Grk); Bezabda (Lat); Jeziret Ibn Umar[8] (Arb), Ain Divar
PERIOD: Arb RATING: T MAP: 74 ITIN: 13b

LOCATION: On the Tigris River, where it forms the Turkish/Syrian border, 116 km east north east of Qamishli via al-Qahtaniye (29 km); left after al-Jawdiye (+28 km); al-Malkiye (+40 km). The bridge is c5 km upstream near the Turkish town of Cizre. The strip of Syrian territory which terminates on the Tigris is called the 'duck's beak'.

Some care should be exercised in approaching this site which is in a sensitive border area. The bridge is on the Tigris (near the point where Alexander crossed in his march towards the Persian heartland in 331) and is heavily watched by Turkish soldiers on the opposite side. Take a local guide and check with Syrian security authorities (the nearest major police station is at al-Malkiye 16 km before Ain Divar) before approaching. It may be advisable to confine your visit to the magnificent perspective over the deep Tigris valley with the mountains of South Eastern Turkey in the distance.

To reach the bridge you will need (besides a police escort) a guide and either to hire a four-wheel drive vehicle (rentable in Malkiye) or be ready for a 10 km round trip on foot from the motorable road. A final problem is that the bridge is only accessible when the river is low (late summer).

The original bridge was Roman (second century) but what survives is largely of Seljuq

---

[8] The site name for the Arab ruins on the Turkish side of the Tigris (see below). Hassan Ibn Umar was a local leader of the 9C - Bell *Desert* p 296.

and Arab origin (11th, 12th century), partly reconstructed in recent centuries by the Turks. It consists of a series of pylons with a single surviving arch in basalt, 20 m wide. One of the piers (on the western end of the south face) carries eight inset sandstone panels representing the signs of the zodiac with explanatory inscriptions in Arabic. Bell observed that the carving was of the same style as the Arab castle on the east bank at Jeziret Ibn Umar (now in Turkey). The castle is situated on an artificial island in the Tigris, formed by the cutting of a canal along the east bank. On the Syrian side of the river, the Roman camp of Bezabde was situated.

REFS: Bell *Amurath* pp 296-7.

Aleppo - Introduction

VARIANTS: Halap (Amorite), Khalap (Hit); Beroia (Grk); Alep (Fr); Haleb (Arb)
PERIOD: All ALT: 390 m RATING: *** MAPS: 2-8

LOCATION: 350 km north of Damascus. Situated where the largely featureless plains of northern Syria begin to rise towards the Taurus mountains, Aleppo marks the point at which the valley of the Quweiq River (the classical Chalus) reaches the plain.

No Eastern city has impressed me with a greater sense of its mystery. To drift with the crowds in the bazaars, those vaulted avenues cool and dim as cathedral naves, is to enter another world: a fatalistic world where violent emotions are covered with a fine veneer of manners.
(H V Morton In the Steps of St Paul p 72)

Aleppo and Damascus vie for the title of 'oldest continuously inhabited city in the world'. Both can claim an impeccably ancient and continuous lineage and it would be a brave outsider who would express an opinion on which city is older until we have firm proof. In fact, neither of these densely occupied sites has offered much opportunity to the archaeologist to penetrate the layers of millennia. It is enough to say that Aleppo is one of the oldest cities on earth, continuously inhabited since the earliest days of settled urban development.

It is a city which, perhaps even more than Damascus, readily leads you back into the past; a sort of time continuum in which flashes of the past, rather than dissipating with time, accumulate in the present. It is still an animated Arab bazaar city where the traditions of the Arab middle ages do not seem all that remote. It still (perhaps more than any other city of the Levant) works according to the conventions of commercial life unbroken since Mameluke times. There are glimpses further back into the past, including the Arab resistance to the Crusades. Less evident is the period of Byzantine, Roman or Greek occupation though their stamp is there in the present street layout and the basic shape of the walled city and *Citadel.

Aleppo may not be the commercial hub it was in the 16th to 18th centuries, when it lay on the land trade routes between Central Asia, Mesopotamia and India, on the one hand, and Europe, on the other. The Suez Canal and superhighways have meant it can readily be by-passed. But its very lack of a modern economic boom has encouraged Aleppo in its old habits of turning in on itself, to preserve its traditional methods of operation and its architecture. Untouched on the whole by the contemporary tourism surge, the rediscovery of Aleppo may come in an age when its past will be more sympathetically preserved. Meanwhile Aleppo remains one of the treasures of the Middle East that should be savoured carefully lest its dignity and fragility be lost.

History

No summary could adequately evoke the complexity of Aleppo's history. Settled since at least eight millennia, its recorded history first comes to light in the archives of Mari and of the Hittites in the early to mid second millennium BC. The Amorite Kingdom of Yamkhad, centred on Halap (Aleppo), controlled many of the cities and towns of northern Syria at the beginning of the millennium but after 1800 BC it was subject to pressures from the east from Mitanni and, eventually, the overall supremacy of the Hittites whose homeland lay in central Anatolia. Unlike Damascus, whose links were largely with Palestine to the south and beyond to Egypt, northern Syria and Aleppo have always been more exposed to events to the north (Turkey) and the east (Mesopotamia). By the 15th century BC, however, the two worlds clashed directly with the short-lived Egyptian bid to extend their direct control to the north. After the catastrophic invasion of the Sea Peoples around 1200 which affected all the eastern Mediterranean, Hittite power revived fitfully a series of small **Neo-Hittite** states (*Ain Dara, *Tell Halaf), one of which was centred on Aleppo.

The Assyrians became the next foreign power to exert their dominance in the area (eighth to fourth centuries BC), followed by the to a Hippodamian grid pattern (cf *Apamea, *Cyrrhus, and *Damascus - Straight Street to Bab Sharqi). As Seleucid control dissolved, the

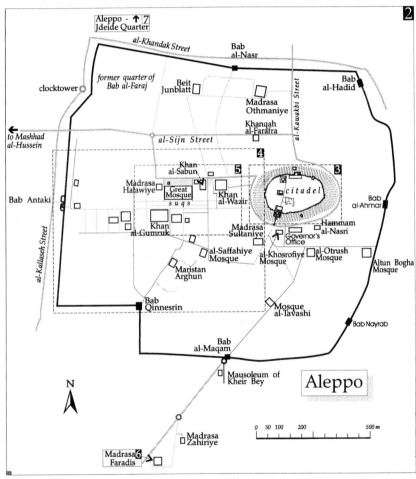

Neo-Babylonians then the Persians (539-333) whose supremacy lasted until Alexander's great campaign cleared the way for the **Seleucids** to establish their claim on the area. Seleucid control, though often tenuous, brought a new dimension to Aleppo's role. It grew from a village centred on a mound near a bend in the River Quweiq to a true urban centre based on the hill to the east which was a natural site for a citadel. The new centre was given the Macedonian place-name, Beroia and was laid out according

city was probably ruled by a separate dynasty from 96 to 69 BC. The **Romans** took control of Syria in 64 BC bringing to an end a period of internal anarchy which had left northern Syria prey to invasions from several directions, including the Armenian kingdom (in present-day eastern Turkey).

Roman control lasted almost 600 years (including the period of **Byzantine** rule from Constantinople) and brought unparalleled prosperity The area became closely settled and highly developed agriculturally. A network of roads was established, the limestone *massif* to the west became the centre of a major olive oil export industry and Beroia was one of the bases for the defence of the imperial frontier to the east and north east. Beroia became an important secondary centre but its role was later limited by the fact that it did not lie on a major transport route, falling between the Antioch/Chalcis (*Qinnesrin) corridor to the south and the trading/military route to Mesopotamia via Cyrrhus and Zeugma to the north.

Aleppo fell to the **Arab** armies without resistance in 637. It played a secondary role to Damascus (under the Umayyads) and Baghdad (under the Abbasids). It became the centre of autonomous power in the tenth century under the swashbuckling dynasty of the **Hamdanids** (944-1003), themselves Arab refugees from Iraq, particularly under Saif al-Daula (r 944-67). However, Saif al-Daula's aggressive style taunted the Byzantines into reasserting their power in the area with an invasion of northern Syria in 962 under General (from 963-9, Emperor) Nicephorus II Phocas who methodically sacked Aleppo. After a period of renewed local rule under the Beduin **Mirdasids** (1023-79), Aleppo was conquered by the **Seljuq Turks** in 1070, the Mirdasids staying on temporarily as vassals. Even the annexation of Aleppo to the Caliphate (now under Turkish dominance) in 1086 did little to end the chaos which peaked just as the greatest threat emerged in the form of the Crusades.

Following their capture of Antioch in 1098, the Crusaders took much of the environs of Aleppo, strangling the city by cutting off its access to the coast. The leadership of the Seljuq governor, Ridwan, proved ineffective in staving off the challenge with the Crusaders installed only 10 km away. It was the city's fiercely orthodox religious leader or *qadi*, Ibn Khashab, who rallied the Muslims and invited Seljuq forces from Mosul (northern Iraq). Their first success was at the battle of Sarmada in 1119. (Because of the Crusaders' extensive losses, the battle was known as *Ager Sanguinis* ('field of blood') in their chronicles - *Harim.) In 1124/5 during a fierce siege by Christian forces under Jocelyn of Edessa, Bursuqi, Atabeg of Mosul, came to the rescue of the city and took the opportunity to stay on. His successor, Zengi, a Mosul Turk, possessed a sense of mission and dedication which most of his predecessors in recent decades had lacked. He built up Aleppo as a centre of resistance to the Crusades. This period of **Zengid rule** (1128-70) continued under

his son, Nur al-Din. Measures were taken to restore the city's crumbling facilities after years of neglect. In order to restore Sunni orthodoxy, the first madrasas and Sufi monasteries were established as centres of counter-propaganda. The union between Mosul's military strength and Aleppo's commitment to *jihad* was the basis on which in the coming decades the Muslim front against the Crusades was slowly forged.

Saladin, initially a Zengid protegé, after 1160 gradually extended his base from Egypt to realise his ambition of uniting most of the central Muslim lands (Egypt to Iraq) under his rule in 1176. Direct control of Aleppo, however, was not secured until after the death of the last Zengid, Nur al-Din's son, al-Salih, in 1183. The **Ayyubid period** (1176-1260) saw the rule in Aleppo of one of its most illustrious governors, al-Zaher Ghazi (effectively ruler (Malik) from 1193 to 1215), a son of Saladin. Ghazi's contribution to the re-fortification of the Citadel is still evident. The work and driving personality of Ghazi made Aleppo one of three premier cities of the Islamic world. Its new international trading role was recognised by a series of treaties with Venice (1207-54) which established in Aleppo a factory (and ancillary church and *hammam*) providing direct access to the Muslim market, leap-frogging the Crusader ports on the coast.

Northern Syria, including Aleppo, was devastated by the Mongol invasion of 1260 which gave the impetus to the Egypt-based **Mamelukes** to seize control of Syria. The Mameluke period lasted from 1260 to 1516. Given Aleppo's exposure to the northern threats, it was many decades (marked by earthquakes, plagues and further Mongol raids) before confidence in the city was restored, one modern historian noting that the early Mamelukes 'virtually abandoned Aleppo to its fate[9]'. The first Mameluke construction projects did not begin until 1313. The collapse of the Armenian Kingdom to the north resulted from a sustained (1335-75) campaign in which Aleppo served as the Mamelukes' base. Subsequent economic recovery in the 15th century owed much to the diversion through Aleppo of the silk caravans that since the Mongol invasions had preferred the more northerly route via factories on the Black Sea or Cilicia. Thus began the era of the great *khans* or warehouses. The spices and fabrics, the gems and precious metals of the camel traffic from the East were traded and re-loaded for the mule trip across the mountains to the Mediterranean while European manufactures (including woollen cloth) were exchanged in the opposite direction.

---

[9] Lapidus p 15.

In 1516, Turkish **Ottoman** forces chased the Mamelukes out of Syria. Aleppo became the seat of a Turkish governor (*wali*). Though it was often subject to the anarchy that beset other Ottoman centres in times of weak government, its commercial role thrived. During the first Ottoman century[10], the earlier Venetian presence was complemented by French, English and Dutch factories and consulates established under 'capitulation' treaties with the Ottomans. Aleppo became the principal entrepot of the Levant, now unified under one power; a role which brought the construction of the great *suqs* which still grace the city. Aleppo met increasing competition from the sea route to India and China but the resulting decline did not become marked until during and after the 18th century with further competition from routes to the east through the Red Sea, the Persian Gulf and across Russia. Even then the city reserved enough of a local entrepot role to remain a centre of prosperity. In particular, the Christian and, to a lesser extent, the Jewish, communities thrived given their protected status under the capitulations, as well as through their favoured position as middlemen and the protective role of the consuls.

The population of the city reflected its more central importance as a trading centre and remained above the level of the more enclosed and orthodox Damascus. Though figures are largely guesstimates, the population of Aleppo which had been around 120,000 at the beginning of the 18th century, declined to less than 100,000 at the century's end - still marginally above Damascus' 90,000, and probably a doubling of the figure two centuries earlier. It was not until the second half of the 19th century that the population curve again rose steadily, reaching 150,000 after World War I with the massive influx of Armenian refugees from Turkey.

The late Ottoman period, an era of tentative reform and Westernisation, saw some new construction of quarters such as al-Aziziye and the linking of Aleppo to Damascus by rail as part of the Hijaz project (1906) and to Istanbul (1912). Ottoman rule lasted until Allied forces occupied Syria at the end of World War I. The political separation of Turkey and Syria has brought a severing of much of Aleppo's natural economic hinterland to the north.

Organisation of Visit

Aleppo is described here in seven itineraries. At least three days are needed for an adequate visit to the town and more time should be allowed for touring in the area (*Saint Simeon, *Dead Cities, *Cyrrhus etc). In addition, some time should be spent savouring the atmosphere of the suqs and of the 20th century city developed under and since the French Mandate, notably the Aziziye quarter (not described here) and the public gardens (1948-50) that border the Quweiq. Aleppo is best visited on foot and few parts of the old city are accessible by vehicle. Although major distances can be covered by car or taxi, parking near the old city is difficult. It is best to avoid high summer or mid winter on account of the heat or the tendency for rain to turn the city streets into sludgy obstacle courses.

REFS: *BG* pp 380 ff; Dussaud *Topographie* pp 472-3; Marcus 1989; Sauvaget *Alep*; Sauvaget *Halab*; Sauvaget *Inventaire*.

Aleppo – Citadel (Front cover)

PERIOD: Arb   RATING: **   MAP: 2 ITIN: 8a

LOCATION: Aleppo - old city (east of the main *suq* area).

It needs an effort of the imagination to appreciate fully the construction as it impressed itself on the citizens of thirteenth century Aleppo: An enormous expanse of bare stone, rising from its base to a total height of 50 metres, shimmering white in the harsh sun. At mid point on its gleaming flanks stood out in stylized black the legend of the fortress' foundation. (Saugavet *Alep* p 146)

History

The small hill on which the citadel is located is a natural feature utilised as far back as the Amorite federation under Yamkhad before the Hittite conquest in the 16th century BC. The earliest remains unearthed, however, relate to religious, not military, use - two lions carved out of basalt, part of a Neo-Hittite temple of the tenth century BC (contemporary with the temple at *Ain Dara).

The first citadel was probably constructed on this site by the Seleucids (333-64 BC), separate from the ancient town to the west. Under the Greeks, the local cult of the god Hadad which had been nurtured here since the time of the Amorites, was taken over and equated with the Greek god, Zeus. It is not clear whether the Romans continued to use the citadel as the military headquarters of their city, called by its Greek name Beroia. In the fourth century of our era, the Roman Emperor, Julian the Apostate (r 361-3), who had abjured the link between

---

[10] France 1535, England 1580; Holland 1612.

Christianity and the Empire established by Constantine, visited the hill to offer sacrifice to the god.

probably that undertaken by Ghazi who dug the encircling ditch, paved the glacis with stone and built the great gateway. As the Mamelukes' control tightened after 1400, the citadel again

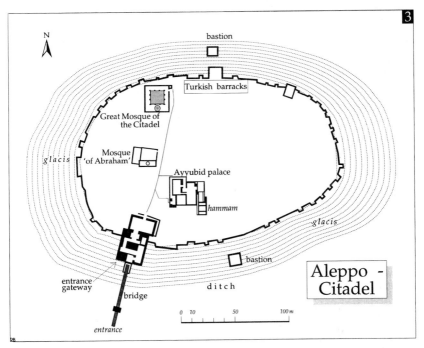

3

Aleppo - Citadel

After the Arab conquest, Aleppo as a whole fell into decline. The role of the citadel is again obscure until the tenth century when it housed a residence for Saif al-Daula whose Hamdanid dynasty gave Aleppo one of its most flourishing periods of activity. Its strategic importance in the struggle against Byzantium continued into the Crusader period when it became the impregnable base for Muslim power in northern Syria. Towards the end of the 12th century, after Saladin's successes against the Crusaders and with the Ayyubids in firm control of Syria, it was made the focal point of the new city established by al-Malik al-Zaher Ghazi, a son of Saladin. Another set-back came, however, with the Mongol invasions. After the first wave in 1260, the citadel was restored in 1292, only to be razed again by the final wave led by Timur in 1400.

The remains that you now see date from various attempts to reconstruct or strengthen the fortress' role between these episodes of devastation. The most enduring work was

assumed a more civilian character. The town had expanded to embrace it on all sides, thus making its role as a bastion against marauders somewhat redundant. The palace of Ghazi, sacked and destroyed by the Mongols, was replaced by the Mameluke staterooms intended to provide a fitting setting for visits by the Sultan.

Visit

The most striking view of the citadel is the approach to the sole entrance bridge and monumental gateway. This masterpiece of Arab military architecture, combines the practical with the flamboyant. The bold sweep of the rising bridge, the depth of the ditch (22 m) and the steepness of the surrounding glacis (48°) culminate in the entrance facade rising several storeys and incorporating a deep arch and a complex range of defensive devices. The effect is emphasised by the window surrounds of contrasting stone in black and white.

The huge ditch, the stone-faced glacis that encircle the lower two thirds of the 55 m high mound and the upper ramparts were originally built by al-Malik al-Zaher Ghazi in the closing years of the 12th century. Note (left) how the lower reaches of the glacis were strengthened against the weight of the upper slope by re-used Roman or Byzantine columns to anchor the skin of stone.

The entry bridge is preceded by a rectangular tower, 20 m high, originally constructed c1211 and refurbished in the 16th century, hence the inscription from the reign of the penultimate Mameluke Sultan Qansawh al-Ghawri, recording the work undertaken by the local governor, Abrak al-Ashrafi al-Saifi (1507). Among the earlier elements included in the renewed tower is the outer door dated by inscription to the early 13th century.

Now cross the bridge which is supported on eight arches and included facilities to carry water to the citadel. Before you enter the great gateway built out from the line of walls note the defensive arrangements. Any attack, having penetrated the outer tower and straddled the gap normally spanned by a draw-bridge (exposed all the while to fire from the walls) would lose momentum as it met the blank face of the citadel wall. The entry door is set on the right, blunting the attack and exposing assaulting troops to the full range of defensive devices above. In addition to a range of slits and parapets, the face of the gateway is furnished half way up with machicolations and strengthened underneath with re-used ancient columns to guard against undermining. Note also 50 m on the right an island bastion, once connected to the fortress by a draw-bridge. This was added in the 14th century to provide flanking cover to the main entrance and (like the corresponding tower on the north side) served to strengthen weak points in the defence of the walls.

Originally, the two entrance towers ended at the level of the machicolations. Major work on the entrance was carried out after the 1260 Mongol attack. The Mameluke Sultan (Governor) al-Ashraf (r 1290-3), had his subsequent contribution grandiloquently commemorated in a long inscription carried on the band that runs around the interior of the great entrance arch. Some further reconstruction work was carried out in the 16th century. The upper facade and deep arch joining the two towers were added during this conversion of the building to more ceremonial purposes.

Above the first doorway, note the intertwined dragons. This gateway brings you to the first of five bends including two more gateways before emerging at the upper defences. As you follow the twists and turns of the passageway, look out for two further carved devices near the next two gateways: the first, above the lintel, two lions facing each other; the second two lions represented frontally, flanking the opening. All three carvings were believed to have some mystical role in guarding entry. The third (cross-vaulted) gateway also provides side-chambers for the guard.

After following the bends of the entrance complex, you reach an ascending passage. On the right are several gloomy rooms, the one near the top leading on to a series of dungeons and a cistern, said to be of Byzantine origin.

You now emerge into the daylight at the top of the mound. Many of the buildings on the summit have recently been excavated or reconstructed. The main points of interest on either side of the alleyway which crosses the mound to the mosque on the opposite (north) side are as follows.

The residence or **palace**, built by the Ayyubid ruler al-Aziz in 1230. What remains (much was destroyed by the Mongols) is on the right, grouped around a series of small courtyards. The entrance (ascend stairs to right to upper level) is decorated with a superb example of *muqarnas* vaulting with a facade in striped stone (basalt and limestone). The first courtyard is built around four *iwans*, a pattern increasingly common in Arab· architecture. Behind it, as part of the complex, is the *hammam* or baths (1367), recently extensively restored. Return now to the main thoroughfare.

10 m on the left is the **Mosque of Abraham** (*Makam Ibrahim al-Asfal*) attributed to Nur al-Din by an inscription dated 1167. The reference is to the tradition that a stone on which Abraham used to sit was preserved on this site, earlier commemorated by a church (of which two columns were preserved in the north wall). The church is also supposed to have contained (yet another) burial place of the head of St John the Baptist moved here in 435 from Baalbek.

At the end of the way, the **Great Mosque of the Citadel**, actually rather small in size but a gem of a building in its austerity and simplicity. This was rebuilt in 1214 by Ghazi. Almost square in external plan, the doorway leads into a stark internal courtyard, beautifully proportioned. The prayer room (south) is equally sparse with a cupola and *mihrab*. The elegant minaret to the north, square in plan, is contemporary with the mosque. From the terrace and parapets above the mosque there are superb 360⁰ views of the city. On the right of the mosque is a barracks building built in 1834 by Ibrahim Pasha who controlled Syria on behalf of Muhammed Ali of Cairo. On the lower slopes of the glacis can be seen the shell of the second tower that complemented the one noted earlier on the south face.

On your way back, ascend to the terrace at the rear of the gateway building from where you enter the large throne room built by the late Mamelukes in their reconstruction of the castle after the last and most devastating Mongol invasion of 1400. It is approached through a courtyard decorated in black and white stone paving. The restored throne room reflects the increasing civilian emphasis of the complex given the encroachment of the town around the walls of the citadel. As in much late Mameluke work, the style is somewhat debased, almost bombastic. Certainly it is grand in its dimensions - 27 m by 24 m. From here, stairs descend through the tower to the entrance.

REFS: Bahnassi *Visite*; *BG* pp 382 ff; Dussaud *Topographie* p 473; Saouaf *Alep*; Sauvaget *Alep*.

Aleppo - Great Mosque (Plate 2a)

VARIANTS: Umayyad Mosque; Jami Zakariye[11] (Arb)
PERIOD: Byz/Arb   RATING: *   MAPS: 2, 4,5
ITIN: 8b

LOCATION: Aleppo - old city, north of the main *suq* area.

The popular attribution of this building to the Umayyads applies only to its basic plan and not to any of the present fabric. It was founded c715 by the Umayyad Caliph Walid I (r 705-15) and probably completed by his brother and successor, Caliph Suleiman (r 715-717). It thus followed by ten years the building by Caliph Walid of the great mosque within the compound of the Cathedral of St John in Damascus and may well have been, on Suleiman's part, a deliberate attempt to echo his brother's achievement in Damascus. In the case of Aleppo, the new mosque was also built in the enclosure of a cathedral, namely the garden or cemetery of the Cathedral of St Helen. (This, in turn, had previously been the site of the *agora* of the Hellenistic/Roman city.)   Of this original mosque, nothing survives, given the amount of subsequent destruction and rebuilding. In 1169 it

was burnt down and Nur al-Din (r 1146-74) rebuilt it entirely with the exception of the tower. Later alterations have in turn replaced most of Nur al-Din's work.

The 45 m tower in its own right is worth particular note. It was erected under the first Seljuq Sultan, Tutush, between 1090 and 1092 and is one of the first notable examples of a growing sense of assured style in Syrian Islamic architecture, heralding the developments of the Ayyubid and Mameluke periods in the next two centuries. It has been described as 'the principal monument of medieval Syria'[12]. The facades are divided into four principal registers, each treated differently but with a strong sense of unity and balance. Note particularly the *kufic* (early stylised Arabic script) inscriptions which run around the bands between the registers. Above a final band of *muqarnas* niches, the gallery for the *muezzin* is covered by a wooden verandah. (The treatment of this top level is almost identical to the tower of the mosque at *Maarat al-Numan.) The stone for the tower may partly have been obtained from the remains of the nearby cathedral.

To enter the mosque proper, you turn right from the parking area and enter the courtyard by the west door. The effect of the white stone flagging and the arcading is pleasing, particularly in strong light. The elements in common with the plan of the Damascus mosque are the broad arcaded courtyard where the majority of worshippers are accommodated and the division of the prayer hall into three transverse aisles with a small dome placed over the middle aisle. The Mamelukes, however, substituted a more ambitious system of cross-vaulted arcades for the original colonnades of the courtyard and prayer hall. The beautifully carved wooden *minbar* (pulpit) is 15th century. The room to the left of the *mihrab* (niche) said to contain the head of Zachariah, the father of John the Baptist.

Opposite the west door of the mosque, the **Madrasa Halawiye** is built on the site of the 6th century Cathedral of St Helen, mother of the Emperor Constantine. The building has recently been restored for use as a mosque after service as a welfare institution. It comprises a courtyard with students' cells on two sides and, opposite the entrance, a columned prayer hall with a dome. This hall incorporates all that remains of Aleppo's original cathedral, a circle-within-a-square plan like that at *Bosra. Only the four L-shaped piers and one of the quatrefoil semi-circular rows of six columns that formed the central part of the church remain intact,

---

[11] After Zachariah, father of St John the Baptist.

[12] Herzfeld *Damascus - I* p 35.

incorporated in the western wall of the hall. The sixth century Byzantine origins of the columns (of which the first third lie buried under the risen ground level) are obvious in the superb, richly decorated capitals. The *mihrab* is particularly noteworthy, dating from a century after Nur al-Din's reconstruction of the building in 1245. The Cathedral of St Helen was used for Christian worship long after the construction of the mosque in the cathedral's garden. It was only in 1124 that it was among six churches seized by the *qadi* of Aleppo and reconstructed as a madrasa in retaliation for the atrocities against Muslims committed by the Crusaders.

REFS: *BG* p 385; Bloom *Minaret* pp 163-4; Butler *EC* pp 170-1; Ecochard *Note*; Elisséeff 'Monuments de Nur ad-Din'; Herzfeld *Damascus I* pp 34-5, Herzfeld *Damascus III* pp 118 ff; Lassus *Sanctuaires chrétiens* p 153; Sauvaget *Alep* pp 59-60.

Aleppo - Suqs and Khans

VARIANTS:
PERIOD: Arb/Ott RATING: ** MAPS: 4, 5 ITIN: 8c

LOCATION: The main *suq* area of the old city.

This tour will lead you through the main area of **covered *suqs*** behind the Umayyad Mosque, visiting some of the old *khans* and continuing to two of the old city gates, Bab Qinnesrin and Bab Bab Antaki (Antioch Gate).

Begin at the square which lies in front of the Umayyad or Great Mosque. 100 m east you will find a smaller square on the east side of which lies the entrance to the **Khan al-Wazir** a 17th century *caravanserai*, one of the finest in Aleppo. The monumental doorway is framed in alternating courses of black and white stone. If you walk through the entrance passageway, look back to the two windows above set in indented and richly ornamented surrounds. On the north side of the same square is the **Matbakh al-Ajami** a Zengid (12th century) palace which formerly housed a small museum of folklore (now in *Aleppo - Jdeide Quarter)

From the west side of the square, take the lane that leads south into the *suq*. After 40 m, on your right, look back to take in the entrance to the famed **Khan al-Sabun** whose gateway is rightly considered one of the greatest examples of Mameluke architecture in Aleppo (constructed in the late 15th, early 16th century by the

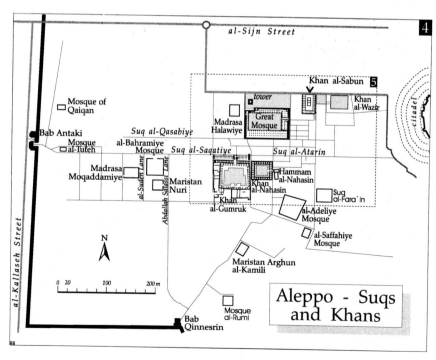

Aleppo - Suqs and Khans

Mameluke Governor, Adzemir). The facade is decorated in a rich variety of carved detailing. Note especially the surrounds of the window above the main entrance particularly the intertwined colonnettes. The courtyard, cluttered by a central warehouse, includes much beautiful arcading and a fine arch (now blocked) on the north.

From here, continue south into the main suq area of the old city. The **suqs of Aleppo** (see map 6) which form a labyrinth totalling 7 km in length are unsurpassed in the Middle East for sheer interest and atmosphere. Largely unchanged since the 16th century (some go back as far as the 13th), they preserve superbly the atmosphere of the Arab/Turkish mercantile tradition. In summer, the vaulted roofs provide cool refuge; in winter, protection from the rain and cold. While many of the products on sale have been updated, there are still areas where the rope-maker, tent outfitter and sweetmeat seller ply their trade much as they have done for centuries. Treasures it doesn't flaunt to any great

from the 12th century, restored in 1357, and are a notable and rare example of medieval sanitation.

The next group of buildings lies to the west of the Great Mosque and represent an extension of the *medina* or central market area undertaken during the period of economic expansion in the early Ottoman period. After 30 m you will reach the main passageway of the *suq*, the *Suq al-Atarin*. This follows the route of the Roman *decumanus* or principal axial thoroughfare, gradually hemmed in over the centuries by commercial buildings and booths. Turn right for 150 m and take the second major side street (left) which eventually leads to the Bab Qinnesrin.

In the 19th century, the Venetian Consulate was located in a small *caravanserai* (**Khan al-Nahasin**), first on the right along this street. In the same 16th century building (which now houses the French consular office), the Belgian consulate was established from the 1930's until the death in the mid-1980's of Adolphe Poche.

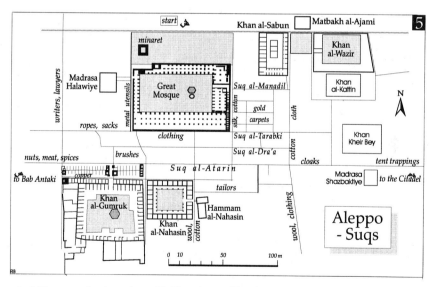

extent. The rug section is poorly provided though the gold suq (*Suq al-Siyagh*) still flourishes. On the whole this is a practical, living bazar, not an upmarket collection of boutiques. Most of all, it is worth simply absorbing the passing parade of faces, a mixture of Arab, Kurdish, Armenian and Turkish with a variety of dress that ranges over several centuries. Even the prosaic is of interest. In the Suq al-Manadil, the public latrines date

(The house, south side of courtyard, which contains many treasures can be inspected by application to the present Belgian Consulate in the Khan al-Kattin, immediately south of the Khan al-Wazir: see map 5 above.)

Almost opposite the entrance to this *caravanserai* is the **Hammam al-Nahasin** or Hammam al-Sitt, 12th or 13th century in origin and still functioning as a public bath. A modern reconstruction has obscured its original treatment.

Continue south 70 m. On the left a rising passage leads to the **Mosque al-Adeliye** built in 1555 by Muhammed Pasha, Governor of Aleppo as part of the mid 16th century expansion into an area previously occupied by a Mameluke exercise field. It is the second oldest Turkish-style mosque in the city, resembling in design its forerunner, the al-Khosrofiye Mosque (*Aleppo - South Quarter). A wide double arcade precedes the prayer hall - note the large dome, the fine *mihrab* and superb faience panels produced locally.

Take the next street left and 100 m on the right you will find the **Mosque al-Saffahiye**. Built in 1425, the mosque is entered through a tall portal decorated in black and white bands. The minaret above is octagonal in shape with beautiful, richly carved decoration.

Return now to the street which led south to the Bab Kinnesrin. 100 m on the left (after the corner of a lane) is the **Maristan Arghun al-Kamili** converted from a house to an asylum in 1354 by the Mameluke Governor, Arghun al-Kamili. The entry is through a tall, honeycombed portal leading through a vestibule to the central courtyard. Diagonally across is a tall vaulted passage leading to a confined octagonal courtyard designed to house the dangerously insane. A central fountain is surrounded by twelve cells, still used to house chained inmates at the beginning of this century. Sauvaget considered this the best preserved Muslim hospital in Syria or Egypt.

The **Bab Qinnesrin** which lies at the end of this street is the most intact of the gates of Aleppo. The tenth century gate was re-constructed in 1256 and restored in 1501 by the Mameluke, Qansawh al-Ghawri.

The present itinerary returns now to the main suq area. Those with some energy to spare might like to trace the line of medieval walls whose ramparts can be seen west of Bab Qinnesrin. After 400 m the walls turn north (right) running as far as the Bab Antaki (described later) though the line is often obscured by ramshackle shops. The area to the east of Bab Qinnesrin is described in *Aleppo - South Quarter.

Return now to the point where you left the main thoroughfare of the *suq*. After another cross street on the left, a high dome over the thoroughfare marks the superbly decorated entrance to the **Khan al-Gumruk**. This is one of the most famous and certainly the largest of the Aleppo *khans*. The whole complex (including the two rows of *suq* at the front) comprised 344 shops spread over 6,400 m^2). It housed after it was completed in 1574 the banking houses and consulates of the French, English and Dutch merchants stationed in Aleppo. The building is still in use for commercial purposes. Go through to the courtyard and turn back to admire the exceptional carved windows with slender columns above the entrance passage. In the centre of the courtyard stands a small mosque obscured by modern buildings.

Keep going to the west along the main thoroughfare (*Suq al-Atarin*). On the left, you will reach after 150 m the **al-Bahramiye Mosque**, a large mosque built in the Turkish style in 1583 by Bahram Pasha, Governor of Aleppo. The tall minaret fell during an earthquake and was reconstructed in 1698. The *mihrab* of the prayer hall rivals that of the Faradis Mosque (*Aleppo - South Quarter) in its bold arabesque decoration. Behind this mosque (70 m on right down the cross street to the left) is the semi-ruined **Maristan Nuri** founded by Nur al-Din c1150-4.

Off the second lane to the left is the entrance (50 m on the left) to the **Madrasa Moqaddamiye,** the oldest madrasa in Aleppo. Formerly a church, it was converted into a theological school (inscription dated 1168) following its seizure in 1124 by the Qadi of Aleppo (Ibn Khashab) as a reprisal for the Crusaders' ruthless siege of the city[13]. The building has a fine porch with two arabesque medallions.

Continue west to the end of the suq[14], Suq al-Bahramiye. Eventually you will reach through a winding passageway the **Bab Antaki** or Antioch Gate. The gateway consisting of two great hexagonal bastions is a 13th century construction by the Ayyubid Governor, al-Nasr Yusuf II (r 1242-60), grandson of Ghazi. It was further reconstructed in the 15th century[15]. Through the earlier gateway on this spot the Arab armies entered Aleppo in 637. (The best perspective is from across the road that runs along the old line of walls.)

---

[13] The Qadi seized other church property including the Cathedral of St Helen - see *Aleppo - Great Mosque.
[14] The survival of the Greek grid plan for Aleppo can be more easily detected in this west end of the old city where many cross streets, especially to the south, still run perpendicular to the main thoroughfare, the *Suq al-Atarin*.
[15] *BG* p 384 notes that some of the stones may derive from the original Roman walls and gateway. It is probable that a Roman triumphal arch stood on this site.

On the intersection 20 m back from the gate is the small **Mosque al-Tuteh** (or 'Mosque of the Mulberry Tree') an Ayyubid building. The west facade of the building incorporated the Roman triumphal arch which marked the beginning of the main east/west *decumanus*. The original mosque on this spot was built in the seventh century, reputedly the first mosque built by the Muslims, to commemorate the taking of Aleppo. The fine Kufic inscription and interlace decoration date from the 12th century (1150) restoration ordered by Nur al-Din.

North of Bab Antaki, the ground rises over the mound of the ancient village which was incorporated in Hellenistic Beroia. If you follow the street that runs just inside the walls, 50 m on the right is the small **Mosque of Qaiqan** ("Mosque of the Crows'). Two ancient columns in basalt mark the entrance. A Hittite inscribed block (14th century BC) was found re-employed in the wall of what is probably an early Mameluke construction. From the top of the rise, a good view of the north western quarter of the city.

REFS: Sauvaget *Inventaire*; Sauvaget *Alep*; Saouaf *Alep*.

Aleppo - South Quarter

VARIANTS:
PERIOD: Arb/Ott RATING: ** MAPS: 2, 6 ITIN: 8d

LOCATION: Those parts of the old city lying to the south of the main *suq* and the Citadel.

This is an extensive walking tour (4 km if you return on foot) that begins in front of the entrance to the Citadel and takes you south as far as the Mosque of Faradis which lies well outside the walls of the medieval city.

Across the road and a little to the left as you look from the entrance to the Citadel lies the **Madrasa Sultaniye** completed in 1223-5 by Governor (Sultan) al-Aziz, a son of Sultan al-Zaher Ghazi, the project having begun under his father. The *mihrab* of the prayer room is particularly commended. To the left lies a modest room which contained the cenotaphs of Sultan al-Zaher Ghazi and his family.

To the west, 40 m right off the street that runs from the gateway, is the entrance to the al-Khosrofiye Mosque built in 1537 by Khosrof Pasha, Governor of Aleppo. Constructed under the supervision of the famous Turkish architect, Sinan, then at the beginning of his remarkable career (*Damascus - Tekkiye), this is the first of

the Ottoman monuments built in Aleppo. Note that the portico, covered by five domes, is wider than the prayer hall. The minaret is distinctly Turkish in style.

The **Governorate** is housed in a 1930 building conceived in a neo-Saracanic style. Beyond it to the east is the **Hammam al-Nasri** (or Hammam Yalbugha) the grandest baths in Syria which since 1985 have been reconstructed and revived for their original purpose by the tourism authorities, having been rescued from service as a felt factory. The *hammam* was built in the 14th century. The restoration has been done in in a sober style and the two domed warm rooms achieve a striking impact.

Immediately south of the post-war Justice Ministry complex behind the baths, is an intersection to the left of which stands the **al-Otrush Mosque** a small funerary mosque commissioned to serve as his mausoleum by Emir Aq-Bogha al-Otrushi in 1403 (and completed by his successor, Emir Damir Dash). The tall entrance portal is richly decorated. Under the minaret, left of the portal, the inscription reads: 'This is the work of God's slave, the famed Aq-Bogha al-Zaheri. God grant him mercy'. The facade is one of the finest of any Mameluke building in Aleppo. From the courtyard inside, a corridor to the north west gives access to the burial chamber, a small square room covered with a dome resting on four honey-combed corners. The prayer hall is divided into five broken-vaulted segments supported by a row of four columns.

From the intersection of the al-Otrush Mosque, continue to the east. 200 m on the right is the **Altun Bogha Mosque** the work of governor Altun Bogha al-Nasiri (built 1318). Impressive in its plain severity – a small courtyard with deep, cross-vaulted arcades.

Return now to the square in front of the Madrasa Sultaniye and take the road that heads south towards Bab al-Maqam. 100 m right (just after a small traffic circle) is the **Mosque al-Tavashi** whose impressive facade is decorated with colonnettes. One carries a windswept Corinthian capital, obviously in imitation of the Byzantine capitals on the portal of *Saint Simeon. It was built in the 14th century but renovated in 1537.

A walk of 300 m south brings you to **Bab al-Maqam**, a project of al-Zaher Ghazi, rebuilt under Qait Bey (1493). From the small tree-shaded square south of the gate, take the street on the right leading south west; 40 m on the left

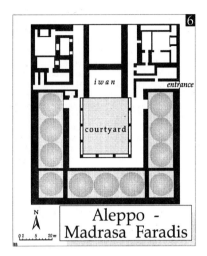

**Aleppo -
Madrasa Faradis**

lies the **Mausoleum of Kheir Bey** commissioned in 1514 by Kheir Bey al-Ashrafi. A Mameluke official, he went over to the Ottomans after 1516 and was transferred to Cairo as Governor thus missing the opportunity to be buried in the mausoleum he had planned.

Continue 300 m south and you will reach a major intersection. To the south east, two roads branch off at a 'V'. 50 m to the left of the V is the **Madrasa Zahiriye**, with an attractive courtyard and fountain, the funerary college of the great builder, Sultan al-Zaher Ghazi constructed in 1217. Ghazi, however, is buried elsewhere (see Madrasa Sultaniye above**).**

Return to the street that came from the Bab al-Maqam. After 250 m, just as the road finishes traversing a cemetery, take the lane left that leads (70 m) to the **Madrasa Faradis** or School of Paradise, truly the most beautiful of the mosques of Aleppo (Plate 3a). The religious school was built by Daifa Khatun, the widow of Sultan al-Zaher Ghazi[16] in 1234-7. She was regent at the time for her grandson, al-Nasr Yusuf II (r 1242-60). The courtyard is a masterpiece of simplicity and balance. An *iwan* at one end looks out on a small pool framed by arcading of simple broken arches supported on fine ancient columns. The capitals are particularly well proportioned, based on a honeycomb pattern. The prayer hall is covered

---

[16] She had two connections to Saladin being the wife of his son and the daughter of his brother, al-Adel.

by three honeycombed domes supported on twelve-sided bases. The central *mihrab* is a restrained but assured masterpiece, decorated in simple interlaced straps of arabesque.

REFS: Sauvaget *Inventaire*; Sauvaget *Alep*; Saouaf *Alep.*

Aleppo - Museum
VARIANTS:
PERIOD: All RATING: **   MAP: -   ITIN: 8e

LOCATION: Central Aleppo, corner of al-Maari and Baron Streets. West of old city and opposite tourist information office.

The Aleppo Museum contains an important collection of items from many periods with a strong emphasis on Iron Age and classical finds. The museum building is a hollow square with two storeys arranged around a central courtyard. To the right of the entrance to the main building is the administration annexe with a mosaic collection yet to be installed on the ground floor.

The main entrance contains elements from the gateway to the temple excavated at *Tell Halaf by a German expedition in the 'twenties. Huge and rather ungainly animals support three caryatids, figures in a style found in a range of statuary from this early first millennium BC site. Around the entrance forecourt are other items of stone sculpture found in the Aleppo region.

After the ticket office, you enter a large foyer in which are often displayed neolithic exhibits or (upstairs) recent finds from foreign expeditions in northern Syria. It is recommended you visit the museum in an anti-clockwise direction, beginning on the right of the ground floor foyer.

The first large hall begins with finds from the Jezira area of north eastern Syria. These include many of the discoveries made by Professor Mallowan at *Tell Brak in the 'thirties among which are examples of the votive offerings found in the Eye Temple. The next section is devoted to finds from *Mari, the early Bronze Age site excavated by Prof Parrot under the auspices of the Louvre from 1933 to 1974. Among the major objects displayed are a superb vase decorated with interlocking snakes (case 1) and the distinctive statues in case 2, including that of King Lamgi-Mari. Beyond are larger statues from Mari including: a black diorite figure of Ishtup-Ilum found in the main throne room of the palace of Mari; limestone statue of the god Shammas; the figure of a spring goddess holding a flowing vase (considered one of the most notable pieces of scupture found in Syria); and a superb statue of a man wearing the leaved skirt or *kaunakes*. A small selection of some of the 20,000 or more early second millennium cuneiform tablets found at Mari are also displayed,

The next room contains objects from **Hama* including finds from the excavations (1931-8) of the Danish archaeologist M H Ingholt on the town's citadel mound. **Ugarit* (Ras Shamra) is the theme of the last section of this hall, displaying many items from this major site of the Late Bronze Age.

You now enter the hall which runs along the rear of the building. This is divided into three sections, each devoted to a different Iron Age site. The first covers ***Tell Halaf** (statues from which you saw at the entrance to the building). Here are displayed several of the huge (and frankly ugly) black figures produced by this Aramean culture of the early first millennium. Several carved stone slabs which once protected the brick walls of the Tell Halaf temple are also displayed, depicting battle and mythological scenes. This style of art strives for monumentality along Assyrian lines but the rendition is clumsy and eclectic; Frankfort has observed that 'there is no pronounced style, either as an imitation of better work or as a result of a vivid original conception of the nature of statuary"[17]

The middle section of the rear hall is devoted to two sites of the northern Jezira, **Tell Hajib** and **Arslan Tash**. The latter is another Aramaean city (ancient name Hadatu) of the early first millennium, excavated by a French expedition from 1928 which also dug the companion site, Tell Hajib, 20 km to the east. The style is also heavily influenced by contemporary Assyria. Note the ivory engravings displayed in the wall cases found at these sites. The work is probably imported from Phoenician (coastal) cities of the period and shows Egyptian influence.

The third section displays finds from another Aramaean site, **Tell Ahmar** (or Tell Barsip) excavated by the French in the 1920's. The site is located on the Euphrates, 20 km downstream from Jerablus (on the Turkish/Syrian border). The palace was built in the Assyrian style in the reign of Salmanasar III (858-824 BC) when Tell Ahmar was the seat of an Assyrian governor. The palace was used as late as the reign of Ashurbanipal (668-29 BC). Wall paintings taken from the palace of the governor have been restored and displayed in this gallery.

---

[17] Frankfort p 291.

Turn the corner and enter the large gallery that runs along the north side of the building. This is used to house finds from several sites including **Tell Mardikh** (*Ebla) and ***Ain Dara** (section of a notable basalt frieze - right).

The first of the major halls upstairs contains an impressive collection of **classical and Byzantine** finds including pottery, statuary (from **Palmyra and *Membij) coins, bronze objects, glass and mosaics. The rear hall is devoted to the **Arab** period including a full model of the city of Aleppo, panels illustrating the restoration work done at **Meskene and *Qalaat Jaber and a wide range of ceramics. (The last gallery displays modern art.)

REFS: Khayyata *Guide*; Saouaf *Alep*.

Aleppo - Jdeide Quarter, North Walls

VARIANTS:
PERIOD: Arb/Ott RATING: *   MAP 2, 7

LOCATION: The traditionally Christian area immediately north of the old walled city of Aleppo and areas along the old line of the north walls.

Jdeide Quarter

This itinerary begins with the Jdeide quarter, which though outside the medieval walls, is one of the most charming areas of the city, with stone-flagged streets and vaulted laneways winding between houses which preserve the best traditions of domestic architecture. The quarter developed during the late Mameluke period (hence its description, 'new quarter'), probably largely in response to the arrival of Maronite and Armenian Christians attracted by employment as middlemen in the Venetian trade. The area is now (late 1990's) being redeveloped with several 'boutique' hotels and restaurants preserving much of the charm of the quarter.

The houses described all bear common features of Arab domestic architecture of recent centuries. The house is oriented around a courtyard at the centre of which stands a pool or fountain. Shade and contrast is provided by planted trees and vines. At one end is an *iwan* or large vaulted room open to the courtyard with a tall arch framing the opening. It is surrounded by benches for guests. Reception and service rooms (usually including a large reception room for winter) surround the rest of the courtyard while upstairs off a gallery lie the private rooms and sleeping quarters for the family. Most of the buildings are now charitable or commercial institutions and gaining entry can be a bit of a lottery.

Begin at the grotesque clock tower (erected under the Ottomans, 1899) which graces the rather disorderly intersection at Bab al-Faraj Square. (The old Bab al-Faraj quarter east of here has been largely demolished for redevelopment.) Head 300 m north and cross Quwatli Street where it becomes (on the right) al-Khandak Street. Cross and continue north (left of the police station) up Tilel Street, the animated pedestrian mall lined with haberdashery and perfume shops. The first sizeable cross street on the right (after 120 m, at the end of the pedestrian zone) leads to the Maronite church. Stop in the square in front of the church which is our starting point before entering this maze of alleys.

The Maronite church is relatively new (1873-1923) as is the Greek Catholic church (1849 - to the right as you look from the square). Some older churches of considerable interest, however, will be found nearby. From the orientation point turn right, following the dog leg turn for 100 m until you reach a T junction. Again turn right and 10 m on the right is the **Greek Orthodox Church** built in 1861 in a consciously Syrian style of decoration - ebony iconostasis, interesting icons; grave of a Russian consul in the courtyard. To reach the **Gregorian Armenian Church of the Forty Martyrs** (15th century - icons and paintings in the Armenian tradition) turn right from the Greek Orthodox Church and follow the bend in the street for +20 m. If you return to the T intersection, the **Syrian Catholic Church** is a few metres left on the left side of the street but is normally now closed due

to the drift of the community to other parts of Aleppo.

Continue east and just before the next cross street, on the left, you will find one of the most impressive traditional houses in Syria, restored in the 1980's and now used as a Museum of Popular Traditions (open 08:00 - 14:00, closed Tuesdays). This is the **Beit Ajiqbash** (Plate 2b), built in 1757 by the wealthy Christian trading family of that name. It has a harmonious courtyard, extravagantly decorated in a style that borrows elements from Mameluke to Rococo, blending them in a exuberant synthesis. The reception room opposite the *iwan* has a superb ceiling in gilded and painted wood.

Turn left into Jdeide Street and after 40 m you will reach on the left the second of our houses, **Beit Ghazale**. This large house of the 17th century has been acquired by the state for possible use as a cultural centre. (Fine polychrome wood inlay in the reception room (domed), *iwan* and waiting rooms; beautiful interwoven designs in the wide frames around the windows of the courtyard; to the west, a bath area.)

40 m on is Jdeide Square which lies at the back (east) of the narrow rectangular block that began with the Maronite church. From the street that runs from the northern side of that block past the church and back to the square where our tour began, a series of three narrow and picturesque streets runs off to the right. The first two will be visited - Sissi and Zabbel Streets.

Taking Sissi Street first, you will find 20 m on the right **Beit al-Dallal** a 17th century house also occupied by an Armenian school. (Large courtyard with fine marble pavement; bandstand in iron; off the *iwan* (to the east) a dining room with polychrome painted ceiling; grand reception room (south) with vault in painted wood; above this a terrace for the women). +20 m left is **Beit Wakil** now a boutique hotel with marvellously decorated walls including stylised gargoyles. The two rooms that flank the *iwan* are beautifully decorated in wood. **Beit Sayegh**, on the left towards the end of Sissi Street, is now also an Armenian school with few signs of any residual decoration.

In the next street (Zabbel) you will find at number 14 **Beit Basil** now a Roman Catholic orphanage. (Early 18th century; fine relief decoration in painted stucco around the *iwan* which has been converted into a chapel.) Opposite (no 12 - Armenian orphanage; also known as the Beit Saghil) is **Beit Balit** - 18th century; painted wood ceiling of room off the *iwan*; courtyard walls elegantly decorated.

North Gates

Return now to Jdeide Street and follow it south until it meets al-Khandak Street. Turn left for 650 m, bringing you along the line of the old ditch (Arb: *al-khandak*) to the **Bab al-Nasr** (Gate of Victory). The gate which is buried amid shops 10 m along a narrow lane on the right (south) side of the road is largely Ayyubid in origin. It was reconstructed by al-Zaher Ghazi, a son of Saladin; an inscription to that effect appears on the gate. The wall between the two bastions has been dismantled to give direct access through the gateway whose original design required two right-angle turns through the left bastion.

Take the first street right after the Bab al-Nasr. After 120 m, turn left then 40 m on the right is the entrance to the **Beit Junblatt** a 17th century house built by a Governor of Aleppo, now a government school. Two *iwans* face each other across the large courtyard, that on the south being exceptionally high and grand. Both carry faience tiles and marble decorations. The area south and west of Beit Junblatt (Bahsita) was the traditional Jewish quarter of Aleppo. The old Synagogue lies in the street that runs behind the Syrian Insurance Company office on Abd al-Munem St. The now badly dilapidated building dates in part from the 12th century. A synagogue probably stood on this site from the fifth century[18].

To reach the **Madrasa Othmaniye** return to Bab al-Nasr and keep going on the continuation street that passes south of the gate. This soon takes a right turn. The madrasa is on the left. The large building (1730-8), endowed by Othman Pasha al-Duraki, is distinguished by the highest minaret of the traditional mosques of Aleppo, in the round Turkish style. A large courtyard has the prayer hall on the south preceded by three large domes and flanked by two *iwans*; 42 student rooms surround the other sides of the court.

100 m to the south (across al-Sijn Street, behind a row of shops) lies the **Khanqah al-Farafra**, a rare example of a Muslim (Sufi) monastery. The rather severe but pleasing building was constructed in 1237 by the Ayyubid Governor, al-Nasr Yusuf II, son of Sultan al-Aziz (Ayyubid Governor of Aleppo 1216-36). Note the honeycombed entrance, the large *iwan* in the

courtyard, and the marble *mihrab*. Cells surround the courtyard.

To reach our final monument, the **Bab al-Hadid**, return to Bab al-Nasr and continue east along al-Khandak Street. After 600 m, the road joins a roundabout in front of the gate. The present remains are largely Mameluke. The Arabic inscriptions refer to the role of Sultan Qansawh al-Ghawri (r 1500-1516), effectively the last Mameluke ruler, in its reconstruction. Two-storeyed bastion with machicolation and firing slits; passage takes a right angled bend.

REFS: Saouaf *Alep*; Sauvaget *Inventaire*; *idem Alep*.

Aleppo - Mashhad al-Hussein

VARIANTS:
PERIOD: Arb RATING: - MAP: - ITIN: 8g

LOCATION: Western outskirts of Aleppo, on the slopes of Jebel Jaushan. Take the Damascus route from downtown. Just after you pass the old stadium (on the right) you cross under the railway viaduct. The street immediately after on the left leads you south. 600 m on the right is the Mashhad al-Hussein, a short walk up the rise.

Aleppo was once a city rich in Shi`ite associations, at least until the 12[th] century. The rise of the great Sunni orthodox dynasties (partly inspired by the need to rally the faithful to the Muslim cause against the Crusades) brought an end to the Shi`ite tradition in northern Syria. These two institutions, however, both linked to the martyrdom of Hussein at the hands of the Umayyad forces, indicate how practices have survived in a remarkable way. In terms of architectural development, they also show an exuberant employment of a variety of dome shapes.

The **Mashhad al-Hussein** (Memorial to the Martyrdom of Hussein) was originally built over the period 1183 to 1260 in honour of Hussein, son of Ali, as a conscious challenge to resurgent Sunni orthodoxy. The building was half destroyed in an explosion in 1920, having served at the time as a munitions store. Shi`ite community contributions brought about its reconstruction using the photographs and plans of the German researcher, Herzfeld, and what remained of the original fabric. The mosque is also called the Masjid al-Mukhtar, commemmorating the spot (*al-mukhtar*) where a drop of blood from Hussein's head is said to have fallen (for background, see *Damascus - Umayyad Mosque).

---

[18] The main synagogue for the residual Jewish community, constructed under the Mandate, is located in the newer residential area south of the post office square.

After passing through the outer courtyard, the reconstructed honeycombed entrance doorway (note the delicate carved frieze) leads you into a large inner court covered by a graceless modern roof. The court is surrounded by: to the west (straight ahead) a large *iwan*; to the south (left as you enter) a prayer hall with three domes; and to the north a portico (behind which lie service rooms and latrines). The stone said to bear the mark of the drop of Hussein's blood is in the grille on the left side of the *iwan*. The *mihrab* of the prayer hall is monumental in size (1.4 m by 3.9 m), a superb example in geometric marquetry flanked by imitations of ancient columns.

Three hundred metres further south along the same road turn right. Straight ahead up the hill is another Shi'ite shrine, the **Mashhad of Sheikh Muhassin** (also known as *al-Dikka* - the platform). Nothing remains of the original shrine built at the peak of Shi'ite influence in the mid tenth century, by the Hamdanid ruler, Saif al-Daula on a site linked to earlier Shi'ite tradition. The present fabric dates from the 12th and early 13th centuries[19] when the building was reconstructed by Zengi, Nur al-Din and the Ayyubids. The entrance gateway (almost a half-dome decorated with honeycomb vaulting) is preceded by a pavement in contrasting basalt and limestone. The large courtyard is flanked on the south (left) side by the prayer hall topped by three domes. Immediately to the left of the gateway is a mausoleum containing a fine cenotaph in carved wood (13th century). The room is covered by twin domes with a central arch terminating in vase-capitals (whose shape is Mesopotamian in inspiration). From the entrance, memorable views over Aleppo.

REFS: Eliséeff 'Monuments de Nur al-Din' in *Bulletin des Etudes orientales* 1951; Sauvaget *Alep* pp 124-5; *idem* 'Deux Sanctuaires'

Amrit (Plate 1b)

VARIANTS: Marathias, Marathos (Grk); Marathus (Lat)
PERIOD: Phn/Grk RATING: * MAP: 8, 67 ITIN: 5a

LOCATION: 7 km south of *Tartus; take old coast road to Tripoli. C 3 kms south of the outskirts of Tartus, fork right along a side road that loops towards the coast.Temple ruins lie just south of the bridge

---

[19] Especially under Saladin's son, Sultan al-Zaher Ghazi. Sauvaget 'Deux Sanctuaires' notes (pp 326-7) that there are many details in common between the two Shi'ite shrines, suggesting perhaps that the same team worked on the reconstruction of the second and the construction of the first.

over the small stream, the Nahr Amrit (classical Marathias).

Amrit was a Phoenician religious centre, heavily influenced in its architectural style by the Achaemenid Persians (who controlled as far west as the Syrian coast and went on to threaten classical Athens). It is the only extant site in Syria whose remains, though fragmentary, convey this mixture of civilisations, reflecting the ability of the Phoenicians to absord and syncretise outside influences. It was also the continental port for the Phoenician settlement on *Arwad, the island 2.5 kms to the west. After the decline of *Ugarit, Arwad had become the principal Phoenician commercial power on the Syrian coast, rivalling Sidon in the south of present-day Lebanon.

History

The earliest constructions on the *tell* date to the end of the third millennium BC. The site was probably founded by people from Arwad and the town virtually functioned as a mainland suburb and religious centre. Many of the buildings date from the period of Persian dominance after Cyrus' conquest of Babylon in 539 BC. The most significant monument, the temple compound dedicated to the gods Melqart and Eshmun, was built at the end of the sixth century BC with

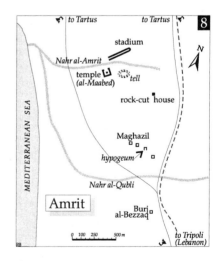

elements freely borrowed from Mesopotamian and Egyptian architecture. It was still functioning as a temple when Alexander the Great paused here in 330 BC, though Dunand believes that the temple may have been desecrated and its statuary thrown into the sacred lake earlier (mid fourth century) during the general breakdown of Persian control in the area. Alexander waited at Marathos, as it was then known, while his army diverted to Damascus. By the Roman period, Amrit had been abandoned, the port of Antaradus (*Tartus) to the north offering better access to larger ships.

Visit

The site of the ancient is large, extending over an area 3 km long by 2 km wide. The most striking remains are those of the Phoenician temple (hence the local name, *al-Maabed*) of the Achaemenid Persian period (late sixth to mid fourth century BC). The **temple** compound dedicated to the god Melqart (assimilated in the Greek period to Hercules) with a secondary association to the Egyptian god of healing, Echmoun, was excavated and partly restored under a Franco-Syrian program undertaken after 1955. The temple was built around an artificial lake (c 48 m by 39 m) with a small sanctuary (*naos*) on a platform of living rock at the centre, topped by an Egyptian-style cornice, terminating in a frieze of stepped triangular merlons. A spring (whose healing properties were the origin of the complex) was channeled towards the sacred precinct from the foot of the *tell* to the east. The rectangular pond was surrounded on three sides by a colonnaded arcade whose facade (formed from plain rectangular pillars in the Egyptian style) was originally topped by a continuous row of merlons (in the Mesopotamian tradition). Two towers flanked the north edges of the east and west colonnades, again reflecting a Mesopotamian inspiration. On the open platform between the towers was a high altar facing south towards the opening in the *naos*.

Traces of a stadium (230 m by 30 m) can be found on the other side of the Nahr Amrit which flanks the compound to the north. Constructed in the fourth century, the stadium remained in use until the following century. 400 m south east of the *tell* lies a house whose 30 m facade and interior walls are cut from the rock.

700 m south (note: area under military control – access may be prohibited), are remains of a necropolis with two **monumental towers** (local name, *al-Maghazel* - 'the spindles'), also fourth century BC but in use up to the end of the first century BC. The northern-most tower is 7 m high, cylindrical with four unfinished lion sculptures around the square base (a Persian motif). The decoration echoes that of the temple compound. Two burial chambers lie in a *hypogeum*. The second tower, also cylindrical, is 4 m high and ends in a five-sided pyramid with a burial chamber below. In 1976, a further *hypogeum* was found 27 m east of the second tower.

A **funerary monument**, with some traces of Egyptian influence is to be found +1 km south (Burj al-Bezzaq, 'snail tower') - a cube formed of massive blocks formerly surmounted by a cornice and ending in a pyramid. Inside were two superimposed funerary chambers. The remains of a fallen obelisk lie further to the south.

REFS: *BG* p 432; Dunand and Saliby; Dussaud *Topographie* pp 123-4; Rey-Coquais *Arados* pp 212-3; Saliby pp 118-20.

Anderin

VARIANTS: Androna (Lat)
PERIOD: Byz RATING: T MAP: 72 ITIN: 11b

LOCATION: From *Qasr Ibn Wardan (62 km north/north east of Hama), the road continues in the same direction +25 km to Anderin, on the west edge of the northern Syrian Desert. (Last 2 km from Maslukhiye dirt track, passable by car if no rain.)

An extensive site scattered over nearly three square kilometres, the only detectable remains being the barracks and a large church. There were once another nine churches in less recognisable condition in what must have been a Byzantine settlement of some religious significance. For the most part, the town was constructed in mud brick with the more significant buildings in stone, the local volcanic basalt. The ruins reveal little of the plan of the city but there were two main cross streets on north/south, east/west axes, intersecting slightly to the east of the cathedral. Sadly, much seems to have been removed since Butler's description and even since the 1965 Blue Guide was prepared.

Butler found inscriptions only from the years 506 to 583 but assumed that many of the construction works (including the walls) were older, some dating back to the second century AD. The town was surrounded by a **wall** 1.5 m thick with rectangular towers. The towers probably fell into disuse in the Christian period and were mined for the construction of the churches.

The **barracks** lie north east of the main intersection and are based on a square plan, each side c80 m in length. They date from AD 558, late in Justinian's reign (d 565) during which he carried out extensive defensive works in northern Syria including *Resafe to the east and nearby at Qasr Ibn Wardan. Parts of the walls are traceable but the interior is a jumble of fallen stones. An inner courtyard was surrounded by a colonnade at the centre of which was a chapel. Hexagonal towers stood at each outer corner. Courses of basalt on the upper walls alternated with brickwork, as at Qasr Ibn Wardan.

Only a few segments of the **cathedral** survive standing. The building was a reasonably typical product of the sixth century Syrian style, triple-naved with an apse ending in a semi-circle, slightly projecting beyond the rear baseline. The overall dimensions were 43 by 25 m. The half-dome of the apse was built of brick. Three vaulting arches separated the naves in the style of the Church of Bissos at *Ruweiha.

REFS: Beyer pp 133; Butler *AE* II/B/2 pp 47-63; Butler *EC* pp 80-2, 158-60, 169; Dussaud *Topographie* pp 211, 266, 274; Mouterde and Poidebard p 174 *et passim.*

Apamea (Plates 3a, 3b, 4a)

VARIANTS: Pharnake, Niya[20] (pre-Grk); Pella[21], Apameia (Grk); Afamia, Fémie, Fémia (Cru); Qalaat Mudiq (Arb); Apamée (Fr)
PERIOD: Hel/Rom/Byz/Arb   RATING: ***
MAP: 7, 68   ITIN: 4

> LOCATION: 55 km north of *Hama. North east exit from Hama by road to Mhardeh (23 km), then +5 km to *Shaizar, +20 km to Suqeilibiye, +5 km to Qalaat Mudiq village. For ruins, sharp turn right north of village takes you behind citadel, from there left 400 m for starting point.
> Also accessible (22 km) from Khan Sheikhun north of Hama on the motorway to Aleppo.

From Apamea, nestled on the east side of the Orontes Plain before the green starts to fade towards the desert to the east, you look out on a stunning sight, over the rich farmlands reclaimed from swamp towards the hazy skein of the Jebel Ansariye to the west.

The early Seleucids chose well in selecting this spot. What it might lose to Palmyra in sheer dramatic contrast between the starkness of the setting and the beauty of the ruins, Apamea makes up in terms of the juxtaposition, no less dramatic, of stone against lush pastures and distant mountains.

Apamea has been excavated since 1934 by the Belgian teams[22], but a good deal of reconstruction work has recently been done by the Syrian Department of Antiquities, particularly in order to restore the columns of the *cardo maximus* (Plate 4a). The results of this work are now evident and the sight of the long stretch of columns, bearing in some cases curious twisted fluting, is giving a new perspective, particularly of the huge scale on which Roman Apamea was conceived.

History

One of the four cities[23] founded by Seleucos I Nicator at the beginning of the third century BC, the name Apameia was adopted to commemorate his Persian wife, Apama. It became one of the four main centres of the Seleucid state in Syria - a satrapal headquarters as well as its forward military base. It enjoyed the particular advantage of rich pasture to provide a breeding centre for the army's cavalry horses and it lay astride the kingdom's main east/west and north/south communications, slightly to the rear of the buffer zone with the Ptolemaic lands to the south. By the second century BC, however, it had fallen well behind Antioch in economic and political importance. In 64 BC, Apamea was taken by the Romans under Pompey and its citadel was razed. Under Roman rule, it was further developed as a military base. The theatre, baths, temples and villas were constructed during the town's period of peak prosperity, the boom years of the second century AD[24]. The first stage of ambitious reconstruction probably came as a result of imperial patronage when Trajan ordered the rebuilding of the city after a severe earthquake in 115. The colonnaded main street was completed in its present form during the reign of Marcus Aurelius (161-80) and served both as axis and as a market, being lined with stalls and shaded arcades[25]. In the third century, the city was made the winter base for the elite II Parthica legion. In addition to its economic and military importance, Apamea became the centre of an influential

---

[20] The name used in the Egyptian account of the expedition of Amenhotep II to Syria in 1447.
[21] A Macedonian occupation (named in memory of Alexander's father's birthplace in Macedonia) pre-dated Seleucus' re-naming of the settlement c300 BC.

[22] The Belgian researches are one of the most prolonged and consistent programs of archaeological work carried out in Syria, apart from *Ugarit. They have been published at length over the half century involved - see Balty, Jean Ch *Guide* pp 218-22 for bibliography.
[23] The other three were Laodicea (*Latakia), Antioch and Seleuceia ad Pieria (the port for Antioch).
[24] One estimate gives the population of the town including extra-mural suburbs as half a million - Klengel *Syrien* p 165. See also Balty, Janine *Apamée.*
[25] Balty describes the *cardo* as 'one of the most esteemed avenues in world architectural history' – 'Apamée' *(Aufstieg)* p 128.

school of neo-Platonic philosophy which flourished particularly under Iamblichos (early 4th century).

later. It fell without resistance, the population – largely converted to Monophysitism by the mid 6th century – already resentful of Byzantium's

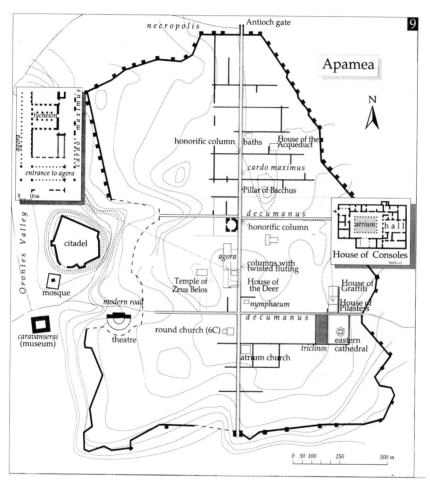

Apamea remained a centre of considerable importance into the Byzantine period when it became a base for adherents of the Monophysite 'heresy'. It was made the capital of *Syria Secunda* province in the early 5th century and was the seat of a Bishop. The Persians sacked and burnt the city in 573 during the troubled century which also saw a succession of major earthquakes. The Persians again held it from 612 to 628 and the Byzantine 'liberation' came just in time to see its fall to the Arabs a decade

heavy-handed imposition of orthodoxy.

The town was under Crusader control (attached to the Principality of Antioch) from 1106 when it was taken by Tancred. In July 1149 it was retaken by Nur al-Din. The castle was fortified during this period but little remains of this phase and later dwellings on the mound have incorporated most of the stones. In 1157, a major earthquake destroyed the city. The settlement within the citadel, however, survived and the 16th century mosque and *caravanserai* indicate the role it later played as a staging post on the pilgrimage route from Istanbul to Mecca.

Visit

The site falls naturally into several groups of ruins:

- The main columned street or **cardo maximus** which runs precisely north/south, bisected by the modern road. This was crossed in ancient times by several east/west axes (less distinguishable) or *decumani*.
- Roman residences and extensive Byzantine **ecclesiastical remains** about 400 m to the east of the *cardo*.
- The **theatre**, between the *cardo* and the modern village.
- The ramparts to the north and west, and the site of the Crusader/Arab castle (where the ancient Seleucid **citadel** was also located) immediately above Qalaat Mudiq. This serves as a landmark as you approach the town from the valley.
- The Turkish *caravanserai* which has recently been converted and restored as a **museum** of mosaics, located on the southern approach to the town of Qalaat Mudiq.

Leave a couple of hours for a leisurely walk along the length of the **cardo maximus** which served as the spine of the typically Hippodamian grid pattern, later retained by the Romans as the standard layout for their military and other colonies. The grid was based on elements 105 by 57 m. Though the *cardo* follows the line of the Hellenistic axis, it is, in its present form, a Roman improvement following the disastrous earthquake of 115. The thoroughfare is oriented precisely north/south and stretches 1.85 km, considerably longer than *Palmyra (1.2 km) or Damascus (1.35 km). It was lined with buildings of civic and religious significance. The street, 37.5 m wide with a carriageway of 20.5 m, was accessible to wheeled transport (you can still see the ruts at some points). Some of the columns along the colonnade carried brackets, a Syrian practice intended to support statues of civic or imperial dignitaries.

Our tour of Apamea will begin where the modern road bisects the *cardo*. It will first survey the northern sector, reserving for later the quarter south of the tarmac road. The northern *cardo* falls into three segments of 400-700 m each, defined by the honorific columns that mark important cross-streets. It should be borne in mind, however, that work on the *cardo* after 115 proceeded from north to south and you will thus

be seeing the thoroughfare in reverse chronological order.

On leaving the point where the tarmac road crosses the *cardo*, head north on foot. 100 m right, the remains of a **nymphaeum** or public water fountain, are seen just behind the main colonnade. Its deeply curved *exedra*, 15 m in diameter, was decorated with statues displayed in niches.

On the left, 150 m to the north, you will see remains of the east side of the **agora** or forum, originally a vast open space behind the main colonnade. The *agora* was approached by two entrances. To the south, a short transverse street lined on each side with seven columns led through a tetrapylon into the south end. Thirty metres to the north are the tumbled remains of a more monumental eight-columned entrance pavilion. The columns were supported on beautifully carved bases, almost Byzantine in their elaboration. The *agora* was a long narrow space, 45 m wide including the porticos on each side and at least 150 m long (the full extent remains unexcavated). It was under construction around AD 130 but, like parts of the *cardo* at this point, the full plan may not have been realised for some decades. Behind the *agora* (100 m on the hill to the left) are the remains of the **Temple of Zeus Belos**, dismantled in 384 by order of Bishop Marcellus.

Returning to the *cardo*, you now approach on the right the section marked by columns with twisted fluting, an effect emphasised by rotating the grooves in alternate directions. This device was a specialty of Apamea for which there are few parallels. The choice of these columns at this point, according to the Belgian archaeologist, J Ch Balty, was perhaps influenced by the siting on the left of the imposing facade of the Temple of the Tyche (or **tycheion**) honouring the city's protecting goddess. The columns and the elaborate entablature with carved trails of acanthus show a baroque taste which foreshadows late Roman style. They probably date from c AD 106.

After 100 m you enter the middle of the three segments of the **northern cardo**. (Note the base of the honorific column marking the intersection.) This is largely devoid of points of interest, except for the remains (in a hollow on the right after 130 m) of a pillar that once supported an arch over a cross street (*decumanus*). The two lower stones depict the legend of Bacchus: Lycurgus entrammelled by Bacchus in the trails of a vine; Pan with a flock of goats. At the end of this second 400 m section, the next major cross street is marked by a reconstructed votive column raised on a triangular base. (Immediately before but 100 m to the right is the House of the Aqueduct depicted in plate 3c.)

Along the final 700 m northern section of the *cardo*, about 150 m on the right past the column, remains of **baths** can be seen. Built in the last year of Trajan's reign (117 AD), they are lavish in scale with two large halls for the cold and warm baths. It is worth noting the richer, more classically portentious lines of the columns in this northern sector, reflecting the imperial inspiration for this early phase of the project as opposed to the more razzle-dazzle style adopted further south where local influences seem more predominant. This reflects Trajan's role in giving impetus to this first phase of the *cardo*. The columns with their beautiful classical entablature above also date from AD 117.

The town was surrounded by 6.3 km of **walls** pierced at major exit points with seven monumental gateways. The walls on the north and west sides are particularly well preserved. (A good view can be had from the road that heads north from the east side of the citadel). Note the effect here of Justinian's rebuilding of the walls and the addition of square bastions. On the inner side of the north wall, you can see evidence of the arcading that once supported the upper perimeter walk. From the second century northern (Antioch) gateway, one of the city's three *necropoleis* extended to the north west.

To visit the remains south of the principal *decumanus* return to the starting point at the tarmac road; 50 m on the right (west) are foundations of a **round church** dating from the reign of Justinian (527-65). The church comprised a circular chamber, 25 m in diameter, extended out to the east to end in a semi-circular apse. Even the foundations suggest in their confident shapes and the four-square precision of the masonry the imperial will that drove so many projects of this era.

A slightly smaller building, the **atrium church,** lies 50 m south but on the east side of the *cardo*. This was an enlargement, from Justinian's time, of a fifth century building. (The latter in turn replaced a fourth century synagogue of which the mosaic floor (391), based on purely geometrical motives, survived the reconstructions and the wear and tear of the centuries and is now located in the *Musées royaux d'art et de histoire*, Brussels). The style of Justinian's church reflects metropolitan rather than local architectural trends, probably resulting

from imperial patronage of the relics of Sts Cosmas and Damien venerated here. Under Justinian, the original chapel was enlarged - two side aisles and a courtyard were added. The remains of the saints were originally contained in two large stone reliquaries found (empty) in the north east chapel in 1934. (One is now in the garden of the National Museum in Damascus).

At the east end of the *decumanus*, 400 m east of the starting point on the *cardo* (follow the modern tarmac road), there is a group of buildings whose significance is still being assessed though it has been said that the most important of them, the eastern cathedral, is 'one of the most significant architectural complexes of the Christian East'[26].

From the modern road, the original *decumanus* ran 20 m to the right, its line marked by a row of excavated columns. The first site you will notice (right, 50 m) are the remains of a large complex of 80 rooms built around a peristyle court (south west corner). There were in addition two subsidiary courts as well as three reception or dining rooms (hence the description, *triclinos*), each ending in an apse. The complex (mid fourth century and later) was richly decorated with marble-clad walls and fine mosaics. (Several are now displayed in the National Museum in Damascus and in the *Musées royaux*, Brussels, including a superb hunting scene mosaic.) J Ch Balty speculates that the house may have been upgraded to serve as the official residence of the Governor of *Syria Secunda* province after its creation at the beginning of the fifth century.

The **eastern cathedral** occupies the next two segments of the city grid to the east. It was approached by steps from the *decumanus* which marked the monumental entrance to the building. This gave access to the *narthex* (the exposed pavement can be seen) and then a large court, originally surrounded by a peristyle. This grand entry court dates from 533. The earliest Christian construction was the centralised church built on the site of an earlier pagan building on the south side of the court. The plan was based on a *tetraconque* or square defined by massive pillars expanded on each side by a semi-circular row of six columns, further carried out to the east by a chapel with semi-circular apse. Most of this plan can be seen in the remains of the walls which reach 4 m. The same shape was employed at other centralised churches in the region, including Bosra (511) and Resafe (520+) though the present example is earlier, probably fifth century.

26 Balty, Jean Ch *Guide* p 115.

A second construction phase, however, was necessitated by the earthquakes of 526 and 528. In 533, a monumental entrance was added north of the *tetraconque*. Advantage was taken of the rebuilding to adapt what had basically evolved as a pilgrimage church housing the famed relics of the True Cross to serve a new purpose as the seat of an archbishop. To the south east, the complex of rooms was built to serve the ceremonies connected with baptism. Most interesting in liturgical terms, however, was the alteration of the open tetraconque shape of the church through the replacement of the east colonnade with a wall, in front of which was built a *synthronon* to frame the archbishop's ceremonial seat. All this, as well as the mosaics[27] and richly decorated capitals of the nave built into the tetraconque were inspired by Bishop Paul who played a strong role in maintaining orthodoxy against the Monophysite 'heresy' at the Council of Constantinople in 536.

On the northern side of the *decumanus*, opposite the eastern cathedral, you will find remains of three **Roman houses** excavated since 1973. The most interesting is the so-called House of Consoles whose facade has been reconstructed on the north side of the grid segment. It is grouped around a large peristyle of six by nine columns. A gallery ran along three sides, the fourth (to the east) opening on to a hall through three doors. In the style later common in the east, the hall was provided with a central fountain, marble paving and wall decorations, high ceiling and benches around the walls. The middle part of the grid segment is occupied by the House of Pilasters. The rooms are grouped around a peristyled courtyard with the main reception rooms off the courtyard to the north, though the plan is less symmetrical and more obscured by later rebuilding. (The third house is less fully excavated, its plan partly concealed by the modern road).

To reach the **theatre**, head back to the orientation point on the *cardo* and follow the modern road west. It is located behind a row of houses in a natural hollow left of the modern road immediately before it reaches the citadel. The ancient remains are rather hard to appreciate from close quarters. Most of the masonry seems to have been carried away to support building activity in the town over the centuries. Some idea of the theatre's scale (it

---

[27] Some of the most significant of the 4C mosaics that predate the Christian cathedral but were found under its structure have been removed, some to the local museum (see *caravanserai* below), some to Brussels or Damascus. They comprise an important indication of the strength of the late Roman neo-Platonist school in Apamea with their concentration on subjects from the Greek myths.

was perhaps the largest in the Roman world - 139 m in diameter with a facade of 145 m) can be guaged by looking back at it from the walls of the castle or citadel site. It has been tentatively dated to the late second century AD.

Qalaat al-Mudiq, the **citadel** of Apamea (100 m north west of the theatre), was in use from Seleucid times and played a particularly important role as an Arab point of defence against the Crusades. The Orontes Valley for long served as the interface between the Frankish and Arab worlds, with most sites on the east side of the valley (notably *Shaizar and *Maarat al-Numan) confronting the Crusader castles on the west (*Qalaat Burzey, *Qalaat Mehelbeh, *Qalaat Abu Qobeis and *Masyaf). The remains of the medieval citadel show no trace of the Crusader occupation (1106-49). The few remains of the later Arab fortress are largely swallowed by the modern upper village but parts of the outer walls of variegated stonework (some re-used from earlier periods) are Mameluke (13th century). There is a beautiful view over the Orontes valley from the gate of the citadel (south side) with the Jebel Ansariye to the west and Jebel Zawiye to the north east. An Ottoman mosque (second half of 16th century) lies on a south west spur of the citadel mound.

The Ottoman *caravanserai* lies on the southern end of the modern village just below the escarpment. It has recently been converted into a **museum** of mosaics, inscriptions, sarcophagi and statuary, many collected from the region of Apamea. The gloomy recesses of the 16th century *caravanserai* are not ideal for their display. The *caravanserai* itself is an impressive building, 80 m square with a vast internal courtyard entered by a single gateway from the north. It is perhaps the most imposing of the surviving caravan stops built in Syria by the Ottomans to service the pilgrimage route from Istanbul to Mecca.

Enter the museum by the door to the left of the entrance passageway and proceed clockwise. As there is no catalogue, the following notes, based on Janine Balty's survey, give a brief account of the more easily identifiable finds displayed:

- The large mosaic set into the floor of the north eastern wing as you enter depicts **Socrates and the Sages** - 2.62 m by 1.3 m, third quarter of fourth century - from the building which preceded the eastern cathedral, dated 362-3. Socrates surrounded by six bearded sages, each wearing the plain *pallium* of a philosopher, seated at a curved table. The faces are superb examples of late Roman mosaic work and reveal the presence in Apamea of a strong centre of neo-Platonic philosophy, attracted by the teachings of Iamblichos. Janine Balty notes the resemblance between this scene and the depiction of Christ at table surrounded by his disciples. Perhaps, she observes, this is Christ 'repaganised', part of a process of rediscovering the Hellenism of the past given new impulse at this time by the decrees of Julian the Apostate (361-3).

- A number of funerary stelae are displayed on the wall to the left. They are set out in chronological order from Hellenistic times to the third century AD.

- In the middle of this (northern) outer wall is a sarcophagus decorated with cupids found in the northern necropolis - second century AD. The Latin inscription is to a 44 year old ex-legionnaire of 22 years' service, dedicated by his wife.

- In the middle of the wall opposite, another sarcophagus from the same tomb, this time dedicated by a centurion in the Second Parthian Legion in honour of his wife of 28 years.

- Turn the corner but stay with the left (outer) wall. The fourth object on the left after the turn is a dedicatory plaque found at pavement level on the *cardo* recording the dedication of a statue installed on the column bracket above, in honour of a Lucius Julius Agrippa.

- Other inscriptions were carved onto the consoles of the columns as can be seen further on to the left.

- Further on again along the left wall, opposite the second mosaic set into the floor, is a statue of a woman (head missing) found near the *nymphaeum* and which probably was part of the decoration of the monument.

- The mosaic just mentioned is a long scene depicting the **Judgment of the Nereides** - 7.69 m by 1.56 m, third quarter of third century - from the *triclinium*. A work of exceptional interest, this frieze of 13 figures depicts a contest between the Nereides and Thetis on the one hand and Cassiopeia on the other to determine who was the most beautiful. The winner, Cassiopeia, is the nude figure second from the right. The judge of the contest, Poseidon, is fourth from the right.

The other wings of the museum are incomplete but the eventual plan include the dedication of the west section to Christian remains including mosaics from the churches at Huarte.

Some 15 km to the north west, in the Jebel Zawiye (tarmac road from north west corner of ruins), the monastery of **Huarte** (fourth or fifth century) has been among a number of Byzantine sites dug by a French expedition since 1973. The remains (which include two parallel churches - that to the north is dedicated to St Michael the Archangel; the larger southern one was built in 483 by Bishop Photios) are largely confined to foundations and lower walls. The existence of two churches is perhaps explained by the need to keep some distance between the official cult (which discouraged giving too much attention to angels) and the popular traditions of the parishioners. Mosaics and other precious finds have been removed to the Apamea Museum and to the Damascus Museum (notably the 'Animal Chase' scene from the upper church - 10.75 m by 2.20 m, AD 472 or 487).

REFS: **Apamea**: *BG* pp 370-2; Balty, Janine (ed) *'Apamée' (73-9)* pp 103-34; Balty, Janine *Mosaïques*; Balty, J Ch *Guide*; Balty, J Ch 'Groupe episcopal'; Balty, J and J Ch; Berchem and Fatio pp 189 ff; Dussaud *Topographie* pp 198-9; Sauvaget 'Les Caravanserails syriens du Hadjdj de Constantinople' in *Ars Islamica* 1937 p 110.
Huarte: Canivet *L'ensemble*; Canivet *Huarte* pp 215-9.

Arwad

VARIANTS: Arvad (Phn/bib); Arados (Grk); Aradus (Lat); Ruwad
PERIOD: Phn/../Arb RATING: T MAP: 66 ITIN: 5a

LOCATION: 2.5 km offshore (south west) from *Tartus. Take ferry service (every 15 minutes) from jetty along the Tartus esplanade (opposite the old fortress walls, south end).

History

At the beginning of his remarkable study of Arwad's role in the classical world, J-P Rey-Coquais notes that on first sight descending the hills towards the coast the tiny island appears lost in a vast sea. Tiny though it is, Arwad has had an extraordinary history. Any place that has its origins written up in Genesis (X, 18) must be destined for a role of some significance. As the sole habitable island off the Syrian coast and the only sizeable natural port between Tripoli and the mouth of the Orontes its inhabitants were able at times to dominate large areas of the fertile coastal region. The island's natural role as a fortress (the name derives from the Phoenician word for 'refuge') were supplemented by a fresh water spring which rose from the seabed between Arwad and the coast, strengthening the islanders' capacity to resist seiges beyond the limits imposed by rainwater resources.

Originally settled as an urban centre by the Canaanites, it was a prosperous trading centre (mentioned in the Amarna archives) by the late second millennium. It was taken by the Pharaoh Tuthmosis III during his fifth campaign in Syria. Under the Phoenicians, it became the base for a series of settlements of the coast as far as *Jeble (25 km south of *Latakia) and inland almost to Homs and to the cult centre at Baetocecea (*Husn Suleiman). Like Tyre (southern Lebanon), its seafaring skills gave it an important role in eastern Mediterranean trade in the first half of the first millennium BC. It used its status in the mainland federation to secure access to timber for shipbuilding.

Arwad was later taken by the Assyrians and the Achaemenid Persians. (Arvadites fought in Xerxes' fleet in 480 BC at the Battle of Salamis - Herodotus VII, 98.) In 333 BC, Arwad's King Gerostratos quickly put his domains at the disposal of Alexander. His voluntary association with Greek rule enabled Arwad to retain a measure of independence under the Seleucids, especially when the Seleucid monarchs needed to engage its support against the Ptolemies to the south. (Like other Phoenician centres, its local monarchy had quietly been dropped by the mid third century.) In the mid second century BC, however, Arwad fell out of favour after siding with the Egyptians, though it later recovered its limited autonomy until the Roman conquest in 64 BC. (It was subsequently punished for siding with Pompey in the civil war of 46 BC and was caught off-side again in 41 when the islanders burned alive an envoy of Mark Antony who had come to demand the return of a brother of Cleopatra.) Its freedom of manoeuvre was further eroded under Roman rule. It lost control of the federated mainland centres and its role diminished with the rise of a new mainland town, Tartus. The island became, in Rey-Coquais' words, a sort of 'museum town'. St Paul is said to have stopped there on his journey to Rome. It was a Byzantine naval base but fell to the Arabs late (640), holding out after mainland Syria. The Templars were given custody of the island during the Crusader presence. From Arwad, the Crusaders made their last stand, hanging on until 1302, many years after the fall of the great mainland bastions - the *Krak (1271), *Qalaat Marqab (1285), Tripoli (1289) - and a decade after the loss of Acre and their last bases on the mainland, Athlit and Tartus (1291). In 1302, however, the last Crusader troops were slaughtered, the surviving Templar knights taken into captivity in Cairo and the Frankish fortress largely demolished.

Visit

Arwad has become something of a local tourist attraction, especially in summer with many visitors to its harbourside fish restaurants. The press of day-trippers plus the over-population of the island in recent decades, makes a visit a bit of a scramble at peak times such as Friday or during feasts.

Oval in shape and aligned approximately north west/south east, the island is small (less than 800 m long; 300 m wide) and can be visited in a couple of hours. The port lies in the north east quarter, its position facing the coast providing relatively safe anchorage from winter storms. The anchorage is divided by a low promontory which was artificially built up to serve as a jetty in ancient times. On the western and south western sides, the island was once protected by a long wall of the Phoenician or later periods. Remnants of the huge retaining blocks can be seen.

There are two small castles. The one in the middle of the island represents only part of the 13th century Crusader fort (nowadays a small museum). Above the gate are the coat of arms of the Lusignan family, Kings of Jerusalem and of Cyprus. The other castle (port side) is Arab.

REFS: *BG* p 437; Dussaud *Topographie* pp 121-3; Grainger pp 92-5 *et passim*; Rey-Coquais *Arados*; Seyrig *Aradus*.

Atil

VARIANTS: Athela (Lat)
PERIOD: Rom RATING: * MAP: 63 ITIN: 2b

LOCATION: 12 km south of *Shahba (6 km north of *Suweida) on the Damascus/Suweida road.

Two apparently identical small temples were constructed here in Roman times. Sources give no explanation as to why the same plan, design and ornamentation were used in each building, one on the north edge of town, the second about 250 m to the south. The southern one is better preserved and the facade is fully exposed. The northern one is still encumbered by part of a modern dwelling and the facade is only extant to a limited degree. It preserves, however, the lateral arch which held the roof. The quality of the detail is quite fine and recalls the temple at *Mushennef.

Like many other settlements in the Hauran (ancient *Auranitis* - see box page 228 under *Suweida), Atil's building programme seems to date from the second century AD when the area was a major source of grain for the Roman market. On the southern temple, an inscription records its construction in the 14th year of the reign of Antoninus Pius (AD 151). The other is assumed to be from the same period, the high-water mark of the imperial classical style in the Hauran.

REFS: Butler *AE* pp 343-6; Butler *PE* II/A/5 pp 355-6; *BG* p 512; Dussaud *Topographie* p 349.

B

Baghuz (Abu Kemal)

VARIANTS: Nagiateh, Corsoteh (anc); Irzi (Arb)
PERIOD: Rom RATING: - MAP: 73 ITIN: 12b

LOCATION: 130 km south east of *Deir al-Zor on the left bank of the Euphrates. Take the Euphrates crossing 4 km before Abu Kemal. From there walk 1 km downstream.

Those with a passion for Roman tower tombs in the style of Palmyra can satisfy their spirit of adventure by visiting the small group on the left bank of the Euphrates at Baghuz, opposite the Syrian/Iraqi border town of Abu Kemal. The tombs lie on the edge of the bluff where the steppe country meets the river flats.

Five extant tower tombs date from before or during the high Palmyrene period when this was probably the necropolis area for a Parthian frontier settlement (first to third centuries AD)[28]. Two towers are in reasonable condition with recognisable architectural detail on their facades (pilasters; staircases rising to upper storeys). The largest is almost 5 m² in plan and has a portico on each face. Unlike most of the Palmyra tower tombs of this period which used a system of niches to hold the remains of the dead in the tower superstructure, the Baghuz towers continued to use vaulted underground chambers for burial. The main purpose of the tower above seems to have been to provide a roof terrace for funerary rituals. Certainly the style, methods of construction and architectural treatment are cruder than at Palmyra though a comparable grade of easily-worked limestone is used.

Baghuz was the site of the even more ancient Nagiateh with pottery remains going back to the fifth millennium BC and an extensive necropolis of the early second millennium BC. The ruins of Corsoteh, mentioned by Xenophon (c 400 BC) were located here.

REFS: Bell *Amurath* p 83-4; BG p 499; Hopkins pp 184-5; Toll *Excavations at Dura-Europos - Ninth Season 1935-36 - Part II The Necropolis* pl LXV 1-4; Will pp 258-312.

---

[28] The tombs could date from anywhere between 1C BC and AD 2C judging by analogies with Palmyra styles. The Parthian town was probably on the river flats and has long since been swept away by the seasonal floods.

Bakas (Shugur Qadim)

VARIANTS: Bakas-Shugur[29]; Bakas Shoqr
PERIOD: Cru RATING: T MAP: 67 ITIN: 7b

LOCATION: Reaching the village of Shugur Qadim is easy enough. Take the Latakia road from Jisr al-Shugur (starting point, main square). At 6.6 km, turn right, following the sealed road +4.5 km to village. Now the hard bit. Though the remains of the castle are almost at arm's length across a ravine from the village mosque, you will need to choose one of two routes to try on foot - either a brief but hair-raising scramble across the rock-face of the ravine; or a longer circuit, looping through the ravine below the village (20 minute hike). A good view of the site (but no access to the castle) can be obtained 1 km before the village by walking down the ridge to the right.

The most breath-taking castle site in Syria. The minimal remains of this Crusader fortress perch precariously on a high promontory hundreds of metres above a sharp bend in the river, the Nahr al-Abiad (a tributary of the Orontes). The nearby village of Shugur Qadim is a stop on the Aleppo/Latakia railway and the ridge that runs down to the castle is pierced by a railway tunnel. While the remains are hard to relate to the original construction, it is worth the effort of the final walk to enjoy the splendour of the scene and the views of the mountainous country to the north, with the river rushing away at a dizzying distance below to the east.

The northern end of the site had been fortified by the Byzantines. It was rebuilt and extended along the southern reaches of the promontory by the Crusaders but the date of their occupation is not known[30] Due to the narrowness of the site, the Crusaders divided the fortifications between two separate compounds. The lower northern keep, Shugur (over 200 m long but only 30 m wide), was separated from the southern fortification, Bakas, by an open space protected by two small ditches. To separate the southern compound from the

---

[29] In recent centuries, the two castles were given different names - Bakas (the Crusader name for the whole complex) was applied to the south and Shugur to the northern part.

[30] There is no mention of the castle in Crusader records. Our information comes from Arab written sources, especially the accounts of Saladin's campaign of 1188.

adjoining heights, a deep trench was cut in the rock.

The twin castles fell to Saladin in his famous

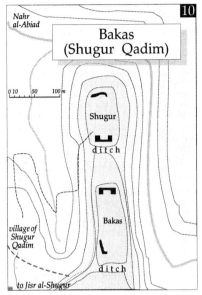

Nahr al-Abiad

10

Bakas (Shugur Qadim)

0 10   50   100 m

Shugur

ditch

Bakas

village of Shugur Qadim

ditch

to Jisr al-Shugur

campaign of 1188 when he rolled back the greater part of the Crusader presence on the eastern side of the coastal mountains (see box on Saladin's Campaign of 1188 in Section 1 - page 13). The attack began immediately after the fall of the Château of Saône (*Qalaat Saladin) on 30 July. The southern compound fell to Saladin on 5 August, the Crusaders taking refuge in the lower redoubt to the north. The garrison surrendered on 12 August having failed in their attempts to attract help from Bohemond III, Prince of Antioch, in whose realms the castle lay. The Mongols took the fortress, probably in 1260, but Baibars seized it from them in the next decade. An earthquake caused serious damage in 1404, beginning the process of decay which has reduced the ruins to a few fragments of walls and cisterns.

REFS: BG p 476; Deschamps *Châteaux III* pp 349-50; Dussaud *Topographie* pp 155-62; Huygens pp 279-80; Runciman II p 470; van Berchem & Fatio pp 251-59.

Bamuqqa

VARIANTS: Bamuka
PERIOD: Rom/Byz   ALT: 590 m   RATING: *
MAP: 69 ITIN: 9b

LOCATION: 55 km west of Aleppo. From the Bab al-Hawa turnoff (starting point of Itin 9b) follow the road to *Harim for c10.5 km until you reach the village of Bashmishli (at the point where the road turns left to Barisha). Keep going to the western edge of Bashmishli and ascend the ridge to the right by foot, heading towards a grove of old oaks on the skyline.

Once you reach it, it is hard to resist the charm of this setting, one of the most perfect picnic spots in all of Syria. The remains are scattered about the oak grove on a ridge that looks down over the Plain of Amuq, east of Antioch. As a place of refuge from the heat on a warm day and to savour the beauty of the 'dead cities' environment, Bamuqqa is well worth the short hike.

Moreover, the site includes a remarkable Roman ruin, a sizeable **villa** with which are associated (140 m to the south) a large cistern and an underground tomb with a pillared facade. There are remains (north) of 16 more modest farmhouses of a later period and, in the same area, a small church (sixth century).

Tchalenko dates the original farmhouse as early as the first century AD and speculates that the easy communications from this area to Antioch and the favourable soil made it one of the first areas settled by the moneyed class which Roman occupation brought into existence. He describes this farmhouse as 'one of the most interesting monuments of the region'. It comprises two rooms, one above the other and connected by an external staircase. The local (Alawi) villagers use them these days to hold fuel lamps as the grove and farm house harbour the tomb of a local saint, Sheikh Khalil Sadeq[31]. The use of the grove for religious purposes has probably discouraged the dismantling of the remains for building materials.

The dating of the villa (and the tomb, probably commemorating the first proprietor) is disputed. Butler believed it dated from the second or third century. Tchalenko prefers the first century because of the earlier style of the decoration: 'Since its characteristics recall no other Syrian building influenced by Roman styles, we have to resort to a local Antiochene tradition of which this is perhaps the sole extant

---

[31] Pena *et al Inventaire* p 53 notes that the *stele* marking the saint's tomb was erected in 1196, some time after Nur al-Din had taken *Harem and the area of Jebel Barisha from the Crusaders.

example. He also compares the tomb to the one in *Beshindlaye but notes the richer but heavier decoration of the latter. Tchalenko surmised that the villa was the occasional residence of a landlord who lived most of the year in Antioch, leaving the running of the olive farm to a local overseer and visiting for the harvest season, one of the first signs of the systematic agricultural exploitation of the mountainous area. (Beshindlaye was probably settled about the same time). Most other Roman sites in the area date from the second century.

No other houses seem to have been built in Bamuqqa until the fourth century. The 16 independent farm houses (north of the Roman villa - see above) established by the fifth century reflect the explosion of small-holder operations in the Byzantine period. After the curiously late construction of the main **church** (apparently not built until as late as the decades immediately before the Muslim conquest - extreme north of the site), the town was abandoned in the seventh century but reoccupied in the 12th century.

REFS: Butler *AE* II pp 63, 79; Pena *et al Cenobites* p 62; Pena *et al Inventaire* pp 52-6; Tchalenko *Villages* I pp 300-18, II pl XCII-XCIX, CXIV, CXXXV.

Baqirha

VARIANTS: Bakirha
PERIOD: Rom/Byz RATING: * MAP: 69 ITIN: 9b

> LOCATION: From the turn-off just before Bab el Hawa (starting point) turn left; go via Sarmada, take right road and ascend steep hill (Harim road); at 9.4 km, a sign in English points right to Baqirha; follow the road (past Babuta on right) for +3 km to Roman temple of Zeus Bombos on the right; churches and town are lower down the slope.

An exceptionally interesting site on the edge of the hills looking over the Plain of Amuq (east of Antioch) and the Amanus Mountains to the north. In the distance are further dead cities up to the Turkish frontier.

The **Roman temple** whose surprisingly intact remains stand on the southern edge of the site consists of a *cella* preceded by a four-columned portico of which one shaky column (with a superb Corinthian capital) is still standing. The surrounding compound wall has been removed except for the monumental gateway dated by inscription to AD 161. The temple is dedicated to Zeus Bombos (Zeus of the Altar) but was probably established on the site of an earlier Semitic cult centre. Butler notes: 'The site may easily have been one of the 'high places' of the early inhabitants which the Roman

conquerors chose further to sanctify by the building of a shrine which should give a Greco-Roman character to this ancient Oriental place of worship and clothe the old tradition with the dignity of classic architecture'.

There were other temples to Zeus in the area, notably the one whose remains can still be traced on the top of nearby Jebel Sheikh Barakat (*Qatura)[32]. The Baqirha temple, however, is the best preserved and is a remarkable sight in this sweeping landscape. Butler described 'the treatment of the whole edifice and its decorative effect (as) the most chaste and dignified in all Syria' - ie lacking the later 'coarse over-elaboration' found at Baalbek. The fact that virtually none of the fabric of the temple *cella* has been removed from the scene makes it a prime candidate for reconstruction one day.

Tchalenko's researches in the area emphasise the importance of the olive oil processing industry in the establishment and subsequent prosperity of the town. He notes that the first presses were probably set up in the second century AD under the auspices of the temple but later greatly expanded in private hands. The industry flourished given the area's easy access to Antioch and the sea. It laid the basis for the later expansion of the settlement during the Byzantine period, hence the remarkable extent of the ruins in the lower town.

Further down the hill from the temple, the jumbled ruins of this extensive Byzantine town contains much of interest but at first sight the confusion seems total. There are two important churches, however, which can be identified relatively easily. The first is the **eastern church** standing on the eastern edge of the town, the western facade and narthex of which have survived almost intact although the rest of the building is in ruins. The church is dated, by inscription, to 546 and is a columned basilica of six bays. Even for the Jebel Barisha region, where heavy use of decoration prevailed, the degree of moulded decorative courses is extraordinary, the effect being somewhat like drooping spaghetti. The interior decoration is also free-wheeling, with considerable departure from classical models in the column bases, capitals and mouldings of the chancel arch. The western portal is a copy of the famous doorways of the architect Kyros.

The second **(western) church** was probably part of a monastic institution. Little survives

---

[32] At Baqirha, Zeus bears the attribute Bombos (Grk: altar), equivalent to the Aramaic version, Zeus Madbachos, on Jebel Sheikh Barakat.

except the eastern wall. The central nave included a *bema*. In date it is earlier (501 according to the inscription on the northern gate, though parts of the compound are perhaps earlier - first half of the fifth century). The compound includes a baptistery, almost a cube in shape and richly decorated with grooved mouldings. Note especially the classic shape of the east door to the courtyard, originally preceded by a portico.

REFS: *BG* p 407; Butler *AE* p 66-9, 190-3, 209-12; Butler *EC* pp 133-4, 139, 145, 148, 153, 157; Butler *PE* II/B/4 pp 195-201; Callot and Marcillet-Jaubert pp 184-5; Lassus *Sanctuaires chrétiens* pp 35, 45, 59, 222, 292; Mattern pp 70-3; Pena *et al Inventaire* pp 72-5; Tchalenko *Villages* I pp 51 n3, 106-7, 110-1; Tchalenko and Bachache pl 323-334.

Bara

VARIANTS: Kapropera (Grk); Kfer al-Bara, al-Kfer (Arb)
PERIOD: Byz   ALT: 670 m   RATING: ** MAP: 11, 70   ITIN: 9c

LOCATION: From Aleppo, follow the main Damascus highway for 67 km, taking Latakia road (right) at Saraqeb junction. Pass the al-Riha turnoff and continue on c+5 km to Urum al-Joz (25 km from Saraqeb). From here take the road south (left) for +14 km to Bara. The site can also be reached (from Damascus) by turning off the Aleppo road at *Maarat al-Numan and taking the road west to Kfer Nabil then north (+5 km) to Bara.

In terms of size and variety of remains, this is one of the most impressive of the dead cities and one which those unfamiliar with the area might choose as a good starting point. The site is huge, extending over an area of 2 km by 3 km and although some motor access roads to the parts of major interest have recently been laid, you need to be prepared for a fair bit of rock fence climbing and walking across often muddy fields.

History

The importance of the settlement resulted from its location between the two major sections of Jebel Zawiye, the trough in which it is located forming a north/south corridor essential for internal access. Though it expanded rapidly during its boom period in the fifth and sixth centuries, settlement at Bara only began in the fourth century. The site was blessed with a plentiful supply of underground water and the first settlers gathered around a church on the eastern edge of the Wadi al-Goz (west of the modern village, running parallel with the main road). At about the same period, a second development, originally isolated in its own compound *(temenos)*, began at the great basilica today called *al-Husn* (north of the main agglomeration).

The settlement rapidly enriched itself through its olive oil and wine industry. By the fifth century, according to Tchalenko, Bara became the processing point for other surrounding villages. An area to the north, called *al-Muallaq*, developed around huge monastic properties. A series of private farms also sprang up in the sectors known as al-Deir, Deir Sobat, Braij, and Deir Debbane. It eventually included five churches which can still be recognised (and another three referred to in sources). The style of buildings was lavish, indicating the high level of prosperity, and the processing facilities, particularly olive oil presses, were built to industrial standard. The people who could finance these buildings could also afford to bury themselves in style and there are two pyramidal-roofed tomb buildings from the sixth century built on a monumental scale.

Settlement here does not seem to have been disrupted by the Muslim conquest, perhaps because the scale of the centre was much greater than the average. Its location on a natural transport route and relatively near the edge of the limestone region gave it a more diversified role. Its economy thus survived the collapse of the export trade to Europe following the disruption of trade routes to the west.

When the Crusaders reached Bara after their capture of Antioch in 1098, they found a Bishop still in residence (affiliated to Constantinople). Raymond de Saint Gilles, Count of Toulouse (later Count of Tripoli) took control of the town on 25 September, 1098, and later installed a Latin Bishop. (The latter distinguished himself by urging on those responsible for the horrendous massacre at nearby *Maarat al-Numan in January 1099 when 20,000 Muslims - men, women and children - were slaughtered by the Crusading forces). The area remained under Crusader control until 1148 but thereafter reverted to the Muslims. They fortified their presence with the building of *Qalaat Abu Safian*.

Visit

Given the difficulty of finding your way between the olive groves, the rock-piled fences and broken terrain, many visitors will be tempted simply to take the site as it comes, which is not a bad first approach. However, for a visit aimed at taking in as many of the main buildings as possible in a period of three or four hours, the following sequence may be useful.

The ruins run roughly north/south, to the right of the Urum al-Joz/Kfer Nabil main road as you head south. A good place to start a tour would be the monastery of **Deir Sobat** which lies on the south edge of the ruins. You reach it by a laneway which heads west out of the south part of the village of al-Kfer al-Bara and crosses the deep *wadi*. The monastery is on the slopes as you ascend the *wadi* and is reasonably well preserved, part of its upper walls having recently

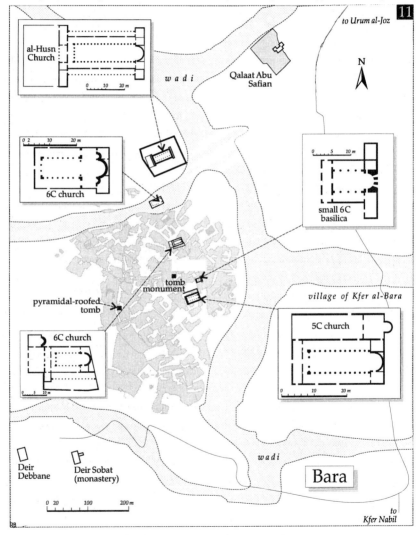

to Urum al-Joz

al-Husn Church

0   10   20 m

w a d i

Qalaat Abu Safian

N

0   5   10 m

small 6 C basilica

0 2   10   20 m

6C church

tomb monument

pyramidal-roofed tomb

6C church

0   5   10 m

village of Kfer al-Bara

5C church

0   10   20 m

w a d i

Deir Debbane

Deir Sobat (monastery)

0   20   100   200 m

Bara

to Kfer Nabil

been reconstructed.

The central building is dated to the sixth century. It comprises a large central chamber off which corridors and rooms are arranged. The room on the east side was probably an *oratorium* for the celebration of Mass. Two other monasteries were located in the south - Deir Debbane and al-Deir - but are in a poorer state of preservation.

Working your way north, you should now head for the first of the **pyramidal-roofed tombs**, visible about 200 m away. (A tarmac road now leads past it; turn off before you descend the wadi again.) This is the larger of the two examples and has a roof based on a considerably elongated pyramid. A beautiful band of carved acanthus leaf decoration surrounds the top of the cubed base and is repeated over the lintel of the door. It is interrupted by the interweaving of the Christian 'chi-ro' symbol. The corners were terminated in pilasters of Corinthian design. Altogether, the effect on a building of relatively exuberant shape is to add an element of restraint and classical balance. Inside, the burial chamber contains five sarcophagi with further decoration. The substantially smaller second tomb is in excellent condition.

The five **churches** of Bara stretch along the central line of ruins from a point roughly 100 m south east of the large tomb monument. The group ends 500 m to the north in the church known as *al-Husn*. You may wish to explore this central area of churches and substantial villas by planning your own fence-hopping.

Beginning from the south, the first church in the sequence is a large (25 m by 17 m) example from the fifth century. Immediately to the north east is a smaller (sixth century), perhaps part of a monastery. Eighty metres north of the large tomb monument is the third church and, 200 m north-north west, the fourth. Mattern notes that the latter, a sixth century construction, barely distinguishable in its ruined state, has each of its three aisles terminate in a semi-circular apse. Continue another 50 m north and you should end up at the al-Husn compound which provided a convenient point for the Arabs to fortify in the late Crusader period. The church of al-Husn is notable for its size (c50 m by 35 m within a compound of 100 m by 60 m), its side porticos and the use of a gallery above the side aisles but very little of this can be appreciated given the lack of walls.

About 400 m to the north east, you will find the remains of another Arab fort **Qalaat Abu**

Safian. It comprises a donjon, protected by walls of 4-5 m and a surrounding wall with bastions in two corners.

REFS: *BG* p 411; Butler *AE* p 97; Butler *EC* pp 66-7; Vogüé I pp 93, 105-6; Tchalenko II pl XII, LXXXI, CXXXVII-IX, CCXII; Mattern pp 35-4.

Barad

VARIANTS: Kaprobarada (Grk), Barade (Brad) (Lat); Brad (Arb)
PERIOD: Rom/Byz ALT: 490 m RATING: -
MAP: *12*, 67 ITIN: 9a

LOCATION: From Deir Semaan, 14 km north along Afrin road. On north edge of al-Barsuta, turn right along a track that ascends the plateau and continues SE for +10 km. (Four wheel drive esential or hire local truck.)

An extensive site (in area, the largest in the Jebel Semaan zone) located on a plateau with a rich variety of remains including a classical tomb, a public bath house, and three churches (one a major basilica). From the second century, Barad was a small provincial city with its own industries, rather than a rural settlement. It was probably the headquarters of an administrative district controlling the northern part of the limestone country. The oil industry was considerably expanded in the fourth century when the principal cathedral replaced the pagan temple. The surrounding terrain offered a variety of crops in addition to olives including grains and grapes.

The only notable surviving building in classical style is the **monumental tomb**, probably dating from the second or the first half of the third century AD and located on the northern edge of the town. The style is rather heavy (not unlike the monumental arch in *Latakia) with four typically Syrian-Roman arches holding up a medium-pitched pyramidal roof. This structure rests on a podium base under which is the burial chamber, originally housing five *sarcophagi*, four within burial niches, one free-standing. Within the open structure itself, two further *sarcophagi* were placed on the podium. It is, says Butler, 'the earliest, and quite the most sumptuous, of this particular type of tomb structure which continued to be built through the fourth century in northern Syria'[33]. The idea of the four-faced arch is essentially classical but much of the detail is oriental in inspiration, particularly the horse-shoe shape of the arches and the moulding of the cornice. At the top of the arches originally stood a series of four busts.

---

[33] Butler *PE* II/B/6 p 299

The ruins of the **baths** complex (northern edge of the settlement, 100 m north west of the mausoleum) provide one of the few examples from the Roman period in Syria. In style the low-vaulted rooms are quite different from the fifth century baths at *Serjilla. Butler dates the building to the third century (cf baths at *Bosra in southern Syria) but Tchalenko believes they were built in the second century as part of the landowner's mansion that preceded the later village.

The great **cathedral** of Barad (or Church of Julianos, centre of the town) is one of the largest church buildings in Syria, apart from the pilgrimage centre of Saint Simeon. Sadly, it is almost a complete ruin and there is little to appreciate beyond a few piers and part of the east wall. The plan is typical of the period (399-402) in northern Syria, the rear wall, for example, being flat and the curved apse accommodated by complicated masonry to square the circle. The arcades of the nave are supported on eight columns and two piers. A *bema* stood in the central nave. There are still some classical touches such as the rectangular west central doorway with dignified jambs and lintel. But above it, the Syrian influence is strong in the more flamboyant use of arches (seen in Butler or Tchalenko's reconstructions). The west entrance was preceded by a colonnaded portico. To the south stood an oblong atrium.

Slightly to the north east lies the northern **church** dated by inscription to 561. Better preserved than the cathedral, the naves are divided by three sweeping arches carried on two free-standing piers, an arrangement more common at this time in the southern parts of the limestone country (*Qalb Lozeh, *Ruweiha) and in southern Syria. The sixth century taste for swooping moulded decoration is indulged in the external treatment of the upper windows.

The south west **church** (sixth century) lies in that quarter of the main quadrilateral of ruins.

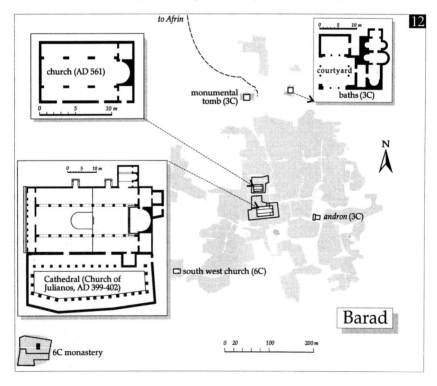

to Afrin

church (AD 561)

0   5   10 m

0   5   10 m

courtyard

baths (3C)

monumental
tomb (3C)

N

0   5   10 m

Cathedral (Church of
Julianos, AD 399-402)

andron (3C)

south west church (6C)

Barad

6C monastery

0   20   100   200 m

The nave is undivided and the sanctuary square in plan. Along the southern wall runs a colonnade. The windows are framed by looping incised decorations, a rather overdone effect in this case.

The **andron** or meeting place lies 100 m to the east of the cathedral. Not unlike a large house in appearance, with double portico along the front, the fact that the lower storey was undivided favours the interpretation that it had some civic purpose. The second storey was supported on three wide (5 m) arches spanning the ground floor. The building is dated to 496. To the east lie the remains of an inn (207-8) and an oil press.

500 m to the south west of the main agglomoration lie the ruins of a sixth century **monastery** (also known as Qasr al-Barad) on the crest of a knoll. The single-naved chapel is reasonably intact and remains can be seen of the high tower (22 m south of the western end of the chapel) and other buildings including the hostelry (17 m east of the chapel).

REFS: *BG* p 403; Butler *EC* pp 109-10, 142; Butler *PE* II/B/6 pp 299-315; Mattern p 140; Tchalenko *Villages* II pl XV, XIX, CXXXIII, CCVII; Tchalenko and Baccache pl 5-32.

Basofan

VARIANTS: Basufan
PERIOD: Byz RATING: - MAP: 68 ITIN: 9a

> LOCATION: Take the road which heads north from the east side of Saint Simeon. Continue for 5 km as the road heads north east.
> NOTE: +1.5 km east are the remains of Kfer Lab.

The remains are not particularly striking at first sight as the scattered ruins are disguised among modern houses. The Church of St Phocas (dated 491-2[34]) is one of the largest churches in the Jebel Semaan area (it measures 15.4 m by 24 m) and was apparently destroyed by fire. The columned basilica is closely related in style to the *martyrium* of *Saint Simeon, particularly in the way in which the curve of the rear wall of the apse is retained on the exterior instead of being filled in by a straight wall between the line of the two side chambers as in earlier examples. Tchalenko speculates that it could have been built by the same craftsmen as Saint Simeon. Butler also draws attention to the two columns

---

[34] The inscription recording the date is in Syriac, the language much more commonly found in the Jebel Semaan area than in the south of the limestone country more directly influenced from Greek-oriented Antioch or Apamea.

with Corinthian (wind blown) capitals and spiral fluting that support the chancel arch framed by piers with facing pilasters. Beyer remarks on the decorative treatment of the south wall and the use of moulded bands to divide the wall and surround the windows with festoons, a style he believed stemmed from the ideas tried out at the nearby church of Saint Simeon.

Butler comments[35] that 'it is a pity this church is so ruinous for in it we have a summing up of the architecture of the fifth century and a carrying to their ultimate forms of expression of a number of motives that have been developing for a century."

To the west is a second church, in ruins, which Butler[36] dates to the first quarter of the sixth century.

REFS: Beyer p 58; Biscop and Sodini p 282; Butler *EC* pp 67-70, 127; Butler *PE* II/B/6 pp 284-7; Krautheimer p 160; Tchalenko *Villages* II pl LXXIV.

Behyo

VARIANTS:
PERIOD: Byz ALT: 720 m RATING: - MAP: 68

> LOCATION: See *Beshindlaye. Before Beshindlaye, stop at 28 km and climb up the steep hill to the left - 10 minute scramble. (The ruins are not visible from this point on the road).

At first sight, this village lying on the crest of the Jebel al-Ala and looking down over the Plain of Self to the east presents an indecipherable jumble of huge rocks, impossibly tumbled in disorder. On closer inspection, you should be able to distinguish two sizeable churches. Why such a large community would have gathered in this isolated spot, surrounded by no apparent plots of arable land, is still difficult to fathom. The researches of Tchalenko have devoted considerable attention to this site. It was apparently a late starter, being developed for olive-growing only after other, more easily exploited, sites had been populated. (The more arable areas such as *Bamuqqa had been opened up as early as the first century AD).

Behyo did not attract settlement until the boom in olive oil prices in the fifth century justified the development of its relatively marginal potential. By this period, the olive oil industry was no longer dominated by the large landlords but had been transformed by the activities of small-holders. According to Tchalenko 'it is probably

---

[35] *EC* p 67.
[36] *EC* p 128.

this village ... which represents most faithfully the changes in the ancient habitat of the region which evolved from the great aristocratic holdings into an agglomeration of small agricultural establishments'.

The ruins include a variety of house types of the fifth and sixth centuries - villas, farmhouses, workers' cottages. Remains of many olive presses are found around the edges of the ruins. The two churches lie to the east of the settlement. The church on the north east corner of the ruins dates from the first part of the sixth century but is badly ruined. It employed the same type of sweeping lateral arches as at *Qalb Lozeh a little to the north but on a smaller scale. The second, older, church lies immediately to the south west, its east wall still relatively intact. It dates from the middle of the fifth century and Tchalenko unearthed in it a horseshoe-shaped *bema*. It takes the form of a basilica with five columns on each side of the central nave. The facades are sober and the scale of the blocks convey an impression of massiveness.

REFS: *BG* p 409; Butler *AE* p 204; Butler *EC* pp 141, 204; Vogüé II pl 113, 137-8; Tchalenko *Villages* I pp 346-72, II pl CIX-CXXIII, CXXXV, CXCIX-CC; Tchalenko and Baccache pl 399-417.

Beshindlaye

VARIANTS:
PERIOD: Rom/Byz RATING: - MAP: 69 ITIN: 9b

> LOCATION: Take the *Harim road for 14.9 km and then turn left. At 22.5 km, turn right up a steep hill and continue through *Qalb Lozeh past *Behyo. At the 30.3 km point, take the road on the right and follow it through Kfer Kila until 32.2 km from starting point.

There is something greatly touching about coming on this Roman tomb of the second century AD among the dross and stench of a modern goat shelter. Here was buried Tiberius Claudius Sosandros and his wife with the following inscription supplied by his son: *Tiberius Claudius Philocles to Tiberius Claudius Sosandros, his father, and to Claudia Kiparous, his mother; witness to his piety and remembrance; in the year 182, 27 Dystros [27 April AD 134]. Sosandros, my father.*

The name has no historical associations but the use of an Emperor's names perhaps indicates descent from a slave freed in the reign of Tiberius Claudius. The surname Sosandros is of Greek origin and it is possible that the family is that of a soldier who was settled in the area on release from military service.

The facade is improbably elaborate, with festooned garlands barely suspended above the muddy courtyard that was the entrance to the underground tomb. If you can manage to make your way through the animals, in the dim light you can discern the three burial niches but no decoration.

Perched above the descent to the *hypogeum* is a curious monolith column, square in shape. The Marquis de Vogüé, who visited in the mid-nineteenth century, describes on it a set of portrait figures but the carvings and inscriptions illustrated in his engraving cannot be distinguished these days.

If you look around the village, you can see remains of olive presses and a sizeable villa (presumably Byzantine) but no interesting church.

REFS: *BG* pp 409-10; Butler *AE* p 60; Dussaud *Topographie* p 219; Vogüé II p 92;

Bosra (Plates 4b, 5a, 5b)

VARIANTS: Busrana (BrA); Bostra (Lat, Cru); Busra Eski Sham (Arb); Bozrah[37]
PERIOD: Nab/Rom/Byz/Arb   ALT: 800 m;
RATING: *** MAPS: *13, 14,* 63 ITIN: 2a

> LOCATION: 140 km south of Damascus. The faster route is to take the motorway to the Deraa/Bosra exit (102 km) and from there turn east on a secondary road (+40 km) to Bosra. A slower trip that enables you to take in other areas of Jebel al-Arab and the Hauran is to take the road to *Suweida (106 km from Damascus). Continue directly south from Suweida for +22 km and turn right (west) +10 km to Bosra.

After Palmyra, Bosra is the most important site of the Roman period in Syria, primarily because of the magnificent and exceptionally intact Roman theatre (early second century AD). The rest of the site, however, is also worth detailed exploration and no visit to Bosra should be crowded into less than half a day, excluding the time needed for the trip to and from Damascus. The sombre and unyielding basalt of this volcanic region may dull for many the impact of the Roman remains (so often associated with bleached stone and marble) but if you visit on a sunny day, especially in winter, the effect can be memorable.

Any visit to Bosra begins with the theatre which, since its restoration (post-1947), has been one of the major monuments maintained and

---

[37] Not to be confused with the Bozrah mentioned in the Bible as one of the towns in Edomite territory (now Southern Jordan).

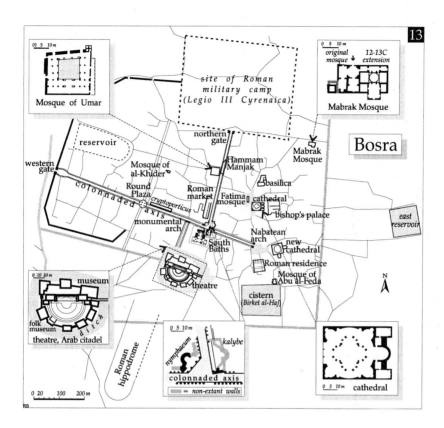

Mosque of Umar

site of Roman military camp (Legio III Cyrenaica)

original mosque / 12-13C extension

Mabrak Mosque

Bosra

reservoir

northern gate

Mabrak Mosque

western gate

Mosque of al-Khider

Hammam Manjak

basilica

Round Plaza

Roman market

Fatima mosque

cathedral

colonnaded axis

cryptoporticus

Bishop's palace

east reservoir

monumental arch

Nabatean arch

South Baths

new cathedral

Roman residence

museum

Mosque of Abu al-Feda

folk museum

theatre, Arab citadel

theatre

cistern (Birket al-Haj)

N

ditch

Roman hippodrome

nymphaeum

kalybe

colonnaded axis

= non-extant walls

cathedral

supervised by the Antiquities Department. The theatre owes its exceptional state of preservation (from both the ravages of earthquakes and the building programs of later centuries) to its conversion into an Ayyubid fort guarding the southern approaches to Damascus. As you enter the theatre from the main square of the town, there is little to indicate its Roman origins. The horseshoe internal shape is jacketted by stout Arab walls with heavy bastions and an imposing gateway. Only when you enter do you realise that the fortifications conceal the underpinnings of a Roman theatre - arches, ribs of tiered seating and curving corridors.

If you follow the itinerary marked by arrows, you ascend the outer rim of this maze and come out on the upper parapets of the theatre. Here a most extraordinary site greets you - a classical theatre more spectacularly and authentically

preserved than virtually any other around the Mediterranean, described as 'the most perfect of all Roman and Italian theatres'[38]. The seating is almost entirely intact, in places up to the last row before the crowning colonnade. The huge facade of the stage and the wings on either side are preserved with much beautiful detail (some unique in style).

History

It is perhaps best to pause here and consider how this splendid monument to the persistence of Roman civilisation got to this bleak spot. While the *Hauran (the classical *Auranitis* - see box page 228) today is an area which is beginning to find a new prosperity, it had until recently been a comparatively backward region, beset, even

---

[38] Rey-Coquais *Bosra* p 159.

during the French period, by banditry and disaffection. Its agriculture had thus been neglected and the stone-littered terrain, the windswept flatness of the volcanic plain and the treeless slopes of the Jebel al-Arab left a harsh impression.

In Roman times, however, the ecology was different and the Hauran was one of the granaries of the Empire - like Egypt but on a smaller scale. Its sudden rise to prosperity as the *Pax Romana* took hold in the first century AD is reflected in the ambitious scale of the civic replanning later in the century. The town of Bosra, however, had played a role in earlier periods. An Early Bronze Age settlement, it is mentioned in Egyptian 18th dynasty records as Busrana. It became part of the Seleucid domains after Alexander's conquests and was seized by Judas Maccabeus in 163 BC[39]. When the Nabatean Kingdom rose to local prominence in the first century BC, Bosra came within the northern reaches of their control though it was later the object of Herodian ambitions from Palestine. From AD 70 to 106, in the final stages of the Nabatean Kingdom (reign of Rabbel II), Bosra was made the capital.

In AD 106 the Romans extended direct rule and established *Provincia Arabia*, a new province with its headquarters at Bosra. Direct Roman control and the implantation of 5000 legionnaires must have fundamentally altered the Nabatean town. It became heavily influenced in its cultural and civic life by Roman models, perhaps even more profoundly than the other major Nabatean centre, Petra. Bosra was made the hub of an important network of trade routes linking Egypt/Red Sea/Syria[40] and the Mediterranean/Mesopotamian regions once the more easily travelled country bordering the desert became a safer option. (The routes closer to the coast had to negotiate difficult ravines and mountainous country).

The city's existing plan was ambitiously expanded. The Nabatean town on the eastern edge of the present ruins, probably centred on a sanctuary dedicated to Dushares, was greatly extended by the establishment to the west of a vast new grid which housed the installations and amenities of the Roman administration, more systematically laid out but continuing the basic

orientation of the eastern quarter. Trajan (AD 98-117), the creator of the new province, particularly favoured the town, renaming it *Nova Trajana Bostra*. It was visited by Hadrian in 129 during his tour of the eastern provinces. Under Alexander Severus (r 222-235), it was made a full Roman colony. It retained strong imperial patronage through to the reign of Philip the Arab (r 244-9) who was born in the neighbourhood (*Shahba) and who declared Bosra a *metropolis*.

It retained its importance through the Christian era of the Later Roman Empire, becoming the seat of an important bishopric (hence the innovative and sizeable cathedral described below - one of the largest in the east). It was, however, a strongly Monophysite centre and thus often at odds with Constantinople. (Monophysitism was adopted by the Christian Arab tribe, the Ghassanids, whose influence was predominant in the region.) The Prophet Muhammed probably visited the city during a trading journey before his religious mission began with the *Hijra* and there are legends of his consulting here a revered Christian monk, Bahira (see basilica, below). Bosra lay on the prime access route into Syria from the Arabian desert and was the first Byzantine city to fall to the Arabs in 632 in the opening phase of Islamic expansion.

After the seventh century, however, Bosra fell on more uncertain times and its fortunes fluctuated for many centuries. The area diminished in agricultural significance as it became prey to political uncertainty. Lying close to Palestine, it was drawn into the long struggle between Crusaders and Arabs, being attacked at least twice (1147 and 1151) by Frankish armies unsuccessfully challenging Nur al-Din's control of the Hauran. It was too exposed on the southern approaches to Damascus to be able to recover its prosperity during the struggles which marked the long rivalry between Cairo and Damascus. The Ayyubid effort to fortify the theatre from 1202 to 1251 (improving on earlier Fatimid and Seljuqid work) only exposed the rest of the area to continued depredations over the centuries not the least of which were the Mongol invasions. The fortress was considerably restored by Baibars in 1261 after the first of these invasions.

Given this perpetual insecurity, the caravan and pilgrimage routes to Mecca gradually moved back to the west where greater security prevailed, out of Bosra's orbit. The area became neglected agriculturally and by the 19th century it was only lightly inhabited, thus making it ripe for new settlement when many thousands of Druze fled Lebanon during the Druze/Christian struggle of 1840-60. Yet the area has retained the more

---

[39] *I Macc* V, 26, 28.

[40] The axis of this network was the *Via Nova Traiana*, Trajan's great trunk road built (probably immediately after 106 - see Isaac p 120) to connect Damascus, through Bosra and Philadelphia (Amman) to the Red Sea at Aqaba. The was protected from the nomadic Arabs to the east by a series of forts of which some remains can be seen in northern Jordan.

traditional elements of its population, including a sizeable Greek Orthodox community which has one of its principal bishoprics at nearby *Suweida.

Visit

Having fixed Bosra's position in history, you may now wish to visit the rest of the **theatre**. It is easy enough to distinguish the original fabric from the reconstructed elements added during the restoration. (Note particularly that the columns of the stage *scaenae frons* are largely careful copies of the rather battered originals, some in pink Egyptian granite). At the beginning of this century, much of the interior of the theatre had been filled with sand deposited by the wind over the centuries, a further stroke of good fortune which accounts for the theatre's preservation. After Syria's independence, a program of clearance work and research was undertaken lasting from 1947 to 1970.

Having removed the debris and some minor Arab additions, the main restoration work was devoted to the stage area and the upper rows of seats. The full extent of the theatre's seating was thus revealed with room for 6,000 spectators distributed over 37 tiers (14 + 18 + 5), plus room for a further 2-3,000 standing. The width of the semi-circular theatre is 102 m. This is one of the handful of Roman theatres which did not take advantage of the side of a hill or natural slope to support its massive proportions (cf *Jeble and *Palmyra). The acoustics are excellent, a voice at normal conversational level rising from the stage can be heard at any point in the theatre.

The auditorium was probably originally covered with a retractable cloth shading (*velum*), the stage being protected by a more permanent wooden roof. Only the lower level of the decoration of the *scaenae frons* remains, the fine Corinthian columns giving some indication of the richness of the treatment, once ornate with coloured marbles, statues, windows and sculptured friezes like the façade of a fantastic palace. The three entrances respected the conventions of the Roman theatre. Opinions vary as to the date of the theatre's construction. Certainly it must post-date the expansion of Bosra following AD 106 and a date, on stylistic grounds, in the mid second century seems probable[41].

---

[41] Finsen, the leader of the team that restored the theatre in the 1960's, 'supposes' that the theatre dates from the time of Trajan (d 117). Dentzer (*Hauran I*) concludes that the theatre dates from the second quarter of the 2C noted in Macadam, 'Bostra Gloriosa' in *Berytus* 1986 p176.

On either side of the stage, the huge crowds required access and exit facilities on a large scale. This accounts for the cavernous courtyard/staircases called, rather inelegantly, *vomitoria*. Behind these and the huge partly reconstructed *scaenae frons* lies a series of Ayyubid-period additions serving as the citadel's headquarters.

In plan, the **Ayyubid fortifications** fit like a jacket around the half-circle of the Roman building, with two major towers at the north east and north west corners, a central bastion along the diameter (north) and five subsidiary towers around the arc of the semi-circle. The first fortifications of the theatre were undertaken under the Umayyads and the first three towers (east and west of the stage and on the south east corner of the theatre) constructed under the Seljuqs (after 1089). However, the greater part dates from the Ayyubid response to the Crusader threat after 1200, particularly under al-Adil (Sultan in Damascus 1196-1218) and his son, al-Salih Imad al-Din, who alternated as Governor of Bosra and Sultan of. Damascus between 1218 and 1238.

The Ayyubid upper ramparts now house a museum (north east tower) a folklore collection (south west tower) and, on the upper terrace, a cafe and a collection of carved remains from the Roman period as well as Roman and Arabic inscriptions. (The difficulties of carving in the dense local basalt are revealed by the ungainly result of many attempts to copy Roman styles, usually worked in kinder marbles and softer stone.) Al-Salih established a palace complex and mosque within the Roman auditorium, remains of which were removed during the reconstruction program. (One surviving remnant is the water basin of the palace *hammam* which has been transferred to the ethnographic (folklore) collection in the south western tower.)

This **folklore museum** can be found as you proceed anti-clockwise around the ramparts to the south. From here you can continue back to the entrance via the Ayyubid parapets, with good views over the modern town and of the area once occupied by the hippodrome (open area to right of Cham Hotel).

Starting again from the main entrance to the citadel/theatre, you can strike out to explore the old town to the north, distributed on either side of the main east/west axis. From the adjacent (north east) corner of the citadel, walk down the alleyway that runs at 90 degrees to the rear wall of the theatre. After 75 m, to the left are the recently excavated remains of the Roman **south baths**. The baths were laid out in a T-shape with an entrance from the north through an eight-columned porch. This leads immediately into a great domed vestibule (*apodyterium* or dressing room), octagonal in shape. The dome, built of volcanic scoria set in hard mortar, has largely collapsed. The vestibule and cold room (*frigidarium*) led into three major chambers furnished with plumbing to serve as warm (*tepidarium*) or hot (*caldarium*) rooms. The date of construction is probably late second or early third century.

Advance a little to the north and you will recognise the once-colonnaded axis of the town, recently cleared of many modern accretions. Take your bearings at this orientation point along this former thoroughfare (*decumanus*) which runs for almost 900 m east/west along the spine of the Roman/Nabatean town. Almost 8 m wide in its original state, it was bordered by a raised colonnaded pavement (5.5 m wide) on each side. Here and there, some of the original columns of the colonnade (with Ionic capitals) can be seen but most have been used in later constructions. To the left you can see 600 m as far as the western gate of the Roman walled town. To the right, the perspective along the axis ends after 250 m in a gateway of the Nabatean period which marks the beginning of the pre-Roman town. (This Nabatean axis, which the Romans extended to the west, was probably originally a *via sacra* leading to the compound of the pre-Roman temple.)

From your orientation point, follow the main axis a few metres to the left and then take the once-colonnaded north/south street (*cardo*) towards the north. On the left lie the remains of a long rectangular Roman marketplace (20 m by 70 m), and behind it remains of a second baths complex, now called the *Khan al-Dibs* (Molasses Caravanserai). At the corner where this market met the main east/west street, four enormous columns, 13 m tall on octagonal bases, are the remains of a public water fountain (**nymphaeum**). The Corinthian capitals of the columns are superbly executed. The *nymphaeum* was probably constructed in the second century AD. The diagonal alignment of the columns reflects the placing of the monument at an angle between two main streets. On the opposite (right) side of the north/south *cardo* stood a structure described in its incription as a **kalybe** and which appears to have served as an open-air shrine for the display of statuary (second century - for a more elaborate example, see *Shahba). It took the form of a half-domed *exedra* with flanking walls provided with niches, the whole slanting towards the *nymphaeum* across the *cardo*. However, only

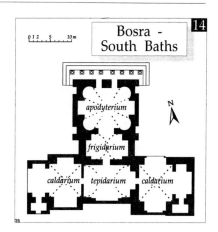

fragments (including two handsome columns) of the *kalybe* survives.

Further on down the main axis to the west, you will see the substantial remains of a gateway or **monumental arch**, built in the early third century AD to honour the III Cyrenaica Legion (which had garrisoned Bosra since 123 and whose base was on the northern edge of the city) as well as to commemorate Cornelius Palma the Roman Governor of Syria (104-108) who oversaw the largely peaceful annexation of the Nabatean Kingdom. The arch follows the traditional pattern of such monuments with the high (13 m) central opening flanked by two smaller arches. The present reconstruction (which may go back to Byzantine or Arab times) probably does not reflect the original design of the upper structure. Originally the central opening would have been framed by a triangular pediment - a typically Syrian device of the period.

At a point beginning 50 m beyond the monumental arch, an underground storage area was built under the raised portico on the right, marked by a series of slit openings in the stairs. This **cryptoporticus**, as it is called, was used for the storage of products before export and can be entered through a door at its western end. The recently opened vault consists of a corridor almost 4 m wide, 4.5 m high and 106 m in length. The 34 openings in the southern wall which were noted from outside were intended to admit light and air. It was probably constructed in the first half of the second century AD. To the north east of the *cryptoporticus*, a large commercial zone merging into the market area is still to be adequately explored. Immediately afterwards, as you proceed west, the next major cross-street was once marked by a **tetrapylon** standing in a circular open space.

It is another 200 m to the **western gate** (Bab al-Hawa or Gate of the Wind) originally preceded by an oval forum (cf the Damascus Gate at *Palmyra). The gate was erected in the early second century AD and shows an unusually sober style for the Syrian environment. The opening is spanned by two barrel vaults, the upper reaching 10.5 m above the ground. The lower vault frames the actual opening and was surmounted by false facades, thus avoiding a huge superstructure imposing a crushing load on the arch. The vaults are supported on towers each flanked by pairs of pilasters totally unadorned by bases or capitals. On each side, the pilasters frame a vaulted niche topped by a small pediment. The simplicity of treatment is striking. Stretching left and right of the gateway, you can still see some of the line of Roman **walls** (third century), its fabric much cannibalised to serve later building programs.

Head back now to the orientation point midway along the main east/west axis. The next group of remains to be visited are those of some important religious buildings to the north. If you take the street following the line of the Roman *cardo* heading north, along the eastern side of the narrow rectangular marketplace, you will come after another 150 m to a sizeable mosque on the left. This is the **Mosque of Umar** (known locally as the *Jami al-Arus*), once considered to be one of the oldest mosques surviving. Though attributed to the great Caliph Umar (Caliph 634-44), responsible for the conquest of Syria in 636, it was probably the work of the later Caliph Yazid II in 720 but heavily reconstructed and enlarged in the 12th-13th centuries under the Ayyubids. Carefully restored between 1938 and 1965, it is the sole surviving mosque from the earliest days of Islam which has preserved its original form.

You enter from the east through remains of the colonnaded *cardo*. Inside, the mosque comprises a courtyard (now roofed) surrounded on two sides (east and west) by double arcades and on the south by the prayer hall, also a double arcade but of wider dimensions. The square-plan minaret on the north eastern corner is fairly intact and, while Umayyad in origin (and one of the earliest surviving dated example of such a structure built to summon the faithful to prayer), was heavily reconstructed in the 13th century. The colonnaded courtyard once gave access to sleeping quarters and a market, illustrating the important link between Islam and commerce.

Immediately to the east lies the recently partially restored **Hammam Manjak**, a Mameluke baths complex in Damascene style inaugurated in 1372 and the last major Islamic addition to the city before its steady decline set in. Described in a recent survey as 'a masterpiece of medieval architectural engineering'[42] it dates from the heyday of the Mamelukes' emphasis on the city's role in servicing the *haj* traffic to Mecca. After two entrance rooms, a corridor leads to the (originally domed) reception room. From the north western corner, a maze-like corridor led the visitor through eleven chambers of the baths proper (left).

About 100 m to the west lies the **Mosque al-Khider** (named after a local Muslim saint) or the Gumeshtekin Mosque. A small building with a bulky tower separated on the west by a narrow gap from the mosque itself, it probably largely dates from the 1133 reconstruction of an earlier mosque. Unlike the more monumental scale of the Mosque of Umar, the al-Khider Mosque is smaller (7 m by 7 m) and follows closely the architectural traditions of the Hauran (transverse arches carry the flat basalt roof), again re-using some classical materials. Nearby are two Roman remains, a house with two courtyards and (to the north) remnants of another set of baths.

If you trace your way back to the Mosque of Umar, you are within 100 m (to the east) of the **basilica**. This building was originally constructed as a civic building in the pagan period (probably third century AD) but was converted for use as a Christian church. It is a large rectangular building with a semi-circular apse on the eastern end. The church is associated with the monk Bahira, the Nestorian holy man who, according to tradition, was consulted by Prophet Muhammed during his visit to Bosra. To his influence, certain elements of the Koran which borrow from Mosaic law and Christianity (at least the Nestorian version) are attributed but the legend seems somewhat tenuous.

If you divert 250 m to the north eastern corner of the city from the basilica (across the Arab cemetery), you will find in the corner near the road that leads to Jemrin, another important early mosque, the **Mabrak Mosque**, restored by the Syrian Antiquities Department and the German Archaeological Institute between 1986 and 1989. According to legend, the first copy of the Koran brought to Syria, rested here, carried on a camel. An important centre of learning grew on this spot. Some idea of the original simplicity and beauty of the early Islamic architectural style

---

42 Meinecke *et al* p 47.

survives despite numerous changes. The building falls into three segments, the earliest (dated by inscription to 1136) being to the west. Its *mihrab* marks the spot where the camel carrying the Koran is said to have rested (hence the Arabic title, 'mosque of kneeling'). The northern wall of this room is one of the best illustrations of Islamic use of Roman/Byzantine styles of sculptured plaster. The northern and central courtyards were added a little later while the larger eastern part of the building was constructed on a more monumental scale in the late 12th-13th centuries. This new wing was cruciform in plan, probably the first manifestation of the new fashion for madrasa of this style during the Sunni revival in medieval Syria.

A little further to the south (back towards the east/west axis) from the basilica, you reach the **Cathedral** of Bosra, a building of considerable importance in the annals of early Christian architecture. The plan is somewhat complex, being basically a circle within a square with the transition from the inner to the outer shapes carried by corner *exedrae* flanked by niches. The plan is extended to the east to take in a choir with four side rooms or chapels. The central chamber was 36 m in diameter (as large in scale as the first version of Hagia Sofia in Constantinople). At its centre stood a sanctuary enclosed by four L-shaped pillars joined by semi-circular colonnades. This complex variation of circular and square shapes is a pioneering masterpiece of early Christian architecture, though rather more heavy and ungainly in its final results than the smaller and slightly later version at *Resafe. (For a more detailed examination of the Bosra cathedral, see the box on Centralised Churches, page 21.)

Unfortunately the remains are badly ruined, some of the worst damage having been done in the last century. Virtually all the walls, apart from the apses, are reduced to ground level by mining for building material. Thus no evidence remains of the roofing of the original church, the assumption being that it consisted of a steeply sloping cupola or dome (a Syrian practice probably borrowed from Persia in late Roman times) rising from the outer walls and the corner *exedra*. The dome itself, 24 m in diameter, sat upon a circular clerestory which housed no less than 50 windows, bringing a high level of natural light into the church, illuminating internal walls which were once probably plastered and painted, perhaps even clad with marble. The external walls are virtually undecorated, in contrast to the contemporary carved stonework of churches in northern Syria.

The cathedral is dated by its dedication in 512/3 by Julianos, Archbishop of Bosra[43] in honour of three of the most celebrated martyrs of early Syrian Christianity, Sergius, Bacchus and Leontius. (Sergius is the saint associated with the great fortress city of *Resafe in northern Syria). Behind the cathedral, and originally linked to it, are the fragmentary remains of the bishop's palace of the Byzantine period.

40 m north west of the cathedral of Bosra you will find the **Fatima Mosque** named after the daughter of the Prophet. A Fatimid period (11th century) building, three arches survive from the original construction, three more having been added in a recent extension. The 19 m minaret (north eastern corner) dates from 1306.

Work your way from the cathedral (head south through the alleyways) to the eastern end of the east/west axis. At its extremity lies the eastern or **Nabatean arch**. The drabness of the basalt stone should not diminish the remarkable effect of this attempt to blend a basically Roman shape with Nabatean-orientalising decoration. While basically conforming to the Roman canon of civic architecture, the arch shows many Nabatean-Syrian touches: the plain undecorated capitals which look like Corinthian blanks left uncarved; the high vaulting central arch which nearly swallows the whole structure; the fascination with semi-circular arched niches; and the (conjectural) addition of triangular indentations to the top of the structure (cf. the crows-feet merlons on the parapet of the *cella* of the Bel temple at Palmyra). These features would date the construction to the first century AD, the high-period for such fashionable touches in Syria. The effect, though, is not inelegant, the division of the facade into two orders being well proportioned. The lower order balances a niche between columns enclosed between pilasters; the upper comprises a plainer niche between two rectangular niches, divided by simpler pilasters. The gateway between the flanking towers was deeply indented but the flanking walls are broken by passages leading to inner rooms on each side. As noted earlier, the gateway probably originally stood at the entrance to the *temenos* of a temple pre-dating the Roman period, foundations of which were recently explored. To the east, recent excavations have revealed a second 'circle in a square' church, even larger than the cathedral described earlier, built after the fourth century.

---

[43] Julianus, known for his courage and forthrightness, was dismissed from his post shortly after the Cathedral's construction, having refused to accept the authority of Severus, Patriarch of Antioch, whom he regarded as an adherant of the Monophysite heresy.

Immediately south of the Nabatean gateway lie the remains of a substantial **residence** which Butler ascribed to the Roman governor of the province of Arabia, but which has more recently been interpreted as the seat of the Christian bishop. The complex was 33 m by 50 m in extent, originally two storeys and arranged around a central court. Two-storeyed colonnades preceded the rooms on the northern and southern sides of the court. On the south, the central chamber or dining room (*triclinos*) was an elaborate hall with semi-circular apses at each end and a central space of grand proportions.

Further south again, it is hard to miss the sizeable **cistern** (known locally as the *Birket al-Haj*), over 120 m by 150 m in extent. A Roman construction, it was originally 8 m deep, the walls being decorated with pilasters. It is one of the largest town water storage facilities found in the Roman east. The supply of piped water to the town was an important preoccupation and much evidence remains throughout the site of the brick and lead conduit system. (There is a further cistern located outside of town 300 m from the eastern limits, together with the remains of a Roman aqueduct which fed it.)

The **Mosque of Abu al-Feda** is situated on the north eastern corner of the Birket al-Haj. Also known as the *Madrasa al-Dabbagha* (Dyers' School - the dying industry probably once drawing its water from the *birket*), it dates from the Ayyubid period (1225 according to an inscription) and was restored between 1982 and 1985. Described by Mougdad as 'one of the finest monuments to Islamic art in Bosra', it was originally a large undivided prayer hall with six pointed arches rising from pylons jutting out from the walls though the placement of the four *iwans* (the southern one being oversized) indicates that the basic *madrasa* plan has been adapted through the use of transverse arches.

Sites of lesser interest on the outskirts of the Roman perimeter include:

* South-south west of the theatre (200 m), the location of the Roman **hippodrome** can be clearly seen from the theatre's parapets (see above page 65). The hippodrome, with its curved end to the south, covered an area 440 m by 134 m and seated 30,000. (Date uncertain, probably second to third century.)
* The base for the Roman legion was probably located on the northern outskirts of the town beyond the remains of the northern gate which is found at the west end of the cardo that passes the Mosque of Umar.

REFS: Abel; *BG* pp 503-6; Butler *EC* pp 124-7; Butler *PE* II/A/4 pp 215-95; Creswell *Early Muslim*; Crowfoot *Churches at Bosra*; *Crowfoot Early Churches*; Dentzer *Bosra (1989)* pp 133-41; Dussaud *Topographie* pp 346 ff; Finsen; Freyburger 'Zur Datierung des Theaters in Bosra in *DaM* 3 1988; Klengel *Syrien* pp 185-9; Freyburger Bostra; Lassus *Sanctuaires chrétiens* pp 150-2; Mango; Meinecke *et al*; Mougdad; Peters; Rey-Coquais *Bosra*; Sartre *Bostra*; Segal; Vogüé I pp 63-7.

Braij

VARIANTS: Breij, Breig
PERIOD: Byz   ALT: 455 m RATING: - MAP: 69 ITIN: 9b

> LOCATION: From the Bab al-Hawa turn-off, follow the road to *Harim. 4 km after the village of Sarmada, the monastery can be seen c450 m across the field to the right.

The remains of the Monastery of St Daniel at the western edge of the Jebel Barisha *massif* are in a surprisingly good state of preservation. The main building is inserted into the cliff face, the first storey being cut out of the rock and the stone used to build the upper two storeys. The complex of three buildings includes some oil presses, cisterns and a conventual tomb.

Tchalenko describes this as 'the most interesting monastic grouping in the area'. It was built relatively late in the monastic 'boom'. Located on the edge of the Dana Plain - an area notoriously infested with Monophysites, heretical in the eyes of the central Byzantine Church authorities. It was probably a Monophysite institution. The building dates from the late sixth century, though sources differ as to whether it was built in one or two phases.

REFS: Mattern pp 88-90; Pena *et al Cenobites* pp 203-212, 261-3; Pena *et al Inventaire* p 84; Tchalenko *Villages* I pp 124-5, 158-9, 173.

Burj Haidar

VARIANTS: Kaprokera (anc), Burj Heidar
PERIOD: Byz RATING: * MAP: 68 ITIN: 9a

> LOCATION: Take the road leading north from the eastern slopes of Jebel Semaan. Follow this towards the north east for c8 km. (Burj Haidar is also c4 km west of *Kharrab Shams.) The villages lying to the north are Kfer Nabo, Kalota.

Burj Haidar's origins go back beyond the adoption of Christianity as the official religion of the Roman Empire (AD 324). A survey mark of 298 indicates that the settlement was registered at that time under the ancient name above. Later, it apparently became a fervent Christian community judging by the unusual number of churches for such a small settlement. The agriculture of the area was based on an extensive basin of arable land below the village.

The columned arcades of a mid fourth century three-aisled church (centre of the village) survive somewhat incongruously, its arcades poking through the chaos of a contemporary farmyard. The two rows of Doric columns are left standing while most of the walls of the church have disappeared. The building was of medium dimensions and typical in style of the period. The exception was the *prothesis*, the chamber to the right of the apse, which has been enlarged during the fifth century, apparently to provide a *martyrium*. The early date is evident in the virtual absence of decoration. Traces of a *bema* were found in the central nave.

Other remains include a tower (75 m north) an *andron* or meeting room and a monastery (sixth century, both on the western edge of town). To the east, the road passes a chapel and a second (**east**) **church** (both sixth century). Of the latter, little is standing. A small court preceded the western entrance and the tower was built on the southern side. The chancel arch, whose basic shape remains, shows early signs of the horse-shoe shape development seen in other late Christian experimentation (*Ruweiha - Church of Bissos) but which is developed much further in subsequent Christian and Islamic architecture.

A more extraordinary survival is the small chapel, also on the eastern edge of town, north of the modern road. The chapel itself is described by Butler as 'one of the most attractive in the Jebel Semaan'[44]. Added to it at a rakish angle is a plain elongated building which was presumably the clerical residence. The chapel is richly decorated on the outside with fluid mouldings. Inside the main decoration is around the extant chancel arch. Note the two bosses sticking out from the arch whose purpose is unexplained and the fact that the sanctuary is raised on three steps. In Butler's day, evidence could be seen of the plastered and painted ceiling of the sanctuary.

REFS: Butler *AE* pp 32, 150; Butler *EC* p 32; Butler *PE* II/B/6 pp 288-93; Tchalenko *Villages* I p 170, II pl CXXIX; Tchalenko and Baccache pl 33-46.

---

[44] *PE* II/B/6 p 290.

Burjke

VARIANTS: Burdjkeh
PERIOD: Byz RATING: - MAP: 68 ITIN: 9a

LOCATION: From Saint Simeon, take the right fork below the east flank. Follow this road as it heads north and east, continuing c4 km before turning right along a good dirt road for +1.5 km.

Just to the left of the road, a sixth century church with meandering band along the side facade and central doorway. Like the chapel at nearby *Surkunya, the chancel is rectangular and had a flat roof of stone.

There is also a tower of the sixth century, 11 m (originally five storeys) high, probably once part of a monastery. In Islamic times, however, it was fortified at the base for defensive reasons.

REFS: Butler *PE* II/B/6 p 329; Pena *et al Reclus* 272-3

Burqush

VARIANTS: ALT: 1850 m RATING: * MAP: 64 ITIN: 3c

LOCATION: 33 km west of Damascus. Take the Beirut motorway. At 17 km from Umayyad Square, right exit then cross over motorway to south. +4 km, left at T junction then immediately right. +4.5 km, right to Burqush. +6.5 km, military check-point. Leave vehicle here. 30 min walk along along dirt road to left.

From this ridge on the lower slopes of Mount Hermon, breathtaking views out to the east provide a setting for the remains of a Byzantine basilica of the sixth century. It is difficult to imagine how blocks of such dimensions were transported to this site, but part of the narrow ridge was cut away to form an artificial platform which was extended to the north by a huge vaulted sub-structure. On this terrace measuring some 46 m by 34 m a three-aisled basilica was constructed on an impressive scale with pillars rounded at each end by half-columns. The basic plan has much in common with other transverse-arched churches of the sixth century. The remains of the capitals which topped these half-columns are scattered about in the general confusion of blocks that litter the site. Most of the southern wall of the sub-structure has collapsed but enough can be seen of the northern wall to reconstruct how the lower space comprised a huge chamber some 6 m wide over which the upper platform was carried on a series of arches supported on consoles. Stairs in the south corner led down from the basilica.

The site had earlier been used for religious buildings in the pre-Hellenistic and Roman periods and traces of an earlier temple (first century AD?) podium can be seen under the Byzantine building. 100 m to the north lies the *cella* of another Roman temple (Krencker suspects it may have been a mithraeum) in a severely plain style. A semi-circular apse was contained within the walls, forming an internal *cella*.

Lower down are the remains of a monastery of which only the foundations survive as well as traces of other religious buildings.

There are a number of other remains of Roman temples in the neighbourhood of Mount Hermon (eg the ruins at Rahleh 8 km north - *distyle in antis* preceding a domed *exedra* - dated by inscription to AD 296-7) but access is currently difficult given military deployments in the area.

REFS: BG p 315; Krencker pp 235-48; Mouterde R 'Antiquités de l'Hermon et de la Beqa'' in *Mélanges de l'Université St.-Joseph* XXIX 1951-52

C

Circesium

VARIANTS: Phalga, Phaliga Rummunidu (anc[45]); Nabagath (anc); Carcis (Grk); Qarqisiye, Buseire (Arb)
PERIOD: Rom RATING: T MAP: 73 ITIN: 13a

> LOCATION: At the confluence of the Euphrates and Khabur Rivers. From Deir al-Zor, cross to the left bank of the Euphrates and take the road to Haseke and Qamishli for c7 km. A track to the right leads +45 km south east.

Circesium once played a role in the defence of the Roman domains in Syria against the Persian and Sasanian threat from the east. In the second century AD, its importance was secondary or complementary to *Dura Europos, the Seleucid foundation on the right bank of the Euphrates, with Circesium offering first haven in Roman territory for caravans proceeding down the Khabur River (the classical Chaboras) from the east. It was essentially a Roman military outpost consolidated under Trajan's policy of pushing out the frontier to the Khabur and later re-fortified by Diocletian who may have revived the Seleucid place name, designating it Circesium. It housed in the fourth century the Legio III Parthica. The defence post was revived under the Byzantine Emperor Justinian (sixth century) as part of his major defensive network in northern and north eastern Syria. It was still in Byzantine hands when it fell to the Arabs in 637. Virtually nothing remains of the Roman fortifications and the course of the river has moved considerably to the west.

REFS: Bell *Amurath* pp 74-5; Chapot 294-6; Dussaud *Topographie* pp 466, 486-8; Musil *Middle Euphrates* pp 334-7; Mouterde and Poidebard esp pp 134, 145; Ulbert 'Euphrate' pp 293-5.

Cyrrhus (Plate 5c)

VARIANTS: Khoros; Kyrrhos, Hagiopolis (Grk); Coricia (Cru); Qurus, Nabi Uri (Arb).
PERIOD: Hel/Rom/Byz RATING: * MAP: *15, 68* ITIN: 10a

> LOCATION: 76 km north of Aleppo, almost on the Turkish border. Take the main north road out of Aleppo that leads to Afrin. At 45 km, right turn to Azaz

(frontier post on the Turkish border). +4 km from the turn-off, at the village of Azaz, follow the rough road to the left +28 km to Cyrrhus (known locally as Nabi Uri). Alternatively, at the 45 km point, continue +5 km along the Afrin road to the turnoff to Bulbul. Follow that road for +16 km, then turn right +16 km for Cyrrhus.

> The first road is more interesting, if only for the experience of crossing two steep hump-backed Roman bridges that still carry traffic. The disadvantage is that this experience is not for the faint-hearted given the sharpness of the hump and the extreme narrowness of the roadway (remarkably slippery in wet weather). The Romans didn't seem to have four-wheeled vehicles in mind when they designed these things - though to be fair the bridges probably originally had parapets.

History

Like many cities that became major bases in the Hellenistic/Roman period, Cyrrhus was founded by Seleucos II Nicator after 300 BC (and named after Cyrrhus in Macedonia) as part of his program of military colonies to secure his share of Alexander's inheritance[46]. It seems, however, to have lacked the economic and security attributes needed to remain the centre of a satrapy under the Seleucids, lying as it did so close to the rival Commagene and Armenian kingdoms to the north. By the late second century BC, it had foundered and in the early first century BC, was absorbed into the Armenian kingdom. It was annexed to the Roman Empire after Pompey's conquest (64 BC) and lost all administrative and political identity. The area was badly affected by invasions from the east and was subject to brigandage. By the first century AD its fortunes recovered. It became both an administrative centre and the headquarters of a legion (the X Fretensis until its transfer in AD 66 to Jerusalem). In the second century, it served as a base for the campaigns against the Armenians to the north.

Its role depended on imperial interest in sustaining its military and commercial advantages rather than on the agricultural resources of the surrounding countryside. It lay on the reasonably secure route from Antioch to

---

[46] There is no documentary reference to Cyrrhus until 220 BC. Grainger p 41, however, deduces that Cyrrhus was probably the headquarters of one of the four original satrapies created by Seleucus before 294 BC on the site of a pre-301 settlement.

the bridge crossing of the Euphrates at Zeugma (a little north of the modern Birecik in Turkey). Its role in supporting the bridgehead to the east, however, was usurped in the third century by Hierapolis (*Membij) which had the added attraction of being a major cult centre.

Cyrrhus was occupied at least twice during the Persian invasions of the mid third century AD. It recovered to become a centre of some importance (under the name of Hagiopolis) in the

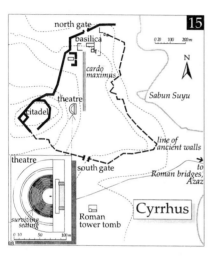

early Christian era, Sts Cosmas and Damian being venerated here. Theodoret, Bishop of Cyrrhus from around 423 to 450, was a prominent early father of the church. Justinian re-fortified and garrisoned it in the mid sixth century as part of his program of frontier works commissioned during the renewed confrontation with the Persians. It fell in 637 to the conquering Arab armies. It was taken for a time by Crusaders (early 11th century) and made dependent on Edessa under the name Coricia. Nur al-Din took it back in 1150 but it must subsequently have lost its strategic significance and the site is now virtually uninhabited though the area is being developed for olive farming.

Visit

The two second century AD **Roman bridges** on the road to Cyrrhus are worthy of particular note. Though much modified in Byzantine and Arab times, the construction is basically late Roman, a singular tribute to the era's engineering skills. Coming from the south east (Aleppo), the first

bridge crosses the upper reaches of the Afrin River and employs three arches. The second, 1 km later and less than 1 km from the edge of Cyrrhus, crosses the stream of the Sabun Suyu River with six arches. The carriageways are 5 m wide and the slope of the rise does not exceed 15 percent.

Cyrrhus has less to show above the ground than other major Hellenistic/Roman cities in Syria but it is situated in a wild and romantic setting and has sufficient of interest to justify a visit for which you will need a good six or more hours, including the trip to and from Aleppo. Spread out between the citadel hill and the Sabun Suyu River to the east, the site bears traces of the main attributes of a planned settlement of the period. These include a grid pattern centred on a colonnaded main street (**cardo maximus**) and major amenities including a theatre. The grid is followed in the centre of the city, with the cardo maximus running north/south, 7 m wide and paved with basalt. At the southern end of the cardo, a monumental gate formed one of the principal entrances to the city (recently partly reconstructed). Lower down the valley, near the northern gate, are some sketchy remains of a church and a basilica. Part of the northern limit of the cardo is also exposed in this area.

Cyrrhus has been dug by the French in several campaigns since 1952. Further work is being done to reconstruct parts of the town which have succumbed to earthquakes or been mined for building materials. The reconstruction effort has concentrated particularly on the **theatre** which probably dates from the mid second century. At 115 m in diameter, it is after Apamea (139 m), one of the largest examples in Syria, its original dimensions slightly larger than the contemporary theatre at *Bosra (102 m). The stage wall seems to have fallen pell mell into the cavea during an earthquake. Only the first fourteen rows of seating embedded in the earth have been preserved, the free-standing upper structure that once provided eleven more rows has collapsed and the stones have been re-used elsewhere.

The **citadel** (on the hill to the west of the theatre) gives sweeping views of the countryside and the outlines of its heavy fortifications (including an inner keep) can still be traced. The **walls** are extensive, the lines being determined by the shape of the site - two saddles radiating from the low hill on which the citadel was built. Much of the work that can now be traced belongs to Justinian's re-fortification of the site in the sixth century, with the Byzantine walls strictly following the Hellenistic foundations.

600 m to the south west (visible on the left of the access road) is a curious hexagonal **Roman tower tomb**, a good example of the eclectic tastes of the period (probably second or third century AD). The upper storey is formed by a six-sided pyramidal roof topped by a knosp of carved acanthus leaves. Inside, the upper storey is surrounded by arches separated by marble monolith pillars ending in Corinthian capitals. It has been made even more eclectic, however, by the conversion of the lower floor in the 14th

century into the burial place of a legendary Muslim saint and the addition of a pilgrimage mosque. Behind the tower is the first of two *necropoleis* associated with Cyrrhus, the other lying to the north west.

REFS: *BG* p 427; Dussaud *Topographie* pp 470-1; Frézouls *Cyrrhus*; Frézouls *Mission archéologique* pp 175-80; Klengel *Syrien* pp 168-70; Tchalenko *Villages* II pl LXXXVI/10.

D

Damascus - Introduction

VARIANTS: Dimashqa, Dimaski (BrA); Arsinoia,
Demetrias (Grk - Ptolemaic); Damascus (Lat); al-
Shams, Dimashq (Arb)
PERIOD: All ALT: 691 m RATING: *** MAPS:
16-26 ITIN: 1a-j

LOCATION: Capital of Syria, occupying the ancient site
which lies in the oasis fed by the Barada River flowing
from the Anti-Lebanon Range.

*If Paradise be on earth, it is, without a
doubt, Damascus;
but if it be in Heaven, Damascus is its
counterpart on earth.*
[12th century Spanish Muslim traveller, Ibn
Jubair[47]]

*She measures time not by days and
months and years, but by the empires she
has seen rise and crumble to ruin. She is
a type of immortality. ... Damascus has
seen all that ever occured on earth and
still she lives. She has looked upon the dry
bones of a thousand empires, and will see
the tombs of a thousand more before she
dies.*
[Mark Twain *Innocents Abroad*]

Preamble

Damascus is described in ten walking itineraries
in this guide (the order described depending on
their distance from the heart of the city, the
Umayyad Mosque). The exploration of
Damascus in this detail amply repays the effort
for it is one of the rare historical centres which
has managed to preserve much of its
atmosphere in the face of mounting population
pressures.

Nestled at the foot of the Anti-Lebanon
Range where the waters of the Barada (the
Abana River (Barada) of antiquity) rush out of the
mountain gorge to water an oasis of 30 km or
more in extent, it is easy to appreciate how this
city has come to play such a continuous role in
history. This is perhaps best appreciated by
beginning your visit with a taxi trip up to the
lookout points along the slopes of Mount Kassiun
which dominates the city and oasis. The

mountain itself has attracted several legends
including the belief that here Abraham had the
unity of God revealed to him[48]. It is from this
point, too, that legend has the Prophet
Muhammed looking down upon Damascus for
the first time and proclaiming that if man could
have only one paradise, he would have to forego
the earthly paradise of Damascus in favour of
the other.

Looking south and east from the lookout
point, you see how the desert which has swept
relentlessly from southern Arabia and the Indian
Ocean abruptly ends at this fragile band of
cultivation as the Barada fans out into the semi-
wilderness. This accounts for Damascus' abiding
importance; like a port on the edge of this harsh
sea of infertility, it is the natural first landing for
the desert traveller.

From Kassiun, you can also gain a good
appreciation of the Anti-Lebanon Range which
stretches to the west and north. At the south
extremity lies the peak (often snow-covered - alt:
2814 m) of Mount Hermon (Jebel al-Sheikh).

History

No large scale systematic excavations have
been possible in a city so continuously and
densely inhabited as Damascus. Much of the
evidence for the earlier phases of its history are
thus fragmentary, resulting from either literary
sources or fortuitous archaeological digs. The
settlement of the oasis, however, clearly goes
back to the earliest phase of post-nomadic
economic development - the fourth millennium or
before - making Damascus one of the oldest
continuously inhabited urban centres in the
world.

The first historical records of 'Dimashqa'
(Damascus) are in the *Mari tablets (c2500 BC)
and a little later as 'Dimaski' in the Ebla archives.
Amorite settlement began around the beginning
of the second millennium BC. Later in the
millennium it came into the Egyptian sphere of
influence and is mentioned in the Amarna
archives (18th dynasty – 14th century BC). After
the great disturbance of the Sea Peoples'

---

[47] Quotation adapted from Ziadeh *Mamelukes* p 24.

[48] A mosque at Berze, north of the city, commemorates the
reputed birthplace of Abraham. Other legends which have passed
into Muslim tradition include the belief that Jesus and his mother
found refuge there (*Koran* XXIII, 50).

invasion c1200 BC, it recovered under the **Arameans**. They established here their principality of Aram-Damascus which took a leading role in checking the expansion of the biblical kingdoms of Israel and Judeah. The city fell to the **Assyrians** in 732 BC. In 572, the neo-Babylonian (or **Chaldean**) King, Nebuchadnezzar, conquered Syria and Palestine but the Chaldean dynasty itself was overwhelmed shortly after in 539 when the Persian King, Cyrus, took the whole region in the course of his sweep towards the Aegean. Damascus was the seat of a Persian governor or satrap.

Alexander's great campaign brought Damascus under Greek control in 332 following the battle of Issus. Though Alexander's own path took him directly along the Phoenician coast, a small contingent under one of his generals, Parmenion, secured Damascus. The subsequent

(including a period of Nabatean domination) that was ended by the Roman conquest in 64 BC.

Roman rule lasted (in one form or another) 700 years. Though Damascus was not a major centre for Roman administration (Antioch in modern-day Turkey was the third city of the Empire for the Romans and the base for the administration of Syria), Damascus flourished under Roman rule. From 37 BC to AD 54, the Romans accepted continued Nabatean control of Damascus. It remained a city-state and kept its major trading role given the importance of the eastern route via *Palmyra. The cult centre, originally a ninth century BC Aramean temple dedicated to the god Hadad, was taken over by the Romans through the syncretisation of Hadad with Jupiter. From the first century AD, the temple compound was rebuilt to a grandiose imperial plan (*Damascus - Umayyad Mosque). The town plan was improved further, an

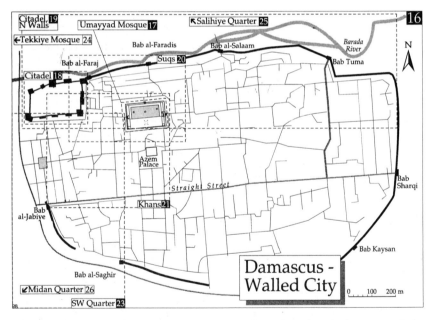

Damascus -
Walled City

rule by **Greeks** brought town-planning to Damascus (*Damascus - Straight Street) but wrangling for control between Seleucids and Ptolemies weakened Greek authority and the lack of effective administration by the first century BC introduced a phase of uncertainty

aqueduct system brought the waters of the Barada to homes and baths and the city was walled and furnished with seven or eight gates (see box on page 77).

Damascus, which housed an important Jewish colony, was associated with the earliest phase of the spread of **Christianity** and the mission of St Paul (see *Damascus - Straight Street). Hadrian gave it the rank of *metropolis* (117), later raised to *colonia* under Alexander Severus (222). After the adoption of Christianity as the imperial religion in the fourth century AD, the Temple of Jupiter-Hadad was adapted to house the Cathedral of St John. In 635-6 the city surrendered twice to a Muslim army, the second time to Khalid Ibn al-Walid after a six month seige. It was made the capital of the **Umayyad Empire** under the fifth Caliph, al-Moawiya, in 661, thus ending a thousand years of western supremacy.

The Umayyad Empire survived only 90 years but it provided Damascus with the most lasting and impressive monument to its fame, the great Mosque of the Umayyads, built by the Caliph al-Walid after 706 on the site of the Cathedral of St John. Little else remains of the Umayyad period in Damascus (the great palace complex, for example, built to the south east of the Great Mosque, has been obliterated).

Under subsequent **Arab dynasties**, Damascus' importance was eclipsed by other centres associated with the regimes that sprang up in Baghdad, Mosul, Aleppo and Cairo, Damascus standing at the intersection of competing spheres of influence. The Abbasids, successors to the Umayyads, based their rule on Baghdad and deliberately defaced or dismantled much of the Umayyad city on the grounds of the alleged apostasy of the earlier Caliphs. The fall in population and status continued under the turbulent days (tenth-12th centuries) of the competing Tulunid, Ikshidid, Fatimid, Hamdanid and Seljuq dynasties which struggled for control of Syria from their power bases in Cairo and Aleppo/Mosul. There are virtually no remains in Damascus of these centuries of disruption which gave the main impetus to the process by which the open grid plan of the Greco-Roman city was broken up into self-contained quarters, each walled for protection of communities segregated along confessional lines. (The Muslims congregated around the great mosque and the citadel to the west; the Christians to the north east; the Jews to the south west.) The street plan was further modified by the narrowing of thoroughfares and the creation of meandering laneways.

THE GATES OF DAMASCUS

The walls of the old city of Damascus are described in three itineraries (*Damascus - Citadel and North Walls; *Damascus – South West Quarter; *Damascus - Straight Street to Bab Sharqi). The following provides a consolidated listing of the city gates which interrupt the 5 km or more of wall (excluding the gates to the citadel itself which were preserved for the army or ruling class). Cross-references are given to the gates' locations on the separate itineraries. A walk around the full circumference of the walled city would be feasible in a rather long morning or afternoon but would not allow time for the exploration of buildings en route. The nine gates (eight are extant) are listed clockwise, starting at the citadel, at the north west corner of the city walls.

Arab Name	Translation	Roman Name (i)	Itinerary
Bab al-Faraj	Deliverance	*(no gate)*	Cit
Bab al-Faradis	Orchards	Mercury	Cit
Bab al-Salaam	Peace	Moon	Cit
Bab Tuma	St Thomas	Venus	Cit
Bab Sharqi	Eastern	Sun	St
Bab Kaysan	*(proper name)*	Saturn	St
Bab Saghir	Small	Mars	SW
Bab al-Jabiye	Water Trough	Jupiter	SW
Bab al-Nasr[1]	Victory	*(not known)*	-

Cit = *Damascus – Citadel; St = *Damascus - Straight Street; SW = *Damascus – South West Quarter
(i) As cited in Arab chronicles (Sauvaire p 371).

What is remarkable in following the walled enclosure is the extent to which the city plan over the centuries continued to observe its basically Hellenistic/Roman outline. The walls retain the position of the Roman gateways (except that Nur al-Din moved part of the northern alignment up to the banks of the Barada) though they do not always follow the Roman alignment between the gates. Where the alignments correspond, however, many of the original Roman blocks can be found at the base of the walls, in spite of much mining and plundering in the last 2000 years.

The Muslim resistance to the **Crusades** began the reversal of this decline. It brought a concentration on Damascus as a bastion of the Muslim cause and thus of Sunni orthodoxy. The refugee influx (particularly after the barbaric slaughter associated with the Crusaders' taking of Jerusalem in 1099) began the process by which the city's population spread beyond the walled city into the Salihiye quarter along the lower slopes of Kassiun and later towards the Midan to the south. To this era belongs the reconstruction of the defenses of the city including the major gateways (see box on page 77), the Citadel and its surrounding walls.

Damascus was twice attacked by Crusader forces (1129, 1140) before the first serious effort to take it was mounted in 1148 during the Second Crusade, under Conrad, King of the Germans. The Crusaders abandoned their seige after a sustained two-day battle on the west outskirts of the city, having been alerted to the expected arrival of further Muslim forces from Aleppo. Under the **Zengids**, Nur al-Din took the city more by charm than by arms in 1154. During his reign, but particularly under his successor (and founder of the **Ayyubid** dynasty), Saladin (1176-93), Damascus again became a political centre of note and its economy recovered much of its vigour. Contemporary European travellers noted that the city was considerably larger than either Paris or Florence. It attracted leading theological and philosophical figures, as well as poets, from the more troubled environments of Baghdad and Palestine. This was the great age of the *madrasa*, the number more than quadrupling in the 13th century in order to reinforce Sunni orthodoxy (see box on page 24). The later Ayyubids' family quarrels, however, weakened the dynasty's cohesion and insecurity prevailed in the face of the first of several Mongol invasions (in 1260 under Hulaga - later invasions which did much to raze the fabric of the city came in 1299-1300 under Ilhan Ghazan and in 1400-1 under Timur).

Gradually, however, the **Mameluke** dynasties based in Cairo restored prosperity to the city after 1260 and put a final end to the Crusader presence in Syria. The early phase of Bahri Mameluke rule was a third golden age for Damascus, particularly during the rule of Baibars (1260-77) who spent much of his time in the city, and under the Governorship of Tengiz (1312-39). Some of the most resplendent monuments of Islamic Damascus date from these decades when the city was the second capital of the Mameluke Empire. It began to expand further beyond the confines of the walled city of Roman times and a new era of endowments resulted in the construction or restoration of 43 institutions between 1260 and 1311. However, internal Mameluke feuding became an increasingly debilitating distraction and in 1400 a campaign against Cairo by the Damascus Governor, Tanabiq, left the city undefended against the worst of the Mongol invasions, that of Timur. Mameluke rule was restored after the unprecedented devastation and depopulation but the city did not recover the sustained confidence it had gained under the early Mamelukes. Instead a phoney 'boom economy' developed in supplying the Mameluke ruling class and soldiery (the rest of the population being left to struggle under the increasing burden of taxes and extortion).

In 1516, the **Ottoman** Turks conquered Syria and incorporated it into their Empire. At first relatively enlightened and progressive, Ottoman control varied in its effects with the capacities of its Governors. A Governor such as Assaad Pasha al-Azem (the Azem family, originally prosperous landholders from *Maarat al-Numan in northern Syria, monopolised the post of Governor of Damascus for the greater part of the 18th century) did much to improve the amenities of the city as had earlier Governors such as Darwish Pasha and Murad Pasha. Much of the importance of the city for the Ottomans lay in its position as the last of the major population centres where travellers could provision themselves before the *haj* from Turkey set out on its arduous three week crossing of the desert to Mecca. Ensuring the security of the *haj* and provisioning it with mounts, camping material and food was an essential element in the Ottoman claim to the caliphate and the growth of the Midan quarter to the south of Damascus went in step with the increasing emphasis on the pilgrimage.

The 19th century was a more troubled period with local resentment against the Ottomans rising and the city readily supporting the cause of Muhammed Ali (who had led a revolt against Istanbul from Cairo). Ibrahim Pasha was his lieutenant in Damascus and he concentrated on administrative and military reform which have left their mark on the area west of the old city. Direct Ottoman rule was restored in 1840 but in the face of the rise of Arab nationalism in the late 19th century, continued Turkish rule had little to offer except stagnation in economic terms and Damascus was rapidly overtaken by Beirut as the economic and intellectual centre of the region. In 1860, serious rioting touched off by Druze/Christian tensions in Lebanon led to a massacre of Damascus Christians. In spite of some 19th century civic improvements which tended to move the city's centre of gravity towards the newly-built Merje Square, by the time of the French Mandate, old Damascus was a rather dilapidated version of its former self. Some expansion of the city was undertaken under the French mandate, especially in the quarters south west of Salihiye where a garden suburb based on the Abu Roumaneh axis was developed by French planners.

Figures recording the population of Damascus across these millennia are virtually non-existent. The city perhaps reached its peak of prosperity under the Romans but declined thereafter for many centuries. Its population was still only 52,000 at the end of the 16th century and that figure was achieved after a reasonably long period of regeneration. It grew to 90,000 by the

end of the 18th century, expanding only slowly for
the first half of the 19th century. Clearly, historic
population growth rates are outstripped by this
century's explosion of the city's size from around
150,000 (1900) through 300,000 (1946) to over
2.5 million today.

The evidence of the history of the city can
still be traced in its topography: hence the
residual broad divisions into quarters associated
with significant minority populations (Christians in
the eastern quarter (Qaimariye and Bab Tuma);
Jews south of the central part of Straight Street;
Shi'ites to the north east of the Umayyad Mosque
(Amara quarter) or the close association
between religious, charitable and trading
institutions in the orthodox Sunni heartland
between Suq al-Hamidiye and Straight Street in
the western part of the city. Over the centuries,
the city's commercial heart had been steadily
moving westward since Greek-Roman times
when civic life was centred on the *agora* that
once lay east of the Temple of Jupiter. After
shifting to the middle of Straight Street by the
Arab middle ages, the commmercial heart
moved to the quarter south west of the Umayyad
Mosque when that area housed the first
Mameluke and Ottoman *khans*. The westward
trend was locked in with the construction of the
Suq al-Hamidiye in the late 19th century thus
switching to the west the axis which had once
linked the *agora* to the temple.

In recent centuries, its conquerors tended to
expand further west beyond the walls to gain
space for their new institutions, for their
bureaucratic and military presence, or for
recreation - the Turks along the present Sharia
Quwatli; the French, as noted above, to fill in the
space between the Turkish city and Mount
Kassiun. The city acquired room to move without
the need to cannibalise its past. Damascus has
thus guarded its traditions perhaps more than
any other of the great cities of the Middle East
outside Cairo, unconsciously preserving in the
process much which in other centres has been
imprudently abandoned, especially this century.

REFS: *BG* pp 282 ff; Dussaud *Topographie* pp 291-3,
315-9; Elisséef *Dimashq*; Rihawi *Damascus*; Sack
Entwicklung; Sauvaget *Esquisse*; Schatkowski
Schilcher.

Damascus - Umayyad Mosque (Plates 6a-7b)

VARIANTS: Jami`a al-Umawi (Arb)
PERIOD: Rom/Byz/Arb/Ott   RATING: *** MAP:
17 ITIN: 1a

LOCATION: Damascus old city - eastern end of the
Suq al-Hamidiye.

This itinerary is principally devoted to the great
Mosque of the Umayyads but includes as options one
or two sites to the east of the mosque which are not
easily reached from other routes. It can be combined
with *Damascus - Suqs.

*In Damascus, there is a mosque that has
no equal in the world.*
[al-Adrissi, 1154]

The Umayyad Mosque sums up in one site much
of the complexity and continuity of Syrian history.
The effect is almost overwhelming on first sight;
scarcely less so on repeated visits. Along with
the Dome of the Rock in Jerusalem (691), it is
one of the great monuments to the ingenuity of
early Islam.

History

This site been marked by sacred enclosures as
far back as the second millennium BC. The
worship on this spot of the Semitic god, Hadad,
assimilated to the Greek Zeus or the Roman
Jupiter, was promoted under imperial patronage.
The temple was developed on lavish lines in the
first century AD. Restored and redecorated
under Septimius Severus (r 193-211), it formed
part of his program of public works to underline
his authority following the civil war of 193. In
accordance with Syro-Phoenician tradition, the
temple compound consisted of a large open
enclosure with a central chamber and sacrificial
altar. The compound extended over an area
even larger than the present mosque, the inner
enclosure (*temenos*) being surrounded by an
outer *peribolos* of which a few traces can still be
observed in the surrounding streets of the old
city.

After the adoption of Christianity as the
imperial religion, the temple was converted to a
Christian church dedicated to John the Baptist.
This is often attributed to the Emperor
Theodosius (r 379-95) who is said to have
ordered the tearing down of the inner shrine of
the pagan temple in 379. With the taking of
Damascus by the Arabs in 636, the Christian
population were generally allowed to continue to
use their churches and Muslims were settled in
new areas of the city. At least for the first 70
years, the Church of St John the Baptist

remained as the principal Christian place of worship though it seems likely that the extensive compound was for a time shared with Muslim worshippers whose prayers were oriented towards the south wall which faced Mecca.

The embellishment of the huge sacred area for the glory of Islam, however, proved a tempting objective for the first of the great

soaked up seven years of the state's revenue[50]. The Caliph used local Syrian (and imported Byzantine[51]) craftsmen to execute much of the glorious mosaic work which survives only in part. The prayer hall was based on the mosque built by the Prophet in Medina. The southern half of the temple courtyard was covered by a massive roof supported on an elongated basilica plan (three aisles separated by two rows of internal

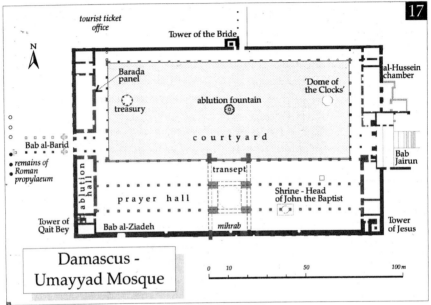

Damascus - Umayyad Mosque

Umayyad builders, the Caliph al-Walid (r 705-715). As the Muslim population of Damascus grew - and perhaps recalling the resistance Damascus had initially offered to the Muslim invaders - he recognised the need for a congregational assembly area capable of accommodating the entire community. The obvious place was the Greco-Roman temple compound, which had by then been converted to a Christian church. He negotiated with the Christian community for the ceding of the church and converted the inner compound into the magnificent mosque that you see today[49]. The work was commissioned in 708 and construction finished in 714-5, the year of al-Walid's death. It

columns). In order to re-orient the building to the south, a central transverse aisle terminated in the *mihrab* and was topped by a central dome.

The rest of the mosque consists of a huge courtyard (now paved in white marble) and surrounded by a colonnade that borrows elements from several periods from Roman to Arab. This pastiche of elements comes together with striking effect.

The mosque has survived the intervening 1200 years with surprising integrity in spite of successive invasions, Mongol sackings and the ravages of earthquakes and fire. Perhaps most devastating was the fire in 1893 which destroyed much of the old fabric of the prayer hall, leaving the outer walls and the courtyard intact. The Ottomans replaced the interior columns, the

---

[49] Several accounts (eg al-Asakir pp 36-8) relate that the Christians were compensated with permanent rights to four church sites elsewhere in the old city including the site of the present Greek Orthodox Patriarchate. For the architectural and symbolic background see Grabar's article in *Synthronon*.

[50] Muqadassi quoted in Creswell *Early Muslim* p 151.
[51] See Gibb pp 219-33.

churches in that area. The Patriarchate of the Greek Orthodox lies immediately to the left beyond the arch. A Christian church was located on this site as far back as the Byzantine period. The immediate quarter is named *al-Mariamiye* after the church dedicated to the Virgin Mary (*al-Mariam*). The buildings and patriarchal church are largely modern but the church has a fine marbled *iconostasis* of the 18th century.

The area to the right has traditionally been inhabited by Jews (*Haret al-Yehud*). One of the most accessible buildings in this area is the Palais Dahdah which has been in the Dahdah family for 65 years. To reach it, take the laneway on the right immediately before the arch. Continue 150 m, then turn right, looking for the small sign pointing to the Dahdah Palace. The house is an excellent example of Syrian domestic architecture of the 18th century with its large summer *iwan* at the western end decorated in superb style. The large reception room on the north side is unusually large for a private house.

Continue your walk eastwards. The remaining stretch of Straight Street (550 m) brings you to the east gate of the city, **Bab Sharqi** (the Gate of the Sun to the Romans). This is the oldest extant monument in Damascus and the only one of the Roman gates of the city to preserve its original form. The gate comprises a triple passageway, the central one for wheeled traffic, the outer two corresponding with the arcaded passages along the colonnaded street reserved for pedestrians. Note the beginnings of the colonnades that once carried the arcading. From Arab times until this century, the two side passageways had been blocked by masonry but the gate was cleared and restored under the French Mandate. The treatment of the facades is rather plain but well balanced. The gate formerly attributed to the period of Septimius Severus or Caracalla (late second, early third century) is more recently attributed to the reign of Augustus (d AD 14). It is through this gateway that the Arab commander Khalid Ibn al-Walid entered Damascus in 636. The mosque perched on the northern side of the gateway dates from Nur al-Din's rebuilding of the city's defences. (To the south of the gate lie two other Christian patriarchates, that of the Armenian Orthodox and of the Greek Catholics.)

While you are in the vicinity, there are two other monuments worth visiting at the east end of the city both of which are associated with St Paul and the story of his visit to Damascus (Acts 9). In brief, Saul (as he was before his conversion to Christianity) a Jew from Cilicia, was brought up as a Pharisee and thus a confirmed opponent of the followers of Christ. He was instructed to go to Damascus to arrest followers of Jesus. As he approached the city[70], 'a light from heaven shone all around him'. He fell to the ground, and then heard a voice saying 'Saul, Saul why are you persecuting me?' Saul was blinded and was led into Damascus by his companions. At the same time, a Christian called Ananias was directed by a vision to go to a house in Straight Street, where he met Saul, sheltered him in his house and initiated him into Christianity. Saul began preaching in the synagogues proclaiming 'Jesus the Son of God', thus arousing the resentment of the Jews. Eventually made aware of a plot by Jews to kill him, Saul evaded capture by having himself lowered over the walls of Damascus in a basket.

The first site associated with these events is the **Chapel of St Ananias** which can be reached by going down the lane on the left immediately before the arch. The chapel is at the end of the lane (150 m) and is reached by descending the stairway in the corner of the small court. The chapel reputedly includes on the right a part of the house of Ananias where Saul took shelter[71].

The second site is more clearly apocryphal, namely the chapel (**St Paul's Chapel**) said to mark the spot where Saul was lowered over the walls in a basket. To reach it you leave the old city via Bab Sharqi and take the broad and busy street to the right that leads after 400 m to the roundabout from which the road to the airport originates[72]. (Note the Roman blocks at the base of this stretch of wall, the upper courses dating from Nur al-Din's time. The Arab re-fortification followed the Roman lines but added seven towers and a major bastion of which only one tower survives.) Set into the walls is a 20th century chapel built and maintained by the Greek Catholics. Inside the chapel near the street entrance is an arch which is clearly the remains of the Arab gateway that stood on this spot (*Bab Kaysan*). The original Roman gateway reflected the *cardo* that ran from Bab Tuma through the eastern quarter of the city. Whatever was left of the Roman gate must have been removed when the aperture was filled in 1154 under Nur al-Din.

---

[70] The exact spot is only conjectural but the Franciscan order recently erected a chapel 15 km SW of Damascus on the road between Kisweh and Artus to commemmorate the incident.

[71] There is some archaeological evidence that the remains of the house could indeed date back to the AD 1C. A Byzantine church known as al-Musallaba was built on the site.

[72] The line of Arab walls at this point cuts the corner off the original Roman rectangular city, rejoining the Roman alignment briefly at Bab Kaysan. The rest of the south walls (between Bab Kaysan and Bab al-Saghir - see *Damascus - SW Quarter) bulge out from the Roman alignment and are in a poor state of preservation.

It is the Mameluke gate built in 1364 whose traces are incorporated in the chapel.

There is no historical evidence that this is the spot where St Paul was lowered and the tradition ascribing it to this section of the wall seems recent in origin, perhaps not much older than the chapel. The incident, of course, could have happened at any point on the 8 km or more of Roman wall. As Saul may well have lodged in the eastern quarter and took off in the direction of Jerusalem, this is as likely a site as any; but who could say?

REFS: Peters; Freyburger 'Jupiter-Heiligtums' in *DaM* 2 1985; Rihawi *Damascus*; Sack *Damaskus - Beitrag*; Sauvaget *Monuments*; Sauvaget *Plan*; Sauvaget *Esquisse*; Wulzinger and Watzinger *Damaskus - islamische*; Wulzinger and Watzinger *Damaskus - antike*.

Damascus - South West Quarter - Old City

VARIANTS:
PERIOD: Arb/Ott RATING: * MAP: 23 ITIN: 1f

LOCATION: The area extending south from the western entrance to the Suq al-Hamidiye, including the cemetery of Bab al-Saghir. This itinerary involves a walk of c 3 km. It is preferable to avoid undertaking it during the heat of the day or when commercial activity is at its peak.

The tour begins at the western entrance to the Suq al-Hamidiye. As you face the entrance to the *suq*, take the road that leads south (right), officially named Zaghlul Street but later becoming Midan Street as it eventually leads to the pilgrim quarter known as the Midan (*Damascus - Midan). Walk along this busy street for about 75 m. The first **mosque** on the right commemorates the Ottoman Governor of Damascus from 1571-4, **Darwish Pasha,** who built it in 1572-5 and whose tomb lies in the small octagonal domed building (1579) to the south, joined to the mosque by an arch. The entrance, consciously Syrian in style, leads you into a small courtyard with the portico (note decorative faience panels) and entrance to the prayer room on the left, following a Turkish domed plan.

The quarter which lies to the west is known as **Qanawat** (canal or aqueduct). This is a reference to the ancient water intake which entered Damascus at this point. Remains of the Roman aqueduct can still be seen in the Qanawat quarter whose houses are largely the product of the 19th century. Take the side street that runs between the Mosque of Darwish Pasha and the tomb. After about 120 m take the

winding lane to the left which eventually brings you to a short flight of steps which rise onto a street. In fact, you have just emerged under one of the arches of the Roman aqueduct whose course can be traced in the embankment supporting a row of white-painted houses. This was part of the aqueduct system which brought water to the city from the Barada River. Return now to Midan Street by continuing east. Double back north a few metres to reach the next mosque on the itinerary along Midan Street.

A rather striking facade frames the entrance on the left (a little raised above a row of shops) of the **Madrasa Sibaiye**, a funerary college commemorating Sibai, Governor of Damascus (constructed 1509-15). Built at the very end of the Mameluke period, the architecture shows a rather debased and heavy version of the style, the minaret in particular being rather lumpy and

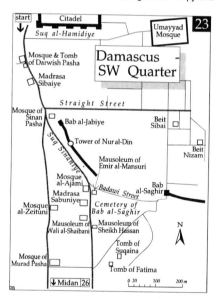

earth-bound. The facade follows the Mameluke preference for alternating bands of black and white stone with *muqarnas* treatment of the doorway. Inside, the prayer hall includes elements taken from earlier buildings (*kufic* inscriptions on marble altar tops (11th century); marble mosaics).

Continue another 35 m south, crossing to the left hand side of Midan Street. Just past the entrance to Straight Street, another small street runs parallel eastwards. On the corner is the **Mosque of Sinan Pasha** (Jami al-Sinaniye). Sinan, Governor of Damascus (late 16th century) was Governor of Damascus and the mosque was completed in 1590 under an endowment which also included a *hammam*, school and market. The minaret is distinguished by its colouring of green-enamelled brick. The courtyard is small but charming, an oasis from the chaos outside. Though none of its parts are particularly striking, the overall effect is a pleasing blend of Ottoman and Syrian. Note particularly the faience panels in the arcade, of local manufacture but in the tradition of Iznik. The prayer hall is exceptionally beautiful, a miniature Turkish domed chamber with galleries. The old windows and the sculptured plaster in the pendentives of the dome are especially fine.

Some remains of the Roman/Arab western wall of the old city lie behind the buildings that now line Midan Street. Immediately behind the Sinaniye Mosque (first right past the mosque's side entrance) can be seen what remains of the **Bab al-Jabiye** (Gate of the Water Trough), though you will have to hunt among the crowds and stalls of the second hand clothes market (known picturesquely as the *Suq al-Kumeile*, 'louse market'). As with other gateways (*Damascus - Citadel, Northern Walls), its reconstruction, partly using the original Roman blocks, dates from the era of Nur al-Din (1164) with further work completed in 1227. The Roman gate on this site marked the western end of the *Via Recta* the main colonnaded axis of the city (*decumanus maximus*) which ran 1.3 km to Bab Sharqi (*Damascus - Straight Street).

40 m south of the Sinaniye Mosque, look for a narrow-arched entrance in zebra-stripes leading to a hotel (*Funduq Islakh*). In the courtyard are the remains of the **Tower of Nur al-Din**, a round structure built in surprisingly small blocks with a bold inscribed band, as part of his improvements to the defences of the city in 1173.

Midan Street now continues south via a suq covered by a curved roof of corrugated iron (*Suq Sinaniye*). A little further, on the right lies the **al-Ajami Mosque** (or Turba Afriduniye) intended both as a tomb (*turba*) and Koranic school (*madrasa*). Built after 1348, the building commemorates the Persian merchant Afridun al-Ajami. The plan is a rare example (for Damascus) of the cruciform mosque. The facade is in the familiar Mameluke striped masonry with door and windows surrounds in *muqarnas*. Frankish capitals are employed in the *mihrab* of the prayer hall.

At this point, another road (al-Badawi Street) diverts to the left off Midan Street and follows the south limits of the old city around to the east. Where it forks, the intersection encloses another Mameluke monument, the **Mausoleum of Emir Saif al-Din Bahadur al-Mansuri**, a military leader in whose honour the twin-domed tomb was built in 1329.

On the land behind this mausoleum lies the extensive **Cemetery of Bab al-Saghir**. This is the most notable of the cemeteries surrounding the old city and contains several tombs of interest. Before visiting them, however, you may wish to note two other funerary buildings along Midan Street.

On the right side of the street as you continue south is the **Madrasa Sabuniye**, a Koranic school founded as a funerary endowment in 1459-64 by a rich merchant, Shihab al-Din Ahmed Ibn al-Sabuni. Highly-patterned facade with black and white banding; medallions over each set of windows; tall stalactited doorway; - minaret; dome decorated inside with painted floral designs.

20 m after, still on the right side of Midan Street, you come to the **Mausoleum of Wali al-Shaibani**. The name apparently refers to the Mameluke Governor who had the building erected but the name of the citizen buried there is not clear. Sauvaget proposes Emir Saif al-Din Ibn Jian (d 1353). (Facade with black stone banding and decorations; entrance with stalactited treatment and arms of the founder.)

50 m west along a small side street is the Mosque and **Mausoleum of Murad Pasha**, built in 1575-6 by the Ottoman Governor in a style that still follows that of the late Mameluke period.

Returning to the left side of Midan Street, another mausoleum backs on to the cemetery a little beyond the point you have reached. This is the **Mausoleum of Sheikh Hassan**, an unremarkable building.

To enter the cemetery, take the street to the left (al-Jarrah St) that cuts through it and enter by the gate 120 m on the right. Two tombs are worthy of particular note, both reached by continuing south through the cemetery towards the central cluster of tomb chambers. As the Cemetery of Bab al-Saghir has been in use since the time of the first Caliphs, it has, not unnaturally, attracted a store of legends relating to its early tombs. The first **tomb** to note has become a centre for Shi`ite pilgrimage as it is held in popular legend to be the burial place of

Fatima, daughter of the Prophet and wife of the Shi'ites' revered Ali. Sauvaget preferred to see it as the tomb of another Fatima, the daughter of one Ahmad al-Sibti who was perhaps a descendant of Ali. In any event, the tomb attracts considerable crowds of pious visitors, particularly from Iran.

A little towards the north is the second **tomb** of note, that **of Suqaina**, a daughter of Hussein and great-grand-daughter of the Prophet. The attribution of this twin-domed building, however, also appears doubtful. Suqaina died in Medina (after many marriages) and the coffin and inscription are dated a good deal after her lifetime. Nevertheless, the coffin, decorated with kufic lettering (which it is difficult to appreciate displayed behind glass in the confined space) is noteworthy and has been dated to the first half of the 12th century.

150 m to the south of Fatima's tomb lies the reputed site of the burial of the founder of the Umayyad dynasty, Moawiya Bin Abi Sufyan (Caliph 661-81). Virtually all trace of the Umayyads was later fiercely effaced by their Abbasid successors but it is not impossible that sufficient memories remained of the approximate spot where the founder of the Umayyid dynasty was interred to have allowed his cenotaph to be located with reasonable accuracy in later centuries[73]. The site is now marked by a simple mud-plastered cube.

At this point, the energetic visitor may want to continue 400 m down Midan Street to pick up the starting point (Bab Musalla Square) for *Damascus - Midan described separately but this would add considerably to the distance covered and time required.

We return by tracking further to the east to take in part of the south walls of the city. Return to the road that crosses the cemetery. At its end, it joins Badawi Street, the thoroughfare that you earlier saw forking away from Midan Street at the Mausoleum of Bahadur al-Mansuri. Walk 50 m east along Badawi Street then 20 m left along a side street to the remains of another Roman gateway, heavily reconstructed in Ayyubid times. This is the **Bab al-Saghir**[74] or Bab Shaghur (Little Gate), reconstructed as part of Nur al-Din's defences of the city in 1156 but on the foundations of the Roman Gate of Mars. The scale is small (as the name implies) and the Arab work sits rather awkwardly on the large

Roman blocks. The minaret on top adds a final bizarre touch.

Continue north through the gate and along the widened street (Hassan Kharrat St) that leads 300 m to Straight Street. To the right are two old houses of considerable interest though access is sometimes difficult to arrange. For the first, turn right at 150 m, left at second cross street and 10 m on the left is the Beit Nizam (Plate 8b), an 18th century house that probably served as the French Consulate for part of the last century[75]. For the second, go back one street towards Hassan Kharrat Street and turn right, left, then right. Immediately on the left is the Beit Sibai (1769-74), recently restored.

Resume your walk northwards to the intersection that leads to the spices suq (Suq al-Bazuriye) and the Azem Palace (*Damascus - Khans). You can return to the starting point by turning left along Straight Street. This 300 m stretch of corrugated iron-covered suq, also known as the Suq Midhat Pasha after the Governor of Damascus who had it constructed in 1878, is described in *Damascus - Khans. The area immediately east of Midan Street is covered in *Damascus - Straight Street.

REFS: De Lorey, Eustache & Wiet, Gaston 'Cénotaphes de deux dames musulmanes à Damas' in *Syria* II 1921; Moaz & Ory *Inscriptions arabes de Damas - Les stèles funéraires - I Cimetiére d'al-Bab al-Sagir* Damascus 1977; Rihawi *Damascus*; Sack *Damaskus - Beitrag*; Sauvaget *Monuments*; Wulzinger and Watzinger *Damaskus - islamische*.

Damascus - National Museum (Plate 9a)

VARIANTS:
PERIOD: All RATING: ** MAP: - ITIN:: 1g

LOCATION: Al-Quwatli Street, east of the Damascus Fairgrounds and west of the *Tekkiye Mosque.

The National Museum of Damascus is one of the world's great collections of archaeological and historical material and it would be impossible to do it justice in a few pages. This survey is intended only to introduce the scope of the collection and its broad layout. A thorough visit is best facilitated with a copy of the Museum's *Concise Guide*.

The museum was founded in 1919 and was originally set up, along with the Arab Academy, in the Madrasa al-Adeliye (*Damascus - Suqs). In

---

[73] Moaz & Ory *Inscriptions arabes de Damas - Les stèles funéraires - I Cimetiére d'al-Bab al-Sagir* Damascus 1977 pp 146-7.

[74] The Arab army of Yazid Ben Abi Sufyan camped outside this gate during the first siege of Damascus by the Muslim armies.

[75] The reason for the use of 'probably' is outlined in Brigid Keenan's forthcoming book on the houses of Damascus – *Inside Damascus*.

1936, the east wing of the present complex was built. From 1939 to 1952, the building's entrance was embellished by the reconstruction of the gateway from *Qasr al-Heir West, an Umayyad desert palace of the eighth century. The three-storeyed west wing of the Museum was added in 1953 and expanded from 1956 to 1961.

OPENING HOURS	
Wed-Mon	0900-1600 hours
	(Summer 0900-1800)
Fri	closed 1100-1300 hours
Tues	closed
Note: Special hours are adopted in Ramadan with the Museum generally opening an hour earlier than the above schedule.	

The archaeological and historical collections of the Museum are arranged in four Departments: Pre-historic; Ancient Syrian; Classical; and Arab-Islamic Antiquities. (There is a fifth department, not covered here, for Contemporary Art.) The layout of the building, however, does not strictly follow chronological sequence.

You may wish to start by taking in the formidable array of largely classical-period sculpture in the gardens of the Museum, left of the entrance avenue. Continuing down the avenue from the ticket office, you enter the building through the monumental **gateway of Qasr al-Heir West**, a superb example of the eclectic Umayyad style. It borrows elements from Persian, Byzantine and local Syrian sources but provides its own synthesis. The gateway comprises two semi-cylindrical towers enclosing a rectangular portal, the latter surmounted by a large blank Syrian arch, familiar in the local repertoire for several centuries. The *tympanum* above is embellished with niches, false windows and colonnettes.

The gateway has been described as 'as extravagantly sham as anything built by Ludwig II of Bavaria', pointing out that the various visual images of the facade are thematically unrelated[76]. Yet the effect is not frenetic and chaotic. The concern with restless decoration applied on every surface, apparent in Arab art of later periods, is already evident. The stucco surfaces are divided into panels of distinct elements, each treated according to a geometric or floral theme. The whole develops a rather weird harmony in spite of the two-dimensional nature of the decorative skin. This is perhaps due to the strong basic shapes adopted for the

architectural elements - semi-cylinder, triangular crenellations, Syrian arch, rectangular doorway and copious niches and colonnettes.

Once inside the vestibule (decorated with other elements from the Umayyad palace), the building offers you two choices. To the right is the new (west) wing with its collections of pre-classical and Islamic art. To the left are the classical and Byzantine collections in the original part of the building. It is suggested you begin to the left though this means that you will have to double back chronologically when you come later to the pre-classical rooms.

The elements of the east wing will be taken in the following order:

- entrance hall
- second corridor
- galleries of Jebel al-Arab and the Hauran (left of corridor)
- main corridor
- galleries of Palmyra and Dura Europos (off the corridor, to the right)
- Dura Europos synagogue (through vestibule at the end of the corridor, then across a small courtyard)
- Tomb of Yarhai from Palmyra (down stairs off the same vestibule)
- Hall of Byzantine art (behind Palmyra and Dura-Europos galleries; also reached off the small entrance hall).

Begin with the **entrance hall** immediately to the left of the vestibule, containing classical statues.

The corridor to the left off the hall is the **second corridor** in the Museum handbook. In it are displayed pottery and glassware of the classical period. Two large **galleries** extend off it to the left, largely covering the **Hauran**. Finds displayed include a mosaic found at Shahba ('Glorification of the Earth'), a mosaic pavement depicting the Orontes as a god (from Latakia), basalt statues, several bronze helmets from the Hauran, and a magnificent marble sarcophagus with a complex battle scene found at Rastan and dated to AD 3.

Return now to the first hall and begin the Palmyra wing with the **main corridor** that leads through directly from the entrance. This is devoted to sculpture and bronzes of the classical period found at Latakia, Apamea and Palmyra. Especially notable is the superb bust of a woman (case no 6) which stands out from its circular frame and the statue of Aspasia from Hama (case 1).

---

[76] Hillenbrand *Dolce Vita* p 7.

The first room off to the right is the **Hall of Palmyra** which contains many items of sculpture, usually busts or groupings taken from tombs. Note on the south wall (right) the superb mosaic of a nude Cassiope revealing her beauty to the Nereids (from a house of the third century AD, Palmyra). Second to the right is the **Hall of Dura Europos** in which are displayed jewellery (see especially works in gold in case no 2), ceramics, bronzes and frescoes from this Hellenistic/Roman site on the Euphrates.

The most celebrated 'find' from Dura Europos, however, is the reconstructed **synagogue** found during the excavations under Cumont in 1931-2 and transported to the Museum later in the decade. The circumstances of its discovery are related in *Dura Europos. The synagogue can be visited across the small vestibule and courtyard that lie at the far end of the wing. (The synagogue is usually kept closed to prevent light fading the wall paintings. A guardian holds the key and may have to be tracked down.) This is a remarkable building not only in itself, by the very fact that a Jewish synagogue of the mid second century has survived at all, but also for the fact that its walls are covered in representations of the human form in scenes from scripture depicted in a unique mixture of Parthian and local painting styles. The shape of the building is itself of interest, prefiguring many aspects of later church and mosque design.

Off the same vestibule, reached by a descending staircase is the *hypogeum* (underground tomb) **of Yarhai** the Palmyrene, reconstructed from the Valley of the Tombs in Palmyra. You enter through stone doors carved to imitate wood. In the alcove to the right is a carved banquet scene topped by two niches. The main vault is to the right and ends in the customary *triclinium* with officials of the temple preparing the funeral ceremony. The two side walls are covered with funerary busts. The tomb was dedicated in AD 108 and used during the following two centuries by members of the family.

The **Hall of Byzantine Art** is divided into several sections representing jewels and coins, Syriac manuscripts and other works including pottery. Note especially the treasury from Resafe (first case on left in first room), a remarkable find of 1982 which comprises sacred vessels which somehow reached Resafe from Europe.

To reach the west wing of the Museum return to the main entrance vestibule and continue though to the other side. After a courtyard in the Arab style, you enter the first of the rooms devoted to **Ras Shamra** (*Ugarit). Exhibits display the high standard of craftsmanship in various materials and a sample of the important archives in syllabic cuneiform, a system of writing which foreshadowed a true alphabet. A second room devoted to Ugarit is found through the doorway.

Follow now the long gallery which continues on from the second Ugaritic room and keeps to the western wall of the building. This covers a variety of Bronze Age sites of the inland and coastal regions of Syria. Double back now along the next series of rooms beginning with the **Hall of Mari**. *Mari on the Mid Euphrates is another Bronze Age site of major importance. The style of art shows much direct influence from Mesopotamia as revealed in the rich variety of pottery, cylinder seals and statuary. Note especially the beautifully worked lapus lazuli statue of an eagle inlaid with gold (case no 6, Treasure of King Cansud).

You now reach a vestibule off the first courtyard displaying finds from *Raqqa. From here, again change direction along the corridor along the right side of the building, the area devoted to Islamic collections of the museum. This contains collections of coins, jewellery and arms.

Beyond lies the reconstructed 'Damascene hall' based on a room taken from a palace of the 18th century in the old city of Damascus. The room was reconstructed in 1958-62 following a gift of the marble and timber panelling by Jamil Mardam Bey, a former Prime Minister. The hall does not follow the dimensions of the original and has been considerably extended and supplemented with reconstructed panels. Among the original sections are the central element of the ceiling (raised section); the marble basin; the two niches surrounding the fountain; and the chimney.

Return now to the main entrance along the same Islamic corridor, this time visiting the rooms to the left that contain specialised collections including manuscripts, pottery, ceramics and stone and stucco carvings.

REFS: Arush *et al*; Arush *Antiquités arabes*; Hillenbrand *'Dolce Vita'*; Lambert.

Damascus - Tekkiye Mosque

VARIANTS: Tekke Mosque
PERIOD: Ottoman RATING: ** MAP: 24 ITIN: 1h

LOCATION: The most notable buildings of the Turkish period in the area between al-Quwatli Street (east of the National Museum) and the entrance to the Suq al-Hamidiye are covered in this itinerary.

The Tekkiye Mosque is the most gracious and perhaps the most under-rated monument in Damascus. It was the work of the foremost architect of the Ottoman period, Sinan. The complex was intended to service the great

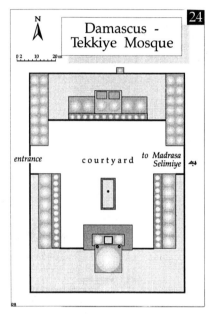

annual pilgrimage to Mecca whose custody was one of the most important duties of the Governor of the *vilayat* (province) of Damascus and the income from which was one of the city's major sources of prosperity. The complex was built on the site of the *Qasr al-Ablaq*, a Mameluke palace built by Baibars. (Earlier, the area from here west to the International Fairgrounds had served as a parade or exercise ground (Midan al-Akhdar) for Ayyubid and Mameluke troops and is assumed to be the site of a Roman hippodrome.)

Though modest in scale by comparison with many of Sinan's other projects (for others in Syria see *Aleppo - South Quarter; *Damascus - Salihiye Quarter), it was begun in 1554 to honour the great Sultan Suleiman I (Suleiman the Magnificent r 1520-66). The work of Sinan is prominently represented in Istanbul, particularly in his superlative Suleimaniye Mosque, and in

other parts of Turkey and in the Balkans. The assurance and sensitivity of his style can be seen on a small scale in this Damascus project but the effect is nevertheless as striking as in his more monumental achievements.

The complex consists of three main parts:

- the mosque itself, still in use;
- the arcaded buildings which enclose the courtyard on the north, east and west sides, forming a *khan* to house the pilgrims. (The northern half, once the kitchens and refectory, now accommodates a rather tatty Military Museum); and
- the compound to the east, now used as a handicrafts suq, the *Madrasa Selimiye*, actually built as a Koranic school (or hostelry) a decade after the Tekkiye and not the work of Sinan.

Relying to a great extent on Ottoman Turkish designs (the domed prayer hall), Sinan has skilfully added local Syrian features including the function and shape of the courtyard and its central tank, the use of *muqarnas* work over the entrance to the prayer hall and the alternation of light and dark courses in stone. (In fact some of it is coloured plaster skilfully applied). The overall effect is calm and magical with the trees providing a cool oasis on a hot day.

In 1553-4 the contract for the construction was given to Sinan by Sultan Suleiman I ('the Magnificent'). The construction took six years. The use of the slim Turkish minarets gives the complex much of its careful sense of proportion. The *khan* consists of a series of chambers each covered by a dome and provided with a chimney.

The **Madrasa Selimiye** was added under Suleiman's successor, Sultan Selim II (Sultan 1566-74). Its style, though more distinctly Syrian, blends well with Sinan's work. The prayer room of the school (off the small courtyard to the south of the main *suq*) is still used for that purpose.

Note too the recently restored **Turkish Law Institute** (1911) on the north eastern corner of the block, now the headquarters of the Tourism Ministry. Among other buildings of the Turkish period in the neighbourhood (continue east up the hill past main Post Office, the Damascus terminus of the Hijaz Railway (1913 - still used for services on the narrow gauge line to Zabadani) is worth noting. The building, though small in scale, is notable for its successful interweaving of Turkish and Syrian elements. Note especially the intricate ceiling, in Damascene style, in the ticket hall.

A short continuation to the east (towards the entrance to the Suq al-Hamidiye) will take you past some other notable buildings which line the street (Sharia al-Nasser) which was widened and straightened under the late Ottoman Governor, Jamal Pasha, just before the First World War. This marked the central administrative headquarters of the late Turkish and French administrations. On the left is the headquarters built for the Societé des Eaux Fijeh, a pleasant late Ottoman building (1906) which originally housed the company that provided Damascus with piped drinking water from the Anti-Lebanon. 100 m, still on the left, is the Mosque of Tengiz, Mameluke Governor of Damascus (r 1312-39). The present appearance of the mosque owes much to the construction under Ibrahim Pasha (r 1832-40) of a military school restored for use as a msoque after 1932. The mosque (original minaret in lane to rear) is rich in historical associations, having been built in 1317 on the site of the former church of St Nicholas. Opposite was once the military headquarters of Ibrahim Pasha and further on, just before the Suq al-Hamidiye, is the impressive civil *serail* (now the main courts complex).

REFS: *GB* pp 304-5; Goodwin p 256; Sack *Damaskus - Entwicklung*; Sauvaget *Monuments* pp 78-81.

Damascus - Salihiye Quarter

VARIANTS:
PERIOD: Arb/Ott RATING: * MAP: 25 ITIN: 1i

LOCATION: The Salihiye quarter lies 2 km north of the walled city on the lower slopes of Mount Kassiun. The following itinerary begins at the busy traffic intersection where Salihiye Street reaches the lower slopes at the square known as Jisr al-Abiad (White Bridge' denoting an original crossing of the Tura arm of the Barada), or simply as al-Jisr.

History

The more gently sloping ground on the lower reaches of Mount Kassiun has long been used to take some of the spillover of population from the walled city of Damascus, to house the tombs of pious benefactors, or to accommodate the wealthier class seeking a more salubrious climate. It has also provided a refuge to new immigrant groups, particularly non-Arabs (Kurds and Cretan Muslims) or refugees from persecution elsewhere. The settlement in the Salihiye area has thus been unplanned compared to the relatively ordered beginnings of the old city which, at least from the Greco-Roman period, was provided with a grid plan and a systematic water reticulation system. The historic importance of the quarter is indicated by

the 70 monuments officially recognised, a significant proportion of the 250 or so for Damascus as a whole.

The area to be visited in this itinerary is a 1.4 km segment of the extensive arc of settlement spread across the lower slopes of the mountain, reaching areas where the ground is precipitous and wheeled traffic impossible. This segment (also known as al-Chaharkasiye) lies between al-Muhajirin (the quarter established between 1895-1911 to settled Muslim refugees from Crete; on the left as you face the mountain) and al-Akrad (Kurdish quarter, established 19th century; on the right). Lying at the end of the main access route from the old city, it represents the first part of the Kassiun slopes to receive permanent settlement in Arab times and which thereafter continued to attract major building projects. The first impetus to the development of civic services, however (including the channelling of the Tura and Yazid arms of the Barada River), came in 1159 under the patronage of Nur al-Din. He settled Hanbalite refugees from Crusader-occupied Jerusalem, under the leadership of Sheikh Abu Umar Muhammed al-Maqdisi, in the Salihiye quarter[77] to prevent rivalries in the old city where adherents of the Shaffi school were dominant. The Hanbalites consolidated themselves around the Hanbila Mosque, founded in 1202 as the first Friday mosque outside the old walled city. In the Ayyubid period, further development was sponsored by endowments from leading figures of the ruling class, usually for the establishment of funerary mosques or *madrasas* (Rukniye 1224; Maridaniye 1227; Sahibiye 1233-45; Morchidiye 1252). The area also served as a place of burial, including for the notable mystic Mohi al-Din Ibn al-Arabi (d 1240) whose tomb (Mosque of Mohi al-Din) still attracts crowds of pilgrims to the quarter.

The Salihiye quarter, essentially without defensive walls or strongpoints for refuge, was sorely affected by the three great Mongol invasions (1260, 1300, 1400) of the Mameluke period as well as by internal strife. Its development thus slowed, at least until private endowments from prominent trading families gave new impetus to the quarter in the late 14th century. In the early Ottoman period, the quarter benefited from the works to enlarge the tomb of

---

[77] The name derives from Abu Salih al-Hanbali, the early Islamic scholar associated with Hanbalite sect whose followers constructed the Hanbali Mosque described in this itinerary. Salihiye became a centre for Hanbalite influence in Damascus, especially after the arrival in the 13C of a large number of Hanbali refugees from Harran in Mesopotamia, fleeing the Mongols. It is also popularly taken as a reference to the number of devout (*salihoun*, 'saints') buried there.

al-Arabi, as well as charitable projects such as the Imaret of Sultan Suleiman of 1552 (see below). After the 16th century, however, it largely stagnated, a process hastened by the earthquake of 1759.

Visit

The following itinerary surveys the major historic monuments of the Salihiye quarter but it should be noted that many are open only irregularly or are used for other purposes (e.g. schools). The majority of mosques (apart from the Hanbali and Mohi al-Din Mosques) are closed except, in some cases, at prayer times. However, given that the facades are usually the aspect which retain most of the original character of a building, even a short visit conveys a good deal of the atmosphere of this richly historic quarter.

The tour begins with the building which stands on the north side of the intersection at Jisr al-Abiad, the **Madrasa Maridaniye**.

entrance) was probably built around 1413 by the Mameluke Amsanak Ibn Uzdamur who is buried in the mosque.

There are two streets which branch from the north side of the Jisr al-Abiad square near the Madrasa Maridaniye. Take the left street (al-Afif Street) and ascend for c120 m. The road veers left across a triangular intersection but instead of following it, continue to ascend 20 m to the next cross street to the left. Immediately to the left are two buildings of interest. The first is the **Mausoleum of Emir Kajkar** (1322) (*Turba al-Kajkariye*). Small building - dome with two side arches; long carved inscription on the façade. Now used as a centre for a government welfare agency but inspection is possible. Under the side arches, close examination will reveal the crumbling remains of a sculptured frieze. The four coloured glass windows under the dome may be modern. Almost immediately next to the left is the **Turba Amat al-Latif**, tomb of a Hanbalite sheikh. Next on the right, a domed

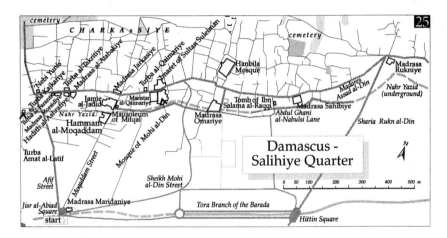

Unfortunately much of the impact of the original Ayyubid building erected after 1213 but endowed in 1227 has been lost with later additions. The title refers to the benefactor, a princess of the house of the lords of Mardin, south eastern Turkey - Ikhshawra Khatun, the wife of Ayyubid ruler, Malik al-Moazzam Issa and probably a niece of Nur al-Din. She died in Mecca and was thus not interred in the building she had endowed. The entry is on the north side and includes a fine lintel in carved wood. Note the carved wooden panels in the prayer hall and three early coloured glass windows. The funerary chamber is to the left. The minaret (right of

mausoleum, Qubbat Raihan (1243).

Heading uphill (north), take the first street on the right. You will now find the majority of buildings described in the rest of the itinerary along this main thoroughfare (Madares Assaad al-Din) which cuts across the Chaharkasiye quarter for 1.4 km from west to east.

Second building on the left is the anonymous **Mausoleum** sometimes given the name **Nebi Yunis**, an attractive dome resting on *muqarnas* squinches; probably late 13th century. After 30 m, on the right is the **Mausoleum al-**

Faranti (Turba al-Farnatiye), the tomb of Sheikh Ali al-Faranti (d 1224) - with a small dome; restored since 1981.

Immediately after, on the right, **Madrasa Morsidiye** (1252). Funerary college commemorating Khadija Khatun, daughter of the Ayyubid leader, Malik al-Moazzam Issa (whose wife was commemorated in the Madrasa Maridaniye above). The simple square minaret is the only example surviving from the 13th century in Damascus. The building now seems to be used as a kindergarten.

10 m on the left, the **Turba al-Takritiye** (or Madrasa Tabutluk), the mausoleum of Taqi al-Din al-Takriti (d 1299). Recently under reconstruction, the building comprises a *muqarnas*-treated entrance doorway, a domed funerary chamber on the right and a small prayer room to the left. Most of the building follows Syrian tradition of the time but the decoration of the prayer room shows Andalusian influence. Opposite is the Hadith al-Ashrafiye (1237).

On the opposite corner, is the **Madrasa Atabakiye**, a building with honeycombed entrance erected in memory of Tarkan Khatun, daughter of a ruler of Mosul and grand-niece of Nur al-Din who married Malik al-Ashraf Mousa (d 1242).

You now enter Salihiye's Friday market. 100m on the right is a street which descends to the Jisr al-Abiad square. On the left at this T intersection is the **Madrasa Jarkasiye** founded by the Ayyubid Emir, Fahr al-Din Jarkas, commander of Saladin's *mamelukes*, (d 1211) and enlarged by the former *mameluke* Hutluba (d 1237). The prayer room contains some old woodwork; two funerary chambers (domed) are attached.

25 m down the street on the right, a gateway leads into the compound which houses the **Jami al-Jadid** (the New Mosque) and, straight ahead, the **Turba Khatuniye.** This is the mausoleum of Ismat al-Din Khatun who was the wife of Nur al-Din and of his successor, Saladin (d 1185/6). The site was incorporated into the mosque in the 14th century. The burial chamber is richly decorated in sculptured plaster. In the separate prayer room, note the Crusader capitals.

On the opposite side of this street, you will notice the remains of another **mausoleum** now in crumbling disrepair, that **of Emir Sabiq al-Din Mitqal**, a *jamdar* (knight) of Saladin who died in 1224. Though the dome has collapsed, the tomb

is intact and the inscription commemorates his service including at Saladin's great victory over the Crusaders at the Battle of Hattin (1187) and at the subsequent capture of St John of Acre and of Ascalon.

Continue to descend. The building on the next corner (lower right) is the **Hammam al-Moqaddam** (late 14th century?), still in use as a bath house. The original layout is preserved but covered, in a recent renovation, with a violent concatenation of new bathroom tiles in showroom-style profusion.

Return now to the main street and continue your walk across the slope to the east. At 70 m on the left, you will notice the red-domed **Turba al-Qaimariye**. The Emir Saif al-Din Qaimari (d 1256) in 1248 endowed the nearby Maristan al-Qaimariye. His son who died in 1260 at an early age, is also buried in the building. The **Maristan al-Qaimariye**, is 10 m further on, on the right side of the street. The plan shows the development of the earlier design of the Maristan Nur al-Din (*Damascus - Suqs*). Note particularly the honeycombed entrance doorway with supporting colonnettes and the sculptured plaster decoration of the main *iwan* (south) which also contains two large medallions and an elegant inscription. There is a good view of Damascus from the window of the *iwan*. The *maristan* was originally supplied with water from the Yazid stream of the Barada by the water wheel whose remains survive nearby.

Next, almost immediately on the left, is a small building of singular interest, the **Imaret of Sultan Suleiman**. This was the work of the famous Ottoman architect, Sinan, who was also responsible for one other building in Damascus, the superb Tekkiye Mosque (*Damascus - Tekkiye*). The architect of some of the most famous mosques of Istanbul, Sinan's building was commissioned (possibly to replace a building burnt in a fire) by the great Sultan Suleiman (1520-66) for the distribution of food to poor pilgrims visiting the tomb of al-Arabi opposite. It was completed in 1552, two years before the Tekkiye. It comprises two domes over a central chamber surrounded by service rooms. It is still in use as a bakery.

Immediately on the right stands one of the most interesting mosques in Damascus, the **Mosque or Mausoleum of Sheikh Mohi al-Din** or Jami al-Selimi. This includes the burial chamber of the celebrated Sufi mystic, Mohi al-Din Ibn al-Arabi (b 1165 in Andalusia, d 1240). The four-aisled mosque above was built in 1518 by Sultan Selim, the first of the Ottoman rulers of

Syria, and widened and restored in 1947/8. The style is an amalgam of late Mameluke (the minaret) and early Ottoman influences.

SUFISM

The has always had an ambiguous relationship with Sunni Islam since the rise of Sufism in the 12th century in parallel with the efforts of the Zengids and Ayyubids to restore orthodox Islam in the face of prevailing Shi`ite beliefs. Sufis attempt to create, through a life of self denial and piety, an individual link to the Creator through *gnosis* or knowledge as opposed to the more communal basis of Sunni mainstream Islam. It has often been rejected by the orthodox as verging on polytheism though a synthesis of Sunnism and sufism was achieved by the notable *alim* (theologian), al-Ghazzali, in the early 12th century. Ibn Arabi was the great Sufi mystic of his age., Born in Andalusia in 1165, he moved gradually east, settling in Damascus which provided a freer atmosphere for his teaching than Cairo or the Muslim west. He died in 1240 in Damascus. His writings drew together the mystical speculations of a wide range of Sufi and other religious sources.

Al-Arabi is buried behind a silver grille in the domed chamber reached by descending the staircase to the left of the entrance courtyard. Described as the 'greatest speculative genius of Islamic mysticism'[78], his shrine is still a centre for the Sufis (see box above) as well as attracting a constant stream of women. A second tomb of interest is that of the Algerian patriot, Abd al-Kader al-Jazairi, who resisted the French conquest of Algeria from 1830 to 1847. After his eventual surrender, he went into exile in Damascus,. (The body was transferred to Algiers following Algerian independence.) Other tombs include those of two sons of al-Arabi; of a devoted follower and fellow mystic, Sheikh Muhammed Kharbutli; and of a son-in-law of an Egyptian Khedive, Mahmud Pasha Sirri al-Khunaji.

Continue now past the street vegetable market (Suq al-Jumaa), keeping left at the V intersection (25 m). After +75 m, take the small street ascending the slope to the left; +30 m on the right you will come to another major mosque, the **Hanbila Mosque** (or Jami Mozafari). This was built between 1202 and 1213 for the Hanbalites[79] of Damascus under Sheikh Maqdisi's patronage (see next building), and

---

[78] Hitti p 652. Hitti claims that much of the schematisation of hell in Dante's poetry can be traced to al-Arabi's writing.

[79] Followers of the Hanbali school of Islamic jurisprudence *(madhabs)*. The other schools are Shaffi (most widespread), Hanifa and Maliki. See also footnote on the origins of the quarter's name (p 104).

completed by Mozafar al-Din Gokburi, a prince of Irbil[80].

The street facade is exceptionally dull but the interior, including the extensive courtyard, is worth close inspection. The courtyard uses six classical or Crusader columns and capitals and the tall minaret is particularly striking in its four-square simplicity. The prayer room (note basilica plan, timber roof) suffers from a 1970s treatment but note the *minbar* of 1207/8 said by Sauvaget to be of a 'fine style' and the beautifully carved window over the first door into the courtyard.

Return to the main street but cross it to continue descending the hill. 50 m on the left lie the badly decomposed ruins of the **Madrasa Omariye**, the oldest building in the Salihiye area whose origins go back to the exodus of Muslims from Jerusalem after its capture by the Crusaders in 1099. On this site, refugees from the terrible massacre that the Crusaders carried out in Jerusalem built an Islamic school named in honour of the leader of the original refugees, Sheikh Abu Umar Muhammed al-Maqdisi (d 1210/11). The school once comprised two courtyards, the one on the west dates from the 13th century reconstruction (student cells; prayer room; *mihrab* with Crusader capitals); the eastern one (behind) from the first years of the 13th century (lined with student cells and an *iwan*).

Return now to the main transverse street. Continue eastwards 120 m. On the right beside an archway is the **Tomb of Ibn Salama al-Raqqi** (1213 - identity unknown) with a dome typical of the period.

Another 30 m on the right, the **Madrasa Sahibiye** built between 1233 and 1245 by Rabia Khatun, a sister of Saladin and wife of the benefactor of the Hanbali Mosque, Prince Gokburi. It was established under a *waqf* for the benefit of the Hanbalite sect. Sauvaget notes that this alone of the madrasa of Damascus preserves its original plan unchanged. The style of the facade is northern Syrian: fine honeycombed portal; restrained geometric decoration around the door and windows. The courtyard includes two *iwans*. Herzfeld notes that 'the building uses no cupolas, but only barrel vaults, cloisters and cross vaults. It is built in the very best Ayyubid style, with conscious simplicity, displaying perfect mastery over stone'. Now a primary school.

---

[80] He was married to Rabia Khatun, sister of Saladin, and was one of the foremost proponents of the restoration of Sunni orthodoxy to Syria.

To reach the final building on our itinerary, continue 200m along the lane until it widens and joins a descending road amid modern apartment buildings on the edge of the al-Akrad quarter. Turn right and 25 m on the left is the **Madrasa Rukniye**, the funerary college of Emir Rukn al-Din Mankuris, a Governor of Egypt under his brother, the Ayyubid Sultan al-Adil (one of Saladin's sons). Recently reconstructed and given a new minaret, the *madrasa* includes a mosque and the mausoleum of its founder. The facade is most impressive for its geometric decoration and *kufic* lettering (lintels of the doorway and windows). The long inscription on the tomb (dated 1224) praises the many qualities of the founder and lists the endowments whose income funded the *madrasa*.

REFS: Sauvaget and Ecochard; Herzfeld *Damascus - III* pp 1-71; Hitti; Meinecke *Survey* pp 189-241; Sauvaget *Monuments*; Wulzinger and Watzinger *Damaskus - islamische*.

Damascus - Midan Quarter

VARIANTS: Meidan
PERIOD: Arb RATING: - MAP: 26 ITIN: 1j

> LOCATION: South west of old city of Damascus. Begin at Bab Musalla Square, 700 m south west of old city. (Can also be reached as a continuation of the itinerary *Damascus – South West Quarter).

This itinerary takes you through the extension of the old city of Damascus that developed through the Arab middle ages and continued under Turkish rule to cater for the growth in the pilgrimage traffic to Mecca. The name (from *midan* – Arb: field) resulted from the use of the area in the middle ages as an exercise field (Midan al-Khasa). (A second midan was established by Nur al-Din in the area west of the city later occupied by the *Damascus - Tekkiye*.) This open area, probably once an ancient hippodrome, later attracted pilgrim caravans from the north keen to rest and provision themselves before the difficult desert journey to Mecca. The main street leading off the old city became lined with shops, houses, mosques and schools to cater for the overflow of services.

The pilgrimage was a 'gigantic enterprise', particularly important to the economy of Damascus, especially under the Ottomans whose claim to most of the Muslim world meant that a great deal of the Empire's credibility and its claim to the Caliphate depended on escorting the pilgrimage safely to Mecca and back each year[81]. Up to 30,000 pilgrims would converge on

the assembly point in the Midan quarter to join the consolidated caravan for the six week journey across the desert to Mecca. The Governor of Damascus was himself commander of the caravan and accompanied it to the Hijaz where his authority prevailed even over the local guardians of the Holy Places.

Today, Midan Street is a rather straggling thoroughfare which pays little respect to the old buildings that appear between the modern apartment blocks and shops. It is also now chopped in two by the city ring road system. Nevertheless, there are some buildings of interest and it gives a chance to savour an old quarter of Damascus which is not strangled by intense traffic. This is a long itinerary on foot, particularly if combined with *Damascus – South West Quarter and the final mosque is only practicable by taxi.

We begin at the busy traffic circle, Bab Musalla Square which lies c400 m south of the Bab al-Saghir cemetery (*Damascus – South West Quarter).

Upper Midan

The first mosque actually lies north of the square (100 m on the right on the road that leads one-way north to the old city), the **Mosque of Musalla** whose facade provides the main interest. The mosque was built in 1209 during the reign of al-Adil Saif al-Din (Saphadin). Inside, the prayer hall is surprisingly large and elongated with a sloping wooden roof structure.

Cross now to the south side of the traffic circle, selecting the street diagonally opposite the one you have exited. 150 m on the right is the **Mosque Abu Fulus** of which little survives from the original construction of the first part of the 13th century.

On the right, opposite the Abu Fulus Mosque is the **Mausoleum of Arak** (1349), named after a former Governor of Safad (d 1349) - two-coloured façade with turquoise faience inlay around the honeycombed doorway. The two domes cover a double mausoleum with a fine cenotaph in carved wood under the north dome.

50 m on, on the right, is the **Hammam Fathi** built in 1743 by Fathi al-Daftari, a senior official under Suleiman Pasha al-Azem, now disused and with a badly dilapidated facade.

100 m further, on the left, is the substantially more intact **Hammam Rifai**, a 14th or 15th

---

[81] Barbir p 177.

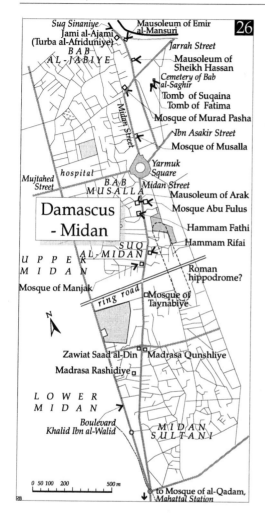

grand Mameluke style. The beautiful minaret is the major point of interest.

Lower Midan

Beyond the huge elevated structure of the Damascus ring-road lies the lower Midan. As you resume your course along Midan Street, opposite the modern police station, take the lane left that leads to the **Mosque of Taynabiye** (or Mosque of Yashbak) the 1399 mausoleum of the Governor of Damascus, Yashbak al-Hasani. Two domed halls - prayer hall (south); mausoleum (north); fine facade with honeycombed gateway, polychrome decoration and coats of arms. The domes rest on honeycombed bases.

300 m south, on your right, is the **Zawiat Saad al-Din** (or Mastabat Saad al-Din) planned as a tomb but converted before completion into a meeting room for the society of Jabbawiye (1570); Turkish style with twin domes; under the south dome, stucco medallion and fine faience panels. Left of the road, just around a corner, is the **Madrasa Qunshliye** a small mausoleum of the 14th century.

100 m further along Midan Street take a small street to the right. 20 m on the left, behind modern shop facades, is the **Madrasa Rashidiye,** the mausoleum of Isiqtamur al-Mardini with twin domed chambers, probably 14th century. The entrance doorway has the arms of the founder set in interlaced decoration, topped by a stalactited frame.

Our final monument lies 2 km south, 500 m beyond the new Damascus railway terminal. The **Mosque al-Qadam** (16th century) comprises an irregularly shaped court (*iwan* on south) at the centre of which stands an octagonal prayer hall covered by a dome. In the centre of the prayer room, the tomb of Ahmet Pasha (1636) is topped by a large stone turban. This mosque was used by the governors of Damascus as they waited for the pilgrims to assemble in what has been described as 'one of the greatest of medieval pageants'[82].

REFS: Atassi 1994; Ecochard and le Coeur; Rihawi *Damascus*; Sauvaget *Monuments*; Wulzinger and Watzinger *Damaskus - islamische*.

century building of 'an extraordinarily picturesque and unusual design' (Sauvaget), still a good example of a functioning Damascene *hammam*. The entrance is narrow and leads into a dressing room probably re-built after the 1925 bombardment by the French.

70 m on the right behind a modern facade, lies the **Mosque of Manjak** a 14th century building commissioned by Emir Ibrahim, son of Emir Saif al-Din Manjak (1368), and built in the

---

[82] Barbir p 152.

Dana (South)/Qasr al-Banat

VARIANTS:
PERIOD: Byz RATING: * MAP: 70 ITIN: 9c

LOCATION: Take main road from *Maarat al-Numan to Aleppo. 2 km north of Maarat, turn left (west) and take the side road which heads into the Jebel Riha. +3 km to Dana (South).

The village was called Dana **(South)** by Butler to distinguish it from the other Dana, on the plain below Jebel Sheikh Barakat, south of Saint Simeon (*Roman Road - Bab al-Hawa).

The style of the remains at Dana (South) are strongly reminiscent of *Bara. There are three buildings of note:

- a **pyramidal-roofed tomb**;
- a third century or fourth century **tomb monument to Olympiane** comprising four columns with a low pyramidal canopy;
- and a 'monastery' or 'convent' (**Qasr al-Banat**), 500 m north of the village.

The **pyramidal-roofed tomb** (recently reconstructed) is a remarkable building especially on account of its state of preservation. The roof is steeply pitched. It is preceded by a small portico supported on four elegant Ionic columns, a graceful touch a little out of character with the towering roof. This building is dated by inscription to 324 (the year of Constantine's adoption of Christianity as the official religion of the Roman Empire). It is thus considerably earlier (and totally pagan in inspiration) compared with the sixth century re-creations of this basically Hellenistic concept at *Bara.

The **tomb monument to Olympiane** nearby comprises four smooth shafts with Ionic capitals supporting a stone canopy and was dated by Butler to the 3rd or 4th centuries on the basis of a comparison with architectural details found in southern Syria.

The remains of **Qasr al-Banat** (500 m north) are also surprisingly intact. The building is compact but three storeyed, the lower two levels on the south faced with a double portico in square, simplified columns. The style is unreservedly plain and severe. The plan resembles somewhat the monastery known as Deir Sobat at Bara but given the small scale of the rooms, the lack of courtyards and the small size of the chamber that might be seen as a chapel, Butler prefers to see it as an inn, perhaps with a small room set aside for prayer, rather than the monastery or convent of tradition.

Scattered remains including a sixth century church.

REFS: Butler *AE* II p 73; Butler *PE* II/B/3 pp 138-142; Tchalenko *Villages* I pp 178-9; Vogüé I 106.

Dayhis

VARIANTS: Daes, Dehes, Dahe
PERIOD: Rom/Byz   ALT: 606 m RATING: -
MAP: 69 ITIN: 9b

LOCATION: From the Bab al-Hawa turnoff, follow the road to Harim for 10.2 km. Turn left to Barisha. After +2 km, (or 1 km before Barisha), take the sealed road to the right. Follow this (which continues on, after 2.5 km, to Khirbet Hassan) for c+1 km looking out for the ruins on the left.

The ruins of Dayhis extend over a considerable area and are accessible from the new sealed road either from the eastern or western edges. Situated on the crest of the Jebel Barisha, and not far from *Bamuqqa (2 km north), Tchalenko compares its economic base to its north neighbour. Intensive agricultural exploitation dates from the first century AD, like Bamuqqa, taking advantage of an arable zone of 2000 ha. Its main period of prosperity, too, was in the fourth to sixth centuries. The village was inhabited long after the Muslim conquest, probably until the tenth century. In the late tenth century, the area of Jebel Barisha became the frontier between the Byzantine Antioch and the Muslim Emirate of Aleppo and there are signs of military occupation.

The extensive remains include a badly ruined **basilica** (north east quarter) with *martyrium* (late fifth or early sixth century - a columned basilica with *bema* and rectangular sanctuary, adjoining baptistery to the south east) and another church (**west church** - sixth century, to the west, also a columned basilica with rectangular sanctuary). Butler also describes tomb reliefs in a rock-cut tomb from the Roman period but all are badly weathered. There is a variety of villas scattered between the religious buildings as well as some monumental tombs and a cistern covered with a low-arched vault.

The **monastery** lies 700 m south east of the main ruins. (Take the second tarred road on the left to reach it). Its remains include a tower, church (another columned basilica with rectangular sanctuary) and an inn for pilgrims (*pandocheion*).

REFS: Bavant *et al* pp 189-94; Butler *AE* II pp 46, 72, 205-8, 274-6; Butler *EC* pp 134-5, 153, 209, 215, 237,

250; Pena *et al Reclus* pp 196-9; Pena *et al Inventaire* pp 93-6; Sodini *et al*; Tchalenko *Villages* II p 191 pl CXXXVI; Tchalenko and Baccache pl 335-360.

Dead Cities (Belus Massif) - general note

VARIANTS: PERIOD: Byz RATING: ** MAPS: 68-70, 78 ITIN: 9a-c

> LOCATION: The so-called 'Dead Cities' are found in the elevated limestone country (sometimes known as the Belus Massif after the classical name for the area) between the Orontes and Afrin Rivers to the west and the Aleppo/Hama highway to the east. Approximately 20-40 km in width, the zone spreads over a much greater length, covering most of the 140 km between Cyrrhus in the north and Apamea in the south. This limestone region lies at 400 to 500 m in elevation, with some crests up to 800 m.
>
> The Belus Massif can be divided into three reasonably distinct groups of hills (see map 78) running from north to south:
>
> - Jebel Semaan with Jebel Halaqa as a subsidiary (Itin 9a;
> - Jebel al-Ala with Jebel Barisha running parallel to the east (Itin 9b). The two are separated by the Plain of Self;
> - Jebel Riha (or Jebel Zawiye) (Itin 9c).

The Belus Massif contains one of the great archaeological puzzles of this century. How is it that this extensive area, once the heartland of Greek and Roman influence in Syria, was apparently so abruptly abandoned that much of the visible remains of its culture survive to this day?

The Belus Massif can present an inhospitable facade to the visitor. The limestone hills are usually denuded of vegetation and often of soil. There are small patches of arable land in the valleys and closer to the plains but few permanent streams. Agriculture today has begun to revive as population pressures has brought new migrations into the upper reaches of the hills but the appearance is still often forbidding and windswept.

Because agricultural life was largely abandoned since the tenth century, the area provides a rich source of insight into Roman and Byzantine rural life, comparatively undisturbed by subsequent settlement and rebuilding. Moreover, the fact that the peak of agricultural exploitation (fifth to sixth century) came at a time when life in most parts of the later Roman or Byzantine Empire was severely disrupted adds to the inherent interest of the area.

The main phases in the occupation have recently been summarised as follows:

- First century to AD 250[83] -- first settlement
- AD 340-550 - intensive exploitation (with a significant increase in the quality of life in the fifth century)
- mid sixth century - saturation point
- seventh century - life undisturbed by Arab conquest
- eighth century - decline coinciding with Abbasid takeover
- tenth century - region deserted, becomes a frontier zone between Byzantines and Arabs.

The prolific range of remains is partly a result of the materials used. The scarcity of wood meant that most permanent buildings were made of stone. Architectural styles, perhaps partly because of the limited choice of materials, evolved conservatively. Especially in domestic architecture, there was little outside influence and while the results are stolid and somewhat inflexible, they pass on to us an incomparable picture of a culture that might have departed only a few decades and not thirteen centuries ago.

Only a selection of the seemingly limitless number of sites are described here - 32 out of over 100 sizeable sites and a theoretical total of 780 settlements. In the past, historians have sought a single coherent explanation why the sites were abandoned during the eighth to tenth centuries. The single-purpose explanations (Muslim invasion, Byzantine persecution of Monophysites, nomad incursion destroying the forests and leading to erosion of the arable land etc), however, are almost all fanciful.

Tchalenko's masterly study completed in the fifties under the auspices of the French Institute for Near Eastern Archaeology (IFAPO) in Beirut gives the best (and simplest) explanation. Though the ground was marginal compared with the rich Plain of Amuq below, over-population of the latter stimulated exploitation of the uplands based on the export of olive oil to the Mediterranean world through Antioch. Once that trade was disrupted by the Arab/Byzantine confrontation, the peasants moved to the outer edges of the zone where they had access to grain-growing terrain, having been forced back to self-sufficiency. There was some resettlement after the Muslim recapture of the area in 1164

---

[83] Some (eg Tate 'Villages du massif') believe settlement began as early as Hellenistic times though the first villages date from the AD 1C. Around AD 250, much of the Roman Orient was devastated by the plague named after St Cyprien. This probably brought an abrupt slowing of the development of the area.

but this was reversed under the Ottomans until it resumed this century.

Though the area was heavily hellenized, the architectural methods used were essentially rustic - reflecting, perhaps, the discrepancy in backgrounds between the wealthy Antiochene (hellenized) upper classes who were the landlords and the impoverished peasants of local (Syriac-speaking) stock. Masonry walls are built without cement to bind the blocks; stone is used for almost all purposes - stairs, porticos, balconies, benches, cupboards, ceilings and roofs. Vaulting is replaced by stone slabs supported on arches. The only exceptions are the roof tiles and wooden framework which supported them. There has been much debate as to how the local architectural and decorative styles evolved and whether they were essentially native to the area. Certainly they are distinct from the practices followed in other areas of Syria at this time. The style of houses (which showed little change over the five centuries or more of settlement) and public buildings reflected both local circumstances (village rather than urban settlement, lack of wood, ready availability of stone) and a mix of Roman/metropolitan and eastern traditions. In the more ambitious public buildings of later centuries (particularly the great basilica complex at Saint Simeon) imported craftsmen and architects were no doubt employed, though probably operating within the Antiochene tradition rather than further afield. This issue is examined in greater detail under Churches in section 2 (page 20).

IFAPO has commissioned further studies since 1975 to follow up Tchalenko's work in northern Syria. Publications resulting from these wide-ranging researches on the region are now appearing but it will be many years before a full picture of the life of this totally inappropriately-named 'dead' zone is available.

REFS: Bavant *et al* pp 187-208; Mattern ; Pena *et al* *Cenobites*; Pena *et al* *Inventaire*; Pena *et al* *Reclus*; Pena *et al* *Stylites*; Sodini *Eglises*; Sodini *et al*; Sournia; Tate *Villages du massif* pp 263-6; Tchalenko *Villages*.

Deir Mar Mousa

VARIANTS:
PERIOD: Byz/Arb ALT: 1500 m; MAP: 75 ITIN: 3b

LOCATION: From Nabk (81 km north of Damascus on the Homs motorway), take the road which heads north east in the direction of the desert for c+14 km. (The area is known as *Jebel Deir Atiye*). When you reach the edge of the escarpment which borders the desert, the chapel is 1.5 km walk down a fairly steep ravine.

It may be necessary to make prior arrangements to collect the key (and a guide) from the Syrian Catholic church in the centre of Nabk.

After a long period of neglect, the sixth century monastery and chapel of Mar Mousa (an Ethiopian saint revered in the Syrian rites) is being restored through the efforts of an Italian Jesuit (Paolo dell'Oglio) and the Syrian Catholic communities of Nabk and Damascus. The church, though small, is divided into three aisles and contains some extraordinary frescoes dating back possibly as far as the seventh century (probably some of the earliest Christian frescoes extant in Syria). Dating, however, is not easy as the style employed is rather untutored and naive, thus offering little opportunity for stylistic analysis. The state of preservation is not good but the effect of the frescoes in their remote and forbidding location, in the gloomy confines of the chapel, is striking.

The monastery is said to have been founded by Mar Mousa (St Moses the Ethiopian) (feast day 28 August). In addition to the early frescoes, there are others of the 11th century in a peculiarly Syrian style. The monastery was abandoned in the 17th century. From the terrace, there is a superb view eastwards into the desert below the escarpment.

The trip can be an arduous one, especially in summer and should not be undertaken without a guide. In Nabk, the *caravanserai* is mid 17th century or later.

REFS: *BG* p 341; Sauvaget 'Les Caravanserails syriens du Hadjdj de Constantinople' in *Ars Islamica* 1937 p 117.

Deir Semaan

VARIANTS: Telanissos (Grk); Tell Neshe (Syriac); Deir Sema`an (Arb)
PERIOD: Byz ALT: 495 m RATING: * MAP: 27, 68 ITIN: 9a

LOCATION: At the foot of the hill on which the Church of *Saint Simeon is located.

History

Originally, Deir Semaan (the Greek name *Telanissos* means 'mountain of women') was founded to exploit the two neighbouring fertile plains on the route from *Apamea to *Cyrrhus. This primitive agricultural community (probably located at the northern end of the later settlement) was transformed in the beginning of

Ottomans replaced the interior columns, the central dome and most of the roof in a rather severe and simplified style but the original plan has been retained.

Visit

HOURS:
09:00 - 17:00 every day (Friday 12:30 - 14:00 closed)

There is no better way to prepare yourself for the experience of visiting the Mosque than to approach it along the 500 m length of the Suq al-Hamidiye. Though the hubub of the *suq* may grate at times and its wares seem tawdry, it is the life blood of Damascus and represents what has drawn people here for thousands of years: commerce, banter and the street life that goes with them. As the long stretch of *suq* comes to an end, you see dramatically rising from the chaos the bizarre remnants of a grand and classical order: fragments of the geometry of the tall *propylaeum* or triumphal arch that proclaimed the western outer entrance to the Temple of Jupiter. The *propylaeum* took the common Syrian form of a huge semi-circular arch framed by a triangular entablature, the whole supported on four soaring columns (almost 12 m high) and two semi-columns, topped with superb Corinthian capitals. After this a few arches of a Byzantine arcade (built as part of a shopping complex of 330-40 that linked the outer and inner enclosures) bring you past the Koran sellers to the newly opened square that reveals the full extent of the west wall of the mosque.

Pause here and get your historical bearings. You are now between the outer and inner enclosures of the ancient temple. The outer complex was built in the first to third centuries of our era, at a time when the stability and prosperity introduced by Roman rule had taken hold. The outer perimeter of the compound (*peribolos*) was a vast rectangle measuring 305 m on the eastern and western edges and 385 m on the northern and southern sides. A monumental gateway stood on each side of the outer enclosure, each preceded by a tall *propylaeum* (the remains of the western one have just been noted). In ancient times, a portico ran around the inner side of the outer wall giving protection to an extensive bazar.

The inner Roman compound or *temenos* originally also had entrances on all four sides (cf *Husn Suleiman), though the principal religious axis was based on the eastern entrance. The

enclosure whose west wall you see in front of you measures nearly 100 m by 150 m and is the cumulative result of all the construction phases since Roman times. The large lower blocks show the Roman mastery of scale and precision. (Note the use of 18 shallow pilasters on the west wall to relieve the massive effect of so much masonry.) The upper reaches of the wall show Arab patching and reconstruction. The beautiful tower above the south western corner (described later) is the work of the late Mameluke period, constructed on the base of one of the smaller Roman/Byzantine towers which were possibly set at each corner of the compound.

The tourist entrance to the Mosque was moved from the eastern to the northern side in 1997. The ticket office (female visitors are required to hire black cloaks for the tour of the Mosque) is on the north west corner of the compound. Continue on to the door in the centre of the north wall. From there, enter and head across the great courtyard (*sahn*) towards the south western corner to begin our tour of the interior at the great western door, the Bab al-Barid.

Immediately inside the Bab al-Barid ('Postal Gate') is the magnificent vestibule of the mosque which retains many remains of the earliest phase of the mosque's construction. The patterned roof in painted wood (restored) dates from the 15th century and is supported on arcading (possibly Byzantine). Note particularly on the upper parts of the walls and above the western doorway remains of the earliest phase of mosaic work (the overall design is discussed later), probably executed by Byzantine craftsmen working for the Umayyads. The magnificent doors of the Bab al-Barid decorated with bronze panels are dated by inscription to 1416.

Return to the great **courtyard** where the full splendour of the mosque's design has lost little of its impact over twelve centuries. This huge space (approximately 50 m by 122 m) is flagged in stark white marble (a late 19th century project in place of the 11th century stone or baked tiles that had replaced the original mosaic paving), thus reflecting the intensity of the sun with brilliant effect. Except on the southern side where the prayer hall is located, the courtyard is arcaded - or rather double arcaded with an upper row of smaller arches resting on the lower. On the lower course, 47 supports comprise a mixture of columns and piers[52]. Note the use of

---

[52] Creswell *Early Muslim* pp 170-3 notes that the original pattern was: pier/column/column; pier/column/column etc but that the columns on the north side were progressively replaced over the centuries with stouter piers.

slightly horseshoe-shaped arches, a design that was found in some late-Byzantine churches (Church of Bissos at *Ruweiha) but, while it was transmitted to Muslim architecture in Umayyad Spain, did not survive in later Syrian Islamic architecture.

Before you leave the western side of the courtyard, note the small domed octagonal building of delicate design raised on a cluster of eight truncated columns with Corinthian capitals, all obviously recycled from antiquity. This was the mosque's **treasury** (Kubbet al-Kazneh or Beit al-Hal), raised above the ground for security reasons. The beautiful mosaic decoration probably dates from the 13th or 14th century restorations of the original early Abbasid building[53]. Little else disturbs the dramatic simplicity of the paved court except for the relatively modern central ablution fountain and on the eastern side another domed pavilion dating from either the 18th or 19th century employing eight Byzantine columns with diverse capitals. (Until 1958, it was used to store the mosque's clock collection, hence its popular title, the Dome of the Clocks.)

The original decorative scheme for the walls of the arcaded areas and the prayer hall facade is now only a faded version of its original splendour. To imagine the richness of the original, you have to picture virtually every surface of the courtyard covered in patterned marble and glistening **mosaics** of unparalleled richness. What you see is partly the result of an unsatisfactory reconstruction of the mosaic work in the 1960's but enough remains of the original mosaics and marble panelling to convey the extraordinary richness of treatment. There can have been few buildings anywhere in the world which employed mosaic decoration on this scale[54]. The unbroken pattern weaved across walls, arcades, arches and under porticos without once resorting to the human figure for dramatic relief or emphasis: an extraordinary tribute to the vitality of the Umayyad synthesis. The mosaics still lead the eye through groves, orchards, fields, cities, rivercourses, pavilions and palaces, creating a universe of fantasy threaded by lush vegetation and stylized trails of acanthus leaves in a treatment that hovers between classical and oriental. For generations

of desert dwellers or travellers, these mosaics fixed in two dimensions the Koranic vision of paradise:

> Such is the Paradise promised to the righteous; streams run through it; its fruits never fail; it never lacks shade.
> [*Koran* Sura 13 (Thunder), 35]

Much of the mosaic work has been lost in fires and reconstruction efforts over the centuries but a good appreciation of its original condition can be gained from the sections under the western arcade (near the entrance), under the western portico (note especially the 1964 restoration of the Barada panel on the western wall) and in the darker, unreconstructed sections of the facade of the transept mid-way along the wall of the prayer hall. Restoration work carried out after 1963 has been criticised for its unsympathetic adaptation of the original styles and techniques and the use of garish and stereotyped designs.

For those interested in a more detailed examination of the mosaics, the provenance of the main panels are:

- vestibule leading to the western portico - cleaned and restored 1929 with later work pre-1963, otherwise untampered;
- outer facade of the western portico - partly restored pre-1963;
- inner facade of the western portico - restored pre-1963;
- soffits of the western portico - uncovered 1929, restored pre-1965;
- inner wall of the western portico, facing the court - the '**Barada panel**' (34. 5m by 7.3 m) - Umayyad work with some patching under Baibars (late 13th century) - uncovered 1929, restored post-1963;
- walls of the 'Treasury' - Abbasid period;
- facade of the northern portico (right) - three fragments, restored c 1954;
- facade of the transept of the prayer hall - except for two (darker) sections, the facade was much restored in the 1960's;
- within the prayer hall - inner face of the transept - largely restored in the Seljuq period (late 11th century);
- upper facade (left) of the east portico - fragments only, some restored under Nur al-Din (mid 12th century).

On all surfaces, the mosaic extended down to a level 6.5 m above the ground. Below this, the Umayyads had decorated the arcades and other facades with patterned **marble panelling**. Most of the geometrically-patterned cladding you now see is post 1893 but fragments of the

---

[53] Dussaud attributes the treasury, on the basis of an Arab historian's account, to the work of the Abbasid Governor of Damascus, Fadil Ibn Salih in 788 - Dussaud *Topographie* p 23.

[54] A singular exception is the great Cathedral of Monreale built in 1172-6 by the Norman king of Sicily, William II, near Palermo which clearly borrowed from the same decorative tradition as the Umayyad mosque through the Arab craftsmen employed on the project.

original treatment can be detected in the eastern vestibule, around the southern lateral door (*Bab Jairun* - discussed later). This would have been interrupted by small pilasters and marble grill panels based on elaborate geometrical patterns (among the first use of such geometrical designs later to become a hallmark of Arab decoration).

As you walk around taking in the details of this great monument, note particularly the three **minarets** that crown the walls of the inner compound. The standard theory that the minarets were erected on the truncated bases of earlier Roman/Byzantine corner towers is currently under debate. The lack of towers on the northern corners has been seen as resulting from the extensive restructuring in the Arab middle ages of the whole northern wall including the addition of a single central minaret. In any event, the southern towers were probably the earliest versions of the minaret in Syria and proclaimed the presence of the Islamic community in a city which was still largely Christian. The existing minarets are:

- Immediately to the right of the western entrance (south west corner), the **Western Tower** (*Madhanat al-Gharbiye*) built by the Mameluke Sultan in 1488 in the Egyptian style.
- On the south eastern corner, the tallest of the minarets, the **Tower of Jesus** (*Madhanat Issa*). According to Islamic popular tradition, Jesus will descend from heaven via this tower in order to combat the Antichrist before the Last Judgment. The minaret was built in 1247 on the site of an Umayyad structure but the upper part is Ottoman.
- On the middle of the northern wall, the **Tower of the Bride** (*Madhanat al-Arus*). The lower part dates from the ninth century but the upper structure is from the late 12th century when the northern wall was extensively reconstructed.

At the western and eastern ends of the courtyard is a series of narrow rooms, dating from the Roman construction. On the western side lies the former tourist entrance and ablutions hall. On the east, the larger room to the north of the eastern entrance leads into an inner chamber which has become a major Shi`ite place of pilgrimage (**Mashhad al-Hussein**) associated closely with the powerful tradition of the martyrdom of Hussein at Kerbala (modern Iraq) at the hands of the Umayyads. Legend has it that the head of Hussein was brought here

from Kerbala and placed by the Caliph in a niche, with the aim of ridiculing Hussein and the supporters of Ali[56]. In some accounts, the Umayyads later sent the head to Medina for burial but there are also legends (unsupported by any physical evidence of a grave or shrine) that the head was buried in the mosque precinct.

Before entering the prayer hall of the mosque, pause again in front of its northern **facade** to take in the overall shape of the great chamber. Note how the long (137 m) arcaded facade is broken by a central transept, the facade of which carries some of the most spectacular of the mosaic work already described. The transept facade, clearly based on Byzantine precedents, consists of three lower arches topped by three smaller ones framed within a sweeping arch. This lower area is bordered by two stout pilasters to provide stability. Above, a triangular entablature surmounts an extensive panel of mosaic work.

You should now enter the **prayer hall** by one of the doors at either end. (The addition of doors was not, incidentally, part of the Umayyad building which had no fixed panels between the arches separating courtyard and prayer hall.) Though elements of the chamber may have Roman or Byzantine precedents, the overall plan is a departure from the earlier triple-aisled basilica plan. Its length and relatively narrow proportions are broken by the central transept, the purpose of which is to orient the worshipper towards the middle of the south wall rather than the east or west ends which are blank. At this focal point, the *mihrab* oriented towards Mecca was placed, the first recorded use of this device. The transept (rare in buildings to that date and usually confined to a narthex at the western end of Byzantine religious buildings) was further emphasised by the use of a dome to crown its centre. The design was thus an Umayyad adaptation of various elements found in the wider Mediterranean and eastern traditions[57].

The modern (post 1893) building broadly follows this plan but the dome has been reconstructed in a Turkish style adapted from

---

[56] Hussein's sister Zeinab and his son, Ali were also brought back to Damascus to participate in this humiliation. Zeinab's burial mosque on the SE outskirts of Damascus (a largely modern re-housing) is another major centre of Shi'ite pilgrimage). Hussein's daughter, Roqayya, is also commemmorated in a new mosque in the Amara quarter.

[57] Grabar *Grande Mosquée* p 38 notes the influence of the first mosque, at Medina, with a Byzantine basilica plan for the prayer room substituted for the hypostyle hall. He believes the transept or axial nave was intended to emphasise the area reserved for the Caliph.

European models. (Its predecessor was itself an 11th century replacement in stone of the Umayyad original in wood.) The columns are neo-classical in their origins and the arcading of the aisles is a simplified version of the Umayyad original. A few remnants of the inner structure of the pre-1893 building remain, notably the beautiful wood panelling of the transept ceiling on the courtyard side and the fragments of mosaic work (probably 11th century) on the northern wall. Note too the six eighth century windows at both ends of the transept enclosed by marble grills. They are the earliest Islamic examples of geometric interlace-patterned marble.

The site of the legendary burial of the head of St John the Baptist[58] is commemorated by the extravagant marble monument to the east of the transept. The monument is late Ottoman, having been constructed in place of a wooden mausoleum destroyed in the fire of 1893.

Those interested in further exploring the history of the mosque may wish to make a tour of the **outer walls**. Exit by the northern entrance and turn left, following an anti-clockwise direction to the long southern wall of the prayer hall[59]. Note that all the mosque windows are placed high (8 m at least above the ground). This reflected the fact that the Roman inner *temenos* wall was kept intact and the mosque's windows placed above it. On the left of the transept facade (partly covered at the moment by an electricity sub-station building) is the original southern entrance to the Jupiter temple inner compound, a triple doorway whose upper moulded lintel can still be seen. When the mosque was constructed, the Roman doorway was blocked as part of the new arrangement orienting the prayer hall towards Mecca (south). Before that time, Creswell believes, Christians and Muslims used this same doorway to gain access to their separate mosque and church within the temple compound. The inscription in Greek over the central doorway reads:

Thy Kingdom, O Christ, is an everlasting Kingdom, and Thy dominion endureth

throughout all generations[60].

A left turn at the next corner brings you to the eastern **facade** of the inner compound and the great gateway now known as **Bab Jairun** or Bab al-Nawfarah (Fountain Gate). In Roman times the monumental main entrance, a triple doorway, was preceded by an imposing *propylaeum* 33 m wide jutting out 15 m from the eastern wall. With its fifteen steps, this massive gateway must have been a near-overpowering climax to the colonnaded axis that led up to the temple from the *agora* to the east. To trace the axis, go down the stairs (note the fountain dating from 1026, the gift of a Sharif of the Hussein family), past the coffee shop (right) and follow the street (Badreddin al-Hassan St) that heads directly east for 120 m. You will come to the triple gateway of massive proportions that led into the outer compound. Two monoliths form the sides of the central passage but the rise in the level of the ground in the past 1700 years has left the side doorways almost buried beneath the surface.

South of the point you have reached is the probable site of the Umayyad palace, al-Khadra, erected shortly after the Arab conquest in the mid seventh century. From the gateway, the broad colonnaded street once led a further 250 m east to the *agora* of Hellenistic/Roman times[61]. No trace remains of this open gathering space in the maze of houses. This avenue between temple and *agora* provided a second west/east axis to complement the commercially-oriented thoroughfare perpetuated to the south in Straight Street.

There is an interesting mosque worth the short diversion from Bab Jairun along Qaimariye St which, after a short dog-leg to the right, continues the axis eastwards (see map 9). 150 m past the propylaeum, on the right, lies the entrance to the **Mosque al-Qaimariye** built in 1743 by Fathi Effendi, an Ottoman treasury official. 'A plan of obviously Ottoman origin (a portico of three domes giving access to a prayer hall covered by a large dome) but with a decor so profoundly influenced by Syro-Mameluke traditions (stone of alternating white, black and ochre colours) that the imported character of the architecture is somewhat overshadowed by the local exuberance of the patterns of colour'

---

[58] There is no evidence at all that the head of St John was bought to Damascus though many legends have sprung up on the subject. An Arab historian, Ibn al-Asakir, recounts (pp 15-8) many versions of the discovery of the head by the Caliph al-Walid who ordered that the spot be commemorated by the placing of a distinctive column above it. The head was left in place and the spot commemorated by the Muslims on account of St John the Baptist's role as a precursor of Christ, one of the Prophets recognised by Islam.

[59] The door immediately after the corner is the *Bab Ziadeh*.

[60] The translation of the inscription adapted from Psalm CXLV,13 (Septuagint) comes from Creswell *Early Muslim* p 164.

[61] The quarter is now called Zukak al-Saha. Elisséeff disputes Sauvaget's earlier thesis that the *agora* was established in Hellenistic times, preferring to attribute it to the monumental building projects of the Romans. See his article in Hourani *Islamic City* p 170.

(Raymond). The effect of the quiet courtyard, the vegetation and the mellowed stone is striking. One street to the north is the Madrasa al-Qaimariye (possibly Mameluke).

To return to the north wall of the Umayyad Mosque, you need to enter the alleyways second right west of the Roman gateway and skirt the north eastern corner. Turn left immediately before the Epigraphy Museum (Madrasa Jaqmaqiye - *Damascus - Suqs) (map 20). Here (as in the western entrance), part of the Byzantine arcade joining the outer and inner walls remains but (as noted earlier) most of the Roman wall on the north side has been replaced over the centuries. You are now back at the northern doorway of the mosque (Bab al-Amara or **Bab al-Kallaseh**, to the left of the Tower of the Bride.

REFS: *BG* pp 286-7; Bahnassi *Damascus* pp 93-5; Bahnassi *Great Umayyad*; Creswell *Early Muslim*; de Lorey; Dussaud *Temple*; Etinghausen and Grabar pp 37-45; Freyburger *Jupiter-Heiligtums*; Gibb; Grabar *Grande Mosquée*; Raymond p 101; Sack *Damaskus - Beitrag*; Sack *Damaskus - Entwicklung*; Sauvaget *Monuments* pp 12-38; Wulzinger and Watzinger *Damaskus - islamische*.

Damascus - Citadel and Northern Walls

VARIANTS:
PERIOD: Rom/Arb   RATING: * MAP: 18, 19
ITIN: 1b

> LOCATION: The itinerary begins with the citadel, just to the left of the western entrance to the Suq al-Hamidiye. It then follows a clockwise direction along the branch of the Barada that flows besides the northern walls, ending at Bab Tuma.

> [NOTE: This is a somewhat long walk (3+ km) and, especially in hot weather, is better done in the morning.]

To orient yourself, you may wish to begin by visiting the Museum of Damascus which is located in the Beit Khalid al-Azem, 200 m north of the citadel. (Take al-Thawra St, turn right just as the overpass ends. Museum is immediately behind the high-rise building guarded by soldiers.) The palace (donated to the state by a former Prime Minister follows the Turkish pattern of two distinct zones, *haremlek* (for the family - north) and *selamlek* (for reception of visitors - south). The *haremlek* court is used for the museum and includes several salons ranged around the open space. That on the north of the western side contains an interesting fountain in the form of a double meander course, used for competitions between floating objects - a sort of

early pin-ball machine. The room to the east contains several models of the old city which will usefully give visitors a perspective on its layout.

Return now to the citadel. If you wish, cross al-Thawra Street just as you reach the citadel, to inspect the Mosque of Sanjaqdar - early Ottoman (1540) but altered in the last century). On the left of al-Thawra Street is the Suq al-Khail (horse suq - re-planned since the French of 1945) and the vegetable and saddlery markets (Suq al-Srujiye).

Citadel – History

The Damascus citadel may disappoint those who would expect to see a formidable Arab military fortification on a par, for example, with Aleppo. Given its setting on flat ground, hemmed in by cluttered urban surrounds, the fortifications never presented the same forbidding front. In fact, the size of the citadel is vast, though the full dimensions are only revealed inside the walls. Most of the construction is from the Ayyubid and Mameluke periods but heavy use since then (in the Turkish, French and independence periods) has not been kind to the fabric. The citadel was only abandoned as a prison in 1985.

There is no firm evidence of the use of this site as a military base as early as Roman times and suppositions about the existence of Roman remains within the citadel structure have recently been disproved. While it is not inconceivable that the site was used for military purposes since antiquity, the theories must await the results of the current excavations in the citadel courtyard.

The remains recognisable today largely date from the 13th century and later. When the new fortifications were undertaken by Sultan al-Adil in 1207, Damascus had become the key centre of Arab resistance to the Crusader presence, a role built up particularly under the leadership of Saladin (r 1176-93). The city had experienced Crusader attacks three times in the 12th century. Al-Adil (a brother of Saladin who replaced the latter's son, al-Afdal, in Damascus in 1196 and ruled until 1218) spent twelve years on the project. It included, besides the expansion of the Roman *castrum* and Seljuq fortifications to a rectangle 220 m by 150 m, a new palace complex in the south western sector. The whole, however, was badly damaged in the first of the great Mongol invasions in 1260. The original 16 towers and walls with three levels of firing slits were dismantled. Baibars, the Mameluke Sultan (r 1260-77) rebuilt most of them. Just as well, otherwise later Mongols - particularly Timur during the fierce siege of 1400 - would have had nothing to knock down; which they did with ruthless efficiency. The Turks over 500 years made less than a 100 percent effort to repair the damage though they continued to use the citadel as a military base.

Citadel - Visit

At the time of writing, the citadel is under extensive reconstruction which will also allow, for the first time, excavations to uncover evidence of its history. For some years, therefore, visitors will have to confine themselves to an external circuit

southern wall are three (two well-preserved) towers with fine machicolations which can be observed from the Suq al-Hamidiye.

Continue your tour along the northern side where the river divides the walls from the *Suq al-Srujiye* mentioned earlier. The partly ruined double towers in the centre of the north wall protected the Gate of Iron (*Bab al-Hadid*) whose twisting passages required any attacker to negotiate five closely-defended bends. [Immediately inside the gateway on the left is a

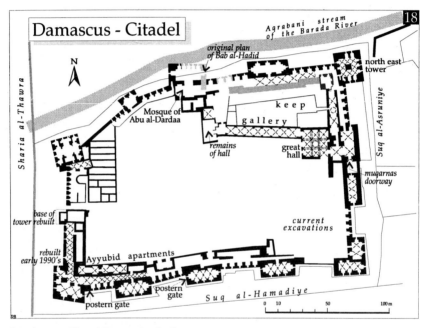

Damascus - Citadel

to gain some idea of the massive fortifications and towers. [Areas which are not visible from the outside will be recorded below in square brackets.] The citadel is roughly a rectangle in shape but with the north western corner cut off. It is protected by twelve surviving towers, that on the south western corner having recently been heavily reconstructed. The work shows the features typical of the Ayyubid masons - large rusticated blocks, massive regular towers, vaulted interiors and use of machicolation and arrow slits.

Begin with the western side, north of the entrance to the Suq al-Hamidiye. [To the right, along the southern face, are the two-storeyed remains of the Ayyubid palace.] Along the

long vaulted hall which served until recently as part of the prison. It leads at its east end to a square chamber, probably the great hall, with surmounting dome over four thick central pillars (recycled from antiquity). The courtyard enclosed by these rooms attracted the heaviest cluster of fortifications around the north eastern corner, forming a keep.] The key element in the north eastern defences was the corner tower dated by inscription to 1209, the most massive (21 m by 23 m) in the complex.

Continue around to the east where a central gate was protected by two salients. Its lack of heavy protection (being on a less exposed side) allowed for a more aesthetic treatment. [The entry vestibule (1213) is a beautiful example of honeycombed vaulting (*muqarnas*). This northern Syrian device, until then rarely used in Damascus, was employed here with striking effect.]

Walls - History

Though there are some traces of Roman work on the lower courses, the city walls as you see them today are largely the work of the Arab period after the 11th century. They reflect the greater need for security in the face of Crusader incursions and Mongol attacks (1260-1400). The gates, however, largely coincide with Roman gateways. There were nine gateways in the Arab period of which seven (and traces of an eighth) remain (see box under *Damascus – Introduction on page 77).

The city's defensive plan was probably largely the achievement of Nur al-Din in the mid 12th century. Much of the work of that period, however, had to be extensively reconstructed under the Ayyubids during the next century, particularly under Sultan al-Salih Ismael (Sultan

recent legislation controlling the modernisation of the streetscape.

Walls – Visit

It will be some distance before the line of walls becomes evident as you head east, taking the street which leads from the north eastern corner of the citadel. Almost immediately, you turn left, through the double gateway, the **Bab al-Faraj** (Gate of Deliverance). The inner doorway dates from the earliest phase of Ayyubid reconstruction (1239-41). The 1154/5 outer door, around a double bend, was reconstructed in the 15th century. There was no Roman gate on this site where the first opening in the wall dates from the time of Nur al-Din.

Continue east, by going straight ahead, not through the outer gate, skirting the Shi`ite quarter of the old city (*Amara*) which lies behind the 1154-74 walls of this sector. 250 m along a picturesque, often-vaulted alleyway (Bein al-Surain St), you reach a modern Shi`ite mosque in the Iranian style. Turn left to the second of the

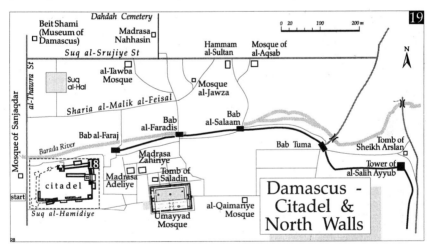

twice, 1237-45). Generally, the phases of construction can be recognised by the quality of the masonry. The Roman blocks are large and precise. The work of the mid 12th to mid 13th centuries follow regular courses 50-60 cm high. Mameluke courses are smaller (20-30 cm) while later Turkish work is largely irregular in pattern. Much of the fabric of the walls has been lost to domestic building in recent centuries, though the practice has now ended given the exodus of population from the narrow confines of the old city (largely impossible for car access) and

gateways, the **Bab al-Faradis** (Gate of the Orchards) named after the extra-mural district to the north. The Roman gate stood a little to the south of this site but the present structure dates from the Ayyubid efforts to rebuild the city's fortifications (1132-42). Originally a double gateway, only the outer door is intact. The inner door was reconstructed in the 15th century but only an archway survives.

Those interested in exploring some of the mosques to the north of the walls should at this point follow the itinerary described at the end of this entry.

Another 250 m walk to the east along the lane left of the Shi'ite mosque (passing after 50 m the house on the left that once was the winter residence[62] of the Algerian patriot, Abd al-Kader al-Jazairi - see *Damascus - Salihiye quarter) brings you to the most impressive of the Arab gateways, the **Bab al-Salaam** (Gate of Peace). Stones from the Roman gate were re-built in the present form by the Ayyubids in 1243 following a 1171/2 reconstruction. The long inscription on the lintel records the extravagant attributes of the Ayyubid ruler, Sultan al-Salih Ismael (Sultan twice, 1237-45).

From the Bab al-Salaam, the road continues to the east for another 300 m at last rejoining both the line of walls and the rivercourse (which has only been glimpsed to the north since leaving the citadel). The wall is well exposed on the right and the different types of masonry can be distinguished.

At the end of this stretch, the road brings you to the square that opens around the fourth of the gateways, **Bab Tuma** (Saint Thomas' Gate). Bab Tuma has become synonymous with the Christian quarter of Damascus which has spilled over from the north east and east of the city into the new areas around Sharia Baghdad. The gate itself is now stranded in a busy square and traffic circle. It consists of a 1227 Ayyubid reconstruction of the Roman gate with the machicolation added during the restoration of 1333/4 by Tengiz, the Mameluke Governor of Damascus. The Roman gate marked the northern end of the eastern *cardo maximus*.

The eastern and southern limits of the old city are described elsewhere (*Damascus - Straight Street; *Damascus - South West Quarter) but you may wish to round off this tour with the **Tower of al-Salih Ayyub** whose remains (base and first storey only) stand at the north eastern corner of the walls (100 m to the east). The tower dates from the final (1243-4) Ayyubid re-fortification of the city. The relatively open area to the east (agricultural land still almost touches the old city here) marks the point where the Arab armies camped before the taking of Damascus in 635-6. Across the road immediately east (behind a modern mosque) is the Tomb of Sheikh Arslan (original parts are 13th-14th century), a local saint and poet (d 1146)

whose reputation for piety and asceticism earned him the title of 'protector of Damascus'.

The tour finishes here and those who are returning on foot to the starting point at the Suq al-Hamidiye may want to make their own itinerary through the winding streets of the old city.

Mosques North of the Walls

As noted above, a short excursion from Bab al-Faradis takes in several mosques in the busy commercial quarter north of the walls along al-Malik al-Feisal Street. Head directly north along the *suq* until it meets the tree-lined street (which comes from Suq al-Srujiye and marks the southern limit of the course of the Hellenistic hippodrome). Turn left and follow the main road for 150 m until you reach a mosque on the left, the **al-Tawba Mosque**. This mosque was built in 1234 on the site of a *caravanserai* which had become a house of ill repute, hence the Arabic name, Mosque of Repentance. The facade is the most noteworthy part of the building - particularly beautiful honeycombed doorway on the right.

Double back now along to where the *suq* brought you from the Bab al-Faradis. Take the narrow, partly-vaulted street to the north. At 100 m, after a dog-leg left turn, you will find the facade of the **Madrasa Nahhasin** (1457/8) (School of the Copperworkers) with a fine stalactited entrance portal. Behind the madrasa lies the Dahdah Cemetery whose origins probably go back beyond the Islamic conquest when this was the only burial ground for the city.

Return to al-Malik al-Feisal Street and walk eastwards for 100 m. You come to a Y intersection which encloses a small minareted mosque, the **Mosque al-Jawza** of 1676 (note Roman monolith column in the courtyard). Return to the main road and continue east (right) for 200 m. Look carefully for the narrow facade of an old bath house, the **Hammam al-Sultan.** The coat of arms of the Mameluke Sultan Qait Bey (r 1468-96) decorate the honeycombed doorway, but inside the changing room of the baths is now in ruins and what remains serves as a furniture factory. The rest of the baths (probably early 14th century) are reached by the entrance in the side street to the left that leads to Bab al-Salaam.

60 m on, on the right, is the **Mosque al-Aqsab** (also called the Mosque al-Zainabiye) founded in 1301[63] and reconstructed in 1408 after the last Mongol invasion by one Nasr al-Din Muhammed, son of Manjak. The square minaret

---

[62] The house in described in an article by Simone Zakri in *Qantara* (issue 9, Paris Oct-Dec 1993).

[63] Herzfeld p 125 cites evidence, however, that the origins go back even further, perhaps to pre-Islamic times.

is the most notable feature. Beautifully constructed in contrasting stone, it is divided into several layers by cornices. The windows of the top layer comprise twin enclosures within a single frame, a design not unlike Gothic windows though the decorative treatment is purely Arab. . Two Roman columns are re-used in the courtyard (left arcade). The *mihrab* is decorated with marble mosaics encrusted with turquoise faience, a masterpiece of Mameluke decorative treatment. This was once the site of a Byzantine church.

Until 1975, the Mosque al-Qadam stood a little further to the east along al-Fesial Street but was entirely destroyed in an ill-advised effort of urban reconstruction.[64]

REF: Ecochard and le Coeur; Herzfeld *Damascus Studies* IV; Cathcart King 'Defences of the Citadel of Damascus' in *Archaeologia* XCIV 1951; Omran & Dabboura *The Citadel of Damascus* Damascus 1997; Rihawi *Damascus*; Sack *Damaskus - Beitrag*; Sauvaget *Monuments*; Sauvaget 'Citadelle' in *Syria* 1930; Wulzinger and Watzinger *Damaskus - islamische*.

Damascus - Suq al-Hamidiye area, Old City

PERIOD Arb/Ott RATING: * MAP: 20 ITIN: 1c

LOCATION: The old city immediately north and south of the Suq al-Hamidiye. Begin at the open area in front of the western entrance to the Suq.

This itinerary covers the busiest section of the old *suqs* of Damascus. The route involves around 1.5 km of walking with some poking into obscure corners and alleyways. You may wish to combine this itinerary with *Damascus - Umayyad Mosque.

The **Suq al-Hamidiye** is built along the axis of the Roman city that originally matched on the western side the eastern monumental approach to the great Temple of Jupiter-Hadad. This 500 m thoroughfare became confined over the centuries and it was not until 1873 and the subsequent reign of the Ottoman Sultan Abdel Hamid II (r 1876-1909) that the then Suq al-Jadid was expanded by efforts of the Governor, Rashid Nasha Pasha, lined with two-storeyed shops with offices and storerooms above and given its existing corrugated iron arched roof (later peppered with the ` evidence of French bombardments or aerial machine-gunning of the suq area). The resulting thoroughfare was then re-named in honour of the reigning Sultan.

The west end of the *suq* also marks the site of the former Bab al-Nasr (Gate of Victory), an Arab gateway which was pulled down in 1863 (see box page 77).

Head down the *suq*, counting the cross streets on the right as you go. At the fifth (about 250 m, just where the roof gives way to clear sky), turn right. After about 75 m on the left, you will notice a white-painted honeycombed arch over a gateway. This is the entrance to one of the most remarkable Islamic institutions in Damascus, the **Maristan Nur al-Din**[65] (Hospital of Nur al-Din).

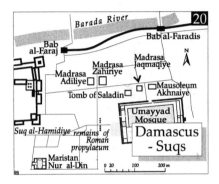

The building has been used since 1978 as a museum of Arabic medical and scientific history. The institution was originally founded as a hospital and medical teaching centre by Nur al-Din in 1154, immediately after adding Damascus to his domains. The *maristan* functioned as a healing centre until the construction of the National Hospital in the 19th century. . The building as you see it now owes much to the restorations of 1283 and of the 18th century.

The dating of the honeycombed gateway is not certain. The lintel of the outer doorway is recycled from antiquity. Note the disused fountain to the right. The outer door panels are encrusted with geometric decoration executed in copper nails with carved wooden panels on the inside. The honeycomb or *muqarnas* dome above the entrance is a Mesopotamian feature introduced to Syria by the Seljuq Turks. The dome is supported on two semi-domes, an arrangement which is also Mesopotamian in inspiration.

The courtyard of the *maristan* (15 m by 20 m) provides a beautiful retreat with *iwans* on each side. The principal *iwan* (opposite the

---

[65]   There were two others in Damascus - Maristan Dakaki; Maristan al-Qaimari (Salihiye quarter, constructed c1256).

entrance) served for consultations and lessons in medicine. Though smaller, the south *iwan* which houses the *mihrab* is more richly decorated. The *mihrab* includes a semi-circular table in white marble decorated with cornucopias overflowing with vines and grapes. More marble is used to provide a frieze and below it, patterned marble on the walls include four large slabs, two of which seem to have originally come from Byzantine altars.

Return now to the main *suq* and continue towards the Umayyad Mosque for another 200 m. As you reach the remains of the Roman arch, take the cross street on the left and follow it for about 100 m. This will bring you to a point where two grand entrances face each other across the narrow street.

That on the right is the **Madrasa Zahiriye** or Mausoleum of Baibars which contains the tomb of the Mameluke Sultan who did more than any Muslim leader to secure the Crusaders' final departure from the east. On the death of Baibars in Damascus in 1277, his son acquired the building (then a private house, the *Beit Akiki*, in which Saladin's father, Ayub, had lived) and converted it into a funerary college or *madrasa* by adding the gateway and domed burial chamber (recently restored). The entrance is a singular masterpiece, executed in contrasting black and yellow stone, with marble inserts which carry three bands of finely executed inscriptions. (The top two relate to the endowments that funded the *madrasa*, the lowest one to the date of construction.) The *muqarnas* work which supports the shell half-dome over the entrance is particularly impressive, falling in a cascade of shells and arches to make the transition between semi-circle and rectangle. Note too the superb geometric medallions on the entrance facade and the south wall.

The madrasa is today a library but it is usually possible to inspect the inner courtyard and the burial mausoleum of Baibars and his son, Muhammed Said - a domed chamber with four shallow *iwans*. The chamber contains much detail of interest: the polychrome patterned marble on the walls is striking in its boldness; several friezes of gilded plaster or wood; an extraordinary *mihrab* in marble framed by colonnettes; perhaps most striking is the wide band of mosaic work. The latter is executed in a style which imitates that of the Umayyad Mosque 500 year beforehand, though in a somewhat coarser treatment.

The baths to the left of the *madrasa*, Hammam al-Malik al-Zaher, have recently been restored and again function for their original purpose. They may in part date from the original Beit Akiki (tenth-12th century). The dressing room is new in its treatment but the warm and hot rooms behind survive from earlier centuries.

The entrance already noted on the western side of the street leads to the **Madrasa Adiliye** which housed the Arab Academy now part of the Arabic manuscript collection of the National Library. The name refers to the burial in this building of Sultan al-Adil Saif al-Din (d 1218), the brother of Saladin and the man who contributed most to the re-fortification of Damascus. The construction of the *madrasa* began earlier (1172-3), however, and was left unfinished until al-Kamil completed it in 1222-3 to serve as the burial place of his father. In style it is purely northern Syrian, with many features in common with the Madrasa Nuriye (*Damascus - Khans). The entrance is a fine example of honeycomb technique with a hanging keystone and bold decorative treatment but not a rival to the doorway to the Mausoleum of Baibars opposite. After a narrow vestibule, you reach the courtyard, once surrounded by the rooms of students and teachers with an open *iwan* to the right (now the reading room of the library). In the near left corner is the burial chamber of al-Adil whose large dome rests on unusual sloping honeycomb supports.

The next group of buildings lies on the north side of the Umayyad Mosque. Retrace your steps as far as the southern wall of Baibars' Mausoleum, then follow the broad street to the left for about 100 m. Here amid a small oasis of trees and foliage you will find on the right, almost against the northern wall of the Umayyad Mosque, the enclosure which houses the Tomb of Saladin.

Most of the original Madrasa Aziziye which housed **Saladin's tomb** has disappeared, leaving an isolated arch and the burial chamber (completed 1196 after the death of Salah al-Din Yusuf Ibn Ayub (Saladin) in 1193). Certainly it is one of the most understated tombs of any great historical figure, perhaps befitting the unassuming pretensions of this outstanding Muslim leader who died without personal wealth though his writ ran from northern Iraq to Libya. The modesty of the site perhaps contributed to its neglect over the centuries. En route to the Holy Land in 1898, the German Kaiser Wilhelm II passed through Damascus and funded the restoration of the chamber as a tribute to the Ottoman Sultan, Abdel Hamid II. (A new cenotaph had already been provided by Sultan Abdel Hamid in 1878). The silver lamp over the new tomb bears the monograms of the Kaiser and of the Sultan. The French General,

Gouraud, following the Allied victory at the Battle of Maysaloun in 1918, is said to have made his way to Saladin's tomb and proclaimed: 'Saladin, we're back again!'. Sultan's cenotaph is in white marble but the remains of the original in humbler wood (with intricate floral design) can be seen to the side. The inscription reads: *Oh Allah, be satisfied with this soul and open to him the gates of paradise, the last conquest for which he hoped.*[66] The faience panels are 17th century.

If you return to the street which brought you from Baibars' Mausoleum and continue along it a little way to the right, you will reach the building which serves as the Museum of Epigraphy. The Museum is housed in the **Madrasa Jaqmaqiye** built in 1418-20 by the Mameluke Governor of Damascus, Jaqmaq al-Argunsawi (who later went on to become Sultan in Cairo, 1438-52). The facade is a beautiful example of polychrome work of the period. Inside, the marble and pearl shell mosaics are striking but the wood and marble sculpture are mediocre. The museum has a collection of Arabic inscriptions including some early examples in *kufic* lettering.

Adjacent to the east (a side street separates them) is the **Mausoleum of Akhnaiye** dedicated in 1413.

REFS: *BG* pp 286-92; Kayem; Sack *Damaskus - Beitrag*; Sauvaget *Monuments*; Sauvaget and Ecochard; Scharabi; Wulzinger and Watzinger *Damaskus - islamische*.

Damascus - Khans, Azem Palace

VARIANTS: -
PERIOD: Arb/Ott RATING: * MAP: 13 ITIN: 1d

> The area south of the east end of the Suq al-Hamidiye and the Umayyad Mosque, extending to Straight Street.

The itinerary begins at the square in front of the western entrance to the Umayyad Mosque, at the eastern end of the Suq al-Hamidiye. In addition to the most outstanding of the Ottoman residences of Damascus (Azem Palace) it covers the main concentration of traditional *khans* - the warehouses for the receiving, storing and sending of trade goods and the provision of accommodation to traders. The Damascus *khan* follows the broader Mameluke and Ottoman traditions. Earlier types (eg Khan Jaqmaq) were arranged around an open rectangular court; later examples (eg Khan Suleiman Pasha) usually

centred on a central area covered by soaring domes, often now in ruins or only partially restored, and were thus covered halls in the Persian tradition rather than courtyards. (See also section on Khans on page 25.)

The 18 surviving principal *khans* were mostly constructed in the Ottoman period and are concentrated in the area to be described. This development represented a westward movement of the main bazar area of the city which had previously been concentrated on Straight Street south east of the Umayyad Mosque but many examples have been obliterated by subsequent development, including the 19th century construction of the Suq al-Hamidiye (*Damascus - Suq Area). (Other old commercial structures were lost when the entire Hariqa quarter, immediately south of the Suq al-Hamidiye, was destroyed by a French bombardment during the revolt of 1925. The area was later reconstructed along geometric lines.) Not all the khans mentioned here are worth detailed examination, many barely surviving in dilapidated conditions.

Buildings of major interest are marked with a ➔.

Start to head west along the Suq al-Hamidiye but turn left immediately after the Roman gateway whose remains poke above the intersection. Take the street (Suq al-Haiyetin - Tailors' Suq) which heads south (eventually towards Straight Street). 50 m on your left is the first of the *khans*, **Khan al-Haramain** or Khan al-Juwar. The original building dates from 1630 but was substantially reconstructed in 1900 when the area was reorganised. Immediately opposite, a 10 m corridor leads off the Suq al-Haiyatin to the small **Khan al-Saih Qatana** (18th or 19th century) whose dome and pendentives have been restored. 20 m further down the same street on the right is the striped stone gateway to the ➔**Khan al-Gumruk** (Customs Khan) an L-shaped gallery constructed in 1608/9 under Murad Pasha), covered with six large domes resting on pendentives.

Opposite the Khan al-Gumruk is a smaller *suq* which was once the changing room of a 16th century public bath, the ➔**Hammam al-Qishani** (Tiled Bath) - domed with modern painted decoration in the pendentives; tiled panel above inside doorway. 25 m further on from the Khan al-Gumruk down a stone passage (right) is the 19th century **Khan al-Zafaranjiye** - arcaded courtyard. About 30 m further south, on the left, lies the ➔**Khan al-Harir** (Silk Suq) built by the Ottoman Governor of Damascus in 1573/4,

---

[66] Adapted from translation in Herzfeld *Damascus - III* p 47. For Baha al-din's account of Saladin's death, see Gabrieli pp 246-52

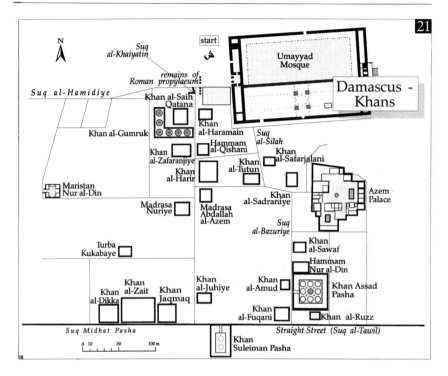

Darwish Pasha - rectangular court; upper gallery covered by domes.

Return to the street heading south. At the next corner, note traces (above and right) of masonry from a Roman gateway, once part of the outer limits of the Temple of Jupiter. Turn left (east) down a narrow street (Osman Aidi St) that is often clogged with motor vehicles. 20 m on the right, is a former *madrasa* (1779), the →**Madrasa Abdullah al-Azem Pasha** built by the man who later became the last of the illustrious Azem Governors; now an antiquarian shop with a superb courtyard - uncovered; double arcading (third storey in timber relatively modern); good view of Umayyad Mosque from terrace.

Continue to the east. After 80 m, the street reaches another crowded crossroad. Take a left turn into the Suq al-Silah (or Assagha - once the weapons' market) which leads back towards the southern wall of the Umayyad Mosque to visit two further *khans* of lesser interest. The first, 15 m on the left is the **Khan al-Tutun** (18th century - of the three original domes, central one is almost

closed, outer two open). 50 m down the Suq al-Silah, on the right, is the entrance to the **Khan al-Safarjalani**, dated 1757/8 - 10 m corridor leads to a rectangular (5 m by 16 m) courtyard covered with three part-domes.

Return now to the southern end of the Suq al-Silah and turn left. The road follows a dog-leg immediately to the right (south) but ignore that for the moment. On the left is the **Khan al-Sadraniye** also built in 1757/8 in two segments, the first a 15 m domed corridor and behind it a small courtyard originally covered with twin domes. Now pass into the small square that terminates Osman Aidi Street and in which on the right stands the antique shop named after its original founder, George Dabdoub. This unprepossessing forecourt brings you to one of the major points of interest in the old city.

This is the →**Azem Palace** (*Beit al-Azem* – Plates 7c, 8a) built in 1749-52 by the Ottoman Governor of Damascus, Assaad Pasha al-

Azem[67]. (Officially, the building is now the Museum of Popular Arts and Tradition.) The Azem Palace displays all the notable features of Arab/Turkish domestic architecture in a restful and harmonious setting. The building (originally erected on the ruins of the Palace of the Mameluke Governor, Tengiz) has been carefully preserved, even though the original 18th century construction was twice partly rebuilt after renovations in the 1830's and a fire in 1925. After 1930, the building served to house the French Institute but reverted to the Azem family on independence. The palace was purchased by the Syrian Government in 1951 and opened as a museum three years later.

Opening Hours:
Wed-Mon   08:00 - 16:00 [Fri   closed 12:00 - 14:00]

Follow the red arrows which lead you first to the north west corner, leading off a western extension of the main *selamlek* (public entertainment area). This corner comprises mostly service rooms not now open to the public including the kitchen and a vaulted storeroom. Continue clockwise around the principal court whose rooms are used to display the museum's collection of household and decorative items as well as furniture of the 18th and 19th centuries. The marked tour takes you successively to a school room and a series of rooms behind a long columned portico along the north wall - a drawing room, a *diwan*, and a library with stucco and painted wood decoration (note especially the latter with geometric carved decoration on the ceiling). Next is a room set up as a 'marriage chamber' with marble inlay, stucco and painted wood decoration.

At the narrow (eastern) end of the court, three more rooms, the first of which has a fine ceiling with relief geometric decoration (1750). Along the south wall, as you continue clockwise, an *iwan* faces on to the court, flanked by two rooms decorated in painted wood. Continuing clockwise, you will find across the wide passage that once led to a smaller court to the left a small

entrance leading to the palace baths. After the large domed room for changing and relaxing, a succession of warm and hot rooms led to the central steam room (domed roof). Behind this is a cleansing room with two massage chambers to the left.

Next in sequence is the main reception hall (*qa`a*) of the palace, with a fountain in the centre of its marble floor and raised wings on each of the three enclosed sides. Note particularly the south wing - painted ceilings; three superb stalactited niches; Delft porcelain panels in the waterfall of the central niche.

The last section of the palace visited is the *haremlek* or private quarters (access by following the arrows through the 'Jebel al-Arab' room off the reception hall). The central courtyard of the haremlek is unusually large with a water pond and a cooling canopy of citrus trees. This area was much affected by the 1925 fire but parts have since been restored.

As you leave the Azem Palace, take the broad street on the left that leads south towards Straight Street. 30 m on the left along this spices and confectionary *suq* (Suq al-Bazuriye) a small sign indicates the entrance to the badly deteriorated Khan al-Sawaf (date not determined). 20 m further on, still on the left, signs indicate the →**Hammam Nur al-Din** or Hammam al-Bazuriye which still functions as a public bath. The *hammam*, one of the oldest in Damascus, was founded between 1154 and 1172 by Nur al-Din in order to provide income to his funerary *madrasa* which you will visit in a moment. Though much restored over eight centuries (it was a soap factory earlier this century), it is still a good example of a classic Arab public bath. The domed chamber immediately inside the entrance is unusually grand and dates from the Ottoman period. To the left lie successively an octagonal *maqsura* and a warm room.

The building 40 m to the left along the spice *suq* towards Straight Street was undergoing extensive reconstruction at the time of writing, the →**Khan Assaad Pasha**. This, conspicuously the boldest and most striking of the Damascus khans, is another project (dated 1752) of the remarkable mid 18th century Ottoman Governor of Damascus who built the Azem Palace. The *caravanserai* was conceived on a grand scale with an uncovered central space flanked by eight domes, the whole covering 2500 m². The monumental effect is increased by the use of severely contrasting stonework in basalt and limestone. A central fountain lies under the

---

[67] There were five Azem Governors of Damascus at nine different periods between 1725 and 1809 - (1) Ismael Pasha (Gov 1725-30); (2) his brother, Suleiman Pasha (Gov 1734-38, 1741-43; (3) Assaad Pasha (Gov 1743-57 - son of (1) - builder of the Azem Palace), (4) Muhammed Pasha (Gov intermittently 1771-83 - nephew of (3)); and (5) Abdullah Pasha (Gov 1795-9, 1805-7 - son of (4)). For a complete genealogy, see Barbir; Schatkowski Schilcher. The period of the Azem governors is examined in Rafeq, Abdul-Karim *The Province of Damascus 1723-1783* Beirut 1966.

circular aperture in the roof. There are current plans to turn the complex into a tourist bazar.

Opposite lies the entrance to the **Khan al-Amud** a badly dilapidated 17th century building formed around two courtyards (the first iron-roofed), still serving as a warehouse.

Before continuing 60 m on to Straight Street, you may want to divert 20 m before the intersection down a small lane to the left. 20 m on the right is the **Khan al-Ruzz** - 18th century; square courtyard of 9 m by 9 m once covered by twin domes.

Straight Street - known in Arabic as the *Suq al-Tawil* (Long Street) - is the *Via Recta* of the Roman city, the main transverse thoroughfare whose fame has been amplified by the account in Acts of St Paul's eventful sojourn in Damascus. (Full details in *Damascus - Straight Street).

There is a further khan of limited interest in this area. 12 m to the right behind a grille doorway as you turn right along Suq al-Tawil is the **Khan al-Fuqani**, another 18th century construction, sometimes known as the Khan al-Sanaubar and now in a bad state, used as a coffee-roasting plant - rectangular courtyard, once covered by triple domes.

Continue right (west) along Straight Street along the section known as the **Suq Midhat Pasha** (cloth, cotton articles, bedding, household items, oils, soap). About 50 m on the left is the striped entrance doorway to the **➔Khan Suleiman Pasha** built in 1732 by the Ottoman Governor, Suleiman Pasha al-Azem (Governor 1734-43). A 15 m gallery leads to an ambitious central courtyard once covered by twin domes with a broad upper gallery.

About 20 m further along Straight Street (continuing west) is the entrance on the right to the street (Suq al-Haiyatin) which you followed at the beginning of this itinerary and which leads eventually back to the Suq al-Hamidiye. If you wish to inspect three further khans in the next block to the right along Straight Street, ignore this turn for the moment. The first *khan* (20 m, right) is the **Khan Jaqmaq** founded by the Mameluke Emir, Saif al-Din Jaqmaq al-Argunsawi, (Governor of Damascus, 1418-20). 40 m further on the right is the **➔Khan al-Zait** - late 16th century; once the depot for the olive oil trade. One of the most pleasant of the khans, it has a partly tree shaded open courtyard enclosed by vaulted arcades with an upper gallery in semi-circular arches. 20 m further

along Straight Street on the right are the fragmentary remains of the **Khan al-Dikka** (date uncertain).

Returning to the Suq al-Haiyatin, follow this north for 20 m. On the right are the remains of the Hammam al-Haiyatin, possibly part of the endowment of the first of the Azem Pashas, Ismael (d 1723/4), now a market - painted dome. A further 20 on (right) is the **Khan al-Juhiye**, or **Khan al-Khayatin**, built in the mid 16th century by the Ottoman Governor, Ahmad Samsi Pasha - collapsed twin dome. 25 m further on, still on the right, is the entrance to the Madrasa Assaad Pasha al-Azem (1748), originally endowed by the builder of the Azem Palace.

A further 60 m along the street, just after the thoroughfare narrows, look out for a long stone wall and the unheralded entrance on the left to a *madrasa*. The (**➔Madrasa Nuriye al-Kubra**) houses the tomb of one of the great Muslim rulers of the middle ages, Nur al-Din, whose achievements united Syria behind the anti-Crusader cause and paved the way for the accomplishments of his nephew, Saladin. The original building (1167-72) survives only in part, notably along the street frontage. The tomb itself is to the left of the entrance. (If it is locked and unattended, the white cenotaph can be seen through the grille behind the drinking fountain). The funerary chamber is covered by a *muqarnas* or honeycomb dome, one of the few examples of this Mesopotamian device in Damascus (cf. the entrance to the Bimaristan Nur al-Din - *Damascus - Suq al-Hamidiye). A recent restoration has served further to disguise the original four-*iwan* plan, the *iwan* on the right having earlier disappeared, the space was later re-used for the widening of a modern road.

To reach the last monument on our tour, double back a few metres towards Straight Street, taking the first street on the right. A little way to the right lies the **➔Turba Kukabaye**, the mausoleum built for Sotaita (d 1330-1), wife of Tengiz, a noted Mameluke Governor of Damascus. The honeycombed entrance at the centre of a simple and symmetrical facade leads to a twin-domed interior decorated with sculptured plaster.

If you return along the street you have just entered and turn left, continuing past Nur al-Din's *madrasa*, you can follow the Suq al-Haiyatin back to the area of the Suq al-Hamidiye where the itinerary began.

REFS: *BG* pp 289; Omiry, Ibrahim & Jabbour, Khousama *Khan Asa'ad Bacha* Damascus nd; Sack

Damaskus - Beitrag; Sauvaget Monuments; Scharabi; Wulzinger and Watzinger Damaskus - islamische.

Damascus - Straight Street to Bab Sharqi

VARIANTS: Via Recta (Lat); Suq al-Tawil (Arb)
PERIOD: Rom/Arb RATING: * MAP:22 ITIN: 1e

LOCATION: A walk along the main thoroughfare of old Damascus from west to east. Begin 250 m (fourth intersection) south of the western entrance to the Suq al-Hamidiye. This is a somewhat long walk (3+ km) through difficult traffic conditions. There is a lot to be said for doing it on a Friday when commercial traffic is light, preferably avoiding the heat of the day.

Since Hellenistic and Roman times, this has been the major west/east thoroughfare of Damascus. When it was taken by the Greeks after Alexander's conquests, the already ancient city (centred on a hillock just north of the central section of the street) was re-oriented on a grid pattern. The **Hippodamian grid** (based on the

The Greek city as expanded by the Nabateans (to the east) and the Romans, largely corresponded in its limits to the old city within the current walls though the edges probably conformed more strictly to a rectangle (some 1330 m by 850 m) than the present more rounded shape. (See also Box: 'Gates of Damascus' page 77.)

The Romans who were considerably more ambitious in their civic embellishments and more concerned to display in public works the sense of a new imperial order, added many improvements to the Greek grid and its Nabatean adaptations. In the first century AD, they expanded enormously the compound of the Temple of Jupiter (*Damascus - Umayyad Mosque), established a military compound possibly on the site of the present Citadel (*Damascus - Citadel and Northern Walls) and widened Straight Street (*Via Recta*) to serve as a broad axis with much the same purpose as the colonnaded streets that can be seen in the remains of *Palmyra or

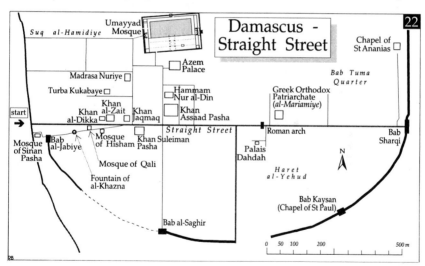

ideas of the fifth century BC Greek, Hippodamus of Miletus) reflected the sense of order the Greeks sought to bring to many centres throughout the east (including *Apamea, *Latakia, *Aleppo, and *Cyrrhus). Little of the orthogonal plan survives to the earth-bound eye though topographical surveys indicate the extent to which the seemingly random web of streets and alleyways of old Damascus still conforms at many points to the ancient plan. The segments of the grid (*insulae*) were based on rectangles each 45 m (east/west) by 100 m (north/south).

Apamea. It became a principal thoroughfare (*decumanus maximus*) lined with solidly built stalls, the whole overshadowed by the forest of columns that lent dignity at the same time as supporting a cloth canopy. But even the Greeks and Romans had to bend to the logic of the existing street pattern at some points. Straight Street followed the path of an existing east/west thoroughfare that dodged the low hills and existing settlements in its passage, hence the slight deviations which aroused Mark Twain's sense of irony: *The street called Straight is straighter than a corkscrew, but not as straight as a rainbow.*[68]

Alas, the dignified ambience of the Roman thoroughfare has gone. The broad Roman street (at 26 m it was four times the width of the present roadway) has over the centuries (especially since Abbasid times - eighth century) gradually been encroached upon by the building line on each side. Commercial establishments and workshops now crowd the thoroughfare allowing only one lane of vehicles with barely room for pedestrians at the sides. All the columns are gone, as have the stone-framed shops and the cloth shadings[69]. You are now left to brave alone the elements, the noise and impatient traffic. Nevertheless, the experience of Straight Street is an indispensable part of a visit to Damascus, and the intense commercial life continues the role the street has played for most of the last 2000 years.

You may notice that Straight Street for its first 400 m runs parallel with two (later one) narrow *suqs* to the south. In Roman times, the *decumanus* embraced this whole width. As the buildings encroached on the pedestrian and wheeled thoroughfares the width, at this western end, was divided into several narrow thoroughfares by the encroachment of stalls.

The market area immediately south of the beginning of Straight Street is described in *Damascus – South West Quarter*. For our present purposes, locate the Arab gateway (Bab al-Jabiye) that lies 20 m south of the start of the street, immediately behind the Mosque of Sinan Pasha (green ceramic-tiled minaret). Continue along this clothing market for 100 m until you spot, on the left, the **Fountain** *(Sabil)* **al-Khazna** (1404/5) erected by Emir Saif al-Din Jarkas, a Grand Chamberlain of Damascus under the Mamelukes. The mouldings inside the arch are said by Sauvaget to derive from a Crusader monument.

A minaret, attached to the **Mosque al-Qali** (1470) is found 70 m to the left along what has

now become a cotton suq. Note the blue faience decorations left incomplete on the south side. Another 100 m on the right is the fine octagonal minaret of the **Mosque of Hisham**, built in 1426/7 by a chancellor of Damascus under the Mamelukes and decorated with fine *muqarnas* work. Though no traces remain and the choice of its location is conjectural, it is generally supposed that the theatre that Herod the Great had built in Damascus (first century BC), mentioned in literary sources, must have been located south of the Via Recta a little east of this point.

Take any passage to the left that brings you back into Straight Street. This section, the Suq Midhat Pasha, is described under *Damascus Khans*. Pass along it quickly until you reach the south entrance to the spices suq (Suq al-Bazuriye) on the left (leading to the Azem Palace and the Umayyad Mosque) and the wide street leading to the Bab al-Saghir on the right. You are now at the beginning of the long (1 km) stretch that takes you through the edges of the Jewish and Christian . quarters, past many shops established for the tourist trade, particularly in brass and wood mosaic wares. 100 m left, amid the densely settled laneways, you can just distinguish the mound (*Tell al-Samaka*) which marks the original settlement of the pre-Hellenistic period. The area to the right of the road was the site of the pre-Hellenistic royal palace.

The next landmark as you proceed east (450 m) is the ·small **Roman Arch** (*Bab al-Kanise,* partly reconstructed in newly cut stone) that stands in a minute oasis of park. The triple arch stood on the *decumanus* at the intersection of a major cross street (*cardo maximus*) but such has been the rate of accumulation of debris over two millennia that by this century, the arch had been buried and forgotten below the surface of the modern street. It was excavated and re-erected at surface level during the French Mandate. The original arch was probably constructed in the third century AD and may have been part of a tetrapylon.

The intersection where the arch stands is a useful orientation point for those who wish to explore more of the neighbouring back streets of the old city. Facing east, the traditionally **Christian quarter** of Damascus begins to the left (north east segment) with the area known as *al-Qaimariye* (and beyond that Bab Tuma - *Damascus - Citadel and North Walls*). The concentration of Christians in the eastern part of the city reflects the decision of Khalid Ibn al-Walid, the Muslim conqueror of Damascus in 636, to confirm their continued access to their

[68] Twain does exaggerate a bit. Along its 1.35 km length, Straight Street makes two slight changes of alignment, both originally marked by an arch placed at a major intersection. Twain went on to observe in *Innocents Abroad* (1869) that 'St Luke [assumed author of *Acts*] is careful not to commit himself; he does not say it is the street which *is* straight, but the ·street which is *called* Straight'. It is a fine piece of irony; it is the only facetious remark in the Bible, I believe.' (Quoted in Yapp *The Travellers' Dictionary of Quotations* London 1988.)

[69] Not to mention the civic facilities including a theatre and an *odeon* that once stood to the right of the first stretch of Straight Street where the Suq Madhat Pasha now runs.

the fifth century AD by the establishment of a monastery. In 412, an ascetic who was later to become famous as Saint Simeon Stylites, joined the monastery. In search of a more arduous life-style, he later abandoned the community and took up residence on the hill above, confining himself to a small platform perched on a tall pillar. His presence attracted a stream of pilgrims from 425. After his death in 459 and certainly by the end of the fifth century, a major centre of pilgrimage under imperial patronage had come into being in the lower village with hostelries, a church and three major monasteries. The village was joined to the huge new basilica on the hill by a triumphal way marked by an arch.

Construction seems to have taken place over several phases. In 470-80, three hostelries were constructed. The northern church was built in 491-2, along with the south western monastery. The period of peak activity was the sixth century when the large *pandocheion* was built. The centre continued to be mentioned as a pilgrimage destination until as late as the 12th century.

Visit

The ruins seen today cover an extensive area, almost two third of a square kilometre and roughly rectangular in shape. The best place to gain an appreciation of their layout is from the hill of St Simeon's Church. The following groups of ruins can be recognised, scattered between the fields:

- **monumental arch** marking the beginning of the *via sacra* ascending to the Cathedral of St Simeon;
- the **small pandocheion** (hostelry) and **bazars** (where the *via sacra* begins);
- the **north church** (100 m to the right);
- the **north west monastery** (450 m west of the north church);
- the **south west monastery** (400 m WSW of the bazars);
- the **large pandocheion** with tomb chapel to the rear (150 m to the south, nestling into the base of the hill).

In between are remains of many hastily and poorly constructed dwellings and of a few more substantial private houses or smaller inns.

The **monumental arch**, recently reconstructed from the tumbled stones, marks the beginning of the ascent along the sacred way.

The **north church** preserves much of its west facade. The plan is typical, with the addition of a tower above the *prothesis* (chamber right of the apse) and small portals each supported on two columns over the south and west entrances. The decoration is restrained.

The central grouping of **pandocheion** and **bazars** includes a building called by Butler a basilica (perhaps an *andron* or law court - 50 m left). The interior was supported by a high transverse arch. Though somewhat classical in style and civic purpose, it probably dates from the fifth century . To the west of this building is the *pandocheion*, dated by inscription to AD 479 - ie just after St Simeon's death (459) had begun to attract the major pilgrimage traffic to the town. Just to the south is a long row of eleven bazar stalls built along the main east/west axis of the settlement.

About 80 m to the west of the bazar stalls, Butler's **house no I** (probably early fifth century) can be identified. Originally three storeyed, each level bearing a colonnaded porch, it must have been a substantial building for a private residence.

The **south west monastery** consists of three colonnaded buildings (at least two of them - north and west sides - probably serving as pilgrim accommodation) grouped to form a courtyard. From the south east corner protrudes a sizeable chapel, remarkably well preserved. The building to the east (joined to the chancel end of the chapel) and that to the south (both tri-roomed structures) provided further accommodation, the former probably for the monks themselves. Butler dates the complex to the sixth century.

The **north west monastery** is described by Butler as 'an exceptionally fine group of buildings in a remarkable state of preservation'. It consists of an irregular collection of hostel buildings grouped around a mid fifth century church (south side) of some size (18 m by 22 m). East of the church was a burial ground, a rock-hewn colonnaded court preceded by an entrance narthex.

The **Great Pandocheion** lies on the lower slopes of St Simeon's mount on the eastern edge of town and comprised the major accommodation complex for pilgrims. The remaining ruins make a remarkable sight with many stretches of arcading and parts of the huge structure still intact. It comprises two separate buildings set 70 m end to end, both surrounded by wide porticos in two storeys. Both are typical shapes for this type of accommodation for pilgrims but the north example is considerably larger than usual. The south building is the better preserved, with large stretches of its porticos intact. A stone bridge at the rear leads from this building to a terrace carefully cut from the rock.

At the back of this terrace stands a tomb chapel, half hewn out of the rock. Into the chapel wall (and along the rock side of the terrace) is set a series of *arcosolia* or burial niches. This burial facility gives some substance to the view that the complex (in spite of its modern description) was intended to house a monastery (with pilgrim accommodation), rather than solely as an inn for passing pilgrims.

REFS: Butler *EC* pp 105-9; Butler *PE* II/B/6 pp 266-80; Mattern pp 135-8; Saouaf *Saint Simeon* pp 45-52; Tchalenko *Villages I* pp 205-222; II pl LXVII-LXX, CXXXII.

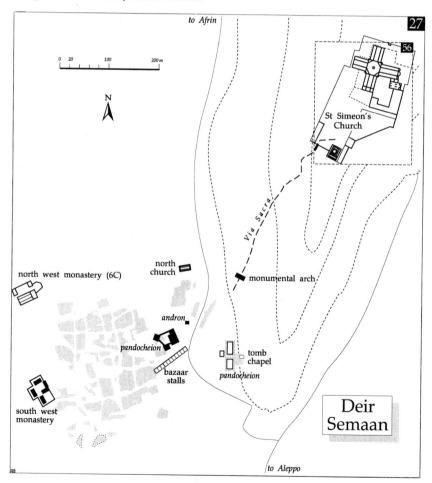

Deir Soleib

VARIANTS:
PERIOD: Byz RATING: - MAP: 65 ITIN: 4

> LOCATION: c4 km south of the Hama/Masyaf road. From Hama continue west 30 km (or from Masyaf, 10 km east on Hama road). Sign points left c+4 km south to Deir Soleib. Church 1 km on left before village. A second church can be reached on foot, 30 minutes walk south east of the village.

The first church (Mattern's **west church**) is an interesting basilica which gives a different perspective on Syrian church building from that provided in the contemporary *Dead Cities further to the north. The dating of the church is not entirely clear. It is probably, judging by its style, from the sixth or second half of the fifth century.

The church is surprisingly good condition, the semi-dome of the apse and the lower walls largely intact. The entrance porch or *narthex* is large and has a baptistery off the south end (note the cross-shaped font). The surrounding compound is large (65 m by 45 m) with an atrium (30 m by 26 m) in front of the narthex and to the south a mausoleum which contains three monolith sarcophagi placed in niches.

Internally, the church is a basilica in plan but almost square in shape. The semi-circular apse protrudes beyond the rear wall of the building, whereas buildings before the sixth century usually enclosed the curved shape behind a straight external wall at the back, thus requiring a good deal of fill-in masonry. The windows are much larger and based on bolder shapes than in earlier examples in northern Syria and the pillars are thin enough to bring the naves together rather than form a barrier between them. There is virtually no decoration except the capitals and the occasional carved crosses in the Byzantine style. The two side rooms, the *prothesis* and the *diaconicon* were not placed in the normal positions at the end of the side aisles but are positioned on the north eastern and south eastern corners of the church. A gallery probably ran around the upper level of the side aisles and the narthex and was usually reserved, in Byzantine rites, for women.

A second church (**eastern church**) is found 2 km south east of the nearby village which lies at the end of the road; but you must go on foot. It comprises a basilica with three naves, the arcades carried on pillars. The semi-circular apse (with three windows) is enclosed in a five-sided chevet. An inscription above the central portal dates it to 604-5, only three decades before the Arab conquest of Syria. The construction is more heavy than that of than the west church and the ruins are in a considerably more depleted condition.

REFS: Mattern pl LIV, pp 151-9; Mattern, Mouterde and Beaulieu.

Dumeir (Plate 9b)

VARIANTS: Thelsae (Lat), Dmeir (Arb)
PERIOD: Rom RATING: ** MAP: 64 ITIN: 3a

> LOCATION: 40 km north east of Damascus. Take *Palmyra road (leave Damascus/Homs motorway 24 km north of Damascus). Continue +16 km. Do not take the diversion which goes to the left and skirts Dumeir but go straight into town. Before you reach the centre, look out on the right for the outline of the temple (first street on right after crossing the wadi).

The **temple** as seen today restored after much research and reconstruction work in recent years, represents one of the fruits of the intensive phase of construction activity in third century Syria. It was dedicated as a temple to Zeus Hypsistos in 245 during the reign of the Emperor Philip the Arab (Emperor 244-9) who was born in the Hauran region of Syria (*Shahba). (Butler believed the portraits carved in relief in the south *tympanum* are of the Emperor and his wife, Otacilia.) However there was an earlier reference to the building in a document relating to a law suit in 216. There may thus have been some changes of plan during the long construction period. An earlier altar dedicated to the Semitic deity, Baal-Shamin, in AD 94 (now in the Institut du Monde Arabe in Paris) indicates that a Nabatean religious building previously stood on the site.

The genesis and original purpose of the building are not clear. The shape is highly unusual. Construction may have commenced as a public fountain or as a staging post on the intersection of two important caravan routes (hence the quadrilateral plan and four entrances)[84]. Perhaps it was even an elaborate triumphal arch or an entrance gateway to a now-buried (or never realised) sacred compound. The argument for seeing it as a temple, at least in its final form, is underlined by the use of corner towers and staircases giving access to the roof for ritual purposes in the Syro-Phoenician tradition while the use of four entrances and exits might be explained by ritual needs peculiar to

---

[84] Dumeir was the crossroads for the E/W route (Emesa (*Homs)/*Palmyra) and the N/S *Strata Diocletiana* (*Resafe/Damascus).

this shrine. It was fortified in the Arab period; the arch on the rear wall remains completely filled in with stones and defensive devices.

About 5 km to the east of Dumeir, on the road to Palmyra, are the remains of a late second century **Roman military camp** to the right of a road leading (south) to a Syrian air force base. The remains can be seen from the road but soldiers guarding the air force approach road do not seem to mind if you park on the highway (away from their barrier) and walk down the slope into the remains, some of which are surprisingly intact. Each side is pierced by a central door guarded by twin semi-circular towers; round towers on each corner.

REFS: Amy *Temples; BG* p 500; Brümmer; Butler *AE* II pp 400-2; Dussaud *Topographie* pp 263, 300; Klinkott; Nasrullah 'Le Qalamoun à l'époque Romano-Byzantine' in *AAAS* 1952, 1958; Poidebard *Trace* p 43.

Dura Europos

VARIANTS: Dura (pre-Grk); Dura Nicanoris (Grk); Salihiye (Arb)
PERIOD: Hel/Rom   RATING: ** MAP: *28*, 73
ITIN: 12b

LOCATION: From Deir al-Zor, follow the main Abu Kemal highway for 93 km south east along the right bank of the Euphrates. Sign points left to Dura and ruins can be seen across the plain.

When the first wall paintings at Dura were uncovered by accident by a British expeditionary force in April 1920, few could have expected that the incident was about to provide a new perspective on early Christian and Judaic art. Dura's remains would not only illustrate the part it played in the drawn out struggle between cultural, political and military influences between east and west but shed an unexpected new light on early representational art of the Christian and Jewish traditions. This 'Pompei of the Syrian Desert' (Rostovtzeff) is thus of major historical and artistic interest even though most of its more important treasures have been moved elsewhere (Damascus; the Louvre; Yale University). Nevertheless, a visit is well worthwhile if you gain some impression beforehand of its historical importance and acquaint yourself with some of its major finds, notably the Dura synagogue which has been installed in the National Museum in Damascus.

History

Dura Europos was established at the beginning of the Hellenistic period when the empire of

Alexander was divided among his heirs and northern Syria/Mesopotamia was apportioned to Seleucos I Nicator. Initially probably founded as a fortress guarding the river route to Lower Mesopotamia, it was (according to the most recent research) not established as a planned city until the mid second century BC. Dura was the focal point of a network of military colonies implanted to secure Seleucid control of the Mid Euphrates. The troops were given land in the area as far as 80 km to the north along the Khabur River. Dura ('the fortress' in Old Semitic) formed a defensive strongpoint on the access route between the two major military centres, Apamea and Seleucia-on-the-Tigris (southern Iraq). The typical grid plan city was established and the name chosen, Europos, referred to the birthplace of Seleucos I Nicator in Macedonia. The ambitious plan for the city was probably never completed in view of the political uncertainties that dogged the Seleucid Kingdom in the short period before the Parthian takeover. Even under the Romans, the replacement of the mud-brick upper courses of the walls with stone was not fully realised and the Seleucid citadel was left unfinished long before it was abandoned.

Seleucid control wavered after 185 BC and the area was continually threatened from the east with the rise of the **Parthians**. After the Parthians pushed their frontier westwards to the Euphrates in 141 BC, Seleucid control was further constricted. The town, in effect, was dominated by Parthia, probably from 113 BC on and the townspeople made the necessary concessions to both sides to avoid a show-down over the issue. Its population, originally based on the Macedonian/Greek settler element, were increasingly outnumbered by people of Semitic stock and by the first century BC, the city was predominantly eastern in character. Dura did not transfer to the Romans' domain when they took control of Syria in the first century BC. It remained a Parthian city to the end of the first century AD, the Romans later establishing themselves at *Circesium to the north east near the junction of the Euphrates and Khabur Rivers. A 'live and let live' policy along the Euphrates was recognized by a treaty with the Parthians signed under Augustus in 20 BC.

Trajan, however, occupied Dura in AD 115 as part of his ill-advised attempt to take control of Parthia and push the frontier across the Euphrates into Mesopotamia. He briefly took over the Parthian domains as far south as modern Basra (southern Iraq) but the conquered population in the north quickly revolted and the campaign turned into a shambles. Exhausted and demoralised, he stumbled back towards

Europe but died at Selente in southern Turkey en route[85]. Trajan had left his nephew and adopted heir, Hadrian, as Governor of Syria. On succeeding his uncle, Hadrian reverted to a softer policy on the frontier and gave Dura back to the Parthians.

In 161, an earthquake severely damaged the city and three years later Rome again took direct control under Lucius Verus (co-Emperor with Marcus Aurelius), stationing its own troops there and for the first time incorporating Dura into the province of Syria. It was declared a Roman colony in 211. After that date - and especially after 227, as the more aggressive Sasanians replaced the Parthians in the east - Rome built up its garrison (using as its initial core a Palmyrene cohort) and began a substantial building program in the northern quarter to provide them with home comforts in the form of a theatre, baths and barracks. The local commander was given the title of *Dux Ripae*.

The period of full Roman control saw a remarkable flourishing of religious architecture in pagan, Jewish and Christian styles, with some notable similarities between the three. The town remained dominated by its Greek cultural origins and the language of civic life, as in most of Syria, was Greek. Greek influences served as the common thread that joined the syncretist elements in all three religious traditions in a remarkable way, with some addition of Parthian artistic styles. The Roman military camp preserved its separate identity based on its imperial connections such as the officially-encouraged Mithraic cult and with institutional links to the garrison at *Palmyra to the west.

Dura was a polyglot town by nature of its mixed origins, its location on the frontier between east and west and its trading function. The latter was particularly important as Dura at its height was not simply a fortress city but an emporium for the trade along the Mid Euphrates. Though the great bulk of east/west trade by-passed Dura, heading directly across the desert to Palmyra from a river crossing further south around Abu Kemal, Dura's merchants played a role in local facilitation and had their own direct interests in trade and shipping as far as the mouth of the Tigris/Euphrates river system.

The days of unbridled mercantilism, however, ended when the Sasanian Persians

emerged after 224 as the new threat from the east. The Sasanians regarded themselves as the heirs to the Achaemenid realms and thus sought to press the terms of the 20 BC treaty between Rome and the Parthians. Having made several thrusts against Dura in the preceding decades (and indeed as far as Antioch in 238) a major assault in 256 by under Shapur I resulted in the fall of Dura and ended the brief and uncertain *Pax Romana*. The Romans had spent the last few years in a hurried effort to build up the long and vulnerable walls of the city and had strengthened its Palmyrene garrison with detachments from the Syrian legions and even that at Bosra.

Shapur I decided to destroy the town and banish its people rather than make it a Sasanian fortress. Except for a brief occupation by the Palmyrene Arabs (whose power was at its zenith in 260-73) the Mid Euphrates was left for centuries without a substantial strongpoint to stabilise the shifting frontier between east and west. Justinian preferred to locate his defences of the Byzantine Empire further to the north (along the Khabur ˉ from Circesium and at *Halebiye) and when the real threat to the area developed the next century, the Arab armies poured into Syria without real hindrance.

Excavations

Dura was painstakingly excavated from 1922 to 1923 by a French team and from 1928 to 1937 by a Franco-American expedition whose work is surveyed in a book published in 1978 by one of the American directors, Hopkins. He evokes the importance of the finds unearthed, particularly the second to fourth century religious buildings. Most remarkable was the synagogue, one of the few examples from the period identified anywhere. The synagogue owes its survival to the fact that the defenders of the city against the Sasanian threat in 256 piled sand against the inner face of the walls to prevent mining. The sand covered part of the inhabited quarters of the city against the west wall, including the area of the synagogue and the Christian chapel.

Even more notable was the fact that the synagogue bore frescoes which carried human representations, largely in the Parthian manner - clearly a break with traditional rules on representational art. Hopkins' excitement on discovering the find is conveyed in the following passage describing how the synagogue was released from its overburden: *But I clearly remember when the foot of dirt still covering the back wall was undercut and fell away, exposing the most amazing succession of paintings! Whole scenes, figures and objects burst into*

---

[85] Perowne (*Hadrian* London 1960) depicts the tragedy of Trajan's blunder in the following terms: *The scene might have come from a Greek play. Amid the ruins of Babylon, already a by-word for beauty made desolate, the Roman conqueror confronts failure where his Greek model had encountered death.*

view, brilliant in colour, magnificent in the sunshine.

The paintings from the Dura synagogue were transferred to the National Museum in

of a liberal policy towards non-Iranian religions adopted by Shapur I. A corresponding shift towards Sasanian/Parthian styles influenced Mesopotamian Jews to abandon the traditional injunctions against pictorial representation. The

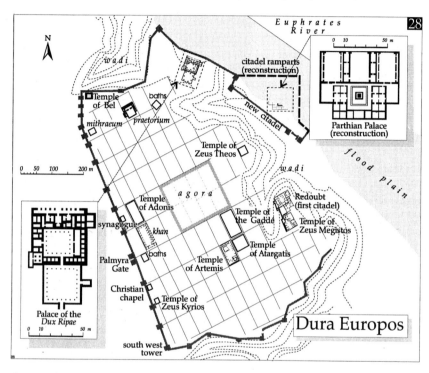

Damascus after the building's excavation in 1932-3 and carefully reconstructed in a courtyard off the wing devoted to Roman and Palmyrene remains (see page 102). The synagogue comprises a columned forecourt beyond which is a hall of assembly. It is dated to the second year of the reign of Philip the Arab (244-9). At this time, the Roman suppression of the two major Jewish revolts had left few remains of Jewish culture in Palestine and the Dura find is an important indication of its survival in an eastern environment even though the overall style of the paintings is almost entirely local in inspiration.

The building as reconstructed represents the synagogue after its refurbishment in a more opulent style after its modest origins as a house-synagogue in the late second century. Hopkins sees the building as inspired by a resurgence of Judaism in the Mesopotamian region as a result

Dura Synagogue has had a major impact on the appreciation of the development of religious iconography in the first centuries of our era, before the Roman Empire went over to Christianity after 312. Dura's significance was reinforced by the discovery of a house converted into a Christian chapel – the earliest recognisable Christian cult centre in Syria, also richly decorated with wall paintings.

On the whole, though of immense historical interest, the local style is rather heavy and crude with little of the technical skill and greater feeling for psychological insight found in Palmyra where a more successful synthesis of oriental and Roman art was developed.

A re-examination of the Dura site is currently underway through the work of a joint Franco-Syrian mission, one of whose more urgent tasks is to arrest the damage done to the site since the exposure of many of its buildings to the elements since the 1920's.

Visit

If you start out from Deir al-Zor, it would be worthwhile to visit the town's museum which contains some of the finds unearthed at Dura, as well as from other sites along the Mid Euphrates including *Mari and *Halebiye.

Though little remains of Dura Europos above the ground, a visit to the site takes a good two to three hours if you wish to gain an impression of its layout and the scale of the walls and the citadel. The walled area covers 80 ha and is based on a very approximate square, the shape being distorted by the need to accommodate natural features. On all but the west side, the site is bordered by natural *wadis* or the river itself.

The original **walls** were probably built by the Seleucids at the same time as the grid plan of the city was drawn up, rather than added as an afterthought. To some extent, the river on the east and the wadis on the north and south gave a degree of natural protection to the site. The perimeter was fortified by a system of stone towers (of which 26 remain) joined by curtain walls 3 m thick. The walls, reinforced with mud brick in the Roman period, still stand, in places, to a height of 9 m. The more substantial stone walls were probably built as part of the original Greek walled city, according to recent research. The long west side open to the desert was the most vulnerable and it was here that the Sasanian forces concentrated their effort in 256. The Sasanians mined the towers, even though the defenders had massively strengthened the walls by piling sand against both sides. The mining of tower 19 (second to the left of the main gateway) was met by counter-mining by the Romans, the two sides meeting in hand-to-hand combat. The mines collapsed, burying the troops. Their corpses were found by excavators this century still carrying their last pay, the date of the latest coin giving the year of the city's fall.

As you approach by the track from the west, you pass the remains of a Roman **triumphal gate** built in honour of the III Cyrenaica legion during Trajan's brief imposition of Roman direct rule (115-7). You enter the city by the 'Great Gate' or **Palmyra Gate** on the west side. The remains are reasonably substantial, measuring over 20 m square. It comprised two stout bastions each with two guard rooms, the top rooms being linked by a passageway over the inner archway. The gateway was defended by three successive doors. Hopkins believed the gateway dates as early as 16-17 BC, from the period of Parthian dominance, but more recent research ascribes it to the second century BC.

From here, the main street, originally a colonnaded *decumanus*, twice as wide as the other principal streets, crossed the city towards the river. This was the main axis of the town, leading caravans towards the *wadi* that descended to the port area (long since swept away) and to the main military facilities. The city was laid out according to the strict grid plan invariably employed in the Macedonian cities founded in the east though the *insulae* or blocks employed were rather smaller (30 by 60 m) than other examples while retaining the 1:2 ratio.

Immediately inside the Palmyra Gate, the original layout of several of the third century religious buildings can be discerned. 100 m north, on the left against the wall, (in the middle of the second *insula*) is the site of the **synagogue** (see above). On the right, after one of three Roman bath sites, the Christian **chapel** (AD 232) and the **temple to Zeus Kyrios** were located against the wall at 50 m intervals.

Heading east (to the river), half way along the *decumanus*, you will find on the left the site of the *agora*. In the original Hellenistic plan, this served as a large open space in the centre of the town, grouping eight normal blocks. Around it clustered the main civic institutions, the whole plan of the city at that stage filling less than half the area enclosed by the outer walls. However, this Greek concept of open space encouraging free assembly became obscured under the Parthians who allowed the area of the *agora* to be over-built with bazar buildings and oriental clutter during the three centuries of their control.

We might digress here to mention several pagan era religious buildings dotted around the area south of the *agora*.

- Separated by one block to the south is the **Temple of Artemis**[86]. The layout is that of the 40-33 BC Parthian rebuilding of the Greek original. This served as the centre of the city's principal official cult throughout the Greek, Parthian and Roman periods. Not only was the cult of Artemis merged with that of her Persian equivalent (Nanaia) but the temple was built along Parthian lines (with some Greek elements), originally a simple layout of entrance, altar and *cella* divided into three.

---

[86] A statue of Aphrodite recovered from this temple can be seen in the Louvre, Paris.

- On the next block directly east of the Artemis/Nanaia temple, a **temple** was built in AD 31-2 to a similar plan in honour of the '**Syrian Goddess**', Atargatis. (On the cult, see *Membij).
- On the block, between the Atargatis temple and the agora, a third **temple** (pre-AD 159) served two Palmyrene gods of the Baal family, the **Gaddé**.

Another cluster of pagan religious buildings lay further to the east.

- A **temple to Zeus Theos** (AD 114) north of the *cardo*, on the edge of the main ravine and opposite the south end of the citadel.
- The **temple of Zeus Megistos** (AD 169) south of the redoubt palace (described below - first citadel) originating, in its earliest form, from 95-70 BC in the hybrid Parthian/Greek style.

Resuming the walk along the decumanus, the **first citadel** complex established by the Greeks, perhaps as a *strategion* (residence for the *strategos* or chief magistrate) or as an inner redoubt, lies across a *wadi* that cuts into the south eastern sector of the city, branching off the main ravine. This early acropolis built on this natural prow-shaped site was later superseded in its military role by the fortress across the principal ravine to the north east but it may have remained in use as the residence of the civil governor of the city.

None of these remains, frankly, will cause much excitement, except to the specialist, consisting largely of foundations scratched out of the desert sand. The main point of interest beside the walls is the *new citadel* just mentioned, along the city's river frontage. Here the part of the new citadel which has not been swept into the river over the years consists of stonework which is more robust and massive in scale, reflecting the citadel's purpose as the main defence against a concerted attack.

The earlier theory that this second or new citadel was largely the work of the period of Parthian dominance in the first century AD, though built on the site of an earlier Seleucid palace, has been disproved by recent research which attributes the whole building to the Seleucids (early second century BC). The conscious use of 'orientalising' features is particularly clear in the triple *iwans* - arched reception rooms opening on to a courtyard, a practice still used in Arab domestic buildings. Similar buildings are to be found at the Parthian capital, Hatra, and at Ctesiphon (both in Iraq). Unfortunately, the plan has had to be reconstructed from only partial evidence as the western face of the citadel is virtually all that remains. Almost 300 m long, it includes three towers over 20 m high with crenellated terraces. There are three gates with semi-circular arches.

Further to the north along the river bank, on the other side of the deep ravine that divides the citadel from the city, you should be able to identify the later palace erected for the Roman garrison commander, sometimes called the **Palace of the *Dux Ripae*** (Commander of the River Bank). This was part of the post-227 military quarter mentioned earlier, and marks the phase of full militarisation of the city in the struggle against the Sasanians. The palace was grouped around two internal courtyards with an arcaded front to the east looking out over the sweep of the river.

The rest of the **Roman military camp** occupied the area between this point and the western and northern walls. This is a rare example of an encampment inserted into an existing town plan, most being located outside the established perimeter. It was a virtually self-contained military colony with its own *praetorium*, exercise square, baths and temples. Of the latter, two should be mentioned, both in the north west corner.

- In the north western angle of the walls, the Temple of Baal or **Temple of the Palmyrene Gods** (mid first century AD).
- A little further around to the south, a **mithraeum** (209-11), a centre devoted to the Persian cult whose practice spread throughout the Empire in the late pagan period and was particularly favoured in the legions.

REFS: *BG* pp 491-6; Downey; Dussaud *Topographie* p 456; Hopkins; Kennedy and Riley pp 109-14; Klengel *Syrien* pp 159-63; Lambert pp 67-72; Leriche and al-Mahmoud pp 121-6; *idem Catalogue* 1966; Perkins; Perkins *et al*; Rostovtzeff *Caravan Cities*; Rostovtzeff *Dura Europos*; Matheson pp 368-74.

E

Ebla (Plate 10a)

VARIANTS: Tell Mardikh (Arb)
PERIOD: EBA/MBA   RATING: * MAP: *29*, 72
ITIN: 11a

LOCATION: Leave Aleppo on the Damascus road. At 51 km (6 km south of Saraqeb interchange where the Latakia road diverges), turn east (left) at the signpost marked Tell Mardikh/Ebla. +3 km on a good sealed road to the *tell*, just past the village.

This may be one of the most important Bronze Age sites discovered since the Second World War but it yields few of its secrets to the naked eye. During an hour's walk around the site, some impression can be gained of the scale of the ancient city and the siting of its main defensive works including the citadel area. The importance of Ebla, however, is more to be judged in the material slowly emerging from painstaking research.

History

The history of Ebla and its place in the Bronze Age civilisations of the area (including its relations with the Old Testament world) is a fascinating piece of historical reconstruction marked by considerable controversy. The discovery in 1975 of a major archive of clay tablets at Ebla should throw much light on the period and the inter-relationships between the kingdoms and city/states of the area but the work of translating and publishing the tablets is making slow progress.

Nevertheless, it is clear that Ebla was an important power in northern Syria in the late third and early second millennia, particularly as a trading hub. The

discovery of Ebla thus fills an important gap in our understanding of the third millennium BC, revealing a Syrian counterpart to the major centres of Sumer and Akkad in southern Iraq with links which spread into Mesopotamia, southern Syria and as far as Anatolia (central Turkey). Ebla was probably founded by people of Amorite (Western Semitic) descent. Their archives were written in a language dubbed Eblaite which was recorded in Akkadian cuneiform.

The sweeping plains of northern Syria at this time encompassed an advanced network of urban societies whose sophisticated political and economic systems were based on the area's

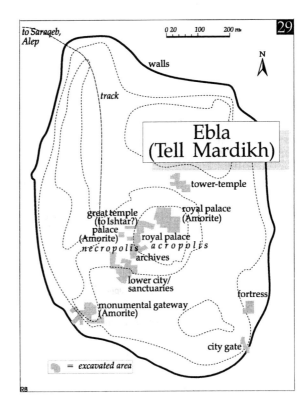

0 20   100   200 m

walls

N

track

to Saraqeb, Alep

Ebla (Tell Mardikh)

tower-temple

great temple (to Ishtar?)
palace (Amorite)
necropolis

royal palace (Amorite)

royal palace
acropolis
archives

lower city/sanctuaries

monumental gateway (Amorite)

fortress

city gate

= excavated area

29

RB

considerable agricultural potential. Ebla reached the peak of its prosperity in the period 2400-2250 BC, bringing under its control most of the western part of northern Syria and enjoying close relations with Mari to the east. Ebla's days of glory were brought to an end either by Sargon, the first great Akkadian ruler or his grandson, Naram-Sin (c2250 BC). Though the city survived for another 600 years, it never regained its central role. It was sacked around 2000 BC and incorporated into the Kingdom of Yamkhad (Aleppo). After a new flowering under the hegemony of Yamkhad in the 18th-17th centuries, a final blow was delivered by the Hittites in c1600 BC.

The last historical mention of Ebla is from c1450 BC when the Egyptian Pharaoh, Thutmose III recorded on a monument at Karnak that the Egyptian army marched through Ebla on its way to the Euphrates. There are some remains of a fortress from the ninth to eighth centuries BC and limited remains from the Persian and Byzantine periods but otherwise the city was largely abandoned.

Visit

The remains of Bronze Age *tell* are of enormous dimensions (50 ha) and only a small fraction has been exposed in the Italian excavations since 1964. The donut-shaped outer mound and its sizeable central citadel area give one a good impression of the scale of Ebla. (Its population has been estimated at 30,000 at its maximum.) The outer **walls** were up to 30 m thick (and still stand up to 20 m high), pierced by four gateways flanked by wide bastions topped with towers. It is worth taking the time to inspect the Middle Bronze Age **gate** footings whose monumental proportions have been exposed on the south western side of the outer defences.

The **citadel** (located in the centre of the donut) includes two extensive residential areas (palaces) on the north and west sides of the acropolis. The best preserved remains are the segments of the **royal palace** so far exposed on the west side of the citadel, giving some idea of the city's splendour during its apogée. These remains include the royal quarters on the upper part of the west side; on the slopes, an administrative area linked to a monumental audience court and stairway; and a residential district (MBA) linked to the palace at the foot of the citadel. Three underground chambers formed out of natural caves lay beneath the administrative area and were later (18th century BC) used for princely burials during the period 1825-1650 BC. (The location of the burials within the palace is explained by Prof Matthiae, the

chief Italian excavator, in terms of an official ancestor cult - possibly a hallmark of Amorite societies). The palace archives were found in the southern part of the administrative zone.

North of the mound are remains of an Amorite palace under a Persian/Hellenistic villa and (to the north) a temple to the sun god, Shamash.

A good collection of finds from Ebla is displayed in the new museum at Idlib, the provincial headquarters town located a little north of the Latakia road.

REFS: Bermant and Weitzman; Matthiae; Pettinato ; Weiss and Kohlmeyer pp 213-6.

Ezraa

VARIANTS: Andrea Zorava (Grk); Zor`ah, Zorah, Zurca (Arb)
PERIOD: Byz RATING: ** MAP: 63 ITIN: 2a

> LOCATION: 80 km south of Damascus on the west edge of the volcanic wilderness area, the Ledja (ancient *Trachonitis*). Take the main motorway from Damascus south towards Deraa and Amman and turn off left to Ezraa (look for a huge grain silos complex), heading east then north into the town. Stop on the northern outskirts and inquire; someone will bring the key for the Church of St George (*Mar Georgis*).

What was once an abode of demons has become a house of God; where once sacrifices were made to idols, there are now choirs of angels; where God was provoked to wrath, now He is propitiated.
[Inscription dated 515 over the middle portal of the west entrance.]

In its historical and religious associations this is perhaps one of the most remarkable buildings in Syria. The Greek Orthodox Church of St George is one of the oldest churches still in use in Syria, its architecture has been largely unaffected by its changing fortunes. It is certainly more interesting than the reputedly earlier chapels in the pilgrimage centres nearer Damascus, *Seidnaya and *Maalula. The signs of previous fortification of the building attest to the difficulties of maintaining the community in the face of fourteen centuries of often tumultuous change.

The church (which stands on the site of an ancient temple) is dated to 515 from the long inscription on the lintel over the main door (quoted above). Architecturally, the sixth century **Church of St George** is notable as one of the earliest examples of a basilica constructed on an octagon-within-a-square plan, surmounted by a cupola (see box on page 21). (The external shape is a rectangle, the line of the basic square being extended to the east to accommodate a chancel with apse and two flanking side-chambers. This extension is enclosed in three sides of a hexagon protruding from the east wall.) The 10 m dome, a relatively modern re-construction covered externally by a metal shell, follows the pointed ellipse shape still seen in mud houses in northern Syria. (The original shape of the dome can only be conjectured but may have been a masonry structure, semi-circular in plan.) The sombre stone arcaded interior was probably once covered with painted plaster but the effect is still impressive.

The internal octagon is formed by cutting off the corners of the square, filling the angles with semi-circular chapels. Within this octagonal enclosure, a second octagon (9 m wide) is formed by eight angle piers carrying soaring arches of impressive simplicity. The masonry rises above these arches, rapidly transforming itself from an octagonal to a circular cross-section until it culminates in the tall dome atop a drum pierced with eight windows. The circumambulatory aisle (and the east apse) were covered by flat stone roofing. The main entrance (west) comprises three arched doorways.

A second sixth century church of equal architectural interest is found 200 m on the left as you return to the centre of town though recent work needed to restore the badly deteriorated structure has given it a more bland and austere appearance. The Greek Catholic **Church of St Elias** is dated by inscription over the main south doorway to 542. The basic shape is a rare example for Syria of a cruciform plan oriented east/west with an apse protruding to the east. The modern dome over the crossing replaces the original wooden dome.

In the same area are remains of buildings (probably domestic) going back to the Roman period.

REFS: *BG* p 508; Butler *AE* II pp 411 ff; Butler *EC* pp 122-5; Dussaud *Topographie* pp 374-5; Krautheimer pp 136, 147, 253; Lassus *Sanctuaires chrétiens* pp 139-142, 148; Lassus *Deux églises* pp 1348; Vogüé I pp 61-2.

F

Fafertin

VARIANTS: Fafirtin, Fafartin
PERIOD: Byz RATING: - MAP: 68 ITIN: 9a

LOCATION: See directions for *Burjke (Jebel Semaan). Continue 2 km to the south along a good dirt road. Surkunya lies over the rise to west.
Note: 3 km walk south are the ruins of Batuta.

A Kurdish village largely devoid of charm, built on a shelf underneath a crest and overlooking a valley which descends to the east. The chief point of interest is the remains of the oldest dated basilica church in Syria. What is left is meagre, however, consisting only of the stubs of the columned aisle. terminating in the intact semi-dome of the apse. The building is dated by inscription to 372, making it also one of the oldest churches surviving anywhere. A *bema* was once located in the centre of the main nave.

If you walk up the hill to the right immediately before reaching Fafertin you will come after 400 m to the ruins of Surkunya. In the centre lie the remains of a small single-naved church of the fourth century. 200 m south is another single-naved church whose rectangular apse still preserves its sloping stone roof. The chancel is formed by a single but elegant arch. The external window frames carry the drooping decoration typical of the period. Underground burial chambers and remains of villas lie scattered about.

REFS: **Fafertin**: Butler *EC* pp 33-4; Butler *PE* II/B/6 pp 327-9; Tchalenko *Villages* II pl CXXVIII; *Tchalenko and Baccache* pl 80-96.
Surkunya: Butler *PE* II/B/6 p 326.
Batuta: Butler *PE* II/B p 330; Tchalenko *Villages* II pl CXXVIII.

H

Halebiye (Plate 10b)

VARIANTS: Birtha (Grk/Lat); Zenobia(Lat)
PERIOD: Rom/Byz RATING: ** MAP: *30*, 72, 73
ITIN: 12a

LOCATION: On the right bank of the Mid Euphrates, 100 km south of Raqqa or 66 km north of Deir al-Zor. From Deir al-Zor, take the Raqqa/Aleppo highway north as far asTibne (46 km). +12 km north of Tibne, turn right at sign-posted intersection and follow sealed road north west +8 km.

'the strangler'), allowing river traffic to be more readily supervised. When the Romans responded to Zenobia's rebellion by occupying the Palmyrene domains in 273, they took Halebiye (which had been named after the Palmyrene Queen). Diocletian may have rebuilt the fortifications as part of his defences of the *limes* from Palmyra north and a further rebuilding in the reign of Anastasias (491-518) is probable.

The great consolidation of the site, however, dates to the reign of the Byzantine Emperor Justinian (r 527-65) as part of his pursuit of a forward defence policy on all the Empire's frontiers, including through the recovery of North Africa and Italy. In Syria, he put considerable store by retaining control of a region which had become an important centre of Christianity and securing it against the Persian threat. His general Belisarius carried out several important campaigns in Syria during the early years of his reign and the series of fixed fortifications were intended to secure the gains the army had made. Halebiye (probably re-fortified after 650) along with the earlier fortification of the pilgrimage city of *Resafe were the most conspicuous results of this policy.

Halebiye was one of the most formidable Byzantine fortifications in Syria, the culmination of Justinian's ambitious policy of securing the frontier of the Later Roman Empire on the Euphrates. Time has disturbed the fortifications only cursorily and what is left makes a singular impression. The site is particularly splendid at sunset when the shadows fall across the stark hills and the sun strikes a warmer luminiscence in the stone.

History

Though what you now see is basically Byzantine construction of the sixth century, Halebiye was first fortified during the apogée of the Palmyrene control in the area, in the mid third century. The choice of this site probably reflected the fact that the river at this point runs confined between substantial hills (known locally as al-Khanuqa,

Such a bold project seems to show the hand of a master builder in its design. Procopius cites two architects as responsible, one being the nephew of Isidorus of Miletus, the architect who rebuilt the dome of Hagia Sophia in 532-7 after the original had collapsed.

In fact, Justinian's grand strategy was eventually a failure. The fixed defences, undermanned, could do little but survey the contraband traffic. Certainly the effort involved in their construction and mistakes in eastern policy of the subsequent Emperors (Maurice, r 582-602, excepted) helped to drain resources and encourage local disaffection in the crucial decades before the Arab conquest swept past these purely symbolic monuments to Byzantine glory.

The Arabs used the great fortification from time to time but on the whole, the sealing of the Euphrates frontier was no longer the preoccupation it had been to Rome and Byzantium; indeed quite the opposite, given the Arab interest in opening up contact between Syria and Mesopotamia. The great fortress was thus largely left to decay. The lack of significant population in the area meant that the stone of the defensive walls was not carried away for other buildings, the main deterioration resulting from earthquake damage.

The scale of the fortifications is remarkable, especially given the remoteness of the site and the paucity of settled population centres. The blocks were of huge dimensions and little effort was spared to tame the irregularities of the terrain. The stretch of wall along the river was partly designed to contain the river's floods but has been badly eroded over the centuries. On the other two sides, the walls converge from two points along the river towards a focal point on the citadel. The resulting triangular shape has survived well due to the quality of the stone and the care taken to secure firm footings.

Visit

The fortifications originally contained a small **garrison city** with the usual range of amenities within the 12 ha walled area. In times of peace, access was relatively open with three gates along the 385 m river frontage and one large one on each of the north and south sides (350 m and 550 m respectively) where the main routes entered the city. They were joined by the main north/south street which was met at its central point by an east/west axis, probably colonnaded. The remains of most of the buildings within the walls are largely foundation courses only and are hard to distinguish. The baths lay a little to the north east of the crossing point while the forum was to the north of the east/west axis. Two churches can be traced: one to the north of the east/west axis, a little west of the forum, dates from Justinian's time; the other, the smaller one to the south east, is earlier.

It is the **walls** themselves, built of a flinty-grey gypsum which provide the main interest. You may wish to trace them by beginning with the gate on the north side of the site. Heading towards the apex on the hill, you pass four of the massive square bastions - more or less identical in design - which date from Justinian's time. They were an attempt to outdo the scale of earlier Roman examples. From their two-storeyed strongholds, archers could fire arrows at those trying to assault the walls. The towers are inter-connected by a series of internal

corridors running on the city side of the walls and by staircases giving access from the bastions. You will soon come to a point in the wall where the bastion shape is considerably extended to contain a three-storeyed building, the *praetorium* for the housing of the troops also dating from Justinian's reign. Much of the groin vaulting in gypsum and brick that supported this massive construction remains.

Continuing up the slope from the inside of the fortress, a steep climb will bring you to the **citadel**. Much of this has been modified by Arab occupiers who made use of the fortress for a time because of the mastery it gave of movement on the Mid Euphrates. The keep commands all approaches to the fortress including from the desert via the Wadi Bishri to the rear.

You can descend by the longer south **wall** to the river. Here the construction may have been undertaken somewhat earlier. The bastion towers (ten excluding the south gate itself) use the same design as the northern examples.

To the north of the city, about 1 km along the dirt track along the river, you can see remains of three **funerary towers** and rock-cut tombs of the late Roman period.

REFS: *BG* pp 485-6; Lauffray *Halabiyya*; *idem* 'Halebiye' in *Contribution*; Procopius II, viii.

Hama

VARIANTS: Hamath (IrA); Epiphania (Grk, Lat); Emath (Byz)
PERIOD: var/Arb RATING: * MAP: *31*, 65
ITIN: 4

LOCATION: 47 km north of *Homs (226 km from Damascus).

In the past, Hama enjoyed a reputation as one of the more charming of the Syrian towns, more successful than most in making of its environment a pleasant and picturesque setting through the use of the Orontes (Arb: *al-`Assi*[87]) as the city's lungs and cooling device. Some of that changed after the events of 1982 which destroyed or damaged large parts of the city including some of its most treasured buildings. Yet the tensions brought out in these

---

[87] It is ironic that the Arabic name for the river is taken from the first name given by the Greeks, Axios, after a river in Macedonia. The Greeks later conferred the name Orontes which has taken hold in the classical and later English, traditions. (Frézouls 'La Toponomie de l'Orient Syrien et l'apport des élements macedoniens' in *La Toponomie antique* Strasbourg 1977 p 239.)

events had long existed under Hama's tranquil surface. The 1932 *Guide Bleu* observed that while Hama was 'at the same time the most picturesque and the least touched by the West' of the towns of northern Syria, it was a 'very enclosed town, unforthcoming to strangers, whose inhabitants border on the fanatic'.

Constant settlement has effaced much of the remains of previous occupation and virtually nothing survives of Hama during the Bronze and Iron Age, or during the Seleucid, Roman, Byzantine and early Arab empires. The citadel hill which you will find to the north west of the centre of the city (today a park crowns the

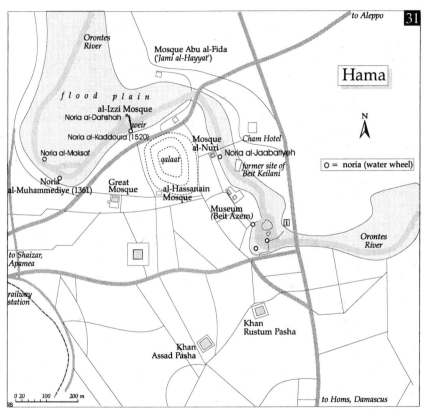

The town is now in the process of reconstruction with a large part of the old city being replaced by a new development. A visit could be combined with a meal by the river banks watching some of the enormous wooden water wheels (*norias*) creak with the flow of the Orontes. Even on the hottest day, the slow grinding of the *norias*, the splash of the water and the drifts of spray suggest some of the refreshing environment that this town traditionally drew from its river location.

History

summit) has been exhaustively researched over the years, particularly by a Danish expedition. Traces have been found of all periods as far back as the neolithic, including the 11th century BC when Hama was the centre of the small Syro-Hittite or Aramean kingdom of Hamath. Some of the evidence is now on display in the museum.

For a while, Hamath was obliged to pay tribute to the Israelite kingdom under Solomon but recovered full independence in the ninth century and joined the federation led by Damascus. The city was destroyed by the

Assyrians in 720 and, like the rest of Syria, came under Assyrian and Persian rule. The Seleucids established a presence after 200 BC and renamed the city Epiphania after one of their foremost rulers, Antiochos IV Epiphanes (r 175-64 BC). It remained a centre of Roman and Byzantine administration, falling to the Arabs by capitulation in 636-7. The city, being on the interface between northern and southern Syria, was often contested by rivals dynasties in Damascus and Aleppo, especially in the troubled 11th and 12th centuries. The Ayyubid period was particularly prosperous and saw the construction of the first of the existing *norias*, reconditioned and supplemented in the Mameluke and Ottoman periods. A period of decline began in the late 16th century and from the 18th century, Hama was under the control of Damascus in an effort to maximise the returns from the pilgrimage - hence the strong link between the two towns through the Azem family.

Visit

You will find a good sample of the town's 17 *norias* in the centre of town, around the little park in front of the Governor's office. A walk around the banks of the river to the west will take you past a number of others. The great wheels, up to 20 m in diameter, were designed to raise water from the Orontes. The river's flow is channelled by a dam into a sluice which drives the wheel. This raises the wheel's wooden box devices that trap water and discharge it at the top of its rotation into towers at the side. From the towers, the water flowed through stone aqueducts into the town or surrounding agricultural areas, each consumer being allocated a portion of the flow over a period of time. Hama and its region specialised in these devices (first developed as far back as the Byzantine period) to overcome the depth of the river banks in this area which required elaborate means of raising the water to a height where it could be used. The largest example of this central group (west bank of the Orontes) is known as al-Mamuriye and dates from 1453.

Your tour will later take you to the northern end of the citadel from where you can continue downstream to a further grouping of *norias*. The largest of all is located 250 m west of the citadel and is known popularly as al-Muhammediye. It dates back to the 14th century (inscription on the aqueduct) and has been restored since 1977. About 1 km in the other direction from the central park (to the east) is another cluster of *norias* which you can take in at your leisure from a group of outdoor restaurants.

The **museum** (in the quarter a little north of the central concentration of *norias* on the left bank of the river) is housed in the Hama Beit Azem (Azem Palace), the 18th century mansion of a former *wali* (governor) of Hama, Assaad Pasha al-Azem (1705-57 - *wali* of Sidon, of Hama pre-1742 and of Damascus 1743-57)[88]. Damage caused by the 1982 events required extensive reconstruction of the upper levels on the river side (the room with the cupola was particularly badly hit) but the singular charm of what must be one of the loveliest Ottoman residential buildings in Syria remains, especially the *haremlek* (area right of the entrance). The collection of objects is displayed in a number of rooms in addition to the Roman and Christian remains found in the lower courtyard. An annexe to the north houses the palace baths and beyond that the public reception area (*selamlek*) with an almost Italian upper *loggia*. (Upper rooms badly charred.)

Particularly worthy of note in the room off the river side of the lower courtyard is the mosaic transferred from a house excavated in the village of Mariamin (west of Homs, on the edge of the Jebel Ansariye). The work is from the last quarter of the fourth century AD and measures 5.37 m by 4.25 m. It depicts a group of female musicians and has been described by Janine Balty[89] as 'one of the most significant finds of recent years, as much for the quality of its execution as for the originality of its subject'. It is a rare example of a work devoted to a domestic rather than an allegorical or mythic theme and was presumably chosen to decorate a dining room or *triclinium*. Six women perform on various instruments while two infants (dressed as Eros) work the bellows. The woman second from the left plays the organ while others play the flute, lyre (or zither), castanets and six metal bowls placed on the central table. The ensemble is conducted, it would appear, by the woman on the far left holding the cymbals. The mosaic sheds a unique light on musical instruments used at the time. The organ, in particular, is the clearest evidence we have of how this instrument was employed in antiquity.

100 m north of the Beit Azem, the **Mosque al-Nuri** stands on a square where a small bridge crosses the Orontes. The mosque was completed in 1163 by Nur al-Din following the severe earthquake of 1157. The admirable minaret, banded with black basalt and yellow limestone, is original. The *minbar* within (12th

---

[88] In Damascus he built the even more splendid Azem Palace located in the central *suq* - see *Damascus - Khans. For a list of the Azem Governors, see footnote under *Damascus – Khans.
[89] Balty, Janine *Mosaiques* p 94.

century), a gift of Nur al-Din, is worth noting. The Beit Keilani (another 18th century palace) once stood on the opposite bank south of the Cham Hotel.

There are some other mosques worth noting in this area. Follow the road that runs east of the *qalaat* until it meets a modern bridge approach. On the north side is the **Mosque al-Izzi**, a small Mameluke building of the 15th century. Cross the small bridge left of the modern one and ascend by the road to the left. On the left is the **Mosque and Mausoleum of Abu al-Feda**, the noted Arab historian and poet (d 1331) who was appointed Emir of Hama under the Mamelukes (c1320). The building is sometimes given the popular name, *al-Hayyat* ("Serpents' Mosque') on account of the interlaced stonework around the windows of the courtyard.

The **al-Hasanain Mosque** stands at the south west corner of the *qalaat*, not far from the road to the summit. An earlier mosque on this spot fell in the great earthquake of 1157. Nur al-Din had it rebuilt in its present form. 100 m west of here stands the **Great Mosque of Hama**. An almost total ruin after the 1982 bombardment, it has been superbly reconstructed by the Antiquities Department in its earlier form. An Umayyad foundation, it incorporates elements of a pagan temple and Christian church though much of the earlier structure was destroyed during the Byzantine re-occupation of northern Syria in 968. The original basilica plan is reflected in the three aisles of the prayer hall topped by five domes in the shape of a cross. The courtyard (north) is surrounded by vaulted porticos and contains an elevated treasury (cf *Kubbet al-Khazneh* in *Damascus - Umayyad Mosque). There are two minarets - one, east of the prayer room, has an inscription of 1153; the other, near the north doorway, is Mameluke.

In the commercial centre of the town, to the south of the *muhafez's* office, two **Ottoman khans** can be seen. The 1556 Khan Rustum Pasha is currently being restored by the Ministry of Tourism - large courtyard; vaulted arcades on four sides; central mosque. The huge facade of the Khan Assaad Pasha (1738), 300 m on the right along the road heading south west, now houses a technical school.

REFS: *BG* pp 365-9; Dussaud *Topographie* pp 233-44; Nour pp 316-325; Sourdel *Hamath* pp 119-21; van Berchem & Fatio pp 173-77.

Haran al-Awamid

VARIANTS:
PERIOD: Rom RATING: - MAP: 64 ITIN: 3a

LOCATION: Town on the eastern edge of the Ghouta. It can be reached directly from Damascus (exit via the glass factory road), via the airport road (via Hejaneh then north) or from *Dumeir.

From Dumeir, proceed as follows: from the Damascus side of the town, take the road going directly south for c+20 km; turn left for +2 km; turn right and continue for c+5 km. This brings you to the town of Haran al-Awamid ('Village of Columns').

A largely mud-brick Ghouta town with two items of interest - a mosque which is clearly a pastiche of many centuries (it uses Roman columns and seems to be based on a Roman basilica plan) and an incongruous group of three tall basalt Roman/Nabatean columns nowadays stranded in a domestic courtyard.

Butler says that the column remains are 'structurally and artistically closely allied to the buildings of (the Hauran)'. The columns belonged to a temple which stood on a high podium preceded by a columned vestibule. The capitals are of the Ionic order, similar to the style found in the colonnades of Philippopolis (*Shahba - mid third century). No clue has been found as to the temple's dedication but Weber speculates it may have been a centre for the worship of the gods who assured the fertility of the Ghouta oasis.

REFS: Butler *AE* pp 398-9; Dussaud *Topographie* p 303; Weber 'Haran al-Awamid'.

Harbaqa Dam (Plate 11a)

VARIANTS: Kharbaqah
PERIOD: Rom RATING: * MAP: 75

LOCATION: From Damascus, take the Palmyra road (turnoff 24 km north on Damascus/Homs motorway). At the point (+130 km) where it joins the road coming from Homs, take the Homs road for +10 km, heading north west. At this point, take left V fork along a faint track curving around a low line of hills. Follow track for c+1.5 km down the *wadi* to the north, skirting the swampy remains of the now-silted lake.

This massive project dates from the Roman period (probably first century AD), though its offtake was improved and adapted during Byzantine and Arab times. The survival of the dam wall is remarkable evidence of the solidity of Roman construction techniques. Virtually the whole wall is intact - 20 m high, 18 m thick at the base, 345 m long and constructed of a solid stone skin with rubble fill. The lake behind has largely silted up with centuries of accumulated sand.

It is difficult to discern the traces of the canal system which took the water away towards the north but evidence is said to lie near the course of the river downstream. The water was channelled to irrigate the area around *Qasr al-Heir al-Gharbi. The irrigation offtake was considerably changed during Umayyad times to improve the water supply to the gardens of the Qasr.

REFS: BG p 323; Calvet & Geyer 1992 pp 79-92; Kennedy and Riley pp 79-80; Schlumberger *Qasr el-Heir el-Gharbi* Paris 1986.

Harim

VARIANTS: Castrum Harench, Harrem (Cru)
PERIOD: Arb RATING: * MAP: 32, 69 ITIN: 9b

LOCATION: Just before Bab el-Hawa (Syrian-Turkish main frontier post, about 40 km west of Aleppo) turn left at the main intersection then immediately right through the village of Sarmada and follow the main road for 20 km until it brings you to Harim.

Harim is today a small provincial town, Sunni in population, almost on the Turkish frontier, overlooking the rich Plain of Amuq to the east of Antioch. The houses are a little more colourful than most villages in northern Syria, the locals having a preference for the application of blue paint to bare concrete. The town dates back at least to late Byzantine times but its main asset is a rather dilapidated 12th century Ayyubid fortress that dominates the centre of the town from an artificial mound.

Its strategic importance resulted from its control of the main route between Aleppo and Antioch (it protected the eastern approaches to the important Orontes crossing at Iron Bridge, *Jisr al-Hadid*, 20 km west-north west of Harim) as well as the route which branched off to the south to Jisr al-Shugur and the Orontes Valley. The modern road from Antioch to Aleppo runs about 5 km to the north on a more direct route across the Amuq Plain but Harim marks the southern limit of the corridor between these two major centres. Harim was occupied by the

Byzantines in 959 during Emperor Nicephorus II Phocas' campaign to regain control of the deep hinterland of Antioch. The Byzantine castle which Nicephorus established fell in 1084 to the Arab, Suleiman Ben Qutulmish who seized Antioch in the same year. Shortly afterwards, in 1086, the Seljuq Turks took control.

When the Crusaders arrived in the area it took them a nine month seige to capture Antioch in 1098. Harim threatened the rear of their beseiging forces and was taken first in November 1097. It was retaken by the Muslim coalition in February 1098 but was abandoned to the Christians before the fall of Antioch (June 1098). It was subsequently held by the Crusaders for over half a century as part of the outer defences of Antioch. In 1119, Crusader

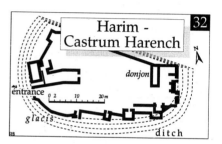

Harim - Castrum Harench [32]
donjon
entrance
glacis
ditch

forces under Roger, Prince of Antioch, suffered a serious defeat at the nearby battlefield later termed *Ager Sanguinis*[90] at the hands of the Muslim forces of Aleppo.

Nur al-Din took Harim twice, first in 1149. It was recaptured by the Crusaders in February 1158 after a two month seige mounted by a coalition headed by Baldwin III, King of Jerusalem which included the then Prince of Antioch, the odious Renaud de Châtillon. (Deschamps points out that this was the last major assault mounted by Crusader forces to the east of the Orontes.) In 1164 Harim fell again to Nur al-Din during the first concerted Arab attempt to dislodge the Crusaders from their inland positions. Nur al-Din broke off the seige when threatened by a coalition of Crusader forces (Prince Bohemond III of Antioch, Count Raymond III of Tripoli, Hugh of Lusignan and the Byzantine, Constantine Coloman). He drew the Christian forces into battle on 10 August on the Plain of Artah. The Christians suffered a

---

[90] 'Field of Blood'. The actual location is a little east of the village of Sarmada, not far from the turn-off from the Bab el-Hawa road (see directions above).

disastrous defeat and the four leaders were taken into captivity in Aleppo[91].

Harim remained in Arab hands right up to the fall of Christian Antioch a century later (1268), a thorn in the side of the Crusader presence in the rich Plain of Amuq below. Just as full Muslim control of the area was restored, however, the Mongol invasions of the late 13th century resulted in the destruction of much of northern Syria, including the Harim fortress. The fortress was restored and re-used for a time by the Arabs but before long fell into neglect.

The present fortress dates from the long period of Arab confrontation against the Crusaders (1164-1268). The Crusader castle was rebuilt by the Ayyubid Governor of Aleppo (and son of Salah ed-Din), al-Malik al-Zaher Ghazi, in the year 1199, according to the Arabic inscription over the entrance gate. The existing mound was pared away to give the truncated cone shape. The sides were covered with a glacis consisting of slabs of smooth stone to deny purchase to assailants. (Only a fragment remains, near the main approach from the south west quarter but the technique is comparable to that of the Aleppo citadel.) The glacis is broken on the north by the natural rock escarpment which was defence enough. The whole was then surrounded by a moat (again, like Aleppo) of which the outline can be seen in part today.

The poor state of preservation of the Harim fortress robs it of its impact as a good example, on a relatively small scale, of Arab military architecture of the period, before the degeneration evident in the hastier work of the Mamelukes and early Ottomans. You approach the castle from the south west up a steep climb, entering through an entrance gateway defended by two salients. The basic shape of the castle is semi-circular with the straight wall on the north. On the side opposite the entry, the only substantial ruins are the remains of the north eastern keep, also the work of Ghazi, placed at this point to strengthen the defences against attack from the facing hillside.

REFS: van Berchem and Fatio pp 229 ff; *BG* pp 408-9; Deschamps *Châteaux - III* p 341; Dussaud *Topographie* pp 191 ff; Lawrence p 57; Pena et al 'Inventaire du Jebel al-A'la' pp 203-12.

Homs

VARIANTS: Emesa (Lat); Hims (Arb)
PERIOD: var   ALT: 400 m   RATING: -   MAPS: *33, 65*   ITIN: 4

LOCATION: 165 km north of Damascus.

Homs is strategically placed at the intersection of the natural north/south corridor and the access route from the Syrian desert to the coast through the break in the coastal mountain chains known as the Homs Gap. (The gap lies between the Lebanon range to the south and the Jebel Ansariye range in Syria to the north). Homs' siting is also determined by the Orontes River which flows through the city. Today it is a key point in the Syrian road and rail networks and the base for several major industries.

Though its siting has placed it across many of the major currents of Syrian history, little of that past has survived in what is today a rather drab city[92]. The French historian, Seyrig, wrote in a 1959 study that 'the history of Emesa amounts to no more than a long career of obscurity from the middle of which emerges three centuries of remarkable opulence'. Even that period of prominence in Roman times yields few remains. Beyond some columns in the central mosque, the Roman era in Homs has left no witness to the fact that one of the major imperial dynasties had its origins here. The continuous historic role of the city has meant that its fabric has constantly been redeveloped and renewed, a more effective method of obliterating the past than earthquakes and war.

History

Homs' prosperity, based on the irrigated plain fed by the Homs dam, was probably more enduring than Seyrig argued. The existence of a *tell* in the centre of Homs attests to the antiquity of the city going back well before Roman times. It was, however, overshadowed in the pre-Roman period by larger centres in the region, including Qatna (Mishrifeh), Arethusa (al-Rastan) and Qadesh (the classical Laodicea ad Libanum and present *Tell Nebi Mend). After 145 BC, it became the base for the Arab dynasty of the Samsigeramos, one of several pretenders to the crumbling remains of the Greek kingdom. Augustus in 20 BC restored the brother of the

---

[91] See *Qalat Areimeh for the story of the capture of Raymond III of Tripoli during this battle and its consequences.

[92] Nothing has improved in this respect since the *Blue Guide* (*Middle East*) of 1965 languidly recorded (p 343): *Homs offers nothing of very special interest... . You quickly get tired of the depressing streets and the monuments are almost all uninteresting.*

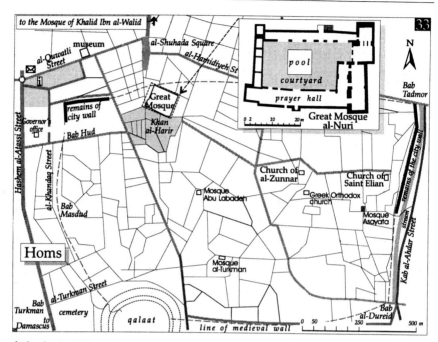

Great Mosque
al-Nuri

Arab ruler, Iamblichos, who had been executed by Antony in 31 BC and the principality was one of the last to be incorporated into the province of Syria (AD 78). The territory of Homs (Latin: Emesa) remained hemmed in by its traditional urban rivals. However, to the east, Emesan influence seems to have extended far into the desert. Control of the desert tribes became crucial to the city's fortunes in the first three centuries of Roman rule[93]. Its destiny marched closely with that of Palmyra with which it enjoyed close ties (witness the number of references to the leading family of Emesa on third century Palmyrene monuments). As long as Palmyra helped to control the security of the central desert and keep the tribes in check, the caravan route based on Homs was viable. Once the desert became unsafe, the caravans by-passed it, preferring the safer reaches of the traditional northern route via the upper Euphrates and Aleppo.

Emesa first claim to wider fame was its connections with the Severan dynasty, the ruling family of early third century Rome. Julia Domna, a daughter of the High Priest of Emesa, married Septimius Severus, the future Emperor (r 193-211) around AD 187 following a period in which he was stationed in Syria as a commander of the IV Scythica Legion[94]. She was described by Gibbon as deserving 'all that the stars could promise her'. She possessed 'the attractions of beauty, and united to a lively imagination a firmness of mind, and strength of judgement, seldom bestowed on her sex'. Following Septimius' coup of 193, Julia Domna became a central personality in the new dynasty's fortunes. Four of her offspring (or those of her sister, Julia Maesa) and their descendants went on to become Emperors - Caracalla (r 211-7); Geta (co-Emperor with Caracalla in 211); Marcus Antoninus (Elagabalus - r 218-22); and Alexander Severus (r 222-35).

The most notorious of the line was Elagabalus, proclaimed as Emperor at the age of 14 by the III Gallica legion based at Raphanea, in the Orontes Valley west of Emesa. His nickname derived from the Baal deity whose emblem, the black stone from the sun temple in

---

[93] The desert Arabs provided the corps of mounted archers (the *Hemeseni*) much prized by the Roman army.

[94] Recalling stories of a woman in Syria whose horoscope predicted she would be married to a king, Septimius contracted to marry her by correspondence from Lyons following the death of his first wife. Birley *Septimius Severus - The African Emperor* New York 1972 pp 123-4.

Emesa, was transferred to the Temple of Vesta in Rome as the basis of a new solar cult. He rapidly declined into insanity, his reign dissolving into four years of chaos and depravity. He was murdered by the praetorian guard; the stone was sent back to Emesa where the sun cult continued at least until the end of the fifth century. (Aurelian took time off from his campaign against Zenobia to visit the Emesa temple and secure the sun god's support for his victory.)[95]

Homs became an important centre after the Arab conquest, rather more fervent and puritanical in its attachment to Islam than the Umayyad court at Damascus. (500 of the Prophet's companions were said to have been settled there.) It later avoided attack by the Crusaders in spite of their strong presence at the nearby *Krak des Chevaliers. Less prosperous than Hama in the Arab and Ottoman eras, it had fallen into a steep decline by the 18th century. By 1914, it had a population of no more than 5000. Its revival this century reflects its key geographical location.

Visit

It is not suggested you spend too much time attempting to unearth Homs' charms. Begin in the centre of town, the area around Quwatli Street where the tourist information office is located. An unremarkable provincial museum is housed in a building on the north side of Quwatli Street.

The **Great Mosque al-Nuri** is found to the south, off the square which runs to the right from the west end of Quwatli St. A vast rectangular building with an oblong courtyard, oriented east/west, it lies on what was probably the site of the pagan sun temple and the later Church of St John.

East of here lies the quarter in which most of the older churches of Homs are located. 400 m east is the **Church of al-Zunnar** (Church of the Virgin's Belt). The curious name derives from the discovery under the church's altar in 1953 of a textile belt said to have belonged to the Virgin. The belt is believed to have been placed in the first church on this spot in the late fourth century. Most of the present church's structure dates from the last 100 years.

More inherently interesting are some newly revealed frescoes in the **Church of St Elian** (continue east for 200 m). The Church of St Elian is dedicated to the son of a Roman officer from Emesa martyred at the end of the third century for refusing to renounce Christianity. The *martyrium* at the end of the right hand nave is the burial place of St Elian and other saints and houses a remarkable set of mural paintings of the 12th century and earlier which were discovered in 1970. They had been covered by a coating of plaster and thus preserved. The church is still a pilgrimage centre due to the miracles associated with St Elian and its renewed fame has resulted in an expansion and redecoration of the main nave. The modern painted frescoes are devoted to the life of St Elian.

Estimated by some to be as early as the sixth century (and thus the oldest surviving in Syria?), there is no definite information as to their dating. (There is no historical mention of the church itself until the 16th century). Some alcoves were re-painted in the 12th century. The remaining paintings represent:

- Christ in majesty with the Virgin and Mary Magdalene on one side and John the Baptist and one other (St Elian?) on the other.
- In the side niches, St Luke, St John (left); St Mark, St Matthew (right).
- Medallions of the prophets and apostles.

The walls of the city and its seven gates were largely demolished in the Ottoman period. Remains of two of the gates survive in Bab al-Masdud (west) and Bab Tadmor (north east). Only a few glimpses of the old walls survive, the most accessible being the short stretch exposed by recent re-development two streets south of Quwatli Street. The remains of the citadel of Homs can be seen on the mound which marks the south west corner of the old city.

The **Mosque of Khalid Ibn al-Walid** stands, set back to the right in a park, 500 m north of Quwatli Street on the road north to Hama. The mosque, completely rebuilt in the late Turkish period (1908-13), is on a site dating back to Ayyubid times and contains (right) the reputed tomb of one of the early followers of Muhammed, Khalid Ibn al-Walid, whose military campaigns in Syria led to the Islamic conquest. He died in 642 his exploits having been eclipsed by his sworn enemy, the Caliph Umar.

18 kms north east of Homs on the road to Selemiya is the bronze age site of Qatna

---

95 For the sun cult see Seyrig *Culte* p 340. Aurelian gave it new impetus in the late 3C. Attributing his victory over Zenobia to the god's intervention, he built a new temple to *Sol Invictus* in Rome and raised the cult to official status. Elagabulus' temple, the Elagaballium, was located in the NE corner of the Palatine Hill.

(modern name, Mishrifeh). The 100 hectare ruins, originally protected by square ramparts in earth, were excavated by a French expedition in the twenties including remains from the Amorite and Mitannian periods.

REFS: *BG* pp 342-4; du Mesnil du Buisson, Comte 'La basilique chrétienne du quartier Karm al-Arabis à Homs' in *Mélanges* XV 1930-31; Dussaud *Topographie* pp 103-5; Elisséeff *Hims* pp 409-15; Gatier 'Palmyre et Émèse, ou Émèse sans Palmyre' in *AAAS* 1996; *GB* pp 114-7; Sa`ade *St Elian*; Leroy, Jules 'Decouvertes de peintures chrétiennes en Syrie in *AAAS* XXIV 1974; Seyrig *Caractères*.

Husn Suleiman (Plate 11b)

VARIANTS: Baotocecea (Lat); Baotocécé (Fr)
PERIOD: Rom RATING: ** MAP: *34*, 66 ITIN: 5a

LOCATION: Reaching Husn Suleiman can be confusing. The most straightforward access is from *Safita taking the road which heads north. After c500 m (northern edge of town) take the right fork and continue +20 km, then left +3 km for the village of Husn Suleiman (check road by asking as there are a number of possibilities). Pass through the village and then continue to the top of a narrow valley.

It may be more convenient (though a little more difficult to orient oneself) to approach from *Masyaf which lies c30 km north. Leave Masyaf by the road that goes south, turning right just out of town, after an elaborate outdoor restaurant. Keep heading south west (road eventually goes to Dreikish). After c20 km a large television relay mast; Husn Suleiman is just down the valley to the south west of this. Keep going towards Dreikish for c+3km but take small road which leads left precipitately over the saddle into the site (ask for directions as there are no signs).

Husn Suleiman (Suleiman's castle) is one of the most extraordinary set of ruins in Syria. The remains are exceptional for the juxtaposition of the gigantic and the aesthetic: the cyclopean scale of the component blocks set against the tranquility and beauty of the setting in one of the remote stretches of the Jebel Ansariye.

History

A cult centre has existed here for millennia. The first temple was probably constructed under Persian domination when the area known now as the Meshta was settled. The present remains are Roman but occupy the site of a Semitic/Canaanite cult to the local version of Baal whose worship was later merged with the Greek equivalent, Zeus, under the title Zeus Baotocecian. Astarte was also associated with the centre, perhaps because of the spring which

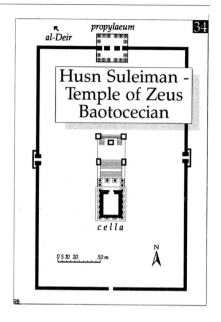

flows through the site. The cult was promoted and flourished during Roman times.

The Roman construction probably began in the first century AD but the greater part of the effort to monumentalise the cult centre took place at the end of the second century, under Severan rule. The Syro-Phoenician cults were still practiced on the site as late as the fourth century, well after the adoption of Christianity as the official religion of the Empire by Constantine. Much of the surrounding countryside belonged to the temple which collected the revenue and enjoyed immunity from taxes.

Visit

The enclosure consists of a large compound (approximately rectangular, c134 m by 85 m) open to the sky with a small central *cella* to house the altar. This is a typical plan for Syro-Phoenician temples (see box on page 18), merging concepts from the Syrian, Roman and Mesopotamian worlds. The same plan is employed in the Bel temple at Palmyra where the scale is much larger. Some of the cyclopean stones used in the compound wall measure up to 10 m in length and over 2.5 m in height. The taste for huge stones seems to have begun in the late first century AD and is paralleled at Baalbek.

There are four gates centrally placed in each face of the outer wall. The *propylaeum* in front of the north gateway is the most elaborate, 15 m wide, with porticos of eight columns on each side of the triple entrance doorway. The outer portico was adorned with two niches, two side entrances and a Syrian-style relieving arch over the elaborate lintel. At both ends of the north wall, the carved figures of lions can be seen. An inscription was added around 255 during the reign of the co-emperors, Valerian and Gallienus, recording their confirmation of the privileges originally granted to the local citizens by the former kings of Syria.

Visit

To the east and west, the doorways practically mirror each other with two *aedicule* (niches) and an elaborately-carved lintel supported by winged victory figures on the sides. On the eastern version, the portrait head of a man can still be distinguished. On the same (east) doorway, there is a Greek inscription dated 171 which records the dedication of the complex by the local people.

All the four gates were adorned with the figures of eagles on the soffits of the lintels, remains of which are still seen in different stages of preservation (the south gateway being practically effaced).

The present grand design was probably never finished, though it is difficult to tell what is what among the jumble of stones that now comprise the remains of the *cella*. This central building took the form of a *pseudo-peripteros*, half columns ranged along each side to simulate the surrounding colonnades seen at Palmyra or the Temple of Jupiter at Baalbek. The entrance (north) is marked by a portico of six free-standing columns preceded by 39 steps divided by a platform. An altar for offerings originally stood on the front of this platform. (A larger altar stood to the east of the *cella*). From inside the *cella*, a narrow staircase rose within the walls from the right near corner as you enter. Amy believes it continued to ascend through the rear and eastern walls, eventually coming out on a roof terrace as in many other temples in the Syrian tradition.

It is difficult to describe exactly the purpose of the second compound (across the tarmac road, north west). Described in some sources as *al-Deir* (the monastery, possibly because it later was used as a Christian monastic building), it has a small temple (two columns, Ionic, between *antae*) in the near corner. The portico of this temple is quite charming, especially the eagle over the lintel. The rest of the compound, however, is largely bare, except for traces (now overgrown) of a Christian basilica north of the temple and the scanty remains of a building on the north side. This may have been a *nymphaeum* (water fountain) housed in an *exedra* preceded by an entrance hall, though there is no trace of a water source.

REFS: Amy *Temples*; *BG* pp 442-3; Klengel *Hosn es-Suleiman* pp 166-70; Krenchker and Zschietzschmann; Rey-Coquais *Arados* pp 213-4; Rostovtzeff *Social* I p 266; Seyrig *Aradus*.

I

Isriya (Plate 12a)

VARIANTS: Seriana (Lat); Esriye (Arb)
PERIOD: Rom RATING: * MAP: 72, 75 ITIN:
11c

LOCATION: Northern reaches of the Syrian Desert.
Take Selemiya exit from Hama. 33 km, Selemiya -
continue to Sabbura (+27 km), Saen (+20 km),
Sheikh Hellal (+23 km) then new sealed road 30 km
to Isriya.

Nothing shows better to what extent
human effort has transformed the Syrian
desert than the beautiful Roman temple
that is to be found here.
[Blue Guide 1966]

The ancient Seriana was once a crossing point
for several Roman routes including that from
Chalcis (*Qinnesrin) to *Palmyra and from
*Resafe to Selemiya, passing through
countryside which was considerably more fertile
than it is today.

This beautiful temple stands alone on the
south of the former citadel promontory, its four
intact walls of mellowed limestone isolated in a
moonscape of scattered, flinty stones. It was
soundly built in solid limestone blocks,
resembling in many ways the techniques used
with the same type of stone in Palmyra. The
pseudo-peripteral temple is oriented to the east
and the walls carry elegant pilasters with capitals
in the Corinthian order. There is little trace of
either the *pronaos* that preceded the *cella* or the
stairs that led up to it. The wide eastern doorway
is richly decorated with a typically Syrian semi-
circular relieving arch above. A staircase
embedded in the masonry to the right of the
doorway ascends to what was once a terrace. A
temenos wall would have surrounded the temple.
The building dates from the early third century,
the style of the doorway bearing the same
elaborate treatment used in contemporary
Baalbek. It seems likely that it was erected by an
imperial offical at an important crossroads of the
Roman road system. Alternatively, but probably
less likely, it was an initiative by local interest
groups concerned to display their 'Roman-ness'.
There is no firm evidence as to the identity of the
god to whom the temple was dedicated but the
German researcher (Gogräfe) has oscillated
between an astral divinity or the local equivalent

of the classical Apollo, Nebo, whose staue was
found nearby. In the Byzantine period, the
settlement was enclosed by walls which
incorporated the temple as a fortified watch
tower. In the Abbasid and Mameluke periods, the
remains served as a way-station on the Sultan's
travels between Damascus and the Jezira.

En route to Selemiya, you may wish to
inspect the striking remains of the Ayyubid fort
on the left of the road 5 km west of Selemiya,
today called Qalaat al-Shmemis (Plate 20a). A
road leads north from the western outskirts of
Selemiya to a point where the castle can be
reached by track or by a 15 minute walk. The
castle is difficult to reach, however, because of
the unstable pebbly slope and what remains
inside the outer shell comprises little but rubble.
The walls rise abruptly from an artificial ditch with
the entrance on the south side, flanked by two
rectangular towers. The fort dates from 1231 and
was built on the flattened top of an extinct
volcanic cone by the Ayyubid Prince of Homs,
Malik al-Mujahid Shirkuh II (r 1186-1240). The
castle was destroyed by the Mongols in 1260 but
restored by Baibars, having been incorporated in
the province of Damascus.

Khanazir

The track which leads north west through Sfire
and on to Aleppo passes after c 56 km another
Roman settlement, Anasarthon (also known as
Kunasara or Anasartha), now marked by the
village of Khanazir. The flat conical mound on
the edge of the village was the site of a citadel
which helped guard the channel between the two
natural bastions of Jebel Hass to the north west
and Jebel Sbeit to the east. Some ancient stones
have been re-employed in the village when it was
settled by Circassians at the turn of the century.
The fort was probably set up as part of the
Roman reorganisation of the area in the third
century which also saw the establishment of the
Strata Diocletiana running further to the east
(*Resafe/Palmyra/Damascus). In the Christian
era, the town was sufficiently important to rate
six churches, one dedicated in 426 to St
Thomas.

There are many other sites in this region to
the east of Khanazir but they are largely of
specialised interest, including:

- **Zebed** (20 km east of Khanazir, citadel and two large basilicas - one (possibly fourth century) was built largely in mud brick; the second with some walls in dark basalt still standing);
- **Muallak** (12 km north east of Khanazir, three churches, one dated 606/7).

REFS: **Isriya** - *BG*   p 418: Butler *PE* II/B/ p 76; Gogräfe 'Isriye-Seriana' in *Catalogue 1996*; *idem* 'Die Datierung des Tempels von Isriye' in *DaM* 7 1993; *idem* 'The Temple of Seriane-Esriye' in *AAAS* 1996; Dussaud *Topographie* p 273; *GB* p 161; Mouterde and Poidebard pp 89-91; Mouterde and Poidebard 'Le `Limes' de Chalcis et la route d'Antioche à Palmyre' in *Melanges de l'Université Saint Joseph* XXII 1939 pp 59-69; Musil *Palmyrena* pp 55 ff; **Selemiye** - van Berchem & Fatio pp 167-170; **Qalaat Shmemis** - van Berchem & Fatio pp 171-3.

J

Jebel Seis (Plate 12b)

VARIANTS: Mons Jovis (??Lat); Jebel Sis, Says (Arb)
PERIOD: Arb (Umd) RATING: - MAP: 75 ITIN: 14

> LOCATION: Jebel Seis is 100 kms E-SE of Damascus as the crow flies but a slightly round-about route is recommended. Take the Palmyra road around Dumeir. 50 kms east of Dumeir, take the old road east to Baghdad instead of turning left to Palmyra. You will come after 5 kms to the well and ruins of Khirbet Butmiyat. Follow the general line of tracks heading immediately SE and continue in the direction of Tell Sedriseh (c 28 kms). From there head south, keeping the lava wilderness, Dirat al-Tilul, on the right for c 30 kms until Jebel Seis appears on the horizon.

This Umayyad castle was built on the slopes of the crater of an extinct volcano on the edge of the volcanic wilderness (the Safa) that briefly acquires a patina of vegetation during the spring. The crater is 500 m broad by 2 km long with steep sides covered in dark lava and scoria, a scene described by Sauvaget as 'a truly nightmare vision'. A small spring provides a precarious source of water, sufficient to attract small-scale settlement. Sauvaget, partly on literary evidence, attributes all the buildings to the reign of al-Walid I (r 705-15), the builder of the Umayyad Mosque in Damascus.

The ruins of the Umayyad settlement fall into two groups, both on the south side of the crater - the castle and ancillary buildings, a little beyond the slopes of the cone; a little to the north on the slopes themselves, a group of houses.

The most important building is the **castle**, built, like other Umayyad desert lodges, in the square design borrowed from Roman military encampments. The walls (66 m square; 2 m thick) are strengthened by eight cylindrical or semi-cylindrical towers. Originally the lower courses of stone were augmented by an upper level of mud brick which has since crumbled. Inside, the plan of the living quarters is concealed by the debris of centuries. The sole entry was through the door in the centre of the northern side, the entrance being cut through the semi-cylindrical tower. Only this entrance area was finished to its full height in stone. The central courtyard (31 m by 31 m) was surrounded by porticos leading to double rows of rooms. Other buildings in this lower grouping include the mosque (70 m to the west, divided by a double arch, small niche in its south face) and the baths (150 m to the east of the *qasr*, originally a large tunnel-vaulted hall (10 m by 4.4 m) with a semi-circular exedra).

A smaller fortified castle or large house lies in the second cluster of ruins on the slopes to the north.

Aerial photography in the twenties revealed a Roman road leading to the site, continuing on a further 48 km west to Habra Merfiye al-Smeyr. There is, however, no evidence of Roman remains at Jebel Seis, making the possible identification with Mons Jovis noted above unlikely.

REFS: *BG* p 517; Creswell *Early Muslim* pp 472-7; Kennedy and Riley pp 79-80; Poidebard *Trace* pp 63-4; Sauvaget 'Ruines omeyyades' *Syria* 1939; Sauvaget 'Châteaux umayyades' *Revue des études islamiques* 1967.

Jeble

VARIANTS: Gabala, Jabala (anc); Gabula (Lat); Zibel, Gebel, Gibel (Cru)
PERIOD: Rom RATING: * MAP: 67 ITIN: 6

> LOCATION: Turn-off 25 km south of *Latakia on the motorway to *Tartus. Theatre is in the centre of the town, near the sea and the main *suq* area.

History

Jeble has served as a small port from the Phoenician period to the present, its fortunes a barometer of prevailing trends. It is mentioned in Assyrian records as part of the Assyrian Empire but received a Greek colony (probably eighth century BC). It formed part of the confederation of Phoenician states controlled by *Arwad in the Persian and Seleucid periods. Nominally controlled by the Seleucids, it was overlooked in favour of Latakia. Pompey's conquest brought it under Roman control (64 BC). It was important enough in the early Christian period to serve as the seat of a bishop but passed from the Byzantines to the Arabs in 638.

The Crusaders, under Raymond, Count of Toulouse forced the local Muslim *qadi* (Fakhr al-Mulk Ibn Ahmar) to pay tribute in 1098, shortly after the fall of Antioch. The *qadi* spent the next decade trying to find an effective protector among the Muslim leaders of the area (Tripoli and Damascus) but in 1109, Jeble was incorporated by Tancred into the Principality of Antioch and renamed Zibel. The Roman theatre was turned into a Crusader castle.

The town rated its own duke and bishop by the mid 12th century. Saladin re-conquered it for the Arabs during his extraordinary sweep up the coast in 1188, shortly after the Battle of Hattin but his successors abandoned it (as they did many of his re-conquests) and the Crusaders moved back in. The Hospitallers took control but their command was disputed by the Templars. The Mameluke Sultan Qalaun resolved the squabble by taking it by assault in 1285, shortly after his great victory at Marqab which saw the final defeat of the crusading forces on the Syrian littoral. It subsequently passed into less tumultuous obscurity though it became a centre of trade and religious pilgrimage for the Jebel Ansariye.

While Jeble has played a role in just about every phase of Syrian history, the only substantial remains the past has left it is a small Roman theatre. Much of the *scaenae frons* and the upper structure lie around in ruins between the weeds and flowers but the first eleven rows of seats of this free-standing building have survived, along with the greater part of the next twelve rows and a fragment of the third tier, the whole sustained by the solid network of support piers and arches underneath. In its present state, the theatre gives little indication of its original seating capacity, probably totalling 7,000. The free-standing semi-circle of 90 m diameter is oriented to the north east.

Also worth noting is the mosque at the centre of the town which houses the tomb of a local Muslim saint, Sidi Ibrahim Ben Adham (d 778). The mosque has been much restored but stands on the site of a church constructed by the Byzantine Emperor Heraclius (r 610-641) whose last-ditch effort to recover Syria from the Persians was foiled by the unexpected new threat, from the Arabs.

REFS: *BG* pp 455-6; Dussaud *Topographie* p 136; Rey-Coquais *Arados* pp 214-5.

Jeradeh

VARIANTS: Gerade, Djeradeh
PERIOD: Byz RATING: * MAP: 70 ITIN: 9c

LOCATION: 2 km south east of *Ruweiha; or turn off the *Maarat al-Numan/Saraqeb road 4 km north of Maarat.

These picturesque ruins on the outskirts of a modern village are worth a visit of an hour or so. The most interesting of the remains is the six-storey watch tower (fifth or sixth century - with latrine arrangements gracing the exterior), one of the best surviving examples in the area even if the use made of these structures (religious, security) is not clear. Pena says that Jeradeh was once surrounded by walls, unusually for villages of this period, and speculates that 'the inhabitants must have feared the ravages of the desert'. Tchalenko notes that the villages on the east edge of the limestone country were more open to incursions by nomads from the desert. Notice the lintel which carries the Roman or Byzantine imperial escutcheon.

The sole church dates from the fifth century. The central nave is divided from the side aisles by five columns. A *bema* was located in the middle of the nave. Remains of a tower can be seen at the north end of the narthex.

REFS: Butler *AE* pp 128-9; Butler *EC* p 66; Mattern p 16; Pena *et al Reclus* pp 273-6; Tchalenko *Villages* I pp 30-1; Tchalenko and Baccache pl 481-96.

Jisr al-Shugur

VARIANTS: Seleucobelus (Grk); Seleucia ad Belum, Niaccuba (Lat)
PERIOD: Rom/Arb RATING: - MAP: 67 ITIN: 7b

LOCATION: On the eastern edge of the Jebel Ansariye, on the highway between *Latakia (75 km west) and Aleppo (104 km east).

An important bridgehead on the Orontes carrying traffic from the coast to northern Syria, Jisr al-Shugur has been settled since ancient times, hence its inclusion in early itineraries or geographies. The *caravanserai* in the centre of the old town was originally constructed between 1660 and 1676 and was restored in 1826-7.

Little that is ancient remains in the bustling modern town but incorporated in the bridge that takes current-day eastbound traffic over the Orontes are remains of a much older predecessor, originally built by the Romans. The design forms a broad arrow facing south to withstand the force of the current. This angle and the fact that the bridge was almost horizontal distinguish it from the majority of Roman/Arab bridges. The fabric was much modified in later centuries, its jumbled origins evident in the variety of stones used in the arches and piers.

REFS: Berchem; Fatio pp 260-264; *BG* p 475; Dussaud *Topographie* pp 155-62; Nour 297-8; Sauvaget 'Les Caravanserails syriens du Hadjdj de Constinantinople' in *Ars Islamica* 1937 p 108f.

K

Kharrab Shams (Plate 13a)

VARIANTS: Kharab Shams
PERIOD: Byz RATING: * MAP: 68 ITIN: 9a

LOCATION: Take the road that forks right from the foot of Jebel Semaan (*Saint Simeon) through the Kurdish villages to the north east through *Basofan, *Burj Haidar (8 km) until the country opens out (+12 km). The ruins, dominated by the tall arcaded church nave, lie across the fields 400 m left.

Alternatively, take the Afrin road north out of *Aleppo. At Hayyan (14 km), take the road to the left for +10 km.

The site on the east edge of the limestone country around Jebel Semaan has always rated highly among writers on the 'dead cities' area. There are a few remains (including a rock-cut tomb and lintels) which reveal the origins of the settlement before the classical period. It was probably further developed early in the phase of Roman settlement to take advantage of the transport route on which it lies and to exploit the patches of arable land on the neighbouring slopes and in the valley along the road.

The remains are, on the whole badly damaged, being cursorily built in polygonal, not dressed, stones. Villas appeared during the Christian period. The village perhaps owes most of its interest to the dominant ruins on the southern edge of the settlement, a **fourth century church** whose side aisles have collapsed, leaving the central arcaded nave of five arches topped by ten windows standing alone, almost perfectly preserved. The resulting effect is rather weird, enhanced if you visit the scene at sunset when the slanting light plays on the beautifully mottled stone and the exuberant vegetation that has taken over the scene is moved by the evening breeze.

According to Butler 'this church is one of the best preserved religious edifices in Northern Syria'. Sources differ as to its date. Butler puts it around 372, on analogy with the church at *Fafertin which is the earliest dated church in northern Syria. The style is in many respects remarkably analogous to the equally well preserved church at *Mushabbak which is usually dated to the late fifth century, about the same time as the construction of the great

complex at Saint Simeon. A dating as late as possible would thus seem logical, supporting Tchalenko's view that the fourth century church was rebuilt in the fifth century. The local church architecture is still clearly a developing art and the treatment of the arcading and windows is rather heavy. The different phases of construction are illustrated in the north and south clerestories, the first (older) containing five windows, the second ten. The nave contains a *bema*. The addition of a wall across the nave in Arab times has accidentally preserved the carved chancel rail behind, the only example to survive in Syria.

Standing by itself further up the hill you will find remains of a small **sixth century church** or chapel with a large enclosure and out-buildings. This was perhaps part of a monastery. Note the variety of capitals, largely based on classical themes but simplified. This church too contained a *bema*.

REFS: Bell *Desert* p 283; Butler *PE* II/B/6 pp 322-5; Tchalenko *Villages* II pl CXXIX; Tchalenko and Baccache pl 97-111.

Kirkbizeh

VARIANTS: Qirqbize, Kirk Birzey (Arb)
PERIOD: Byz ALT: 650m RATING: - MAP: 69
ITIN: 9b

LOCATION: See instructions for *Qalb Lozeh. Stop at 24.5 km, just before you turn left for Qalb Lozeh. The ruins are about 2 minutes' walk to the right.

A settlement of moderate interest with houses dating from the third to the sixth century. The site looks out over the Plain of Self to the south. A patch of arable land nearby allowed for the early exploitation of this area for monoculture (olives) but Tchalenko speculates that the settlers, who joined the community established around the dominant land-holder, needed to supplement their resources with exploitation of grain on the plain below.

The buildings include at the top of the rise a house from the third century and adjoining it on the west a fourth century church probably originally a house but large enough to contain a *bema* in the single nave (with its throne still intact at the time of Tchalenko's survey). The church is preceded by a colonnaded portico and a courtyard. There are two other villas which are later in date (fifth to sixth centuries). A little further away are the remains of six modest farmhouses.

Bnabel

3.5 km to the north west (straight ahead at Kirkbizeh intersection instead of left to Qalb Lozeh), an orphaned funerary column and a jumble of ruins hopelessly mixed in with the modern Druze village is all that awaits the visitor to Bnabel. The village was basically late Roman and has no building specifically constructed as a church. Seek out the remains of a sizeable house (two storeyed) with an attractive engaged Corinthian column, one of three said to be from the second century AD. The orphaned column is all that is left of a bicolumnar funerary monument, typical in style of the same period.

REFS: **Kirkbizeh:** *BG* p 409; Butler *AE* pp 114 ff; Tchalenko *Villages* II pl C-CVII, CXXXV; Tchalenko and Baccache pl 381-399. **Bnabel:** Butler *AE* pp 62, 69-71, 75.

Kokanaya

VARIANTS: Kaukanaya, Koukanaya
PERIOD: Byz ALT: 582 m RATING: - MAP: 69
ITIN: 9b

LOCATION: Take directions for Harim but before *Qalb Lozeh, at 22.5 km, continue ahead (not up the steep hill to right). +2 km then sharp right, keeping the swampy lake on your right. Continue +4.6 km, through the village, following the steep roadway to reach ruins marked by a distinctive pyramidal-roofed tomb.

A little far off the main itinerary, Kokanaya is probably not worth visiting for its own sake unless you have a particular interest in its two principal **tombs**. The moderately extensive ruins lie on the edge of a modern village. Near the road lie two open-sided tombs. One with its pyramidal roof largely standing is inscribed 384 and said by Butler to be an example of his first type of 'canopy tomb'. The second houses an open - and beautifully carved - sarcophagus (to Eusebius, a Christian, dated 369 by inscription).

Further up the hill you will find a two-storey **villa** with attractive columns and fine carving. Pena notes that the purpose of this building is not clear (religious or farmhouse) but Tchalenko says it is a guardhouse. Pena opts for a monks' hermitage (hence the tower). He notes that three **churches** were located in the village. They are located on the eastern edge (fifth century), to the

west (sixth century) and on the southern edge (sixth century).

REFS: *BG* p 410; Butler *AE* II pp 104,109 (tombs), 146 (church), 173-4 (houses I-III), 213; Butler *EC* p 136; Pena *et al Reclus* pp 169-74; Pena *et al Inventaire* pp 151-5; Tchalenko *Villages* I p 41, 334n, 387; Vogüé I pp 119, 124.

Krak[96] des Chevaliers (Plates 13b-14b)

VARIANTS: Qalaat al-Husn, Husn al-Akrad (Arb)
PERIOD: Cru RATING: *** MAP: *35*, 66 ITIN: 5b

LOCATION: Take the motorway from *Homs to *Tartus. (From Damascus, use the Homs by-pass which brings you around to the west of the city, near the oil refinery.) 41 km west of Homs, a road branches off to the right (north). Follow this for +4 km then take the road which rises sharply on the left for +5 km bringing you into the village of al-Husn. Kepp ascending to the top of the village. To gain an appreciation of the castle before visiting, go to the west (seaward) side via the circuit road that skirts the north end.

As the parthenon is to Greek temples and Chartres to Gothic cathedrals, so is the Krak des Chevaliers to medieval castles, the supreme example, one of the great buildings of all times.
[T S R Boase[97]]

Many superlatives have been spent on this monument but few do it full justice. The challenge in finding the apt description is that, no matter how many times you visit the great fortress, it never presents the same face. In the winter gales that seek to rend it apart, it is glowering and forbidding; on a spring day, its lovely warm hues blend with the wildflowers and the gentle light; in the heat of summer it broods, indifferent to the sun-blasted bare fields.

History

The Krak is certainly the supreme example of Crusader castle building, showing the full flowering of the Hospitallers' style which went far beyond the stolid adaptations of Byzantine models that had previously influenced the castles of the first half of the 12th century.

The site lies on a hill called Jebel Kalakh, part of the Mount Lebanon/Jebel Ansariye range

---

[96] The origins of the word are intriguing. It could either be a corruption of the Arabic Husn al-Akrad (see footnote 2) with its reference to Kurds or a medieval French borrowing from the Syriac word for fortress.
[97] Boase p 52

near the famous gap that lead to Homs from the sea via the plain called the *Buqeia* (*Homs). This position had long been an important defensive site before the Crusaders arrived. There is some evidence that the Egyptians of the 18th dynasty took an interest in it during their struggle with the Hittites for domination of Syria. Their rivalry worked itself to a climax at the nearby battlefield of Qadesh (*Tell Nebi Mend). Its usefulness was also plain in 1031 to the Emir of Homs who installed a colony of Kurds and constructed the first fortress.

The Crusaders reached here first in February 1099 when Raymond de Saint Gilles, Count of Toulouse, resumed his journey south to Jerusalem after the bloody taking of *Maarat al-Numan. The site was reoccupied by the Emir of Homs when the Crusaders passed on. It was not until 1110 that it was retaken by Tancred, Regent of Antioch. The castle was enfiefed to the Count of Tripoli. But the Crusader presence at this eastern limit of the County of Tripoli was over-extended. Without European colonists, the feudal lords lacked the income needed to consolidate the inland castles to form a solid defence against the growing threats from the Muslim towns along the Orontes.

The rationalisation of the Crusaders' resources came in 1144 when Raymond II, Count of Tripoli, transferred the Krak along with his other dependent castles to the Knights Hospitaller. This secular order, originally founded (as its name implies) to shelter pilgrims reaching Jerusalem, was bound by solemn oaths, sanctioned and encouraged by the Church, to protect the Crusader presence in the east. Founded possibly earlier than the 12th century, its presence was extended to other Crusader principalities as its influence grew and as the need for an organisation devoted to the common defence of the Crusader states became more evident. Its work was complemented by another secular order, often bitter rivals of the Hospitallers, the Knights Templar.

The Hospitallers' decision massively to expand the existing fortress after 1170[98] reflected several strategic considerations.

- The Krak, in conjunction with the defences at *Safita and Akkar (northern Lebanon) was vital to Crusader interests along the coast and thus the land access route between Europe and the Holy Land.
- It prevented encroachment on the rich coastal plains between Tripoli and Tartus.

(The Homs Gap is the most easily accessible route from the coast to the interior between Turkey and northern Palestine.)

- It was, moreover, a forward defence position against the threat not only from the Muslim Emirs of Homs and Hama but their more distant masters in Damascus and Aleppo (or even Cairo and Mosul).
- The fortress provided a secure base in a region largely populated then (as now) by Christians, albeit of the Orthodox persuasion.
- It guarded the exit from the rich Beqaa Valley in what is now Lebanon.

The Crusader castle survived two major Muslim challenges in the late 12th century. Nur al-Din (then nominally the Fatimid ally as Sultan/Emir of Aleppo) was beaten beneath the castle in 1163 by a strong coalition of Christian forces from Tripoli and Antioch. In 1188, moving up the coast after his great victory over the Kingdom of Jerusalem at Hattin, Saladin (who had united the Muslim forces of Egypt, Syria and Mesopotomia) by-passed the castle after a one day trial seige but ravaged the rest of the Count of Tripoli's territory.

During the 13th century, the Crusader presence away from the coast thinned further and the garrison at the Krak dwindled with the lack of new recruits from Europe, especially after the disaster of the Seventh Crusade (1249). Nevertheless, it continued to extract tribute from the Emir of Hama until 1267. In that year, however, the Mamelukes under Sultan Baibars began a concerted effort to assert Muslim supremacy in Syria. Baibars invested the Krak on 21 February 1271 (having already virtually isolated it from 1267). By 31 March he had punched a hole in its outer wall (probably at the south west tower, no 6). Baibars bottled up the Hospitallers in the inner defences. Faced with the awe-inspiring southern battlements, he resorted to a psychological campaign to force the demoralised garrison to surrender which fortunately they did on favourable terms on 7 April. They were given safe conduct to Tripoli in return for a promise that they would remove themselves to a Christian country and not stay in Arab lands. The 'key of Christendom' thus passed into the hands of the Crusaders' most ruthless opponent.

---

[98] Also the year of a major earthquake in this part of Syria - Runciman II 389.

The Mamelukes themselves used the castle as a base for a time, making certain repairs or improvements to the structure, described later. Gradually, however, as the foreign threat disappeared, it fell into disuse as a military strongpoint. Muslim villagers settled in it and remained there until cleared out by the French antiquities administration in 1934. (They were relocated in the present village of al-Husn.) The French arrested the damage (relatively minor) which the centuries of civilian occupation had brought, even declaring the building a 'monument of France'. The castle was ceded to Syria in compensation for the damage inflicted by the French bombardment of Damascus in 1945. Considerable work has been done since

back across the whole expanse of the castle below you.

The Krak is built on a spur running off the higher mountain range to the south and its defences form an elongated loop. The blunt end is to the south from where it was most vulnerable, hence the greater accumulation there of heavy bastions atop an outer ditch dug to isolate the fortress from the connecting spur. There are two distinct lines of fortifications: the outer, a curtain wall protected by round towers; and the inner ring which clusters tightly on the south side around the innermost keep, protected by its great sloping base. In the case of the Krak, the keep or donjon is not physically separated

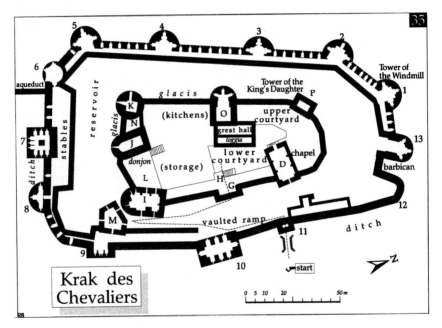

Krak des Chevaliers

1946 to continue the work of restoring and safeguarding the fabric of the building.

Visit

Even a leisurely visit of three or four hours may result in some confusion over the complex layout of the castle. It is wise to gain a good overall appreciation of how the defences are laid out by driving or walking around to the west side of the building as suggested in the location notes above. Stop a little way along the rise and look

within the inner defences but integrated into the south side of the central ring as part of a complex grouping of fortifications. Note especially the western outer ring with its five beautifully balanced and evenly spaced towers along the 150 m stretch of wall that Deschamps has described[99] as 'an architectural perspective based on pefect harmony'.

The two rings of defences were separated by an open space which incorporated many of

---

[99] Deschamps *Châteaux - Crak* p 150.

the refinements in fixed defence that the early 13th century had perfected. A ditch surrounded the inner ring on three sides except on the south where the huge reservoir is located. The talus or glacis behind this fulfilled several purposes: a strengthened footing for the massive weight of wall above, particularly necessary in an earthquake-prone area; solid protection against undermining of the walls; and a smooth surface to discourage scaling. Above, the battlements with loopholes and jutting firing positions as well as the strategically placed bastions delivered fire along the full length of the walls.

This, however, is no theory-based fortress plan. Partly its shape has been dictated by the site. Partly it needed to incorporate the pre-1170 Crusader castle which formed the core of the inner fortress though there is a clear distinction between the scope of the fortress envisaged in the earlier (pre-1170) phase and its subsequent reconstruction and improvement. Above all, it reflected a high degree of expertise combined with imaginative improvisation. This fresh approach to castle building reflected the lessons of the first Crusades, the secular orders' re-examination of the fortress' role in response to the challenge of Saladin, the adaptation of expert advice from Europe and the need to repair the devastation wrought by the severe earthquakes of 1157 and 1170. However varied the influences that contributed, the resulting complex, even allowing for the reinforcements and minor additions of the Mameluke period, is a building of extraordinary symmetry without undue concern for a rigid plan: it fully justifies the precepts about 'form following function' without the least self-consciousness.

Nothing identifiable remains of the castle as it stood before the Hospitallers took over in 1144 and certainly nothing of the Kurdish fortress. Under the Hospitallers, the castle was rebuilt in three main phases.

- 1144-70 - walls of the inner fortress (especially the north side) and chapel.
- Late 12th early 13th century - greater part of the outer walls; talus of the west and south sides of the inner walls.
- After 1250 - east side with its sloping passage, north barbican, lower storage rooms/stables.

The main Mameluke additions or improvements include the three outer towers on the south, the outer parts of the two north towers comprising the barbican, and the three square towers on the east which flank the entrance passage and stables.

Having taken in this view of the castle as a whole (and noted, incidentally, the aqueduct that once fed the castle's reservoir from the upper hills), return to the entrance on the eastern side. The building is maintained by the monuments administration of the Antiquities Department and thus observes fixed opening hours as follows:

HOURS
09:00 – 18:00   Wed – Mon [09:00 – 16:00 Winter]

As you face the entrance, the square tower on the left (no **10**) with the sloping base is Mameluke (as is that further to the south (no **9**), housing, on the upper storey, the Arab baths). The tower immediately in front (no **11**), where the entrance and ticket office are located, is late Crusader but with an Arabic inscription of 1271 commemorating Baibars' restoration of the fortress. It was once probably approached by a drawbridge. The metal-clad door is Arab and brings you into the vaulted base of the tower. From here, the main entry to the upper castle follows a long (130 m) rising passage to the left, vaulted for protection and flagged with low steps to allow horses to negotiate it. (Note too the opening in the vaulting which not only admitted light but allowed missiles or hot oil to be rained upon any attackers who might get this far.) On the way, the ramp passes a gateway connected to tower 10 and then on the left a long chamber built into the outer defences, probably for the housing of guards or horses.

You then reach a point at which the passage turns back on itself in a hairpin bend. We will take that 'V' turn now as it rises hard right, leaving for later the inspection of the area between the two lines of walls (to which you gain access by going through the short passageway heading off diagonally before the main ramp makes its sharp turn). Another steady ascent along a vaulted ramp leads you to a left turn through a tall vaulted gateway, protected by a series of doors, a large machicolation and a portcullis. This marks the point at which you pass through towers **G** and **H** of the second line of walls and enter the inner fortress.

Now it gets really confusing since there is little apparent symmetry to this tightly-packed series of buildings and underground chambers. Orient yourself carefully by stepping into the confined court in front of you. Opposite the entrance gateway (i.e. on the west) is a curious purely Gothic colonnaded building, a vaulted annexe leading into the great hall behind it. Turn right (north) and you are facing steps leading to an upper terrace which we shall explore later. Behind these stairs is the castle chapel. To the left of where you entered, a modern cement roof (reached by the stairs which double back above the gateway you have come through) protects an enormous vaulted hall. If you look above this cement terrace, another terrace gives access to the huge southern towers noted from your initial survey.

Taking all these features in turn, begin with the colonnaded arcade or *loggia* that precedes the great hall, a grouping of which Boase says: 'Apart from the cathedral of Tortosa, nothing of this period that survives in Syria can equal them in faultlessness of charm and elegance[100]. The *loggia* is a product of the late phase of the Krak in the second half of the 13th century. The Gothic style was by then established in France and it was time for it to be tried out in the Frankish east. The stonework is not in good condition (some of it has recently been restored by the Antiquities Department) but it conveys something of the grace and lightness of structure otherwise foreign to the Crusader style. The roof is divided into seven bays of ogival vaulting. Two doorways correspond with the entrances to the great hall beyond and are matched by five windows opening on the courtyard. (The central colonnette and round tympanum above it were characteristic of the new style.) Note the carved Latin inscription on the north lintel of the window furthest to the right: *Grace, wisdom and beauty you may enjoy but beware pride which alone can tarnish all the rest.*

This graceful building was a later addition to the 12th century **great hall**. While hardly cheerful in character, the spacious (27 m by 7.5 m) hall behind it has a certain austere dignity. The two doors leading off the arcaded annexe end in pointed arches. Above are three windows, the main source of light. The ceiling is divided by cradle vaulting into three segments. The ribs come down to capitals embedded in the walls bearing various patterns of leaves, animals and caryatids, all badly damaged (as are the corresponding embellishments of the annexe). A circular opening in the central vaulting could have either served to ventilate the room or was associated with a bell tower. On the north, a double window is externally decorated with trefoiled tympanums.

Behind the great hall, a huge room stretches for 120 m, taking up one whole side of the inner fortifications and looping around to the north to join the chapel. The central part probably served as kitchens (there is also a well and a bread

oven at the south end), storage, accommodation and even latrines (the latter can be inspected at the north end of the outer wall, just before the turn). This structure is within the original early Crusader construction which provides the basic shape of the central fortress.

The **chapel** dates from the first phase of the Hospitaller fortress (1142-70) when Romanesque influence was still evident. The nave, divided into three bays, ends in an apse roughly oriented towards the east. On the southern side (right as you face the apse) are three roughly-carved niches. These (and the *minbar* or pulpit approached by steps) result from the conversion of the chapel to a mosque following the Mameluke occupation and are intended to orient the faithful towards Mecca during prayers. Otherwise it is bare of decoration except for the barrel vaulting, a plain cornice and the slender support pilasters. There is a small window with a pointed arch driven through the thick masonry of the apse (which gives on to the outer wall of the inner fortress). The original doorway to the chapel has been largely covered over by a staircase probably built during the final seige. A makeshift new entrance to the chapel was added via the porch to the south.

Take this staircase to ascend to the upper court. Here you will find on the north western side a building known as the 'Tower of the King's Daughter' (tower **P**). The lower part is 12th century but the upper (with machicolations) is Arab. (The outer face of this tower which you cannot see from here will be described later.) From the nearby parapets, a view across to *Safita and the coast can be obtained.

Return now to the lower court and concentrate on the two levels at the southern end of the inner fortress. First, inspect the cavernous reaches of the pillared area under the modern cemented roof. This space was probably originally divided between a number of purposes - kitchen, refectories, storage of provisions, troop accommodation, A further storage area provided with an oil press is located right at the back but there is no natural light to guide you in the dank interior.

More salubrious is the upper part of the south area. This forms the so-called keep or donjon, a grouping described as 'probably the finest medieval line of defence anywhere'[101] consisting of two towers of enormous strength (**I** and **J**) plus a third (on the west - **K**) meant to provide enhanced security and comfort to the

[100] Boase p 56.

[101] Cathcart King p 84.

senior ranks of the garrison. The central tower (**J** - sometimes called the Tower of Monfret), midway along the south wall, consists of three storeys. In shape rectangular with a round face to the south, it is built of huge solid masonry to withstand heavy bombardment from the high ground to the south. The upper floor has a large mullioned window with, on the south, a single large loophole. The parapet on the roof has disappeared.

The south east tower (**I**) is larger in plan and shows the massive scale of the fortress' defences. Its upper chamber is supported on a central pillar 6 m thick. It likewise presents a rounded face to the south. It was joined to the central tower by a heavily fortified and wide structure, the upper defences of which have not survived. On this bridging platform, engines of war could be assembled to confront invaders from the south and the two towers could be linked by protective parapets.

The third tower (**K**), on the south west corner, is not strictly speaking a part of the heavily fortified donjon, being considerably lighter in construction and different in purpose. (This circular building, however, was also linked to the central tower by a terrace which formed part of the defensive front facing south). This apartment is interpreted as housing on the second floor the lord of the castle. This vaulted room (dated 1260), reached by a spiral staircase, is relatively elegant and light in design, the ribs of the vaults being supported on colonnettes built into the wall. A band of rosettes runs around the walls. Runciman describes this room as 'entirely Western in spirit'[102], a product of the 13th century striving for height and light. The tower's roof (not for the faint-hearted) provides the best vantage point in the castle with stunning views towards Safita and the sea (if haze is not a problem).

We have now finished with the inner fortress. You should retrace your steps along the V-shaped entrance passage until you reach the hairpin bend. From here take the doorway noted earlier which leads south to the space between the inner and outer lines of wall. You come out under a large bastion of irregular shape (**M**) and shortly afterwards will see the almost biliously vivid green of the stagnant waters of the reservoir. Immediately above is the great slope of masonry supporting the three towers (**I,J,K**) of the prestige accommodation wing that you have just inspected. Though you have earlier gained an appreciation of the defences from the upper battlements, it is worth pausing here to admire the great towers surmounting the talus, 'the most striking and unforgettable aspect of this noble building'.[103]

From this point, you should also look back to the bastion through which you passed (**M**). Half way up the wall above you note the two (now headless) lions facing each other. Though they have the same stance as the lions of Baibars' insignia, they are Latin in origin, the odd-shaped building having been erected in the second half of the 13th century to protect the bend in the ascending passage from fire from the south.

Walk across the open space towards the outer southern defences. You will notice in front of you a long (60 m) hall, probably more stables to judge by the loops to accommodate rings for the tethering of animals. Above this is a parapet leading to a substantial square tower (tower **7**), the centrepiece of the lower range of southern defences. This was built in the Arab period (an inscription records that it was the work of Sultan Qalaun in 1285) but probably on a Crusader base. The vast interior room follows the typically Frankish design of a huge vaulted roof supported on a massive central pillar. Flanking this at either end of the lower southern defences (and predating it) are round towers (nos **6**, **8**), both, according to inscriptions, the work of Baibars' reign. The inner room of the tower on the left (no **8**) contains a central octagonal pillar which bears an inscribed frieze in Arabic.

From the west end of the 60 m hall, you can work your way around the reservoir and stroll along the ditch that runs between the full length of the inner and outer walls. On the lower wall are five matching half-round towers (nos **1-5**) that strengthen the curtain wall and whose symmetry was admired in our initial survey. Note too the catwalk with numerous loopholes between the crenellations and below it the protected gallery incorporated in the wall. The wall is Crusader except for the machicolations at the top near the south end. After the outer wall turns the corner to the north, the last half-round tower juts out from a more prominent base than the others. This used to house a windmill and so earned the title *Burj al-Tauneh* (Tower of the Windmill - no **1**). After a gap in which a modern entrance to the castle has been inserted (originally for the convenience of the Arab villagers) the next two rounded bastions (**12, 13**) formed a barbican which once protected a postern gate.

While you are tracing the lower defences, take account of the western face of the inner fortress. The long talus or glacis (smoothly

---

[102] Runciman III 383.

[103] Boase p 54.

surfaced sloping front) runs all along the south and west fronts. North of the tower which housed the master (**K**), there is only one other break in the sheer wall above the glacis, a semi-circular bastion (**O**) which was linked to a 120 m gallery along the top of the wall. This also linked a series of passageways built into the space between the glacis and the old wall, ending up at a sally-port near the base. This network allowed reinforcements to be rushed to the outer defences, if necessary.

On the north western bend, the Tower of the King's Daughter protudes prominently, its great sheer wall dropping straight to the level of the ditch. This huge mass of stone is relieved by a series of blind arches creating a striking effect. Though architecturally impressive, the origins of this arrangement probably reflect several practical changes of plan, the earliest dating back to the origins of the castle. The original three tall arches concealed machicolations at the top to rain down projectiles on potential attackers at the base of the wall, a device which Boase has described[104] as 'elaborate and somewhat ineffective'. The arches were later filled in and the machilocation arrangement moved higher up following the raising of the wall and the addition of an arcade of smaller arches (now also filled in).

From this northern curve in the open space between the two walls, you can either return the same way up the bend half way up the ascending entrance passage or continue clockwise and take a small passage at the left of tower **G**. This leads you back to the top of the vaulted entry passage from where you can descend to the main entrance.

In the town below the castle, little of interest except a minaret of the early 14th century attached to a mosque rebuilt by Baibars, possibly on the site of a church

REFS: *BG* 348-54; Boase pp 51-6; Cathcart King pp 83-92; Deschamps *Châteaux - Crak*; Deschamps *Krak*; Dussaud *Topographie* pp 92 ff; Fedden *Crusader Castles* pp 50-55; Eydoux pp 87-113; Lawrence pp 93-98; Rihaoui *Krak*.

---

[104] Boase p 55.

L

Latakia

VARIANTS: Ramitha or Mazabda (Phn); Laodikeia (Grk); Laodicea, Laodicea ad Mare (Lat); la Liche (Cru); al-Ladhiqiye (Arb).
PERIOD: Hel/Rom/Arb RATING: * MAP: *36*, 67 ITIN: 7a

LOCATION: Major Syrian seaport, 320 km north of Damascus.

ike most other cities of the Levantine coast, Latakia has played its role in entertaining most of Syria's conquerors. Little of that wanton quality remains but there is a residual trace of Mediterranean and Levantine air in the older quarter, conveying a whiff of the Alexandria- or Beirut-that-might-have-been when the sea breeze sweeps through it in the late afternoon.

History

Even before Alexander or Pompey, the town had known a procession of conquerors. It was a Phoenician village nearly a millennium before Christ but fell to the Assyrians and then the Persians who made it part of their fifth satrapy. In 333 BC Alexander took it, just after the great battle with the Persians at Issus not far to the north (near Alexandretta, now in Turkey). It became a major town of the Seleucid Kingdom under Seleucos I Nicator (r 311-281 BC). (Apamea and Antioch were other major Seleucid centres but they were 'new cities' compared with Latakia).

Named in honour of the mother of Seleucos (later modified by the Romans to Laodicea ad Mare), it played a vital role in Seleucid and Roman times. In addition to serving as a port (more reliable than the fickle conditions at Arwad to the south), it was particularly known for its wine and is mentioned by Strabo[105] as the main supplier to the Alexandrian market. Mark Antony whose eventful relationship with Cleopatra sent him storming up and down this coast, won the town's temporary support by granting autonomy and some remission of taxes. By the late second century, Septimius Severus declared it capital of Syria (194-202), snubbing the more degenerate Antioch which had supported the aspirations of its governor, Pescennius Niger, his rival for the

emperorship. His initiative probably resulted in a major upgrading of the city, including the building of four colonnaded main streets, embellishing the Hellenistic grid plan. The role of capital soon, however, devolved back to Antioch. Zenobia seized it in her ill-advised drive to the sea that so provoked Rome's retaliation in 272.

In a region subject terribly to earthquakes, however, its fabric was just as much prey to natural destructive forces as to the fatigues that come from too much history. There were bad earthquakes in 494 and 555, just as it was facing a new Persian threat. Justinian, who fortified many towns in northern Syria against the Persians, rebuilt much of Latakia; he, too, favoured it over Antioch. In 638, Latakia was lost to Byzantium after the Arab armies swept into Syria. The Byzantines mounted a devastating raid in 705 but it was not until 968 that they reasserted their control in the area, fitfully retaining Latakia as their southern most port until it was retaken by the Turks in 1084.

The Crusades again put it on the fault line between Christian and Muslim. It was taken by a Crusader fleet in the autumn of 1097, even before Antioch fell. It lapsed back to local control and became an irritant in Byzantine/Crusader relations, for a while governed in condominium between Raymond of Toulouse and the Emperor. It was retaken by the Crusaders in 1103 and 1108 and incorporated by Tancred into the Principality of Antioch. The city, along with *Jeble, was included in 1126 in the dowry of Alice, daughter of King Baldwin of Jerusalem, who made an unsuccessful bid to assume the regency of Antioch. Later in the century, the town rated a duke who took charge of local affairs.

Saladin took and pillaged it in 1188 and it remained a Muslim enclave on the coast under Aleppo's control until 1260. In that year, in the first of the Mongol invasions, it was returned to the Principality of Antioch whose ruler had shown due deference to the Central Asian invaders. It remained as a truncated Crusader enclave under Bohemond VI even after the fall of Antioch in 1268. But the small Crusader garrison proved incapable of offering effective defence of this last remnant of the Principality and it reverted to Arab hands in 1287 during Qalaun's series of victories following the taking of Marqab (1285). In a gratuitous gesture, the neo-Crusaders, the Lusignans of Cyprus under Peter I, returned in

[105] Strabo XVI, 2, 9.
[106] See *Colossians* 4, 13-16; *Revelations* 1, 11; 3, 14-22.

1367 to sack and burn the city. It housed a Venetian trading colony from 1229 until Sultan Barsbay expelled it in 1436.

to competition from Beirut and Tripoli. By the beginning of this century it was a fishing village (population 7000) with a silted-up harbour barely

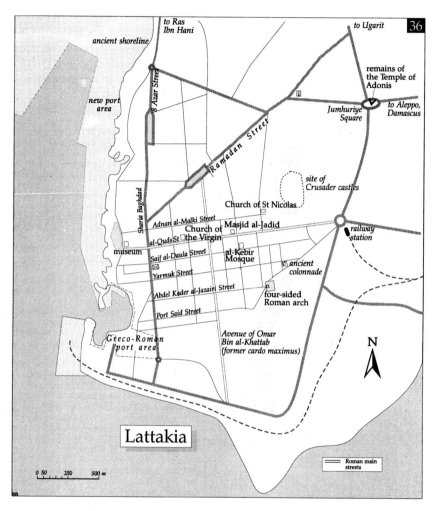

By then in a semi-ruined conditioned, Latakia under the Ottomans became merely a dependency of Tripoli (Lebanon) or *Hama. Its fortunes revived somewhat in the 17th century through the silk and tobacco trade and by the 18th century it had again become a major port, comparable to Smyrna or Tripoli. However, it could not sustain this role in the 19th century due

able to shelter four to six boats. It resumed a more prominent role under the French when it was the capital of the Alawite state set up for much of the Mandate period.

Visit

In spite of this complex history, the physical look of the town is less than romantic. The tightly ordered grid plan of the old city bears witness to a basically Hellenistic pattern. The very consistency of its historic role, however, has meant that its ancient remains have largely been obliterated by continuous re-development over the centuries. There are a few columns here and there (often re-erected in ungainly fashion in the middle of some frantic swirling roundabout), the scrubby remains of the acropolis (east of the town), one or two churches with bits of ancient chapels or Crusader rooms and the four-sided Roman monumental gateway (see below), perhaps erected for a triumph now forgotten.

In the southern part of the old city, one of the few surviving indications of the town's past glory is the **four-sided gateway (tetraporticus)**, erected at the eastern end of one of the main transverse streets (*decumanus*). The French scholar Sauvaget reconstructed the plan of Roman Laodicea in a study completed in the thirties. The city was based on a grid (its elements measured 112 m by 57 m) laid out on a long (1.5 km) axis in the area between the sea (and port) on the west and a low range of hills on the east. The gateway marks the eastern edge of the plan. You can still see on the west face the point at which the colonnade of the *decumanus* terminated. There is little resemblance to the triumphal arches common in the Roman world, the shape being too distinctly cubic to have any direct comparisons among surviving examples[107].

The dome within the arch is intact and is set upon an octagon which provides the transition to the rectangular base. As the sides are not quite square, the pendentives which fill the corners are irregular. The stonework and the construction are not particularly fine but the arch is clearly robust having withstood the ravages of at least seventeen centuries including several major earthquakes since its construction, probably, according to Chéhab, in the early third century.

Remains of the granite columns that once supported the portico of the main Roman streets still appear haphazardly in the central area.

Latakia has a sizeable Greek Orthodox population which has paid considerable attention in recent years to the care and restoration of its churches. Two are particularly worth visiting. (A guide may need to be arranged through the Archbishop's office in the street parallel on the north to al-Qods St.) The **Church of the Virgin** lies in the *suq* in the block south of the Archbishop's office. The original building may go back as far as Byzantine times, its simple single-nave plan being embellished in the 18th century by an ornate marble *iconostasis*. A smaller chapel with an icon of the Virgin believed to have miraculous properties is on the right. The second church (also undated), is the Church of St Nicholas in Maysalun St (one intersection north of al-Qods St), includes a notable collection of icons of the Syrian school of the 17th and 18th centuries and an ebony wood throne dated 1721. Right of the main nave is a chapel to St Moses the Ethiopian.

Several of Latakia's mosques (in the area east and south of al-Qods St - see map, previous page) are worth inspecting, at least for their facades. They include the early 13th century Masjid al-Kebir (Great Mosque) and the Masjid al-Jadid (New Mosque – 18th century), erected by Suleiman Pasha al-Azem.

A **museum** was opened in 1986 in the building along the seafront (east end of al-Qods St, opposite the new port) which formerly housed the residence of the Governor of the Alawite State during the French Mandate. The building was originally a *khan* (perhaps 16th century) serving the tobacco trade and later a private residence.

In Jumhuriye Square (where the Damascus and Ugarit roads start) stand a group of four elegant **monolith columns**, topped with Corinthian capitals. This may have been part of the Temple of Adonis whose myth, sourced to the mountainous region of northern Lebanon, was strong in this area. On one of the two hills to the east were found remains of a sizeable Roman theatre, near the Moghrabi Mosque. These hills (access restricted) bear no evidence of the twin Crusader castles that once overlooked the approach from the interior.

REFS: *BG* pp 459-67; Chéhab *Fouilles de Tyr - la Nécropole - I l'Arch de Triomphe* p 95; Elisséeff 'al-Ladhikiyya' pp 589-93; Rey-Coquais *Arados*; Sauvaget *Plan - Laodicée*.

---

[107] The survey by Maurice Chéhab in *Fouilles de Tyr - La Nécropole - I l'Arc de Triomphe* gives seven examples of 'quadrifons' arches in the Roman world - p 92.

M

Maalula (Plate 15a)

VARIANTS: Calamona (?anc); Magluda (Byz); Maalloula
PERIOD: Byz/Arb ALT: 1650 m; RATING: MAP: 64, 75 ITIN: 3b

LOCATION: Take the Damascus/Homs motorway north for 50 km. As the road ascends an escarpment, look out for a Turkish *caravanserai* (*Khan al-Arus*) just as the two carriageways part. Immediately afterwards, a sign pointing left will give you little warning of the turn-off to Maalula. Follow this road for +8 km. [It can also be reached in conjunction with *Seidnaya.]

Though rich in historical and religious associations, Maalula preserves only a few remains of its past. It is, however, a village of some charm, its tempered houses piled up on the lower slopes of an escarpment rising sheer above the village. There is an uncompromising beauty to the setting and the gorge that cuts into the escarpment at the back.

Maalula has three claims to fame; its setting; its early Christian associations; and the resistance of the villagers (until recently) to the final replacement of Aramaic by Arabic as the language of communication. There may be some doubt about the extent to which Aramaic, the language spoken by Christ and the popular *lingua franca* of the area until the Arab conquest in the seventh century, has remained in active use to the present day. However, even the vestigial survival of West Aramaic (Syriac) as a spoken tongue indicates the tenacity with which the inhabitants of Maalula have clung to their identity[108].

There are two chapels above the village whose loyalty is divided between the Greek Catholic and Orthodox churches. That of the Greek Catholics is on the escarpment left of the gorge. Ask for directions to the church of Mar Sarkis (St Sergius) and follow the steep path which ascends to the plateau from the left hand side of the village. This tiny chapel, probably built on the site of a pagan temple, has architectural

elements which go back to the Byzantine period and may have been constructed even before the Council of Nicaea in 325. Icons dating back to the 13th century are worth inspecting.

On the plateau behind the church (left of the ugly modern hotel/casino), there are remains of ancient rock-cut tombs.

You can descend to the village via the ravine, taking you past the second chapel, located in the lower monastery on the right of the gorge, a Greek Orthodox institution dedicated to Mar Taqla (Saint Thecla). The saint (reputedly a pupil of St Paul and one of the first martyrs of the Church) is believed to be buried in a cave above the monastery. There is no confirmation that any parts of the monastery or chapel date back to the Byzantine period.

There are two parish churches in the village itself. In one (of St Elias), a fourth century mosaic was found.

REFS: *BG* pp 302-3; Dussaud *Topographie* p 281; Nasrullah, Joseph 'Le Qalamoun `a l'époque Romano-Byzantine' in *AAAS* 1952, 1958; Tate 'Ma'lula' in *OE*; Thubron p 59.

Maarat al-Numan

VARIANTS: Arra, Megara (Grk); Marra, la Marre (Cru)
PERIOD: Arb RATING: * MAP: 72 ITIN: 11a/b

LOCATION: The Hama/Aleppo highway passes on the eastern outskirts of Maarat 108 km north of Homs, 73 km south of Aleppo.

History

Maarat lies in a moderately prosperous agricultural belt on the southern edge of the limestone area of northern Syria, the Jebel Zawiye, between the Orontes and the desert. Traces of ancient remains are found in modern habitations, illustrating the antiquity of the town. Though known to the Greeks and Romans as Arra, surviving buildings attest only to its history since the coming of Islam. Its modern name refers to al-Numan Ibn Bashir al-Ansari, a companion of the Prophet who was made governor of the region by the Umayyad Caliph Moawiya (r 661-81).

---

[108] They are, however, not the only community in Syria to have done so. The Syriac-speaking communities (numerous particularly in the North East Province to which they have fled this century from Iraq) speak a more diluted form of neo-Aramaic which was preserved during their long exile in Persia and northern Iraq.

Given its location on the Damascus/Homs/Hama/Aleppo corridor and on the edge of the Belus Massif east of the Orontes, it has been contested several times by forces seeking to control northern Syria. The Byzantines took it in 968 during the attempt by the Emperor Nicephorus to profit from instability in Syria and regain possession of northern Syria for Constantinople. Their destructive occupation was short-lived, however, as the Fatimids moved in by 996 though the town soon lapsed back into Aleppo's orbit. The Crusaders passed this way in 1098 on their initial march south to Jerusalem and halted while they disputed tactics and options. Their three week seige was a particularly frustrating experience, made worse by rivalry between two leaders, Raymond de Saint Gilles, Count of Toulouse, and Bohemond, Prince of Antioch, who had already fallen out over the seige of Antioch. The latter offered to spare the citizens in return for surrender, just at the moment when the impetuous Raymond was successful in breaching the walls. The townspeople were cut down in a famous massacre which saw the slaughter of 20,000 Muslims including many women and children. In the siege and subsequent occupation, Christian troops resorted to cannibalism in the face of starvation.

Our people suffered a severe famine. I shudder to speak of it; our people were so frenzied by hunger that they tore flesh from the buttocks of the Saracens who had died there, which they cooked and chewed and devoured with savage mouths, even when it had been roasted insufficiently on the fire. And so the besiegers were more harmed than the besieged.
[Raymond of Fulchre][109]

Though this point so far to the east into Muslim territory was precariously held, the town did not permanently revert to Muslim control until Zengi reoccupied it in 1135 as part of the first concerted effort to dislodge the Crusaders from inland areas. Under the later Ayyubids, it was dependent on Aleppo and, under the Mamelukes, on Hama. The town is noted by Muslims as the birthplace of the blind poet, Abu al-Ala al-Maari. A modern tomb marks his burial.

Visit

In the main square in the centre of town, you will find a handsome mosque tower (**minaret**) originally erected in the first half of the 12th

century but rebuilt after an earthquake in 1170[110]. The rebuilding is attributed to Hassan Ben Mukri al-Sarman who sought to rival (by imitation) the tower of the Great Mosque of Aleppo. The same architect is responsible for the nearby (south) *madrasa* of the Shaffi tradition dated to 1199 Madrasa Abu al-Fawaris, entry on east side, tre-foiled arch; pyramidal cupola over vestibule; *iwan*; prayer hall to south; tomb of founder to north.

In the south eastern part of the central area, an early 16th century *khan* (Khan Murad Pasha - the largest *khan* in, Syria, 7000 m^2) has been converted to a **museum** with striking effect. It contains an interesting collection of objects including mosaics and pottery from many periods. The mosaics have been transferred from nearby sites and as of 1998, new finds were being installed including a fifth century mosaic from as far afield as Homs. Note especially the mosaic dated depicting Romulus and Remus, found at al-Firkiye (north of Maarat) and dated to 510. A second mosaic of the same date from al-Firkiye depicts animals in a field bordered by vines. A mosaic from the ruins of a church in Selemiya (second room reading anti-clockwise from entrance) carries representations of animals. In the centre of the courtyard is the Tekkiye or foundation for the instruction of initiates of the Dervish sect. A doorway to the left once led to the *hammam* and *suq* attached to the *khan* (now managed separately). Opposite the museum is another Ottoman *khan*, the Khan Assaad Pasha al-Azem (1748) (visit not possible).

On the north western edge of town, near the road to al-Riha and the Jebel Riha, you will find the remains of the medieval **citadel**. The scale is surprisingly small. Although subsequent habitation has almost totally dismantled the original fortifications, the shape of the site is preserved and many of its stones have presumably been re-cycled.

REFS: *BG* p 377; Shéhadé; Dussaud *Topographie* pp 187-90; Elisséeff *Ma`arat* pp 922-7; Maalouf pp 37-40.

---

[109] Quoted (in translation) in Hallam *Chronicles of the Crusades* pp 86-7.

[110] The mosque itself stands on the site of an ancient temple of which only fragments including two small columns (re-used in a courtyard building) and some inscribed portions of architrave survive. Herzfeld, however describes (pp 37-9) a fountain made entirely of recycled ancient stones and columns.

Maraclée

VARIANTS: Maraclea, Maraccas (Cru); Marqiye (Arb)

PERIOD: Cru RATING: T MAP: 66 ITIN: 5c

LOCATION: Just below the waterline, 16 km north of *Tartus; 11 km south of *Qalaat Marqab. Opposite the village of Kharrab Marqiye.

The small **sea tower/fortress** of Maraclée was built by the local *seigneur*, Barthélemy, in 1277 several years after the fall of the *Krak des Chevaliers and at the end of the Crusader period. The tower/fortress in the sea was built in view of the insecurity of the nearby land castle which had attracted the particular hostility of the Mameluke Sultan, Baibars and which he had had destroyed in 1271 (see below). (Baibars was incensed by Barthélemy's consorting with the Mongol invaders of Syria under Hulaga). The next Sultan, Qalaun, took the nearby castle of Marqab in 1285. Having found the sea tower impregnable, he ordered Bohemond VII whose days were numbered as Lord of Tripoli, to have the tower dismantled, holding him responsible for abetting its construction. (Tripoli itself fell to Qalaun in 1289.) Bohemond apparently obliged, ordering Barthélemy to dismantle it.

Certainly nothing of the building remains above the waterline, though from a boat the foundations can just be discerned below the surface of the sea about 180 m from the shore, at the point where the track to the village of Bezzak leaves the old Tartus/Baniyas road. The remains of the 9 m by 15 m tower come to within a few centimetres of the surface. The stream known as the Nahr Marqiye and the hamlet of Kharrab Marqiye or Merakieh lies near this point.

The **land castle** was established long before the tower and was held by a Frankish family with close links to the lords of Marqab. The site of Maraclée was taken in the earliest phase of the Crusades (1099) and was later important enough to warrant a mention in several Crusader records and to have rated a Bishop (shared with Tortosa). It was the subject of a prolonged dispute in the 13th century between the local seugneurial family, the de Ravendels, and the Hospitallers for its possession. A compromise was reached in 1241. The castle, as noted earlier, was largely destroyed by Baibars in 1271 and no traces remain.

REFS: Berchem and Fatio p 96; Deschamps *Châteaux - III* pp 146, 323-6; Dussaud *Topographie* p 126; Eydoux pp 128-132; Gabrieli pp 339-41; Huygens.

Mari

VARIANTS: Tell Hariri
PERIOD: EBA, MBA RATING: * MAP: *37, 38, 73* ITIN: 12b

LOCATION: 12 km west-north west of Abu Kemal (Syria/Iraq border). Take the road from Deir al-Zor south towards Abu Kemal. At 24 km south of *Dura Europos, the tell can be seen across the flat land to the left, between the road and the Euphrates River.

History

Mari is a site of central importance, 'a unique example of a bronze age palace' giving 'an exceptionally concentrated picture of the Syro-Mesopotamian world' in the words of its current excavator, Jean-Claude Margueron. Discovered in 1933, the excavation of this rare example of a Mesopotamian palace found with its accoutrements and archives relatively intact has been one of the keys to the unravelling of the history of the Syria/Mesopotamia region during the early millennia of recorded history. Its excavation rested for many years in the hands of the French archaeologist, André Parrot, who supervised the excavations from 1933 to 1974; a remarkable record. The research was funded partly by the Louvre where many of the most important pre-war finds can now be seen. Since 1978, excavations have continued under Margueron with the aim of embracing Mari's role in the wider Euphrates valley, thus better establishing its place in the Mesopotamian world of the third and second millennia by researching its economic resources and agricultural base.

Mari was the third millennium BC royal city-state *par excellence*. It controlled access between central and southern Mesopotamia and the drier plains of northern Syria and the upper Euphrates/Khabur system. Caravan routes through Mari also brought tin for the bronze industries to the west. Its key position between the confluence of the Khabur and Euphrates and the cliffs further south at *Baghuz explain its choice as the site for a new city built by political decision.

Mari was first occupied at the beginning of the third millennium (2900 BC). Positioned in an area of limited natural agricultural potential, the centre based its foundation not only on its trading position but on a sophisticated irrigation scheme. It was surrounded by a circular rampart and ditch (1.9 km in diameter) through which was dug a canal for the dual purpose of water supply and controlling navigation on the river. Recent evidence indicates further extensive

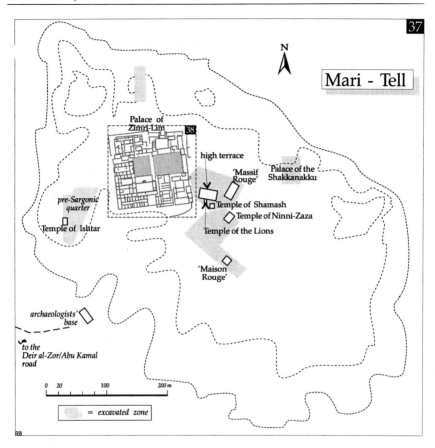

development of canals, including a 120 km navigation link between the Khabur and Euphrates rivers.

The first major period of development (2700-2600 BC) saw the construction of a great palace, the temples of Ishtar, Nini-Zaza, Shamash and the terrace area or 'Massif Rouge'. Mari succumbed to the Akkadian Empire (c2340-2150 BC - founded by Sargon of Akkad) for a while but re-established its prosperity, its population heavily boosted by the arrival c2000 BC of many Amorites (a Semitic people). There followed a period during which a succession of local princes (*Shakkanakku*) perhaps served as governors for a foreign kingdom (Akkad?), building a new palace on the site of the old. Mari lost out in the power struggle touched off by the rising dynasty of Babylon. Occupied for a time by the Amorite

leader Shamsi-Adad (1813-1782 BC), it briefly found its independence under Zimri-Lim (1775-60) only to lose it to Hammurabi of Babylon (r c1792-50) in 1760. It was by sacked by him in 1759. Its walls were razed, its temples sacked and the palace of Zimri-Lim set on fire and dismantled. The city was no longer a centre of any importance from that time though there are signs of limited re-occupation in the Seleucid and Parthian periods.

Visit

While this is the most impressive and best preserved of the MBA palaces unearthed in the region, the largely mud-brick remains which have been successively peeled off to expose the preceding layers beneath, are difficult to appreciate. The task of orienting yourself is especially difficult if the weather is inordinately hot or muddy as, depending on the season, it so often is in this region of Syria. Only a small section of the tell, consisting of the sacred enclosure of the pre-Sargonic palace is protected by roofing from the eroding effects of rain.

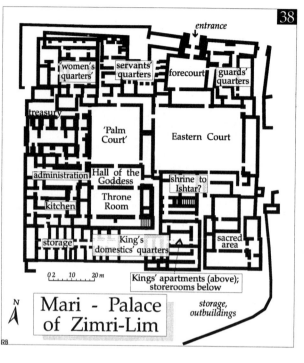

The palace (north west segment of the mound) is one of the most extensive excavated in the Middle East (275 rooms covering 2.5 ha) and was constructed across several centuries though it bears the name of the last ruler, Zimri-Lim. The fact that the building was deliberately destroyed, its mud walls half knocked down to fill in the rooms, accounts for its remarkable state of preservation.

From the palace was recovered a rich variety of finds including the notable statues of Ishtup-Ilum (Governor of Mari) and of a water goddess (now in the *Aleppo Museum) and an archive of 15,000 tablets recording the household accounts of the palace as well as diplomatic and administrative records of the kingdom. The walls of the palace survived in places to a height of 5 m and spread across a formidable range of rooms arranged around two courtyards.

The main gateway to the Palace of Zimri-Lim was on the north eastern side of the roughly square palace compound which was originally surrounded by a mud brick rampart. Moving south, a small courtyard gave access via a zig-zag passage to the larger of the two courtyards (east). At its centre was a reservoir. A sanctuary, probably to Ishtar, lay on the south side of this courtyard. The south eastern corner gave directly on to the area used as a temple within the palace and then to a storage area.

The other (west) courtyard, dubbed the Palm Court, had a more official role, the south facade having borne remains of a frescoe including an investiture scene (now partly preserved in the Louvre). The courtyard gave access (to the south) to a long antechamber

(where the water goddess statue, mentioned above, was found) and then to the rectangular throne room of impressive dimensions (25 m by 11 m and at least 12 m high). The throne itself stood against the west wall. To the west of this second courtyard lies a maze of living, administrative and service quarters with the royal apartment probably located above and to the east of the throne room and a secondary residence (for the wives?) in the north western quarter. There is evidence in many places of a sophisticated plumbing system. Many of the rooms were decorated with wall paintings (partly preserved now in the *Aleppo and *Damascus Museums as well as in the Louvre).

The remains of a high terrace (constructed around 2000 BC to the west of an earlier terrace of red bricks) lie to the east of the sacred enclosure of the palace. Around it are grouped a number of **religious buildings**, including the Temple of Lions (c 2000 BC - east of the palace) and that of Shamash (south of the high terrace). In the Temple of Ninni-Zaza (mid third millennium BC - east of the Temple of Shamash) was discovered a remarkably rich trove of statues including that of the singer Ur-Nanshe, now in the Damascus Museum. An earlier palace of the late third millennium lies underneath the later palace while the Palace of Shakkanakku lies 300 m to the east. The remains of the **Temple of Ishtar** (third millennium) lie on the western limits of the tell. It is a temple typical of Mari in its layout, the inner sanctum lying within a central hall flanked by rooms reserved for the priests. Other facilities included a well, an oven, a libation basin and a table for offerings. Only the priests could enter the inner sanctum. Small votive figures were presented to the priests to represent devotees at the sacrifical rites in the inner sanctum.

REFS: Amiet; Arnaud; *BG* pp 497-9; Margueron *Mari (1983)* pp 103-9; Margueron *Mari (1989)* pp 41-9; Parrot

---

Masyaf (Plate 19b)

VARIANTS: Massya (anc); Massiat (Cru); 'Castle of the Assassins'"
PERIOD: Cru/Ism RATING: * MAP: 66, 67 ITIN: 5c

LOCATION: Masyaf is 51 km inland from Baniyas along a spectacular mountain road, initially clinging to the southern slopes of the deep ravine of the Baniyas or Jobar River (the ancient *Chrysorhoas*) and passing through the village of Qadmus (27 km). Also accessible from *Hama, 40 km to the east.

En route from Baniyas (at c16 km), the vestigial ruins of Qalaat Ollaiqa, an Ismaeli castle (mentioned under *Qalaat Maniqa) can be seen across the ravine to the north.

Masyaf is the best preserved, and probably the most famous, of the Ismaeli castles of the mountainous region between the Orontes and the coast. It is superbly located and the sight of the castle outlined against the green of the Jebel Ansariye behind is striking when seen from the road from Hama.

In the 12th century, a network of fortresses established by the Ismaelis protected their presence in the mountains to which they had fled to escape persecution by orthodox Sunni regimes in Aleppo and Damascus. The site had clearly been used for defensive purposes in Seleucid, Roman and Byzantine times, if one is to judge by the prolific use of stones from those periods incorporated in later buildings[111]. Written

records indicate that it was seized by the Crusaders in 1103, shortly after the establishment of their presence on the coast but it was one of several inland sites that the Crusaders did not have the resources to maintain.

By 1140-1, it had been taken by the Ismaelis and became a chief centre of their sect, particularly under the leadership of Sinan. Sinan's control came under threat from Saladin who, following two assassination attempts by Sinan's followers, sought to assert his mastery over the sect. Saladin aimed to promote Sunni orthodoxy by ridding the country of Shi'ite influence following the ending of Fatimid rule in Cairo. Saladin laid seige to Masyaf in 1176 but suddenly broke off the campaign. It seems he had been the target of another Ismaeli plot, this time in symbolic form through the appearance on his camp bed of a threatening verse, a dagger and a collection of hot cakes. It took another century before the Assassins were subjugated by the Mameluke Sultan, Baibars in the 1170's in a new wave of resurgent Sunni orthodoxy.

Visit

An hour and a half should be sufficient for an inspection of the castle (and a quick circuit of the central parts of the town where some buildings of the Ottoman and Mandate period retain a certain faded charm). You will need to rouse the guardian of the castle if he is not on duty, as the number of visitors is few.

The castle sits on a small elongated rocky prominence (running north/south) on the eastern side of the town. Make a circuit of the outer defences on foot, the relatively open area on the east being a particularly good vantage point to gain an appreciation of the fortifications. The entrance to the castle is on the south. The overall plan is a central keep surrounded by an outer wall strengthened by many square bastions built above the rocky 10 m high slopes. Given the short Crusader occupation of the site, little of the fabric appears attributable to their hand though in general it is not difficult to distinguish their more regular stonework from the smaller, irregular shapes used by the Ismaelis. The whole complex, however, is very much a pastiche, given the re-cycling of ancient elements such as the monolith columns used to anchor the walls to the core of the building.

REFS: *BG* p 450; Dussaud *Topographie* pp 143 ff; Eydoux pp 125-7; Lewis *Assassins*; Maalouf.

---

[111] There are records of Roman legionnaires based in this area and for a time Massya served as the headquarters of the IV Scythica legion.

THE ASSASSINS

The Ismaeli sect originated in Persia. Though first recorded references to the sect dates to the late 11th century, the central element in their beliefs is their devotion to the eighth century leader, Ismael (son of the sixth Imam, Jafar al-Sadiq). An element among the Ismaelis later earned the popular appellation 'Assassins' (*Hashasheen*) on account of their alleged use of hashish in summoning the fierce determination needed to pursue the sect's commitment to murder to advance their ends.

In the late 11th century while the sect was consolidating in Persia, Syria was more than usually fragmented. Nominally under the Fatimids, it was subject to pressures from the Seljuq Turks, Iraq (Mosul) and the Byzantines. The religious scene was in ferment with a proliferation of Shi`ite sects resentful of the increasingly assertive Sunni mainstream. Persia was still the source of much of this Shi`ite heterodoxy and the Ismaelis extended their interests into northern Syria.

The Ismaelis were for a time encouraged in Aleppo by a Seljuq ruler Ridwan (son of the great Sultan Tutush). Ridwan exploited a group of Ismaelis to advance his vendetta against his father-in-law, Jenah al-Daula, whose base was at Homs. The group, however, acquired a fierce agenda of their own, taking on the assassination of orthodox figures such as the respected *qadi* of Aleppo, Ibn al-Khashab (1125). Discredited in the main cities during the 1120's for their blatant courting of the Crusaders in their intrigues against the Sunnis, the group of 'Assassins' retreated to bases in the mountainous areas. Their principal headquarters was at Qadmus on the Masyaf/Baniyas road which they took in 1132 from the Banu Munqidh (*Shaizar). (All vestiges of the Qadmus castle were removed in the 19th century.) After 1142, from their widening network of mountain castles (*Qalaat Abu Qobeis, *Qalaat al-Kahf, *Qalaat Maniqa) they extended their influence by playing off Muslims against Crusaders. Masyaf (also acquired in 1140-1 from Shaizar) was relatively exposed compared with other sites hidden deep in the mountains, notably al-Kahf. *Qalaat al-Kawabi was acquired at a later date.

The sect was particularly vigorous during the leadership (1163-93) of Rashid al-Din Sinan. The Crusaders dubbed him the 'Old Man of the Mountain' out of a mixture of fear and respect for his cunning and ruthlessness. Sinan, born in Basra, Iraq, was a charismatic leader who induced his followers to depart further from conventional Islam into mysticism. He had originally been sent from Persia to govern the Syrian province in 1162. The sect by then controlled the central part of the Jebel Ansariye between Tartus and Jeble. The Crusaders held only a narrow strip to provide access along the coast. At their peak, the Ismaelis controlled a total of ten castles[1], the eastern-most being Masyaf.

The sect's activities continued at a lesser level of intensity after the death of Sinan (1193). Its independence gradually diminished in the 13th century, however, as Sunni control from Damascus and Aleppo was consolidated. Much of their coherence was lost when their headquarters in Alamut (Persia) fell to the Mongols (1260). In 1270, having forced the Ismaelis to renounce the tribute they had paid to the Hospitallers, Sultan Baibars dismissed their Grand Master and the Ismaelis rose in revolt. By 1273, the Mamelukes gained the upper hand and the Ismaelis ceased to retain a political identity, becoming yet another of the minorities (Christian and Shi`ite) whose adherents sought refuge in the mountains. There they survived till present times though often under pressure from the more numerous Alawi population. Many Ismaelis last century fled the mountain altogether, settling around the Syrian desert town of Selemiya.

---

1. Deschamps (*Châteaux – Crac* p 42-3) believes the ten were: *Qalaat al-Kawabi, *Qalaat al-Kahf, Qalaat Resafi, Masyaf, Hadid (near Qadmus), Qalaat al-Qrayte (?Qolai'a), Khariba, Qalaat Ollaiqa and *Qalaat Maniqu. He excludes *Qalaat Ben Qahtan and *Qalaat Abu Qobeis which were Ismaeli strongholds for part of their histories. For locations, see map 79.

Meez

VARIANTS: Ikhkhenis (anc); Maes, Maaz
PERIOD: Rom/Byz   ALT: 382 m   RATING: -
MAP: 69   ITIN: 9b

LOCATION: Jebel Barisha area of the 'dead cities' zone. Take Harim road from Bab al-Hawa turnoff. After 12 km take the road (left) to Kferdaya (Kfer Darian) - +3 km to Meez.

An extensive site, it probably played a central role in the surrounding region from the second century because of its sizeable fertile area. The town grew up around the *agora* and temple of the second century Roman settlement. Other Roman remains also include a nearby *andron* and a water reservoir. Tchalenko notes that its history seems to be marked by two separate periods of prosperity, one at the beginning, the second at the end of the Roman/Byzantine period.

The most notable ruin of the Christian period is the sizeable church to the east which has a richly decorated rear wall including elaborate window placements (first decades of the sixth century). The church compound also includes a baptistery (to the south) and tomb. The second church (mid sixth century, columned basilica) is less lavish and little remains of its structure.

The monastery 1.6 km to the east (local name Deir Aizarara) has an associated monastic tower (probably of the second half of the sixth century), *Burj al-Assafir*, 100 m to the north.

REFS: *BG* pp 411; Mattern pp 95-103; Pena *et al Cenobites* pp 120-2, 160-66, 219-226, 250-1, 266-9; Pena *et al Inventaire* pp 170-1; Tchalenko *Villages* I pp 280-4; II pl LXXXVIII-IX.

Membij

VARIANTS: Manbog, Mabog, Bambyce (Br/IrA); Hierapolis (Grk); Bumbuj (Arb).
PERIOD: Hel/Rom/Arb   RATING: -   MAP: 71
ITIN: 10b

LOCATION: 88 km north east of Aleppo.

Manbij. May God protect it. ... its skies are bright, its aspect handsome, its breezes fragrant and perfumed, and while its day gives generous shade, its night is all enchantment.
[Ibn Jubair]

Nothing (Ibn Jubair) wrote about Menbij had prepared me for it. If every town on earth were vying for the name `nowhere', a mere two or three could hope to compete with Menbij.
[Charles Glass *Tribes Without Flags* London 1990]

Membij has seen better days. Little now remains in this alternately dusty or muddy town in the midst of the northern Syrian grain belt of the famed cult centre whose origins go predate Greco-Roman times. Travellers such as Gertrude Bell had equal difficulty in relating Membij to its days of glory. Perhaps just as well. Under the ancient name of Hierapolis, the fame of Membij spread throughout the Roman Empire. The cult - celebrated, or rather parodied, in the work of the ancient author, Lucian, *De Dea Syria,* 'The Syrian Goddess' - centred on the worship of Atargatis (originally a Mesopotamian goddess) and her consort Hadad. The divine pair were appeased by notoriously bloody and sadistic practices, including the sacrifice of children. In the centre of its sacred lake (once 100 m wide and surrounded by porticos; now simply a broad depression in the town park) stood the altar to Atargatis.
The religious significance of Membij pre-dated the Seleucids and Romans, a local

dynasty having sponsored the cult in Persian times. It was thus a sizeable town when Seleucos I Nicator hellenized it as Hierapolis after 300 BC. Its abundant water supply fed by underground channels (*qanats*) assisted it to become perhaps the chief religious centre of Syria. Its growth was complemented by an important military role as an assembly point for Roman campaigns beyond the Euphrates, a major preoccupation in frontier policy of the second and third centuries. The rotation of soldiers through Hierapolis helped spread the fame of its cult throughout the Empire as far as Gaul but it had aroused interest at the highest level even from the time of Nero (mid first century). A sanctuary to Atargatis (second, third century) has been found on the Janiculum hill in Rome.

Hierapolis remained a centre of importance into Christian times, becoming the seat of a Bishop. Justinian fortified it as he did many centres west of the Euphrates. It achieved new fame in the dying days of Byzantine rule when the Emperor Heraclius came here in 630 to recover the True Cross, apparently taken by the Persian invaders during their sack of Jerusalem in 614. Heraclius' restoration of Byzantine rule in the area was short-lived and two decades later, northern Syria followed the south in falling easily to the Muslim forces.

Membij (having returned to its pre-classical name) remained a sizeable centre in the early Islamic period and up until the times of the Zengids (11th and early 12th centuries) when Ibn Jubayr was so impressed by it. The Crusaders from Edessa reached as far as Membij briefly in 1168, 1110 and again during the period 1119 to 1124. Nur al-Din built a *madrasa* (1156), of which the tower added by Saladin (1185) was a notable example of the development of the minaret in 12th century Syria.

Not only the temple of Atargatis and the sacred lake but virtually all the other vestiges of Membij's past have disappeared – the Roman baths and theatre, the Byzantine fortress and churches, the medieval minaret and madrasas. Membij's decline, however, now seems to have been arrested. The region, settled earlier this century with Circassian and Armenian refugees, is gaining a new prosperity through irrigation of the rich farmlands of the Sajur River to the north. Membij's Syriac linguistic root, 'gushing water', is again becoming appropriate.

REFS: *BG* p 419; Bell *Amurath* pp 23 ff; Dussaud *Topographie* pp 474-5; Elisséeff *Mandbidj.*

Meskene

VARIANTS Emar (LBA); Barbalissos (Grk); Barbalissus (Lat); Balis (Cru); Eski Meskene, Meskene al-Qadimeh (Arb)[112].

PERIOD: LBA/Byz/Arab RATING: *   MAP: 72
ITIN: 12a

> LOCATION: From Aleppo, take the road south east towards *Raqqa (same exit from the city as the airport road). Pass through the modern town of Meskene (90 km from Aleppo). After +2 km, at the point where a sign on the right points to Joumanie, head left at ninety degrees to the road across the desert following the unmarked tracks towards the minaret +2 km away.

Meskene marks the site of an important crossing and transit point on the Euphrates where caravan traffic on the Mediterranean/ Mesopotamian route transferred from land to river transport. The creation of Lake Assad as a result of the first phase of the Euphrates scheme, however, has totally changed the sleepy remains of the ancient caravan stop. Formerly perched on a small plateau bordered by a cliff overlooking the river valley, the site has become a lakeside promontory with the waters lapping at the Byzantine fortification walls.

Meskene has been a fortified point since the Middle and Late Bronze Ages. Known as Emar, it was mentioned in the Mari, Ebla and Babylonian archives. A palace and three temples from this period were discovered and excavated in great haste in 1973-6 before the greater part of the site was covered by the lake waters. An archive of over 300 tablets in Akkadian and Hittite was found.

Written records corroborate the Hittites' conquest of the site in the Late Bronze Age during their period of dominance in northern Syria. The town was destroyed, however, around 1175 BC at a time when population movements brought great disruption to Syria as to other parts of the eastern Mediterranean.

The site was re-settled in Seleucid times (third to first centuries BC) and was fortified under the Romans. (In the fourth century AD, the *Equites Dalmatae Illyriciani* was garrisoned there.) The greater part of the remains still visible, however, date from the Byzantine period when the settlement (then known as Barbalissos) was re-fortified by Justinian as part of his major program of fortress cities to hold the

line along the Euphrates against the Persians. The remains of this period include a *praetorium* or fortified housing for the imperial troops and the walls built in the massive style of Justinian's engineers. In the end, of course, it was a threat from another direction, the Arabs, which overwhelmed the area in the next century and, like most Syrian towns, Barbalissos fell easily to the Muslim armies.

The site was again contested during the Crusades. As part of their ill-fated push from Edessa into northern Syria, the Crusaders took the town, then known as Balis, around 1100 but were over-extended and soon lost it. The Mongol invasions of the 13th and 14th centuries finished it off and it fell into disuse as a fortified settlement.

When the site was threatened in the early seventies of this century, a rescue campaign was undertaken to move to safety the superb brick minaret of a 13th century mosque. This can now be seen on arriving, carefully and expertly restored in its new location. The simple and striking style shows the strong influence of the Iranian tradition in northern Syria at the time of the Ayyubids. An internal staircase gives access to the top of the minaret.

REFS: BG pp 483; Dussaud *Topographie* pp 452-3; Hillenbrand *Eastern*; Margueron *Emar*.

Mushabbak (Plate 15b)

VARIANTS:
PERIOD: Byz RATING: * MAP: 68 ITIN: 9a

> LOCATION: 25 km west of Aleppo. Take the road from Aleppo direct to Deiret Azze (and Saint Simeon). Turn right from the Damascus road at the Aleppo Scientific College roundabout (starting point). After 400 m, turn left and continue to 25 km point. Take new dirt road to left which leads directly to church (+1 km).
>
> NOTE: The road on the right about 3 km back towards Aleppo leads to the deserted settlement of Sheikh Suleiman, 3 km to the north. Its ruins include the remains of a church of St Mary which closely resembles the church of Mushabbak.

The church at Mushabbak, as noted in Butler's survey at the turn of the century, is 'one of the most perfectly preserved of all the basilica churches of Northern Syria and one that seems typical of the ecclesiastical architecture of the third quarter of the fifth century in this province. The replacing of the fallen stones of the gables, and a restoration of its wooden roofs, are all that would be required to make it a practicable house of worship'.

---

[112] 'Old Meskene', to distinguish it from the new town created after the filling of the lake.

1a - Ain Dara

1b - Amrit

2a - Aleppo Great mosque Minaret

2b - Aleppo - Beit Ajiqbash

3a - Aleppo - Madrasa Faradis

3b - Apamea - *cardo columns*

3c - Apamea - House of the Aqueduct

4a - Apamea - *cardo maximus*

4b - Bosra - Roman theatre

5a - Bosra - nymphoeum

5b - Bosra Nabatean arch

5c - Cyrrhus - Roman bridge

6a - Damascus - courtyard of Umayyad mosque

6b - Damascus - Umayyad mosque - Mosaic

7a - Damascus - Mosaics of prayer hall facade

7b - Damascus - Treasury of the Umayyad Mosque

7c - Damascus - Azem Palace - *iwan*

8a - Damascus - Azem palace - *qa'a*

8b - Damascus - Beit Nizam

9a - Damascus - Qasr al Heir Gateway

9b - Dumeir - Roman temple

10a - Ebla - Staircase of Royal Palace

10b - Halebiye - Justinian's walls

11a - Harbaqa Dam

11b - Husn Suleiman - gateway to the *temenos*

12a - Isriya - remains of the Roman temple

12b - Jebel Seis - gateway to the Umayyad castle

13a - Kharrab Shams - 4th century church

13b - Krak des Chevaliers - western face

14a - Krak des Chevaliers - southern inner bastions

14b - Krak des Chevaliers - *loggia*

15a - Maalula - Monastery of Mar Taqla

15b - Mushabbak - Byzantine church

16a - Palmyra - Valley of the Tombs

16b - Palmyra - Bel Temple - eastern columns of cella

16c - Palmyra - decorative detail of monumental arch

17a - Palmyra - Monumental Arch

17b - Palmyra - Qalaat Ibn Maan

18a - Khan al Hallabat

18b - Qanawat - *seraya doorway*

19a - Qalaat Jaber

19b - Qalaat Masyaf

20a - Qalaat al - Shmemis

20b - Qasr al - Heir East - eastern castle

21a - Qasr Ibn Wardan - basalt lintel, southern entrance to church

21b - Resafa - St. Sergius basilica

22a - Saint Simeon - courtyard and remains of saint's column

22b - Saint Simeon - chevet of eastern basilica

23a - Serjilla - sarcophagus

23b - Serjilla - baths and *andron*

24a - Shahba - Roman theatre

24b - Tartus - Cathedral facade

The three-aisle columned basilica borrows several eclectic architectural ideas. The internal dimensions are almost 18 m by 12 m and the use of nine semi-circular arched windows in a clerestory supported by five 4.5 m columns adds a sense of height which echoes the main church at *Kharrab Shams. The more lavish use of windows is also found on the western facade where six openings above the portal and two on each side are complemented by a further three in the triangular entablature. The decoration is minimal, restricted largely to the varied carvings of the column capitals. The overall effect shows a considerable evolution from the earlier stodgy church designs based on enlarged house architecture. The striving for greater light and height achieves some success. As usual, two annex rooms lead off the side aisles, but the north one (a *martyrium*) also has a door leading off the apse.

At the time of construction, nearby *Saint Simeon was being developed as a centre of pilgrimage. Mushabbak was possibly built to serve as a way-station on the pilgrimage route (this would explain the lack of other substantial buildings in the area) thus benefitting from the more advanced architectural concepts tried out in the great basilica by metropolitan builders.

REFS: *BG* p 396; Beyer pp 55-7; Butler *AE* II p 143-7; Butler *EC* pp 62-4; Butler *PE* II/B/6 pp 341-2; Mattern pp 115-7.

Mushennef

VARIANTS: Nela, Nelkomia (Grk)
PERIOD: Roman RATING: * MAP: 63 ITIN: 2b

LOCATION: At the roundabout in the centre of *Shahba (87 km south of Damascus on Suweida road), turn left. Take the road down the hill and through the gap in the Roman wall that still marks the town limits. Follow this road which skirts to the east of the Jebel al-Arab for +25 km, keeping the slopes of the Jebel on your right.

A typically bizarre mixture of ancient and modern in a rather harsh Jebel al-Arab setting with the predominant colour coming from the black basalt stone of this volcanic region. (Beyond to the east begins the volcanic-wilderness area known as the Safa.) In the centre of Mushennef is a small Roman temple constructed on the edge of an artificial lake. In spite of the setting and the sombre stone, it manages to suggest a sense of delicacy through its fine architectural decoration (meanders, rosettes, Corinthian capitals) in the dark unyielding stone. The temple was originally enclosed in a courtyard. The porticoed front of the *cella* has been reconstructed and filled in for defensive purposes in a hopelessly dyslexic style - a random Lego-like composition that adds to the bizarre effect.

The temple of Mushennef carries an inscription dated AD 171 on the north gate referring to the Emperor Marcus Aurelius. However, the site was probably used for religious purposes long before that. Another inscription, to Herod Agrippa I, indicates was in use in the first half of the first century AD. Butler compares the temple in style to the twin temples at *Atil and recent researchers date its decoration to the decades 20-01 BC.

This was a flourishing area in Roman times, as can be seen in the amount of ancient stonework incorporated in modern buildings. If you continue south, two other sites are worth visiting. 6.5 km south is Busan where part of a Roman temple survives amid stone houses. 4 km further on at Saleh (classical *Salamanestha*) - a Roman fountain has been dismantled and partly re-assembled on a concrete base to serve as the centre-piece in a stockyard.

REFS: *BG* p 545; Butler *AE* pp 346-51; Butler *PE* II/A/5 p 380; Dussaud *Topographie* p 359.

P

Palmyra (Plates 16a – 17a)

VARIANTS: Palmyre (Fr); Tadmor (Arb)
PERIOD: Rom/Arb ALT: 600 m RATING: ***
MAP: *39, 40, 41, 42, 75* ITIN: 14

LOCATION: In the central Syrian Desert, 235 km north
east of Damascus, on a good sealed road. Turn off
Aleppo motorway 24 km north of Damascus and
follow direction signs for the Cham Hotel, Palmyra.

Palmyra is one of the great sites of the ancient
world. The remains of this oasis city, midway
between the Mediterranean seaboard and the
thin cultivated zone of the Euphrates, seem
suspended in time in this harsh desert
environment. An elusive and highly romanticised
goal of European travellers over the centuries,
even today a visit to Palmyra is an experience
which alone makes the trip to Syria worthwhile.

History

Palmyra owes its origins to the extensive oasis to
the south of the ruins. The date, olive and
pomegranate orchards are watered by
underground springs emerging from the
mountains that enclose it to the north and west.
For this reason, it was settled as long ago as the
end of the third millennium BC and is mentioned
in archives of the period from *Mari (18th century
BC) and as far away as Kultepe (in Cappadocia,
modern Turkey). The Semitic name Tadmor is
mentioned in Assyrian archives and is listed in
the Bible as within Solomon's sphere of influence
though the reference is based on a confusion of
the name with Tamar in the Judaean desert[113].

The Seleucid settlement has recently been
identified as lying south of the main Roman city.
The early Romans found Palmyra an elusive
prize. In 41 BC, Antony attempted to seize its
riches but arriving in the oasis found it deserted
by its inhabitants and thus devoid of booty. It
probably owed nominal allegiance to Rome
under Augustus, developing closer links
(including Roman city-state political institutions)
under Tiberius (r AD 14-37). It was probably

integrated into the Province of Syria by the reign
of Nero (54-68).

Though its rise to prosperity reflected its
trading role, Palmyra is not on the natural trade
route between the coastal/Orontes area and the
Mid Euphrates. The natural link arches to the
north, following the curve of the Fertile Crescent
and skirting the uplands of Turkey. In the first
century BC, that route fell prey to the instability
that brought the Seleucid Kingdom to an end. A
coalition of Arab interests was formed between
Homs and Tadmor to secure a new short-cut
across the desert. It was an instant success.

Given the conditions of sustained security
under the Empire and the impetus to east/west
trade resulting from the exotic tastes of the
Roman and provincial upper classes, Palmyra
continued to flourish. Much of the trade between
the Mediterranean and the east - India (via the
Persian Gulf) Trans-Oxiana and China - flowed
through Palmyra. As long as the Arab dynasties
could control the desert tribes, the commercial
viability of the route was assured given the
considerable time and effort saved compared
with the northern route or the more arduous
desert journey via Nabatean territory to the
south. But prosperity depended, too, on good
relations with the Parthian kingdom to the east
and for the century and a half of nominal Roman
rule, Palmyra retained a close understanding
with the Parthians (with whom they had many
traditional links) while respecting Rome's overall
supremacy. It prospered as a sort of neutral zone
'wherein the goods of these two officially hostile
powers, Parthia and Rome, might be
exchanged'[114], with a suitable rake-off arranged.
(The rates are set out in the Palmyra Tariff - see
page 170 below.)

At the height of its prosperity in the second
century Palmyra was a centre rivalling Antioch, at
least in economic importance, perhaps the most
active entrepot in the eastern Empire. It was
particularly favoured by Hadrian during his tour of
the eastern provinces in AD 129, being declared
by him a free city (*civitas libera*) and renamed
Palmyra Hadriana. Though basically Semitic in
population, it increasingly turned to Roman
political, social and cultural models while

---

[113] 2 *Chronicles* 8,4. The original meaning of the Semitic and
modern-day Arab name for the town is probably 'guard-post' -
Starcky and Gawlikowski p 33. The Greeks and Romans adopted
Palmyra in the belief that Tadmor was a reference to the local date
palm (the Semitic root being *tamar*).

[114] Rostovtzeff quoted in Huxley *From an Antique Land* Boston
1966 p 155.

retaining predominantly eastern styles of art and dress. In 194 the city was transferred to the new province of *Syria Phoenice*. The second century was the high period of its prosperity as reflected in the present-day remains and the evidence of the *nouveau riche* lifestyle of its ruling families. The veneer of Roman culture, however, only superficially cloaked a society still basically tribal and mercantile rather than urban and aristocratic, in spite of all the money sunk into prestige civic projects.

Empire following successive power struggles in Rome. Palmyra had become a more vital strategic prize as a result of the rise after 227 of the more centralised and aggressive Sasanian dynasty in Persia, founded by Ardashir with its capital at Ctesiphon. At the same time, the Palmyrene economy suffered from the Sasanian seizure of the territory at the mouth of the Tigris/Euphrates from where Palmyra had previously controlled traffic on the Indian Ocean thus securing the cross-desert caravan trade at its source.

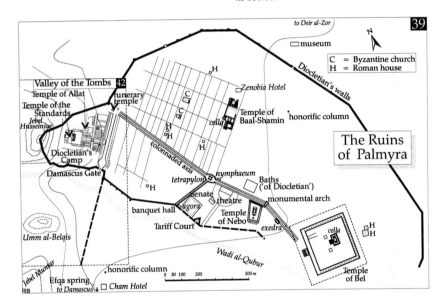

Although the first Roman garrison was installed in the 150's, Roman control until the late second century was lightly wielded. After the Parthian wars of 162-66, however, the army took a greater role in the affairs of the Empire and by 212 under Caracalla the city was declared a Roman colony (*colonia*). This new period of uncertainty was reflected in the decline of the caravan trade. Palmyra's closer association with imperial strategic interests also reflected the Syrian links of the Severans, Caracalla's mother being a daughter of the High Priest of Emesa (*Homs). Major building programs from this period include the extension of the colonnaded axis to the Bel Temple.

In the second half of the third century, however, the rulers of Palmyra began to re-assert their independence. Partly this reflected the breakdown of central control throughout the

With that trade effectively strangled, the mercantilist ethic in Palmyra weakened, making more difficult the city's attempts to act as a go-between linking east and west. The oligarchical rule of the good times gave way to the dynastic ambitions of one family, the Julii Aurelii Septimii. Their leader, Septimius Odainat (Odenathus - r 252-67) rose to prominence as the local strong man by seeking and exploiting Rome's favour. He was apparently put in charge of Rome's legions in the area when appointed Consul and Governor of *Syria Phoenice* (256/7) by the Emperor Valerian (r 253-60) at a time of intense Sasanian pressure. (*Dura Europos fell to them in 256.)

Rome was happy to encourage Odenathus, anxious in particular to reverse the disaster brought about by the capture of Valerian by the Persians in 260 and his brutal and humiliating murder. In 266/7, Odenathus campaigned as far as Ctesiphon on Rome's behalf. No doubt his intervention saved Roman fortunes in the east at a vital moment when central authority was at crisis point but in pursuing Rome's security interests against the Sasanians, he inevitably became a power in his own right beyond the traditional perimeter of the oasis state.

PALMYRENE ART

Something needs to be said about the style of art, particularly architecture and carved relief sculptures, found at Palmyra, if only to head off any assumption that it represents a provincial (and thus debased) version of Roman styles of the first to third centuries AD. True, much of the art (including the overall architectural conventions based on Roman and Hellenistic repertoires) does strive for a metropolitan or standard style. But the differences are significant; and consciously so. The Roman/Hellenistic framework had already been adapted to local usage and tradition through several centuries of blending oriental and Mediterranean styles. This Arab/Parthian synthesis reflected the ripples left by Alexander's great campaign of the fourth century BC as seen in the succession of Nabatean, Bactrian and Greco-Buddhist (Gandara) styles that spread towards the east, including the orientalised Parthian forms found at *Dura-Europos and Hatra (Iraq).

We are thus not simply dealing with a provincial Roman phenomenon but with a Greco-Persian-Parthian synthesis whose roots go back deep into the hellenized traditions of the east, long before Roman influence became prominent in the first century AD. This semi-'orientalising' or 'other-worldly' element, common to several traditions, involves concentration on frontal representation; timeless rather than realistic expressions; oriental dress in a heavily stylised treatment; and restless, almost baroque, application of decoration. To some extent, the obsessive formalism of the local style gradually broke down under more direct Roman influence. Realism, introspection and psychological insight in the expressions depicted on late funerary sculptures are thus all the more striking. Ironically, the final victory went to the orientalised/formalised tradition which penetrated even the art of the imperial centre following the move to Constantinople, setting the style for over a millennium of Byzantine art.

Palmyra's ambitions, however, were to assert themselves even more aggressively after the murder of Odenathus in 267/8[115] during the

regency of his wife, Zenobia, on behalf of her son, Vaballath (Vabalathus). Determined to realise on her husband's inheritance and to by-pass the constrictions on Palmyra's commercial interests resulting from Sasanian control of the Tigris/Euphrates mouth, she asserted Palmyrene power westwards, taking Bosra and venturing as far as Egypt in 269-70. Anatolia followed and she began squeezing Antioch from 270. It seems for a time she entertained ambitions of sharing the Roman world with the new Emperor, Aurelian (r 270-5): she (with the title of *Augusta*) would reign in the east, leaving the western Mediterranean provinces to him.

Clearly, for the Romans, things had got out of hand. Aurelian, at first prepared to be flexible, met the new challenge as a cavalry man. He took to the field himself to put down the threat. In 272 he recovered Anatolia and Antioch and defeated a large Palmyrene force outside Emesa (*Homs). He went on to attack Palmyra. Queen Zenobia attempted to flee eastwards on a dromedary (probably to seek Sasanian support) but was captured by the Romans trying to cross the Euphrates. She was taken back to Aurelian's camp where she formally surrendered Palmyra to the Emperor. According to the *Augustan History*, she was later taken to Rome to grace Aurelian's triumph in 274 in sumptuous bondage[116]. Before that, however, in the spring of 273, the garrison Aurelian had left at Palmyra was overwhelmed in a local revolt and a new and more brutal action against the city was undertaken in 272/3. Aurelian rushed back from the Danube to meet the emergency. This time, he drove home the lesson of Roman power by allowing his troops to massacre indiscrimately and to sack much of the city. Even the Bel Temple was pillaged, its treasure confiscated.

Roman control now became even more tight, Palmyra becoming even less a trading centre and more a strategic asset - the nodal point in a network of strategic roads that secured Rome's eastern frontiers. The city was expanded under Diocletian (r 284-305) to encompass an enlarged quarter to house Rome's legion and was walled against the Sasanian threat (given the lesson of Dura's fall in 256). In the Byzantine period,

---

[115] He and his elder son Herodianus were murdered in Cappadocia (where they were stemming, again on Rome's behalf, a barbarian threat) sometime between August 267 and April 268 (Starcky *Palmyre* 1952 p 57). A disaffected soldier did the deed, but on whose behalf, if not his own? Some theories accuse

Zenobia herself, others (eg Ruprechtsberger p 129) the Emperor Gallienus (260-8).

[116] The Augustan History (*Life of Thirty Tyrants* XXIX - not necessarily a reliable source) describes the theatrical cortege, complete with elephants and gladiators, culminating in Zenobia, weighed down with gold chains and exotic jewelry. Aurelian's willingness so to humiliate a woman was questioned at the time in the Senate. She was kept in captivity in the neighbourhood of Rome, near Hadrian's villa at Tivoli. The circumstances of her death are not clear.

several churches were constructed in the northern area and the walls further strengthened under Justinian (r 527-65) though much of the city was by then in ruins. In 634 It was taken by Khalid Ibn al-Walid, one of the military leaders under the first Caliph, Abu Bakr, but later played only a minor role in the Islamic period though the Umayyads built their desert castles at nearby *Qasr al-Heir East and *Qasr al-Heir West. In 745, a local revolt resulted in the dismantling by Caliph Marwan of the walls rebuilt by Justinian. The area still had some minor defensive role as is illustrated in later centuries by the fortification of the Bel Temple (12th century) and the Arab castle (*Qalaat Ibn Maan). By the Ottoman period, the ruins had been surrendered to the desert.

Visit

The ruins which spread over ten square kilometres are described in the following order:

- Temple of Bel;
- main colonnaded street and associated public buildings;
- Diocletian's Camp;
- museum;
- Temple of Baal-Shamin and area north of colonnade;
- Valley of the Tombs;
- south west necropolis;
- south east necropolis.

Though the broad outline of the city suggest some initial grand design, the evidence indicates that it was more the sum of its parts than a strict town plan. Whatever basic plan existed (evident more in the western quarters) was much modified and extended by later religious and civic improvements. When, after the first century AD, some attempt was made to imitate the rigid grandeur of Greco-Roman town planning by imposing a colonnaded axis on this higgledy-piggledy design, the successive changes of mind about the basic alignment were evident in the erratic course of the axis as it dodged existing obstacles.

To take in·most of these areas, a full day should be allowed. Two days would not be excessive for a more leisurely visit, especially in summer when you need to avoid the heat of the middle of the day (which is also unsuitable for photography due to the intensity of the light). A day trip out from Damascus allows only for a superficial impression of the ruins and doesn't give an opportunity to experience them either by moonlight or at dawn when they reserve a special magic for visitors.

HOURS - TEMPLE OF BEL, MUSEUM, LOCKED TOMBS
Summer (May - Sep) 08:00 - 13:00; 16:00 - 19:00
Winter (Oct - Apr) and Ramadan 08:00 - 16:00

The **Temple of Bel** (broadly oriented towards the compass points) stands in its enormous compound at the eastern end of the main colonnaded street. The temple is certainly the most important religious building of the first century AD in the Middle East and is one of the few early imperial projects in the region to survive. The complex was built in several stages:

- Hellenistic temple - only fragments of stones incorporated in later walls survive;
- central shrine or *cella* dedicated AD 32 but probably under construction since AD 17 or 19;
- AD 80-120 - *peribolos* enlarged, surrounded by double colonnaded portico on north, east and south;
- late second century - west portico and *propylaeum*.

The undertaking of such a project on a truly imperial scale and to a high standard of craftsmanship reflects both the ubiquity of the Hellenistic tradition which inspired its architecture as well as the prosperity of the late Augustine period and the early years of his successor, Tiberius (AD 14-37), which provided the wherewithal to construct it.

Before you enter through the ticket office on the west side, note the massive scale of the second-third century walls, reinforced and converted to defensive purpose during Arab times. In some places, earthquake damage has been reconstructed in a rough and ready manner, Roman details such as niches, pediments and pilasters being reinserted in random order. The general pattern of the Roman walls can still be observed (eg the north western corner, left of the ticket office) with pilasters alternating with framed windows topped by triangular pediments. The artificial terrace was built up to the level of the mound on which the original temple had been placed.

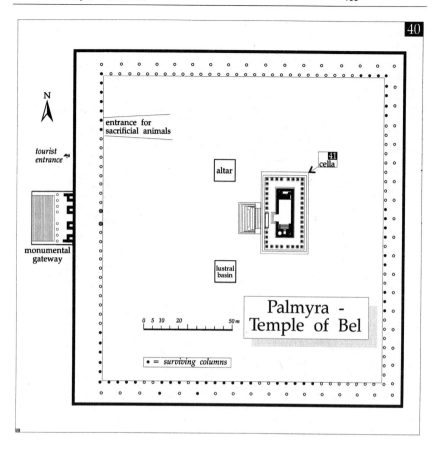

40

entrance for
sacrificial animals

tourist
entrance

monumental
gateway

N

altar

41
cella

lustral
basin

0 5 10   20   50 m

**Palmyra -
Temple of Bel**

• = *surviving columns*

To the right of the ticket office stood the great triple entrance gateway (late second century) - 35 m wide, a broad flight of stairs leading up to a *propylaeum* with a tall central portal. The impressive scale of the west facade reflected a new peak of Roman prestige and prosperity in the Antonine period. The *propylaeum* originally carried eight columns with a huge central arch but the remains were removed in the 12th century during the Mameluke fortification works, bringing the facade of the gateway back to the level of the flanking walls. The Arab builders constructed in utilitarian style with two sets of machicolation above the recessed central doorway.

Having entered the compound, it is worth looking back to the right to gain an internal perspective of the great gateway. The central

opening in the *temenos* wall is extant, along with the subsidiary doors and niches. The western portico along this side of the compound was considerably larger in scale than its counterparts on the north, east and south. The pillars are higher (some remain at either end of the portico) and the internal space is uncluttered by the second row of pillars that supported the roof on the other three sides.

Though the grandeur reached its climax in this Antonine addition to the first century temple it in no way overshadowed the Augustan *cella* that formed the centrepiece of the complex. The tradition of the Syro-Phoenician temple is traced elsewhere (see box in Section 2, page 18). After Baalbek, the Bel Temple in Palmyra is the supreme realisation of the tradition with its huge compound, surrounding peristyle and relatively small central *cella*. The *cella* is offset somewhat to the east in the compound whose main axis extends from the great gateway and ascends to the centrepiece by a broad flight of stairs.

As you approach the central chamber, two common features of Syro-Phoenician religious architecture can be traced: the ritual pool for ablutions (right); and the altar for sacrifices (left). A subsidiary feature also worth noting is the passageway that enters the compound left of the tourist entrance. Designed as a ramp to lead animals up to the sacrificial altar, after passing under the compound wall the entrance rises through an arch supporting the columned portico above. A little to the right of the passageway's end, and in front of the altar, are the remains of a long rectangular banqueting hall.

Before approaching the *cella*, take in the scale of the compound (205 m by 210 m) and the beauty of the north, south and east peristyle colonnades (AD 80-120). The columns are relatively intact on the south side and are fine realisations of the Corinthian order (the purpose of the column brackets will be discussed later).

BEL

Bel is a Semitic god of multiple manifestations, whose name ('lord') is Akkadian in origin but which was later found in the Ugaritic pantheon as Baal and eventually equated with the Greek Zeus (as Zeus-Belos). He was often accompanied by subsidiary Palmyrene gods representing the sun (Yarhibol) and moon (Aglibol).

One of the manifestations with whom Bel was linked was the Canaanite god, Baal-Shamin (*Ugarit) who was likewise equated with Zeus in Seleucid/Roman times and with Hadad whose cult was widespread in Roman Syria (*Damascus - Umayyad Mosque). Baal-Shamin duplicated to some extent the role of Bel as master of the heavens.

Given the mix of populations at Palmyra, hundreds of other gods were honoured, not least several of Arab origin, including Allat ('the goddess' who took on many of the attributes of the 'Syrian goddess', Atargatis, worshipped at *Membij) and Shamath, a sun god probably linked to the cult at Emesa whose statue Aurelian had transferred to Rome as the centrepiece of the cult of *Sol Invictus*.

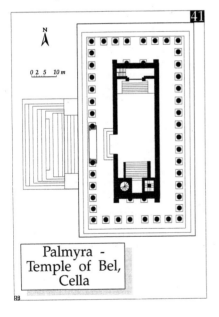

Palmyra - Temple of Bel, Cella

centres of the period, the architectural treatment owes much to the Greek tradition as passed on by Rome. The eastern and western traditions vie brilliantly for the last word. In the Semitic tradition, the scale and function of the *cella*, a single chamber enclosed by a colonnaded peristyle, should merely be part of the vast surrounding sacred enclosure. The builders, however, have emphasised its centrality by the bold adaptation of the classical temple concept. The north and south walls of the *cella* are restrained in treatment, furnished with four square or round pilasters in the Ionic order. It is with the peristyle that the oriental opulence begins. The outer columns (eight survive on the east side) were originally capped with metal capitals in the Corinthian order probably plated in gold or silver. But it is the sheer height of the peristyle (18 m – Plate 16b) which still impresses, particularly the soaring entrance portal set between two of the columns on the west side. And to top the effect, the lower cornice around the peristyle was crowned with crow-feet merlons, a Mesopotamian device repeated in the four towers that jutted above the roofline of the *cella* itself. This may have been echoed in the frieze of merlons which crowned the whole of the outer wall of the complex. The neo-Hellenistic bravuro with which the project was realised marked Palmyra's assertion of its new economic power on the fringes of the Roman world; a brilliant synthesis symbolising the city's role between east and west.

The *cella*, as noted earlier, was dedicated in AD 32 but the site had been used for religious purposes as long ago as 2200 BC. Though it follows the pattern of other Syrian religious

The fact that the entrance is off-centre and not on the narrower end of the building further emphasises the variation on classical tradition. Opinions vary as to why the main axis of the compound, traditionally oriented north/south, seems to have been switched to the west. The change was evidently made after the construction of the *cella*'s peristyle had commenced. Perhaps it became clear that to the south, the steep walls of a *wadi* prevented the creation of a monumental entrance to the enlarged terrace of the *temenos*. However, the reorientation may also have been required for ritual reasons, to provide two internal chapels within the *cella*.

The present rather wobbly reconstruction of the portal was undertaken by the French in 1932. The carved decoration is again typical of the Syrian adaptation of Roman styles. Some may find the effect rather overblown or baroque with no surfaces left unadorned but the style, though exuberant, is controlled and departs judiciously from the classical tradition. The addition of decoration wherever possible is even achieved in the beams that joined the cornice of the peristyle to the top of the *cella* and supported the sloping peristyle roof. Some of the beams that have fallen now lie to the right of the portal and the typically Parthian stylised carving, depicting local gods, is vividly preserved in the crisp limestone.

As you enter the *cella*, you find yourself off-centre within the 10 m by 30 m chamber. Even more confusing is the fact that the chamber has two focal points, namely two shrines for the worship of images of the gods. This lack echoes the multiplicity of deities embraced within the Mesopotamian/Semitic concept of Bel. A trinity of gods was worshipped in the compound, Bel himself and two Palmyrene divinities affiliated to him, Yarhibol (a solar god) and Aglibol (a lunar god). The setting of the images of the gods in an enclosed *adyton* is a Semitic concept, the Romans preferring to place images of their gods on plinths or pedestals.

The normal place for the statue of the god would be in the north *adyton*. This is where the trinity was worshipped in the Semitic predecessor of the cella. The ceiling of the niche is a single stone carved with images of the seven planetary divinities encircled by the zodiac. Superimposed on the carved mouldings of the lintel is an eagle with wings outspread across the soffit, representing Bel controlling the movements of the heavens. He is accompanied by Yarhibol and Aglibol. To the right and left of the *adyton*, the sanctuary facade concealed two side chambers. Through that on the left, a staircase (one of three) ascends, emerging

through a tower at the corner of the *cella* roof which, unlike the surrounding peristyle roof, is flat. This use of the roof as a liturgical platform (for purposes still not clear) is a common feature in Syro-Phoenician temples, probably continuing the earlier tradition of conducting sacrifices in 'high places'.

The south *adyton* is somewhat simpler, comprising a smaller niche flanked by two pilasters and a half pilaster on each side. The entablature and the frame of the niche are richly carved. The pillars may once have supported a cornice that would have balanced the rather earth-bound proportions of the current arrangement. Note the gradually sloped stairs leading up to the niche, perhaps intended to facilitate the carrying of the god's image for it is assumed[117] that this niche contained a statue of Bel used in ritual processions. Take particular note of the remarkable monolith ceiling of this south *adyton*. In spite of its soot-stained condition, the superb detail and balance of this design (a central *fleuron* surrounded by a meander band and border rosettes) is òne of the great examples of ancient sculptural decoration that influenced the classical revival of the 18th century[118]. To the right and left of the south niche are the other two staircases which originally ascended to the roof.

Until the villagers of Tadmor were dislodged from the Bel Temple compound by the French antiquities administration in 1929, the *cella* was used as a mosque, hence the *mihrab* in the south wall and a number of inscriptions going back as far as 728-9.

If you walk around to the back of the Bel Temple compound, you will come upon the remains of two patrician **houses** of the third century AD. Both contain rooms grouped around central courtyards. Mosaics of fine quality were found here and have been reassembled in the Palmyra and Damascus museums.

The next stage of our description covers the full length of the **colonnaded street** that serves as the main axis of the Roman city running 1.2 km approximately north west/south east in its orientation. For the sake of simplicity, however, the following description will assume a broadly east/west orientation with the Arab castle as the western orientation point and the Bel Temple on

---

[117] Starcky *Palmyre* p 17.

[118] The pattern was carefully reproduced by the English travellers Wood and Dawkins in their work on Palmyra published following their visit in 1751. Browning pp 124-5 notes the important influence which the design had on English decorative arts in the second half of the 18C.

the east. Note, too, that you will be following the colonnaded axis in reverse chronological order, the western end being the first to be developed.

Start your walk from the entrance to the Bel Temple or from where the asphalt road cuts across the ancient axis. This first section of the street was constructed in the late second or early third century to link the new grand entrance to the Bel Temple to the existing axis. The plan was probably never completed but the first notable embellishment (left) is the *exedra* or semi-circular wall flanked by niches and preceded by a portico with four tall and elegant columns. Such monumental flourishes often served in Roman/Syrian cities to display statuary of civic notables.

60 metres further on, you come to the first of two bends in the central axis at which point stands the **monumental arch** (Plates 16c, 17a), an achievement of considerable architectural interest. It resolves with masterly confidence the problems posed by the street's marked change in direction (30⁰). The solution was a wedge plan, thus facing two directions while preserving the facades of the traditional type of arch, a high central opening flanked by two smaller ones. The decoration is rich, in the Syrian style, with much resort to the niche, either with the semi-circular Syrian arch or a classical entablature above it. The arch was erected under Septimius Severus (Emperor 193-211), more or less the *apogée* of Palmyra's prosperity when extensive civic improvements were undertaken in the city.

Just after the arch, on your left as you continue west, you will find the remains of the **Temple of Nebo** or Nabu, comprising only the podium of the temple measuring 20 m by 9 m and the bases of the surrounding colonnade which forms a trapezoid. The plan is basically eastern in inspiration, comprising a peristyled *cella* opening towards an outdoor altar, with a columned *propylaeum* forming the main entrance from the south. The scale is much smaller than the Bel Temple. Nebo was a Mesopotamian god of wisdom and oracles, equated with the classical Apollo. The compound was thoroughly researched by a Franco-Syrian team in the 1960's who dated the temple to the last quarter of the first century AD with work continuing on the surrounding complex until the third century.

Leaving the temple and heading west, you are now well into the main **colonnaded street** (technically, the *decumanus*) at its best-preserved point. The street as you see it here was the work of the mid to late second century. The central carriageway is 11 m wide and was not paved, thus facilitating access for camels. It

was flanked by porticos each 7 m broad. In several places behind the colonnaded porticos, the foundations of the market shops can be seen. Note how each of the columns carries a protruding bracket on which originally were placed statues of civic notables. While to the modern observer this may rob the classical columns of their commanding simplicity of form, the Palmyrenes could not conceive of civic life without sponsorship and fanfare - hence the constant reminders of the civic notables to whom everyone was indebted.

In addition to shops, civic amenities were concentrated in this area of the principal axis. An example of the latter is the entry to the **Baths of Diocletian** whose location is signalled on the right hand side by four tall monolith columns in Egyptian red granite jutting from the line of arcading. Diocletian's reign (284-305) came after the destruction that followed the defeat of Zenobia. The decision to build up Palmyra as a military centre also brought a new range of civic improvements. Behind the colonnade, the outline of the baths (which probably existed for almost a century before being provided with a more sumptuous entry and attributed to Diocletian) can be traced in the foundations, including surviving columns of the atrium peristyle.

Shortly after on the left, you will notice a semi-circular arch which marks the junction of a cross street which was also colonnaded, at least on one side, and curves around behind the semi-circular enclosure of the theatre.

Until recently, the remains of the **theatre** gave little hint that it was once in the same league as several other major examples in Syria (*Apamea, *Bosra, *Cyrrhus) in terms of size. Until the 1950's, the theatre was largely buried under the sand. Its lower levels have since been excavated and restored to give a greater idea of its original appearance and the *scaenae frons* or stage facade has been reconstructed. (As there is no sign of any substructure for seating beyond the first 12 rows, it has recently been argued that the upper levels of seating must have been constructed in wood.) The stage area of the theatre is separated by only a narrow portico from the main street. The Polish archaeologist, Michalowski, dates the theatre to the first half of the second century AD, earlier than the improvements to the colonnaded street. The *scaenae frons*, however, is later (late second or early third century) and lacks the usual facilities for crowd handling and rooms for the actors. This sequence might account for the rather cramped arrangement if compromises had to be made in order to rebuild the stage area in the narrow space left by the late second century widening or realigning of the main thoroughfare.

Inside, the theatre is restored up to its ninth row of seating. The stage is preserved to the first level of entablature over the lowest series of columns, giving some idea of the elaborate *scaenae frons*. The central doorway is set in a half-oval instead of the usual half-circular *exedra* and there are five doorways leading behind the stage instead of the usual three.

If you walk round to the back of the theatre, you will see on the west side of the semi-circle the remains of what was possibly the **Senate**. This was a small building consisting of an entrance hall, a peristyled court and a chamber with an apse at the end around which were arranged rows of seating. The rather truncated form of the building is probably due to the amputation of its north side during the building of the colonnaded street that enclosed the theatre.

Immediately south of the Senate is a large courtyard area known as the **Tariff Court** in which an inscribed stone was found setting out a decree of AD 137 listing the Palmyrene tariff arrangements[119]. It seems reasonable to deduce that it was here that caravans paid the taxes stipulated. The southern entrance to the court (which was not paved) is rather grand in treatment, two of the triple doorways being extant. The outer entrance to these openings was once marked by a monumental portico but the arrangement was partly dismantled at the end of the third century during the building of **Diocletian's wall** which cut across the facade at this point.

To the west of this court, you enter the *agora*. This large rectangular enclosure (48 m by 71 m) dates from the first part of the second century AD and has been extensively restored since its excavation in 1939-40. The open space was surrounded on four sides by columned porticos. The walls were decorated with windows with richly decorated triangular pediments. The usual brackets for statues of local dignitaries are found on the columns and walls (there must have been more than 200 in total in this space). The doorway to the Tariff Court to the east was known as the Senators' Gate and was decorated with statues of the family of Emperor Septimius Severus (Emperor 193-211) who was married to Julia Domna, daughter of a High Priest of Emesa. In the south west corner of the *agora* are the remains of a banquet room or *triclinium* with benches around the walls for reclining guests.

Head back now directly to the main colonnaded street. Almost immediately on your left, you should find the group of four clusters of columns (tetrapylon*)* which marks the major crossing point. Leave this for the moment and note, on the north side of the axis, the remains of the *nymphaeum* or public water fountain. This takes the form of a columned portico behind which is a curving *exedra* to accommodate a semi-circular water basin. The portico was carried on four tall columns standing on pedestals, the whole protruding a little from the line of the axis.

On the southern side of the cardo at this point note the last eight columns as the cardo approaches the tetrapylon from the east. The seventh, counting from the tetrapylon, originally carried a statue of Zenobia. On the supporting console is an inscription in her honour dated 271 from which Zenobia's name was effaced in Roman times. The preceding (sixth) column carried a statue of her husband Odenathus. The Romans (perhaps recalling his earlier service to the Empire) left his inscription intact.

At the end of this second section of the main axis, a second, less severe (10°) change of direction is marked by the **tetrapylon** which stood in an oval place. Reconstructed by the Syrian Antiquities Department since 1963, this comprises a stepped platform on which are grouped four sets of four columns, each set standing on a plinth and topped by an entablature. Statues originally stood in each of the groupings. The columns were of pink granite from Aswan in Egypt but only one has survived, the modern reconstruction using compounded concrete substitutes.

The remaining 500 m of the colonnaded street to the west is less marked by public buildings and has only been partially excavated. It represents the first stage of the axis developed (first half of second century). Browning[120] has noted that the axis may originally have been designed to continue this alignment by driving straight across the city to the entrance to the Temple of Bel. This plan may have been subsequently modified by pressure to preserve the *cella* of the Temple of Nebo and the practical difficulties of cutting into the *cavea* of the theatre, hence the two changes of direction.

An *exedra*, probably marks the site of a second *nymphaeum*, just beyond the tetrapylon on the left. The remaining 500 m brings you to the **funerary temple** (late second century). This is actually more an elaborate temple tomb or

---

[119] The 5 m long stone was found in 1881 and is now in the Hermitage Museum, Saint Petersburg.

[120] p 84.

burial centre preceded by an elegant portico with six columns and with a vault below. The portico was standing before the modern reconstruction effort but the rest has been restored in recent times with rather lavish use of concrete where insufficient ancient stones survive.

The next part of our description covers the area to the left as you face the funerary temple, commonly called **Diocletian's Camp**. This is reached by the broad transverse street to the left (originally constructed in the second century) some of whose columns can still be traced. After about 300 m, you will come to the remains of another columned avenue leading to the right. This was the principal axis of the Roman camp constructed by Sosianus Hierocles, Governor of Syria under Diocletian (r 284-305), the Emperor who did much to stabilise Rome's eastern frontier after the Sasanian incursions and Zenobia's revolt. Half way along the 90 m avenue, at the junction of the main cross street, a tetrapylon was constructed on a massive scale. (Some bases and two of the columns which supported the grand entablature remain).

At the end of the main avenue stood a forecourt followed by the culminating vista of the Temple of the Standards or the legion's *principia*, also the work of Sosianus carried out between 293 and 303. What remains of the temple and its entrance portico is preceded by a huge flight of stairs, intact except that they seem to have collapsed into a melting heap like an ambitious but unstable blancmange. Behind the portico was a hall, only 12 m deep but 60 m wide, at the rear of which was the inner shrine. This shrine or *cella* for the housing of the Roman legion's standards was a rectangular chamber ending in an apse and flanked on either side by administrative rooms. Above it was an upper chamber and roof reached by a winding staircase. The purpose of the complex seems to combine several ends including the accommodation of the troops and their weapons and the promotion of a military cult on pseudo-religious lines. The building's regularity, and imperial scale, however, pay tribute to the confidence of the Empire under Diocletian who had his own palace at Split (Croatia) built to a similar plan.

Two other parts of the area called Diocletian's Camp are worth noting. If you return to the main cross street where the four-way arch was situated, continue to the north a little way and you will see on the left the remains of a door frame and several fluted columns. This was part of the **Temple of Allat**, constructed during the second century AD (on the site of a first century BC sanctuary) before the adaptation of the area

as the *principia* for the Roman troops. (*Cella* with a *pronaos* framed by six columns, within a *temenos*). Allat ('goddess') was Arab in origin, equated with Ishtar in Mesopotamia, Atargatis in Syria (see *Membij) and Athena. A statue of the goddess as Athena copied from a version by the Greek sculptor, Phidias, was found on the site. A giant lion figure of strikingly modern, partly stylised appearance was incorporated into the temple compound wall, and is today in the front garden of the Palmyra Museum (it probably dates from 50 BC).

Return to the main transverse street that led off the main axis and turn to the south (right). After 60 m you will come to an oval forum (a minor version of the one at Jerash in Jordan) that lay just inside the **Damascus gate** of the city. The arcading in the Corinthian order was carefully coordinated in a perspective that framed the gateway.

You have now finished with the areas south of the main axis. For the next stage, areas **north of the axis**, return to the east and head for the group of ruins immediately south and west of the Hotel Zenobia.

Immediately south of the hotel are the remains of the **Temple of Baal-Shamin** (Lord of the Heavens in the Semitic pantheon, responsible for rain and thus fecundity). The complex history of the various phases of its construction is still being unravelled. The first work (the northern courtyard) dates as early as AD 17. Further construction was carried out in the early second century AD funded by a private bequest but improvements were made in the third century under the rule of Odenathus. The small *cella* (AD 130, immediately after Hadrian's visit) is a charming building, none the less so for the foliage it has acquired since its restoration by a Swiss mission in 1954-6. (The restoration has brought out the almost fanciful or baroque style of the central *exedra* flanked by side chambers - cf the temples at *Suweilim and *Qanawat.) The *cella* is preceded by a six-columned vestibule, the side walls decorated with pilasters, all in the Corinthian order.

Colonnaded courtyards lay to the south and north of the temple. The court to the north is larger and (as has already been noted) mostly belongs to the earliest phase of construction, except for the west portico which was completed under Odenathus. Whereas the earlier columns were in the classical Corinthian style, the western capitals show an interesting variation. The Corinthian acanthus leaves have been highly stylised and simplified in a distinctly Roman-Egyptian manner. This is one of the few instances of Egyptian influence on the architecture of Roman Syria. The south court is smaller but was also surrounded by a portico. The sole column which remains intact bears an inscription recording the building of the court, commemmorated in AD 149.

Though little is left above the ground, other remains in the area north of the main axis include:

- 150 m behind the Baal-Shamin Temple the remains of a Christian basilica, typical in plan of buildings of the sixth century. Six columns separating the central from the northern side aisle remain standing and had been recycled from an earlier period;
- a smaller Christian basilica 100 m to the south of the first;
- 200 m to the west of the larger basilica, the peristyle of two Roman houses can be seen, one virtually intact though the rest of the houses have largely disappeared;
- sweeping around the edge of this area are remains of the north wall, possible constructed as part of Diocletian's fortification of the city but reinforced under the Byzantine Emperor Justinian (r 527-65);
- outside the wall and well to the north west of the two peristyle houses stands the fairly intact Marona House Tomb, built in 236 as a mausoleum for a patrician merchant of that name.

The most prolific aspect of the collection displayed in the Palmyra **Museum** (founded 1961 – north west of ruins, at entrance to Tadmor town) is the religious and funerary art. The latter, in particular, depicts in all its richness the sculptural tradition by which patrician and wealthy families commemorated their dead. The eastern affinities of the society are clearly shown both in their appearance and, most immediately, in their dress; the men in Parthian costume, over-embroidered and complemented by patterned worked leather; the women in simpler almost Greek robes but veiled and at the same time bedecked with heavy jewelry and head-bands.

Also worthy of note are the mosaics recovered from a private house east the Bel Temple. Some have been transferred to the Damascus National Museum but among the most notable sections retained in Palmyra is **Achilles at Skyros** - 1.70 m wide, end of third century AD. Achilles' stay on Skyros is a common theme of Roman art, here depicted in the company of the King's daughters in a style strictly metropolitan in its inspiration.

Before leaving the museum, you should arrange the services of an accredited guide to gain entrance to the underground tombs described in the following section.

Tombs

The prosperity of Palmyra during the years of its pre-eminence in the caravan trade is reflected in its funerary art. The exploration of the tombs can be divided into three sectors - the so-called Valley of the Tombs (western necropolis) and the south western and south eastern *necropoleis*

PALMYRENE TOMBS

The Palmyrene upper classes seem to have put a great deal of effort into arranging their decent interment and the range of burials from which they could select were diverse. Several broad categories apply:

Tower tombs were developed earliest, possibly as far back as the Hellenistic period, with the last example dated to AD 128 (though existing tombs were used for later burials up to the third century AD). On each floor of the multi- (up to four) storeyed structure, a central corridor gives onto narrow side passages into which the remains were stacked in layered *loculi*, usually faced with a carved limestone relief or stucco portrait of the deceased.

- Underground chamber (or *hypogeum*). Dated examples ranging from AD 81 to 251. (Comparable styles are found in Phoenicia and Egypt.)
- Combination of *hypogeum* and tower - a transitional phase between tower and underground types. For a while, tower and underground burials were carried out concurrently, bodies sometimes being buried first in underground chambers and later transferred to tower tombs with their economical 'filing cabinet' methods. Later, *hypogea* became the norm and the same efficient methods of stacking remains were extended to the underground chambers.
- House or temple tombs (eg Marona Tomb above). A late fashion (AD 143 to 251).

Within these categories, many variations in style are found. Our survey will be restricted to a few representative examples, particularly given the difficulty of access to the many scores of tombs in the area. Access to the locked tombs needs to be arranged through the museum.

areas.

Valley of the Tombs (or Western Necropolis)

The Valley of the Tombs (Plate 16a) spreads west from Jebel Husseiniye behind Diocletian's camp and stretches 1 km down a barren and forbidding valley. It is an eerie sight at the best of times, even more so under moonlight or at first or last light. Orient yourself by standing on the western slopes of the *jebel*. Around the

the Parthian rigidity of style later softened by Roman techniques.

You will see 300 m away a row of relatively well preserved tower tombs standing on the slopes of another hill, Umm al-Belqis, to the east of which runs the road to Damascus. Immediately below this row, a track leads right along the Valley of the Tombs. The most prominent of the tombs along the slopes of Umm Belqis is the **Tower Tomb of Iamliku** (or Yeliku,

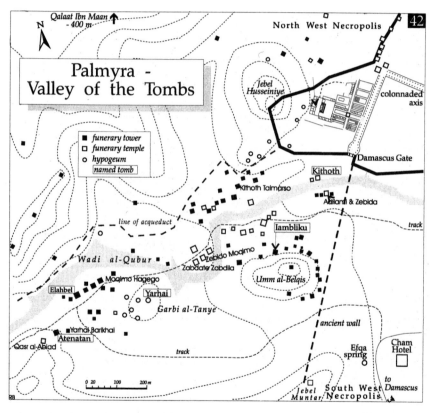

immediate northern slopes of the hill are signs of underground tombs. South of Jebel Husseiniye is a group of tower tombs spread out along the edge of the *wadi*. Head for the eastern-most tower, 120 m west of the Damascus Gate, the **Tower Tomb of Kithoth**, built in AD 40 and standing 10 m high. A relief of a burial feast carved into a niche of the eastern façade is the earliest example found at Palmyra and shows

AD 83), a handsome and imposing family tomb on the right of this grouping. The first of the tombs to be built in dressed stone, it was restored in 1973-6 by the Syrian Antiquities Department. The ground floor is impressive with Corinthian pilasters supporting a fine cornice. Three upper storeys survive giving a total capacity of 200 burials. After Elahbel's Tomb (below) this is the most intact among the tower tombs. The tombs to the left in this grouping are of lesser interest but can be inspected.

Head 600 m west along the valley to the level area in the distance. Here you will find another group of tombs of which the most notable is the **Tower Tomb of Elahbel** and his three brothers. This is the largest (capacity 300) and most famous of the tower tombs and is distinguishable by its well-preserved lines and the arched niche above the doorway which contains a representation of a sarcophagus. It was built in AD 103 according to the plaque above the door by four members of a family. It incorporates a *hypogeum* underneath (entrance from the north) with four storeys above. The ground floor outdoes even the tomb of Iamliku in its rich use of classical (Corinthian) architectural decoration. 100 m south west is the **Tower Tomb of Atenatan**[121] (9 BC - the earliest dated tower tomb, partly collapsed to a conical shape).

A great number of *hypogea* can be found in this area including the site of the **Hypogeum of Yarhai** (close to Elahbel Tower) which has been dismantled and partially reconstructed in the Damascus Museum.

South West Necropolis

The south west necropolis area is reached along the Damascus road, a short distance on the right after the Cham Hotel. The tower tombs in this area are somewhat stubby, the most interesting tombs being the *hypogea* for which a museum guide will be needed. The **Hypogeum of the Three Brothers** (mid second century, restored 1947) offers rich insight into Palmyrene painting styles. (Situated just to the west of the asphalt road, 150 m from the hotel.) You descend a short flight of stairs, noticing the inscription that informs us that three brothers built the tomb as a commercial arrangement. Inside, the main corridor is preceded by two wings. The whole layout provided 65 side-corridors each of which contained five burial niches or *loculi*.

At the end of the main corridor is a fresco in Syro-Roman style showing the three principal sponsors in circular frames carried by winged victories. Other paintings convey the theme of the spirit rising above death: Ganymede raised by the eagle of Zeus (ceiling); Achilles gaining immortality in battle (inspired by the valour of Ulysses) having thrown off the garments and the company of women (the daughters of the King of Skyros). In the right wing, a dining setting; in the

left wing, a funerary monument to Male, one of the brothers (d AD 142/3). Subsequent burials in the tomb span the period up to AD 259.

The **Hypogeum of Atenatan** (AD 98) lies 150 m north west of the Three Brothers Tomb. The original tomb dates from AD 98 but the main point of interest is the *triclinium* added in 229 by one Maqqai who is depicted on the couch above the sarcophagus at the back. He and the other figures of the group are treated with a subtlety of style associated with the late phase of Palmyrene sculpture.

The **Hypogeum of Hairan** is found a little to the west of Atenatan. Built in 106/7 with a well-preserved frescoe from AD 149/50. The **Hypogeum of Dionysos** lies a little to the south of Atenatan (second half of the second century). It contains a fine frescoe of the god after whom the tomb has been named.

South East Necropolis

The south east necropolis area lies south of the main oasis. Most noteworthy is the **Tomb of Artaban** (second half of the first century AD), discovered in 1957 during construction of an oil pipeline under which you descend to gain entry. The main gallery leads off into four side ones and is covered by a cradle vault. 56 niches each contained five *loculi*. Also noteworthy is the **Tomb of Breiki** (early second century AD – 25 m on right), restored by the Antiquities Department following its discovery in 1958. The architectural treatment is on a par with the Yarhai tomb. The neighbouring **tomb** (15 m on right) is the **Tomb of Bolha** (inscription of AD 88).

Finally, you should not forget the source of it all, the **Spring of Efqa** which emerged into an extensive cavern under Umm Belqis, opposite the entrance to the Cham Hotel, and surfaced just to the left of the hotel entrance. The spring unfortunately dried up in the mid 1990's but it once supplied 60 litres per second of water, at a consistent temperature of 33°. Although sulphurous, it was suitable for agriculture and said to be good for a number of complaints.

A little way back towards the ruins, on the rise to the right, are the remains of one of four solitary honorific columns known in Palmyra. Originally they would have been topped by statues of town notables.

31 km south east of Palmyra (10 km north of highway) are the remains of a typical Roman desert fort (second century - probably the classical *Veriaraca*) at **Khan al-Hallabat** (Plate

---

[121] Not the Atenatan whose tomb is described later in the SW necropolis.

18a). The building. with substantial walls (47 m square) and four round corner towers has been restored since 1978.

For a description of the Arab castle see *Qalaat Ibn Maan.

REFS: As'ad & Schmidt-Colinet 'Tadmor-Palmyra' in *Catalogue 1996*; *BG* pp 325-9; Bounni and Alas`ad; Bounni *Sanctuaire*; Fourdrin; Browning; Colledge *Art*; Ecochard *Consolidation* pp 298-307; Michalowski *Palmyra*; Millar *Paul*; Richmond pp 43-54; Ruprechtsberger; Seyrig *Palmyra*; Starcky *Palmyre* (1941); Starcky *Palmyre* (1952); Starcky and Gawlikowski; Teixidor; Will *Développement*.

Q

Qalaat Abu Qobeis

VARIANTS: Bochebeis, Bokebeis (Cru)
PERIOD: Ism/Cru ALT: 930 m RATING: - MAP:
65, 67 ITIN: 5c

LOCATION: Only 25 km north of *Masyaf but access is
by a rather confusing pattern of roads. Best and
simplest is to take the road leading to Hama from
Masyaf. After 7 km, turn left (north) along the edge of
the Jebel Ansariye for +17 km to Tell Salhab from
where take road west for al-Dalieh. At 6 km (village of
Abu Qobeis) continue straight for 1 km. At the picnic
spot near the river which flows between a steep
gorge,a track leads left c+2 km south east around the
side of a mountain, past a small Alawi shrine and on
to the *Qalaat* which looks out over the Orontes Valley.

A small, compact castle, round in shape with five
towers and a central but badly ruined building. It
affords a superb view over the Orontes Plain
towards *Shaizar and *Hama. It gives every
appearance of an Ismaeli work, judging by the
rough stonework and method of construction.

The site had earlier been utilised by the
Byzantines in the 999 campaign of Emperor
Basil II to recover Syria. In 1133 it was held by a
local Emir, Ibn Amrun. When the Ismaelis moved
into this area (see box on 'Assassins' under
*Masyaf – page 158) the Emir sold them the site,
along with Qadmus and *Qalaat al-Kahf.

Bokebeis (to use its Crusader name) may
have been occupied for a time (during the first
half of the 12th century) by the Crusaders, before
the Ismailis were present in strength in the area.
There is, however, no evidence of Crusader
construction and little reference to the castle in
the historical record though it was believed for a
time to have paid tribute to *Marqab. (The annual
tribute for Abu Qobeis was 800 gold pieces).
Under the Ismaelis, the canton of Abu Qobeis
may have retained a degree of semi-autonomy
from the rest of the Assassins' territory (see
footnote on Ismaeli castles in box on
'Assassins', page 157).

Even more elusive is another Crusader site
in this area, **Hosn al-Khariba**. Ceded to the
Crusader leader, Tancred, in 1105, it was
guarded by the Hospitallers from 1163, being

handed over to them by the Seigneur of
*Maraclée (Guillaume). Like other Frankish posts
in the mountains, Khariba would have
maintained the watch on Shaizar, north of Hama,
from where a fierce Islamic resistance to the
Crusades emanated.

REFS: *BG* p 451; Dussaud *Topographie* pp 145-7;
Eydoux p 158.

Qalaat Areimeh

VARIANTS: Arima (Cru); `Areima (Arb)
PERIOD: Cru RATING: - MAP: *43*, 66 ITIN: 5a/b

LOCATION: Take the motorway from *Homs to
*Tartus. After you have passed through the 'Homs
gap' and descended through the low hills, you arrive
at the coastal plain, c72 km from Homs. At this point
(c20 km from the *Safita turn-off outside Tartus),
start looking on the right for a sign in English which
points the way to Deir Mar Elias. Follow this road as it
crosses the old Homs/Tartus road and continue +2 km
stopping when the track to the monastery forks right
to ascend a hill. Instead, you should take the left fork
+1 km until you come to the edge of a village called
Sefsafe. Ascend on foot the fairly steep hill to the left
of the road. (The best path is from the village itself or
by circling around to the western edge of the rise).

Arima was built as a Crusader castle, to help
safeguard the routes between Tortosa and
Tripoli, to protect the coastal plain leading to the
Homs Gap (*Buqeia*) and to strengthen the outer
defences of Tortosa (*Tartus).

Little remains of the original fabric though
the scale of the defences can be seen and part
of the walls show the quality of the Frankish
work. The dates of the original construction are
not known but it was presumably begun even
before 1177 when the Templars were given
responsibility for the security of the region around
their base at Tortosa.

Certainly the castle was there in 1149 when
Bertrand of Toulouse seized it from Raymond III,
Count of Tripoli, whom he suspected of having
murdered his (Bertrand's) father. Raymond was
so determined to retrieve it that he sought an
alliance to this end with the Muslim ruler of
Damascus, Unur. Unur in turn sought the
support of Nur al-Din and the two Muslim leaders
dislodged Bertrand and went on to destroy and

sack the castle. Bertrand was sent into captivity in Aleppo, together with his sister. (Legend has it that the sister was made a wife of Nur al-Din and bore him a son.) Raymond was captured by Muslim forces in northern Syria in 1164. In 1171, Nur al-Din returned and destroyed what was left of the fortifications as part of the same campaign

The two are divided by an open courtyard and two ditches, originally surveilled by a tower in the north west corner, of which traces can be seen.

Even if you find the remains disappointing, the trip is worth the outlook from the ramparts. Located in beautiful olive-growing country, on a

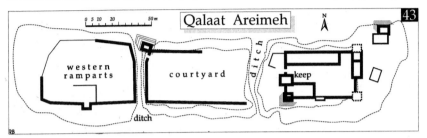

that saw Safita's original castle razed. The area apparently reverted to Crusader hands the next year with the restoration of Raymond on his release from captivity in Aleppo, but his debts to the Hospitallers (who seem to have paid the ransom for his release) resulted in the transfer of the castle to the Order. The site was briefly retaken for the Muslims by Saladin in his famous campaign of 1188.

Thereafter, the castle apparently remained in Crusader hands until after their general retreat (1291). Much of the present fabric dates from the Arab rebuilding on the Crusader remains but the difference in quality and durability of stonework is readily apparent.

The ruins cover an area of 80 m by 300 m on the crest of a small rise. The land falls away steeply to the east. The site is roughly defined by the confluence of two streams, the Nahr al-Abrash and the Nahr Krach. To approach the ruins, you should work your way through the scrub to come out on the west or north side of the castle. This will bring you to the extensive courtyard or bailey that lies between the two main fortified compounds. The two distinctly Crusader elements are:

- the **keep**, which lies on the east side. Rectangular (75 m by 45 m) in plan, it included two towers which can still be noted (the one on the south was probably the donjon) and several (half-buried) vaulted chambers;
- the west **ramparts** (only a little of the south wall remains).

good day the castle enjoys breath-taking views towards the usually snow-clad peak of Mount Lebanon well to the south. Often, haze veils the mountain but it is worth persevering to detach from the misty envelope the outline of the peak dominating the whole coastal plain as far south as Tripoli. In theory, you should also be able to pick out from here, preferably with binoculars, the Castle at Akkar in northern Lebanon which shared with Arima - and, of course, the great fortress of the Krak - the responsibility for preventing incursions from Muslim-held Homs and Damascus through the Homs Gap.

Calvet and Geyer have described a number of ancient irrigation works, remains of which can be found along the Nahr al-Abrash.

REFS: *BG* p 431; Calvet & Geyer 'Barrages antiques de Syrie' Lyon 1992 pp 53-63; Deschamps *Châteaux - III* pp 313-6; Dussaud *Topographie* p 120; Lawrence p 87; Runciman II pp 387, 395.

Qalaat Ben Qahtan

VARIANTS: Bikisrael, Castellum Vetulae, Château de la Vieille (Cru); Qalaat Beni Israel (Arb)
PERIOD: Cru RATING: - MAP: 67 ITIN: 6

LOCATION: 24 km inland from Jeble. Coming from the north, turn off the old *Latakia/Baniyas road 25 km south of Latakia where a signpost indicates (on the left) Ain al-Sharqiye, just south of the turn-off (on the right) for *Jeble. Follow the Ain al-Sharqiye road for 10 km, but turn left 3 km before the village and head north through Zama (+1 km), al-Thawra (+4 km) then ask for final directions for the last 8 km to Qalaat Ben Qahtan.

Though the trip is worthwhile for the beauty of the mountain countryside in the region, the remains on this site are minimal. There are few references to the castle in the historical records, most from the 12th century. It lay on a traditional route between the port of Jeble and the Orontes towns of *Hama, *Apamea and *Shaizar. It is first mentioned as taken by Tancred, Prince of Galilee in 1111 as part of an attempt to counter the Arab presence at Shaizar.

The subsequent history of the castle is by no means clear. It was seized briefly by a Turcoman adventurer in the 1160's. Recovered by the Crusaders, it seems to have passed to the Ismaeli sect (see box on 'Assassins' page 158). However, in 1188, during the course of his sweep up the coastal range, Saladin accepted the castle's submission from the Ismaelis. For a while it was linked to the port of Jeble (also temporarily in Muslim hands) to give the interior towns direct access to the sea, the local chieftains having found it expedient to make their peace with the Ayyubids.

If the medieval names listed above are accurate, however, the site reappears in Christian hands as the castle ceded in 1211 by Rupin, Prince of Antioch, to the Hospitallers who had by then assumed responsibility for some of the strategic strong-points in the region, including Marqab and the Krak. This was possibly only a notional transfer of ownership involving occasional payments of tribute from the Ismaelis for the reality was that by the 13th century, the Muslim hold on the area was increasingly unassailable.

Even more difficult to unravel is the other historic name for the site listed above, Qalaat Beni Israel. This implies that there was a Jewish settlement there at some time though Dussaud speculates this might have been as far back as Pompey's time (first century BC) when there was some evidence of local dynasts espousing Judaism (cf Lysias - *Qalaat Burzey).

REFS: *BG* p 455; Dussaud *Topographie* pp 140-1; Runciman II pp 118, 120.

Qalaat Burzey

VARIANTS: Lysias Bourzo (Grk); Borzé, Bourzey, Borzeih (Cru); Rochefort (?Cru); Qalaat Marza or Barzuya (Arb)
PERIOD: Cru ALT: 480 m RATING: ** MAPS: *44, 67, 78* ITIN: 7b

If I had to pick a spot to build a Frankish castle, this would be it. In a wildly romantic location on a

LOCATION: Locating Burzey can be a challenging exercise. Although it commands a sweeping view of the Orontes Plain and marshes (*Ghab*) from the inland side of the *Jebel Ansariye), it does not stand out from its surrounds.

There are two options from Latakia:

- Take the Hafeh road (for exit from Latakia, see *Qalaat Saladin) and continue on to Slenfe (40 km). Go past the village and continue straight up the hill (TV transmitter on right). The road curves left along the ridge of Nebi Yunes (alt 1583 m). Keep to the sealed road which will descend after c+5 km by a new stretch of broad, curving tarmac to the Orontes Valley floor. At this point, a T junction, turn left along the edge of the mountain for c+2.5 km. After passing a lake, you should be able to pick out the castle on a spur coming off the lower line of hills. Be warned: a stiff 45 minute climb over steep and heavily boulder-strewn ground. Keep ruins to your left for easier climb.
- An alternate way of reaching the same point to begin your climb is to take the Aleppo road almost to Jisr al-Shugur (Itin 7b). Take road south 1 km west of Shugur for +15 km.

There is also a donkey track which brings you to the castle from a village half-way down the mountain road described under (a). The village is called Qalaat Marza and someone there should be able to guide you to the track.

rocky crag on the steep side of the Jebel Ansariye, the castle is described by Deschamps as resembling 'the prow of a fantastic ship launched for an assault on the clouds'. The experience is only improved by the relief of arriving after a vigorous and precipitous scramble up the rocky slope. Once you reach it, the scattered remains spread over 3 ha of grassy meadows afford breathtaking 360⁰ views of the mountains and the Orontes Plain 500 m below, with only the tinkling of goat bells to disturb the peace.

History

What remains of the castle is minimal. Clearly it was once a sizeable complex; surprisingly so given its remoteness from the main Crusader centres on the coast. It served as the forward defence post, confronting Arab held positions on the eastern side of the valley - Qalaat Mudiq (*Apamea) is 34 km to the south east - and marking the easternmost line of control held by the Crusaders on a consistent basis along the Orontes Valley.

References to the site as Lysias are found in Strabo's *Geography*. It presumably played a role for the Seleucids in protecting their communications between Laodicea (Latakia) and their military base at *Apamea. Pompey at the beginning of his campaign (65-64 BC) which resulted in the Roman occupation of Syria, had to dislodge a Jewish partisan (Silas) from the site. The Byzantines fortified it and as late as 975 it was retaken by the Emperor Tzimisces from the Hamdanids of Aleppo. It was probably taken

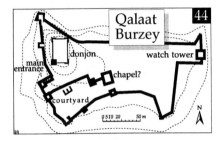

by the Crusaders in 1103; five years after they had seized Antioch and shortly before the taking of Latakia by Tancred.

The castle whose ruins you see today dates from the 12th century and (like *Qalaat Saladin) marks the first phase of Crusader building in the area. On 23 Aug 1188 it was taken by Saladin during the whirlwind campaign in which he swept up the coast, besieging Tartus, and took the forts at *Safita, *Jeble, Latakia, Saône, Mehelbeh and Shugur-Bakas (July/Sept 1188). (See box page 13.) Though Burzey had the reputation of being impregnable as no engines of war could be brought near its walls, Saladin struck from the west ridge. His engines indeed having failed to get close enough to make any impression on the walls, Saladin resorted to successive charges by three waves of troops against the western wall, thus wearing down the thin ranks of the defenders and apparently making good use of intelligence from the commander's wife transmitted to her sister, Sybilla, third wife of Bohemond III, Prince of Antioch. (Sibylla was an agent in the pay of Saladin.) The garrison surrendered under the pressure of Saladin's human wave tactics.

While Saladin's rather hit and run strategy did not permanently dislodge the Crusaders from their main defences on the coast, it certainly hemmed in their territory for the second century of their presence and inland sites such as Qalaat Burzey played no continuing role in the Frankish defences.

Visit

If you arrive by the ascent from the valley, you will reach the fortified area on its eastern side. Your scramble should bring you out at the watch-tower which marks the eastern extension of the outer enclosure. (This is probably an Arab reconstruction of an earlier tower.) From here, work your way round to the south (left) which should bring you into the area between two levels of fortifications. On the way you may notice the remains of a relatively large (22 m by 17 m) building whose purpose is not entirely clear but may have been the castle chapel.

You are now within the court that lies between two lines of walls on the south face. The fortifications follow a rather random plan resulting from the irregular shape and levels of the crest. The land falls away steeply on most sides but its slope is relatively gradual on the south and west where the main defences are concentrated. The outer walls on the vulnerable aspect of the south face were ranged on two levels with a gateway on the westernmost corner giving entry to the inner enclosure. The lower wall consists of four towers with a joining curtain wall.

The main keep was located on the west side and is recognisable today. Also Arab in its present form, it consists of a rectangular base with square towers on the corners. To the west of the keep, the castle was most exposed to relatively level ground and was thus protected by five towers and a curtain wall partly faced with a talus. The main entry to the castle was through the central tower on the west side.

8 km north of Burzey, also on the east edge of the Jebel Ansariye, are the remains of the Crusader fortress of **Sarmaniye** which was taken by Saladin at the same time as Burzey.

REFS: *BG* pp 471; Boase pp 78-80; Deschamps *Châteaux* - III pp 345-8; Dussaud *Topographie* pp 151-3; Eydoux pp 321-2; Runciman II p 470; Saadé 'Chateau de Bourzey' *AAS* 1956.

Qalaat Ibn Maan

VARIANTS:
PERIOD: Ayy RATING: * MAP: 75 ITIN: 14

LOCATION: 2 km north of the main ruins of Palmyra. It can be approached by vehicle (track from the north west outskirts of Tadmor); but that is spoiling the fun. The climb up the pebble-strewn slope (150 m above the valley) takes about 40 minutes.

While the castle itself is rather poorly constructed, it is well preserved and a visit is an essential adjunct to any exploration of Palmyra. The splendour of the scene either at sunset or at dawn as the sun rises over the ruins and the mountains behind is a memorable souvenir of Palmyra.

The castle has for long been attributed to the Lebanese Maanite Emir, Fakhr al-Din (1590-1635), who tested the limits of Ottoman flexibility in the early 17th century by expanding his area of direct control well beyond Mount Lebanon as far east as the Syrian desert, hoping to present the Ottomans with a *fait accompli* that they would be too weak-willed to reverse. His calculations were wrong. He was pursued and arrested by the Ottomans in 1635 and kept in captivity in Constantinople until executed later in the year.

Recent Polish research has confirmed, however, that Fakhr al-Din made use of an earlier Arab castle on the site, a late Ayyubid construction of around 1230 (contemporary with the fortification of the Bel Temple at *Palmyra).

Relatively small in size, the fortifications are based on an original triangular fortress of seven towers (1230), extended later in the 13th century with second curtain walls to the east and west, the whole ringed by a deep ditch. The effect, emphasised by the crumbling of much of its fabric down the steep slope of the ditch, is spectacular. You enter from the south east corner via a metal bridge that brings you to a landing between two towers. Like many Arab castles, the internal arrangement of chambers and defences is compact, with a steep passage taking you up to the internal court. This is surrounded by battlements with a substantial thickening of the defences on the south side where the highest terrace is located. There are memorable views for 360° around but perhaps the most striking is the view to the north along the spine of the Jebel al-Tadmoria as the rising sun begins to colour its rugged slopes.

REFS: *BG* p 339; Bounni and Alas'ad p 92; Bylinski in *PAM* 1990-95.

Qalaat Jaber (Plate 19a)

VARIANTS: Dausara (Lat); Qalaat Jaabar, Jafar
PERIOD: Arb RATING: * MAP 72 ITIN: 12a

LOCATION: North eastern shore of Lake Assad. From the new town of al-Thawra (incorporating al-Tabqa) built to service the Euphrates Dam, cross the dam wall to the north bank. At 3.5 km from dam wall, turn left. +7 km to castle via road curving back towards the lake and the promontory on which the castle is located.

Like other Arab fortresses of the period, Qalaat Jaber uses a central core of high ground, tightly circumscribed by defensive walls and a ditch (*Aleppo Citadel is the classic example). Today, though there has recently been considerable restoration work by the Antiquities Department, much of the fabric of the upper fortress is simply rubble. However, the entrance gateway and ramp and much of the largely brick walls are worth inspection. Moreover, the building is dramatically sited. It once overlooked an important crossing point on the Euphrates; it has, if anything, gained in visual impact with the encroachment of the waters of Lake Assad to the base of the castle. The rise on which the castle stood is now an island joined to the shore by a causeway. You look out from the battlements over the intensely blue waters of the lake hemmed between bare promontories.

History

The history of the castle is largely confined to the Zengid, Ayyubid and Mameluke periods in northern Syria and to the build-up of Arab resistance to the Crusaders. It is not known what previously may have stood on the site though it was known to be held by the Arab tribe, the Banu Numeir until taken by the Seljuq Sultan, Malik Shah, in 1087. During the First Crusade, probably in 1104, it was incorporated into the territory of the Count of Edessa, the Crusader principality in the mountains of south eastern Turkey. Edessa (today the Turkish city of Urfa), however, fell to Zengi, the Atabeq of Aleppo, in 1144 and the subsidiary fortress at Qalaat Jaber reverted to the Arabs by 1149. However, in an earlier (1146) attempt to dislodge the Crusaders, Zengi was killed before its walls after a quarrel with a Frankish eunuch.

The remains which are seen today date from the rule of Zengi's son, Nur al-Din who, as his father's successor in Aleppo, fulfilled his vision of bringing Syria (less the coastal strip held by the Crusaders) under united Muslim rule by 1154. His rebuilding of the castle began in 1168. It remained in Ayyubid hands under

Saladin and his successors (1176-1260) but it fell victim to the repeated Mongol waves whose incursions, particularly in northern Syria, caused so much devastation between 1260 and 1400. There was, however, some reconstruction in 1335-6 during the rule of the Mameluke Governor of Damascus, Tengiz.

Visit

A visit to the **castle** requires 30-45 minutes. The fabric is entirely brick in the upper levels, reflecting the Mesopotamian tradition whose influence was strong in Syria at the time of the Zengids (*Raqqa). The main parts of interest are the **entrance gateway** and the corridor which takes you within the battlements to the upper level of the fortified walls. You can then make a circuit of the **walls** in a clockwise direction. Much of this upper brickwork has been restored post-1972. On the broad summit, (oval in shape, 130 m by 250 m) little remains above the ground except for a fine brick cylindrical **minaret** (the rest of the mosque has disappeared) which recalls others of the 12th century in northern Syria (*Raqqa, *Meskene) probably erected by Nur al-Din. Note the effect of wind erosion on the square brick base. The outlines of a palace with baths may be discerned near the lake end of the summit.

On the right bank of the river at this point lay the Plain of Seffin, where the famous confrontation took place between Moawiya and Caliph Ali, son-in-law of the Prophet, in 657. The forces confronted each other for some months before the issue (the Umayyads' demand that Ali punish the murderers of Othman) was put to arbitration which broadly went against Ali and led to the final undermining of his leadership.

The legendary forefather of the Ottoman sultans, Suleiman Shah, reputedly drowned in the Euphrates near this spot in the thirteenth century. His tomb was marked and guarded by a contingent of Turkish troops (a clause allowing for this arrangement was negotiated at the 1919 Versailles Conference following the end of Ottoman rule). The practice continued after Syrian independence but as the lake filled, the tomb (and its small garrison) were moved upstream (*Qalaat Najim).

REFS: *BG* p 484; Bell *Amurath* pp 49-51; Hillenbrand *Islamic Influences*; Runciman II pp 112, 239.

Qalaat al-Kahf

VARIANTS: Khaf
PERIOD: Ism RATING: ** MAP: 66 ITIN: 5c

LOCATION: Finding Qalaat al-Kahf can be a major exercise and the Ismaelis did well in searching out a location deeply hidden in the folds of the Jebel Ansariye. It can be approached from several directions: from *Masyaf, Baniyas (both via Qadmus) or *Tartus. One proven route is to take one of the Sheikh Badr roads from the coast (turn off either from Tartus or c10 km north). From Sheik Badr, ask for directions north to Ain Breisin (4 km) then al-Nmreije (+7 km). This will take you along narrow tarmac roads, up and down several ravines. Al-Nmreije lies c2 km east of the castle. A new road was recently built to the castle from the village.

History

While Masyaf, which also served as an Ismaeli headquarters, may be in a better state of preservation, al-Kahf enjoys an equally rich history for the short period of its prominence.

The castle was originally established by a local lord who in 1132-3 sold the fortress of Qadmus to the Ismaelis from where they began to establish themselves in the area. (See box on 'Assassins', page 158). His son later sold al-Kahf to the sect, part of their program of rapid acquisition of eight castles in the area from 1132 to 1140.

From 1164 to the early 1190s, the Ismaeli leader, Rashid al-Din (known to the Crusaders as the 'Old Man of the Mountain'), operated from this remote mountain fastness. The castle is mentioned in the historical records of the 12th century Crusaders in connection with exchanges between the sect and the Knights Templar with whom they shared an unspoken entente. In 1197, Henry of Champagne, Regent of Jerusalem, sought an alliance with Sinan's successor to counter Muslim pressure on the fragmented Crusader state. He was invited to el Kahf where, to demonstrate the fanatical devotion of his followers, the Assassin leader bid two of them to hurl themselves from the castle parapets, which they did without hesitation.

This ambiguous relationship with the Crusaders continued the next century particularly under St Louis of Acre, the French King who led the disastrous Sixth Crusade against Egypt in 1249. The Ismaeli leader set up an assassination attempt on St Louis but his agents were detected and sent back to al-Kahf with gifts to illustrate Louis' magnanimity. Later Louis sent an envoy, Yves le Breton, to al-Kahf bearing presents, as a result of which an alliance was concluded. Yves was the first Western visitor to the Ismaelis to take an interest in their doctrines.

JEBEL ANSARIYE
VARIANTS: Nusayri, Alawi or Bargylos Mountains.

Seleucus called them the Pieria Mountains but by the time of Pliny (V.78) they were known by the name Bargylos. Pliny located there the Tetrarchy of the Nazerini (V.81-2), a name reflected in the description, Nusayris, applied earlier this century to the Alawi inhabitants. The Nazerini probably organised themselves into a principality in the Seleucid period and retained a separate status into the first century of Roman rule.

The mountain range remained a refuge for groups seeking to avoid outside authority and imposed orthodoxy, especially after the arrival of the Sunni dynasties of the 10th century and after. Hence the presence of groups such as the Alawis and the Ismaelis (*Masyaf). The isolation of these groups was often exploited by outsiders seeking to engage cheap labour or to take on recruits for military service.

The background to the Ismaelis is explained on page 151. The Alawis trace the origins of their sect to the ninth century figure, Muhammed Ibn Nusayr al-Namiri whose teachings emphasised the inexpressible nature of the One God from whom a heirarchy of beings emanated, chief among whom was Ali (from whom the sect takes its name). Both sects were for many centuries cut off from mainstream Islam and so evolved practices different from the majority, a situation which in turn provoked further hostility and even persecution from the Sunni regimes.

Not surprisingly, al-Kahf was the last of the Ismaeli strongpoints to fall to centralised Arab control. It was not until 1273 (two years after his successful siege of the Krak) that Baibars captured the castle as part of his final elimination of the Ismaeli presence. The castle remained a military post into Ottoman times, probably serving as a usefully remote place of detention. In 1816, the British resident of Lebanon, Lady Hester Stanhope, took up the cause of a French captain who had been taken captive and held in the castle. He was rescued at her behest by the Ottoman Governor of Tripoli who also carried out her wish that the castle be razed.

Visit

Of all the mountain castle sites, this is probably the one most marked by a raw and untamed beauty, the environs unsoftened by the cultivation of crops and orchards. The mountain

country is either forested or too steep for cultivation in this place where three rivers meet. The castle sits on a ridge, nestled between wild gorges, its fragmentary walls clinging to the rocky flanks. From its elongated heights (running east/west), precipitous cliffs provide their own natural protection. What remains of the castle buildings is merely some debris spread along the 300 m by 50 m site. Most remarkable is the entrance passageway (approached by taking the path which skirts the north side of the ridge) carved into the solid rock with an Arabic inscription to the left. (The artificial 'cave' gives rise to the Arabic name for the castle, Castle of the Cave). Legend has it that the Sinan was buried near the craggy fortress, the reputed site lying near the north eastern face by which you approach the castle.

REFS: *BG* p 450; Burman p 139; Eydoux p 127; Lewis *Assassins* pp 108, 110, 122-3; Runciman III.

Qalaat al-Kawabi

VARIANTS: Coïble (Cru)
PERIOD: Ism RATING: T MAP: 66 ITIN: 5c

LOCATION: About 20 km (45 minutes' drive) from the coast, Qalaat al-Kawabi is reached by turning off the *Tartus/Baniyas motorway 10 km north of Tartus. The turn-off is marked (in Arabic only) *Sheikh Badr* but is readily recognisable as the road that branches at the north edge of the cement works. Follow this road inland for c+10 km, passing Dweirtah to reach al-Soda. From here take the road heading east for Oaro (+3 km) and Albatteye (+8 km). This road winds on +2 km, around a series of ravines until it comes within sight of the *Qalaat* perched on a narrow summit amidst a modern village.

History

The castle (in Arabic, Castle of the Ewes) is a purely Ismaeli structure, though well enough known by the Crusaders to have been given a Frankish name, Coïble. The ruins are pretty dilapidated, not helped by being continuously occupied and thus constantly mined (particularly during the 19th century) for building materials for local houses. It is the surrounding scenery (as usual, castle builders in the Jebel Ansariye knew how to pick their site) that impresses most. Located in a ravine, it is perched on a narrow summit surrounded by four hills that tower some 400 m or more above. At its base runs the Nahr Hussein. Olive groves in profusion soften the countryside and provide an idyllic setting. There is even a certain charm in the way the modern village houses improvise around the remains of the medieval fortress.

The history of the Ismaeli presence in the mountains is sketched in the entry for *Masyaf. The historical references to Coïble are scanty but it appears to have been acquired from the local lord in the 1140s. It was certainly well established as an Ismaeli centre early in the active career of Rashid al-Din Sinan who rebuilt it after 1160. In 1213, Bohemond IV of Tripoli (later of Antioch) laid siege to Coïble following the murder by Assassins of his son Raymond in the Cathedral of Tortosa. The seige was a determined one and the Ismaelis, then in alliance with the successors of Saladin, called on the aid of forces from Aleppo and Damascus. Eventually the Crusader seige had to be called off in the face of this coalition. The castle does not seem to have been used by later Arab rulers for defensive purposes once the Ismaeli presence in the mountains had largely been rooted out by the end of the 12th century.

Visit

It takes only half an hour or so to inspect the remaining ruins. A short walk over the Nahr Hussein and up the stone path along the south side of the crag brings you to the gateway which still controls access to the village. The single village street takes you from one end of the narrow castle to the other with diversions down alleyways to gain some impression of the remains of the defensive walls. However, only fragments of the castle buildings survive amid the houses and it is difficult to relate anything to a coherent plan. The quality of the stonework, as is often the case in Ismaeli constructions, is not particularly fine.

REFS: *BG* p 443; Burman pp 105-6, 119-20; Dussaud *Topographie* pp 139-40; Lewis *Assassins* 1967; Runciman II p 138.

Qalaat Maniqa

VARIANTS: Malaicas, Castellum Malavans (Cru); Qalaat Ksabiye, Hisn al-Mainakah (Arb)
PERIOD: Cru/Ism RATING: * MAP: 67 ITIN: 6

LOCATION: 22 km south east of *Jeble in the Jebel Ansariye. From Baniyas (mid-way between Tartus and Latakia) take the old road north to Latakia for c12 km. Follow the road leading right +10 km to Duweir Baabda then the road heading south east (not the direct road east to Adele), to the village of Wadi al-Qalaa (+6 km). The castle can be seen looming above the small settlement, a steep 15 minute walk.

This castle, originally Ismaeli, is set amid some of the most beautiful tobacco-growing terraced country in the Jebel Ansariye. The drive from the coast is equally scenic, particularly the last few kilometers winding through the mountain scenery and ducking at one point along a convenient ledge behind a waterfall.

The history of the castle is very sketchy. It was originally constructed by local Arabs in the early 11th century but soon was taken over by the Byzantines. The Franks took control at some stage in the 12th century (perhaps as early as 1118) but sometime after 1160[122] it was re-fortified by the Ismaelis when Rashid al-Din ('the Old Man of the Mountain') became active in the area (see box on 'Assassins' under *Masyaf, page 158). Somehow, it passed back into the hands of the Crusaders, perhaps as part of their accommodation of interests with the Ismaelis against their common enemies, the Sunni Muslim forces of Damascus and their allies. By 1186, it had been entrusted to the Hospitallers by Bohemond III, Prince of Antioch[123]. The Hospitallers maintained largely amicable relations with the Ismaelis and the castle may have stayed effectively under the control of the sect for it was in Ismaeli hands again in 1270-3 when it was taken by the Mameluke Sultan, Baibars, during his suppression of the Ismaeli presence in the Ansariye Mountains.

The castle, more or less rectangular in plan, is located on a ridge running north east to south west between two streams feeding into the valley of the Nahr Hussein. As you ascend, chose the path on the left that will take you to the west face, entering the fortifications through a break in the north western wall.

The site is naturally defended by the steep slopes on all but the north eastern side. Here, a lower ridge joins it to the mountain and the defenders cut a ditch in the rock to provide a steep face to discourage assault. This was topped by a formidable wall of solid basalt construction. The defensive positions, notably the keep, were concentrated here, affording commanding views over the spectacular terraces and the mountain ravines to the north.

While the defences to the north are relatively intact the rest of the walls skirting the central court are in a poor state of preservation. Three underground chambers remain, however, including two apparently used for the stabling of horses, judging by the loops provided to attach rings to the stonework. Much of the stone is roughly dressed and has not survived well above the base level. There is, however, some finer work around the windows that survive. Part of a

---

[122] Perhaps as late as 1180, giving the Ismaeli period of control a span of only six years - Deschamps *Châteaux* - III p 335.
[123] At the same time, Marqab was handed to the Hospitallers.

tower is preserved on a lower level in the south eastern corner (overlooking the village). You can descend to the village from this point.

Another Ismaeli castle lies c20 km south east via winding roads, Qalaat al-Ollaiqa. The fortress was built on a narrow triangular plateau atop a conical prominence.

REFS: **Qalaat Maniqa**: *BG* p 454; Burman p 105; Deschamps *Châteaux* - *III* pp 335-6. **Qalaat Ollaiqa**: *BG* p 449.

Qalaat Marqab

VARIANTS: Margat (Cru)
PERIOD: Cru/Arb RATING: *** MAP: *45*, 66, 67
ITIN: 5c

> LOCATION: Currently no direct exit to the castle from the Latakia/Tartus motorway. You will need to take the Baniyas exit and proceed south through the town, turning east (left) on the southern edge. Follow ascending road for c6 kms reaching the inland side of the castle, then skirting it to the south and park on the west (seaward) side.
>
> It is worth pausing on the way up at the point where you make the right turn, to gain an appreciation of the southern defences of the fortress, discussed in detail below.

'The triumph of the gigantic'. The description of Eydoux, a French writer on the Crusader castles of the east, just about sums up the first impression of this formidable castle: predominantly black, the colour of the extinct volcanic peak on which it sits, scowling over the narrow coastal plain and the Mediterranean far below. Located at the point where the plain narrows to a precarious passage between the sea and the mountains, Marqab is in many ways the most baleful of the Crusader fortresses; or at least the most sombre. From it, access along the principal route connecting Asia Minor (Turkey) with the Holy Land could be controlled and its commanding battlements offer superb views over the sea and Jebel Ansariye inland.

History

The site is the natural location for a fortified post but it does not seem to have been used for this purpose until the Muslims built there in 1062. Baniyas, at the foot of the mountain, has a much longer history, dating its foundation to the Phoenicians and may have played the defensive role later assumed by the massive castle. Baniyas is referred to in Strabo's geography (c 58 BC to c AD 24) as Balanea. It was used by the Greeks, Romans and Byzantines and

became the seat of a bishop. The Crusaders installed themselves first in Baniyas which they knew as Valénie (Valenia). They reached the town in November 1098, shortly after the fall of Antioch, and slaughtered its inhabitants.

The Crusader presence quickly faded away and it was the Byzantines who took the site of Marqab from the Arabs in an expedition of 1104. The date of the return of the Crusaders is unclear but at some stage between 1108 and 1140 the site of Marqab passed to the Principality of Antioch. It was maintained on behalf of the Prince by a prominent family (Mansoer or Mansour) in recognition of its strategic potential particularly in response to the Assassin threat after 1140.

Later, it was sold by the family to the Knights Hospitaller (1186). Marqab avoided the fate of other castles still held in private hands which lacked the resources to withstand Saladin's 1188 raid. Following his victory over the Crusaders at Hattin (Palestine), Saladin marched past the fortress of Marqab in his sweep up the coast in 1188 but, consistent with his strategy of probing only weak points, did not attack it.

The Hospitallers converted the fortress into one of the Crusader strong points, their main construction effort probably being concentrated on the years 1186 to 1203. They employed new concepts in military fortification still only tentatively being exploited in Europe and exceeded them in scale and boldness, anticipating many of the achievements of the military engineers of Philippe-August in 13th century France. In doing so, they eschewed the adaptation of Byzantine concepts which had marked Crusader defensive works of the first half of the 12th century. Marqab is thus much less of a pastiche of different styles than the more complex fortress, the *Krak des Chevaliers (also entrusted to the Hospitallers). T E Lawrence saw in it 'all the best of the Latin fortifications of the Middle Ages in the East ... informed with the spirit of the architects of Central and Southern France'.

Properly manned, there was no reason why the castle should not have been considered impregnable. It withstood attacks from the Emir of Aleppo (Malik al-Daher) in 1204 and by the Turkoman Emir, Saif al-Din Balban, in 1280. The fatal flaw in the Hospitallers' strategy, however, was their dwindling manpower resources as the 13th century brought increasingly fewer volunteers from Europe. By 1271 its status had already been eroded when, following the fall of the Krak to Baibars, the Mamelukes of Cairo enforced an agreement for a sharing of the revenues of Marqab's dependant lands between the Hospitallers and the Sultan. It was besieged, bombarded and undermined by Baibars' successor, Qalaun, beginning on 17 April 1285. One mine brought down the great south tower, convincing the defenders that their resistance was useless. The fortress surrendered on 25 May after a month of bombardments without the need for a final assault, the knights being allowed to retreat to Tartus and Tripoli. Within the next six years, the remainder of the Crusader presence on the coast unravelled, deprived of the strategic strongpoints which had ensured their defences. With the fall of Tripoli in 1289 and Tartus in 1291, the ethos which had sustained such gigantic ambitions ended.

Qalaun retained the fortress and he and his Arab successors strengthened some of its defences, including the south tower. It remained in military hands until Ottoman times but it ended up as a repository for discredited former governors.

HOURS
09:00 - 16:00 Wed - Mon

Visit

On the ascent by the approach road, take time to gain a good appreciation of the fortress (Arabic name, 'castle of the watchtower'). The site itself is a natural defensive position, taking advantage of a ridge-like feature (alt: 360 m) which falls away to the north. The plan is basically a huge but narrow triangle, the sharp end pointing south where the line of the narrow ridge which joins it to the Jebel Ansariye is partly interrupted by an artificial ditch. The natural weakness of this southern aspect is the reason for the concentration of the complex defences on this rounded salient (called in the Middle Ages 'the spur').

Here most of the castle's defensive weight is deployed to afford protection against the vulnerable southern ridge. The great donjon serves as the central anchor point and the refuge of last resort in the event of the overrunning of the castle. At this point, the second enclosure wall was enormously thickened by the accumulation of functional and defensive constructions making a formidable arrow-head and giving the fortress much of its impression of strength and bulk.

The **south tower** of the first enclosure wall echoes the great donjon

tower above. Note the band of white marble running around the upper part of the outer wall (this can only be observed from the approach road). This typically Arab or rather Mameluke stylistic flourish (stark white on black) carries an Arabic inscription dating from Qalaun's reconstruction of the south defences. Above it can be found contemporary machicolations or protuding slots for the pouring of boiling oil on potential invaders.

Having reached the main entrance, you will need about two hours to explore the castle adequately. You enter through the **west (tower) gate**. The Arab bridge leading up to it is covered with gradually rising stairs leading you via a 90⁰ turn over the ditch and into the entrance gateway (13th century - note the stone brattices and the portcullis) looking out over the Mediterranean. The outer wall to the left is interrupted by round bastions every 20 or 30m and the line of the ditch that rings it can still be identified.

After passing through the recessed double-arched gateway, you find yourself in a vaulted entrance vestibule which leads via a right-hand turn into the inner defences. Immediately inside the 12th century outer wall of huge blocks of dark volcanic basalt joined by white mortar is a second defensive wall, somewhat badly preserved in most places. If you continue 30 m between the lines of the two walls, you will reach a **barbican** entrance **gate** (1270). From the

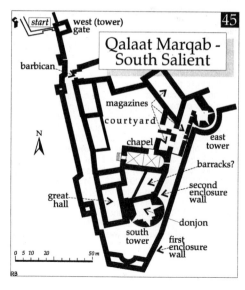

cross-vaulted entrance chamber, stairs and an archway on the right lead via a subsequent left turn and ascending vaulted stairway into the main **courtyard** of the keep.

Before entering the barbican and the inner keep, you may wish to continue on to explore the line of the outer wall as it heads south, eventually leading you to the southern spur discussed above. Note the protected gallery and circuit walk built into the outer wall.

Having reached the courtyard, the principal parts of the castle to be visited are located around this point, on which you should orient yourself. On the west side is a building recently restored to house a tea room.

At the south end of the courtyard, the castle **chapel** can be readily identified. Aligned east/west, its main entrance is on the west (sea) side with a side door to the north. It dates from the initial phase of Hospitaller control (end of 12th century) and is a gem of austere Crusader architecture, inspired by the transition to the Gothic style in France. The beautiful doorways on the northern and western sides are similar in their rich mouldings and elegant colonnettes (only those on the north survive). The interior is divided into two bays by the cross-groined vaulting. The central arch dividing the vaulting meets the wall and terminates with two columns encased in pilasters with simplified Corinthian capitals. The absence of internal columns adds a feeling of space in what is a relatively small structure, typical of the striving for openness and light in the Gothic period. At the east end of the chapel, the rounded apse is raised two steps above the level of the rest of the chapel. Two small rooms or sacristies are embedded in the thick wall behind the curving apse.

South of the main steps to the chapel, you will find the remains of a two-storeyed building which was probably the **great hall**. It was built over a cistern used to store water to provision of the garrison and civilians. The southern end of the building is missing. It was linked to the complex of buildings around the **donjon**, the great central tower with walls of massive thickness (5 m in places) probably constructed between 1186 and 1203. Over 20 m in diameter, constructed of dark granite, its three storeys were pierced with loopholes surveying the perimeter of the southern defences. Another two-storeyed building joins the donjon on the north to the chapel on the south and was probably used as **barracks**.

More than any other site in Syria, the grim but impressive symmetry of this late 12th century construction underlines the determined resourcefulness of the Crusaders' search for security. Ironically, it was not the crumbling of the defences under fire but their undermining by the simple expedient of tunnelling from below which brought the Crusader presence to an end.

Returning to the main courtyard, another series of great chambers north east of the chapel continues the line of the fortress defences. They were probably used as **magazines** for storage (though some describe the 46 m long outer room (12th century) which gives on to the second enclosure wall on the east as the great hall). This latter room also leads to the great **east tower** of the castle (built at the same time as the donjon) which gave flanking protection to the south eastern corner and guarded the small postern gate leading to the circuit walk above the first enclosure wall.

This south salient or 'sharp end' of the fortress comprises the main areas of interest. The rest of the triangular site to the north and east would probably have been occupied by more flimsy civilian housing and was certainly heavily built upon in Arab and Ottoman times. Although the greater part of the inner enclosure wall has been dismantled for later housing, you can still make a circuit of the blunt end of the fortifications to gain some impression of the original extent of the fortified area. An Arab cemetery and remains of an Ottoman-period *seraya* occupy the central part of the site.

A little to the south west of the main castle, an isolated watchtower still stands to the east of the new highway as it passes below the castle. Called **Burj al-Sabi** ('Tower of the Youth'), it protected the access to the castle's port and the coastal route. It comprises a stout tower in basalt, 15 m square, topped with machicolations supported on consoles. Within were two storeys of accommodation and a basement. It was probably built at the same time as the castle itself, namely the end of the 12th or beginning of the 13th century.

Baniyas

Of the town of Baniyas (the Crusaders' Valénie[124]), little of historical interest remains. It is now a small fishing port, commercial centre and base for nearby industries. As late as the mid 19th century, substantial remains of the medieval Valénie were described by European travellers but all have disappeared in the further development of the town.

---

[124] Possibly also the site of the ancient Leucade.

REFS: *BG* pp 445-6; Boase pp 56-60; Deschamps *Châteaux* - III pp 259-85; Dussaud *Topographie* p 127; Eydoux pp 113-133; Lawrence pp 98-103; Runciman II, III.

Qalaat al-Mehelbeh

VARIANTS: Platanus (Lat), Balatonos (Cru)
PERIOD: Cru ALT: 774 m RATING: - MAP: *46*, *67* ITIN: 6

LOCATION: Leave Latakia by the old Tartus road. After c17 km, after the village of Snobar, turn left along the road which heads for Jobet Borghal. Follow this for +22 km into the hills. At the point where, after a distinct descent, the road again ascends a hill recognisable by a trig station on the right (11 km before Jobet Borghal), look carefully for the barely distinguishable outline of castle ruins on the left, the hill being known as Jebel Arbaine. Keep going up the hill, asking if necessary, for the village of Mehelbeh (3 km past Beit Salame). Walk (c15 minutes) up to the ruins.

Qalaat al-Mehelbeh is situated in wild and beautiful mountain scenery, in one of the innermost recesses of the Jebel Ansariye. From here there are commanding views over the plain towards Latakia and over the northern reaches of the range, as far as Mount Casius. The scene is unspoilt and rarely visited. Even though the ruins are at best vestigial, the one hour trip from the coast (perhaps en route to other sites such as Qalaat Saladin or Burzey) is well worthwhile.

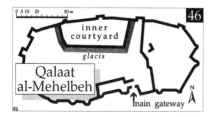

History

As with many Crusader sites, the choice of this high ground for a fortification pre-dates the Frankish presence. The local mountain clan, the Banu al-Ahmar, built a fortified post here at the beginning of the 11th century to guard the point at which the route over the range from the Orontes Valley divided into branches leading either to Jeble or Latakia, the two nearby ports on the Mediterranean. The Byzantine governor of Antioch took the post from the clan in 1031 and completed the original fortress. At some stage

during the next 80 years, it again seems to have lapsed into the hands of clansmen (the Banu Sulaia), Byzantine control in the area having weakened in the wake of the Muslim resurgency.

After the Crusader presence was progressively established in the area beginning with the capture of Antioch in 1098, Mehelbeh fell into the Crusaders' sphere of interest. The then Prince of Antioch, Roger, took it from the clans in 1118 and made it a dependency of Robert, Lord of Saône, whose castle lay 12 km to the north (*Qalaat Saladin). It remained a Crusader possession for 70 years, affiliated to Antioch via Saône and part of the system of inland castles (Burzey, Saône, Qahtan, Boqabeis) which guarded the passes leading to the Orontes, from where the threat to the coastal Crusade presence seemed most real.

In the end, though, the Crusaders lacked the manpower to maintain a presence in strength away from the coast. Balatonos, like many of the lightly guarded inland posts, surrendered to Saladin during his sweep through the mountains in 1188, three days after Saône. Under the Ayyubids it was incorporated after 1194 into the possessions of the Governor of Aleppo, al-Malik al-Zaher Ghazi (see *Harim).

Local tribal chiefs regained control of it in the mid 13th century probably as a result of the disruption brought on by the first Mongol invasion (1260) but in 1269 it was again brought under centralised control by Baibars as part of his campaign leading to the capture of the Krak (1271). Some work was done on it during the Arab period but its importance dwindled as the threat from the alien presence on the coast disappeared and the fabric of the fortifications gradually decayed.

Visit

The castle lies on a rocky prominence at the top of a low mountain. Slightly elongated east/west, its maximum length is 170 m. An enclosure wall runs (or rather ran, since much of it has crumbled away except at the base) around the crest. The wall was broken by square, round or polygonal bastions. Below the walls, the natural escarpment falls away except on the west side where a ditch was used to supplement the natural defences of the site.

You enter by the main gate, on the south, which is still marked by the remains of a flanking tower, polygonal in shape. This brings you into the main courtyard, now much overgrown and where care needs to be taken to avoid cistern and cellar openings. What might have been the barracks area lies to the right of the gateway. On the north side, note the fine piece of Frankish stonework in the form of a glacis, the remains of an inner defensive wall protecting the redoubt. The rest of the stonework is a mixture, the finer more regular work (especially the great bossage blocks) being Crusader period, the rest Arab. By curving around to the right, you can gain the upper level which includes another, smaller courtyard, but much of the fabric is in ruins.

On descending, if you can work your way through the underbrush, it is worth heading for the west (seaward) end of the fortification to follow for a while the line of wall and towers. It is just possible to make your way around via the north, circumnavigating the walls. If you follow the natural line of descent of the goat paths, you will probably come across a small local (Alawi) shrine of curious but charming origins set, as usual, in an oak grove. Built upon a spring, the shrine has re-used some of the stones from the castle including a whole arch and part of a scupture of a lion, undoubtedly the work of Baibars' reign of which the Venetian-type lion was a symbol. The shrine is a mausoleum of a local holy man, Sheikh Yunis. An inscription on the water trough is dated to 1285 during the reign of Sultan Qalaun (r 1280-90).

REFS: *BG* pp 457-8; Deschamps *Châteaux* - III pp 339-40; Dussaud p 150; Runciman II; van Berchem & Fatio pp 283-88.

Qalaat Najim

VARIANTS: Caeciliana (Lat); Qalaat Nadjim (Arb)
PERIOD: Arb RATING: * MAP: 71 ITIN: 10b

LOCATION: Take the new highway to the Jezira which heads north east out of Aleppo (*Raqqa road, then left turn at airport interchange). After *Membij (71 km), continue +17 km (12 km before new bridge crossing of the Euphrates) then turn south east (right) for +3 km. The castle is located on the right bank of the Euphrates.

Caeciliana, an important Euphrates port and crossing point in this area, was also the bridgehead for *Membij, the assembly-point for Roman forces preparing for campaigns against the Parthian/Sasanian threat in the region of Mesopotamia.

Today, while the precise location of Caeciliana is not clear, the chief point of interest in the area is the remarkable Arab castle of the 13th century which is being carefully restored by the Antiquities Department using mostly original methods and materials. Though the wear and

tear on the castle over the years has been great, enough remains, aided by the reconstructed elements, to give you a better idea of Arab fortification techniques than at any site outside the *Aleppo Citadel.

The existing remains largely date from the 13th century rebuilding of the fortress erected by Nur al-Din (r 1146-74) who in turn reconstructed an earlier fortress. The remains largely reflect the concepts of Arab military architecture realised from 1208 to 1215 by the Ayyubid Governor of Aleppo, al-Malik al-Zaher Ghazi. This Ayyubid Governor of Aleppo whose main achievement was the great rebuilding of the fortifications of the Aleppo Citadel, was a son of Saladin. By the next century, however, Qalaat Najim was already in decline, a victim, like other sites, of the neglect and disruption which attended the Mongol invasions of the late 13th and 14th centuries.

The castle follows the Arab style and takes full advantage of an existing highpoint in the terrain. The rocky crag is in itself a natural defence, towering steeply above the river plain. On the river side, a cladding of dressed stone provides an effective glacis and two towers further discourage scaling of the heights and defend the entrance gateway. Above the entrance, an Arabic inscription pays tribute to the building efforts of Ghazi.

A great vaulted central passage leads up from the gateway with chambers on either side. The castle spreads over a series of these underground rooms and passageways (some reputedly giving secret access to the river) and two upper floors. Some pattern to the chambers and battlements on top of the mound is gradually emerging from the reconstruction. Remains include a small palace with a central courtyard with *iwan*s and a mosque.

To visit the modern monument commemorating the re-entombment of the Suleiman Shah, forefather of the Otoman Sultans, who perished in the Euphrates downstream at a·site now covered by Lake Assad (*Qalaat Jaber), return to main Jezira road but turn right (instead of left for Membij) and continue 12 km to Euphrates bridge. Tomb is on right bank of the river, guarded by a small contingent of Turkish troops.

REFS: *BG* pp 419-20; Dussaud *Topographie* pp 449 ff.

Qalaat Rahba

VARIANTS: Qala`a al-Rehaba (Arb)
PERIOD: Arb   ALT: 244 m   RATING: *   MAP: 73
ITIN: 12b

LOCATION: Take the Abu Kemal road south of Deir al-Zor. After 45 km, you will reach the village of Mayadin on the river. Castle +1 km south on the right of the road, accessible by a dirt track.

This small, almost fairy-tale, castle presents an unreal impression when seen from afar. Constructed eight centuries ago, its masonry was never particularly robust. Given the harsh environment, the fabric of the five-sided donjon (137 m along its longest side) has been literally crumbling to pieces ever since. As the fabric disintegrates, the dust accumulates around the walls above the ditch, the effect perhaps emphasised by the piling up of desert sand around the periphery. Yet it still retains enough of its shape to be readily distinguishable.

The first fort at Qalaat Rahba was constructed on this spot by Malik Ibn Tauk during the Caliphate of al-Mamun (813-33) but was destroyed by an earthquake in 1157. A new castle was built during the reign of Nur al-Din (r 1146-74) by one of his officers, Sirkuh (uncle of Saladin), as part of the ruler's grand design for the unification of Syria under a single Muslim ruler (a goal already largely realised in 1154). In 1264, the Mameluke ruler, Baibars, appointed an Egyptian as Governor. As the successive Mongol invasions ravaged Syria (1260-1400) its usefulness lapsed given the damage inflicted by the invaders.

Although contemporary with many of the major Crusader castles of Syria, the approach taken was altogether different. Instead of a massive keep area surrounded by complex rings of curtain wall, bastions, and ditches, Qalaat Rahba concentrates on a centralised mound, ringed by a high but simple set of walls (a pentagon roughly 270 m by 95 m) protected by a huge ditch. Enough remains of the inner fabric to give you an impression of the scale of the defences. The central donjon echoes the five-sided shape of the outer wall on a smaller scale (c 60 m by 30 m). This donjon had its largest side to the west and on three levels, the lowest comprising a huge cistern. Some of the brickwork in geometric designs is characteristic of Arab architecture of this period which was heavily influenced from Mesopotomia and Persia.

Since 1978 a Franco-Syrian mission has been excavating the fortress and the remains of two associated town sites, one at the foot of the castle (on the river side), the other the mound which is found on the river bank and dominates the village of Mayadin.

REFS: *BG* p 490; Bianquis pp 220-6; Elisséeff and Paillet; Musil *Middle Euphrates* pp 7-8; Toueir, Bianquis & Rousset in *Catalogue 1996*.

Qalaat Saladin

VARIANTS: Sigon (Grk); Château de Saône , Saona, Sehunna (Cru); Qalaat Sahyun, Qalaat Salah al-Din[125] (Arb - mod)
PERIOD: Byz/Cru/Arb   ALT: 400 m   RATING: ***
MAP: *47, 67*   ITIN: 7a

LOCATION: In the mountains 24 km east of *Latakia. From Latakia (Jumhuriye Square, starting point) take southern exit for *Tartus. At 4.5 km, as the road to Aleppo turns left, the Tartus road passes under a railway bridge. Immediately past that, take road that branches left. +0.5 km, fork left of a large factory, continuing on to Hafeh (+15 km). Above Hafeh (+2 km), a sign in English points right to the castle. +1.5 km, then turn left to follow the spectacular and circuitous road (+2.4 km) that leads across the ravine forming the northern perimeter of the fortress. It is worth pausing before descending the ravine in order to gain a full appreciation of the layout of the site and to admire the dramatic setting.

It was I think the most sensational thing in castle-building I have seen: the hugely solid keep upstanding on the edge of the gigantic fosse.
[T E Lawrence - Letter to his Mother, Aleppo, September 1909[126]]

While its defences are less intact than the unstudied symmetry of the *Krak des Chevaliers and it is less sombre and brooding in its aspect than *Marqab, this is an example of Crusader castle-building at its most romantic. Much of this is due to the site, a ridge between two spectacular ravines leading down from the commanding reaches of the Jebel Ansariye. (Nebi Yunes, the highest peak in the range - alt 1583 m - is immediately behind). The fall of the land takes the eye down to the coastal plain and beyond it the Mediterranean sparkling in the distance. The castle represents the flamboyance

---

[125] This is the official title bestowed on the castle in 1957 to commemorate Saladin's capture of the fortress in 1188. It might misleadingly convey the impression that Saladin founded or built part of the monument - which he didn't.
[126] Quoted in Boase p 49.

of the Crusader enterprise - perhaps folly is a better word - in a raw and beautiful location, softened today by the peaceful setting and, on a spring day, the profusion of wildflowers that cover the scene.

History

Long before the Crusaders, the site was chosen for its defensive properties. From this secluded spot could be surveyed the access routes between the Orontes Plain and the coast via the Bdama Pass to the north that today carries the main road from Latakia to Jisr al-Shugur and Aleppo. While not directly on this route, the presence of a formidable strongpoint in the area was a severe impediment to anyone trying to challenge control of movement. Moreover, its commanding location protected the sweep of the broad plain behind Latakia, the reason which probably led to the earliest fortification by the Phoenicians (early first millennium BC) who were holding it when Alexander reached Syria (333 BC).

extensive domains (which stretched from Balatonos in the south (*Qalaat Mehelbeh) to Sardone (east of the Orontes)) perhaps explain how they found the resources to undertake the greatest Crusader building enterprise of the 12th century. As Deschamps has observed, other Crusader leaders had built economically; at Saône, everything was 'big, solid and magnificent'.

Saône (as it was known to the Crusaders) was unlike the other major Crusade strongholds in two other respects. It was never entrusted to one of the major orders, the Knights Templars or the Hospitallers; and its construction dates entirely from the early phase of the Crusader presence in the east, namely the years between 1100 and 1188. In the latter year, it fell to Saladin, the first major casualty of the Crusader's fundamental problem, the lack of sufficient manpower to protect their far-flung positions.

Confident after his major victory over the Crusaders at Hattin in Palestine in 1187 which resulted in the Arab recovery of Jerusalem,

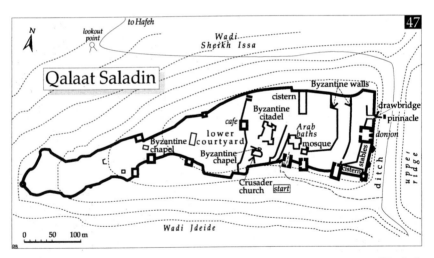

When the Byzantines moved back into Syria in the second half of the tenth century, the Emperor John I Tzimisces seized this site from the Hamdanid dynasty of Aleppo and began the first substantial defensive works after 975. It is not known precisely when the Crusaders took it over, probably in the first two decades of the 12th century. Certainly by 1119, a castle on this spot, a feudal endowment from Roger, Prince of Antioch, is recorded in the possession of a local seigneur, Robert of Saône. The family's

Saladin took his army on an expedition to the north to probe Crusader defences and block the prospective access route for a fourth Crusade bent on re-liberating Jerusalem. He contented himself with softer targets, especially the smaller, more lightly-defended castles. He took all but the inner redoubt of Tartus but moved on when resistance stiffened. Safita fell to him but he marched straight past the great fortress of Marqab. On 23 July 1188, Latakia surrendered.

He moved on the next day to Saône, arriving on the 26th and beginning his seige on 27 July. Saladin's forces pounded the castle from the plateau to the east while his son, al-Malik al-Zaher Ghazi, moving in from Aleppo, took up position across the north ravine. The Crusaders resisted fiercely but two days later the walls were breached by bombardment from the mangonels of Ghazi, the weak point proving to be the elongated and relatively thin walls of the lower court. Muslim soldiers stormed the breach[127], gained the lower court and from there swarmed over the narrow and incomplete ditch into the upper fortress. The garrison, overwhelmed by the swiftness of events, surrendered after barely a fight. The vast area of the fortress had proved too much for them to defend. Moreover the easy victory by Saladin at Latakia gave little point to their further resistance to an Arab leader who had established his prowess by his triumph the previous year against the united forces of the Jerusalem kingdom and who enjoyed a reputation for magnanimity.

Unlike the other major fortresses seized by the Arab leader (*Tartus, *Safita, *Latakia), Saône did not lapse back into Crusader hands. It was lost to the cause, along with other smaller strongpoints along the mountain (*Qalaat Burzey and *Qalaat al-Mehelbeh are nearby examples). It was controlled from 1188 to 1272 by a local family, that of Emir Nasr al-Din Manguwiris, but in the latter year it was ceded by the family to Sultan Baibars as a contribution to his campaign against the Crusader presence; a campaign which also asserted central authority in the mountain region. It was occupied from 1280 by the rebel ex-Governor of Damascus, Sonqor al-Ashqar, but was regained for the Mameluke Sultan Qalaun in 1287 after another seige. In the course of these Arab occupations it acquired a range of Ayyubid and Mameluke additions, including a mosque built by Sultan Qalaun. Though the lower enclosure housed for a time a small town, it was gradually deserted in favour of more convenient locations once the security of the area was assured. Commenting on its neglect as late as 1967, Boase observed: 'It still today keeps something of this remoteness, its solitude rarely disturbed, its secrets not wholly explored'.

Visit

HOURS
Summer - 10:00 - 18:00 Wed – Mon;
Winter 10:00 – 16:00 Wed - Mon

As the site is not an easy one on which to gain a perspective, it is suggested that you pause on the other side of the ravine as you approach and take note of its complex layout. The narrow ridge between two ravines runs approximately east/west and was once joined on the inland (eastern) side to the mountain spine. Probably in the Byzantine times, however, this link was broken by a formidable 156 m long ditch cut from the living rock, 28 m deep and 14 m to 20 m wide.

Along this elongated triangular site which follows the remainder of the ridge down to the west the Crusader castle was built on several levels stretching 740 m and covering a total of 5 ha. To the east (left) is the main keep, deploying the castle's most formidable defences against a potential enemy utilising the high ground. Next, moving westwards, is a courtyard that precedes the core of the Byzantine fortress, preserved by the Crusaders. West of the knoll on which the earlier fortress stands, a ditch separated the upper and lower courts. The elongated circuit wall followed the site down the hill, encompassing further strongpoints or gateways in the lower court, including a small chapel at the narrowest point. These somewhat thin outer defences petered out with a Byzantine round tower at the sharp end where the two ravines meet.

What you see is 'the finest and best-preserved of the feudal castles built in the East before the profound modification of military architecture at the end of the 12th century'[128]. After the great victories of Saladin in the 1180s and the loss of Jerusalem, the defence of the Crusader realms was undertaken with a new sense of purpose. The Templars and the Hospitallers were given a key role in the professional management of the main defensive positions and a new look was taken at military architecture. The result was the superb and formidable work realised at Marqab and the vast improvements made at the Krak. But this came too late for Saône already irretrievably lost. Its construction had been part of the more spontaneous phase of Crusader enterprise when urgency required an improvisatory approach adapting local and Byzantine techniques.

---

[127] The point at which the breach was made, notes Sa`adé *Histoire* p 999, can be traced today in a section (partly repaired) of the north wall of the lower court, a little to the west of the point at which the walls narrow. Boase p 51, however, prefers to locate the breach at the NE corner of the walls where the ditch reaches the natural *wadi* to the N.

[128] Fedden *Crusader Castles* p 49.

The road continues down, across the stream and up the other side of the ravine. After crossing the ridge via the ditch (to be inspected on foot in a moment), you park on the right hand side. You may wish to take a closer look at the walls on the south and east sides where they are best preserved. The fortifications here formed the line of defence against the relatively open and thus vulnerable south eastern approach. This outer line of walls, combining round towers to the east and the stouter square bastions on the south, show the transition from Byzantine to Crusader work. The three relatively slender round towers (east) are Byzantine in origin, adapted and strengthened in the Crusader rebuilding of the 11th century. In the massive square towers (south), the stone is laid in large blocks finished with neat bossage detailing in a typically precise Crusader style.

If you walk back to the east face, a close examination of the ditch will convey a striking impression of how much labour went into carving it out by hand with relatively basic tools. It is not entirely clear whether this work was substantially or entirely completed by the Byzantines before the Crusaders arrived. Most likely, it was a Byzantine achievement which the Crusaders deepened and widened. Note especially the 28 m tall needle of rock which was left at the northern end of the ditch to support the drawbridge leading to the postern gate (a secondary entrance to the castle). The postern gate is flanked by another two round towers.

To gain entry to the castle, you need to return to the main entrance on the south side. A path leads you via a dog-leg turn to the third of the square bastions. The door is located on the left flank of the bastion where it gained most protection from bombardment. It was once protected by a slot either for a portcullis or to rain down burning oil from the first floor of the tower. You enter a vestibule from which a second door opens to the north leading into the castle compound. (Notice the huge monolith stone which forms the lintel of the second door - 3.25 m in length, topped by a shallow relieving arch.)

The tour described below will take you in an anti-clockwise direction around the fortifications. The first tower on the right after the entry is marked by two doors on the north face, one leading to the ground-level hall, the other to the underground storage area. 50 m east, you come to a second square bastion. It is similar in style to the other Crusader bastions on the south side but includes a secret sally port to facilitate covert exit. Note that there is no access direct from the towers to the battlements between, a feature which displays the Byzantine origins of the defensive concept.

From this point, you reach the **courtyard** flanking the main donjon (or keep) situated in the middle of the east side, above the huge ditch. As you work around from the tower just described, there are two other buildings worth noting. The first is the **cistern** at the south east corner, one of several for the storage of water. Between the cistern and the donjon is a building in the form of a pillared hall which housed the castle **stables**.

The eastern donjon is built on a massive scale with walls over 5 m thick on a base 24 m square; as formidable as the great donjons at *Marqab or *Safita. Designed for a last-ditch defence of the castle, it presents a largely blank front even to the inner courtyard. The keep contains two storeys topped by a terrace. The entry is by a very plain doorway on the west with a straight lintel above, a feature borrowed into Crusader architecture from Byzantine examples. The first storey is 11 m high but presents a gloomy appearance due to the restricted light from the slit loopholes or *archères*. The groined vaulting is supported on a single central pillar. A staircase built into the north wall gives access to the upper storey which duplicates in plan the hall below except for the addition of three windows. A further staircase leads to a panoramic view from the roof parapets.

As you move northwards around the defences, you will reach the postern gate where the **drawbridge** led into the castle. The doorway was protected by two round towers already noted. Below this level, the building housed a domed room of Byzantine origins.

At this point, you should gain some appreciation of the Byzantine core which the Crusader castle profoundly modified. On the rise to the west of the courtyard you can see the remains of the **Byzantine citadel** including, beyond the mosque tower, the central rectangular tower of the Byzantine fortress. The Byzantine design relied essentially on a series of three or possibly four concentric defensive walls as opposed to the massive concentration of Crusader defenses on the most vulnerable point to the east. The outer line of Byzantine walls was superceded, at least on the east, by the Crusader keep. To the north, however, much of the Byzantine wall survived though the two huge cradle-vaulted cisterns towards the middle of the north wall are Crusader insertions. The largest **cistern** is 32 m long and 10 m deep. To the west, the Byzantine defenses followed the line of the wall between the upper and lower fortresses which you can reach by skirting anti-clockwise around the central rise.

You will reach a point where the upper terrace looks directly down to the lower courtyard and a tea house is located in a Crusader defensive building. Below it you can detect the outline of the ditch which complemented the inner dividing wall between upper and lower courtyards. (Saladin's forces gained entry to the castle across this ditch, having forced the weaker lower walls. The forces concentrated in the upper keep then surrendered.)

If you feel like bashing your way through the heavy (and prickly) undergrowth, you can descend to the lower courtyard. After 150 m, at the point where the thin-walled defences (Byzantine in origin) narrow, there is a small but charming **chapel** (also **Byzantine**), much overgrown with vegetation. There is also a cluster of square towers to protect the twists and turns of the walls at this point and to guard the postern gates giving direct access to the lower town from both north and south.

Returning to the tea house, continue in an anti-clockwise path to take in the rest of the inner Byzantine fortress. As you head back towards the entrance gateway, you will pass on the left the remains of the principal **Crusader church** of the castle. Between the ruins of the church and the south wall of the Byzantine fortress, lies another small **Byzantine chapel**.

Keep to the higher reaches between the Byzantine fort and the main east courtyard of the keep and you will come across the main additions of the Arab period. These include a **mosque** (with minaret) probably dating from the time of the Sultan Qalaun (r 1280-90) and a palace complete with **baths**, recently partially restored. The baths include an attractive courtyard with four *iwan*s. The palace entrance is marked by a superb gateway in stalactited carving (probably late 12th, early 13th century). It lies almost opposite the entrance gateway from which the tour began.

REFS: *BG* pp 467-70; Boase pp 49-51; Deschamps *Châteaux* - III pp 217-47; Dussaud *Topographie* pp 149-50; Fedden *Crusader Castles* pp 46-50; Eydoux pp 67-87; Lawrence pp 60-63; Sa`ade *Histoire* pp 980-1015; Smail *Warfare* pp 236-43.

Qalaat Yahmur

VARIANTS: Jammura (anc); Castrum Rubrum, Chastel Rouge (Cru)
PERIOD: Cru RATING: - MAP: *48*, 66 ITIN: 5a

LOCATION: 12 km south east of Tartus. From *Tartus, take the road to Safita. At c10 km (village of Beit Shalluf) a small track leads off to the right for +2 km.

There are sites in the environs earlier than the Crusades, including some Roman tombs. The site of the present small keep, however, was probably not fortified until the tenth century. The Byzantines under the Emperor Nicephorus (who reinstated Byzantine authority in this area, three centuries after the Arab conquest) built the first fortification.

It is not clear how much of the present keep dates from this construction and how much belongs to the Crusader period. The early Crusader fortress was in 1177 transferred to the Hospitallers who had been given the job of ensuring the defence of the hinterland of Tartus. Applying their skills in fortification and defensive technology, the Hospitallers improved on the Byzantine effort. Certainly, the architecture looks typically Crusader in its present appearance. Chastel Rouge temporarily fell to the Muslims in 1188 during Saladin's campaign in the area. The Crusaders recovered it and it remained in their hands for another century. It fell, in the end, in 1289, two years before Tartus, to the forces of the Mameluke Sultan, Qalaun.

The keep, essentially a fortified watch-tower with a surrounding wall, was built as part of the outer defences of Tartus, complementing the larger fortified points in the area, Safita and

Arima (*Qalaat Areimeh). The three points were in line of sight, enabling contact by signal fires.

The construction is basic but solid, typical of Frankish work of the mid 12th century. It consists of a stubby square tower with a lower room now used for village cattle surrounded by an outer wall obscured by modern housing. On entering the tower, if you can nudge the beasts out of the way, it is worth peering into the gloom of the lower chamber to observe the solid construction with the arched vaults coming down to a central pillar (cf the donjon at *Qalaat Saladin). This gave sturdy support to the upper storey which can be reached by a staircase built into the north wall. The terrace gives a commanding view of the countryside. The square enclosure wall, now employed as a domestic courtyard, is marked by two watch-towers at the south eastern and north western corners. The latter is still reasonably intact.

REFS: *BG* pp 438; Boase p 43; Deschamps *Châteaux* - III pp 317-9; Dussaud *Topographie* p 120; Eydoux p 224; Lawrence p 67; Runciman II pp 132, 134n, 188, 190.

Qalb Lozeh

VARIANTS: Qalbloze
PERIOD: Byz ALT: 683 m RATING: ** MAP: *49*, 69 ITIN: 9b

LOCATION: Follow directions for Harim. After 17.4 km, take the left turn (instead of continuing on to Harim). You should reach Qalb Lozeh on the top of a ridge, after +5 km.

The church at Qalb Lozeh (in Arabic, 'the heart of the almond'), is one of the most celebrated ecclesiastical monuments in Syria. Though there are earlier churches which survive in reasonable condition, this is the first example which realises on a monumental scale the Syrian model of the broad-aisled basilica church. It anticipates (possibly only by a decade or two) the bold experiment at *Saint Simeon and its decoration is of the same order of sophistication. It represents, in short, the full development of a Syrian style as an offshoot from Byzantine models and anticipates many of the features which were to find their way eventually to Europe in the Romanesque period (eg the dramatic entrance arch and flanking towers).

Qalb Lozeh is one of a group of Druze villages which have survived in the Jebel Ala since the tenth century, considerably isolated from the main concentrations of Druze in the area of Jebel al-Arab south of Damascus and the Golan region near Mount Hermon.

Visit

The church is the only ancient remains surviving in this mountain hamlet and it is not difficult to find it as the road winds its way between the dwellings. You will come upon the church from the north side. If you walk around to the right, you will see the entrance just noted with the three-storeyed towers to each side. These towers once framed a huge semi-circular arch topped by a terrace but only the footings on the left of the arch survive. Behind is the entrance doorway where the arch theme is continued, relieving the weight of masonry above the door. Reconstructions of the main arch show how this bold effect virtually brings to a climax several centuries of Syrian fascination with this device, seen also in the local adaptation of Roman styles in such centres as Palmyra or even the monumental arched entrance *(propylaeum)* to the Temple of Jupiter in Damascus.

To complete a circuit of the exterior, continue anti-clockwise to the south side, marked by three decorated entrance doorways and the newly-developed volute band flowing around the windows. Continue on to the east end (behind the altar) and you will come to the semi-circular *chevet* which takes the apse out beyond the rectangular lines of the building. This too is a new development, most Syrian churches having embedded the semi-circular apse inside the outer rectangular shape of the building, using complex and massive stonework to accommodate the incompatible shapes. The chevet is finished off by a device soon to be further developed at Saint Simeon, the use of two tiers of colonnettes topped by a classical cornice to embellish the curved wall.

Completing the circuit, you will come again

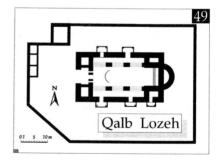

Qalb Lozeh

to the north side from which you can now enter the building. The first thing that will strike you as you enter is the dramatic shape of the three sweeping arches which divide the central from the side aisles and once carried the clerestory and roof. This practice of substituting piers for columns, thus integrating the side aisles more fully with the nave became a feature of later Syrian church building (Basilica Church of St Sergius at *Resafe (480-500) or the Bissos church at *Ruweiha (sixth century) are good examples). To support the huge weight of masonry at the critical points, relatively slim piers are used but in later examples, the piers become considerably more massive.

Thankfully, much of this structure survives in a remarkable state of preservation at Qalb Lozeh and even some of the stone roofing slabs of the side aisles are still intact. By providing the side aisles with a flat roof, the builders of Qalb Lozeh allowed considerably more light to enter the church by the clerestory windows. Note the elegant treatment of the these windows, separated by small brackets and colonnettes which once supported the wooden structure of the roof over the main aisle. The semi-circular apse preserves intact its vaulted semi-dome and the choir in front (raised five steps above the level of the nave) is flanked by two side rooms (the *prothesis* on the left accessible to the faithful; the *diaconicon* on the right reserved for clergy).

The standard of decoration framing the apse's semi-dome is particularly worth noting, rising on each side from beautifully treated pilasters and capitals of almost classical simplicity. Mattern rightly observes that the architects of Qalb Lozeh show an ability to use classical Greek norms 'with unexpected effect ...to give them a new application, even a new life'. Certainly the overall effect is more harmonious than the over-achievement which later churches strive for, often heavy-handedly mixing styles and shapes with ungainly effect.

The dating of the church has been much debated in recent decades. Butler had dated the church to around 480. The late expert on the villages of the limestone country, Tchalenko, argues that by comparison with the nearby dated church at Bettir (2 km north), Qalb Lozeh must have been built before 469. Most likely, he feels, the church was built during the lifetime of St Simeon (d 459) or immediately after. Many aspects of the Qalb Lozeh basilica were repeated, often in a more refined way, at the great quadruple basilica erected on the site of St Simeon's column, probably after 475.

Except for a few olive trees, the village consisted of little but the church, there being no sizeable patches of arable land on the limestone ridge. The fact that the church was surrounded

by a walled compound supports the likelihood that it was intended not to serve a village but to provide a stop for pilgrims, perhaps those bound for the already flourishing pilgrimage centre at Deir Semaan, at the foot of St Simeon's pillar. Whatever, the explanation, clearly a number of seminal influences came together on this site with an unusually productive blending of metropolitan and local Syrian influences most likely inspired by the pilgrimage role. Krautheimer may be right in criticising the unneccesarily monumental treatment of a relatively small-scale building and ascribes this and the emphasis on classical decoration to the Emperor Zeno's attempts to revive the classical heritage.

REFS: *BG* p 409; Butler *AE* II pp 221-5; Butler *EC* pp 71-3; Krautheimer pp 160-4; Mattern pp 107-14; Tchalenko *Basilique*; Tchalenko *Travaux*; Tchalenko *Villages* I pp 343-4; II XXII, CVIII, CXXXVI; Tchalenko and Baccache pl 418-25; Vogüé I pp 135-8 (pl 122-9).

Qanawat (Plate 18b)

VARIANTS: Kanatha, Kenath, Nobah (Bib[129]); Canata, Canatha (Grk); Kanawat
PERIOD: Rom/Byz RATING: ** MAP: *50, 51*, 63
ITIN: 2b

LOCATION: 100 km south east of Damascus. Leave Damascus by the *Suweida road. Pass through Shahba (87 km) and at +10 km (*Slim on right) turn left for +4 km then left again and ascend +2 km to Qanawat.

Qanawat ('canal' in Arabic[130]) is a site of considerable interest. Though its foundation probably goes back earlier, first historical mention of the town dates to the reign of Herod the Great (first century BC) when Nabatean Arab forces inflicted a humiliating defeat on the Jewish forces. (The campaign was the result of pressure on Herod from Antony who wished to restore the area to Cleopatra's realms.) It remained an issue of contention between the Nabateans and the Jewish kingdom to the south. From Pompey's time until the period of Trajan (r 98-117 AD), it was listed as one of the cities of the Decapolis, a loose federation allowed by the Romans to retain some degree of civic autonomy[131]. Incorporated into the province of

---

[129] *Numbers* 32, 42 relates its conquest by Nobah who renamed the settlement of Kanatha or Kenath after himself. It is later mentioned in *Judges* 8, 10-12.
[130] Perhaps a play on words, referring both to the remains of a Roman water reticulation system and to the pre-Roman Kanatha.
[131] Most of the Decapolis towns were in northern Jordan. The only other towns in present-day Syria listed in the Decapolis was Damascus.

Syria (first century), it was titled Septimia Canatha by Septimius Severus (late second century) and transferred to the province of Arabia at end of the second century. Christianity flourished (as elsewhere in the Hauran) in the fourth and fifth centuries and it became the seat of a bishop. The town fell to the Arabs in 637, after Damascus' capture, and then declined. It was virtually deserted by the mid 19th century.

The central ruins (popularly called the **Seraya** or palace) are set in a beautiful grove of oak trees and consist of two basilica-shaped buildings. Both are grouped around an atrium and were originally oriented north/south. They are Roman in origin (probably largely second century AD) but were adapted to Christian purposes in the fourth and fifth centuries. To gain the best perspective, go first to the central atrium that lies in the angle between the two buildings. From here looking west (back towards the square) is the first Roman construction. The second, larger, building, sometimes called the basilica, lies to the south through an imposing doorway.

the building was re-oriented east/west to conform to religious custom where the altar is set against the east wall. The south wall with three semi-circular niches as its focal point which had been added to the building in the early third century, was covered by the side wall of the new church and probably used as a *martyrium*. The Christian building thus turned the basic basilica plan around 90°, with three naves separated by two rows of columns oriented east/west and a semi-circular apse around the altar.

The origins of the atrium and the south building have most recently been explained by a group of French scholars[132]. The plan originated in the third century AD in a long open courtyard (18.5 m by 57 m) oriented north/south and surrounded by a colonnade, enclosed later at the south end by an apse and two side chambers. The purpose of this construction is unclear; perhaps it served as a civic building or a temple. The long courtyard was cut in two, probably in the fourth or fifth century by the monumental wall with three doorways, elaborately decorated. The reason for this change is not known. Later in the Christian period, the north section was kept as an atrium, the south being converted to a second church. The altar was placed to the east, at the centre of a *synthronon*. Behind the altar (east wall) a tomb was added. The narrow room to the east of the atrium seems to have been a baptistery. Recent research has speculated that the Qanawat complex became a centre of pilgrimage in the early Christian period, perhaps associated with the legend of the Old Testament Prophet, Job.

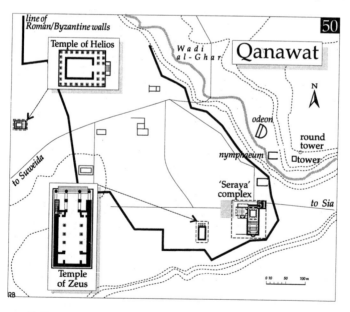

Taking the west building first, this was originally a basilica of the second half of the second century AD (possibly used as a *praetorium*), oriented north/south and preceded by a columned portico on the north. In the Christian period (probably fourth or fifth century),

The ruined remains to the north east of the *seraya* belong to the Christian period (episcopal palace or monastery?). The remains of the tower

132 Amer *et al.*

on the far corner of the complex represents a late addition in the Christian period, presumably at the time when towers were common in monastic establishments of northern Syria.

Along the road that ascends the rise to the *seraya* square you will see on the right after 200 m the fairly substantial remains of a Roman mausoleum, vaulted with multiple burial compartments.

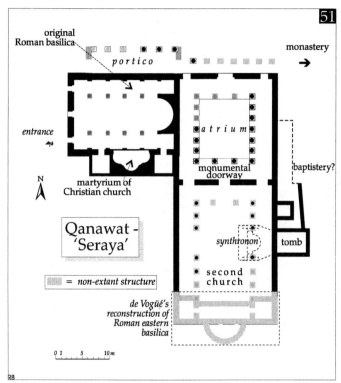

Further scattered remains of the Roman period can be explored on foot from the *seraya* square. Walk a little to the east, towards the monastery tower and then take the road descending sharply to the left. This takes you along the south west side of the gorge of the *Wadi al-Ghar*. After 120 m you will notice a park bordering the stream which contains along the opposite bank the remains of an **odeon** or small theatre (46 m diameter) with nine rows of seats built into the rise. A litle further upstream is a curious building which was probably a *nymphaeum* (water fountain) or a temple. Further upstream, the remains of a tower are incorporated into a modern house. On the top of the rise to the left, another tower, round, whose provenance is unexplained.

Besides the charm of the location amid its grove of trees, the decoration is of a high standard, the Christian buildings having simply re-used much of the classical stonework.

If you take the first turn left from the square, you will come after 100m to the remains of a **temple** of the second half of the second century AD, dedicated to **Zeus**. The temple (which stood near a square within the gateway of the ancient route to *Sia) consists of a *cella* with a four-columned portico, not unlike the temple at *Mushennef. The dimensions, however, are larger (15 m by 30 m in plan) and the interior was supported by six internal columns with a rectangular sanctuary at the south end.

On a knoll to the north west of the town 200 m on the right as you descend on the way back to the main road is the **peripteral temple** to the sun god Helios. It commands an impressive view across the flat plain of the Hauran to Mount Hermon. Built during the hey-day of the sun god cult on a high platform surrounded by a colonnade on all sides, it is a sort of minor version of the Palmyra and Baalbek temples. Little of the building is extant though the surviving columns indicate that the decoration was rich, in the Baalbek/Palmyra tradition.

REFS: Amer *et al*; Amy *Temples*; Baedeker pp 166-8; *BG* p 510; Butler *AE* pp 351-61; 402-8; 418-9; Butler *PE* II/A/5 pp 346-51; Donceel 'L'exploration de Qanouat (Qanawat)' in *AAAS* XXXIII 1983 pp 129-139; Donceel-Voûte 'Deux grands centres..' *AAAS* XLI; Dussaud *Topographie* pp 362 ff; Klengel *Syrien* pp 189-191; Sartre *Territoire* pp 343-57.

Qara

VARIANTS: Ocurura (Lat), Cehere
PERIOD: Byz/Umd Rating: - MAP: 75 ITIN: 3b

LOCATION: 97 kms north-north west of Damascus on the Homs road. On left, 15 kms north of Nabk.

During the doctrinal differences which split the church in the fifth and six centuries, Qara was a bishopric which resisted the Monophysite trend that swept over much of Syria. Most remarkable of the Christian remains are the beautiful frescoes (tenth century) found in the Greek Orthodox Church of Sts Sergius and Bacchus (last street on the right before the main square), though some have been transferred to the National Museum in Damascus. The great Basilica of St Nicholas has long since been converted to a mosque (1260) which can still be found occupying the centre of the southern ridge that runs through the old town, its Byzantine facade preserved intact.

One km to the west of the town are the striking remains of a fifth century Byzantine monastery to St Jacques built on the remains of a Roman fortlet. Inside are frescoes of the 13th century.

REFS: Nasrullah, Joseph 'Le Qalamoun à l'époque Romano-Byzantine' in *AAAS* 1952, 1956, 1958

Qasr al-Heir East (Plate 20b)

VARIANTS: Qasr al-Zeitouni (?Arb); Qasr al-Heir al-Sharqi (Arb)
PERIOD: Byz/Umd RATING: * MAP: 75 ITIN: 14

LOCATION: From Palmyra, take the road towards Deir al-Zor via Sikne. (Starting point Cham Hotel.) At 110 km (35 km past Sikne – site of a Roman fort), a sign in English and Arabic points across the desert to the *qasr* but no consistent track or improved road is available. Follow the sketchily-defined tracks keeping in the general direction north by north west. The surface is rough but not impossible in dry weather. After rain, a four-wheel drive vehicle would be essential. At c30 km (a good 60 minutes at slow speed), you should see the *qasr* in the distance.

The purpose of the two desert castle complexes at Qasr al-Heir (in Arabic, 'walled castle') East and West has stimulated much debate in recent decades. In 'City in the Desert'[133], recording the results of an American expedition of 1964-72, Grabar *et al* note that the monumental facades of these two palaces are not commensurate with the more mundane internal structures and the utilitarian nature of most of the items found. They see the buildings as lacking any grand purpose as would be the case if they had been supervised by a major patron (as in, for example, the Mosque of the Umayyads in Damascus). Moreover, they see a confusion of styles - Byzantine, Mesopotamian/Persian and local - which in this case resulted more in an unresolved pastiche than the triumph of synthesis realised in the Umayyad Mosque. There is, they conclude, 'something grandiloquent, *nouveau riche*, and provocatively expensive about the site'. Nevertheless, it is a bizarre ruin of great interest and although one should not expect another Palmyra or even a Resafe, the one hour diversion each way is well worthwhile.

History

Earlier studies this century tended to emphasise the possible pre-Islamic or Byzantine origins of the complex, citing the presence of architectural elements such as capitals. Grabar *et al* believe, however, that the Byzantine and Roman period stonework had been transported from neighbouring sites (some around Palmyra) or was provided by Christian craftsmen using Byzantine techniques. However, when work commenced on the Umayyad complex (728/9 under Caliph Hisham), it may already have been in use for oasis gardens. The water supply that made settlement possible was based on a water-course leading from a dam at al-Qawm, 30 km to the north west. The gardens, 850 ha in extent, were surrounded by 22 km of largely mud-brick walls (the remains of which can still be traced in places).

Like the companion castle, Qasr al-Heir West (200 km west), the scale of the *qasr* owes a good deal to the edifice complex that marked the second half of the Umayyad dynasty, particularly under Caliph Hisham. Other castles of the Syrian-Jordanian desert have attracted equal speculation as to their purpose. Traditional explanations have covered a range of possibilities from pleasure (a hunting lodge with oasis gardens) through practical (intensive agricultural development; *caravanserai* or *khan*) to military (defence of the Umayyad realm

---

[133] Harvard University Press (2 vols) 1978..

against fractious tribes and the threat from Mesopotamia).

The American expedition is inclined to plumb for a combination of several practical explanations, speculating that the site was probably originally built as a grandiose agricultural settlement intended to cower and help control warring desert tribes. It later acquired a more distinctly economic purpose with the addition of the east building or caravanserai to encourage commercial traffic. The original motivation for the settlement (probably around 700) was the need to pacify the area after a series of murderous tribal wars. As the Umayyads consolidated their rule in the region, they concentrated on developing the 'fertile crescent' link between Mesopotamia and Syria, particularly through ambitious schemes on the Mid Euphrates and the new province of the Jezira (north east Syria). This new order required a more effective means of controlling the caravan traffic across the desert, along the short-cut route from Damascus via the Jezira to Mesopotamia and Persia.

Shortly after the end of Hisham's caliphate, the Umayyads were overturned and replaced by the Abbasid dynasty ruling from Baghdad. Syria was purposefully neglected, increasingly a backwater and a hotbed of discontent and factionalism. The *qasr*, however, was not abandoned, there being signs that the Abbasids saw economic advantage in bringing it to fruition, albeit on a reduced scale. There was further minor building works up to the tenth century but the area by then had largely been abandoned to the nomads. Renewed settled occupation seems to have taken place in the 11th century, lasting until the 13th century after which (presumably due to the effects of the Mongol invasions) the site was again abandoned for permanent settlement.

Visit

If you approach the ruins from the south, look out for the remains of the outer walls which are as far as 5 km distant from the *qasr*. The outer walled garden area measured 3 by 6 km. Closer in was the palace garden and the civilian town. An inner enclosure wall surrounds the two castle buildings about 200 m out.

The central complex consists of two distinct castles, 40 m apart and carefully built from fine-grained grey limestone. The two gateways guarded by semi-cylindrical towers on each side face each other with a minaret between.

The gate of the **eastern castle** is reasonably well preserved and is the most interesting architectural feature of the complex.

The decoration is clumsy but shows a conscious juxtaposition of styles (Mesopotamian, Byzantine and local), a practice much encouraged under the Umayyads (cf the gateway of Qasr al-Heir West in the National Museum, Damascus). The two half-circle towers found on each wall are on the entrance side moved in to flank the gateway. This is decorated with a simple framework of a semi-circular arch above, the architectural device beloved of Syrian builders since Roman times. (The Palmyrene inspiration is repeated in the two semi-circular niches flanking the arch). The upper frieze is in brick (a Mesopotamian touch probably added after 760, the first known use of brick patterning in Syria). A jutting machicolation (also a new device in the military context, later much favoured by Arab military architects) protects the gateway.

This smaller eastern castle (c 70 m square) has been judged to be the more military in purpose, perhaps because its defences are more intact and it has a single entrance. In fact, it was almost certainly built as a khan or caravanserai, possibly as an afterthought after the agriculture-based settlement under official sponsorship had been initiated. It largely retains its outer walls, 2 m thick and once 12 m high, topped by a circuit walk and fortified with twelve cylindrical towers. Inside, however, its remains are in ruins, the courtyard deeply covered in rubble. The structure once consisted of a series of 12 m deep chambers, vaulted in brick in order to support a second storey, probably roofed in timber. The central courtyard was based on an irregular square with sides varying from 28 m to 36 m, once surrounded by a colonnade. The use of brick to finish off the upper level of the walls and for vaulting probably indicates that this building was completed under the Abbasids for whom brick was a more natural material.

The **larger castle** (167 m^2) on the west had six times as much space for habitations and common facilities but its walls (with 28 rounded towers) and five gateways are less well preserved. The east entrance gateway opposite the minaret consists of a rectangular aperture topped by a blind arch. The tympanum inside the arch was originally filled with a marble decorated panel. Above this is a heavy machicolation, the doorway being flanked by semi-circular towers now ruined. Inside, the original plan comprised a central square with streets leading to it from each of the four cardinal gateways. The square was surrounded by a portico and provided with a covered cistern for the storage of water. The buildings comprised twelve segments each roughly a square - six were living quarters of approximately the same plan; three were ancillary service areas; one was an official building; one housed olive presses; and the last was a mosque (south eastern corner). They formed a small urban centre with limited commercial facilities.

The **minaret**, placed between the two castles, is not adequately explained. Assumed to be contemporary with the rest of the complex, it would be the third oldest minaret in Islam. Yet there is no mosque to which it was attached unless one sees it as related to the mosque in the south eastern quarter of the larger palace.

Remains (to foundation level only) of reasonably spacious baths were discovered 60 m to the north of the area between the two enclosures.

REFS: *BG* p 357; Creswell *Early Muslim* pp 522-44; Etinghausen and Grabar; Grabar *et al*; Hillenbrand *Dolce Vita*; Holod-Tretiak.

Qasr al-Heir West[134]

VARIANTS: Heliaramia (Lat); Qasr al-Heir al-Gharbi (Arb)
PERIOD: Byz/Umd RATING: - MAP: 75 ITIN: 14

LOCATION: Damascus/*Palmyra road. At c153 km from Damascus, the road from Homs joins from the left. Follow this road back towards Homs, passing after c+10 km the turn-off for *Harbaqa Dam. Continue +20 km north - castle is +2 km to the east across the desert.

See remarks below about the monumental gateway re-erected at the National Museum in Damascus (*Damascus - Museum) before visiting the Qasr.

History

The existence of a settlement in this bleak spot in the desert has always depended on the supply of water to its gardens from the nearby dam at Harbaqa. Water was brought by canal and pipe from the dam (17 km south). The Palmyrenes established the first settlement here in the first century AD but it was abandoned after their revolt in 273. The Byzantines (under Justinian) and their local Arab allies, the Ghassanid tribe, re-occupied the site in 559 and established a monastery, some of the remains of which still survive. (At the time, the eastern desert was a favourite area of monastic concentration - eg *Mar Mousa).

The Umayyad Caliphs, who sought to retain their roots in the desert, established here a retreat from the environment and pressures of Damascus. But this 'hunting lodge' reflected the Umayyads' judicious cultivation of both leisure and practicality. It was built on the Byzantine site by the last great Umayyad Caliph, Hisham (r 724-43). Construction began in 727-8, about the same time as the more ambitious project at *Qasr al-Heir East 200 km across the desert, beyond Palmyra. As well as pleasure, the complex served the practical purposes of facilitating contact with the tribes, as a post-house for communications and as a means of consolidating defensive arrangements in the desert.

The more spartan Ayyubids and, many centuries later, the Mamelukes, used the site for military purposes but after the 14th century Mongol invasions, it was again deserted.

Today, the remains are a disappointment, though it is a worthwhile short diversion (30 minutes in each direction) for travellers visiting Palmyra who may also wish to see the more interesting phenomenon of the surviving Roman dam at Harbaqa. The castle is on the edge of a stock control station and modern additions such as power facilities and shabby buildings do little to enhance the scene. Moreover, most of the surviving remains of the curious Umayyad building were (probably wisely from the point of view of conservation in this harsh environment) taken away to be re-assembled to form the striking main entrance to the National Museum in Damascus.

A visit to the Museum should therefore precede any call at the ruins of the *qasr*. The huge monumental gateway (*Damascus – National Museum) constructed largely in stucco and fired brick of a fine consistency is a remarkable testimony to the cultural diversity of Syria at the time of the Umayyads. The patterns of the two large semi-circular towers and the joining gateway are largely geometric, in accordance with Islamic norms but the style juxtoposes elements of Persian, Byzantine and local traditions.

Visit

What remains on the ground gives an indication of the size of the Umayyad **lodge** (measuring c70 m square) which partly incorporated the remains of the Byzantine monastery. The most prominent feature of the latter is the north western tower which rises three storeys above the ground. The rest of the compound was originally two-storeyed, made of brick on a lower

---

[134] The Arabic name translates as 'Western Walled Castle', the *heir* being an archaic word referring to the walls of the gardens.

2 m course of limestone and with a colonnaded internal court. Except at the north west, the corners ended in round towers. In the middle of each face, semi-circular towers provided protection for the walls, except on the east side where the central gateway (now in Damascus) was flanked by twin towers.

To the north, remains of a *hammam* were excavated by the French under Schlumberger. The small reservoir for collection of the waters channelled from the Harbaqa Dam are found to the west. From here the gardens of the lodge (1050 m by 440 m in extent) were irrigated. A *khan* was built at a distance of 1 km in 727 and its entrance has been re-erected in the garden of the National Museum in Damascus.

REFS: Arush pp 155-161; *BG* p 322; Creswell *Early Islamic* pp 506-18; Hillenbrand *Dolce Vita*; Sauvaget *Châteaux Umayyades*; Schlumberger.

Qasr Ibn Wardan (Plate 21a)

VARIANTS:
PERIOD: Byz RATING: * MAP: 72 ITIN: 11b

> LOCATION: In the north steppe 62 km north east of *Hama. From central Hama (starting point) take Aleppo road but 100 m before motorway, turn right along the perimeter avenue for 1 km then left onto Hamra road. At Bardurah (22 km) continue straight to Qasr Ibn Wardan (+40 km).

History

The Byzantine Emperor Justinian (r 527-65) did much to set his stamp on northern Syria. During his long reign, he followed a policy of restoring to the eastern Empire much of the territory lost since the high point of Rome in the second century. Syria was the strategic depth for the defence of the Empire's heartland against Persia to the east. Justinian's military commander, Belisarius, conducted several campaigns in the area and in order to secure the fruits of his achievements, a series of impressive fortifications was constructed, largely along the north reaches of the Euphrates (*Halabiye, *Resafe, *Meskene).

Completed in the last full year of Justinian's reign (564), Qasr Ibn Wardan was in architectural terms perhaps the most remarkable of these defensive creations though it lacks the sheer size and stolidity of the more distinctly fortress-like cities elsewhere. The overall design is more graceful and flamboyant, partly reflecting in concept and choice of materials the high art of the capital at the time, rather than the more prosaic provincial models common in Syria.

The complex of palace/church/military barracks on the edge of the great Syrian Desert were as much intended to control the nomadic Arab population of the desert zone as to meet the more strategic threat from Persia. The scale of the buildings and their defences is thus considerably smaller than in the fortresses along the Euphrates and its hinterland. This allowed for greater freedom of expression, elegance of style and lightness of touch. The results are still obvious in this extraordinary complex with its broad-banded brick and stonework silhouetted against the harsh desert landscape. The old Blue Guide does not exaggerate when it calls these ruins 'among the most impressive, and perhaps even the most outstanding, in the whole of northern Syria'.

Visit

The largest part of the complex is the **palace** (east side) (dated by inscription AD 564). This was presumably built to house the military governor of the region. The south side, through which you enter, is the best preserved facade. The complex of rooms on this side reached two storeys and much of the fabric damaged largely by the work of nature over the years has been recently restored by the Antiquities Department. After noting the carved basalt lintel and the bold brickwork of the facade, you can enter through a broad vaulted vestibule. On both left and right are vaulted apsidal rooms each with annexes to each side, probably ceremonial chambers. Stairs from the right chamber lead to an upper (dormitory) area. On the west side of the courtyard is a large cross-vaulted chamber said to be a school.

The courtyard is extensive and contains a variety of service annexes including the stables along the north wall and wells. The north and east sides, until recently in a considerably worse state of preservation than the rest of the complex, have also been heavily reconstructed.

The building of greatest interest is the **church** which lies to the west of the palace. The church still impresses today, in spite of the collapse of most of the dome, the south western corner and parts of the soaring *triforium*. The basic shape is a building square in internal plan, surmounted by a dome but conforming to the three-aisled Syrian format, a difficult combination of shapes that Byzantine architectural practice was still trying to get right. The solution to the problem of squaring the circle – i. e. supporting the round dome on the square base - was to connect the two elements by devices called pendentives, triangular segments of a sphere which lead down from the base of the dome to the corners of the square. Actually, in this case, the solution is made even more complex by the addition of gallery rooms (or *triforia*) running around three sides of the church and overlooking the central nave. This meant that the dome's weight had to be distributed through the arches supporting the upper storey to the north and south as well as to the substantial piers that carry the main arches across the nave. The total height of the dome was 20 m but the building has a sense of harmony and compactness resulting from the variety and rhythm of the complex internal shapes. (The same effect is sought on a much larger scale in the profusion of shapes supporting the great dome at Hagia Sophia, an earlier project of Justinian.)

The nave itself, excluding the side aisles, measures almost 7 m by 10 m and ends in the customary semi-domed apse. It had entrances to the north, south and west, the latter leading through a wide but shallow lobby or *narthex* into the main nave. From the narthex, a staircase on the north western side led to the upper storey which, in the Byzantine tradition, was probably reserved for women. The extensive use of brick (including the only baked brick dome found in Syria) and the use of many different types of stone (including columns and capitals probably recycled from *Apamea, local lava or basalt and imported gypsum, limestone and marble) underlines the exotic nature of the project. Yet though there is much in the structure and the use of materials that recalls metropolitan models, it is likely that the building was largely local in execution. Mango points to the unusual proportions of the building (it is uncommonly tall), the placing of pendentives and the crude style of carving on the capitals, door jambs and lintels as evidence of a Syrian architect imperfectly following Byzantine models.

The third building in the complex was the military **barracks** to the south of the palace (probably AD 558). Of this nothing remains of any significance.

REFS: *BG* pp 373-4; Butler *EC* pp 168-9; Butler *PE* II B 1 pp 26-45 (plans); Klengel *Syrien* p 200; Lassus *Sanctuaires chrétiens* pp 146-7; Mango pp 150-1.

Qatura

VARIANTS: Qatoura
PERIOD: Rom/Byz   ALT: 485 m   RATING: -
MAP 68 ITIN: 9a

LOCATION: Just south of *Saint Simeon. Follow the directions for *Mushabbak (25 km) then go on to Deiret Azze (+5 km). As the road leaves Deiret Azze and heads north towards Saint Simeon (the peak of Jebel Sheikh Barakat is on the left) it passes over a saddle and begins to descend quite steeply before crossing a small fertile valley. Immediately at the bottom of this descent, a dirt road branches off to the left. Follow this for c1 km.

The village and its environs contain a number of late Roman and Byzantine remains. If you continue just past the village, you can see on the left, carved into the rocky hillside, roughly cut rock tombs with carvings from the Roman period. The sculptural style is a rather crude version of classical funerary art, but there are also touches of Palmyrene, though less stylized and without its oriental embellishments. Tombs in the locality are variously dated between AD 122 and 250. The last tomb on the road that heads around the Jebel towards *Zarzita shows a rather decomposed low-relief of a draped figure lying on a banquet couch. The inscription in Greek and Latin refers to one Titus Flavius Julianus, a veteran of the VIII Augustus Legion and his wife Flavia Titia. The tomb probably dates from the late second century.

On the southern edge of the village, a subterranean burial chamber is marked by a two-column funerary monument. This is the tomb, dedicated in AD 195, to Aemilius Reginus. The design is not unlike the nearby bi-columnar monument at *Sitt er-Rum devoted to Isidotos.

Tchalenko's study of the 'dead cities' zone brings out the sudden onset of prosperity in the region in the second century, as illustrated in the adoption of monumental tombs in settlements as small as this one. On the whole, construction techniques as seen in the extant fragments of ancient housing are not sophisticated, using stones irregular and polygonal in shape. There is no church. Remains of two quadrated stone villas are found in the surrounding fields, one to the north, both probably dating from the fifth or sixth century. The earliest Christian inscription found in the limestone country (dated 336/7) was noted in the northern sector of the settlement.

Those interested in a vigorous climb might consider visiting the nearby second century AD Roman temple site on the top of **Jebel Sheikh Barakat** (alt 870 m) to the north. A track leads to the summit from the village of Qatura. This was a major pilgrimage centre in Roman times (known as Mount Koryphaios), the most important of the 15 or more temples in this area (see also *Baqirha). The temple was dedicated to Jupiter Madbachos (Jupiter of the Altar) and the local god, Selamanes. It was built on a partly artificial terrace 68 m square. The surrounding wall (whose construction was spread over the period mid first century to AD 170) was lined with an internal portico pierced by central doors and ramped entrances on three sides. At the centre stood a *cella* preceded by four columns. Foundations only remain. It may be no coincidence that nearby Saint Simeon took over from this pagan site as a major focus of pilgrimage. The summit has become a Muslim place of pilgrimage and the tomb of the venerated Sheikh Barakat is built against the north wall of the temple compound.

REFS: **Qatura**: Butler AE II p 61, 272; Butler AE II pp 61,273-4; *idem* PE II/B/5 pp 249-51; *GB* 396; Sournia p 112; Tchalenko *Villages* I pp 183-94, II pl LVII-IX, LXI, LXII; CXXVII. **Jebel Sheikh Barakat**: Callot and Marcillet-Jaubert pp 181-6; Tchalenko *Villages* I pp 106-7, II pl XLII, CXXXI; Vogüé pl 94.

Qinnesrin

VARIANTS: Chalcis ad Belum (Lat); al-'Iss (Arb)
PERIOD: Rom/Byz   RATING: T   MAP: 72   ITIN: 11a

LOCATION: 31 km south west of Aleppo, known by the modern name of al-'Iss. Take the main Damascus road south from Aleppo Scientific College roundabout (starting point). Turn left after 25 km for the village marked as al-'Iss (+6 km).

Though Chalcis ad Belum[135] was an important centre on Roman itineraries, more central as a hub than Aleppo, the modern-day visitor should not approach it with any great expectations. The present village marks the point where the Quweiq River (east of the site), having struggled to maintain a trickle as it flows through Aleppo, peters out in the marshes of the *Madkh* before surrendering to the desert. South of the village, the citadel once occupied the 30 m high *tell*.

The great advantage of the location was its commanding views over countryside which, as in Roman times, is still a flourishing agricultural area as a result of recent efforts to drain the marshes. Qinnesrin, the traditional Arab place name, reflects a pre-Hellenistic (Aramean) name meaning 'eagle's nest'. From here views could be obtained as far as Jebel Hass to the north, to Jebel Zawiye in the limestone country to the east, and to Jebel Isriya to the south east. It thus surveyed not only the desert margins but the rich undulating country around Aleppo and the hill country east of Antioch. No wonder it was made the junction point of major routes including Antioch-*Palmyra, Aleppo (Beroia)-*Apamea (and south to *Hama, *Homs and Damascus),

the east route to Anasartha and Zebed (see *Isriya) and the road south east to Androna (*Anderin).

Few traces remain of the thick pattern of Roman roads and defensive positions which kept guard over the outer approaches to Antioch. The Roman settlement of Chalcis was divided between the acropolis and the lower town to the north, the whole being surrounded by a 4 km wall. The site had been founded earlier under the Seleucids by Seleucos I Nicator. By the end of the second century BC, the city may have fallen under Arab control as Seleucid authority weakened. The substantive fortification work, however, was begun by the Romans, primarily to defend the settlers against marauding nomadic Arabs to the south. Justinian (r 527-65) re-fortified it in 550-1 as part of his extensive works in the desert fringes intended to ward off the Persian threat. It was destroyed in the first shock of the Arab invasion (637), but was revived as an administrative headquarters of the new Umayyad province covering northern Syria. It was depopulated by Saif al-Daula (963) during his struggle against the Byzantines. By 1200 the town was permanently abandoned.

A few stones of the Roman/Byzantine walls survive, mainly on the western edge of the citadel. The citadel (southern side of the site) was once surrounded by two lines of walls, the inner (fortified by square bastions) ran around the edge of the plateau, the outer around the base. The lower town extended as far as the hill to the north called Nebi 'Iss (hence the modern place name) on the southern slopes of which are quarries and a number of underground tombs.

REFS: *BG* pp 414-5; Dussaud Topographie pp 476-7; Monceaux, P & Brossé, L 'Chalcis ad Belum' in *Syria* VI 1925; Mouterde and Poidebard I pp 7-9.

---

[135] The *ad Belum* was added to distinguish this Chalcis from *Chalcis ad Libanum* in the Beqaa Valley of Lebanon. For *Belus*, see *Dead Cities - General Note.

R

Raqqa

VARIANTS: Nikephorion, Leontopolis (Grk); Callinicum (Lat); al-Rafiqa (Arb)
PERIOD: Arb (Abd)   RATING: - MAP: *52, 72*
ITIN: 12a

LOCATION: On the left bank of the Middle Euphrates at its junction with the Balikh River (the classical Balissus), 193 km south east of *Aleppo (134 km north west of Deir al-Zor).

History

Founded, according to Pliny, by Alexander the Great (but named after one of his general, Seleucos I Nikator), the settlement was located south of Tell Bia, the mound 2 km east of the present walled city. (The Latin name Callinicum probably commemorates its real founder, Seleucos II Callinicos, who established the centre around 244-2 BC. Another foundation legend ascribes the name to a Greek sophist Callinicos who was murdered there.)   In Byzantine times, it was an important fortress on the front line between the Persian and Christian empires. (Remains of the Byzantine fortifications have been found between Tell Bia and the river.) Belisarius, Justinian's famous general, who did much of the campaigning against the Persian threat in Syria, was defeated near the town in 531.

After falling peacefully to the Muslim forces (639-40), written records indicate that the Umayyad Caliph Hisham chose the flat land to the west of the classical town as the site for two palaces. From 772, the Abbasid Caliph al-Mansur (r 754-75) commissioned the architect, al-Rabah, to rebuild the town as a second capital to control the province of the Jezira (north eastern Syria) and serve as a forward headquarters against the Byzantines, giving it the prosaic name al-Raqqa ('the morass'). Al-Mansur's horse-shoe shaped design (1500 m in diameter) was a modified version of his earlier circular plan for Baghdad.

The great Abbasid Caliph Harun al-Rashid (r 786-809) favoured the area and built alongside the old Raqqa a new capital (al-Rafiqa - 'companion') from 796 which served as his base until 808 and which gradually acquired the old

town's identity. The new building program in Raqqa was intended not simply to reinforce the town as a frontier fort but as a symbol of Abbasid hegemony, deliberately not choosing an area which had been central to the Umayyads' power base. As the Zengids' and Ayyubids' traditional connections with Mosul (northern Mesopotamia) emphasised the role of the Jezira, the symbolic and defence roles of Raqqa remained important. Saladin (late 12th century) started the glazed ceramic industry for which Raqqa became famous. After it was ravaged by the Mongols in 1258 at the time of the catastophic sacking of Baghdad, it fell into ruin and ceased to play a major role until its recent elevation to the status of provincial capital in 1960.

Visit

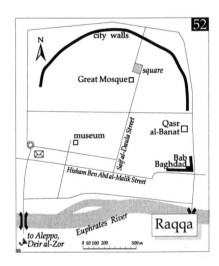

Though Raqqa has been intermittently dug by archaeological missions since 1906, much of what has been unearthed has proved perishable or is of specialised interest. Greek and Roman remains consist solely of a few architectural fragments incorporated in later buildings. Raqqa preserves only a few inadequate remnants of its former glory under the Abbasids. These glimpses, however, are enough to reveal the extent to which the Islamic world, after the Arab-

Hellenistic blending of the Umayyad period, became more heavily influenced by the Persian traditions in art and architecture, particularly through the development of the pointed arch.

There have been recent efforts to build up again the semi-circular baked and mud brick **walls** of the Abbasid town of which two thirds of the length survive (the exception being the south side parallel to the river). The walls were originally of double thickness, strengthened every 35 m by more than 100 round towers. In the south eastern corner of the walled city lies the **Bab Baghdad** (Baghdad Gate) which recent research indicates may date from the mid 12th century, rather than the original construction phase under the Abbasids. It conveys some idea of the effective use of decorative brickwork (eg the frieze of patterned blind arches above the gateway) which closely followed Mesopotamian styles whose influence in Syria was largely confined to the Jezira.

One of the most famous remains within the old city is the **Qasr al-Banat** ('Palace of the Maidens') the purpose of which is not clear. The building is centred on a courtyard with fountain, with an *iwan* (high-arched and open hall) on each side, all richly ornamented in brick. It dates from the ninth century and is a rare example outside Iran of the four-*iwan* plan.

You can also find in the centre of the walled area some remains of the **Great Mosque** (or Friday Mosque) whose construction was originally undertaken in 772 under Caliph al-Mansur. The courtyard was rebuilt (1165-6) by Nur al-Din who seems to have devoted a good deal of attention to building projects in the Jezira. The remains comprise only two elements: an uncompromisingly plain 25 m tower, Mesopotamian in inspiration but probably dating from Nur al-Din's restoration; and part of the courtyard colonnade in mud-brick Arab arches including the inscription recording Nur al-Din's contribution. The mosque was originally almost 100 m square with 11 towers around the periphery. Creswell notes that the square plan and the bastioned walls were Mesopotamian in inspiration while the triple-aisled prayer hall and its parallel gabled roofs are Syrian in origin (cf *Damascus - Umayyad Mosque). 1 km north east of the walled town, remains of two **Abbasid palaces** have been excavated - one attributed to Harun al-Rashid, the second probably of his successor, al-Maamum.

To the north and north east of the town, there are extensive remains of earlier settlements including Tell Bia where a MBA palace was unearthed and which resembles the Palace of Zimri-Lim at Mari. A guide is needed, though, to unscramble the several sites, only a fraction of which have been excavated.

Heraqla

Eight kms to the west lie the remarkable ruins of Heraqla, once thought to be a Roman military camp or *castrum*. Later research has unearthed an Arab enclosure which has no parallel in Islam. Clearly not intended for habitation but as a monument, Toueir believes it may have been built by Harun al-Rashid to commemorate his victory over Byzantine forces at Herakleon but was never completed. Each side is 103 m long and includes a vaulted hall or *iwan* opening to the outside as well as towers on each corner. The whole stands on a terrace which is in turn enclosed in a circular stone-walled compound 500 m wide. Four gates (each based on a different plan) mark the cardinal points of the outer enclosure.

REFS: *BG* pp 362-3; Creswell *Early Muslim* pp 183-91; Hillenbrand *Eastern Islamic*; Honigmann pp 1108-10; Meinecke in *Near East in Antiquity* II; Toueir *Raqqa/Rafiqa*; Toueir 'Heraqlah'.

Ras al-Basit

VARIANTS: Posideiôn (Grk), Posidium (Lat)
PERIOD: LBA/Hel RATING: T MAP: 67 ITIN: 7c

LOCATION: 53 km north of Latakia. Take northern route from Latakia towards the hill resort of Qasab (Casambella to the Crusaders), an Armenian village near the Turkish border. At 40 km, turn left and descend +13 km to the coast, weaving through pine forests. The archaeological site, a 25 m *tell*, lies about 500 m east of the lighthouse that marks the cape (turn left c+1 km when you reach the beachfront road).

The French excavations of 1971 to 1984 revealed a small settlement with citadel founded (like *Ras Ibn Hani) as an outpost of Ugarit during the Late Bronze Age, surviving into the Iron Age. It had strong links with Phoenicia and Cyprus and received a Greek colony in the seventh century BC but was destroyed during the Persian period (539-331 BC). Alexander passed this way in 333 BC (the Battle of Issus took place not far to the north, near modern-day Alexandretta) and it became a Seleucid settlement after 313 BC under the name of Posideiôn with a fortress on its small acropolis (southern end of the tell). A new phase of development began with the re-fortification of the town in the third century AD. A basilica was erected at the foot of the acropolis (north end), the port facilities improved and houses for the wealthy constructed. The port was still in use during the Crusades and was a destination for Venetian ships in the 15th to 16th centuries. By the 19th century, it was used only by the local fishing community.

To the north is **Mount Casius** (Jebel al-Aqra). At 1728 m, it is the highest peak on the coast. It was known in Hittite records as Mount Hazi or Nanni. The summit was sacred to the Phoenicians (*Ugarit) and the Greeks (Zeus). The Emperors Hadrian and Julian (the Apostate) climbed to worship on the peak. The Crusaders knew it as Mont Parlerius or Parlier.

REFS: Courbin pp 102-6; Dussaud *Topographie* pp 418-21.

Ras Ibn Hani

VARIANTS: Diospolis (?Grk)
PERIOD: LBA/IrA/Hel   RATING: T   MAP: 67
ITIN: 7c

LOCATION: 10 km north of *Latakia on the northern side of the promontory occupied by the Cham Hotel. Low tell on right 100 m past hotel entrance.

Ras Ibn Hani was dug from 1975 to 1982 by a Franco-Syrian mission. The site complements *Ugarit/Minet al-Beida, continuing the chronological sequence from the end of the Bronze Age until the Byzantine period (13th century BC to sixth century AD).

It was founded by a King of Ugarit, probably to survey maritime access to the main port but also to provide a cooler summer residence. The settlement is based on a regular grid angled at 45° to the compass. The palace area (east side of the site) is in total larger than the main palace at Ugarit, covering over 8000 m². It is divided into two segments, north and south, the latter including an industrial quarter in which were discovered a supply of copper ingots, probably from Cyprus. A library of tablets in Ugaritic and Akkadian was discovered in the north palace. The original palace was probably destroyed in the Sea Peoples' invasion of 1200 BC after being evacuated by its inhabitants .

Ras Ibn Hani thus sheds some light on the otherwise obscure period after the great invasion and reveals a resumption of indigenous Syrian influences, reversing the heavily Mycenaean links of the LBA. The link to Greece revived with renewed strength in the third century BC with the foundation of a major Hellenistic fortress on the site, probably by Ptolemy III Euergetes (r 246-21

BC) who campaigned in northern Syria in 246 BC. The town covered most of the neck of the peninsular and was taken by the Seleucids under Antiochos III the Great (r 223-187 BC) after his victory at Panion. The fortress (north east - square plan, square corner towers) was razed but the site again fell into the hands of the Ptolemies under Antiochos IX Cyzicenus (r 115-95 BC) and a small fortress was erected in the south eastern corner of the ruined compound. This in turn was razed a half-century later. The last significant phase of occupation was during the fourth to sixth centuries AD when the centre's major importance appears to have been industrial.

REFS: Bounni and Lagarce pp 91-7; Bounni *Ras Ibn Hani* pp 144-6; Dussaud *Topographie* pp 416-7; Lagarce; Leriche, P 'Urbanisme defensif ' in *Sociétés urbaines* Strasbourg 1987.

Refade

VARIANTS:
PERIOD: Byz   ALT: 509 m RATING: * MAP: 68
ITIN: 9a

LOCATION: On the western slopes overlooking the Plain of *Qatura. Follow directions for *Sitt al-Rum, then continue a few hundred metres further up the hill. The site is also accessible from Qatura from where it can be seen 1.5 km away on the skyline to the north.

Though it demands a short hike, this site is well worth visiting. Butler describes it as 'the most picturesque of all the little deserted cities of the hill country' and Tchalenko saw it as 'an aristocratic village for big landowners'. The striking appearance of the village derives from the intact nature of the houses, their elegant decoration and the appearance on the skyline of an isolated tower, evoking a deserted Tuscan hill village.

The buildings are almost entirely domestic but are in a variety of styles, including some built in the early method with polygonal stones. The village contained no church (perhaps the isolated church at Sitt al-Rum below served its needs). The large number of lavish houses, mostly from the sixth century but with some evidence dating back to the first century AD, indicates a sustained high level of prosperity. The agricultural exploitation of this area was begun early compared with the rest of the limestone country and the settlement seems to have been continuously inhabited from the first to the seventh century.

There is no clear consensus as to the purpose of the tower (sixth century – south west corner of the village). Between watch-tower or monastic recluse, the purpose is more likely to have been the former. The tall (9 m) four-storeyed structure (which has been reconstructed since Butler's study) includes a very obvious latrine arrangement protruding from the upper storey. Pena laconically notes that it is 'a rare example in the history of hygiene'.

The double-towered house is clearly a domestic villa (possibly incorporating an earlier independent watch-tower), grouped in a compound with a second, smaller dwelling. The towers were of three storeys with a double portico on the facade between. Other dwellings worthy of particular note are a house with a well-preserved double portico (*stoa*) facing south (dated 516); and one with a lighter and more graceful colonnade, plainer in decoration.

REFS: Butler *PE* II/B/5 pp 254-8; Pena *et al Reclus* pp 259-62; Sournia p 85; Tchalenko *Villages* I pp 194-7, II pl LX, LXIII, CXXVII; Vogüé II pl 110-1.

Resafe (Plate 21b)

VARIANT: Rasapa, Receph (bib); Resapha (Lat/Grk); Sergiopolis(Byz); R'safah; Risafe (Arb)
PERIOD: Byz/Arb RATING: ** MAP: *53*, 72 ITIN: 12a

LOCATION: The nearest main town is *Raqqa. If you head north from Raqqa on the road to Aleppo you will reach at 26 km the village of al-Mansura from where a road leads left c+28 km to Resafe. 200 km south east of Aleppo.

History

Although associated essentially with the Byzantines, the site of Resafe was mentioned in earlier sources, both in Assyrian texts and in the Bible (as Receph - 2 *Kings* XIX, 12; *Isaiah* XXXVII, 12). The Roman Emperor, Diocletian (r 284-305) established here a frontier fortress to meet the Sasanian threat. (*Dura Europos had already fallen to the Sasanian Persians in 256). The *Strata Diocletiana*, named after the Emperor, ran from Sura (on the Euphrates – see below) via Resafe south to *Palmyra and on to Damascus via *Dumeir.

For the Byzantines, the original settlement of Resapha took on a new importance with the growth of the cult of St Sergius. A Roman soldier serving as a court official, Sergius was martyred here during Diocletian's persecution in 305 after refusing to sacrifice to Jupiter. His cult attracted

followers from throughout Syria. Whether to help handle the crowds and their needs or to service the garrison which was stationed there, the town's amenities were considerably expanded under the Byzantine Emperor, Anastasius I (r 491-518) who officially renamed the city Sergiopolis in honour of its patron saint. A large basilica was constructed and cisterns and ramparts provided.

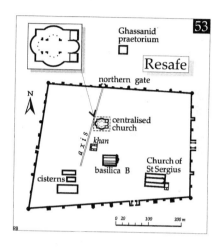

The sixth century brought a new and more persistent Persian threat. The town became a new focal point of Justinian's great program of military works in Syria (*Halebiye) towards the end of his reign 527-65. Perhaps slightly before the rebuilding of the great fortress of Halebiye, the walls of Resafe were reconstructed on an ambitious scale; stone replaced mud-brick and state-of-the-art military architecture introduced, for example the galleries to allow movement within from strong-point to strong-point. What had begun as a pilgrimage town dedicated to the memory of a former soldier took on a much more heavily military character, reflecting the frontier nature of the Christian presence in this area in the latter days of Byzantine control.

The policy of forward defence was, however, only partially successful. The Persians penetrated the screen on several occasions in the sixth century (reaching as far as Antioch in 540). Sergiopolis held out against the Persian raids but with great difficulty, notably during the campaigns of Chosroes I. Later it succumbed to the greater Persian compaigns of the early seventh century and was sacked by Chosroes II in his campaign of 616 which did so much fatally to weaken Byzantine control of Syria, softening it up for the Arab invasion two decades later.

Under the Umayyads Resafe was for a time favoured by the Caliph Hisham (r 724-43) who restored its facilities and erected a palace. After the Abbasid conquest in 750, it suffered the vengeance of the new regime's troops who destroyed Hisham's tomb in the city. Further damage was done by a serious earthquake at the end of the eighth century. Though it continued to support a token population, including a sizeable proportion of Christians, into the 13th century, it was depopulated by Baibars (r 1260-77) who sent the remaining inhabitants to Hama. By the time the Mongols laid waste northern Syria on several expeditions in the 13th and 14th century, there wasn't much left at Resafe for a decent sack.

Visit

You will need a good three hours to see the site properly. As you approach by road, the fortress walls look forbidding across the bare plain. Nothing suggests why such a monumental project was conceived in this bleak spot. After perhaps driving around the road that encircles the site to gain an appreciation of the size of the fortified area, you should approach the ruins via the great north gateway.

The city is laid out in a huge rectangle, approximately 550 m by 400 m. The **northern gate** is slightly to the west of the mid-point of the wall. Described by Musil as 'among the most beautiful as well as the best preserved products of Byzantine architecture', the protected arrangement of the gateway proclaims the semi-religious purpose of the settlement. The gate juts out from the line of the wall, a single outer entrance (now gone) sheltering a rectangular court whose inner triple gateway with its rich decoration would not have been seen until the outer gateway had been crossed. The impact of the complex confection of columns and arches would thus have been all the greater, with their typically Syrian embellishment of late Roman ideas. The central passage is flanked by two side doors decorated with friezes, the details of which are now hard to distinguish. As a reminder of the second purpose of the city, defence, the towering bastions enclose the entrance gateway on each side.

From the north gate, you may wish to explore a little from the inside the **city walls** to the right and left. You can see the intricate nature of the facilities built into the structure including the protected upper gallery and passageways to enable movement from bastion to bastion without coming under fire. The stone used is a local gypsum not dissimilar to the originally sparkling but somewhat friable stone used at Halebiye. Round and square shapes alternate erratically in the layout of the bastions. The walls along the north side are the best preserved and little remains of the gates which once gave entry on the other three sides. The total length of the walls is almost 2 km. Fifty towers or bastions of assorted sizes and shapes strengthen the line of walls.

Once you enter the enclosure, the size of the city is apparent together with the bareness of the site. Only a fraction of the surface has been excavated, largely concentrating on the main churches. The rest lies as undisturbed as it was after the last Mongols left, except for the steady encroachment of desert sands protecting what remains underneath. The task of fully excavating the site would be a daunting enterprise.

From the north gate, you can just discern the path of a main thoroughfare that crossed the city roughly north/south, veering a little to the west as it goes. Given the size of the site, you may wish to orient yourself on this axis until you are familiar with the layout. Head south and you will reach, on the left after 100 m, the outline of a curious **centralised church**. The Byzantine love for rather phantasmagoric shapes in church architecture comes out here. There are other Byzantine 'circle within a square' churches in Syria (see box on page 21). All appear to come from the same period, the first half of the sixth century though there is little to indicate any common inspiration. The Resafe example, however, is a tour de force. The basic basilica shape (three naves) is broken up by the clever use of curves to bend outwards the inner and outer rectangles. Three arcaded semi-circles expand the inner area; while the rear and side outer walls are gently taken out to accommodate them. The eastern end of the church adopts the familiar Byzantine design of a central apse with semi-circular seating flanked by two square side chapels. These, according to Musil, once provided bases for the east towers.

This building has been dated by style to the 520's which would put it slightly after the bold experiments with circular shapes achieved at *Ezraa and *Bosra. Klengel argues that the *sarcophagi* for the burial of local bishops indicates that it was the metropolitan church as opposed to the two more sizeable pilgrimage churches examined below. The building was constructed in a fine gypsum stone in comparatively small blocks. The ornamentation was restrained.

Resume your walk along the north/south axis. After 100 m you should see on the left the remains of a market. The shape is basically that of the later Turkish *caravanserai*, seen all over Syria. In this case, the building is actually from the early Byzantine period.

After another 100 m, shortly before the south wall of the city, you should note on the right the first of a series of three huge **cisterns** (one with a double row of chambers). Signs indicate the danger of going too close to the apertures which lead into the underground chambers. If you look in carefully, however, the sheer size of the cavernous interiors is astonishing. The largest of the three, that to the south, is almost 58 m long and 21.5 m wide. The depth of water was 13 m and capacity over 15,000 m^3. The need for such enormous storage capacity is explained by the fact that Resafe has no permanent water supply. It does, however, receive the considerable run-off from the Jebel Bishri and Jebel Rujmayn ranges to the south. This collects in pools which could be channeled to the cisterns which held a reserve supply capable of sustaining the city during a prolonged siege or drought. The roofing system is in itself a major achievement. The cisterns are ascribed by the Byzantine historian Procopius to Justinian but there is evidence that they were begun earlier.

Slightly to the east of this point you can see the remains of a building called prosaically **basilica B**. Though later replaced as the main pilgrimage church of the town by basilica A, it was virtually as big. Most of the walls are gone. Begun probably in the late fifth century, the church was originally a basic three-aisled Roman/Byzantine basilica plan, extended (probably in Justinian's time) with a fourth aisle on the south side and a broad entrance chamber or *narthex* on the west. The main horse-shoe shaped eastern apse included a chapel that once contained the remains of a martyr, possibly the original burial place of St Sergius.

If you continue 120 m towards the south east corner of the site, you reach the prominent remains of the building once known as basilica A or the **Basilica Church of St Sergius** but, since the discovery in 1977 of a dedicatory inscription, now termed the Basilica of the Holy Cross. This was the focal point of the religious pilgrimage in the last decades of the Byzantine period. The inner walls of this sizeable building have been partly reconstructed in recent years giving you some idea of its scale and grandeur. The basic plan (31 m by 20 m) is basilica-shaped: two side aisles are separated from the central nave by three enormous semi-circular arches resting on cross-shaped piers. The building was dedicated in 559 when the bold use of broad leaping lateral arches to divide the nave from the side-aisles had been tried elsewhere (*Qalb Lozeh). In such late Byzantine buildings, the huge weight which had formerly been taken by relatively thin and vulnerable pillars now rested on stout piers. (There is another example in the Church of Bizzos at *Ruweiha). Apparently, however, the engineering principles had not been perfected at the time of construction for 20 years later (probably as a result of an earthquake), each of the broad arches and their superstructure had to be supported from underneath by two smaller arches resting on three columns. The basic insecurity of the sweeping arches was not to be resolved until many centuries later with the full development, in Byzantium and Europe, of the supporting pier and buttresses.

Above the arches, the upper or clerestory level provides a row of arched windows to allow light to enter, interspersed with small columns resting on jutting corbels. The apparent lack of transverse arches indicates that the original roof of the main aisle⁻ was a wooden structure supported by wide beams. The nave terminates in a semi-circular apse which is relatively well preserved. As is usual in churches of this period, the apse is located between two side chapels of rectangular design. The one on the right, however, is extended out towards the east. A large and complex *bema* was located in the nave, occupying most of the space between the central piers. It was provided with a central baldachin, side seating for 28 and a throne surrounded by additional stone seating set in a semi-circle.

In the atrium north of the church, German researchers discovered a small treasury of superbly crafted religious vessels, votice offerings for the grave of Sergius buried here just before a Mongol invasion. They are now in the *Damascus Museum.

If you return to the main north gate, outside and further to the north is a curious building, partly preserved in a sand drift. This is a palace or *praetorium* of the **Ghassanid** period. Built around 560-81, it recalls the alliance in the sixth century between the Byzantine imperial power and the Christianised Arab tribe, the Ghassanids. On behalf of Byzantium, they kept control of the central Syrian desert tribes. The building is of somewhat unusual design based on a large central banqueting hall with a semi-domed apse to the east. Some other examples of this cross-in-square shape have been found in the Byzantine world and further east.

On the south side of the city, outside of the walls, are sparse remains of several palaces, including the so-called **Palace of Hisham**, an Umayyad building of typical square design based on the Roman *castrum* or military enclosure plan.

Sura

The Roman town of Sura (northern-most point of the *Strata Diocletiana*) has not yet been researched. The ruins with a central square fortification lie 5 km north of al-Mansura, between the main road and the river. The river once flowed past the town and 2 km to the south evidence has been found of a Roman bridge[136]. Procopius lists this as one of the towns re-fortified by Justinian.

REFS: **Resafe:** *BG* p 360; Butler *EC* pp 161-3, 166; Dussaud *Topographie* pp 251-5; Klengel *Syrien* pp 195-9; Krautheimer; Lassus *Sanctuaires* pp 154-6; Mango; Musil *Palmyrena* p 300; Procopius 'De Aedificiis' II, ix; Tchalenko and Baccache pl 499-543; Ulbert *Resafe*; Ulbert *Rusafa-Sergiopolis*. **Sura:** Procopius *On the Buildings* II, 9; Ulrich 'Villes' in *Archéologie et histoire* p 287.

Roman Road - Bab al-Hawa

PERIOD: Rom RATING: * MAP: 68 ITIN: 9b

> LOCATION: 40 km west of Aleppo. Take the main road from Aleppo towards the Bab al-Hawa check point on the Turkish border. At Urum al-Sughra (23 km) where the road to Idlib branches left, take the right fork and continue +17 km. At this point the modern road intersects a stretch of Roman road climbing a slope. (The village at the top of the slope is called Tell al-Karameh.)

Syria was once criss-crossed with substantial roads during the Roman period (see box on page 7). Most of them have vanished, except where aerial photography, traces of installations (water holes and milestones) and written records enable us to reconstruct their path. This 1200 m section of **Roman road**, however, was built on a more solid scale to take the roadway up the steep slope.

This road formed part of the route from Antioch (the capital of the province of Syria) to Chalcis ad Belum (*Qinnesrin), Beroia (*Aleppo) and on to Mesopotamia. There is no direct evidence for the date of its construction though a nearby inscription at Qasr al-Banat inside the Syrian/Turkish no-man's-land has Marcus Aurelius taking the credit (r 161-80). Certainly the

later part of the second century saw the peak in Roman construction and road-building activity in Syria.

The road is supported on a base held within containing walls filled with rubble with limestone paving on top. This provides a good illustration of Roman road-building techniques, though the road was partly reconstructed during the French period.

A little to the south east of the Roman road is the village of **Tarib** in the centre of which stands an ancient mound. This was mentioned (under the same name) in Assyrian archives of the ninth century BC. Tarib was known as Litarba in Byzantine times and became the nearest point to Aleppo fortified and defended by the Crusaders, later destroyed by the Zengids.

If you are continuing on to Saint Simeon, the turn-off is 1 km further on (turn right). The road takes you almost immediately through the village of **Dana** (not to be confused with *Dana (South) near Maarat al-Numan). This village contains a remarkable Roman tomb of the second century in the form of a pyramidal canopy supported on four Ionic columns. The tomb is located at the northern end of the settlement to the left of the main road. Nearby to the west is a cistern carved from the living rock covered with stone slabs, probably once associated with a bath house.

The **Plain of Dana** lies across the two most important access routes through the Belus Massif. The Antioch/Aleppo road crosses the massif at its narrowest point and here meets the north/south axis of the hill country, the ancient route from *Apamea to *Cyrrhus. It has thus been a strategic crossroads throughout many epochs and is cited as far back as the Egyptian and Assyrian archives. The plain attracted a large number of monastic institutions (80 is Tchalenko's estimate) in the ascetic 'boom' of the late fifth and sixth centuries. 4 km south of Dana is the peak of Jebel Srir (alt 558 m) on which can be found remains of one of the small temples to Zeus contructed in the area in the first to second centuries AD, probably when the road from Antioch to Beroia (Aleppo) began to be developed for military traffic to support campaigns to the east. (Track to the summit begins at the village of Tell Aqibrin.) To the north west of this peak was the scene of the battle known as *Ager Sanguinis* which resulted in the Crusaders' major defeat at the hands of Zengid forces from Aleppo in 1119. (The actual site was to the south, near the village of Sarmada on the Harim road. Further details under *Harim.)

---

[136] For a full survey of historic references - Musil *Middle Euphrates* pp 323-5.

REFS: *BG* p 404; Hadjar; Klengel *Syrien* pp 24-5; Saouaf *Saint Simeon* pp 2-5; Tchalenko *Villages* I p 141.
Dana: Butler *AE* II pp 29, 73; Dussaud *Topographie* pp 221, 239, 243; Tchalenko *Villages* I pp 117-9; Vogüé II pl 93.

Roman Road - Wadi Barada

VARIANTS: Abila Lysaniae (Lat); Suq Wadi Barada (Arb)
PERIOD: Rom RATING: T MAP: 64 ITIN: 3c

LOCATION: 35 km west of Damascus. 1.5 km east of the point where the new Zabadani road meets the old Barada River road. From Damascus (starting point, Umayyad Square), there are two choices:
- Follow the new motorway to Lebanon, taking (at 33 km) the branch to Zabadani then +4 km to the crossing of the Barada River near the old dam. Turn right (east) for c+2 km along the old Barada road until you see the tomb entrances about 100 m up the steep sides of the gorge on the left.
- Alternatively, follow the slower old road from Damascus (via Dummar) until 1.5 km beyond Suq Wadi Barada (c34 km - the ancient Seleucid-Roman town of Abila Lysaniae).

Along the steep northern side of the Barada gorge, remains can be seen of several Roman burial places as well as traces (over some 200 m) of a cutting for the Roman road which led from Hierapolis (Baalbek) to Damascus. A quick (seven minute) scramble up the mountainside takes you to the cutting. The Roman road clung to the upper side of the gorge to avoid raging torrents during floods but the cutting, restored in Roman times on at least one occasion, has partly been swept away by later rock-slides.

Two versions still exist of a Roman inscription (in Latin, for once) recording that Julius Verus, legate of the province of Syria, restored the road after a rock-slide 'at the expense of the people of Abila' (Suq Wadi Barada). The inscription is dated to the reigns of '*Emperor Caesar M Aur Antoninus Aug Armeniacus and Emperor Caesar L Aurel. Verus Aug Armeniacus*' - ie Marcus Aurelius (r 161-80) and his co-Emperor Lucius Verus (r 161-9). The restoration must thus have been carried out between 161 and 169.

By following an old aqueduct cut into the rock a little lower down, the courageous can head to the east to inspect the rock-cut tombs each of which contained multiple burials.

There are legends associating this area with the Old Testament story of Cain and Abel (hence the Roman *Abila*). The summit to the west of this site (*Tell Habil* - or *Nebi Habil*) is the legendary place where Cain buried Abel after murdering him (*Genesis* 4). A Druze holy place marks the reputed spot. (Bad road access from Zabadani turn off from motorway.) Legend relates that St Helen built a church there, on the site of an earlier (AD 29) Roman temple to Zeus Kronos.

The ancient Abila (of which the only traces are a few re-cycled stones in the houses of modern-day Suq Wadi Barada) was a Hellenistic foundation. It was part of the Iturean principality whose ruler, Lysanias (a son of the King of Chalcis), was killed by Antony in 36 BC. It briefly became a substitute capital for what remained of the kingdom of Chalcis which had covered the Beqaa and part of the Ledja (see box on 'Hauran' under *Suweida, page 228) after Augustus relieved the tetrarch of his original seat. (Chalcis was located at modern Anjar, just over the border in Lebanon.) The city was later among lands presented by Claudius and Nero to the pro-Roman clients, Herod Agrippa I and II (r AD 37-44, 52-93 respectively). The tetrarchy was absorbed into the Roman administrative system at an unknown date and controlled a district extending across the Qalamoun as far as *Yabrud to the north. Abila's strategic importance for the Romans reflected a combination of factors including its location on the road between Heliopolis (Baalbek), a Roman military settlement) and Damascus.

REFS: Baedeker pp 297-8; Dussaud *Topographie* pp 287 ff; Jones 'Urbanization'; Mouterde R 'Antiquités de l'Hermon et de la Beqa' in *Mélanges de l'Université St.-Joseph* XXIX 1951-52; Porter pp 99-100; Thubron pp 20-3.

Ruweiha

VARIANTS: Ruwayha, Rouweiha
PERIOD: Rom/Byz RATING: ** MAP: *54*, 70 ITIN: 9c

LOCATION: Eastern slopes of Jebel Riha/Jebel Zawiye. Coming from the north, go through Riha and head up the hill. Continue c+5 km down the other side into a more desolate landscape.

This site is well worth a visit and comprises extensive ruins with two major churches as well as interesting vestiges of the Roman period. Moreover, the setting in sweeping, open countryside on the edge of the plateau adds a dramatic effect. The town was largely the product of the fifth and sixth centuries.

Near the road which intersects the southern part of the town, you will notice a church of the fifth century, a columned basilica built in a severe style. The church compound to the south includes the remains of a strange structure perched on eight columns. This may have been a tower to house a recluse.

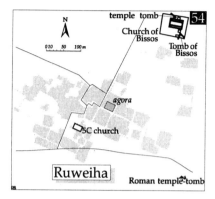

A little to the east, note the tiny **Roman temple tomb**, dated by inscription to 384. The portico includes two columns with Doric capitals and an enclosed burial chamber behind. (In the necropolis to the south east, there is another classical tomb, underground with a columned entrance.)

The **agora** (in the centre of the main cluster of ruins) is built on an ample scale for a rural setting and was surrounded by a two storey portico. In addition to the great number of villas in the style typical of the region, the agora also attracted a concentration of high-density construction.

Especially notable on the northern edge of the town is the **Church of Bissos**, named after its sixth century benefactor. The largest church in the Jebel Riha, it is said by Butler to be the second largest in the limestone country of northern Syria. It is clearly a notable architectural milestone with its bold use of two high transverse arches spanning the central nave (not found in Europe until several centuries later) as well as the three more traditional longitudinal arches springing from four massive T-shaped piers. Sadly, though, the transverse arches were not matched by any buttressing in the form of side arches over the outer aisles to transfer the weight to the external walls. The high nave and the structure supporting the clerestory windows above it have thus almost entirely collapsed. At the entrance, the use of horseshoe-shaped arches above the two flanking doorways anticipates later Arab use of this device. The central arch of the *narthex* is more traditional and two towers rise above the outer doorways. The use of ornamentation is restrained, as in most of the churches of this southern part of the 'dead cities' zone.

The church is flanked by two tombs, the one with a dome being in honour of Bissos himself. Butler emphasises the unique status of this stone-cut dome, thè only extant example in Syria, foreshadowing later Muslim domed saints' tombs (*turba* or *weli*) which employ this basic design. Left of the door on the west facade, the inscription reads: *'Bizzos (son) of Pardos. I lived worthily, died worthily and rest worthily. Pray for me.'* This is the only tomb of a church founder recorded in the 'dead cities' and it is possible that Bizzos was a local priest or bishop. The second tomb (unattributed) in the form of a small but not very graceful Greek temple (*distyle in antis*) stands symmetrically on the north side of the church. The church compound is surrounded by a walled enclosure.

REFS: *BG* p 414; Butler *AE* pp 84, 99-102, 106, 113-4, 120-3; Butler *EC* 145-8; Butler *PE* II/B/3 pp 142-8; Pena *et al Reclus* pp 174-9; Mattern pp 19-26; Tchalenko *Villages* II pl CXLI; Tchalenko and Baccache pl 462-80; Vogüé II pl 68, 69, 91.

S

Safita

VARIANTS: Argyrocastron (Grk); Chastel Blanc (Cru)
PERIOD: Cru   ALT: 380 m RATING: ** MAP: 55. 66 ITIN: 5a

LOCATION: From *Tartus, 30 km by a good road, somewhat winding as you get into the foothills of the Jebel Ansariye.

Safita is one of the most picturesque towns in as the Krak and Tartus. The area fell early into Crusader hands and is mentioned in Arab sources as part of the domains of the Count of Tripoli from 1112. The building of the first castle probably dates from that time, part of the defence in depth for Tartus. In 1167 and 1171, Nur al-Din took advantage of Crusader unpreparedness, occupying Tartus, destroying Areimeh (*Qalaat Areimeh) and largely demolishing the first version of the Safita fortress, partly out of anger at Crusader piracy against Egyptian merchant ships.

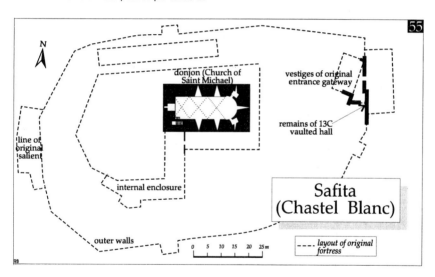

Syria, set in beautiful orchard and olive-growing country dotted with historic sites. It is equally accessible from Tartus, the *Krak and Dreikish and the surrounding valleys contain many picnic spots, idyllic particularly during the spring when the countryside is covered in wildflowers. Many of the villages suggest more the atmosphere of the old Lebanon or even southern Europe and the bustling town perches on a hill in an almost Tuscan scene.

History

At the top of the ridge along which the town sprawls, the blunt square Frankish **donjon** or keep still stands watch, visible from as far away

Either around this time, or later after Saladin's assault (1188), the Knights Templar were given responsibility for securing the Tartus area, having made their second headquarters in the port city. They took control of Chastel Blanc and the major work on the present keep probably dates from their reconstruction of the earlier fortress. Damage from an earthquake in 1202 probably intensified the need for major improvements and the present building dates largely from the 13th century.

The castle fell into Muslim hands with barely a fight in February 1271, taken by the Mameluke Sultan Baibars en route to the Krak. The evacuation of the castle was ordered by the Master of the Templars in Tartus, even though the garrison numbered 700 knights at the time. Its fall certainly left Tartus, one of the last Crusader stronghold on the mainland, increasingly exposed, contributing to its abandonment in 1291.

The plan chosen is a typical Frankish design, a stout central tower surrounded by two series of walls. The tower of the donjon or keep is in its own right a work of some note, one of the highpoints of the Crusader style in Syria. It housed the garrison as well as a church. The standard of construction was high with massive walls and stout internal pillars. In spite of earthquakes and the varied purposes to which it has been put, the donjon has survived in an almost perfect state.

Though the town was almost totally Greek Orthodox Christian in the late 19th century, the Christian community had only begun to settle there from the Hauran early in the previous century, gradually displacing the Alawi inhabitants. Today the population is again mixed.

Visit

You gain access to the keep by ascending from any of the alleyways leading off the circular main street that runs around the ridge. Arriving at the square on the west of the small plateau, it will be immediately obvious that the castle still serves as the main Greek Orthodox church (dedicated to St Michael - *Mar Mikhael*) for the town. You may need to knock on a few doors to find the guardian if the priest is not in attendance.

The exterior of the building (18 m wide by 27 m high) is typically blank, presenting as few weak points as possible to assailants. You enter by the west door (note the machicolation set in the vault of the doorway) straight into the church which occupies the lower storey (10 m by 24 m internal dimensions). The vault of the nave is divided into three sections by two arches that rise from pilasters in the side walls. A moulded band passes under the west window and does a circuit of the interior. The apse at the east end is curved and is flanked by two sacristies built into the massive thickness of the walls. There are only five 'windows' - really firing slits in the 3 m masonry. The height of the nave is almost 18 m, giving the church a surprising feeling of space, in spite of the restricted sources of light. In the south west corner (hard right as you enter), a narrow staircase built into the walls leads to the next storey.

The staircase brings you out in a large (13 m by 26 m) and surprisingly elegant room used to house the garrison. The walls are slightly less thick than in the church below and the system of arches is different. Three central cruciform pillars divide the room into two parts, each with four bays comprising cross-groined arches. From each bay, a firing point looks over the surrounding countryside. Another staircase leads to the terrace. From this point, commanding a sweeping view of the hill country as far as the Krak and Tartus, signal fires could be exchanged with other watch points. The parapet consists of alternating loopholes and crenellations. A cistern beneath the chapel was used to store water for times of seige.

If you return to the ground and walk round to the back (east) of the church, a path into the town passes, after 10 m, one of the gateways of the outer defences and part of a wall which originally belonged to a mid 13th century building. If you skirt around to the south from here, taking the lower path back to the western entrance of the church, you should be able to see some of the glacis of the outer protective wall which formed an oval-shape (160 m by 100 m) with the tower at the centre. On the north side of the plateau are other remains of the outer wall and a salient. Originally, an inner wall lay between these defences and the tower but no vestiges remain.

REFS: *BG* p 439; Boase pp 60-1; Deschamps *Châteaux* - III pp 249-58; Dussaud *Topographie* p 119; Eydoux pp 177-9; Lawrence pp 67-73 (plans).

St George Monastery

VARIANTS: Deir Mar Georgis; al-Houmayra (Arb)
PERIOD: Arb RATING: - MAP: 66 ITIN: 5b

LOCATION: In the deep valley north west of the *Krak des Chevaliers. From the Krak, take the road north to Marmarita (5 km) but fork left immediately before the town.

This Greek Orthodox monastery was originally founded in the sixth century AD probably at the time of the Emperor Justinian. It has two chapels of which the older (reached from the lower courtyard) dates from the 13th century with an *iconostasis* in ebony wood (18th century). The new chapel (right off first courtyard) was built in 1857. The lower court also includes remains of the Byzantine monastery.

The monastery is located in the Wadi al-Nasara (Valley of the Christians) which has been a centre of Greek Orthodox Christianity since the early Christian period. Its feast day (attended by Christians from all over Syria and Lebanon) is held on 14 September.

REFS: *BG* p 354; *GB* p 94.

Saint Simeon (Plates 22a, 22b)
VARIANTS: Qalaat Simaan
PERIOD: Byz RATING: *** MAP: *56*, 68 ITIN: 9a

LOCATION: From Aleppo, take the new road which leads directly to Deiret Azze by turning right at Aleppo Scientific College, then at 400 m turn left again - 30 km to Deiret Azze. Go through village, take right turn +6 km to Saint Simeon.

Butler, who led the famous Princeton expedition which surveyed Syrian antiquities at the turn of the century, summed up the importance of Saint Simeon as follows[137]:

As all roads in Northern Syria lead to Qalaat Semaan, so does the history of Syrian architecture lead up to the building of the great church and monastery which were erected at the foot of St Simeon's pillar. ...

The great cruciform church is unique in the history of architecture and is not only the most beautiful and important existing monument of architecture between the buildings of the Roman period of the second century and the great church of Santa Sophia of Justinian's time, but also ... is the most monumental Christian building earlier than the masterpieces of the eleventh and twelfth centuries in Northern Europe.

High claims indeed but few will find the complex of buildings and the magnificent setting a disappointment. The church is notable not only for the boldness of its scale but the classical refinement of its detail.

History

Unlike the later cathedrals of medieval Europe, the great church was conceived and executed more or less as a single project over a short space of time. The cruciform church comprising four separate basilica buildings was probably constructed shortly after the death of the ascete, St Simeon. Born in the area of Antioch around 389-90, Simeon joined the community of monks at Telanissos (*Deir Semaan, at the foot of the present site) around 410-2. He spent the rest of his life in the area, moving only to isolate himself more effectively from the rest of the community.

He finally took up residence on a platform atop a column (12 to 18 m high, 1.5 to 2 m in diameter) around the remains of which the great building is centred. He died on this spot on 24 July 459, having already become a figure of reverence attracting pilgrims from many parts of the Byzantine world, particularly from neighbouring Antioch.

Construction of the great basilica complex began a few years after St Simeon's death (probably from 476 to 491). This was a time of great ferment in the Antiochene church and the controversy over the Monophysite heresy was at its height. Much of this tension, based on pseudo-theological and contradictory interpretations of the emphasis to be given to Christ's human and divine natures, was in effect a revolt by local (Syriac-speaking) Christians against domination from Constantinople. The ascetic and monastic movement was in essence a revolt against the metropolitan church. The cause of St Simeon, however, was tolerated and eventually promoted by the imperial authorities partly as a way of harnessing simple piety to distract attention from the theological/political controversies. Both Constantinople and Antioch vied to honour his memory. Against local (Monophysite) resistance to the removal of his remains, Simeon was buried in Antioch[138], only to be later transferred to a new *martyrium* in Constantinople. Meanwhile, the column and the site of his ascetic deeds was commemorated under imperial patronage (the Emperor at the time was Zeno - r 474-91) thus encouraging the continuation of the cult of St Simeon through pilgrimage.

The colossal scale of the pilgrimage centre reflected the availability of outside resources under imperial patronage with architectural ideas and tradesmen brought in from a wide area. The plan of the building has precedents elsewhere and metropolitan influences and classical styles of decoration are blended with more typically Syrian elements. The ambitious design of the complex thus reflects several architectural styles. The basic concept of the three-aisled basilica already had a long tradition going back to Roman times. The idea of the centralised church focussed on a pivotal point was soon to be seen in other manifestations in Syria (*Resafe, *Bosra, *Ezraa, *Apamea). The idea of laying out the buildings in the shape of a cross was more novel and was not established as a tradition until the

---

[137] *EC* pp 97-8.

[138] In 459 Simeon's body was virtually seized by a Byzantine military excort and transported to Antioch by 600 soldiers where he was buried in the city's cathedral. The church of St Simeon is thus not strictly a *martyrium* but 'a commemorative shrine centred around Simeon's pillar of forty cubits' (Mango p 79).

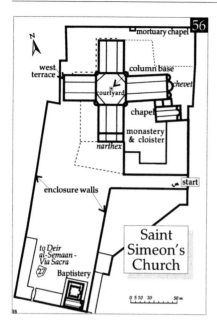

great European religious buildings of the Middle Ages.

The ridge in its pre-479 state had to be levelled and extended to the west by artificial terracing and arched support to accommodate the enormous scale of the four-basilica plan. On this platform, the complex was arranged in several groups of buildings:

- the four basilicas meeting in the central octagonal courtyard;
- the U-shaped monastery complex, adjoining the basilicas to the south east;
- the baptistery, 150 m to the south;
- annexes to the baptistery.

In Tchalenko's study of the 'dead cities', he reconstructs the sequence of construction as follows:

- 476-92 - the basilica itself and baptistery;
- 490+ - monastery; annexes to baptistery;
- 500-525 - all other parts of the complex including two hostelries and the monumental arch leading from Deir Semaan.

In 526 and 528, violent earthquakes destroyed Antioch and probably brought down

the roof over the central octagon between the four basilicas. The hillside was fortified when the Byzantines retook the area from the Arabs in the tenth century. It was retaken and sacked in 985 by the Hamdanids (Said al-Daula's forces) and again in 1017 (by an Egyptian army). It was subsequently abandoned as a monastic/religious centre.

Visit

Hours:
09:00 - 18:00 summer
09:00 - 16:00 winter

After passing through the ticket office, you ascend to the ridge on which the church is located, arriving at the point on the ridge mid-way between the baptistery (to the south, left) and the four-basilica church (right). Before you, the Afrin Valley and the Plain of Amuq stretch westwards to the environs of Antioch with the Kurd Dag line of hills and the Amanus Mountains, lost in the haze to the north west.

Turn right to the main church, approaching it by the great south *narthex*. You now gain a closer appreciation of the distinctive plan of the church. Four basilica buildings, each big enough to be a major church in its own right, are laid like a cross roughly oriented to the cardinal points. (The overall dimensions of the complex are 100 m east/west, 88 m north/south. The total area enclosed by the cruciform is 3840 m^2.) The four buildings (each 24 m wide) meet in a central court at whose focal point stands the stub of the column on which St Simeon's platform was poised. (The rest of the column has been chipped away by pilgrims over the centuries.) This court is rounded off by exedra-shaped devices to form an octagon. The monumental portals lead into the four basilica. Though no direct evidence remains of the original roof of the court, it is believed to have been erected in wood, perhaps with a dome or a central conical lantern. The design, however, was too ambitious and, after tumbling in the earthquake of 528, was not restored, the court being left uncovered. Though now striking for the simplicity of its pristine, honey-coloured limestone, the building was once ornately decorated with polychrome pavements, plastered and painted walls and encrusted decoration.

The eastern basilica, slightly larger than the other three (43 m long, nine bays; as against 30 m, seven bays), was naturally the most important and would have accommodated the major ceremonies in honour of the saint. In practical terms, the other three buildings had little perspective into the main basilica and were probably used for assembly and organisation of the pilgrims rather than for religious ceremonies. The observant visitor will notice that the east building is slightly off axis, being bent fractionally towards the north in order to orient the east apse towards the true east.

The detail of the church is worth close examination. The sculptured decoration is superbly executed, extraordinary in its richness and variety Indeed almost all the concepts exploited later in the churches of the Antioch hinterland are already found, usually in a more classical form, at Saint Simeon. Some features are of necessity experimental and having been tried out on a building of such huge scale are not always fully successful. Note, for example, the way in which the four basilica are joined by the device of the corner *exedra*. The square is transformed into an octagon at the points of which stand eight complex piers in line with the columns of the naves. From these piers spring the four arches leading into the basilicas as well as the arches framing the *exedrae*. These framing arches enclosing the trapezoidal *exedrae* are somewhat heavy, more like the local rural churches of the era in their preference for massive monumentality.

Though the architectural ideas are post-Roman, the treatment of the decoration is almost classical. Pillars are used to round off the piers and help support the arches. The capitals are variations on classical orders, with the occasional Byzantine flourish.

While you will want to wander around by yourself to take in the scale and detail of the building, three points are worthy of particular note.

- The first is the narthex by which you entered, a beautiful Byzantine adaptation of Roman concepts. The classical detail, including the grooved pilasters facing the piers, and the swept acanthus motif of the capitals, is particularly noteworthy. The latter device, first employed in this building, is later commonly adopted in the Byzantine world.
- Second, the great west **terrace** which looks down over the rich plain. The *loggia* is built upon an enormous artificial platform constructed over the steep slope of the ridge (cf the similar arrangement at *Burqush near Damascus.) This was necessary in order to balance the length of the eastern and western basilicas, the central position of the column determining the focal point on the narrow ridge.

- The third point of particular interest is the outer wall of the **chevet** of the eastern basilica. To inspect it, you will have to walk around the outside of the cathedral to the east, through the remains of the attached monastery. The chevet echoes some of the ideas employed a few years beforehand in the church at *Qalb Lozeh, notably in allowing the curve of the apse to project beyond the rear line of the building and in decorating the drum wall with two tiers of colonnettes. Note too that the windows' decorated mouldings are passed continuously from frame to frame without interruption.

If you walk around to the north end of the cruciform cathedral, the upper remains of the enclosure give commanding views of the complex and the surrounding countryside. The tenth century enclosure wall was hastily constructed in a slapdash technique during the Byzantine re-occupation of the area. Just within the wall are the remains of a mortuary chapel, the lower level being carved out of the rock, probably for the storage of skeletal remains.

The segment between the south and east basilica is occupied by the ruins of a **monastery**, apparently intended for resident and visiting clergy. (The general public were accommodated at the foot of the hill in Deir Semaan.) The remains include a small chapel, the whole group forming a great courtyard around the south eastern walls of the cathedral itself.

To visit the rest of the complex, exit the main cathedral by the south narthex and continue south along the ridge. This was the great central processional way (*Via Sacra*) for pilgrims. 200 m south stands the baptistery, in which new converts were sacramentally initiated into Christianity. The main processional path skirted this building to the west, having ascended the ridge at an angle to its slope.

The **baptistery** dates slightly after the main cathedral but is an essential part of the pilgrimage complex. Described as 'one of the finest remnants of Christian architecture in the whole of Syria'[139], it was built in two phases - the baptistery itself first; the associated small basilica later. The octagonal drum which externally tops the square base of the building was once crowned by a wooden roof shaped either like a cone (cf the cathedral courtyard roof) or a dome. The inner octagon (15 m) was enclosed in a rectangular outer building. The two shapes are resolved by arches cutting across the corners of

---

[139] *BG* p 400.

the square, linked to the outer walls by pilasters. At the east end of the chamber is a semi-circular *absidiola* which includes a curious channel with steps leading down to it. This was clearly the walk-through baptismal 'font' intended for the mass baptism of converts. The remains of the associated basilica to the south are minimal.

South west of the baptistery, you can trace the remains of ancillary buildings which provided accommodation and facilities to pilgrims. The **processional route** entered the complex from this direction, passing through the great monumental arch lower down the slope (described in *Deir Semaan).

REFS: Bavant *et al* pp 194-8; Beyer pp 60-2; *BG* pp 397-402; Butler *AE* II pp 97-109,156, 184-90; Butler *EC* pp 97-105; Butler *PE* II/B pp 281ff; Delehaye pp LIX-LXXV; Mango; Saouaf *Saint Simeon*; Sodini pp 277-8; Tchalenko *Villages* I pp 223-76; II pl LXI-III, LXXV-IX, LXXXI-IV; LXXXVII; Mattern pp 118-34; Vogüé I pp 141 ff, II pl 139-50.

Salkhad

VARIANTS: Salchah (bib)[140]
PERIOD: Arb   RATING: -   MAP: 63 ITIN: 2b

LOCATION: From Damascus, reach *Suweida (128 km) then continue +30 km south east.

The main item of interest is the Ayyubid citadel built (in conjunction with the fortification of the theatre at *Bosra) in 1214-47 to serve as the southern defence of Damascus against the Crusader presence in Jerusalem. The site was probably earlier occupied by a fort built by the Egyptian Fatimid Caliph, al-Mustansir, in 1073/4. The citadel was renewed in 1277 by the Mameluke Sultan, Baibars. The fortress was built into the crater of a volcano but the walls which slope steeply down the outer face of the vent are now badly crumbled. The building is now used by the military and is surrounded by barbed wire. There is apparently little to see from the crest and access is in any event forbidden.

There are remnants of a minaret (erected 1232) in the mosque in the town's main square. The lower 20 m of the tower located next to the bus terminal dates from the Ayyubid period. Hexagonal in shape (a plan unique in Islamic architecture but probably borrowing from Roman models), it is largely made from the local basalt (black, with a dark red section at the top), interrupted by two bands of white with finely inscribed Koranic passages and niches on each face. The original mosque has disappeared but

resembled in style the Mosque of Umar in nearby Bosra.

REFS: *BG* p 506; Butler *PE* II/A/2 pp 117-9; Meinecke 'Salkhad, exemple de ville-forteresse islamique' in Dentzer & Dentzer-Feydy (edd) *Le Djebel al-'Arab 1991*; Meinecke in *AAAS* XLI (special edition 97).

Seidnaya

VARIANTS: Sardeneye (Cru)
PERIOD: Byz/Arb ALT: 1415 m; RATING: -
MAP: 64, 75 ITIN: 3b

LOCATION: On the edge of the Anti-Lebanon Range, 27 km north of Damascus. Take the road to al-Tal (turn-off at 11.5 km) and continue north +15 km.

Seidnaya is more notable as a place of religious pilgrimage than for any outstanding remains. In fact, few reminders of its origins can be distilled from centuries of legends.

The chapel and convent is perched on an outcrop of rock, looking rather like a castle from some angles. Legend relates that the monastery was founded by Justinian (r 527-65). The miracles associated with the image of the Virgin brought the chapel wide fame particularly during and after the middle ages. It became the most famous centre for pilgrimage in the east, after Jerusalem. The Crusaders were fascinated by the legends of 'Notre Dame de Sardeneye' associated with a painting of the Virgin said to have been executed by St Luke the Evangelist. Even in times of open hostility between the Franks in Jerusalem and the Muslims of Damascus, Christian pilgrims reached Seidnaya.

After entering through the confined doorway, the interior leading up to the chapel of the Virgin is a maze of indeterminate origins. The shrine itself contains many mementoes of recent pilgrim traffic. The concealed image of the Virgin is said to be an early copy of the one reputedly painted by St Luke (cf *Tartus) and there are other icons said to date from the fifth and seventh centuries. The shrine is usually crowded; perhaps most remarkable is the number of non-Christians, particularly on a Friday, reflecting the long tradition of Muslim interest in the shrine and its attendant legends. The convent is in the care of the Greek Orthodox Church. The main day of pilgrimage is 8 September (Birthday of the Virgin).

---

[140] *Job* XII, 5; XIII 11; *Deut* III 10.

On the right of the car park, the chapel (dedicated to St Peter - *Mar Boutros*) is a converted Roman tomb. The design is superbly austere - only a doorway and a deep cornice relieve the basic cube shape (9.5 by 9.5 by 7.9 m). The interior is cruciform.

There are other minor sites of historical interest in the area, some associated with the monastic tradition of the early Church. To the north east (St Thomas Chapel and Cherubim Monastery on Mount Qalamun) and the south (Deir Mar Elias on the escarpment overlooking the great Syrian Desert), caves of holy men and remains of monasteries can be visited. You will need to ask for keys and a guide from the Greek Orthodox church. The Cherubim Monastery is a recycled Roman temple on a commanding peak (1910m).

REFS: *anon Recueil historique*; *BG* p 304; Dussaud *Topographie* p 283; Keriaky, Rama Elias *Saidnaya - History and Ruins* Damascus nd; Lassus '*Deux églises*' Appendice II; Thubron pp 55-6

Serjilla (Plates 23a, 23b)

VARIANTS: Serdjilla; Sergilla
PERIOD: Rom/Byz   RATING: ** MAP: *57*, 70
ITIN: 9c

LOCATION: Turn east immediately south of *Bara. 4 km to Bauda then +3 km to Serjilla.

One of the most interesting and visited of the 'dead cities', Serjilla, located in a natural basin opening out to the south, comprises extensive remains of houses, a church, baths, tombs and sarcophagi - a complete Byzantine settlement in a superb and isolated setting. A perfect spot for a picnic or camping.

Near the road, on the left, you will notice a necropolis area with a **sarcophagus**. Beyond this and a little to the south east (downhill) lie the substantial remains of the **baths** and meeting house. A floor of the baths is dated to 473 and their existence in this remote locality indicates the degree of prosperity in the community at the time. The baths are one of the most intact examples found in Syria and are particularly interesting given their origins in the Christian period, as opposed to earlier Roman examples. The main hall of the baths (the largest room, along the north side of the building) measured 8 m by 15 m. The American expedition at the turn of the century found a large mosaic in this room (since destroyed[141]) dedicated by one Julianos

and his wife Domna. In appearance, the building is rather severe, the only decoration being the moulded cornice on top of the walls and gables.

Immediately to the south east lies an outbuilding, an *andron* or men's meeting place. The building on its south frontage is marked by a double portico, each level having three columns. It is described by Butler as 'one of the most perfectly preserved structures in all the ruined and deserted towns in Syria'.

East of the andron and half way up the rise, you will find a small **triple-naved church**. The chamber (*prothesis*) on the north side of the apse is unusual in being enlarged beyond the line of the north wall of the church. On the south side, there is an additional room off the right nave. This communicates with a longer room to the south which gave on to a cloistered court of irregular shape. Beyond this room is a chamber which contained three sarcophagi. Such a mortuary chapel is unusual, possibly intended for ecclesiastical dignatories or town notables rather than venerated saints. Butler judges the church on stylistic grounds to be one of the oldest in the region, perhaps begun earlier than the inscribed

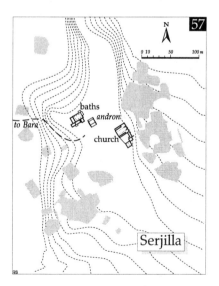

date of 372. The building was remodelled and enlarged in the fifth or sixth century.

---

[141] In fact, most of the mosaic disappeared in the six years between the first and second American expeditions (1899-1905) -

a sad commentary on the destructive consequences of archaeological research!

A little further to the east and up the rise, there are extensive remains of **housing**, mostly of the detached villa variety. Most are ranged along an arc extending from the south to the east, with colonnaded fronts facing a court. Some were large in size, with 16 rooms, allowing for up to four families. The most extensive is 50-60 m north of the church, a double-fronted villa of the fourth or fifth century with a colonnaded facade (modified Corinthian capitals) giving on to a courtyard. Two ancillary houses were grouped around this triangular space. The house immediately behind the church to the east is also of interest. Its facade, now blank, once bore a double colonnade in addition to the then-fashionable decorative mouldings around windows and doors. The building, somewhat analogous to the andron described above, is probably from the late fifth or early sixth century.

The housing spreads downhill towards the south east with one house still inhabited by a local family and their domestic animals. Other houses are found on the other side of the valley (south west of the baths). This group terminates with an isolated pyramidal tomb. A small square chamber is partly cut out of the rock with a front of cut stone. This was once topped by a pyramidal roof, like many other funerary monuments of the area.

Other sites within walking distance include a Crusader stronghold, **Rubea** (1.5 km to the south west).

The village of Bauda passed en route includes another pyramidal-roofed tomb.

REFS: *BG* p 412; Butler *AE* II p 124; Butler *PE* II/B/3 pp 113-133; Krautheimer pp 147-8; Mattern pp 49-55; Tchalenko *Villages* II pl CXL; Vogüé I p 80.

Shahba (Plate 24a)

VARIANTS: Philippopolis (anc), Shehba, Shuhba PERIOD: Rom ALT: 1100 m; RATING: * MAP: 58, 63 ITIN: 2b

> LOCATION: 87 km south of Damascus on the *Suweida road. Take the Damascus airport highway; turn right opposite the Ebla Cham Hotel and head south.

A curious town located between the volcanic region of the Ledja to the west and Jebel al-Arab to the south east. It is nearly 100 percent Druze, a fact apparent from the dress of the inhabitants. It is dominated by the nearby cone of an extinct volcano (*Tell Shihan*). From an archaeological point of view, it is the only town in the Roman Hauran (the ancient Auranitis) - apart from the capital, *Bosra - built to a grid pattern and the walls are broadly oriented towards the cardinal points of the compass. (The terrain of other towns such as *Qanawat was probably too broken to lend itself to a geometric layout.) It is also the only 'new town' in Syria established according to a purely Roman plan (the others being Hellenistic, Nabatean or pre-Hellenistic in origin). Finally, the architectural style adopted at Shahba was not found elsewhere in the Hauran which largely lacks buildings of the mid third century.

Its square shape and the remains of its Roman walls give it a much more 'imperial' feel than other towns in the area and it was in fact founded by the local boy made good, Philip the Arab, who was Emperor from 244 to 249[142]. The Italian origins of many of the concepts and techniques is revealed in the lavish scale of the baths, the use of barrel vaulting and concrete domes and the extensive use of marble cladding on interior walls. The purpose of the project is not entirely clear but it was perhaps intended as a symbolic capital to serve as a monument to Philip's family and receive his ashes. It is likely that the design was not completed on Philip's death and the project was abandoned. Less than half of the walled area was built upon and only a small community continuing to inhabit the town in the late imperial period. It was only in the last century that the town was re-populated with the influx of Druze from Lebanon.

The **walls** of the town still exist in outline with monumental gateways at the four main entrances. The town forms a rough square, the actual dimensions of the walls being north 800 m, east 800 m, south 900 m, west 1000 m. The two main axes which join the gates were originally 11 m wide excluding the colonnaded pavements (4 m on each side). The *insulae* depart from the Greek pattern, being more square (c 100 m by 130 m) than the proportions adopted under the Hippodamian system. The gates followed the usual imperial pattern of a large central arch flanked by two smaller ones. Attempts have been made to reconstruct them, without decoration, at the north and south entrances to the town. (That to the south is the best preserved).

The main cluster of ruins is 100 m along the cross street to the west of the main intersection

---

[142] It seems that Philip was born somewhere in the Roman province of *Arabia* but there is no information on exactly where. It seems a reasonable assumption that he came from the area of present-day Shahba. He was proclaimed Emperor on the death of Gordian III, killed in battle near Baghdad.

in the centre of town (right as you come from Damascus). The ruins centre on the rather pompous square which is dominated by the facade of the **exedra building**. This was an eye-catching facade comprising an elaborate niche area 30 m wide and 20 m deep meant, apparently, to display statuary. Some (including the 19th century visitor, the Marquis de Vogüé) saw this curious building with its large central *exedra* as a *nymphaeum* (water fountain). There is, however, no evidence of a water source or associated channelling. Butler concluded that it was a *kalybe* (open-sided shrine) or 'great open-air state apartment ... where, perhaps, the Arab

Emperor sat upon his throne'. More recently, researchers prefer to see the arrangement as an elaborate frame for statuary depicting the divinity of Philip's ancestry:

> The great exedra dominating the town from its esplanade took the place of a capitol in other Roman colonies. Thus on the eve of the celebration of the thousand years since Rome's foundation (247), the Emperor's native land was endowed with a unique form of sanctuary, a striking proclamation of the glory of the local boy risen to be master of the eternal city.
> [Amer and Gawlikowski *DaM* 1985 p 15]

To the right but not directly connected with the monumental *exedra* are the remains of the palace.

The simple but impressive **temple** (between the square and the theatre to the south) was probably erected in honour of Philip's father, Julius Marinus. This consists of an almost square chamber interrupted only by a broad and lofty entrance doorway on the north side. On the other three sides, groups of blind arches are set in the walls, each consisting of a broad recess flanked by narrow arches. These niches were presumably once filled with statuary, probably again of the Emperor's family. The holes found in many parts of the walls and niches indicate the original use of marble revetments to decorate the interior. The rear (south) wall is considerably thicker in order to accomodate a staircase ascending to the roof. The exterior is austere, relieved only by slight corner pilasters with Ionic capitals and bases. The doorway, 5.5 m high and 3 m wide, is impressive in its restrained moulding. The two brackets which flank the door were intended for statues, one of Philip's father.

The **theatre** (immediately south of the temple) is small, rather stolid and without decoration but is one of the best preserved in Syria (though with a diameter of 42 m it is not in the same league as the superb example at Bosra to the south). The vaulted passages underneath (based on an unusual and complex arrangement of semi-circular and radial vaults) and access to the seating are well preserved, along with the lower rows of seats and the stage front. This is the last of the Roman theatres constructed in the east.

The **baths** (turn left at 80 m as you go south from the intersection of the two main Roman axes) are on a remarkable scale for a town of this size and the only identifiable remains in this style in the Hauran. Butler observed that the quality of construction is much higher than, for example, the Baths of Caracalla in Rome. The domes were constructed of a light concrete, mixing small stones and high quality cement. The interior walls were clad with marble and alabaster and the domes faced inside with painted plaster. The plan was complex: to the south, a series of three rectangular rooms (two *apodytaria* flanking a *caldarium* - that on the right was never completed); two round *caldaria* in the centre; and a long room with semi-circular ends to the north, the *tepidarium*. An aqueduct led into the baths from the south east.

In the street running alongside is a **museum of mosaics** which contains some of the best examples of the art of the late Roman period in Syria. They were found on this site in the remains of a private house and date from the Constantinian renaissance of the second quarter of the fourth century. The scenes depicted include:

- **Orpheus surrounded by animals** - 3.1 m by 3.1 m - second quarter of fourth century. Orpheus, dressed in a Phrygian cap and oriental attire, is sitting on a rock, playing the lyre. He is surrounded by animals entranced by his music. The importance of the mosaic is described by Janine Balty as 'a major resource in the history of pagan religiousity of the first decades of the fourth century, this mosaic, at the level of art history, impresses as one of the most powerful and sensitive in the whole history of late Roman mosaic work'.

- **The Wedding of Ariane and Bacchus** - 3.14 m by 3.14 m. Second quarter of fourth century - Bacchus and Ariane are seated on a rock (both provided with halos) in a scene typical of the 'love conversation' tradition. Behind stands Hymen carrying a flaming torch symbolising desire. At their feet lies a rather enebriated Hercules. On the left, an aged Satyr-like figure labelled Maron seems to be lunging towards Ariadne's cup. Balty notes that: *The composition of the scene, the relatively frozen attitudes of the figures - they pose rather than seem caught in realistic action - the bare decor, the absence of any anecdotal details, confer on the grouping a rather strange character that might be described as didactic or symbolic.*

- **Aphrodite and Ares** - 3.04 m by 3.04 m. Second quarter of fourth century - The scene is from *The Odyssey* VIII. 266-270. Aphrodite and Ares in their love tryst before Hephaistos takes his revenge, ridiculing them before the gods of Olympos. Aphrodite, barely covered but richly bejewelled, stands opposite Ares attended by a rather severe-looking woman, labelled as Charis. Cupids divest Ares of his arms and armour and dispute possession. Balty sees this depiction (particularly the presence of Charis and two other women attendants) as a more prudish interpretation of the 'erotic-idyllic' theme of adultery.

- **Tethys** (goddess of the sea) - 2.66 m by 2.65 m. Second quarter of fourth century. The goddess bears in her thick tresses, various manifestations of sea life. A favourite theme of artists from Antioch, the goddess is often depicted as the consort of Oceanos. Not a major deity, she was used as a vehicle for depicting the rich variety of fish life of the region. Balty notes, however, that the work here is of unaccustomed vigour and richness.

There are other odd remains here and there: note, for example, the five Corinthian columns, beautiful fragments of a portico that once provided the entrance to a **hexastyle temple** or shrine, 50 m on the right as you go up towards the palace/theatre area from the main crossroads.

REFS: Amer and Gawlikowski 'Le sanctuaire impérial de Philippopolis' in *DaM* 1985 pp 1-15; Balty, Janine *Mosaiques* pp 44-69; *BG* p 513; Butler *AE* II pp 369-70; 376-96; Butler *PE* II/A/5 pp 359-60; Freyburger 'Die Bauten und Bildwerke von Phillippolis.' in *DaM* 1992; Hatoum *Philippopolis* Damascus 1996; Maqdisi 'Chronique' in *Syria* 1995; Segal *Town Planning* 1988; Segal *From Function to Monument'* 1997.

Shaizar

VARIANTS: Sinzaru (BrA); Larissa (Grk); Cesara (Lat); Le Grand Césaire (Cru); Seijar, Qalaat Shaizar (Arb)
PERIOD: Cru/Arb   RATING: * MAP: 65 ITIN: 4

LOCATION: 28 km north east of *Hama on the road to Qalaat Mudiq (*Apamea) and *Jisr al-Shugur. 27 km south east of Apamea.

History

Shaizar is located at a vital crossing point on the Orontes. Here the river, after rushing around a bend through a confined gorge to the east, returns to the more leisurely pace of the plains. The settlement has classical origins, local legends recorded by Diodorus Siculus (first century BC) claiming its foundation by a regiment of Thessalonian cavalry from Alexander's forces.

In the early Arab period, a Fatimid castle stood on the site but was seized in 999 by the Byzantines in their effort to reassert their control in Syria against the Fatimids. As the Byzantine hold weakened, a local clan (the Banu Munqidh) seized Shaizar in 1081. By the time the Crusaders had installed themselves briefly in Qalaat Mudiq to the north, the clansmen used Shaizar as a base to harass their presence. It formed a strongpoint of the Arab frontline against the Crusaders. (An interesting Arab perspective on this confrontation is given in the memoirs of a member of the Banu Munqidh family, Usamah (see Bibliography page 286).

Shaizar grew in importance as a centre of Arab resistance, so much so that the Crusaders set up positions in the mountains on the opposite side of the plain to observe and contain Shaizar (*Qalaat Abu Qobeis, *Qalaat al-Mehelbeh). Tancred unsuccessfully sought to take it in 1108 but after another feint in 1110 was forced to settle for a treaty with the Emir of Shaizar agreeing to live-and-let-live within existing spheres of influence. The Byzantines attempted in 1134 and 1138 to take the castle but failed. Much of it was destroyed in 1157 by the severe earthquake which affected the greater part of Syria. The Crusaders tried to profit from the decimation of the clan owners in the destruction by moving on Shaizar, occupying the lower citadel. But by then Nur al-Din was active in northern Syria. He expelled them, repaired the damage and installed his own governor.

In 1170 another earthquake did further damage. Saladin's incorporation of northern Syria after 1174 brought it under his control. A new keep was constructed under the Ayyubids (1233). The first Mongol invasion of Syria in 1260 brought renewed destruction but Baibars (1260-77) who did much to revive Syria after the Mongol wave had passed, garrisoned it. He and his successor, Qalaun, were probably responsible for the substantive rebuilding of a good deal of the castle as seen today (especially the northern defences and the reconstruction of the keep). The castle subsequently fell into disuse as a military post but came to shelter the village inhabitants whose building activities helped erode its fabric until they were moved out in recent decades.

Visit

The elongated (300 m) crag on which it sits provides a natural setting for a fortress. As you pass the village, take a close look on the right at the south end of the crag where a great ditch has been dug out of the living rock to isolate the defences from the connecting hill and give the main castle keep greater elevation. (Similar arrangements were employed at *Qalaat Saladin and *Bakas-Shugur.)

A visit to the castle requires only an hour or so and is a convenient stop on the way from Hama to Apamea. The castle is entered from the north, near the old Turkish bridge and *norias*. The bridge which gives entry is not medieval. It leads into a salient of the castle built in 1290 (according to the Arabic inscription above the rear arch of the vestibule) which juts out from the northern walls at an angle and was originally skirted by a glacis. The salient's construction is solid with large bossaged blocks anchored through the use of classical columns. The upper tower is partly missing but one storey and several windows survive.

A vaulted passage takes you through to a relatively open space, the jumbled remains of various epoques left after the villagers were evacuated. There is not much that is identifiable but the views west over the plain or east over the Orontes gorge 50 m below are worth taking in. Head straight for the south end of the ridge, towards the prominent remains of the keep or donjon already noted, towering above the artificial ditch. Poised at the weakest point of the castle's defences, this was originally built in 1233 by the Ayyubids using large bossaged blocks and strengthening columns. The quality of work is superior to the entrance gateway. There is an entrance on the north but access is difficult. Inside, the tower comprises a *cellar* area with vaulted rooms, two large floors and a roof platform. The architecture and siting of the keep has much in common with Crusader techniques though the proportions are not always as regular, especially in the pillars holding up the vaulting.

REFS: *BG* pp 369-70; Bevan I p 205; Boase pp 72-4; Eydoux pp 328-30; Dussaud *Topographie* pp 145 ff; van Berchem & Fatio pp 177-87.

Shaqqa

VARIANTS: Saccaia, Maximianopolis (Grk); (Grk); Shakka.

PERIOD: Rom/Byz RATING: - MAP: 63 ITIN: 2b

LOCATION: From Damascus, take the road to *Shahba (87 km). Immediately before Shahba, a large volcanic cone (*Tell Shihan*) on the right is being mined for bitumen. At the check-point a little south, turn left and follow this road for +8 km. The ruins lie at the centre of the older part of the village.

The scale of its buildings indicates the degree of importance Shaqqa once had, its decline symptomatic of the general neglect of the area once its wider markets were cut off and insecurity prevailed. (It had been one of the principal sources of grain for the Roman market.) It had the status of a colony in Roman times and was the seat of a bishop in the Christian era.

On the west of the square are the remains of an impressive Roman palace (dubbed in early sources the *Kaiseriye*). A forecourt preceded a broad hall spanned by five closely spaced wide arches supporting a flat ceiling, a common roofing system in the Hauran reflecting the difficulty of cutting the local basalt into roofing slabs longer than 2 or 3 m. South of the same square is part of the facade of a basilica of the pre-Christian era, probably either a judicial building or a cult centre. 300 m to the east are

the remains of a monastery tower of the fifth century incorporated into a farmyard. Right off the second cross street on the way to the tower you can see the base of a Roman tomb, a rectangular cavity within an octagonal base with *exedrae* on four of the sides.

Further up the hill to the west (guide needed) you will find a chamber now used as a Druze meeting hall that clearly has classical or early Christian origins. Termed *al-Maabed*, this centralised structure with four internal columns was probably part of a fourth century house. A little way south east of this is a private house in what may once have been a *kalybe* or a chapel.

REFS: *BG* pp 514; Butler *AE* pp 370-5, 396-7; Butler *EC* pp 22, 84-5 ; Butler *PE* II/A/5 p 360; Dussaud *Topographie* pp 367-8.

Sia

VARIANTS: Seia (anc); Si, Siah, Si`a
PERIOD: Rom   RATING: - MAP: 59, 61
ITIN: 2b

LOCATION: 3 km south east of *Qanawat in the Jebel al-Arab. From the square in front of the Qanawat *seraya*, head down the road which goes past the precariously-poised fragment of a tower east of the main ruins. Continue about 3 km until the road turns sharp left, running below a ridge. It then heads right and ascends steeply to the village of Sia. Stop just as you enter the village and go through the first farmyard to the jumbled remains of a temple on the right (at first rather hard to distinguish amid the dark natural rock).

Even in terms of the many survival stories of the Jebel al-Arab, Sia is a remarkable site, providing some insight into the pre-Roman Semitic architecture of Syria and its adaptation under Roman influence.

In the first decade of this century, the Ottoman Turkish forces dismantled entirely the temple of the Nabatean period at *Suweida to provide stone for their new barracks. Thus was lost an important (and, until then, largely intact) example of the Nabatean architectural tradition. The same barracks project also inspired the mining of a considerable part of the temple complex at Sia, though enough remains of its plan and lower courses to give some idea of this second major example of Nabatean temple architecture and its adaptation under later Roman influence. Fortunately both the Suweida and Sia temples had been recorded in some detail by the French Marquis, Melchior de Vogüé, who visited the site in the mid 19th century. The remains he described were considerably more substantial than those seen today, though he had to employ the villagers to dig much of the temple facade out from its covering of earth and scrub.

The temple complex had its axis along the crest of the small ridge running east/west, beginning with a monumental gateway. To reconstruct the site needs a little imagination. The sequence involves a gateway, two inner courts divided by a secondary gateway, culminating in a *cella* preceded by a peristyle court.

History

Sia began as a Semitic 'high place' attracting worshippers from the surrounding agricultural region. The area came under the influence of the Nabatean Arabs (from present-day Jordan and Saudi Arabia) who promoted the local cult in the form of a temple to Baal-Shamin (for Bel/Baal-Shamin, see box on page 167). Sia did not become a site for settlement until the village sprang up nearby to service the burgeoning pilgrim traffic inspired by peaceful conditions and prosperity in Roman times. There is evidence of three construction periods:

- 50 BC to AD 50 - At this time, Sia marked the northern limit of Nabatean rule as Roman control of Damascus after 64 BC had pushed the Nabatean controlled area back to the Hauran. The Nabateans came under constant pressure from the Romans to hand the area over to Herod the Great's kingdom. The original Baal Temple is from the late first century BC (in a hybrid Persian/Greek style).

- AD 50 to 106 - Additions were made to the Nabatean cult centre when the area fell under more direct Roman control. Roman influences in the architecture became more prominent.

- AD 106 to 200 - The creation of the Roman province of Arabia made Roman influence even more direct, as seen in the second century forecourts.

Visit

You enter the complex from the east side, after passing through the farmyard. The first remains are the ruins of a Roman bath on the left and a gatehouse on the right. After 150 m, you reach the tumbled ruins of a monumental **triple-arched gateway** in classical imperial style of the Roman period. Immediately inside this gateway was a paved second **courtyard** with terraces on either side artificially cut out of the ridge, held behind thick retaining walls. On the elevated south

terrace (left) stood a small **temple**, classical in design but with Nabatean ornamentation, probably dated to the period of the last Nabatean King, Rabbel II (AD 71-106).

At the end of the court is another gateway, also fragmentary. This was a Nabatean construction with triple entrances dating probably

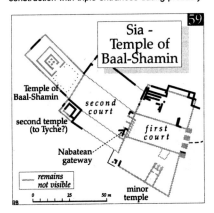

Sia -
Temple of
Baal-Shamin

Temple of
Baal-Shamin

second temple
(to Tyche?)

second
court

first
court

Nabatean
gateway

remains
not visible

0   25   50 m

minor
temple

from the first century AD. Again, the gateway leads into a courtyard flanked by terraces, the upper 1 m above the level of the avenue, the lower 6 m below. On the upper terrace (left) stood another small temple, to the Tyche of the area (previously described by Butler as a temple to the Semitic god, Dushara). This was constructed in the period of Agrippa (AD 50-95)

At the end of this second court, the processional way entered the forecourt of the **temple of Baal-Shamin** by means of a rectangular recessed gateway (late first century AD) topped by a semi-circular arch richly embellished with carvings. Butler found in 1909 that much of the main sanctuary had been carried away in the ten years before his arrival and little now remains of its splendid decorations in a florid Nabatean style not found on any other remains of this period. His reconstructions, however, based on fragments found at the site indicate a temple (built between 32 and 1 BC) preceded by a shallow portico with two columns, flanked on each side by pilastered towers of two storeys. The columns supported a triangular pediment with a sculptured *tympanum*. A statue of Herod, according to Butler[143], stood in front of the *cella*. The main door was decorated with vines and the lintel carried a bust of Baal-Shamin (now in the Louvre). Within the temple was an

---

[143] Butler *PE* II/A/6 p379.

inner chamber, square in plan enclosing a group of four pillars set in another square (perhaps supporting an open space in the roof).

REFS: *BG* p 512; Butler *AE* pp 334-40, 421; Butler *PE* II/A/6 pp 366-402; Dentzer *Fouilles* pp 142-50; Dentzer, J M & Dentzer-Feydy, J 'Fouilles et prospections a Si' 1977-1982' in *AAAS* XXXIII 1983 pp15-25; idem 'Le site et le sanctuaire de 'Si' in *Le djebel el-'Arab*; Dussaud *Topographie* pp 368-9; Rey-Coquais *Seia*; Vogüé I pp 31-8.

Sitt al-Rum

VARIANTS:
PERIOD: Rom/Byz   ALT: 482 RATING: - ITIN: 9a MAP: 68 ITIN: 9a

LOCATION: From the road 1 km south of *Saint Simeon (2 km north of Deiret Azze) ,walk hard left towards the lower group of ruins in the distance, c 600 m. The site can also be approached via the road to *Qatura.

The ruins of Sitt al-Rum ('Our Lady of the Greeks') consist of an isolated church and a Roman tomb. The **church** or rather monastery chapel is dated to the fourth century and is virtually devoid of decoration. In plan it is a simple rectangle with one nave but the walls are tall in proportion to the width and the windows are placed high. The sanctuary is set in a rectangle which protrudes beyond the east wall. The chancel arch is low and stolid with three windows above to augment light. The chapel was surrounded by a monastery complex of which the double arcading of one building survives precariously but the rest is barely recognisable.

The **tomb** is across a small valley (south). It is marked by two monolith pillars, square in shape, which once carried a classic entablature. Near the top of each column is a framed sunken panel which originally bore bronze plaques or low-reliefs. Butler notes that 'it is interesting to find so chaste and well-studied a design in Classic style at so early a period, and at such a distance from the great artistic centres' and assumes it is an example of contemporary work in Antioch. The tomb (entrance 6 m to the north) is rock-cut and dates from AD 152. It was a family burial place as 15 *sarcophagi* were found in the chamber but the inscription gives a particular dedication to one Isidotos with explicit directions as to where his body would be found ('the third in the first *arcosolium* on the right as you enter'). Isidotos was a man of 21 who had already done five years of military service as an auxiliary attached to the Governor of Syria. It is hard to see the common thread in these remains. Possibly this is the site of an early (first

century) estate of a Roman landholder, later overtaken by the nearby developments at Qatura and *Refade and used to house a monastic community.

REFS: Butler *EC* p 149; Butler *PE* II/B/5 pp 258-261; Sournia pp 85, 112; Tchalenko *Villages* II pp 198-200.

Suweida

VARIANTS: Dionysias (Grk); Soada (Lat)
PERIOD: Rom RATING: * MAP: 63 ITIN: 2b

LOCATION: 128 km south east of Damascus. For exit, see directions for *Bosra or *Shahba.

A Nabatean town dating back probably to the fourth century BC, Suweida would have been ruled by an independent prince until the area was handed by the Romans to Herod the Great in 23 BC. In AD 92, it was annexed to the Roman province of Syria and in 106 was incorporated in the new province of Arabia. Under the Romans it was an important market town subordinate to *Qanawat. It was given the name Dionysias under Commodus (r 180-85) in honour of the Roman god of the grape, one of the main products of the region.

Nowadays, Suweida is again a major centre which serves as the capital of the increasingly prosperous province of the Hauran. Unfortunately, most of its ancient remains were used by Turkish troops for building material for their new barracks in the first decade of this century. A new museum (1 km on right on road to Qanawat) includes, however, an exceptional collection of sculptures and Roman mosaics from *Shahba (Philippopolis). The sculpture dates from the Nabatean to Islamic periods but the most striking items are those demonstrating that even the heavy basalt of the Hauran could not defeat the creative capacities of the sculptors of Roman Syria.

Like those in the Shahba museum, the mosaics reveal an extraordinary degree of expressiveness. Those worthy of particular note are:

- **Artemis Taking Her Bath** - first on right from door - mid third century - 4.3 m by 4.3 m - Artemis crouches near a spring, leaning on her left leg. The naked goddess is bejewelled and crowned with a diadem of pearls. She is surrounded by four nymphs. The head of Acteon emerges from the shrubbery. The scene is bordered by a superb frieze of garlands of fruit and foliage.

- **Venus at her Toilet** - second on right of door of central hall - mid third century - 3.24 m by 3.23 m - Venus, framed within a shell, holds in her right hand a tress of her hair and in her left a mirror to adjust her coiffure. Two cupids attend her and she is flanked by two marine divinities. The figure is naked but richly adorned with jewels.
- **Banquet Scene** centre of opposing wall - first quarter of fourth century - 6.5 m by 6.62 m - circular banquet scene enclosed within a square frame.

Suweilim

VARIANTS: Selaema (Lat); Selim (Arb)
PERIOD: Rom RATING: - MAP: 63 ITIN: 2b

LOCATION: 6 km north of *Suweida on the Damascus road. The ruins are conspicuous on the north west side of the village in the form of the corner pilaster of a temple facade, visible above the houses.

Selaema was originally a Nabatean settlement later incorporated into *Provincia Syria* but transferred to *Provincia Arabia* in the late second

---

HAURAN

This basalt plain, the result of relatively recent volcanic activity, forms an area (100 km north/south, 75 km east/west) of fertile land south of Damascus between Mount Hermon and the desert with the Jordanian border as its southern limit. The plain is protected from the encroaches of the desert to the east by Jebel al-Arab (alt c1500 m), the Mount Bashan of the Psalms (Asalmanos in Greek/Roman times) noted for its oak.

The Hauran was colonised by the Greeks but with the collapse of Seleucid rule by the first century BC, was raided by rival Jewish and Nabatean groups. The semi-hellenized local kings were overthrown and in the confusion the area largely fell under the control of Arab shepherds and bandits. Herod the Great, as King of Judaea (r 37-4 BC) was given most of the area in 23-20 BC as a reward for his last-minute switch to Augustus' cause after Actium (31 BC). It remained in the hands of Herod's son, Philip until his death in AD 34. Still subject to Nabatean and Bedouin designs, it was annexed to *Provincia Syria* in 34 but handed by Caligula to Herod Agrippa II. By AD 70 Bosra had become the capital of the Nabatean kingdom but controlled only the southern part of the Hauran, the rest (including Suweida and Canatha) being included in Syria. The whole area, however, was transferred to *Arabia* in the late second century. Stable Roman control brought new life to the economy of the Hauran and cultivation of corn was pursued by pushing back the desert limits (*Bosra).

The ancient Hauran in its wider sense was divided into several sub-regions (modern names in brackets):
- Gaulanitis (Jaulan or Golan) - the area between the Damascus/Deraa road and the Golan Heights
- Batanaea (Nuqra) - capital Deraa (ancient Adraa)
- Trachonitis (Ledja or Leja - the refuge) - the lava-strewn semi-wilderness area north west of Jebel al-Arab
- Auranitis (Hauran proper, mainly Jebel al-Arab plus the plain as far as Bosra) - capital *Bosra

To these is sometimes added the area north of Gaulanitis, namely:

- Ituraea west and south of Damascus which was for a time associated with Chalcis (modern Anjar, central Beqaa Valley in Lebanon)

There are few remains in the older part of town of the Roman or later periods. Near the central square south west of the Governor's office are the remains of four columns (only three visible), all that has survived of a temple of Nabatean times. To the west, remains of a five-aisled basilica (fifth century) which recent research indicates may have been a pilgrimage church constructed on an enormous scale.

REFS: *anon Le musée de Soueïda* Paris 1934; Balty, Janine *Mosaïques*; Brünnow & Domaszewski pp 88-102; Dentzer (ed) *Hauran*; Dussaud *Topographie* p 333, 369; Rey-Coquais *Dionysias*; Sodini 'Monuments chrétiens du Mohafaza de Suweida' in Dentzer & Dentzer-Feydy *Le djebel al-'Arab* 1991.

century. The rather scanty remains of a small Roman temple consist of the corner of the badly decomposed facade poking up rather incongruously. It is hard to reconstruct in the imagination the few stones left on the site but illustrated reconstructions of the temple reveal a building of some considerable size and interest with a number of features in common with the Syro-Phoenician tradition. Robert Amy's study of step temples indicates that the building originally included towers on either side of an entrance portico comprising two pairs of pillars set in a 5 m wide staircase. The small *cella* behind included a semi-circular chamber set between two flanking rooms, a plan later employed in the Baal-Shamin temple in Palmyra and in many church buildings, particularly in northern Syria. Above the corners of the facade the stonework continued upwards, rising above the level of the entablature richly decorated with maeanders, roses and garlands, to support a giant Corinthian capital, probably ending with a further entablature enclosing a flat open platform-roof, en effect described by a recent researcher as a 'totally unorthodox way to achieve an eclectic effect'. Acroteria adorned the lower corners of the pediment. Much of the carved decoration is of a high standard. According to K S Freyberger,

the temple dates from the reign of the Roman Emperor Augustus (d AD 14) and may have been dedicated to Baal-Shamin.

REFS: Amy; Butler *PE* II/A/5 pp 356-9; Freyburger 'Der Tempel in Slim: Ein Bericht' in *DaM* 1991 pp 9-38; Rey-Coquais 'Selaema'.

T

Takleh

VARIANTS: Taqle
PERIOD: Byz ALT: 520 m RATING: * MAP: 68
ITIN: 9a

LOCATION: From the road 1 km south of *Saint
Simeon (coming from Deiret Azze), walk up the steep
hill on the right, aiming towards the three-storeyed
facade of a church on the skyline, 800 m away.

This village seems to have comprised a group of
reasonably prosperous farmers who exploited
the fertile Plain of Qatura below to the west.
Tchalenko notes that the houses all belong to the
same period (mid fifth century), modest in scale
and of middling execution.

The settlement was grouped around the
church of the same date. The plan of the church
is typical of the columned basilicas of the mid
fifth century with the apse flanked by two side
rooms - a *diaconicon* or sacristy (north) and
martyrium or burial chamber for a saint (south).
Most striking is the west facade which preserves
its three tiers of windows. On the south side of
the church an arcade leads to a baptistery in the
annexe. Note also the two olive presses, one
attached to the church, the other accessible to all
inhabitants.

REFS: Butler *PE* II/B p 284; Tchalenko *Villages* I pp
200-4, II pl IX, LVII, LXIV-VI, CXXVII.

Tartus

VARIANTS: Antaradus, Constantia (Lat);
Antartus, Tortosa (Cru)
PERIOD: Cru RATING: ** MAP: 60, 66
ITIN: 5a

LOCATION: On the coast 220 km north west of
Damascus.

Tartus has been rapidly developed in recent
decades as Syria's second port city, with a
number of major industries to the north. It has
been connected to the national rail and road grid
and the expansion of the city has robbed it of
much of its sleepy charm as a small
Mediterranean fishing port with its roots firmly
planted in the past. Nevertheless, the old city
retains some of its character and the former
Cathedral of Our Lady of Tortosa is one of the
most remarkable surviving remains of the
religious architecture of the Crusades outside
Jerusalem.

History

Tartus was originally founded by the Phoenicians
to complement the more secure but less
accessible settlement on the island of Arwad.
Tartus for a long time thus played a secondary
role to Arwad, a major centre in Seleucid and
Roman times. The classical name, Antaradus
(*anti-Aradus* – 'the town facing Aradus' or Arwad)
reflected this secondary role. Constantine (306-
337) made it a separate city and his successor,
Constantius renamed it Constantia in 346 as he
favoured its Christian inhabitants over the
pagans of Arwad. The town was already famed
for its devotion to the cult of the Virgin, one of the
earliest chapels in her honour having been built
there before the fourth century. (Legend had it
that St Peter himself had consecrated the first
church in honour of the Virgin.) The altar of the
chapel is believed to have miraculously escaped
destruction by an earthquake in 487. An icon,
said to have been painted by the evangelist St
Luke, was also venerated there (cf *Seidnaya).

After passing into Muslim hands with the
Arab conquest in the 630s, Tartus was one of
the towns the Byzantine Emperor Nicephorus II
Phocas retook in his effort to reassert Byzantine
sovereignty in Syria in 968. The Cairo-based
Fatimids sought to take it in 997 during Caliph
Aziz's push into Syria. By the time the Crusaders
arrived in 1099, it was subject to the Emir of
Tripoli. The Governor was tricked into surrender
by the Crusaders for whom the acquisition of the
port and its easy communications to Cyprus and
Antioch greatly helped them establish their
foothold in the area.

Tartus quickly reverted to Muslim hands but
in 1101, Raymond de Saint Gilles, Count of
Toulouse began his concerted campaign to take
Tripoli and the areas connecting the coast and
the Orontes near *Homs. He turned Tartus into a
fortress city owing allegiance to Tripoli. The
Franks strongly promoted the Marian pilgrimage
and after 1123 began construction of the

cathedral church of Our Lady of Tortosa, presumably in order to house the venerated altar. The military role of the Frankish city was underlined when the Knights Templar took control after 1152. It became the order's principal fortress after the headquarters at Acre in Palestine. They improved its defences considerably and fortified the harbour as part of their ambitious program of defensive works in the region.

The decision of Baldwin IV, King of Jerusalem, to hand Tortosa over to the Templars followed the temporary occupation of the city by Nur al-Din (1152). Nur al-Din's incursion profited from the confusion sown by the murder at the hands of the Assassins of Raymond II of Tripoli at the gates of that city. In 1188, Nur al-Din's nephew, Saladin followed up his major victory over the Crusaders at Hattin in Palestine by raiding much of the countryside north of Tripoli. In most cases, he did not press engagements if serious resistance were offered but at Tartus in 1188, he occupied most of the city from 3 to 8 July. He failed, however, to take the donjon in which the Templar garrison had taken refuge (an episode which did little credit to their reputation as fearless defenders of the Christian realm). Saladin took the opportunity to destroy a good deal of the occupied town including the cathedral, for the first time offering a serious challenge to the Crusader presence in the area.

Taking note of the lesson, the Templars thereafter took the defence of the region more seriously. By consolidating a chain of outer defences - *Safita, Chastel Rouge (*Qalaat Yahmur), Arima (*Qalaat Areimeh), Akkar (in northern Lebanon) not to mention the other substantial fortresses at Tripoli, Marqab and the Krak - Tartus was no longer a soft target[144]

Despite attacks by the Mameluke Sultan Baibars in 1267 and 1270, Tartus remained in Templar hands until the last days of the Crusader presence on the mainland. A 1282 truce between Sultan Qalaun and the Knights Templar prolonged the fortress' survival until after the fall of the great fortress of Acre in May 1291. It finally succumbed on 3 August 1291, by which stage its forward defence posts in the area had all fallen and even the great castles of the Krak and Marqab were in Mameluke hands. Except for Athlit (the last remnant of the

---

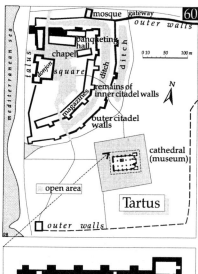

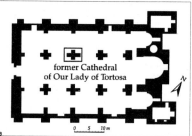

former Cathedral
of Our Lady of Tortosa

Jerusalem Kingdom evacuated 14 August, having become untenable with the fall of Acre), Tortosa was the last point on the mainland held by the Crusaders.

The knights slipped away to the nearby island of Arwad without resistance, taking with them the revered icon of the Virgin. From Arwad, they conducted a last-ditch harassment campaign for another decade but by 1303, the last Crusaders had withdrawn to Cyprus from where their descendants carried on the cause through the Lusignan dynasty. For centuries, the cathedral fell into neglect. In 1851 it was use as a mosque and, after 1914, as a Turkish barracks but was restored under the French and used as a museum in the independence period.

---

[144] Another factor assisting its defence in depth may have been the presence of a considerable number of Christian villages in the mountains behind Tartus. This presence has survived to this day, especially in the so-called 'Valley of the Christians' around the Krak. The town of Tartus, however, has for long been substantially Muslim.

Visit

It may be simplest to begin your visit with the **Cathedral of Our Lady of Tortosa**. You enter it from the west, the exterior wall being a blank but powerful expression of simple Crusader-period style. This dates entirely from the 13th century improvements to the original Crusader redevelopment. It has lost most of its two corner towers (the west walls of the tower up to the level of the side aisles remain) which gave the building more the character of a fortress than a church. The eye is now drawn in to the entrance doorway surmounted by twin windows framed with elegant colonnettes and topped by a third matching window. Two small windows to the side mark the axes of the side naves.

Inside, the effect of the simple Crusader style is most impressive - 'the most beautiful interior from the Crusader period in Syria' (Odenthal). The plan is a straightforward three-aisled basilica. Each aisle has four bays and ends in an apse, the central one being preceded by a short choir. In the eastern corners, two more towers are located, reached through passageways off the apses.

It is worth paying particular attention to the north aisle. Note the pillar between the central and north aisles which rests on a cube of masonry, pierced by a transverse passageway. This is assumed to represent an attempt during the 12th century rebuilding to preserve some elements of the earlier Byzantine chapel. (The passageway would originally have given entry to the chapel below). Note also the carved figure of a bird (head missing) at the top of the north apse - presumed to represent the Third Person of the Trinity, the Holy Ghost.

Though the work on the Cathedral church was begun in the 12th century (1123 on), it was interrupted in the middle of the century. After Saladin's attack (1188), much damage had to be reconstructed. When major work resumed in the 13th century, under the Templars' guidance, the church took on a more defensive character lying, as it does, just outside the main walls of the fortress. The exterior was reinforced, the nearly blank western wall was built and the towers were probably added. (You can still see in the east towers the reinforced firing positions.) It was probably at this time that the traces of the Byzantine chapel were built over, bringing the level of the north aisle up to that of the rest of the church. The transition from Romanesque to Gothic in contemporary Europe is also reflected in the new style, particularly in the mix of treatment of the capitals. In looking around the church, note traces of more ancient stones used

in its construction, presumably from classical buildings. From the terrace, to which the eastern towers give access, a view of the town is obtained.

The **museum** contains a number of objects of interest from various periods, notably: Syro/Phoenician finds; some *Khoroi* figures from fifth century Greek colonisation; Roman glass, bronze and sculptures; as well as later remains.

Taking your bearing from the church, you should now head for the remains of the **fortress** itself. Tracing the inner walls of the Crusader city amid the tangle of later buildings can be a challenge. The first defence wall of the castle lay c100 m north west of the church. Behind it, traces of the Crusader inner walls poke here and there through the houses.

At this point, however, some appreciation of the layout of Tortosa's defences is needed. The fortress city formed a large, irregular rectangle, its length (350 m) parallel to the sea. The outer (town) wall is difficult to trace but vestiges can be seen along the street which leads from the north western corner of the citadel inland towards the modern main street. From there it ran south about 200 m before curving close to the east wall of the cathedral. The point where it reached the sea and turned back northwards along the coast is marked by the remains of a tower seen along the seafront about 400 m south of the citadel. The walls were 2.5m thick in parts and were surrounded by a rock-cut ditch filled with sea water. The remains of another outer gate are seen on the north western corner.

In the north western segment of this outer compound was the first defence wall and behind it the inner citadel, both roughly semi-circular shape. At the heart lay the donjon from where the Crusaders held out against Saladin. The concentric defences thus consisted of:

- outer ditch and town wall;
- inner ditch and first defence wall around citadel;
- main citadel wall (almost half-circular in plan) with square bastions;
- central donjon.

The point you have now reached is between the second and third of these.

If you keep heading in the same direction inside the walled area, you will come to a relatively open space with a coffee shop. This is more or less in the centre of the fortress area and from here you could explore what traces remain of the original fortress. Little apart from a trace of the north wall remains of the 13th century **banqueting hall** once 44 m long (north of the square). The hall was divided by a central row of five pillars into two naves vaulted in six sections. The chapel is a little more easily identified to the north east, up a short flight of stairs. The remains of the original **donjon** adjoin the square on the west side. What there is of these remains, though, is in an extremely dilapidated state in spite of recent efforts to free the ruins from their modern encrustations.

From this point, if you head a little north you will come to a recognisable gateway on the northern edge of the semi-circular walls. (You may also want to look out for a mosque, a little to the east, which is installed in a former guard room of the Crusader castle.) From here, it is a few metres west to the sea. The fortified half-circle is closed by the line of **walls** along the modern sea-front drive. The mixture of old stonework, later patching and modern dwellings along the line of wall is worth noting. The sloping talus of the donjon survives in part, flanked by two stout towers. The modern sea esplanade has considerably extended the shoreline, dividing the walls, which once were lapped by the sea, from the water. At the base of the donjon there is a small postern gate, across a paved open area just below the level of the esplanade. This was probably the exit the last Crusaders used in 1291 to slip quietly into the water, abandoning without ceremony one of the last vestiges of their 200 year adventure on the Levant coast.

After continuing south to the other end of this stretch of wall, head eastwards again into the town and you will reach the small square in front of the museum from where you started out. (A diversion 200 m to the south will take you to the south west tower of the outer walls mentioned earlier.)

REFS: *BG* pp 433-6; Boase pp 93-6; Deschamps *Châteaux* - III pp 287-92; Dussaud *Topographie* pp 124-5; Eydoux pp 171-7.47

Tell Brak

VARIANTS:
PERIOD: EBA/MBA RATING: T MAP: 74 ITIN: 13a

LOCATION: 40 km north east of Haseke (North East Province). Take the old Qamishli road (fork right c5 km north of Haseke). Turn right at the village of Tell Brak, heading south east to the ancient mound (+2 km) on the banks of the Jaghjagh River (the ancient Mygdonios - a tributary of the Khabur).

Tell Brak is the site of Mallowan's excavations (1937-9) which were an important landmark in reconstructing the history of this area in the Early Bronze Age[145]. The Khabur region was at the time (as it is becoming again) an important centre for dry-land farming, expecially the production of grain given the reliability of the annual rainfall and the benefits of the run-off from the Taurus Mountains in Turkey to the north. Tell Brak sits at the point on the Khabur basin system where the natural communication route from the Jebel Sinjar region of Mesopotamia to the east joins the river before continuing south to the Euphrates.

The tell is one of the largest (43 ha) in the north east region of Syria and since 1976 is again being researched by a British team which is currently concentrating on remains of the **Akkadian fortress** (24th or 23rd century BC) in the south eastern corner of the site. The fortress of the Akkadian ruler Naram-Sin (24th century BC) which assumed the role of the northern Mesopotamian centres such as Mari, was rebuilt in the third Ur dynasty (22nd century BC) but abandoned at the end of the third millennium. The ruins included those of a substantial palace (frontage 90 m long, four internal courts), probably the seat of a regional governor of the Akkadian Empire.

The most celebrated discovery of Mallowan's dig was the 3100-2900 BC Eye Temple found under part of the Akkadian palace complex ('Palace of Naram-Sin') 200 m to the east. The temple was named on account of the hundreds of flat idols discovered there, all bearing an outsized representation of an eye. (They were presumably *ex voto* offerings for the temple which follows a plan typical of Sumerian religious buildings of the period - long central nave, deliberate use of proportion (18 m by 6 m), double entrance, podium at the far end, service rooms to the left, subsidiary sanctuary to the right).

The recent British excavations have also uncovered remains of a third period, a 16th-15th century BC **Mitannian palace** 250 m north of the eye temple (50 m north east of the trig point) on the northern edge of the *tell*. The palace was destroyed by the Middle Assyrian kings and totally abandoned by 1200 BC.

Though it is not possible to pick it up from an earthbound perspective, French aerial

---

[145] Mallowan's wife was Agathie Christie. She has written an amusing account of several seasons spent together in the NE of Syria, including the seasons at Tell Brak - *Tell Me How You Live* by Agathie Christie Mallowan, London, 1946.

surveying in the 1920's revealed a Byzantine fort 91 m square with external semi-circular towers 5 km to the west at Tell Zenbil, surrounded by an extensive outer compound. A Roman legionaires' barracks camp (5 km to the east of Tell Brak, 4 ha in size) had preceded it in defending this access channel from the Tigris to the east. The late Roman/Byzantine line of defence in this area followed the course of the Jaghjagh River from Thannouris (10 km south east of Haseke) to Dara (in modern Turkey, 25 km north west of Qamishli).

REFS: *BG* p 489; Kennedy and Riley pp 187-9, 215; Mallowan; Oates; Poidebard *Trace* pp 143-6; Weiss *Tell Brak*.

Tell Halaf (Ras al-Ain)

VARIANTS: Guzana (anc), Gozan (bib), Resaina, Fons Chaborae (Lat), Theodosiopolis (Byz); Ras al-`Ain(Arb).
PERIOD: IrA/Rom   RATING: - MAP: 74 ITIN: 13a

LOCATION: Tell Halaf (Ras al-Ain) lies on the Turkish frontier at the source of the Khabur River (classical Chaboras). It can be reached from the capital of the North East Province, Haseke, on a good sealed road (74 km north west).

The tell itself is c+2 km to the west of Ras al-Ain town. The sulphurous springs that gush out of the flat terrain lie c+1 km to the south of Tell Halaf. (They can be located by identifying the ruined French-period bathhouse next to a small dam wall). The Roman military camp is on a separate, flatter tell (Tell Fakhariye) on the south western outskirts of the town.

Tell Halaf has been an important site in the development of Middle Eastern archaeology. The story of the excavation and its aftermath is in itself a remarkable saga. In 1899, the tell attracted the attention of Baron Max von Oppenheim, a Prussian engineer involved in surveying the route of the Berlin/Baghdad railway[146]. Von Oppenheim resigned from his appointment and returned to the area to take on the excavation of the site from 1911. Work was interrupted by the First World War but resumed from 1927 to 1929.

The site goes back to neolithic times and has given its name to a type of fourth millennium BC pottery found on the *tell*. The site was then abandoned until the first millennium BC when the

city has been identified with Guzana mentioned in the Assyrian archives. It was the capital of Bit Bahiani, the easternmost of the Aramean states that had spread over Syria at the beginning of the millennium but its independence was curtailed from the early ninth century and an Assyrian governor was installed from 808.

The ninth or eighth century palace of the Kapara dynasty was unearthed with many huge sculptured figures in a somewhat grotesque style found in a less fantastic and prolific form in other sites of the period including Carcemish and *Ain Dara. The greater part of the finds were divided between Syria (now in the *Aleppo Museum) and Berlin where some were set up in a special Tell Halaf Museum. During the Second World War, the building in which they were temporarily stored received a direct hit from an allied bomb and much of the Berlin collection was lost[147].

The palace covered an area 52 m by 30 m on a spur of the citadel mound near the river bank, surrounded by a three-sided fortification with the river forming the fourth (north) side. On the west side of the citadel mound thetemple complex included receptions halls for ceremonial purposes. The facade was lined along the lower course of the 61 m wall with sculptured orthostats, black and red in colour. Other monstrous sculptures stood along the ceremonial entrance passage in black volcanic stone - caryatids, griffins, lions, a bull and sphinxes. The effect is recreated in the replicas at the entrance to the Aleppo Museum which is a reconstruction of the Tell Halaf temple facade. Most of the palace and temple remains, however, have been transported elsewhere or succumbed to the elements over the last 60 years.

The **sulphur springs** to the south (Hammam al-Sheikh Bashir) probably account for the intensity of settlement in this area (which in ancient times supported a considerably more active agriculture than today perhaps because the cutting of the forests in the Turkish foothills to the north have diminished the region's rainfall). The springs are worth visiting for the sight of the huge volume of foul-smelling hot water bursting out of the flat ground. In the French period, the springs were exploited for health cures (hence the ruined bathhouse).

The site of the Roman military post at **Resaina** (the modern Tell Fakhariye) contains little of obvious visual interest. It is hard to think

---

[146] The railway, which was never completed in its more ambitious form, survives in the Aleppo/Mosul link, now disused due to the disruption of Syrian/Iraqi relations. The rail line runs along the Turkish/Syrian border at this point.

[147] Part, however, had been donated beforehand to the *Berliner Museen* and can be seen in Berlin. Four orthostats are also on display in the Metropolitan Museum in New York.

of this remote spot playing any role in the outer defences of Rome but the fortress may date as early as the second century AD. By the late third century, the Roman/Byzantine *limes* were maintained on a line well to the east of here (from Dara - ancient Anastasiopolis north east of modern Nisibis just over the Turkish border - as far south as Thannouris, south east of Haseke). Resaina was for a time an important garrison town (there is evidence that it was the base for the III Third Parthica Legion under the Severan Emperors) and part of the rear line of defence along the Khabur River that provided defence in depth to the *limes* and controlled a reasonably prosperous district which bore the classical name, Gauzanitis. Resaina was re-named Theodosiopolis when city rights were conferred under Theodosius I (379-95).

REFS: **Tell Halaf:** *BG* p 481; Canby pp 332-8; Honigmann *Ras al-'Ain*; Dussaud *Topographie* pp 490-5; Frankfort pp 288-9; Poidebard *Mission*; Sader. **Tell Fakhariye**: McEwan *et al.*

Tell Nebi Mend

VARIANTS: Kinza (Hittite), Qidsha, Qadesh, Kadesh (BrA); Laodiceia (Grk); Laodicea ad Libanum (Lat); Chades (?Cru).

PERIOD: LBA/Rom RATING: MAP: 65 ITIN: 4

LOCATION: As you approach Homs on the Damascus/Homs motorway, watch out for an overhead railway viaduct. Immediately before the viaduct, a secondary road leads off to the left, towards the Anti-Lebanon Range. Follow this for 20 km until you reach al-Qusair. NW +c4 km (towards Lake Homs) until you see a village perched on a mound on the other (W) side of the Orontes River.

The earliest habitation probably goes back to the sixth millennium BC but the site was abandoned and re-inhabited in the Early Bronze Age. After 2000 BC, Qadesh acquired massive fortification walls and was a city of some significance in the Middle Bronze Age, sufficiently prominent for its prince to lead a coalition of Mitannian principalities that was savagely put down by the Pharaoh Thutmose III c1480 BC at Megiddo in northern Palestine.

Two centuries later, north west of this unprepossessing site, 'perhaps the most famous battle of pre-classical antiquity'[148] took place in the early 13th century BC. The battle of Qadesh is still a prominent theme of the surviving propaganda works of the reign of Ramses II in

Egypt (c1290-1237 BC). A scene of the Pharaoh slaughtering his opponents by the score is repeatedly used in the vainglorious monuments at Thebes (Ramesseum), Abydos and Abu Simbel, in Upper Egypt. His opponents were the Hittites under their leader Muwatallis. The two powers, Egypt of the New Kingdom and the Hittite Empire, had for some time disputed control of northern Syria.

Ramses II's claim in his monumental propaganda panels to have eliminated the Hittite threat is somewhat overstated. The Hittites threw everything into an attack by their chariot forces, catching Ramses by surprise and throwing the Egyptians into confusion, though Ramses managed to rally his forces and drive the Hittites back. Both sides subsequently agreed to a balance of power in Syria largely favourable to the Hittites which lasted until the end of the Bronze Age (c1200 BC). The Hittites, from their base in central Anatolia (Turkey), remained a power in the area of northern Syria and had access to the area's important trade (not least through the port of *Ugarit).

A small tributary stream (the Nahr Mukadiye) comes in from the south west and joins the Orontes in a marshy area north of the mound, on the edge of present-day Lake Homs. The location of the battle in relation to the present village was probably the ground to the west and south of the confluence. Part of the Egyptian army arrived from the its base camp on the ridge to the south west and were attempting to set up a fresh camp west of Qadesh when the Hittite cavalry attacked from the east, fording the river and looping around from the south. The Egyptians counter-attacked from the west and brought up their reserve units from the ridge to drive the Hittites back east across the river.

Qadesh was probably abandoned again after the Assyrian period but was revived by the Seleucids around 300 BC when Seleucos I Nicator established the town of Laodikeia south of the tell. The town bore the same name as the port (*Latakia) on the Syrian coast, both being named after the mother of Seleucos. To distinguish the two in Roman times, the full title of Laodicea ad Libanum was used[149]. This town survived through to Byzantine times.

The significance of the site lies less in the size of the settlement and its present remains than in its location at an important cross-roads. Not only is it at the point where southern Syria

---

148 *Encyclopedia Brittanica* Chicago 1983, Macropedia entry 'Syria and Palestine, Early History' p 936.

149 Parr also records an alternative Latin name, *Laodicea Scabiosa*, a title which he speculates may have referred to the malarial conditions emanating from the nearby Lake of Homs.

gives way to the flat grain-growing plains of the north, but it also marks the northern exit from the rich Beqaa Valley in Lebanon, a natural north/south corridor. Moreover, Qadesh lies near the 'Homs Gap', the only point between Turkey and Palestine at which the otherwise unbroken coastal chain of mountains allows easy access between the Mediterranean and the interior[150].

Except for gaining an appreciation of the battle scene (and the views, on a clear winter day, towards snow-clad Mount Lebanon), the site offers little of particular interest to the casual visitor. The 10 ha mound which rises to the unusual height of 30m above the surrounding ground is being dug by a British team but the tell itself was probably never a major urban settlement. The flood plains that surround it, however, were a rich agricultural resource that would have provided excellent supplies for cavalry forces. Immediately west and north of the mound, you will see some gigantic *sarcophagi* scattered about.

Jusieh

Eight kilometres south of Quseir, a turn off to the left immediately before the Lebanese frontier brings you to the small village of Jusieh. Immediately beyond the village (no vehicle access) lie two late Roman/Byzantine fortifications on the lower slopes of the Anti-Libanon. The first (2 kms south east) is a late Roman fort with a 40 m square central citadel. 4 kms south of Jusieh are traces of a Byzantine defensive complex, Juseir al-Harab, probably the ancient Maurikopolis, represents the last attempt, a few decades before the Muslim conquest, to create a hellenic 'new city' in Syria under the Emperor Maurice (r 582-602. Nothing much remains at either site above the foundation courses. The forts would have guarded access between Emesa and Baalbek.

REFS: Dussaud *Topographie* pp 107-8; Mouterde & Poidebard pp 31-5; Parr; Parr in *AAAS* 1983; Parr 'Nebi Mend, Tell' in *OE* 1995; Pézard; Pritchard pp 26-7.

---

[150] One good way of gaining an appreciation of the 'Homs gap;' is to visit the site on a windy day, an option difficult to avoid in any case. The pull of the desert heat often sucks air from the Mediterranean through the mountain gap with incredible vehemence, as evident in the slant of the trees in the vicinity. The significance of the gap is discussed further in the entry for the *Krak des Chevaliers.

U

Ugarit

VARIANTS: Ras Shamra (Arb)
PERIOD: LBA RATING: ** MAP: *61*, 67 ITIN: 7c

LOCATION: Leave *Latakia by the four-lane road
which heads north past the Mediterranean Games
sports complex to the resort Hotels. At c10 km, at the
roundabout in front of the Cote d'Azur Hotel, turn
right c+4 km. The site (known as *Ras Shamra*,
'Headland of Fennel' in Arabic) is clearly marked.

Ugarit is one of the few Bronze Age sites in the
Middle East which offers identifiable remains to
the casual visitor and not simply to the specialist
scholar or those who have the time to familiarise
themselves with the wealth of published
information extracted from the site. Unlike other
centres of the period, the palace and religious
buildings were built in stone. Whereas the mud
brick of cities such as *Mari or *Ebla has quickly
eroded with rain and wind on exposure to the
archaeologist's spade, Ugarit survives with at
least its foundation courses and a good deal of
its walls clearly delineated in stone.

Ugarit has been described as 'probably the
first great international port in history'[151]. Through
its ancillary port at Minet al-Beida, in ancient
times, Ugarit actively participated in trade
around the eastern Mediterranean and from here
much of the later Phoenician commercial and
cultural expansion took its inspiration, not least
through the development of the alphabet.
Admittedly the riches of the palaces are now
elsewhere (including in the *Damascus - National
Museum and the Louvre in Paris) but it is still
possible to get an appreciation of the period by
wandering between the palace walls and
passageways or scrambling up to the acropolis.
Choose a cool day, though, or start early in the
morning. If you visit in spring when the
wildflowers give the scene a patina of colour,
watch out for the vipers that take on the hues of
the mottled stone.

Excavated almost continuously over the
course of 50 years, Ugarit has served as one of
the anchor-points of modern archaeological
research and biblical studies illustrating in
particular the Canaanite *milieu* in which the
Biblical world later emerged. The chance

---

[151] Culican p 153.

discovery of the site in 1928 quickly confirmed
the identity of the remains with Ugarit, mentioned
in the archives of *Mari and of Tell al-Amarna in
Egypt. Exploration began in 1929 under French
auspices and (except for a break from 1939 to
1948) continued until 1970 under the direction of
Claude Schaeffer. They have resumed since
1974 under a series of French directors
(currently Margeurite Yon), thus continuing the
virtual sub-industry of scholarship generated by
this extraordinarily rich site.

History

Though it rose to prominence towards the end of
the Bronze Age (late second millennium BC), the
earliest settlements at Ras Shamra go back
much earlier. Neolithic remains were found at the
base of the tell, dating from the seventh
millennium. The earliest links of the inhabitants
were probably with the Upper Euphrates area. By
the fourth and early third millennium, contacts
extended as far as the lower Euphrates or
Mesopotamia. The city, lying close to Cyprus, a
rich source of copper, shared in the general rise
in sophistication of technology and political
organisation in the area in the Early Bronze Age
(third millennium BC) and through trade was
drawn into the orbit of the Mesopotamian world.
For the Mesopotamians, it offered access for
their goods, a source of permanent building
materials (wood and stone) and a point of
contact with the wider Mediterranean world.

A dark age descended around 2200 BC.
The city at this time seems to have been burnt
and its population probably diminished. A new
wave of migrations in the region, however,
brought fresh infusions of population with the
coming of the Amorites around 2000 BC. The
Canaanites (called sometimes proto-
Phoenicians), a Semitic-language group from the
south, formed the pre-dominant population
during the new millennium.

Ugarit's commercial potential as the key
point on the Mediterranean/Mesopotamian route
was fully exploited during the second millennium.
Moreover, a new economic role was added when
the Egyptians, in a period of increasing
prosperity and stability, turned to Ugarit (along
with Byblos in northern Lebanon) as a source of
timber and other imports. This golden age saw
the establishment of a local Ugaritic dynasty

whose authority was underpinned by the balance struck between Egyptian power under the XI and XII Dynasties (c2000-1800 BC) and Hammurabi's dominance in Mesopotamia.

The diverse influences on this city state are clear from the remains seen today. The walled palaces, almost totally blank viewed from the outside perimeter, show Mesopotamian inspiration but the sheer luxury of their appointments (prolific use of courtyards, pools, internal gardens and light-wells) demonstrates a way of life which has its echoes only in Minoan civilisation on Crete[152]. It was at this time that the working of bronze became a specialty of the city and such value-added exports supplemented its role as an entrepot for local agricultural output.

Even at its peak, the Kingdom of Ugarit did not control extensive territory. The King's writ probably ran no further than the mountain range directly behind the city and the land between the present Turkish border to the north and Jeble, 25 km south of modern Latakia. But the land is exceptionally fertile and the city's prosperity was based on the agricultural riches of its hinterland and its trading role rather than extensive political control.

After a period of renewed uncertainty coinciding with the Hyksos invasion of Egypt (which ushered in the break between the Middle and New Kingdoms), Ugarit flourished once again in the Late Bronze Age (after 1600) in collaboration with the XVIII Dynasty in Egypt. The transition locally may have been marked by the arrival of a Hurrian elite linked to the new power in the northern Syrian region, the Kingdom of Mitanni. The population, however, remained basically Canaanite. Not the least of the new dynasty's skills was its ability largely to stay out of the great power games of the period, poised as it was between Mitanni and the Egyptians.

Ugarit's resilience and economic strength were shown in its recovery from a severe earthquake and tidal wave which struck in the middle of the 14th century BC (1365?) as a result of which most of the city had to be rebuilt. The subsequent golden age (late 14th-13th centuries BC) accounts for much of the building achievements now visible when the city benefited most directly from the Egyptian/Mitannian peace. The warehouses were overflowing and one of the earliest alphabets greatly simplified record-taking and accounting; thirty cuneiform symbols based on the principle of 'one sound, one sign'

were a much simpler method of recording language than the unwieldy pictogram-based cuneiform. The results of this greater facility can be seen in the range of correspondence and archives from this period: political dealings, tax and commercial accounts and religious texts, the latter throwing much light on the Semitic world in which the Israelite colonisation of Palestine was to unfold three centuries later. As well, there was an extensive archive of diplomatic correspondence in Babylonian syllabic cuneiform (the 'diplomatic language' of the time), some scholarly texts in Hurrian and a few in Cypriot-Minoan script.

Once the more remote power of the Hittites (based on Anatolia, central Turkey) came directly into play in the late 14th century BC, the balance was less easily maintained and the correspondence unearthed at Tell al-Amarna in Egypt (the capital of the heretic Pharaoh, Akhenaten) reveals much of the nervous state of mind in Ugarit with the King urging the Pharaoh to appease the Hittites with gifts. Maintaining sound relations with the Hittites (the Ugaritic navy was put at the Hittites' disposal), Ugarit avoided taking the Egyptian side in the century-long struggle which culminated in the great battle at Qadesh, just south of modern Homs in southern Syria (*Tell Nebi Mend).

The 13th century brought other changes, in particular links with the Aegean . But more ominous developments were about to end Ugarit's days of creative prosperity. The secondary effects of the population movements of c1200 BC touched off by the invasion of the 'Sea Peoples', probably accounts for the destruction of the city's palace-based economy.

Though there are later traces of casual or light occupation, the local economy probably reverted to a more traditional village-based system. There are some signs of a prosperous class re-emerging during the Persian period, but the tell was never again to accommodate the sizeable and prosperous urban community that had brought it to prominence for much of the second millennium. The beginning of the Iron Age which the Sea Peoples ushered in demanded new skills and technology and these were found elsewhere.

Visit

You enter the site on the western side. If you turn hard right from the ticket office, you will see the remains of the **fortress, walls and postern gate** which once protected the palace complex on this side of the city. (The gate for commoners has not been unearthed but may have been on the south

---

[152] A point made by Caubet in *Beaux Arts* (Hors Serie on Syria), 1993 p 15.

side of the city.) This defensive work was begun in the 15th century BC, not long after the city's recovery at the beginning of the late Bronze Age, but was later considerably re-built. The city walls were formed by smoothing off at 45⁰ the slope of the mound created by preceding occupation layers and covering this with a stone glacis (a seamless surface intended to give attackers no purchase). At this point (the only surviving section), the glacis was supplemented by a bastion or tower protecting the official entry. The walls of the tower are up to 5 m thick. Defenders could, at a later date, exit to harass besieging forces through a postern gate to the right. A passage to the gate was formed by tunnelling down through the mound and covering it with a corbelled vault.

If you ascend to the left of the bastion, you will come out at the small open area at the entrance to the **main palace** which dates from the second half of the Late Bronze Age phase of the city's occupation (late 14th-13th century BC). In front of you (west) is the outline of a portico (**A** on plan 61) with two pillar bases which marks the main entrance to the palace from the tower. The central passage between the pillars (originally wood on the present stone bases) leads into a small courtyard/reception area for guests from which the palace proper opens to the south (right after you cross the entrance threshold). As you enter this courtyard, the rooms on the left (**B**) were used to store one of the important archives unearthed in the French excavations. A U-turn to the right down a passageway leads to the guard room (**C**).

A 90⁰ turn to the right from the threshold entrance brings you straight into the main courtyard (**D**) of the palace, the paving of which still bears evidence of the channels used to feed water throughout the building. A well in the south west corner was the main water source for the palace. The throne room lay to the south, preceded by a hall marked by two columns.

Before you get further immersed in the maze of 90 rooms and 6500 m^2 comprising the main palace, pause here to note the fine quality of the stonework, showing the increasing sophistication of building methods of the time, including quite advanced plumbing and ornamental arrangements. All of the stonework carried intervening layers of wooden beams. What you see is only the first storey layout of a complex of buildings that often extended by at least another storey (where the bulk of the living quarters were probably located). This is a royal residence of a dynasty which had established itself comfortably in a society based on

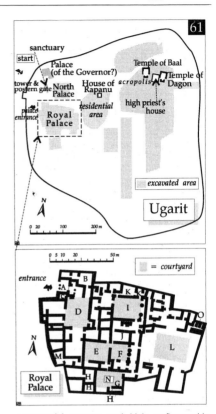

commercial acumen and high craftsmanship. The proliferation of rooms during the two hundred year life of the building reflected the growing administrative burden of its role, the accumulation of extensive archives as well the need to accommodate a growing court. The bureaucracy operated from here on a self-contained basis.

Take time to wander through the rest of the maze, orienting yourself on the main courtyard. If you continue to the next major room, opposite the point where you entered the courtyard, a left turn will take you into a space once thought to be a second courtyard (**E**) but now considered more likely to have served as a banquet hall. A courtyard (**F**) leads off this to the west (opposite to where you have reached). A little way to the south of this third courtyard is a further court (**G**), as large as the main one but a little trapezoidal in shape. It contains the remains of a large ornamental pool (**N**) which was fed by an elaborate water supply arrangement. Archives of political records (**H**) were located in the rooms overlooking this courtyard from the south and west. A final grouping of rooms lies around a fifth courtyard (**I**) separated from the third to the north by two banks of rooms. (The first was actually the palace's central archives (**J**).) Scattered throughout is evidence of the staircases which lead to the upper storeys where the private quarters of the royal family were probably located.

North of court I, a series of five large burial chambers (**K**) dug underneath the rooms served as the palace necropolis. The corbelled vaulting technique seen in the postern gate is again evident. Behind the main palace, to the east, was the royal garden (**L**) with verandahs and pavilions once equipped with ivory furniture.

Immediately to the north and south of the main palace complex, **subsidiary palaces** are found. To the north of the same entrance courtyard that leads to the principal palace lies a complex of buildings including a shrine (far left), a so-called 'Queen-Mother's residence' and to the right the 16th-15th century palace, possibly never rebuilt after the mid 14th century earthquake. The palace south of the principal complex covers 1000 m² and 33 rooms. East of the main palace was a **residential quarter** for the well-connected.

The main temple area or acropolis is on the hill about 200 m to the north east, the highest point of the site. In scrambling through the intervening ruins, you may come across the **House of Rapanu** (75m from the north west corner of the main palace) under which lies a burial vault, a domed rectangular underground chamber approached by a descending corridor (*dromos*).

There are two main temples on the **acropolis,** to Dagon and to Baal. Baal was the patron deity of the city (as distinct from the supreme deity in the Ugaritic pantheon who was known as El) The worship of Baal (originally a lesser god representing strength, fertility and control of the weather) or various local manifestations under this name, became closely associated with Canaanite religion as recorded in the Bible[153]. Baal worship and its attendant fertility rites survived among the Semites of Syria. The cult of the Semitic Baal/Bel ('lord' - see box page 167) in various manifestations continued into Roman times when Baal was syncretised into the local version of the Roman pantheon. Here at Ugarit, the Syro-Phoenician temple tradition (see box on page 18) begins on a modest scale. The **Baal temple** lies on the north western side of the acropolis. Its plan consists of an open courtyard (south) with a central altar. Beyond this on the north, the sanctuary is preceded by a vestibule. The walls of the latter were extraordinarily thick in order to conceal internal staircases on three sides leading upwards to form a tower rising above the *cella*. From this artificial 'high place' sacrifices could be performed, commanding a superb view of the great natural high place on which Baal was believed to dwell, Mount Casius to the north. Between the Baal and Dagon temples, in the remains of the priests' quarters, an archive of religious texts was discovered including chants.

The **temple of Dagon** (god of fertility in the Ugaritic pantheon) is 40 m to the south east. Its outline can only be seen in the foundation remains but it follows much the same basic plan as the Baal temple though the walls are even thicker (4-5 m).

Excavation trenches have been dug to extend knowledge of Ugaritic life into areas occupied by the classes dependant on the court. An area has been unearthed north of the acropolis (a pattern of housing blocks can be discerned) and there are two long extensions of the excavations on the citadel exposing private houses (some with burial vaults). These have provided evidence of the variety of artisanal activity in the city including ceramics, cosmetics, weaving and (in the port area) shipbuilding and the smelting and working of bronze, thus supplementing the wealth generated by the mass exportation of local produce such as wine, grain, dyed fabric and the preparation of dye from the murex shell), wood and salt.

Minet al-Beida

The port (**Minet al-Beida** - 1 km north west) is currently a military area to which access is restricted. Excavations of the mound (1928-32) unearthed buildings of a more mundane nature. This was the Leucos Limen ('white harbour') of Greek sources, reflecting the fact that this port regained a degree of importance up to Seleucid times (330 BC on).

REFS: *BG* pp 462-7; Dussaud *Topographie* pp 417 ff; Margueron *et al Au pays de Baal* pp 135-49; Sa`adé *Ougarit*; Yon M. (ed) *La Syrie au bronze récent*; Yon M 'Ugarit' in *OE* 1997; Yon M *La cité d'Ougarit* Paris 1997.

---

[153] The worship of Baal in this area is associated with the classical Mount Casius now known as Jebel al-`Aqra which rises from the coast to a height of 1728 m to the north of *Ras al-Basit.

Y

Yabrud

VARIANTS: Iabruda (Lat)
PERIOD: Rom RATING: - MAP: 64 ITIN: 3b
LOCATION: 8 km south west of Nabk. Left turn off Damascus/Homs motorway 81 km north of Damascus.

Yabrud lies in a fertile pocket on the edge of the forbidding terrain of the Anti-Lebanon and has evidence of settlement going back tens of thousands of years. It once formed part of the domains of Agrippa II, perhaps ceded to him as part of the Tetrarchy of Lysanias by Claudius in AD 53 (*Roman Road – Wadi Barada). It was the seat of a bishop in the early Christian period. The Greek Catholic Cathedral of Constantine and Helen (100 m on right after start of one-way street) seems to have been built largely with elements of the former Temple of Jupiter. The worship of Jupiter in his local form (Jupiter Yabrudis) seems to have achieved wider fame and an altar to Malekiabrudis has been unearthed in Rome. The church contains a good collection of icons (sacristy to right of altar). The bases of three Roman columns (part of the peripteral arrangement) can be seen to the south. Other remains, perhaps of a temple, are found on the tell to the north, looking out over the Anti-Lebanon, and a single monolith tomb lies on the western edge of town.

There are several Roman tombs 3 km to the west, cut into the limestone rock, one (third century) with two lions in relief besides the door (not easy to distinguish) and eleven carved relief panels. Other rock-cut tombs are found left of the Maalula road (south west).

REFS: BG p 305-6; Dussaud *Topographie* p 284; Nasrullah, Joseph 'Le Qalamoun à l'époque Romano-Byzantine' in *AAAS* 1952, 1958.

Z

Zalebiye

VARIANTS: Annoucas (?Grk); Regia Dianae Fanum (Lat)
PERIOD: Byz RATING: - MAP: 72, 73
ITIN: 12a

LOCATION: Although only 2 km downstream along the Mid Euphrates from *Halebiye (with which it shared control of river traffic), there is no direct access - no boats, ferry or bridge being available on the river near this point. To reach Zalebiye, therefore, you need to cross to the north bank of the Euphrates at Deir al-Zor and follow the sealed road north for about 55 km. (A track leads from the main road to the railway station near the ruins, the remaining short distance needs to be covered on foot.)

Alternatively, you could cross at Raqqa and travel downstream (c70 km). For a good view of the fortifications, the Raqqa/Deir al-Zor train passes quite close.

The history of Zalebiye marches closely with that of the complementary fortress on the right bank of the Euphrates, Halebiye. Being in a worse state of preservation, smaller in extent, and until recently less accessible, Zalebiye has been infrequently visited.

The fortress, like Halebiye, was established in the period when the Palmyrenes were unwisely attempting to assert their control in the area to test Roman dominance (*Palmyra - for Zenobia's rebellion). The fortress was improved as part of the defensive works of the Byzantine Emperor Justinian. The use of less solid construction techniques and the effects of earthquakes and river flooding (not to mention the recent use of its stone as ballast for the railway) have done considerably more damage to the fabric than is the case at Halebiye. The basic plan is an elongated rectangle narrowing to a point at the northern end, strengthened by square towers. Only the eastern half of the rectangle survives, the wall on the west having been swept into the river. The east wall (which carries six towers) gives on to the plateau and is marked by an imposing entrance gateway. To the north and east lay suburbs greater in extent than at Halebiye.

One kilometre upstream from Zalebiye remains can be seen of a dam built across the Euphrates and, on the eastern bank, an off-take canal. These works probably date back at least to the first century AD and probably to the Late Bronze Age. The canal was still in use in the Arab middle ages when it was named after Semiramis, the legendary Arab queen.

REFS: *BG* p 486; Bell *Amurath* pp 67-8; Calvet & Geyer pp 19-26; Dussaud *Topographie* p 486; Lauffray *Halabiyya*; Poidebard *Trace* pl LXXXIII-IV.

Zarzita

VARIANTS:
PERIOD: Byz ALT: 550 m RATING: - MAP: 68
ITIN: 9a

LOCATION: On the western slopes of Jebel Sheikh Barakat in the Jebel Halaqa region of 'dead cities'. Branch left 1.5 km south of Saint Simeon for *Qatura then continue c+1.5 km west.

Rather bleak stone ruins, a few arches but, on the whole, nothing memorable except the splendid view over the Plain of Amuq, the rich plain to the east of Antioch.

Little remains of the sixth century church with a single nave but 30 m south east of the church lies a tower, the two once connected by a *stoa* or colonnade. Built of large stone blocks, the tower measures 4 m by 4 m with the ground floor slightly overhung by the second storey. The lower floor housed a *ciborium* or baldachin, possibly marking the altar of a small chapel. The second storey was presumably a recluse's living quarters. There is an inscription on the cornice which reads: *Simon, priest, built this in the month of June 500. Eusebius, architect, John Mar [...]. Lord, help us.* A small (detached) porch nearby is dated earlier (423).

The village seems to be basically of the fifth and sixth centuries from the period when the local agricultural industry was flourishing and there was surplus to support a large number of monastic communities.

REFS: Butler *PE* II/B/5 pp 246-8; Pena *et al Reclus* pp 165-9.

4. ITINERARIES

4- SUMMARY OF ITINERARIES

1   **Damascus** - ten walking itineraries

    Old City

a   Umayyad Mosque (***)
b   Citadel, Northern Walls, Gates (*)
c   Suq al-Hamidiye Area (*)
d   Khans, Azem Palace (*)
e   Straight Street (*)
f   South West Quarter

    Ottoman City
g   National Museum (**)
h   Tekkiye Mosque (*)

    Extensions to Old City
i   Salihiye Quarter (*)
j   Midan Quarter

2.   **Hauran**

a   Eastern Hauran (Bosra, Ezraa)
b   Jebel al-Arab

3.   **Around Damascus**

a   Dumeir/Haran al-Awamid
b   Seidnaya/Maalula/Yabrud
c   Barada Gorge

4.   **Orontes** Towns

-    Homs, Hama, Apamea, Shaizar, Deir Soleib

5.   **Southern Littoral**

a   Tartus and Inland
b   Krak des Chevaliers
c   Tartus/Ismaeli Castles/Qalaat Marqab/
     Baniyas

6.   **Central Mountains**

-    Qalaat Maniqa/Qalaat Ben Qahtan/
     Jeble/Qalaat Mehelbeh

7   **Northern Littoral**

a   Qalaat Saladin
b   Jisr al-Shugur/Bakas/Qalaat Burzey
c   Ugarit to Ras al-Basit

8.   **Aleppo** - seven walking itineraries

    Walled City

a   Citadel (**)
b   Great Mosque (*)
c   Suqs and Khans (**)
d   South Quarter (*)

    Outside the Walls

e   Museum (**)
f   Jdeide Quarter (*)
g   Mashhad al-Hussein

9.   **Dead Cities** (Belus Massif) - three routes

a   Jebel Semaan
b   Jebel al-Ala area
c   Jebel Zawiye/Maarat al-Numan/Jebel Riha

10. **North of Aleppo**

a   Cyrrhus/Ain Dara
b   Membij/Qalaat Najim

11. **South of Aleppo**

a   Qinnesrin/Ebla
b   Qasr Ibn Wardan/Anderin
c   Khanazir/Isriya

12. **Mid Euphrates** -

a   Qalaat Jaber/Resafe/Raqqa/
     Halebiye
b   South of Deir al-Zor (Qalaat Rahba/Dura
     Europos/Mari/Baghuz)

13. **North East Syria**

a   Circesium
b   Tell Brak/Tell Halaf/Ain Divar

14. **Central Desert**

-    Qasr al-Heir East/Palmyra/Qasr al-Heir
     West/Harbaqa Dam

Quick Itinerary

Most visitors will not have the time to explore more than a selection of the detailed itineraries described in this book. A visit of two weeks or less will need to concentrate on the sites marked *** in the gazetteer. Although a car is the preferred means of getting around, most major sites are reasonably accessible by public transport (tour or inter-city buses or in the case of major cities, train). In some cases, (eg Qalaat Saladin/Saint Simeon) a taxi trip from a major town (Latakia/Aleppo) would be required.

For a quick (seven to ten day) visit, the following sequence of sites might be considered (moving in a clockwise direction around the map):

- Damascus (2 days)
- Krak/Tartus
- Qalaat Marqab/Qalaat Saladin
- Latakia/Aleppo (with possible diversions to either Orontes towns or southern 'dead cities')
- Aleppo (two days - one for diversion to Saint Simeon and northern 'dead cities')
- Hama/Homs/Palmyra
- Palmyra/Damascus

In following this sequence, visitors could be guided by relevant parts of the detailed itineraries below as well as by the location notes for each site.

Instead of visiting Palmyra on the way back from Aleppo, a visitor with a little more time available could supplement the short program with a second 'loop' itinerary (six days) taking in:

- Damascus/Palmyra
- Palmyra/Deir al-Zor
- Deir al-Zor/Halebiye/Raqqa
- Raqqa/Aleppo
- Aleppo/Damascus

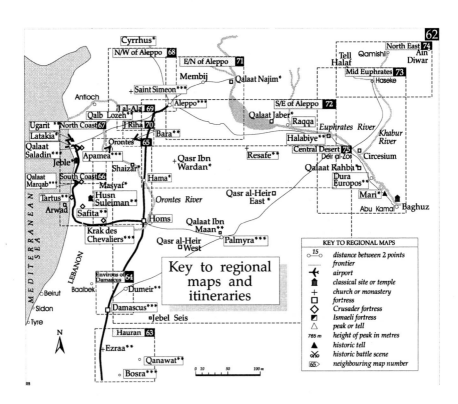

62

Cyrrhus*

N/W of Aleppo 68

North East 74

Tell
Halaf   Qamishli   Ain
Diwar

E/N of Aleppo 71

Mid Euphrates 73

Membij

Qalaat Najim*

Haseke

Antioch

Saint Simeon***

Aleppo***

S/E of Aleppo 72

Tal-Ala 69

Qalb Lozeh**

Qalaat Jaber*

Raqqa

Euphrates River

Khabur
River

Riha 70

Ugarit * North Coast 67

Bara**

Latakia*

Halabiye**

Qalaat
Saladin***

Orontes 65

Central Desert 75
Deir al-Zor   Circesium

Resafe**

Jeble*

Apamea***

Qasr Ibn
Wardan*

Qalaat Rahba

Dura
Europos**

Qalaat
Marqab***

South Coast 66

Shaizar*

Hama*

Mari*

Tartus**

Masyaf*

Orontes River

Qasr al-Heir
East *

Abu Kamal   Baghuz

Arwad

Husn
Suleiman**

Safita**

Homs

Qalaat Ibn
Maan**

Krak des
Chevaliers***

Qasr al-Heir
West

Palmyra***

LEBANON

Environs of
Damascus 64

Key to regional
maps and
itineraries

Dumeir**

Beirut   Baalbek

Sidon

Damascus***

Tyre

Jebel Seis

N

Hauran 63

Ezraa**

Qanawat**

0 10   50   100 m

Bosra***

KEY TO REGIONAL MAPS	
○—15—○	distance between 2 points
—	frontier
✈	airport
🏛	classical site or temple
+	church or monastery
□	fortress
◇	Crusader fortress
◪	Ismaeli fortress
△	peak or tell
765 m	height of peak in metres
▲	historic tell
⚔	historic battle scene
65▷	neighbouring map number

R8

Detailed Itineraries

1. Damascus

The ten walking itineraries described in the gazetteer are largely self-explanatory. Six describe areas of the old city of Damascus and mostly take as their starting point the W end of the Suq al-Hamidiye. Two describe areas in the Ottoman extension of the city (Tekkiye Mosque, National Museum) and the remaining two (Salihiye, Midan) cover older extensions of the

city beyond the Greco-Roman walled area. For the latter, you may need to use a taxi to reach the starting points.

The following is a list of itineraries with starting points and sugested time needed to complete the tour on foot:

ITIN	RATING	SECTOR	MAP	STARTING PT	DISTANCE	Time
Old City (Map 16)						
1a	***	Umayyad Mosque	17	Umayyad Mosque (Western entry)	n/a	1 hr
1b	*	Citadel and North Walls	18, 19	Citadel (West side)	3 km	2 hrs
1c	*	Suq al-Hamidiye Area	20	Suq al-Hamidiye (West)	2km	2-3 hrs
1d	*	Khans, Azem Palace	21	Umayyad Mosque (West)	2 km	2 hrs
1e	*	Straight Street	22	250m S of Suq al-Hamidiye	3 km+	2-3 hrs
1f	*	South West Quarter	23	Suq al- Hamidiye (West)	3 km	2 hrs
Ottoman City						
1g	**	National Museum	-	al-Quwatli St	n/a	2-3 hrs
1h	**	Tekkiye Mosque	24	al-Quwatli St	n/a	1 hr
Extensions to Old City						
1i	*	Salihiye	25	Jisr al-Abiad Square	3 km	2 hrs
1j	-	Midan	26	Suq al- Hamidiye (Midan St)	4 km	3 hrs

2. Hauran

All of the Hauran can be visited in day trips from Damascus. The Hauran is divided between two programs, though it would be possible to see all of the main sites (Ezraa (**), Bosra (***) **(MAP: 8)**, Shahba (*), Qanawat (**)) in one itinerary by combining the two.

2a Eastern Hauran - 320 km round trip - one day. Exit Damascus via Deraa motorway - 80 km S turn off left to **Ezraa** (**) - return to motorway for remainder of distance (25 km) to Deraa - take road 42 km E to **Bosra** (***) - [either: take up Itin 7b at **Suweida** (*) - 7 km E then 40 km N - or return to Damascus either via Deraa road or via Suweida].

2b Jebel al-Arab - 285 km round trip. Exit Damascus ring road via Suweida/Sitt Zeinab road (immediately W of airport road) - 87 km S to **Shahba** (*) - then follow location notes and Jebel al-Arab map for tour around Jebel al-Arab beginning with side trips to **Slim**, **Atil**, **Qanawat** (**) and **Sia** and then anti-clockwise circuit **Suweida**(*)/**Salkhad**/**Mushennef**(*)/**Shaqqa**.

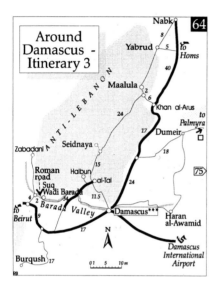

3. Around Damascus

There is limited scope for combining these sites given their location on separate roads radiating from Damascus, but loop itineraries combining small groups of sites might be organised as follows:

3a **Dumeir/Haran al-Awamid** - c90 km - half-day circuit. Exit Damascus via Palmyra road - follow site directions for **Dumeir** (**) (43 km) then **Haran al-Awamid** (27 km) - return via direct road to Damascus.

3b **Seidnaya/Maalula/Yabrud** - 180+ km - half/full-day circuit (full day with picnic/lunch stop). Exit Damascus via road N to al-Tal (turn-off at 11.5 km) - +15 km N, **Seidnaya** - +26 km to **Maalula** (*) - **Yabrud** c12 km N - continue 8 km to Nabk (Damascus/Homs motorway) - possible visits to **Deir Mar Mousa** (*) (14 km NE of Nabk) or **Qara** (15 kms N of Nabk) - return to Damascus via motorway (81 km).

3c **Burqush/Barada gorge (Roman Road - Wadi Barada)/Zabidani** - c125 km - half-day circuit. Follow directions for **Burqush** (*) - return to Beirut highway, continue W 9 km to turn-off to Zabadani - follow directions for **Roman Road - Wadi Barada** - after visiting Roman road cutting, return W 2 km to Zabadani road - turn right at intersection (small dam .) 13 km to Zabadani/Bludan (restaurants, mountain resort) - return to Damascus via Beirut highway.

4. Orontes Towns

Several of these sites can be covered by prolonging the half-day trip from Damascus to Aleppo as few require an extensive diversion from the main N/S highway. Certainly **Homs** (MAP: **21)**, **Hama** (*) (MAP: **20)**, **Apamea** (***) (MAP: **7)** **Shaizar** (*) and Tell Nebi Mend could be covered in this way. **Deir Soleib** (*) is more accessible from Masyaf (*) and could be visited in conjunction with a trip to or from the coastal mountains. However, there are many advantages in a more leisurely circuit of the Orontes area from Hama which could also provide a base for expeditions into the steppe area to the east.

Orontes Towns - 150+ km - full day. From **Hama** (*) - take NW road (to Mhardeh) 28 km to **Shaizar** (*) - after visiting Shaizar,

take road W 20 km to Suq al-Biye, then +7 km N to Qalaat Mudiq (for **Apamea** (***)) - from Tell Salhab (+17 km S of Tell Mudiq) road S leads 38 km to **Masyaf** (*) [*but you may wish to divert into foothills from Tell Salhab to take in* **Qalaat Abu Qobeis** *which, along with Masyaf, is on itinerary 6*] - as you meet Hama/Masyaf main road, turn left (E) c3 km before taking road right (S) for **Deir Soleib**. Return to Hama 30 km.

Further options from Hama include **Qasr Ibn Wardan/Anderin** (*) - Itin 11b - and **Isriya** (*) (see location notes and Map 72).

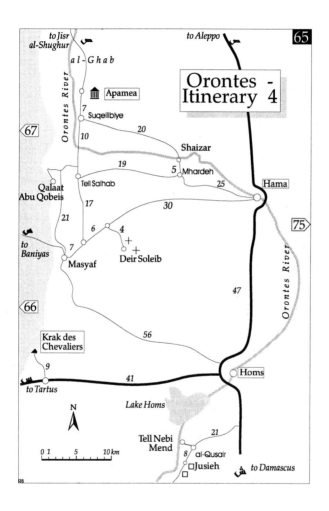

to Jisr al-Shughur

al-Ghab

Orontes River

to Aleppo

65

Apamea

7 Suqeilibiye

67

10

20

Shaizar

Orontes - Itinerary 4

19

5 Mhardeh

25

Hama

Qalaat Abu Qobeis

Tell Salhab

75

17

30

21

6 4

to Baniyas

7

Masyaf

Deir Soleib

66

47

Krak des Chevaliers

56

9

41

Homs

to Tartus

Orontes River

N

Lake Homs

21

Tell Nebi Mend

8 al-Qusair

0 1   5   10 km

Jusieh

to Damascus

RB

5. South Coast

5a **Tartus and Inland** - full day - 162 km - follow directions for **Qalaat Areimeh** - take road back to Tartus as far as the Safita turn-off - follow directions to **Qalaat Yahmur** - return to Safita road and follow directions to **Safita** (**) (164 km) - continue N by following directions for **Husn Suleiman** (**) (27 km) return to Tartus via Dreikish.

5b **Krak des Chevaliers** - half day (full day if combined with parts of 5a). The **Krak** (***) can be visited as a one-day trip from Damascus (and is so described in the gazetteer location notes). It could more conveniently be visited from Tartus, either as a half-day trip or combined with elements of 5a. Leave Tartus by the Homs motorway - after Tell Kalakh turn left, picking up the location guidelines - visit Krak - visit nearby **St George Monastery** - either return to Tartus [*or take direct road W to* **Safita** *(**)* *(continuing on to* **Qalaat Yahmur** *and Tartus) or return to Tartus motorway*].

5c   **Tartus/Ismaeli Castles/Qalaat Marqab/Baniyas** - a long itinerary (190 km if done as a round trip) which you may want to trim to a more comfortable one-day program. Exit Tartus via motorway to Latakia - follow notes for **Qalaat al-Kawabi** (T) (22 km) - visit

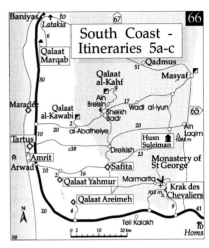

castle and return as far as Sheikh Badr road - continue to Sheikh Badr (10 km) - pick up location notes for **Qalaat al-Kahf** (**) (13 km) - visit al-Kahf and return to Sheikh Badr - take direct road E to **Masyaf** (*) (c24 km - see also itinerary 4) - [*note: possible option to include Qalaat Abu Qobeis - see itinerary 4*] return to coast motorway (54 km), by re-tracing Masyaf direction notes to Baniyas - short side trip (12 km round trip) to **Qalaat Marqab** (***) - return to Tartus via motorway (40 km) or continue N to Latakia (c45 km).

6. Central Coast

6 **Qalaat Maniqa/Qalaat Ben Qahtan/ Jeble/Qalaat Mehelbeh** - full day - 200+ km depending on starting/finishing points. Start either from Tartus or from Latakia - (from Latakia, order of visits could be reversed) - reach Baniyas and follow location notes for **Qalaat Maniqa** (*) (21 km) - return to coastal motorway and continue c+20 km N to just before Jeble turn-off - follow notes for **Qalaat Ben Qahtan** (round trip 48 km) - return to coastal road - visit **Jeble** (*) - continue N on coastal road to Snobar - turn inland following location notes for **Qalaat al-Mehelbeh** (c45 km round trip) - return to coastal road - return to Latakia/Tartus.

7. North Coast

7a **Qalaat Saladin** - use location notes for half day (70 km) round trip from **Latakia**. [*Could be combined with* **Qalaat Mehelbeh** *(*) from itinerary 6 or* **Qalaat Burzey** *(**) from itinerary 7b.*]

7b **Jisr al-Shugur/Bakas/Qalaat Burzey** - c175 km - full day. From Latakia, follow notes for **Qalaat Burzey** (**) (c55 km) - continue 15 km N along road that follows W side of Orontes Plain - visit **Jisr al-Shugur** - take main road to Latakia, following direction for turn-off to **Bakas** (T) (9 km round trip) - return to main road and continue along Latakia road (80 km). [*Note: if Qalaat Burzey is visited with itinerary 7a, remaining elements of this section could be covered during road trip Aleppo/Latakia.*]

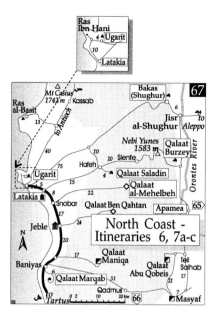

7c Ugarit to Ras al-Basit - 110+ km - half to full day (picnic at Ras al-Basit). From Latakia, follow location notes for **Ugarit** (**) (14 km) - from there, head W to join main Latakia/Kasab road (to Turkish border) and pick up notes for **Ras al-Basit** (T) - return to Latakia.

8. Aleppo - Seven Walking Itineraries

Except for the tour of the Mashhad al-Hussein, all the seven walks described are in the old walled area of the city or the adjoining Jdeide area immediately to the NW. No description is given of the still-charming areas built during the French mandate to the E of the main city park (Aziziye quarter) but as this is the main area for restaurants and outdoor cafes it is where visitors are likely to find themselves more than once during a visit, inspired to wander around the streets absorbing the characteristic blending of Western (from French Empire to art deco) and local architectural influences.

The following list if walking tours summarises practical information needed to plan a program of visits:

ITIN	RATING	SECTOR	MAP	STARTING POINT	DISTANCE	TIME
Walled City						
8a	**	Aleppo - Citadel	2, 3	Citadel - main gateway	1 k	2 hrs
8b	*	Aleppo - Great Mosque	2	Suqs - northern entrance	0.5 k	1 hr
8c	**	Aleppo - Suqs and Khans	4, 5	Suqs - northern entrance	2.5 k	3 hrs
8d	**	Aleppo - South Quarter	2	Citadel - main gateway	4 k	2-3 hrs
Outside the Walls						
8e	**	Aleppo Museum	-	Western edge of old city	-	2 hrs
8f	*	Aleppo - Jdeide Quarter	7	Bab al-Faraj Square	2 k	2 hrs
8g		Aleppo - Mashhad al-Hussein	8	Western outskirts	0.2 k	1 hr

9. Dead Cities (Belus Massif)

There are literally hundreds of so-called 'dead cities' in the limestone country (Belus Massif) W of Aleppo, as explained in *Dead Cities - General Note* The three itineraries described here take in most of the sites selected for this survey, grouping them as much as possible to rationalise a program of visits.

9a **Jebel Semaan area** (map 68, below) - c100 km round trip without diversions. From Aleppo, start with location notes for **Mushabbak** (*) - then pick up directions for

Qatura, **Zarzita**, **Refade** (*) and **Takleh** (*) - visit from there **Saint Simeon (MAP: 29)** (***) - take Afrin road N 14 km to **Barad** turnoff - 10 km bad road to Barad - return to Afrin road [*possible diversion 3 km further N to **Ain Dara** (*) which could also be done with itinerary 10a*] - return to Saint Simeon to pick up directions for **Basofan**, **Burjke**, **Burj Haidar** (*), **Fafertin** and **Kharrab Shams** (*) - return to Aleppo by continuing E to Afrin road and heading S for Aleppo. For a two day itinerary with Barad included, a natural break would come after Saint Simeon.

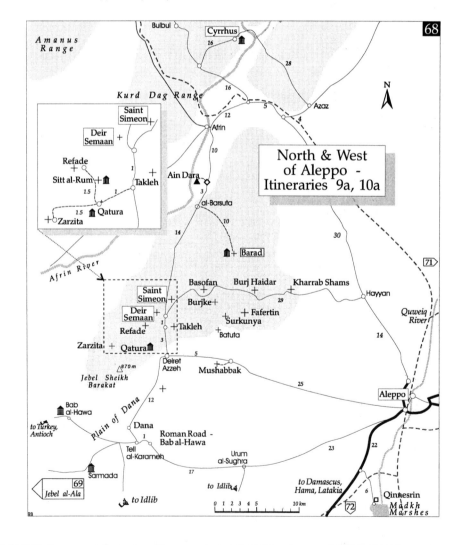

9. Dead Cities (Belus Massif)

9b **Jebel al-Ala** (map 69) 150+ km without diversions - one/two day(s) (one day if you confine your tour to sites with one or more * - ie the Harim road plus **Qalb Lozeh**). A complex itinerary given the bewildering range of roads in the area. To reach the starting point of the tour, exit Aleppo via the Damascus highway, turning right along the road that is sign-posted as leading to the main Turkish border crossing at Bab al-Hawa (40 km) (via Urum al-Sughra, Atareb) - before the border post, turn left at the road junction that also leads S towards Idlib - avoid,

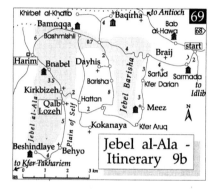

Jebel al-Ala - Itinerary 9b

however, the Idlib road and take the turn-off immediately to the right that goes initially through the village of Sarmada and leads eventually to **Harim** (*).

Using this Bab al-Hawa junction as 'point zero', the following sequence of sites is recommended - **Braij**, diversion to **Baqirha** (*) (+7 km), **Bamuqqa** (*), **Harim** (*) (21 km), **Kirkbizeh, Qalb Lozeh** (**) - [*if you wish to undertake the longer itinerary continue S from Qalb Lozeh for **Behyo, Beshindlaye**, return

to *Kirkbizeh* for **Kokanaya, Dayhis,** and/or **Meez**].

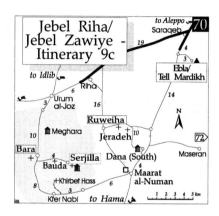

Jebel Riha/ Jebel Zawiye - Itinerary 9c

9c **Jebel Zawiya/Bara/Maarat al-Numan/Jebel Riha** - A relatively long (c200 km if done as out-and-back one-day trip from Aleppo) which can, however, be abridged and made a half-day diversion while travelling Aleppo/Latakia or Aleppo/Damascus. Leave Aleppo via Damascus highway - at Saraqeb junction (c38 km from Aleppo), take highway to Latakia - pass Riha (+19 km) and after +6km, at Urum al-Joz, pick up directions for **Bara** (**) - visit Bara - immediately S, pick up road E towards **Serjilla** (**) - return to Bara road and continue S for 5 km - at Basqala, turn left (E) for **Maarat al-Numan** (*) (10 km) - visit Maarat, then take Aleppo highway N and after 4 km, take left turn for **Dana (South)** (*) - proceed N along Riha road to **Jeradeh** (*) and **Ruweiha** (**) - return to Aleppo or resume journey to Latakia or Damascus.

10. North of Aleppo

10a **Cyrrhus/Ain Dara** - 200+ km round trip - half/full day - exit Aleppo by N road to Afrin - follow location notes for **Cyrrhus** (*) (76 km from Aleppo) - return to Azaz and main road (+32 km), continuing on W to Afrin (+10 km) - take road S +10 km and turn right (W) for **Ain Dara** (*) - visit Ain Dara and return to Aleppo via Afrin or take road S through St Simeon (+17 km - see Ain Dara location notes) and take Deiret Azze/Aleppo road (+36 km).

10b **Membij/Qalaat Najim** - 200 km round trip - full day - exit Aleppo via E (airport) road - at c12k (airport on right) turn left (N) on new Membij/Jezira road - follow direction notes for **Membij** - visit Membij - return to Jezira road, turn right after +17 km for **Qalaat Najim** (*) (+3 km) - return to Aleppo via same route.

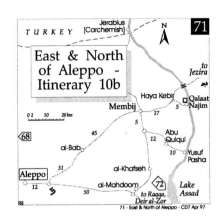

71 - East & North of Aleppo - CD7 Apr 97

11. South of Aleppo

11a **Qinnesrin/Ebla** - 157 km round trip - half-day - exit Aleppo on main road to Damascus - follow location notes for **Qinnesrin** (T) (31 km) - return to main Aleppo/Damascus highway and travel S to Saraqeb junction (50 km from Aleppo) - pick up notes for **Ebla** (*) +9 km - return to Aleppo via main highway or continue with itinerary 11b.

11b **Qasr Ibn Wardan/Anderin** - probably best done as part of a wider itinerary (eg Aleppo/Damascus), this itinerary involves a detour of 162 km from the main Aleppo/Damascus highway at Hama - allow a half day - from Hama by-pass, follow notes for **Qasr Ibn Wardan** (**) - continue NE

following notes for **Anderin** (T) +25 km - return via same route [*though four-wheel drive vehicles would have option of picking up the Khanazir route covered in itinerary 11c*].

11c **Khanazir/Isriya** - 130+ km round trip to Khanazir - full day+ - exit Aleppo by E road (airport/Raqqa) - just as new Jezira road diverges NE, take the road heading S towards al-Sfire (14 km from turn-off) - continue heading SE +40 km along track to Khanasir - *+56 km to Isriya (*) from where options for continuing W (track only) to connect with* **Anderin** *(itinerary 11b) or SW on new sealed road to Isriya/Selemiya*].

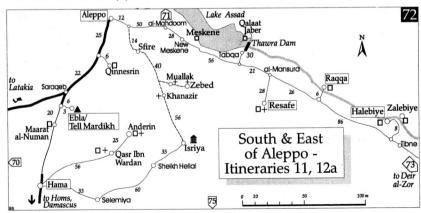

12. Mid Euphrates

12a **Qalaat Jaber/Resafe** - 345 km without diversions - full day. Best covered as one-way itinerary Aleppo/Deir al-Zor (or vice versa) Aleppo/Halebiye 279 km; Halebiye/Deir al-Zor 66 km - exit Aleppo on airport/Raqqa road - 146 km SE to turn-off for Tabqa/al-Thawra (new town for Euphrates dam) - take turn-off

(left) and cross dam wall (permission may be needed), picking up location notes for **Qalaat Jaber** (*) - return to main road - continue SE +21 km to al-Mansura - turn-off to right (S) for **Resafe** (**) +28 km, see location notes - visit Resafe, return to main road - continue +26 km E to Raqqa turn-off - turn left (N) and cross Euphrates to **Raqqa** - return to main road and resume SE road +85 km (12 km before Tibne) - turn-off left 8 km to **Halebiye** (**) - visit Halebiye and return to main road - resume journey SE via Tibne to Deir al-Zor (58 km from Halebiye turn-off).

12b **South of Deir al-Zor (Qalaat Rahba/Dura Europos/Mari/Baghuz)** - full day round trip - 270 km plus diversions - exit Deir al-Zor by Abu Kemal road (right bank of Euphrates heading SE) - 45 km pick up directions for **Qalaat Rahba** (*) - resume SE journey +48 km - pick up directions for **Dura Europos** (**) - return to main road and resume road SE +24 km - turn left, for **Mari** (*) (see location notes) - return to main road, continue SE towards Abu Kemal and pick up location notes for visit to **Baghuz** on left bank of Euphrates - return same road to Deir al-Zor.

13. North East Syria

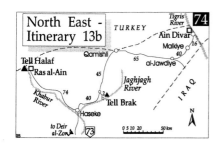

13a **Circesium** - 52 km round trip from Deir al-Zor - see Circesium (T) location notes (and **MAP: 73** above).

13b **Tell Brak/Tell Halaf/Ain Divar** - three destinations difficult to combine into a single itinerary but which could separately be visited from either Qamishli or Haseke using the location notes. Except for **Tell Brak** (T) (42 km NE of Haseke), each requires a good half-day though the roads are relatively fast in this part of Syria.

14. Central Desert

Qasr al-Heir East/Palmyra/Qasr al-Heir West/Harbaqa Dam - 470 km plus diversion - at least two full days needed to include both Umayyad castles and Palmyra (including *Qalaat Ibn Maan (*)). For many visitors, however, Palmyra will be an out-and-back itinerary from Damascus (and it is so described in the location notes). This itinerary includes it as a final prize in the clockwise tour of Syria but the order could as easily be reversed.

Exit Deir al-Zor by Palmyra/Damascus road across the central desert - at c100 km point, pick up directions for **Qasr al-Heir East** (*) - return to main road and continue 110 km to **Palmyra** (***) - after Palmyra (at least one day required for a full survey) continue along road to Damascus, picking up directions for **Harbaqa Dam** and Qasr al-Heir West from the second turn-off to Homs - return to Damascus road and continue via **Dumeir** (see itinerary 2a).

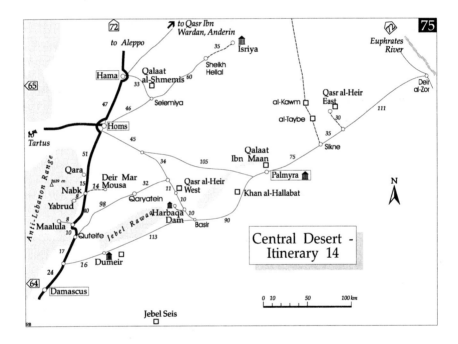

Central Desert - Itinerary 14

THEMATIC MAPS

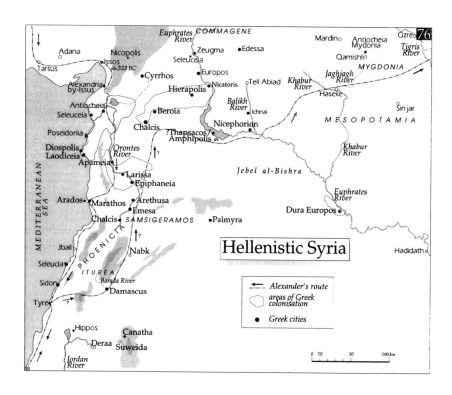

Hellenistic Syria

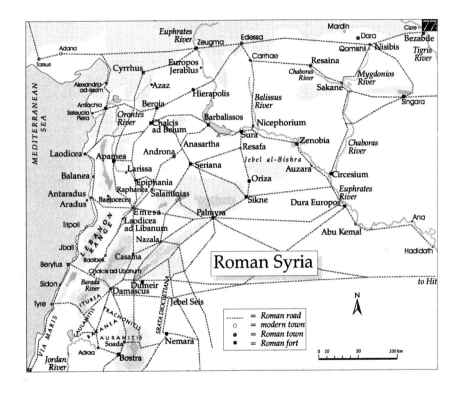

Roman Syria

= Roman road
○ = modern town
● = Roman town
■ = Roman fort

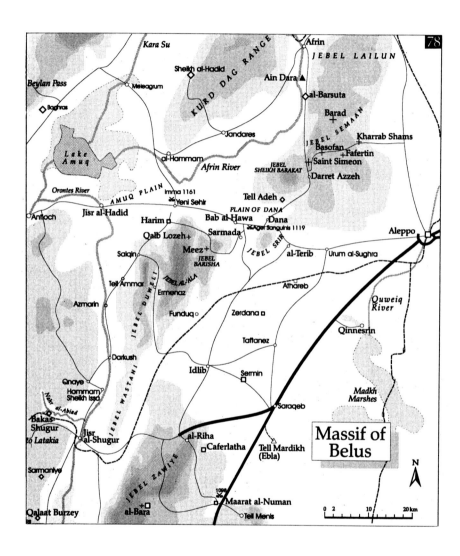

Kara Su

Afrin

JEBEL LAILUN

Sheikh al-Hadid ◇

Ain Dara ▲

KURD DAG RANGE

Beylan Pass

Meleagrum ○

◇al-Barsuta

◇ Baghras

Barad
+

Jandares ○

JEBEL SEMAAN

Kharrab Shams
+

Basofan
+Fafertin

Lake Amuq

al-Hammam ○

Afrin River

JEBEL SHEIKH BARAKAT

+Saint Simeon

◇Darret Azzeh

Orontes River

AMUQ PLAIN

Imma 1161

Tell Adeh ◇

Yeni Sehir

PLAIN OF DANA

○Antioch

Jisr al-Hadid

Harim ◻

Bab al-Hawa

◇Dana

Tell Ager Sanguinis 1119

Aleppo ◻

Qalb Lozeh+

Sarmada

JEBEL SRIN

Meez+

JEBEL BARISHA

al-Terib

Urum al-Sughra

Salqin ◇

Quweiq River

Tell Ammar

JEBEL AL-A'LA

Ermenaz

Athareb ◻

Azmarin ○

Funduq ○

Zerdana ◻

Qinnesrin ○

JEBEL DUWEILI

Taftanez

Darkush ○

Idlib

Sermin
◻

JEBEL WASTANI

Qnaye ◇

Madkh Marshes

Hammam Sheikh Issa

○Saraqeb

Nahr al-Abiad

Bakas-Shugur ◇

to Latakia

Jisr al-Shugur

al-Riha

Massif of Belus

◻Caferlatha

Tell Mardikh (Ebla) △

N
↑

Sarmaniye ◇

JEBEL ZAWIYE

0 2   10   20 km

Qalaat Burzey ◇

+◻ al-Bara

1098
◻ Maarat al-Numan

○Tell Menis

78

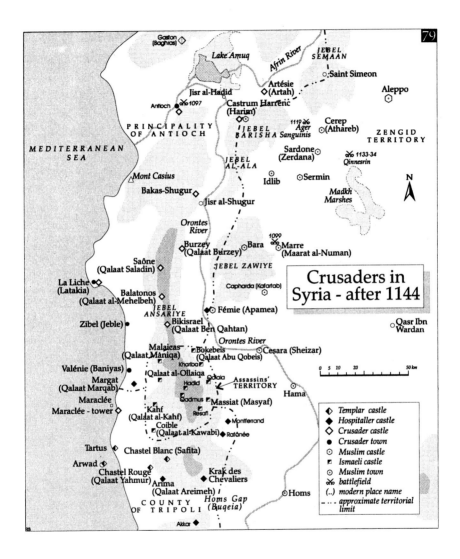

79

Gaston
(Baghras)
Lake Amuq
Afrin River
JEBEL
SEMAAN
Saint Simeon
Artésie
Jisr al-Hadid
(Artah)
Aleppo
Antioch 1097
Castrum Harrenc
(Harim)
PRINCIPALITY
OF ANTIOCH
1119 Ager
JEBEL
BARISHA Sanguinis
Cerep
(Athareb)
ZENGID
TERRITORY
MEDITERRANEAN
SEA
Sardone
(Zerdana)
1133-34
Qinnesrin
JEBEL
AL-ALA
Mont Casius
Idlib
Sermin
N
Bakas-Shugur
Jisr al-Shugur
Madkh
Marshes
Orontes
River
Burzey
(Qalaat Burzey)
Bara
Marre
(Maarat al-Numan)
1099
Saône
(Qalaat Saladin)
JEBEL ZAWIYE

**Crusaders in
Syria - after 1144**

La Liche
(Latakia)
Balatonos
(Qalaat al-Mehelbeh)
Capharda (Kafartab)
JEBEL
ANSARIYE
Fémie (Apamea)
Qasr Ibn
Wardan
Zibel (Jeble)
Bikisrael
(Qalaat Ben Qahtan)
Orontes River
Malaicas
(Qalaat Maniqa)
Bokebeis
(Qalaat Abu Qobeis)
Cesara (Sheizar)
Kharibai
Valénie (Baniyas)
Qalaat al-Ollaiqa
Odaia
Hadid
Assassins'
TERRITORY
Margat
(Qalaat Marqab)
Maraclée
Cadmus
Massiat (Masyaf)
Hama
Maraclée - tower
Kahf
(Qalaat al-Kahf)
Resafi
0 5 10   20   50 km
Coible
(Qalaat al-Kawabi)
Montferrand
Ratânée
Tartus
Chastel Blanc (Safita)
Arwad
Chastel Rouge
(Qalaat Yahmur)
Arima
(Qalaat Areimeh)
Krak des
Chevaliers
Homs Gap
(Buqeia)
Homs
COUNTY
OF TRIPOLI
Akkar

◇ Templar castle
◆ Hospitaller castle
◇ Crusader castle
● Crusader town
⊙ Muslim castle
▨ Ismaeli castle
⊙ Muslim town
⚔ battlefield
(..) modern place name
–··· approximate territorial
limit

GLOSSARY OF ARCHITECTURAL AND OTHER TERMS

ain	spring, well (Arb ''*ain*')
ablaq	alternating courses of contrasting stone, especially in Mameluke or Ottoman periods (Arb)
absidiola	large niche, usually semi-circular, often built into a corner (Lat)
acropolis	elevated (usually fortified) administrative or religious centre of a Greek city (Grk)
acroteria	ornaments placed above the lower angles of a pediment (Grk)
adyton	inner sanctuary within the *cella* of a temple, usually in the form of a broad niche (Grk)
aedicule	niche or shrine housing a cult image (fr Lat)
agora	open meeting place or market (Grk)
aisle	in a basilica, the elements of the building lying either side of the central passage or nave
ambulatory	colonnade with roof encircling a small temple
ambo	pulpit in a Christian basilica (Grk)
andron	men's meeting room in a Greek or Roman city (Grk, Lat)
anta	squared pilaster continuing the line of a side wall, eg of a *cella* (pl *antae*, Lat)
apse	structure (often semi-circular in shape and vaulted by a semi-dome) terminating the east end of the nave of a church
apodyterium	changing room of a Roman bath (Lat)
arcosolium	burial niche, carved into rock with roof in the form of an arch (Lat)
architrave	lowest division of an entablature; or the moulded frame around a window or door
ashlar	square-shaped stones laid in regular courses
atrium	courtyard (in a Roman house) or forecourt (in front of a Byzantine church)
bab	door, gateway (Arb)
baldachin	or baldaquin - free-standing canopy above an altar, tomb, reliquary or throne (fr Itn 'baldacchino')
baptistery	part of a church (or separate building) intended for the baptism of converts
barrel vault	vault in the form of a half-cylinder
barbican	gateway usually defended by twin flanking towers
basilica	building of Roman origins in the form of a central nave flanked by two aisles. The nave is higher than the aisles and is lit by a clerestory supported on double colonnades.
bastion	strong-point in a fortification, usually a fortified tower
beit	house (Arb)
bema	tribune or raised area (usually horseshoe in shape) placed in the chancel of a Byzantine church (Grk)
bimaristan	see '*maristan*"
bossage	practice of leaving the outer surface of a block of stone rough and projecting, thus providing a rusticated appearance
brattice	see 'machicolation"
burj	tower (Arb)
caldarium	the hot room of a Roman bath (Lat)
cardo maximus	main (usually north/south) thoroughfare of a Roman city comprising a wide central carriageway flanked by colonnaded pavements on each side and lined with stalls, shops and public buildings (Lat)
caryatid	figure of a woman or man serving as a column or pier to support an architectural element (roof or portico) (fr Grk)
castrum	Roman fortress, rectangular in shape with corner towers (Lat)
cavea	semi-circular seating comprising the auditorium of a Roman theatre (Lat)
cella	central sacred chamber in a *Syro-Phoenician temple enclosure (Lat)
chancel	section (usually raised by a few steps) surrounding the altar of a church
chemin de ronde	walkway around the battlements of a medieval castle (Fr)
chevet	wall terminating the east end of a church - often semi-circular or rounded in shape (Fr)
ciborium	canopy construction, usually raised over the high altar (Lat)

citadel	stronghold commanding a city (cf *acropolis*)	fosse	ditch surrounding a Crusader or Arab fortification (fr Fr)
clerestory	the upper structure flanking a nave, supported on columns or piers set between the side aisles and the nave. Usually broken by windows to provide light to the interior of a basilica	frieze	middle segment of a clasical entablature
		glacis	smooth sloping surface of stone intended to deter scaling of a medieval fortification and to expose attackers to fire (fr Fr)
colonnade	columns set in rows supporting a roof structure or entablature	groin vault	vault formed over a square bay by the intersection of two barrel vaults
corbel	projecting stone supporting a decorative element or statue on the face of a wall	hammam	public bath (Tur)
		haremlek	private quarters of an Ottoman house (Tur)
Corinthian	type of capital (Grk in origin) decorated with acanthus leaves	Hippodamian grid	
cornice	top section of the classical entablature, usually a projecting moulding		concept of urban planning developed by Hippodamus of Miletus based on a grid with segments (*insulae*) c 110 m by 55 m. Applied by the Seleucids to most of their cities in Syria
crypt	chamber (often underground) set beneath the floor of a church		
cryptoporticus	a dark passage, usually semi-underground, often flanking an open colonnade (*porticus*) (Grk/Lat)	hypogeum	underground tomb chamber (Lat fr Grk)
		iconastasis	screen bearing icons separating nave from chancel in a Byzantine or Orthodox rite church (Grk)
cupola	dome (Itn fr Lat)		
curtain wall	long run of straight wall between towers or bastions		
deir	monastery (Arb)	*in antis*	facade comprising a number of columns set between *antae* (see *anta*, Lat)
decumanus	major cross street (E/W) of a grid-planned Roman city intersecting with the *cardo maximus* (Lat)		
		insula	grid segments of a Greek/Roman city plan (see Hippodamian grid), rectangular in the proportion of 2:1 (Lat, 'islands' pl *insulae*)
diaconicon	small chamber, used as a sacristy, to the left of the chancel of a church (Grk)		
dikkah	platform in a mosque for the recitation of prayers (Arb)	Ionic	style of column capital deriving from one of the three classical Greek orders; the shape is based on a scroll
diwan	see *iwan*		
donjon	central fortified refuge or keep of a Crusader castle		
		iwan (or *liwan*)	large open reception area off a courtyard with high arch opening, usually surrounded with benches and with a fountain at the centre (Arb)
Doric	classical order based on a simple undecorated capital		
distyle	two columns at the front of a temple (Lat)		
distyle in antis	two columns set between protruding pilasters (*antae*) at the front of a temple (Lat)	jamiaa	large congregational mosque (Arb)
		jebel	mountain (Arb)
entablature	horizontal elements connecting a series of columns (comprises cornice, frieze and architrave in the classical order)	juggled voussoirs	
			voussoirs (elements of an arch - see below) the edges of which are not straight but cut to fit together in a dovetail pattern
exedra	a semi-circular indentation in a wall or line of columns; room opening across its full width into a larger space, often furnished with seats (Lat)		
		kalybe	open-fronted shrine with niches for the display of statuary ('hut' or 'cabin' - Grk)
fleuron	sculptured ornament in the form of a flower (Fr)	keep	innermost structure of a castle, strengthened to serve as a last refuge for the defenders
fluting	vertical grooves or ridges set in the surface of a column		
		khan	combined warehouse and hostel for merchants (Arb)
		khanqah	Sufi monastery (Arb)

khatun	princess, especially a woman with elite connections during the time of Nur al-Din and the Ayyubids (Kurdish)
khirbet	ruin (Arb)
kufic	type of script employed especially in the early Arab period with highly stylised and pointed terminals (Arb)
limes	limits of Roman administration or control; military line of control (Lat)
lintel	horizontal member above a doorway or window to support surmounting masonry
liwan	synonymous with *iwan*
loculus	niche inserted lengthwise into wall of a burial chamber or tower to contain a body (Lat)
loggia	a colonnaded arcade providing a sheltered extension of a hall or other entertainment space (Itn)
machicolation	a projection from a masonry wall intended to allow liquids or missiles to be rained upon attacking forces. It usually takes the form of an opening with corbels on each side supporting a surmounting shelf, to which the term brattice is also applied
madrasa	school for the teaching of Islamic law, often endowed by a prominent citizen (Arb, pl *madaris*)
maqsura	washing/scrubbing room of an Arab bath (Arb)
maristan	(*bimaristan*) institution for medical care and training (Arb fr Persian)
martyrium	small chamber or chapel for the burial or preservation of relics of a saint or martyr (Lat)
masjid	local mosque (Arb)
mashhad	building (literally 'place of witness') constructed over the tomb of a religious notable (Arb)
merlon	architectural embellishment rising above a parapet; a Mesopotamian device (often introduced into buildings of the Roman period in the form of a step-sided triangle
mihrab	niche, usually ornately decorated, intended to show the direction (*qibla*) of Mecca (Arb)
minaret	tower of a mosque (fr Arb)
minbar	pulpit in a mosque (used particularly for the preaching of the Friday sermon) situated to the right of the *mihrab* (Arb)
mithraeum	temple devoted to the cult of the Persian god, Mithras (Lat)
muezzin	man who recites the call to prayer from a minaret (Arb)
muqarnas	decorative treatment of an arch or dome support by clusters of triangular segments of a sphere, giving a 'stalactite' effect (Arb)
naos	sanctuary (Grk)
narthex	entrance vestibule located at the west end of a Byzantine church, usually running the full width of the building (Grk)
nave	central part of a basilica between the colonnades dividing off the side aisles
necropolis (-eis)	burial ground (Grk)
noria (nouriah)	large wooden water wheel to elevate water from a river, usually to supply a town via an aqueduct (Arb)
nymphaeum	structure enclosing a public fountain (dedicated to the nymphs), usually with niches for statues (Lat)
odeon	concert hall or small theatre for the performance of music (fr Grk)
orchestra	paved space (semi-circular) between stage and auditorium of a Roman theatre
oratorium	oratory or small chapel devoted to prayer (Lat)
orthostat	large slab of stone (usually basalt) set to line the lower part of a wall
pandocheion	large building to house pilgrims (Grk: 'inn' - origin of the Arab word, *funduk*)
Pasha	Ottoman honorific usually bestowed on the Governor (*wali*) of an Ottoman province (*vilayat*) (Tur)
pediment	triangular, low-pitched gabled end to a classical building, framed by a cornice
pendentive	triangular segment of a sphere, used to carry the transition between a square base and a round surmounting dome
peribolos	outer area of a sacred enclosure, surrounding an inner enclosure or *temenos* (Grk)
peripteral	temple with *cella* surrounded by a colonnade or peristyle
peristyle	colonnaded and roofed corridor running around the edges of an internal courtyard; or the outer colonnade of a peripteral temple

pilaster	engaged pier, usually a shallow rectangle in section		the transition to an octagonal or domed upper structure
portal	doorway, usually treated in a monumental style	stele	upright narrow slab of stone, usually inscribed (fr Grk)
portico	porch or structure sheltering the outer part of a doorway, usually supported on columns	stoa	porticed structure supported at the front by columns, at the rear by a wall (Grk)
portcullis	heavy wooden grill gateway designed to drop from within a tower, preventing access by invaders	synthronon	raised platform or semi-circular bench, often intended to frame a bishop's throne in the apse of a Byzantine or Orthodox church (Grk)
praesidium	camp or military headquarters (Lat)	Syrian arch	broad semi-circular arch, usually framed within the pediment of a building or arch, with an ornately decorated architrave
praetorium	residence of a Roman governor; barracks for Roman troops (Lat)		
principia	headquarters building for Roman troops (Lat)	talus	synonymous with glacis
pronaos	porch at the entrance to the *cella* of a temple (Grk)	*tekke*	Dervish monastery (Tur)
propylaeum	monumental pillared entrance to a *temenos* or sacred precinct (pl *propylaea* - Lat fr Grk)	*temenos*	sacred enclosure providing space (mostly outdoors) for worshippers to gather. See also *peribolos* (Grk)
prothesis	small chamber on the right of the chancel of a church (cf *diaconicon* on the left) used in the preparation of the liturgical offerings (Grk)	tell	mound or artificial hill formed by the accumulated debris of centuries of occupation (fr Arb)
pseudo-peripteros		*tessera*	small pieces of stone used in mosaics (Lat fr Grk)
	use of pilasters on the outer wall (e g of a *cella*) to resemble a peristyle	tetraconque	shape which results when a square described within columns or piers billows out on each side to form semi-circular lines of columns (fr Grk: 'four shells')
qa`a	reception room (Arb)		
qadi	Muslim judge (Arb)		
qalaat (qalaa)	castle, fortress; also refers to any old remains assumed to have served that purpose (Arb)	*tepidarium*	the warm room of a Roman bath (Lat)
qibla	place towards which prayer is directed in Islam - ie the wall of a mosque which faces in the direction of Mecca (Arb)	tetrapylon	arrangement of columns (often in four groups of four) used to mark a major intersection of a Roman city (fr Grk)
qubba	dome (Arb)	*tetrastyle*	four columns at the front of a temple (Grk)
redoubt	central place of refuge in the event of a Crusader castle being overrun (cf keep)	transept	a transverse section inserted in a basilica plan, usually between the main nave and the apse, thus transforming the rectangular plan into a cross shape
scaenae frons	elaborate stone facade behind the stage area of a Roman theatre, usually richly decorated with columns and niches (Lat)		
selamlek	public entertainment quarters of an Ottoman house (Tur)	*triclinos*	Grk equivalent of *triclinium*
		triclinium	dining room of a Roman house (originally with three divans) (Lat)
sentry walk	see *chemin de ronde*	*triforium*	gallery above the arches flanking a nave (Lat)
serail, seraya	palace; headquarters of a governor or senior administrator (Tur)	turba	tomb or mausoleum (Tur)
		tycheion	shrine or temple in honour of a city's protecting goddess (Tyche) (Grk)
soffit	exposed lower surface of a lintel or ceiling beam	vilayat	see *wali*
suq	market (Arb)	vomitorium	corridors and stairway system enabling a large number of spectators to enter/exit a theatre (Lat)
squinch	a small arch or niche placed across a corner in order to carry		

voussoir	wedge-shaped stone used to form the components of an arch (fr Fr)	*wali*	governor of a Turkish province (*vilayat*) (Tur)
wadi	valley or watercourse, dry except during rain (Arb)	*waqf*	endowment intended for the upkeep of a mosque or *madrasa* (Arb)

CHRONOLOGY OF MAIN EVENTS

The list does not attempt to give comprehensive details of rulers, confining itself to those who are mentioned in the text or who made a substantial impact in their Syrian domains.

Entries in *italics* are references to major building programs or external historical events affecting Syria.

Bold is used for references to significant battles, and to major headings, places or personalities.

BC

c3100-2150 - Early Bronze Age

c2900	founding of Mari, Ebla
post 2500	development of Mari
2340-2150	*Akkadian Empire - Sargon of Akkad (r 2340-2284)*
2400-2250	*apogée of Ebla*
c2250	Mari and Ebla razed by Akkadians

c2150-1600 - Middle Bronze Age

c2100	arrival of Amorites
2050-1786	*Middle Kingdom in Egypt*
c2000	Ebla rebuilt
1900-1759	Mari's second golden age - Amorite dynasty (Zimri-Lim (r 1775-60)
18C	Amorite kingdoms of northern Syria
c1792-1750	reign of Hammurabi of Babylon
1759	Hammurabi of Babylon razes Mari - **Amorite Kingdoms** of north Syria escape direct Babylonian rule
1674-1567	*Hyksos period in Egypt*
c1600	*Ebla destroyed - by Hittites*

c1600-1200 - Late Bronze Age

1595	***Babylon falls to Hittites***
1567-1085	*New Kingdom in Egypt*
1550	Hittites arrive in Syria
post 1500	Egypt, **Hittites** and Mitanni compete for control of Syria
c1450-1360	Kingdom of Mitanni flowers
1425-17	*Thutmose IV Pharaoh of Egypt*
1417-1379	*Amenhotep III Pharaoh of Egypt*
1400-c1365	Ugarit's golden age - development of the alphabet
14C	Egyptian campaigns in Syria
1350	Hittites dislodge Mitanni in Syria
1304-1237	*Ramses II Pharaoh of Egypt*
1286	**Battle of Qadesh** - Ramses II vs Hittites
1284?	Egypt/Hittite peace treaty settles spheres of influence in Syria
13C	Ugarit in contact with Mycenaen Greece

1200-539 - Iron Age

c1200	**Sea Peoples invade Syrian coast**
12C	*period of prophets in Israel*
1200-1150	Aramean people arrive in Syria

970-931	*Solomon King of Israel*
9C	Arameans establish 'Neo-Hittite' city states in the North
890-842	Kingdom of Aram-Damascus resists expansion of Israel's influence northwards
856-612	Assyrian dominance
853	**Battle of Qarqar** - Assyrians defeat Aramean states' combined forces
732	**Assyrians take Damascus** - end city-state of Aram-Damascus
605-539	**Neo-Babylonians** (Chaldeans) control Syria
604-562	*Nebuchadnezzar neo-Babylonian (Chaldean) ruler*

539-333 - Persian Period

539	Cyrus takes Babylon and acquires Neo-Babylonian realms in Syria
521-486	*Darius I ruler of Persia*
490	*Greeks defeat Persians at Battle of Marathon*
486-463	*Zerxes ruler of Persia*

333-64 - Hellenistic (after 301, Seleucid) Period

333	**Battle of Issus** - Alexander of Macedonia defeats Persians under Darius III
323	death of Alexander
311-281	Seleucos I Nicator
301	army of Seleucos Nicator occupies northern Syria
223-187	Antiochos III Megas (the Great)
198	Antiochos the Great seizes Southern Syria from Ptolemies
175-164	Antiochos IV Epiphanes - raids Egypt
164-138	**civil wars** bring breakdown of Seleucid control

64 BC – AD 395 - Roman Period

64	**Pompey annexes Syria** - creation of *Provincia Syria* but with considerable local autonomy (eg Nabatean control of Damascus)
51-30	Cleopatra VII Philopater, Ptolemaic ruler
43-36	Mark Antony Governor of Syria
37-4	*Herod the Great's rule in Judaea*
31	***Battle of Actium*** *(Octavian defeats Antony)*
27-14 (AD)	*Octavian (Augustus) Emperor*

20	Roman/Parthian treaty establishes agreed boundary

AD

14-37	*Tiberius Emperor*
24-37	*Pontius Pilate Procurator of Judaea*
41-54	*Claudius Emperor*
54-68	*Nero Emperor*
66	*Jewish revolt against Roman rule - Vespasian appointed by Nero to suppress it*
69-79	*Vespasian Emperor (Flavian line begins)*
70	*Romans (under command of Titus) take and destroy Jerusalem*
81-96	*Domitian Emperor*
98-117	*Trajan Emperor*
105	Trajan annexes Nabatean kingdom - creates Provincia Arabia based on Bostra
113	Trajan annexes Dura Europos
114-6	Trajan's agressive policy in East against Parthians results in annexation (temporary) of Mesopotamia and Armenia
117-38	Hadrian Emperor - less agressive policy in East, moves frontier back to Euphrates
117	Damascus raised to *metropolis* by Hadrian
119	Hadrian visits Palmyra - renames city *Palmyra Hadriana*
138-61	*Antoninus Pius Emperor (Antonine line begins)*
161-80	*Marcus Aurelius Emperor*
late 2C	major Roman road-building projects in Syria Husn Suleiman - major construction phase Apamea - colonnaded main street built
162-6	major campaign against Parthians - Dura Europos retaken
180-92	*Commodus Emperor*
187	Septimius Severus marries Julia Domna (daughter of High Priest of Emesa)
193-211	Septimius Severus Emperor (Syrian line begins)
193	Governor of Syria, Pescennius Niger, revolts against new Emperor
194	Syria reorganised into four provinces

211	Dura Europos declared Roman *colonia*
212	Palmyra declared Roman *colonia*
211-17	*Caracalla Emperor*
212 *constitutio*	*antoniniana* declares all free inhabitants of Empire Roman citizens
218-22	*Marcus Antoninus (Elagabalus) Emperor*
222-35	*Alexander Severus Emperor*
224	Sasanian dynasty under Ardashir (r 224-41) takes power in Parthia
241-72	*Shapur I ruler of Sasanians*
244-9	*Philip 'the Arab' Emperor*
244	founding of Shahba to commemorate Philip's family
249-51	*Decius Emperor*
253-60	*Valerian Emperor*
256	**Dura Europos falls to Sasanians**
260	amid anarchy in Syria (Shapur I conquers as far as Antioch), Valerian captured (and later killed) by Sasanians at Edessa
260-8	*Gallienus Emperor*
260	Gallienus seeks help of Odenathus (Palmyrene leader) in pushing Sasanians back to Euphrates
267/8-72	**Zenobia** takes control on Odenathus' death
270-5	*Aurelian Emperor*
272	**Aurelian takes Palmyra - Zenobia captured**
273	Aurelian puts down second rèvolt in Palmyra
284-305	*Diocletian Emperor*
305-11	*Constantius Emperor (west), Galerius (east)*
306-37	*Constantine I Emperor*
313	*Edict of Milan recognises Christians' right to practice their faith*
325	*First Ecumenical council - Nicaea*
326	pilgrimage by Helena (Constantine's mother, later St Helen) to Jerusalem
330	Constantine dedicates **new capital - Constantinople**
337-61	*Constantius II Emperor*
361-3	*Julian 'the Apostate' Emperor*
375	*Arian schism in church*
379-95	*Theodosius I Emperor*
381	*Second Ecumenical Council - Constantinople*

395- 636 - Byzantine Period

395	Roman Empire formally split between east and west
395–408	Arcadius Emperor (east)
389–459	life of St Simeon 'the stylite"
422	'One Hundred Year Peace' with Sasanians
post 423	rise of Nestorianism
431	Third Ecumenical Council, Ephesus - condemns Nestorians
451	Fourth Ecumenical Council, Chalcedon - condemns Monophysites
474–91	Zeno Emperor
post 475	pilgrimage centre honouring St Simeon built
518–27	Justin I Emperor
527–65	Justinian Emperor
532	Justinian's 'eternal Peace' with Sasanians
532–7	building of Hagia Sophia, Constantinople
553	Fifth Ecumenical Council - Constantinople - fails to deflect Monophysite split by reviving condemnation of Nestorianism
565–78	Justin II Emperor
573	Chosroes (Persian ruler) raids Syria as far as Apamea, Antioch
582–602	Maurice Emperor
590–627	Chosroes II Persian ruler - gains throne with help from Maurice
602	Maurice murdered by usurper Phocas - Chosroes subsequently breaks treaty and invades Syria in retaliation
610–41	Heraclius Emperor
611–4	Chosroes II takes Syria, including Damascus
622	Muhammed leaves Mecca for Medina - **Hijra**
622–8	Heraclius' counter-offensive against Persians - reaches Ctesiphon
632	**death of Muhammed**
632–4	Abu Bakr Caliph
634–48	Umar Caliph
635	Muslim army takes Damascus for first time
636	**Battle of Yarmuk** results in Arab defeat of Byzantine forces - opens Syria to Islamic rule - Damascus taken
637	Aleppo falls to Muslims
637	**Battle of Qadissiye** - Arabs defeat Persians
638	last Syrian towns fall to Arabs
640–61	Moawiya Governor of Syria
644–56	Othman Caliph

656-61	Ali Caliph
656	Moawiya refuses loyalty to Ali - first Arab civil war
661	Ali murdered

661-750 - Umayyad Period

661-81	**Moawiya Caliph - makes Damascus his capital**
668-85	Constantine IV Emperor
672	Umayyad forces reaches Sea of Marmora - subsequently besiege Constantinople
679	Umayyad/Byzantine truce - Umayyads abandon attempt to control Aegean
680-3	Yazid Caliph
685-705	Abd al-Malik Caliph
705-15	Abu al-Abbas al-Walid Caliph
706-14	building of Umayyad Mosque, Damascus
post 715	construction of Great Mosque, Aleppo
724-43	Hisham Caliph
744-50	Marwan II last Umayyad Caliph

750-968 - Abbasid Period

754-75	al-Mansur Caliph
762	foundation of Baghdad
772	construction of Raqqa
786-809	Harun al-Rashid Caliph
813	Damascus revolts against Abbasids
842	further revolts in Syria - disaffection encourages spread of Shi`ism
868-905	Tulunids in Egypt
935-969	Ikhshidids in Egypt
944-1003	Hamdanid dynasty controls Aleppo
944-67	Saif al-Daula's rule, Aleppo

969-1055 Fatimid Period

969	Fatimids set up rival Caliphate - establish new capital al-Qahira (Cairo)
978-1076	Fatimids control southern Syria
969-997	Byzantine push to regain Syria - ends in treaty recognising Fatimid supremacy
996-1021	al-Hakim second Fatimid Caliph - Druze later revere him as last Imam
1037	Seljuq Turks in effective control in Baghdad

1055-1128 - Seljuq Period

1055	Seljuqs take northern Syria on behalf of Abbasids
1070-72	*Alp Arslan, Seljuq Sutlan*
1071	**Battle of Manzikert** - Seljuqs defeat Byzantine army - Seljuq control of all Syria
1072-92	*Malik Shah I Seljuq Sultan*
post 1078	*Seljuqs begin fortification of Damascus citadel*
1095	*Pope Urban II preaches* **First Crusade** *at Council of Clermont-Ferrand*
1098, March	Edessa taken by Crusaders
1098, June	Crusaders take Antioch after 9 month siege
1098, December	Crusaders massacre population of Maarat al-Numan
1099, July	**First Crusade takes Jerusalem**
post 1100	*first Ismaeli presence - beginning in Aleppo*
1108	Latakia taken by Crusaders
1109	Crusaders take Tripoli
1116-54	Tughtagin dynasty in Damascus - nominally on behalf of Fatimids
1118	al-Ghazi invited by Aleppo to garrison city against Crusader threat
1119	**'Ager Sanguinis'** - battle near Sarmada - Crusader forces defeated by Seljuqs from Aleppo
1124/5	Crusader attack on Aleppo fails

1128-1174 - Zengid Period

1128-46	Zengi Atabeq (regent) of Aleppo
1128-9	first Crusader attack on Damascus
post 1128	*Zengid push to restore Sunni orthodoxy*
post 1130	*Ismaelis (Assassins) move into coastal mountains*
1144	Zengi regains Edessa
1146-74	Nur al-Din's rule
1147-9	**Second Crusade** - unsuccessful attack on Damascus
post 1162	active career of Ismaeli leader, Rashid al-Din Sinan ('Old Man of the Mountain')
1171	*Saladin restores nominal Abbasid authority in Cairo - ends Fatimid Caliphate*

1176-1260 - Ayyubid Period

1176-93	*Saladin's rule - invited to take succession to Nur al-Din*
1186	Saladin takes full control of Aleppo - unites central Muslim lands from Baghdad to Cairo
1186-1216	al-Zaher Ghazi Ayyubid Governor of Aleppo
1187	**Battle of Hattin** - Saladin defeats Crusader army - goes on to take Jerusalem
1187-92	**Third Crusade** - recovers coastal ports
1188	Saladin's campaign along Syrian coast against Crusader positions - Qalaat Saladin (Saône), Burzey fall
1192	Richard Coeur de Lion's truce with Saladin - Christians allowed access to Jerusalem
1193-1215	al-Malik al-Zaher Ghazi Ayyubid governor of Aleppo
post 1193	on Saladin's death, succession disputed, empire fragments
post 1200	*major Ayyubid-endowed building programs in Damascus - especially for promotion of Islamic learning and for fortification of city*
1202-4	*Fourth Crusade - occupies Constantinople*
1217-21	Fifth Crusade - fails to take Egypt
1227	Cairo Ayyubid, al-Kamil, hands back Jerusalem to Christians
1244	Turkish invaders restore Muslim control of Jerusalem
1248-50	St Louis' Crusade in Egypt fails - retires to Acre
1258	Mongols sack Baghdad - Caliph murdered
1260	**first Mongol invasion** - under Hulaga

1260-1516 - Mameluke Period

1260	**Battle of Ain Jalud** - Mamelukes defeat Mongols
1260-1382	*Bahri Mamelukes*
1260-77	al-Zaher Baibars Mameluke Sultan
1261	Baibars installs al-Mustansir in Cairo as Caliph
1268	Antioch falls to Mamelukes
1271	Krak des Chevaliers falls to Baibars
1280-90	Qalaun Mameluke Sultan
1281	Qalaun defeats Mongol invasion
1285	Marqab falls to Qalaun
1287	Latakia falls
1289	Tripoli falls
1291	Tartus falls

1300-3	**fourth Mongol invasion** - Damascus occupied
1302	Arwad, last Crusader position in Syria, falls to Muslims
1312-39	Tengiz Mameluke Governor of Damascus
1382-1516	*Burji Mamelukes*
1400-1	**last Mongol invasion** - under **Timur** - Damascus besieged for 40 days
1453	*Constantinople falls to Ottoman Turks*
1468-96	Qait Bey Mameluke Sultan
1500-16	Qansawh al-Ghawri Mameluke Sultan

1516-1918 - Ottoman Period

1516	**Ottoman Turks** take Syria
1520-66	*Suleiman ('the Magnificent') Ottoman Sultan*
1548	*first Ottoman 'capitulation' treaties with European powers - subsequently led to European consulates being established in Aleppo*
1555	Suleiman undertakes building of Tekkiye Mosque, Damascus

1590-1635	*Fakhr al-Din's rule in Lebanon*
1805-48	Muhammed Ali, Pasha in Cairo
1832-40	Ibrahim Pasha administers Syria on behalf of Mohammed Ali
1840	Ottomans restore their authority in Syria, Egypt
1840	*Druze/Christian tensions in Lebanon break out*
1860	Druze massacre of Christians in Damascus
1863	paved road Beirut/Damascus completed
1893	major fire in prayer hall of Umayyad Mosque, Damascus

1918-present - Modern Period

1918	**Allied forces enter Damascus**
1918-9	Feisal King of Syria
1920-45	French Mandate
1925	revolt begins in Hauran against French rule
1936	France cedes Antioch and Alexandretta to Turkey
1945	Syria admitted to the United Nations
1946	last French troops leave

BIBLIOGRAPHY

The following list of books and journal articles consulted for this survey is in two parts. More specialised works cited in the REFS section at the end of each gazetteer entry are listed in the first section. The second lists works which are of wider background interest or which have been published since *Monuments of Syria* first went to press (1991).

There are few up-to-date and readily available works on Syrian history. Those titles on both lists which are of most interest to the general reader are marked with a ■ before the title though this is not intended to imply that the works are in print.

Three important journals are devoted to the publication of reports on research in Syria - the *Annales archéologiques arabes syriennes* (*AAAS*) published in Damascus by the Antiquities Department, the annual *Syria* published by the Institut français d'archéologie du Proche-Orient (IFAPO) in Beirut and *Damaszener Mitteilungen* (*DaM*) by the German archaeological institute in Damascus.

Works cited in REFS and footnotes

Abel, A   'Bosra' in *Encyclopedia of Islam*
                   - New Edition I Leiden 1960
Abu Assaf, Ali   ''Ain Dara' in *Ebla to Damascus*
                   (Weiss, Harvey ed) Washington
                   1985
Abu Assaf, Ali   *Der Tempel von `Ain Dara* Mainz
                   am Rhein 1990
AE   see Butler, H C
Amer, Gh et al   'L'ensemble basilical de
                   Qanawat (Syrie du sud)' *Syria*
                   1982
Amer, Gh and Gawlikowski, M
                   'Le sanctuaire impérial de
                   Philippopolis' in *Damaszener
                   Mitteilungen* 2 1985 pp 1-15;
Amiet, P   'La Syrie ... l'époque des
                   royaumes Amorites XXe-XVIe
                   siècle av. J.-C.' in *Au Pays de
                   Baal et d'Astarté* Paris 1983
Amy, R   'Temples à escaliers' *Syria*
                   XXVII 1950
anon   *Recueil historique - Couvent
                   Patriarcal Orthodoxe de Notre-
                   Dame de Saydnaya* Damascus
                   n.d.
Arnaud, D   'Histoire et civilisation écrite
                   2200-1600 av. J.-C.' in *Au Pays
                   de Baal et d'Astarté* Paris 1983
Arush, Abu-l-Faraj al-
                   *Musée National de Damas -
                   Département des Antiquités
                   Arabes et Islamiques -
                   (catalogue)* Damascus 1976
Arush, Abu-l-Faraj al- *et al*
                   *A Concise Guide to the National
                   Museum of Damascus*
                   Damascus ?1982
Asakir, Ibn al-   *Description de Damas* (trans
                   Elisséeff, Nikita) Damascus
                   1959
Atassi, Sarab *et al*
                   *Damascus Extra-Muros – Midan
                   Sultani* Damascus 1994
Baedeker   Baedeker's Guide *Syria,
                   Palestine* Leipzig 1908
Bahnassi, Afif   *Damascus* Tunis 1982
Bahnassi, Afif   'Visite archéologique de la vieille
                   cité d'Alep' in *Bulletin d'Etudes
                   Orientales* Institut Français de
                   Damas 1986
Balty, Janine (ed)
                   'Apamée de Syrie - Bilan des
                   recherches archéologiques
                   1973-1979 - Aspects de

l'architecture domestique
                   d'Apamée' in *Actes du colloque
                   tenu à Bruxelles les 29, 30 et 31
                   Mai 1980* Brussels 1984
Balty, Janine   ■*Mosaïques de Syrie* Brussels
                   1977
Balty, J Ch   'Le groupe épiscopal à Apamée,
                   dit "Cathédrale de l'est" -
                   premières recherches' in *Actes
                   du colloques Apamée de Syrie*
                   Brussels 1972
Balty, J Ch   ■*Guide d'Apamée* Brussels 1981
Balty, Janine and J Ch
                   'Apamée de Syrie, archéologie
                   et histoire. I. Des origines à la
                   Tètrarchie' *Aufstieg und
                   Niedergang der römischen Welt*
                   II.8 Berlin 1979
Barbir, K K   *Ottoman Rule in Damascus,
                   1708-1758* Princeton 1988
Bavant, B et al   'La mission de Syrie du nord' in
                   *Contribution française à
                   l'archéologie syrienne 1969-
                   1989* Damascus 1989
Bell, Gertrude   *Amurath to Amurath* London
                   1911
Bell, Gertrude   ■'The Desert and the Sown'
                   London 1985
Berchem, Max von & Fatio, Edmond
                   Voyage en Syrie Cairo 1914
Bermant, Chaim & Weitzman, Michael
                   Ebla - An Archaeological Enigma
                   London 1979
Bevan, Edwyn Robert
                   The House of Seleucous 2 vols
                   London 1902
Beyer, H W   *Der syrische kirchenbau* Berlin
                   1925
BG   ■Blue Guide (Hachette World
                   Guide) *The Middle East
                   Lebanon, Syria, Jordan Iraq, Iran*
                   (Boulanger, Robert ed) Paris
                   1966
Bianquis, Thierry
                   'Mission franco-syrienne de
                   Rahba-Mayadin (1976-1981)' in
                   *Contribution française à
                   l'archéologie syrienne 1969-
                   1989* Damascus 1989
Biscop, Jean-Luc and Sodini, Jean-Pierre
                   'Qal`at Sem`an et les chevets à
                   colonnes de Syrie du nord' *Syria*
                   1984

Bloom, Jonathan
  Minaret - Symbol of Islam
  London 1989
Boase, T S R ■*Castles and Churches of the*
  Crusading Kingdom London
  1967
Bounni, Adnan 'Le sanctuaire du Nabu ...
  Palmyre' in *Contribution*
  française à l'archéologie
  syrienne 1969-1989 Damascus
  1989
Bounni, Adnan 'Ras Ibn Hani' in *Au Pays de*
  Baal et d'Astarté Paris 1983
Bounni, Adnan and Alas`ad, Khaled
  Palmyre - Histoire, Monuments
  et Musée Damascus 1982
Browning, Iain ■*Palmyra* London 1979
Brümmer, Elfriede
  'Der Römische Tempel von
  Dmeir. Vorbericht' in
  Damaszener Mitteilungen 2 1985
Burman, Edward   *The Assassins -*
  Holy Killers of Islam London
  1987
Butler, Howard Crosby
  AE - Publications of the
  American Archaeological
  Expedition to Syria, 1899-1900
  New York 1903, including:
  Part II - Architecture and Other
  Arts
Butler, Howard Crosby
  PE – Publications of the
  Princeton University
  Archaeological Expedition to
  Syria (1904-5, 9) Leiden 1907-20
  including:
  Division II Section A - Southern
  Syria
  Division II, Section B - Northern
  Syria
Butler, Howard Crosby
  EC - Early Churches in Syria, 4th
  to 7th Centuries (re-print)
  Amsterdam 1969
Bylinski, Janusz
  'Survey of the Arab Castle in
  Palmyra' (annual reports) *Polish*
  Archaeology in the
  Mediterranean 1990-95
Callot, O and Marcillat-Jaubert, J
  'Les Temples romains du massif
  calcaire de Syrie du nord' in
  Contribution française à
  l'archéologie syrienne 1969-
  1989 Damascus 1989
Canby, Jeanny Vorys
  'Guzana (Tell Halaf)' in *Ebla to*
  Damascus (Weiss, Harvey ed)
  Washington 1985

Canivet, Marie-Thérése and Pierre
  'L'ensemble ecclésial de Huarte
  d'Apamée (Syrie)' *Syria* LVI
  1979
Canivet, Pierre 'Huarte - l'ensemble ecclesial' in
  Contribution française à
  l'archéologie syrienne 1969-
  1989 Damascus 1989
Cathcart King, D J
  'The Taking of Le Krak des
  Chevaliers in 1271' in *Antiquity*
  XXIII 1949
Chéhab, Kamel 'Le musée de Ma`arat al-
  Numan' *Syria* LXIV 1987
Colledge, Malcolm
  ■*The Art of Palmyra* London
  1976
Courbin, P 'Bassit' in *Contribution française*
  à l'archéologie syrienne 1969-
  1989 Damascus 1989
Creswell, K A C
  Early Muslim Architecture vol I,
  parts 1 and 2, (re-issue) New
  York, 1979
Crowfoot, J W *Churches at Bosra and Samaria-*
  Sebaste London 1937
Crowfoot, J W *Early Churches in Palestine*
  London 1941
Culican, William'The First Merchant Venturers' in
  The Dawn of Civilisation (Piggot,
  Stuart ed) London 1961
Delehaye, H *Les Saints Stylites* Paris 1923
de Lorey, Eustache
  'Mosaics of the Great Mosque of
  Umayyads in Damascus' in
  Creswell *Early Muslim*
  Architecture, New York 1979
Dentzer, J-M (ed)
  Hauran I - Recherches
  archéologiques sur la Syrie du
  sud à l'époque hellénistique et
  romaine Paris 1986
Dentzer, J-M 'Bosra' in *Contribution française*
  à l'archéologie syrienne 1969-
  1989 Damascus 1989
Dentzer, J-M 'Fouilles et prospections à Si`
  (Qanawat)' in *Contribution*
  française à l'archéologie
  syrienne 1969-1989 Damascus
  1989
Dentzer, Jean-Marie and Orthmann, Winfried
  (ed)
  Archéologie et histoire de la
  Syrie Saarbrucken 1989
Deschamps, Paul
  'Le Krak des Chevaliers' in
  Gazette des Beaux Arts Paris
  1929

Deschamps, Paul
Les châteaux des croisées en
Terre Sainte – I - Le Crac des
Chavaliers - étude historique et
archéologique 2 volumes Paris
1934
Deschamps, Paul
Les châteaux des croisées en
Terre Sainte - III - La défense du
Comté de Tripoli et de la
Principauté d'Antioche 2
volumes Paris 1973
Downey, Susan
Mesopotamian Religious
Architecture Princeton 1988
Dunand, Maurice and Saliby, Nessib
Le temple d'Amrith dans la pérée
d'Aradus Paris 1985
Dussaud, Réné Topographie historique de la
Syrie antique et mediévale Paris
1927
Dussaud, Réné 'Le Temple de Jupiter
Damascène' Syria III 1922
EC   see Butler, H C
Ecochard, Michel 'Consolidation et restauration
du portail du temple de Bel à
Palmyre' Syria XVIII 1937
Ecochard, Michel 'Note sur un édifice chrétien
d'Alep' Syria 1950
Ecochard, Michel and le Coeur, Claude
Les bains de Damas Beirut 1942
EI   Encyclopaedia of Islam (new
edition) Leiden 1970+
Elisséeff, Nikita 'Dimashk' in Encyclopaedia of
Islam - New Edition II Leiden
1971
Elisséeff, Nikita 'Hims' in Encyclopaedia of Islam
- New Edition III Leiden 1971
Elisséeff, Nikita 'al-Ladhikiyya' in Encyclopaedia
of Islam - New Edition vol V
Leiden 1982
Elisséeff, Nikita 'Ma'arrat al-Numan' in
Encyclopedia of Islam - New
Edition V Leiden 1980
Elisséeff, Nikita 'Mandbidj' in Encyclopedia of
Islam - New Edition VI (fascicule
103-4) Leiden 1987
Elisséeff, Nikita and Paillet, J L
'Deuxième mission au château
de Rahba' Annales
archéologiques Arabes
Syriennes 1986
Etinghausen, Richard and Grabar, Oleg
The Art and Architecture of Islam
650-1250 Harmondsworth 1987
Eydoux, Henri-Paul
■Les châteaux de soleil Paris
1982

Fedden, Robin ■Crusader Castles - A Brief
Study in the Military Architecture
of the Crusades London 1950
Finsen, Helge (ed)
'Le levée du théâtre romain à
Bosra, Syrie' Analecta Romana
Instituti Danici VI Supplementum
1972
Fourdrin, J-P 'La frons scaenae du théâtre de
Palmyre' in Contribution
française à l'archéologie
syrienne 1969-1989 Damascus
1989
Frankfort, Henri
■The Art and Architecture of the
Ancient Orient Harmondsworth
1970
Freyburger, Klaus S
'Einige Beobachtungen zur
stätdtbaulichen Entwicklung des
römischen Bostra' in
Damaszener Mitteilungen 4 1989
Freyburger, Klaus S
'Untersuchungen zur
Baugeschichte des Jupiter-
Heiligtums in Damaskus' in
Damaszener Mitteilungen 2 1985
Frézouls, Edmond
'Cyrrhus et la Cyrrhestique
jusqu'à la fin du Haut-Empire' in
Aufstieg und Niedergang der
römischen Welt II, 8 Berlin 1979
Frézouls, Edmond
'Mission archéologique de
Cyrrhus' in Contribution
française à l'archéologie
syrienne 1969-1989 Damascus
1989
Gabrieli, Francesco
Arab Historians of the Crusades
London 1984
GB   Guide Bleu Syrie, Palestine,
Iraq, Transjordanie Paris 1932
Gibb, Hamilton A R
'Arab-Byzantine Relations under
the Umayyad Caliphate'
Dumbarton Oaks Papers 12
1958
Goodwin, Godfrey
A History of Ottoman
Architecture, London, 1987
Grabar, Oleg 'La Grande Mosquée de Damas
et les origines architecturales de
la mosquée' Synthronon Paris
1968
Grabar, Oleg et al
City in the Desert - Qasr al-Hayr
East 2 vols Harvard University
Press, 1978

Grainger, John D
    The Cities of Seleukid Syria
    Oxford 1990
Gray, John   *The Canaanites* London 1964
Hadjar, Abdallah
    'Die römischen Straßen in
    Syrien' *Das Altertum* 1979
Hallam, Elizabeth (ed)
    Chronicles of the Crusades
    London 1989
Herzfeld, Ernst 'Damascus, Studies in
    Architecture' I-IV *Ars Islamica* 9
    1942, 10 1943, 11/12 1946,
    13/14 1948
Hillenbrand, Robert
    'La Dolce Vita in Early Islamic
    Syria: The Evidence of the Later
    Umayyad Palaces' *Art History*
    5/1 March 1982
Hillenbrand, Robert
    'Eastern Islamic Influences in
    Syria: Raqqa and Qal`at Ja`bar
    in the Later 12th Century' in *The
    Art of Syria and the Jazira 1100-
    1250* Oxford 1985
Hitti, Philip K ■*History of Syria - Including
    Lebanon and Palestine* London
    1951
Holod-Tretiak, Renata
    'Qasr al-Hayr al-Sharqi - A
    Mediaeval Town in Syria'
    Archaeology 23/3 June 1970
Honigmann, E 'al-Rakka' in *Encyclopaedia of
    Islam* III Leiden 1936
Honigmann, E 'Ras al-`Ain' in *Encyclopaedia of
    Islam* III Leiden 1936
Hopkins, Clark ■*The Discovery of Dura-Europos*
    New Haven 1979
Hourani, Albert ■*The Islamic City - A Colloquium*
    Oxford 1970
Huygens, R B C 'La campagne de Saladin en
    Syrie du nord (1188)' in *Actes du
    colloque Apamée de Syrie*
    Brussels 1972
Jones, A H M 'The Urbanization of the Ituraean
    Principality' *Journal of Roman
    Studies* 21 1931
Kayem, Ali al- *Bimaristan Nur al-Din* Damascus
    (n.d.)
Kennedy, David and Riley, Derrick
    *Rome's Desert Frontiers from
    the Air* London 1990
Khayyata, Wahid
    *Guide to the Museum of Aleppo -
    Ancient Oriental Department*
    Aleppo 1977
Klengel, Horst *Syria antiqua - Vorislamische
    Denkmaler der Syrischen
    Arabischen Republik* Leipzig
    1971

Klengel, Horst 'Hosn es-Suleiman - ein
    Heiligtum in Syriens
    Küstenbergen' *Das Altertum* 22
    1976
Klengel, Horst *Syrien zwischen Alexander und
    Muhammed - Denkmale aus
    Antike und frühem Christentum*
    Vienna 1987
Klinkott, Manfred
    'Ergebnisse der Bauaufnahme
    am "Tempel" von Dmeir' in
    Damaszener Mitteilungen 4 1989
Kohlmeyer, Kay 'Ugarit (Ras Shamra)' in *Ebla to
    Damascus* (Weiss, Harvey ed)
    Washington 1985
Krautheimer, Richard
    ■*Early Christian and Byzantine
    Architecture* Harmondsworth
    1981
Krencker and Zschietzshmann
    Römische Tempeln in Syrien
    Berlin 1938
Lagarce, Jacques and Elisabeth
    *Ras Ibn Hani - archéologie et
    histoire* Damascus 1987
Lambert, E 'La synagogue de Doura-
    Europos et les origines de la
    mosquée' *Semitica* III 1950
Lapidus, Ira M ■*Muslim Cities in the Later
    Middle Age* Cambridge 1947
Lassus, Jean *Sanctuaires chrétiens de Syrie*
    Paris 1947
Lassus, Jean 'Deux églises cruciformes du
    Hauran' *Bulletin d'études
    orientales de l'Institut français de
    Damas* I 1931
Lauffray, J *Halabiyya-Zenobia - place forte
    du limes oriental et la Haute-
    Mésopotamie au VIè siècle* vol 1
    Paris 1983
Lauffray, J *Halabiyya-Zenobia - place forte
    du limes oriental et la Haute-
    Mésopotamie au VIè siècle* vol 2
    Paris 1991
Lauffray, J 'Halebiye-Zenobia' in
    *Contribution française à
    l'archéologie syrienne 1969-
    1989* Damascus 1989
Lawrence, T E ■*Crusader Castles* London 1986
Lewis, Bernard *The Assassins - A Radical Sect
    in Islam* London 1985
Leriche,P and al-Mahmoud, A
    'Doura Europos' in *Contribution
    française à l'archéologie
    syrienne 1969-1989* Damascus
    1989
Maalouf, Amin *The Crusades Through Arab
    Eyes* London 1977
Mallowan, M E L
    'The Birth of Written History' in

The Dawn of Civilisation (Piggot, Stuart, ed) London 1961

Mango, Cyril *Byzantine Architecture* New York 1976

Margueron, J-Cl 'Mari' in *Contribution française à l'archéologie syrienne 1969-1989* Damascus 1989

Margueron, J-Cl 'Emar et Faq`ous' in *Contribution française à l'archéologie syrienne 1969-1989* Damascus 1989

Margueron, J-Cl 'Mari - Le Palais du second millénaire' in *Au Pays de Baal et d'Astarté* Paris 1983

Margueron, J-Cl et al 'Ugarit au IIe millénaire' in *Au Pays de Baal et d'Astarté* Paris 1983

Matheson, Susan 'Dura-Europos on the Euphrates' in *Ebla to Damascus* (Weiss, Harvey ed) Washington 1985

Mattern, Joseph *Villes Mortes de Haute Syrie* Beirut 1944

Mattern, J, Mouterde, R and Beaulieu, A 'Dair Solaib - Les deux églises' *Mélanges de l'Université Saint Joseph* XXII 1939

Matthiae, Paolo ∎*Ebla - An Empire Rediscovered* London 1977

McEwan, Calvin W et al *Soundings at Tell Fakhariyah* Chicago 1958

Meinecke, Michael 'Der Survey des Damaszener Altstadtviertels as-Salihiya' *Damaszener Mitteilungen* I 1983

Meinecke, Michael 'Raqqa on the Euphrates' in *The Near East in Antiquity* vol II Amman 1990

Meinecke, Michael et al *Islamic Bosra - A Brief Guide* Damascus 1990

Meyer, M (ed) *Oxford Encyclopaedia of Archaeology in the Middle East* 1997

Michalowski, Kazimierz *Palmyra* New York 1970

Milburn, Robert *Early Christian Art and Architecture* Aldershot 1988

Millar, Fergus 'Paul of Samosata, Zenobia and Aurelian: The Church, Local Culture and Political Allegiance in Third Century Syria' *Journal of Roman Studies* 61 1971

Mougdad, Sulaiman ∎*Bosra* Damascus 1974

Mouterde, R and Poidebard, A *Le limes de Chalcis - Organisation de la steppe en Haute Syrie romaine* 2 volumes Paris 1945

Musil, Alois *Palmyrena - A Topographical Itinerary* New York 1928

Nour, Antoine Abde *Introduction à l'histoire urbaine de la Syrie ottomane (XVIe-XVIIIe siècle)* Beirut 1982

OE see Meyer, M (ed)

Oates, David and Joan 'Tell Brak - l'empire akkadien' in *Les Dossiers d'archéologie* 155 Dec 1990

Parr, Peter 'The Tell Nebi Mend Project' *Annales Archéologiques Arabes Syriennes* 1983

Parrot, Andre *Mari - capitale fabuleuse* Paris 1974

PE see Butler, H C

Pena, I with Castellana, P & Fernandez, R *Les Stylites syriens* Milan 1975

Pena, I with Castellana, P & Fernandez, R *Les Reclus syriens* Milan 1980

Pena, I with Castellana, P & Fernandez, R *Les Cénobites syriens* Milan 1983

Pena, I et al *Inventaire du Jebel Baricha* Milan 1987

Perkins, Ann ∎*The Art of Dura Europos* Oxford 1973

Perkins, Ann et al (ed) *The Excavations at Dura Europos - Final Reports* 8 vols New Haven various dates

Peters, Frank E 'City Planning in Greco-Roman Syria: Some New Considerations', *Damaszener Mitteilungen* 1 1983

Pettinato, Giovanni *The Archives of Ebla - An Empire Inscribed in Clay* New York 1979

Pézard, Maurice *Qadesh* Paris 1931

Poidebard, A 'Mission archéologique en Haute Djéziré (1928)' *Syria* XI 1930

Poidebard, A *La trace de Rome dans le désert de Syrie - le limes de Trajan à la conquête arabe - recherches aériennes* 2 volumes Paris 1934

Pritchard, James (ed) ∎*The Times Concise Atlas of the Bible* London 1991

Procopius   *Complete Works VII. Buildings*
             London 1940
Raymond, Andre
             ■*Great Arab Cities of the*
             Sixteenth to Eighteenth
             Centuries New York 1984
Rey-Coquais, J-P
             Arados et sa pérée aux époques
             grecque, romaine et byzantine
             Paris 1974
Rey-Coquais, J-P
             'Arados', 'Bosra', Dionysias
             (Soueida)', 'Seia', Selaema' in
             The Princeton Encyclopedia of
             Classical Sites Princeton 1975
Richmond, I A 'Palmyra Under the Aegis of
             Rome' in *Journal of Roman*
             Studies LIII 1963
Rihaoui, Abdulkader
             The Krak of the Knights
             Damascus 1982
Rihawi, Abdulqader
             ■*Damascus - Its History,*
             Development and Artistic
             Heritage Damascus 1977
Rostovtzeff, M *Caravan Cities* Oxford 1932
Rostovtzeff, M *Dura-Europos and Its Art* Oxford
             1938
Rostovtzeff, M *Social and Economic History of*
             the Roman Empire 2 volumes
             Oxford 1957
Runciman, Steven
             ■*A History of the Crusades* 3
             volumes Harmondsworth 1965
Ruprechtsberger (ed)
             Palmyra - Geschichte, Kunst und
             Kultur der syrischen Oasenstadt
             Linz 1987
Sa`ade, Gabriel 'Le château de Bourzey,
             forteresse oublié' in *AAS* 1956
Sa`ade, Gabriel 'Saint Elian de Homs' Beirut
             1974
Sa`ade, Gabriel *Ougarit - Métropole Cananéenne*
             Beirut 1979
Sa`ade, Gabriel
             'Histoire du Château de Saladin'
             Studi Medievali 9 1968
Sack, Dorothée 'Damaskus, die Stadt intra
             muros. Ein Beitrag zu den
             Arbeiten der "Internationalen
             Kommission zum Schutz der
             Altstadt von Damaskus"' in
             Damaszener Mitteilungen 2 1985
Sack, Dorothée *Damaskus - Entwicklung und*
             Struktur einer orientalisch-
             islamischen Stadt Mainz am
             Rhein 1989
Sader, Hélène S
             Les états araméens de Syrie
             Wiesbaden 1987

Saliby, N   'Amrith' in *Contribution française*
             à l'archéologie syrienne 1969-
             1989 Damascus 1989
Saouaf, Soubhi *Alep - son histoire, sa citadelle,*
             ses monuments antiques et son
             musée - Guide des visiteurs
             Aleppo c1983
Saouaf, Soubhi *Saint Simeon* Aleppo (n.d.)
Sartre, Maurice 'Le territoire de Canatha' *Syria*
             LVIII 1981
Sartre, Maurice *Bostra des origines à l'Islam*
             Paris 1985
Sauvaget, Jean 'Deux sanctuaires chiites d'Alep'
             Syria IX 1928
Sauvaget, Jean 'Inventaire des monuments
             musulmans de la ville d'Alep'
             Revue des etudes islamiques V
             1931
Sauvaget, Jean *Les monuments historiques de*
             Damas Beirut 1932
Sauvaget, Jean 'Le plan de Laodicée-sur-mer'
             Bulletin d'études orientales 4
             1935
Sauvaget, Jean 'Esquisse d'une histoire de la
             ville de Damas' *Revue des*
             études islamiques 1934 VIII
             Paris 1937
Sauvaget, Jean 'Les ruines omeyyades du Jebel
             Seis' *Syria* XX 1939
Sauvaget, Jean *Alep - Essai sur le*
             développement d'une grande
             ville syrienne des origines au
             milieu du XIXème siècle 2
             volumes Paris 1941
Sauvaget, Jean 'Le plan antique de Damas' in
             Syria 1949
Sauvaget, Jean 'Châteaux umayyades de Syrie'
             Revue des études islamiques
             (1967) Paris 1968
Sauvaget, Jean 'Halab' in *Encyclopedia of Islam*
             - New Edition IV Leiden 1971
Sauvaget, Jean & Ecochard, M
             Les monuments ayyoubides de
             Damas Damascus 1938-50
Scharabi, Muhammed
             'Der Suq von Damaskus und
             zwei traditionelle
             Handelsanlagen: Han Gaqmaq
             und Han Sulaiman Pasa'
             Damaszener Mitteilungen 1,
             1983
Schatkowski Schilcher, Linda
             Families in Politics - Damascene
             Factions and Estates of the 18th
             and 19th Centuries Stuttgart
             1985
Schlumberger, Daniel
             'Les fouilles de Qasr el-Heir el-
             Gharbi (1936-1938) – Rapport
             préliminaire' *Syria*, 1939

Segal, Arthur   *Town Planning and Architecture in Provincia Arabia* British Archaeological Reports, International Series 419 London 1988

Segal, Arthur   *From Function to Monument* Oxford 1997

Seyrig, Henri   'Palmyra and the East' *Journal of Roman Studies* XL 1950

Seyrig, Henri   'Aradus et Baetocaece' *Syria* XXVIII 1951

Seyrig, Henri   'Caractères de l'histoire d'Emesse' *Syria* XXXVI 1959

Seyrig, Henri   'La culte du soleil en Syrie à l'époque romaine' *Syria* 1971

Shéhabé, Kamel   *The Mosaics of the Ma'arra Museum* Kaslik 1997

Smail, R C   ■*Crusading Warfare (1097-1193)* Cambridge 1956

Sodini, Jean-Pierre   'Les églises du massif de Belus' in *Au Pays de Baal et d'Astarté* Paris 1983

Sodini, Jean-Pierre and Tate, Georges   'Maisons d'époque romaine et byzantine (IIe-VIe siècles) du massif calcaire de Syrie du nord - étude typologique' in Balty, Janine (ed) *Apamée*

Sodini, Jean-Pierre et al   'Déhès (Syrie du Nord) Campagnes I-III (1976-1978) - Recherches sur l'Habitat Rural' *Syria* 1980

Sourdel, D   'Hamath' in *Encyclopaedia of Islam - New Edition* IV 1971

Sournia, Jean Charles & Marianne   *L'orient des premiers chrétiens* Paris 1966

Starcky, Jean   'Palmyre - guide archéologique' *Mélanges de l'université Saint Joseph* Beirut 1941

Starcky, Jean   *Palmyre (L'ancien orient illustré)* Paris 1952

Starcky, Jean & Gawlikowsky, Michael   *Palmyre* Paris 1985

Tate, George   'Les villages du massif calcaire' in *Au Pays de Baal et d'Astarté* Paris 1983

Tchalenko, Georges   *Villages antiques de la Syrie du nord; le massif de Belus à l'époque romaine* 3 volumes Paris 1953-8

Tchalenko, Georges   'Travaux en cours dans la Syrie du nord' *Syria* L 1973

Tchalenko, Georges   'La basilique de Qalb-loze' *Annales archéologiques arabes syriennes* 24 1974

Tchalenko, Georges & Baccache, E   *Eglises de villages de la Syrie du nord* 2 volumes Paris 1979-80

Teixidor, Javier   'Un port romain du désert - Palmyre et son commerce d'Auguste à Caracalla' special issue of *Semitica* XXXIV Paris 1984

Thubron, Colin   ■*Mirror to Damascus* London 1967

Toueir (Tuweir), Kassem   'Raqqa/Rafiqa' in *Ebla to Damascus* (Weiss, Harvey ed) Washington 1985

Toueir, Kassem   'Heraqlah: A Unique Victory Monument of Harun al-Rashid' *World Archaeology* 14/3 Feb 1983

Ulbert, Thilo   'Rusafa-Sergiopolis: Pilgrimage Shrine and Capital' in *Ebla to Damascus* (Weiss, Harvey ed) Washington 1985

Ulbert, Thilo   *Resafe II, Die Basilika des Heiligen Kreuzes in Resafe-Sergiopolis* Mainz-am-Rhein, 1986

Ulbert, Thilo   'Villes et fortifications de l'Euphrate' in *Archéologie et histoire de la Syrie* tome 2 Saarbrücken 1989

van Berchem, Max & Fatio, Edmond   *Voyage en Syrie* Cairo 1914

Vogüé, Melchior, Marquis de   *Syrie Centrale - architecture civile et religieuse du Ier au VIe siècles* 2 volumes Paris 1865-77

Weber, Thomas   'Haran al-Awamid' *Antike Welt* 28 1997

Weiss, Harvey   'Tell Brak' in *Ebla to Damascus* (Weiss, Harvey ed) Washington 1985

Weiss, Harvey and Kohlmeyer, Kay   'Ebla (Tell Mardikh)' in *Ebla to Damascus* (Weiss, Harvey ed) Washington 1985

Will, Ernest   'La tour funéraire de la Syrie et les monuments apparentées' *Syria* XXVI, 1949

Will, Ernest   'Développement urbain de Palmyre' *Syria* 1983

Wulzinger, K and Watzinger, C   **WW - Damaskus – antike -** *Damaskus, die antike Stadt* Berlin 1921-4

Wulzinger, K and Watzinger, C
WW - Damaskus – islamische
Damaskus, die islamische Stadt
Berlin 1924

Ziadeh, Nicola A
■*Damascus under the Mamluks*
Norman, (Oklahoma) 1964
Yon, Marguerite
La Syrie au bronze récent Paris
1982

Books and Articles for Further Reading

anon ■*Au Pays de Baal et d' Astarté*
Paris 1983

anon *Contribution française à
l'archéologie syrienne 1969-
1989* Damascus 1989

anon *Syrian-European Archaeology
Exhibition - Catalogue*
Damascus 1996

Aharoni, Yohanan
*The Land of the Bible - A
Historical Geography* London
1974

Baduel, P R (ed)
'Villes au Levant - Hommage ...
Andr, Raymond' Aix-en-
Provence 1991

Ball, Warwick ■*Syria* London 1994

Bourchier, E S *Syria as a Roman Province*
Oxford 1916

Bowersock, G W
Roman Arabia Cambridge
Massachussets 1983

Bowersock, G W
Hellenism in Late Antiquity
Cambridge 1990

Cahen, Claude *La Syrie du nord à l'époque des
Croisades et la principauté
franque d'Antioche* Paris 1940

Caubet, Annie 'Des premiers villages aux cités-
états' in *Beaux Arts* (Hors Serie
on Syria) Paris 1993

Colledge, Malcolm
'Greek and Non-Greek
Interaction in the Art and
Architecture of the Hellenistic
East' in *Hellenism in the East*
(Kurht, Emilie et al. ed) London
1987

Cotterell, Arthur
■*The Penguin Encyclopedia of
Ancient Civilisations*
Harmondsworth 1988

Dalrymple, Willam
From the Holy Mountain
London 1997

Davis, Ralph *Aleppo and Devonshire Square -
English Traders in the Levant in
the Eighteenth Century* London
1967

Davis, Norman & Kraay, Colin M
*The Hellenistic Kingdoms -
Portrait Coins and History*
London 1980

Degeorge, Gérard
■*Palmyre - Métropole du désert*
Paris 1987

Degeorge, Gérard
■*Syrie - Art, histoire, architecture*
Paris 1983

Degeorge, Gérard
■*Damas des origines au
Mamluks* Paris 1997

Degeorge, Gérard
■*Damas des Ottomans à nos
jours* Paris 1994

Dentzer, J-M & Dentzer-Feydy, J
*Le Djebel al-'Arab - Histoire et
patrimoine au Musée de
Suweida* Paris 1991

Donner, Fred McGraw
The Early Islamic conquests
Princeton 1981

Downey, Michael
*A History of Antioch in Syria -
from Seleucus to the Arab
Conquest* Princeton 1974

Fedden, Robin ■*Syria - An Historical
Appreciation* London 1946

Fowden, Elizabeth Key
*The Barbarian Plain: St Sergius
Between Rome and Iran*
Berkeley (forthcoming) 1999

Fowden, Garth *From Empire to Commonwealth*
Princeton 1993

Freyburger, Klaus S
'Der Tempel von Slim: Ein
Bericht' in *DaM* 5, 1991

Freyburger, Klaus S
'Die Bauten und Bildwerke von
Phillippolis. Zeugnisse imperialer
und orientalischer
Selbstdarstellung der Familie
Kaisers Philippus Arabs' in *DaM*
6, 1992

Frézouls, Edmond
'Recherches sur les théâtres de
l'orient syrien' *Syria* 1959,1961

Frézouls, Edmond
'Cyrrhus et la Cyrrhestique
jusqu'à la fin du Haut Empire'
*Aufstieg und Niedergang der
Römischen Welt* II/8 Berlin 1977

Fugelstad-Aumeunier, Viviane
Alep et la Syrie du Nord Aix-en-
Provence 1992

Gaube, H and Wirth, E
*Aleppo - Historische und
geographische Beitrage*
(Beihefte zum Tübinger Atlas
des Vorderen Orients)
Wiesbaden 1984

Gawlikowski, Michael
　　'Palmyre et l'Euphrate' *Syria* LX
　　1983
Grabar, Oleg　'Islamic Art and Byzantium'
　　Dumbarton Oaks Papers 18,
　　1964
Grabar, Oleg　■*The Formation of Islamic Art*
　　New Haven 1987
Green, Peter　■*Alexander to Actium - The*
　　Hellenistic Age London 1990
Hillenbrand, Robert
　　■*Islamic Architecture - Form,*
　　Function and Meaning
　　Edinburgh 1994
Houghton, L C　'Survey of the Salihiye Quarter of
　　Damascus' *Art and Archaeology*
　　Research Papers 14 1978
Hourani, Albert　■*A History of the Arab Peoples*
　　London 1991
Isaac. Benjamin *The Limits of Empire* Oxford
　　1990
Jones, A H M　*The Cities of the Eastern Roman*
　　Provinces Oxford 1937
Jousiffe, Ann & Peter
　　■*Jordan, Syria and Levbanon –*
　　A Travel Atlas Melbourne 1997
Kennedy, David (ed)
　　The Roman Army in the East
　　Ann Arbor 1996
Kennedy, Hugh ■*Crusader Castles* Cambridge
　　1994
Klengel, Horst　*The Art of Ancient Syria* New
　　York 1972
Kohlmeyer, Kay & Strommenger, Eva (ed)
　　Land des Baal - Syrien - Forum
　　der Volker und Kulturen Mainz
　　am Rhein 1982
konzelmann, Gerhard
　　Damaskus – Oase zwischen
　　Haß und Hoffnung, Frankfurt/M
　　1996
Kuhrt, Amélie　■*The Ancient Near East c 2000-*
　　330 BC 2 vols London 1995
Lapidus, Ira M　■*A History of Islamic Societies*
　　Cambridge 1988
Lassus, Jean　*Inventaire archéologique de la*
　　région Nord-Est de Hama 2
　　volumes Damascus (n.d.)
Lifschitz, B　'Etudes sur l'histoire de la
　　province romaine de Syrie'
　　Aufstieg und Niedergang der
　　römischen Welt II/8 Berlin 1977
Lovell, Mary S　*A Rage to Live: A Biography of*
　　Richard and Isabel Burton
　　London 1998
Lovell, Mary S　*A Scandalous Life: The*
　　Biography of Jane Digby London
　　1995

Marcus, Abraham
　　■*The Middle East on the Eve of*
　　Modernity - Aleppo in the
　　Eighteenth Century New York
　　1989
Margueron, J-Cl and Pfirsch, Luc
　　Le Proche-Orient et l'Egypte
　　antiques Paris 1996
Michell, George (ed)
　　■*Architecture of the Islamic World*
　　- Its History and Social Meaning
　　London 1978
Milburn, Robert
　　Early Christian Art and
　　Architecture Aldershot 1988
Millar, Fergus　■*The Roman Near East 31 BC -*
　　AD 337 Cambridge Mass. 1993
Moosa, Matti　*Extremist Shiites - The Ghulat*
　　Sects Syracuse 1988
Mougdad, Sulaiman A
　　Bosra - Guide historique et
　　archéologique Damascus 1974
Müller-Wiener, W
　　■*Castles of the Crusaders*
　　London 1966
Pirovano, Carlo *Da Ebla a Damasco - Diecimila*
　　Anni di Archeologia in Siria Milan
　　1985
Raymond, André
　　'La conquête ottomane et le
　　développement des grandes
　　villes arabes' in *Revue de*
　　l'Occident Musulman et de la
　　Méditerranée 27 1979
Rey-Coquais, J-P
　　'Syrie romaine, de Pompée à
　　Diocletian' *Journal of Roman*
　　Studies 1978
Riley-Smith, Jonathan (ed)
　　■*The Atlas of the Crusades*
　　London 1991
Riley-Smith, Jonathon (ed)
　　■*The Oxford Illustrated History*
　　of the Crusades Oxford 1995
Rostovtzeff, M　'Syrie romaine' *Revue Historique*
　　CLXXV 1935
Salibi, Kamal S *Syria Under Islam - Empire on*
　　Trial 634-1097 New York 1977
Sartre, Maurice
　　L'Orient romain – provinces et
　　societé provincials en
　　Mediterrannée orientale
　　d'Auguste aux Sévères Paris
　　1991
Sauvaget, Jean
　　L'architecture Musulmane en
　　Syrie' *Revue des Beaux Arts*
　　Asiatiques VIII/1 1934

Scheck, Frank Rainer & Odenthal, Johannes
■*Syrien* (DuMont Kunst
Reisefuhrer) Cologne 1998
Seyrig, Henri   'Seleucus Ièr et la fondation de
la monarchie syrienne' *Syria*
1949
Smail, R C   'Crusaders' Castles of the
Twelfth Century' *Cambridge
Historical Journal* X, 2 1951
Smail, R C   *The Crusaders in Syria and the
Holy Land* London 1973
Stark, Freya   ■*Letters from Syria* London 1946
Stark, Freya   ■*Rome on the Euphrates* London
1966
Stilwell, Richard (ed)
■*The Princeton Encyclopedia of
Classical Sites* Princeton 1976
Stoneman, Richard
*Palmyra and Its Empire -
Palmyra's Revolt Against Rome*
Ann Arbor 1992
Tchalenko, Georges

Eglises syriennes à béma Paris
1990
Usamah Ibn Munqidh (trans Philip K Hitti)
■*An Arab-Syrian Gentleman and
Warrior in the Period of the
Crusades - Memoirs of Usamah
Ibn-Munqidh* London 1987
Weiss, Harvey (ed)
■*Ebla to Damascus - Art and
Archeology of Ancient Syria*
Washington 1985
Will, Ernest   'Damas antique' *Syria* LXXI
1994
Wood, Robert   *The Ruins of Palmyra, otherwise
Tedmor in the Desert* (re-print of
1753 edition) Westmead, Hants
1971

INDEX TO PLACES AND PEOPLE

- Arab and Muslim names are listed by the most commonly recognised part of the name - eg al-Malik al-Zaher Ghazi is listed under **Ghazi**.
- The article 'al-' is ignored for the purposes of establishing alphabetical order.

Quick Index of Gazetteer Sites by Period and Rating

SITE	PERIOD	MAP OR *PLAN*	RATING
Ain Dara	Ira/Grk	68	*
Ain Divar	Arb	74	T
Aleppo	BA/Ott	2, 68, 71-2	***
Aleppo - Citadel	Arb	3	**
Aleppo - Great Mosque	Byz/Arb	-	*
Aleppo - Suqs and Khans	Arb/Ott	4, 5	**
Aleppo - South Quarter	Arb/Ott	2	**
Aleppo - Museum	All	-	**
Aleppo - Jdeide Quarter	Arb/Ott	7	*
Aleppo - Mashhad al-Hussein	Arb	-	-
Amrit	Phn/Grk	8, 66	*
Anderin	Rom/Byz	72	T
Apamea	Hel/../Arb	9, 65	***
Arwad	Phn/../Arb	66	T
Atil	Rom	63	*
Baghuz	Rom	73	-
Bakas (Shugur Qadim)	Cru	10, 67	T
Bamuqqa	Rom/Byz	69	*
Baqirha	Rom/Byz	69	*
Bara	Byz	11, 70	**
Barad	Rom/Byz	12, 68	-
Basofan	Byz	68	-
Behyo	Byz	68	-
Beshindlaye	Rom/Byz	69	-
Bosra	Rom/Byz/Umd	13, 14, 63	***
Burj Haidar	Byz	68	*
Burjke	Byz	68	-
Braij	Byz	69	-
Burqush	Rom/Byz	64	*
Circesium	Rom	73	T
Cyrrhus	Hel/Rom/Byz	15, 68	*
Damascus	All	16, 64	***
Damascus - Umayyad Mosque	Rom/Byz/Arb/Ott	17	***
Damascus - Citadel, North Walls	Rom/Arb	18, 19	*
Damascus - Suq Area	Arb/Ott	20	*
Damascus - Khans	Arb/Ott	21	*
Damascus - Straight Street	Rom/Arb	22	*
Damascus - South West Quarter	Arb/Ott	23	*
Damascus - National Museum	All	-	**
Damascus - Tekkiye Mosque	Ott	24	**
Damascus - Salihiye	Arb/Ott	25	*
Damascus - Midan	Arb/Ott	26	-
Dana (South)	Rom/Byz	70	*
Dayhis	Rom/Byz	69	-
Deir Mar Mousa	Byz	75	*
Deir Semaan	Byz	27, 68	*
Deir Soleib	Byz	65	-
Dumeir	Rom	64, 75	**
Dura Europos	Grk/Rom	28, 73	**
Ebla	EBA/MBA	29, 72	*
Ezraa	Byz	63	**
Fafertin	Byz	68	-
Halebiye	Rom/Byz	30, 72, 73	**

Safita	Cru	*55*, 66	**
St George Monastery	Arb	66	-
Saint Simeon	Byz	*56*, 68	***
Salkhad	Arb	63	-
Seidnaya	Byz/Arb	64	-
Serjilla	Rom/Byz	*57*, 70	**
Shahba	Rom	*58*, 63	*
Shaizar	Cru/Arb	65	*
Shaqqa	Rom/Byz	63	-
Sia	Rom	*59*, 63	-
Sitt al-Rum	Rom/Byz	68	-
Suweida	Rom	63	*
Suweilim	Rom	63	-
Takleh	Byz	68	*
Tartus	Cru	*60*, 66	**
Tell Brak	EBA/MBA	74	T
Tell Halaf	IrA/Rom	74	-
Tell Nebi Mend	LBA/Rom	65	T
Ugarit	LBA	*61*, 67	**
Yabrud	Rom	64	-
Zalebiye	Byz	72, 73	-
Zarzita	Byz	68	-

bold   = UNESCO World Heritage List site;
... /../...   = from ... through to ... (period)